The Cover Story Index™

The
Cover Story™
Index

1960
___
1991

Edited by Robert Skapura

Highsmith®
P R E S S
Fort Atkinson, Wisconsin

Published by Highsmith Press
W5527 Highway 106
P. O. Box 800
Fort Atkinson, Wisconsin 53538-0800

The paper used in this publication meets the minimum requirements of American National
Standard for Information Science – Permanence of Paper for Printed Library Material,
ANSI/NISO Z39.48-1984.

ISBN 0-917846-08-7
ISSN 1054-433X

Acknowledgments

I wish to thank Betty Bortz, Diablo Valley College, and Carol Bartlett, Contra Costa County Public Library, both in Pleasant Hill, California; and Ann M. Smith, John Swett Unified School District, Crockett, California.

I must also thank Carol Shuey who not only entered all of the data but also rigorously proofed the many versions and tracked down the missing issues and the inconsistent references. Thanks also to Monica Ertel at the Apple Computer Library and Dennis Marshall at Claris Corp. for their advice and technical support. I am especially grateful to Catherine, my wife, who proofread the original manuscript and remained cheerful when for months all dinner conversation came around to some major news story of a decade or two ago.

Finally, I owe a special debt to Duncan Highsmith whose vision made the first edition possible and whose insistence on quality guaranteed that the final format would match the original idea. He made the commitment to the second edition before we knew of the success of the first.

Magazines Indexed

Business Week

Congressional Digest

Discover

Life

Ms.

National Geographic

Newsweek

Omni

Psychology Today

Time

U.S. News and World Report

USA Today (periodical)

Table of Contents

Preface

At a time when there is so much emphasis on immediate user access to massive amounts of information, *The Cover Story Index* introduces a new approach to reference materials: a subject index and chronology to the major stories and trends that are now often buried in too much information. The first edition of *The Cover Story Index* included only the three news magazines: *Newsweek, Time* and *U.S. News and World Report.* Coverage went back thirty years. The second edition includes nine additional magazines: *Business Week, Congressional Digest, Discover, Life, Ms., National Geographic, Omni, Psychology Today,* and *USA Today* (periodical).

Life, Newsweek, Time and *U.S. News* are indexed from 1960. For many reasons, 1960 seemed like a good starting point. Many libraries have microforms of magazines that go that far back; the country seemed to take a different direction after 1960; and presently there's a new interest by today's students about that time period. The other eight magazines are indexed from 1981. They were chosen because we found that users were turning to *The Cover Story Index* not simply for a specific topic but because it guaranteed them material of a certain length. Cover stories contain substantial information, more than a short article but less than a book. The additional magazines add depth in the areas of business, science, social sciences, psychology and government.

The idea for such an index grew out of frustration, both mine and my students. In helping students locate materials on controversial topics or important events of the past three decades, I could very often "see" in my mind the cover of one of the news magazines but could not quickly or easily locate it. (Actually, it has gotten more difficult the older I have become.) A story I remembered as happening only a few years ago, I frequently found happened eight or ten years ago. The idea of an index of just cover stories eventually included a 120-page chronology that places the cover stories side by side, month by month, giving the reader a feel for the changes and trends that have been part of each time period.

With many projects this size, it is challenging and exciting at the beginning but drudgery at the end. This was the rare project that was interesting to the last. The meetings with the indexers were part "memory lane," part lively discussion about events from the perspective of a decade or two later, and finally a sharing of patterns that emerged from the vantage point of 1989. In short, creating *The Cover Story Index* was enjoyable because even though each of us had over fifteen years experience answering reference questions, we all came away feeling we had learned a great deal in the doing of it. In looking at the three news magazines (*Newsweek*, *Time* and *U.S. News*), here are some of our collective observations.

It was individual people that dominated the covers of all three magazines. Over 700 individuals have been the subject of cover stories over the three decades. Jimmy Carter, a one-term president, led with over forty cover stories, beating both Ronald Reagan (37) and Richard Nixon (33). But it wasn't just the presidential personality that kept them in the news. All three were plagued by lingering stories. Carter had inflation and the Iranian hostage crisis; Nixon had Watergate and Reagan had the Iran-Contra affair. Pope John Paul II (18) proved that a peripatetic pope gets good coverage, and Henry Kissinger (15) showed that one didn't have to be president to both wield tremendous power and stay in the limelight. Mikhail Gorbachev (23) is ahead of George Bush (14), but Gorbachev has had many more problems that have kept him in the news. There were only five cover stories on John F. Kennedy while he was president, less than two a year. He was on another six as a presidential candidate, but five seems a small number for a man remembered so well. On a lighter side, it was a surprise to see that Twiggy and Max Headroom both made it, but Elvis Presley had to wait ten years after his death for a commemorative story. Movie stars and politicians seem to be the largest two occupational categories. A surprising number of biographical subjects were not at all current, e.g., Johann Sebastian Bach, Albert Einstein, and Sigmund Freud.

The past thirty years have been a very violent period. Riots, demonstrations, assassinations, terrorism, and wars small and large garnered a large number of the cover stories in the 1960s and 1970s. It is not surprising then that voters found Ronald Reagan's words and reassuring style attractive in the 1980s.

Dominating the covers by sheer numbers was the Vietnam War with over a hundred (106) cover stories. When one keeps in mind that *U.S. News* did not begin cover stories until the last year of the war (1974), these one hundred stories were split between *Newsweek* and *Time*. That's almost a year's worth of cover stories each. The Watergate Affair (67) was the second most dominant news story, but its intensity is missed unless one remembers that these all appeared in only two magazines over a short three-year period.

Looking at the entire three decades, it was the Soviet Union and China, especially our changing relationship to those two countries, that captured over 150 covers. Reading the titles of those stories from 1960 to 1991, one can feel the changing public emotion toward both countries (fear, antagonism, anger, competitiveness, cautious trust), changes that frequently were reflected in our government policy.

There have been over thirty stories on drugs and drug abuse, testimony to the prevalence of that social problem. But all the news has not been bad. Various space flights and launchings have made the covers over 60 times, and it's impossible to look at the magazines of the 1960s without feeling the pride of accomplishment and sense of adventure in the early days of space exploration.

Even though the three magazines are viewed as news magazines, a surprising number of "non-news" subjects have made the covers of all three: the Bible, ice cream, Cro-Magnon man, Buddhism, and dinosaurs. Anniversaries have brought to the covers many subjects that we think of as historical rather than current: the 1929 stock market crash, World War II, the Constitutional Convention of 1787, and the Statue of Liberty. Some anniversaries commemorated sober moments (the attack on Pearl Harbor and the bombing of Hiroshima) but many more joyous (America's 200th birthday).

Sports, fads, and entertainment captured many covers, possibly a better reflection of American society than the attention-getting headline stories. Surprisingly, America's pastime of baseball (10) gave way to football (18) as the most covered sport. Muhammad Ali (4), however, was the single athlete most often on the covers , a tribute to both his long career as a boxer (1960 to 1981) and the entertainment quality of his out-of-the-ring life. Disco, Cabbage Patch dolls, and break dancing all had their brief moments on the covers.

Motion pictures and the actors and actresses in them proved that Hollywood still holds some magic. Even here, however, there were some surprises. Cher made the cover twice, but Dustin Hoffman was on only once and had to share the cover with Mia Farrow. In the activist '60s, only three movies were cover stories, but in the 1980s sixteen pictures made it.

There were a number of stories that received wide coverage at the time but have slipped from the public's memory: John Anderson's bid for the presidency, Tom Eagleton's brief spot as vice-presidential candidate, Legionnaire's disease, the U.S.S. Pueblo, and the Symbionese Liberation Army. There were some covers that we found almost embarrassingly dated, for example, a 1967 story titled "The Negro in Viet Nam." Certainly the most quaint was "Girls in College: They Have Scarcely Begun to Use Their Brains," from 1961. And there were two cover stories on building back yard bomb shelters.

Time magazine's "Man-of-the-Year" was almost a barometer of the period. Dwight Eisenhower opened the 1960s; Mikhail Gorbachev and the planet Earth closed the '80s. Only one individual woman has made it (Corazon Aquino). And Deng Xiaoping, Ronald Reagan, and Lyndon Johnson were all selected twice.

A few stories surprised us in that they were not a cover story. John F. Kennedy's assassination was never a cover story the week it happened. Television and newspaper coverage probably made it impossible for a weekly news magazine to seem timely. Woodstock is almost a touchstone when talking about the 1960s, but at the time it was only a short inside article. And more recently, the S&L crisis, which will cost the United States more than the Vietnam War, has been a cover story only once.

Most recently the invasion of Kuwait and the resulting Persian Gulf War stayed on the covers of the three news magazines for almost nine months. Fifty-eight cover stories put it just behind Watergate as the third most dominant news story in the past three decades.

Probably the story that best symbolizes the changes over these thirty years is the Berlin Wall. The first of seven stories appeared in July of 1961 describing the building of the wall; the last in November of 1989 shows people joyously breaking it down.

Robert Skapura
February 1992

Explanatory Notes

Creating a useful index of news magazines requires more than just assigning subjects to a large group of citations. It also requires that the indexers strike a balance between traditional subject headings, the words the magazines used at the time of the event, and the most probable terms patrons will think of when beginning their searches. The nature of the stories that have appeared in these magazines in many respects determined the nature of the index itself.

Structure of the Entries

The coverage by the three major news magazines has a strong emphasis on United States news: the people and events within the United States, the president, government branches, and agencies.

Traditionally, many of these subjects would become subtopics under the main topic UNITED STATES, e.g., UNITED STATES - DEPARTMENT OF DEFENSE. In *The Cover Story Index* this would mean the alphabetical division "U" would be very large and it would make the index cumbersome to use. Instead, it was assumed that the government departments, agencies, elections, movements, and events are specific to the United States and distinctions are made only when they are not. Thus, SUPREME COURT is found under "S" and the DEPARTMENT OF DEFENSE under "D."

An index that spans six presidencies affords distinctions that are not usually found in other indexes. Many of the subjects are divided by administration, e.g., DEFENSE SPENDING - REAGAN ADMINISTRATION, FOREIGN POLICY - NIXON ADMINISTRATION. Every four years the media gears up for a presidential election, covering the campaigns, the debates, and the elections themselves. All of these subjects are divided by election year and listed chronologically, e.g., PRESIDENTIAL CAMPAIGNS, 1976. Non-presidential candidates are put under POLITICAL CANDIDATES and are also separated by year. Non-presidential elections are put under ELECTIONS - UNITED STATES followed by the year.

Many of the cover stories concentrated on the relationships between other countries and the United States. Traditionally, these have been placed under the heading UNITED STATES - FOREIGN POLICY, followed by the name of

1

the country. We have concentrated on the foreign country first and established the relationship to the United States with the word "and." For example, we list CHINA AND THE UNITED STATES as a subject. This places our relationship to a country in the context of other articles about that country.

Most Current Form for Names

Individual people make up the largest single category of subjects on the covers. The various spellings of foreign names and the fact that people occasionally changed their own names posed the possibility of inconsistency. Individuals are listed in *The Cover Story Index* under the name they were known by in 1991, with a "See" reference from an original name or different spelling. Cassius Clay, for example, is listed under MUHAMMAD ALI and Jacqueline Kennedy under JACQUELINE KENNEDY ONASSIS. Foreign names will be found on the covers in many variations which means that, at the time, the news media had yet to decide on a consistent spelling. QADDAFI appears on various covers as Gaddafi and Kaddafi. DENG XIAOPING is found on early covers as Teng Hsiaoping.

Style Variations

A close reading of the citations will show an inconsistency of style as well as spelling. For example, some book titles and plays are put within double quotation marks, others between single quotes, and many with no quotes at all. We reproduce them as they appeared on the original cover.

New Subject Headings

Last, we have created some new subject headings to help the reader see the broader picture over the past thirty years. It is easy to see the changes in the public attitude toward the Central Intelligence Agency by looking at the fifteen articles beginning in 1961. But other subjects, such as RIOTS, are usually subtopics of some major topic. The user would have to search under the names of locations where riots occurred to find information about riots.

To provide easier subject access to this type of information we have chosen to use some topics that would normally not stand alone, permitting the user to see the patterns that have developed over the years. For example, RIOTS is used as a subject and is divided geographically, RIOTS - WATTS (CALIFORNIA). We have made similar divisions for PROTESTS AND DEMONSTRATIONS, ASSASSINATIONS, and ASSASSINATION ATTEMPTS.

In this way we hope we have produced a useful research tool for those interested in what has shaped and reflected the events of the past thirty-two years.

Subject Index

OF COVER STORIES

1960 - 1991

User's Guide to the Subject Index

The Subject Index provides access to people, places, things, and events that appeared as cover stories. **Subject headings** are used to find topical materials in articles that include interviews, photographs, experts' opinions, coverage of diverse viewpoints, and concise summaries of complex events.

Each citation includes: cover story title, magazine, magazine date, and page number on which the article begins.

The citations under each subject heading are arranged in **reverse chronological order**, i.e., the most recent citation on a subject is listed first. This provides an historical view of controversial subjects, such as abortion or capital punishment, and allows the user to see changes in people and countries over the thirty-year period. When more than one magazine covered the same story, the citations are listed in alphabetical order by magazine.

Frequently, the cover story is a collection of individual stories focusing on various aspects of a topic. An eye-catching title for this collection is created for the cover of the magazine. The Subject Index shows this cover title exactly as it appears.

When preparing a bibliography, however, the cover story titles should not be used. Rather, the user should cite the title of the article as it appears inside the magazine.

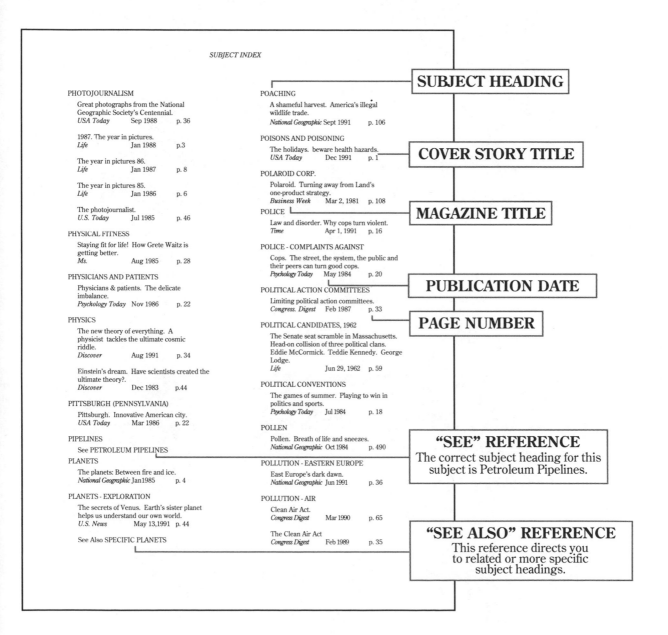

SUBJECT INDEX

PHOTOJOURNALISM

Great photographs from the National Geographic Society's Centennial.
USA Today   Sep 1988   p. 36

1987. The year in pictures.
Life   Jan 1988   p.3

The year in pictures 86.
Life   Jan 1987   p. 8

The year in pictures 85.
Life   Jan 1986   p. 6

The photojournalist.
U.S. Today   Jul 1985   p. 46

PHYSICAL FITNESS

Staying fit for life! How Grete Waitz is getting better.
Ms.   Aug 1985   p. 28

PHYSICIANS AND PATIENTS

Physicians & patients. The delicate imbalance.
Psychology Today   Nov 1986   p. 22

PHYSICS

The new theory of everything. A physicist tackles the ultimate cosmic riddle.
Discover   Aug 1991   p. 34

Einstein's dream. Have scientists created the ultimate theory?.
Discover   Dec 1983   p.44

PITTSBURGH (PENNSYLVANIA)

Pittsburgh. Innovative American city.
USA Today   Mar 1986   p. 22

PIPELINES

See PETROLEUM PIPELINES

PLANETS

The planets: Between fire and ice.
National Geographic Jan1985   p. 4

PLANETS - EXPLORATION

The secrets of Venus. Earth's sister planet helps us understand our own world.
U.S. News   May 13,1991 p. 44

See Also SPECIFIC PLANETS

POACHING

A shameful harvest. America's illegal wildlife trade.
National Geographic Sept 1991   p. 106

POISONS AND POISONING

The holidays. beware health hazards.
USA Today   Dec 1991   p. 1

POLAROID CORP.

Polaroid. Turning away from Land's one-product strategy.
Business Week   Mar 2, 1981   p. 108

POLICE

Law and disorder. Why cops turn violent.
Time   Apr 1, 1991   p. 16

POLICE - COMPLAINTS AGAINST

Cops. The street, the system, the public and their peers can turn good cops.
Psychology Today   May 1984   p. 20

POLITICAL ACTION COMMITTEES

Limiting political action committees.
Congress. Digest   Feb 1987   p. 33

POLITICAL CANDIDATES, 1962

The Senate seat scramble in Massachusetts. Head-on collision of three political clans. Eddie McCormick. Teddie Kennedy. George Lodge.
Life   Jun 29, 1962   p. 59

POLITICAL CONVENTIONS

The games of summer. Playing to win in politics and sports.
Psychology Today   Jul 1984   p. 18

POLLEN

Pollen. Breath of life and sneezes.
National Geographic Oct 1984   p. 490

POLLUTION - EASTERN EUROPE

East Europe's dark dawn.
National Geographic Jun 1991   p. 36

POLLUTION - AIR

Clean Air Act.
Congress Digest   Mar 1990   p. 65

The Clean Air Act
Congress Digest   Feb 1989   p. 35

SUBJECT HEADING

COVER STORY TITLE

MAGAZINE TITLE

PUBLICATION DATE

PAGE NUMBER

"SEE" REFERENCE
The correct subject heading for this subject is Petroleum Pipelines.

"SEE ALSO" REFERENCE
This reference directs you to related or more specific subject headings.

AARON, HANK

    Chasing the Babe. Hank Aaron.
Newsweek   Aug 13, 1973 p. 52

ABDUL-JABBAR, KAREEM

    The towering talent of Lew Alcindor.
Newsweek   Feb 27, 1967 p. 59

ABORIGINES

    See AUSTRALIAN ABORIGINES

ABORTION

    Title X Pregnacy Counseling Act.
Congressional Digest Aug 1991   p. 195

    The Bush court. A move to the right.
What it means for: Abortion, the death
penalty, civil rights.
Newsweek   Jul 30, 1990 p. 14

    Abortion's most wrenching questions.
Should parents have a say? What about
rape victims?
Time   Jul 9, 1990 p. 22

    Repro woman. Pro-choice champion
Faye Wattleton talks tough.
Ms.   Oct 1989 p. 50

It's war. From slavery to voting rights,
the Supreme Court sometimes gets on the
wrong side of history. This could be one
of those times. No matter what the
justices decide, reproductive freedom *is* a
fundamental human right.
Ms.   Aug 1989 p. 38

The future of abortion in America. New
restrictions: How tough will the states get?
A dilemma for doctors. The war within
the Court.
Newsweek   Jul 17, 1989 p. 14

The battle over abortion. The Court
confronts Roe vs. Wade. Justice
O'Connor's key role. Sandra Day
O'Connor.
Newsweek   May 1, 1989 p. 28

Abortion. Will the Court turn back the
clock?
Time   May 1, 1989 p. 20

Abortion. America's new civil war. Say
that one word, and other words fire like
weapons. One side yells bloody murder,
the other insists that a woman presides
over her own body. Political fury in an
election year.
U.S. News   Oct 3, 1988 p. 22

Teen abortions. The story of one girl's
solitary court battle and why she couldn't
tell her parents.
Ms.   Apr 1988 p. 46

Abortion. The moral dilemma. The
medical issues. The turn to violence.
Newsweek   Jan 14, 1985 p. 20

A special poll: How women feel about
abortion. When does life really begin?
Life   Nov 1981 p. 45

Abortion. The battle of "life" vs. "choice."
Time   Apr 6, 1981 p. 20

The ultimate invasion of privacy—and
how to fight back.
Ms.   Feb 1981 p. 43

Abortion under attack.
Newsweek   Jun 5, 1978 p. 36

Abortion and the law.
Newsweek   Mar 3, 1975 p. 18

Abortion and the law.
Newsweek   Apr 13, 1970   p. 53

ABRAMS, CREIGHTON
New man in Viet Nam. General
Creighton Abrams.
Time   Apr 19, 1968   p. 25

ABSCAM BRIBERY SCANDAL, 1980
Operation Abscam. The FBI stings
Congress.
Time   Feb 18, 1980   p. 10

ABU SIMBEL, TEMPLES OF
Moving a 15,000-ton treasure. Feat on the
Nile—to save the temples Abu Simbel.
Life   Oct 29, 1965   p. 28

ABZUG, BELLA
Women in politics. How are they doing?
Where are they going?
Life   Jun 9, 1972   p. 46

ACADEMY AWARDS (MOTION PICTURES)
Rocky KO's Hollywood. Sylvester
Stallone.
Newsweek   Apr 11, 1977   p. 70

How they pick the Oscars.
Life   Apr 7, 1972   p. 46

ACHILLE LAURO SHIP HIJACKING, 1985
Hijack fallout.
Time   Oct 28, 1985   p. 22

Getting even. How Reagan did it. Will
justice be done? The risks ahead.
Newsweek   Oct 21, 1985   p. 20

Turning the tables. The U.S. strikes back
at terrorism.
Time   Oct 21, 1985   p. 22

Will Americans still be terrorist targets?
'We want...justice done.'
U.S. News   Oct 21, 1985   p. 24

ACID RAIN
The acid rain controversy.
Congressional Digest Feb 1985   p. 33

ACKLEY, H. GARDNER
The economy: What's ahead?
Presidential adviser Gardner Ackley.
Newsweek   Jul 18, 1966   p. 67

ACUPUNCTURE
Wonder cures? New respect for fringe
medicine. Acupuncture. Hypnosis.
Biofeedback.
U.S. News   Sep 23, 1991   p. 68

Acupuncture: Pinning hopes on Chinese
medicine.
USA Today   Feb 1988   p. 1

All about acupuncture.
Newsweek   Aug 14, 1972   p. 48

ADAMS, ANSEL
The master eye. Photographer Ansel
Adams.
Time   Sep 3, 1979   p. 36

ADDICTIVE BEHAVIOR
Addictive personalities. Who gets hooked
on drugs and alcohol - and why. Kitty
Dukakis: Her private struggle.
Newsweek   Feb 20, 1989   p. 52

Addictions. Surprising dependencies of
independent women.
Ms.   Feb 1987   p. 35

ADENAUER, KONRAD
Adenauer. End of an era.
Newsweek   May 6, 1963   p. 48

ADOPTION
Want a baby? Not all children are equal
in the joy and anguish of adoption.
Time   Oct 9, 1989   p. 86

The new face of adoption.
Newsweek   Sep 13, 1971   p. 66

ADVENTURE AND ADVENTURERS
The adventurers. Sir Francis Chichester
and Gipsy Moth IV.
Newsweek   Jun 12, 1967   p. 61

ADVERTISING
What happened to advertising? Why a
mild recession unleashed a depression in
ad sales. And what it means for
marketing, media, and Madison Avenue.
Business Week   Sep 23, 1991   p. 66

Advertising's creative explosion.
Newsweek   Aug 18, 1969   p. 62

Commercials: The best & worst on TV.
Time   Jul 12, 1968   p. 55

Going broke. Tangled policies. Failing
farms.
Time   Feb 18, 1985   p. 18

The new U.S. farmer.
Time   Nov 6, 1978   p. 92

AGRICULTURE POLICY - JOHNSON
ADMINISTRATION

The man who wants the government to
get off the farm. Farm Bureau's Charles
Shuman.
Time   Sep 3, 1965   p. 22

AGRICULTURE POLICY - KENNEDY
ADMINISTRATION

Farm trouble. Behind the Billie Sol mess.
Agriculture Secretary Orville Freeman.
Newsweek   May 28, 1962 p. 25

AGRICULTURE POLICY - REAGAN
ADMINISTRATION

The farm credit system controversy.
Congressional Digest Jan 1986   p. 3

AIDS (DISEASE)

'Even me'—Magic Johnson.
Newsweek   Nov 18, 1991   p. 58

Doctors with AIDS.
Newsweek   Jul 1, 1991   p. 48

AIDS: Eye movement can help us see
trouble ahead.
USA Today   Feb 1991   p. 1

How AIDS is changing . . . everything.
Ms.   Jan 1991   p. 16

At last: The first real hope for an AIDS
vaccine.
Discover   Sep 1990   p. 70

AIDS: Redefining medicine.
Omni   Dec 1989   p. 50

The human mouse. In a bold new bid to
conquer AIDS, a visionary researcher has
transplanted our immune system into a
mouse.
Discover   Aug 1989   p. 48

AIDS. What effect on the workplace?
USA Today   Feb 1989   p. 1

Sex in the Age of AIDS. Masters &
Johnson. Excerpts from their
controversial new book.
Newsweek   Mar 14, 1988   p. 42

The runaway epidemic. AIDS on the
streets.
Psychology Today Jan 1988   p. 28

Outcast. How AIDS is tearing apart one
American community.
U.S. News   Oct 12, 1987   p. 62

AIDS. Everything you *must* know.
USA Today   Oct 1987   p. 3

Kids with AIDS. The struggle to care for
the epidemic's youngest victims.
Newsweek   Sep 7, 1987   p. 50

The face of AIDS. One year in the
epidemic.
Newsweek   Aug 10, 1987   p. 22

AIDS. Should you be tested? Why it's
prudent for 30 million Americans.
Turmoil in the testing centers. Answers
about your privacy, your job, your
insurance.
U.S. News   Apr 20, 1987   p. 56

AIDS and business. How companies deal
with stricken employees. New drugs: Are
they helping? Will insurers foot the bill?
A model for corporate policy.
Business Week   Mar 23, 1987   p. 122

The big chill. How heterosexuals are
coping with AIDS.
Time   Feb 16, 1987   p. 50

AIDS. What you need to know. What
you should do.
U.S. News   Jan 12, 1987   p. 60

AIDS. Future shock. How the spreading
epidemic will affect health care,
government policy, civil liberties and
attitudes toward sex.
Newsweek   Nov 24, 1986   p. 30

Viruses. Keys to life and death. Aids:
new research, new danger.
Time   Nov 3, 1986   p. 66

Communicable diseases: Efforts to control
AIDS epidemic hampered.
USA Today   Oct 1986   p. 1

The AIDS doctor. Gerald Friedland has treated nearly 300 men and women with AIDS. More than 200 are dead. The rest are dying. This is the story of his caring and his struggle.
Newsweek   Jul 21, 1986   p. 38

AIDS. The latest scientific facts.
Discover   Dec 1985   p. 28

How to prevent AIDS.
Omni   Nov 1985   p. 76

The fear of AIDS. Ignorance and uncertainty fuel growing public concern.
Newsweek   Sep 23, 1985   p. 18

AIDS. It is the nation's worst public-health problem. No one has ever recovered from the disease, and the number of cases is doubling every year. Now fears are growing that the AIDS epidemic may spread beyond gays...
Newsweek   Aug 12, 1985   p. 20

AIDS. The growing threat. What's being done.
Time   Aug 12, 1985   p. 40

Now no one is safe from AIDS.
Life   Jul 1985   p. 12

Disease detectives. Tracking the killers. The AIDS hysteria.
Time   Jul 4, 1983   p. 50

Epidemic. The mysterious and deadly disease called AIDS may be the public-health threat of the century. How did it start? Can it be stopped?
Newsweek   Apr 18, 1983   p. 74

AIR SAFETY

See AIR TRAVEL - SAFETY

AIR TRAFFIC CONTROL

How safe is the air traffic control system? "We have reached the red line. The people within the air traffic control system —the controllers, the technicians, and even the supervisors—have informed us not only of an erosion of safety, but the fact that safety is at times non-existent."
USA Today   Nov 1987   p. 12

Gridlock. You think it's bad now? Airline delays are going to get worse.
U.S. News   Dec 22, 1986   p. 14

Who controls the air? Reagan's tough line. The strike's impact. The public's view: A poll.
Newsweek   Aug 17, 1981   p. 18

Winging it. Coping without controllers.
Time   Aug 17, 1981   p. 14

Stack-up. Danger and confusion of the air traffic jam.
Life   Aug 9, 1968   p. 38

The split-second jet age. Controlling today's traffic jam in the sky.
Newsweek   Jan 2, 1961   p. 17

AIR TRAVEL

Smart ways to fly. Air traveler's guide. Exclusive airport ratings. On-time airlines. Tips for painless trips.
U.S. News   Nov 26, 1990   p. 68

Fare games. Flying has never been cheaper.
Time   Jan 13, 1986   p. 40

New era in the air. Cheap fares, crowded flights.
Time   Aug 14, 1978   p. 50

Aboard the first flights. Moscow to New York. New York to Moscow.
Life   Jul 26, 1968   p. 20

AIR TRAVEL - ACCIDENTS

Anatomy of a plane crash. Why little Cecelia survived and the other 154 died on Flight 255.
Life   Apr 1988   p. 66

AIR TRAVEL - SAFETY

Finding God on Flight 232. Gripping stories told by the passengers who faced death for a chilling 41 minutes.
Life   Sep 1989   p. 28

Year of the near miss. How to make air traffic safer.
Newsweek   Jul 27, 1987   p. 20

Air travel. How safe is it?
Time   Jan 12, 1987   p. 24

These seats can kill you. Hundreds of people have died needlessly in plane accidents, mostly from seat failure and fire, for when it comes to crashworthiness technology, a mid-'70s economy car is safer than a modern commercial jet.
Discover   Oct 1986   p. 30

Can we keep the skies safe? Intense competition and the drive to cut costs are making it more difficult.
Newsweek   Jan 30, 1984   p. 24

Safer skies. The lessons of Flight 90.
Discover   Apr 1982   p. 18

How safe?
Newsweek   Jun 11, 1979   p. 34

Air travel. How safe?
Time   Apr 11, 1977   p. 22

The drive for air safety. U.S. Airways boss Quesada.
Time   Feb 22, 1960   p. 16

AIR TRAVEL - SECURITY

Bombs on planes. A chilling expose of U.S. airports.
Life   Mar 1989   p. 130

AIRBORNE WARNING AND CONTROL SYSTEM

AWACS. He does it again!
Time   Nov 9, 1981   p. 12

AIRCRAFT CARRIERS

Inferno at sea. Forrestal disaster.
Life   Aug 11, 1967   p. 20

AIRLINE INDUSTRY

Dogfight! American vs. United. The battle for global supremacy.
Business Week   Jan 21, 1991   p. 56

The frenzied skies. Ten years after deregulation, fares are rising, service is erratic, and the number of airlines is declining. Now what?
Business Week   Dec 19, 1988   p. 70

The high flier. Frank Lorenzo's bid for Eastern Air Lines is the latest and most daring move in the restructuring of the airline industry. Will it work?
Business Week   Mar 10, 1986   p. 104

Airlines in turmoil. Labor woes, price wars–and bankruptcy threats.
Business Week   Oct 10, 1983   p. 98

Delta. The world's most profitable airline.
Business Week   Aug 31, 1981   p. 68

Upstarts in the sky. Here comes a new kind of airline.
Business Week   Jun 15, 1981   p. 78

Is the U.S. sabotaging its international airlines?
Business Week   Jan 26, 1981   p. 74

The superjets take off.
Time   Jan 19, 1970   p. 52

What the airlines mean to the country.
Time   Jul 22, 1966   p. 80

AIRPLANE HIJACKING

See HIJACKING, AIRPLANE

AIRPLANES, JET

The superjets take off.
Time   Jan 19, 1970   p. 52

The 747 arrives. Into a new air age.
Newsweek   Oct 27, 1969   p. 95

AIRPLANES, MILITARY

The new era of invisible warfare. The Pentagon reveals the B-2 Stealth bomber. Is it a wonder weapon or a costly waste?
U.S. News   Nov 28, 1988   p. 20

$100 billion shoot-out.
U.S. News   Jan 9, 1978   p. 54

AIRPLANES, SUPERSONIC

The Concorde furor.
Newsweek   Feb 16, 1976   p. 16

The SST. Racing for $25 billion.
Newsweek   Aug 29, 1966   p. 48

AKERS, JOHN

IBM. Big changes at Big Blue. Just as John Akers became chairman three years ago, the computer giant went into its worst profit slide ever. Now his plan to rejuvenate the company is in place. Will it work?
Business Week   Feb 15, 1988   p. 92

ALASKA

Alaska's big spill. Can the wilderness heal?
National Geographic Jan 1990 p. 5

The Alaska spill. What Exxon leaves behind. Is the damage permanent? Cutting through the hype, hysteria and confusion.
Newsweek Sep 18, 1989 p. 50

Alaska. The battle for America's last frontier.
Time Apr 17, 1989 p. 56

Southeast Alaska. A place apart.
National Geographic Jan 1984 p. 50

Alaska: Last chance for the last frontier.
Time Jul 27, 1970 p. 44

Alaska. 49th state. Land of risks and high promise.
Life Oct 1, 1965 p. 64

Alaskan walrus crowd a rocky shore.
Life Jun 27, 1960 p. 63

ALBEE, EDWARD

Playwright Edward Albee. Odd man in.
Newsweek Feb 4, 1963 p. 49

ALCINDOR, LEW

See ABDUL-JABBAR, KAREEM

ALCOA ALUMINUM CO.

The quiet coup at Alcoa. The untold story of how the board ousted the chief executive—and changed corporate strategy.
Business Week Jun 27, 1988 p. 58

ALCOHOLICS' FAMILIES

Alcohol and the family. Growing up with alcoholic parents can leave scars for life.
Newsweek Jan 18, 1988 p. 62

ALCOHOLISM

Addictive personalities. Who gets hooked on drugs and alcohol - and why. Kitty Dukakis: Her private struggle.
Time Feb 20, 1989 p. 52

This is one of the 18 million Americans who have a drinking problem. But there is hope: Science is discovering the causes of alcoholism, and new ways are emerging to cope with the disease.
Time Nov 30, 1987 p. 80

Alcoholism. Getting the monkey off our backs. Is the addiction inherited? Can it be prevented? Getting help for the family.
U.S. News Nov 30, 1987 p. 56

Getting straight. How Americans are breaking the grip of drugs and alcohol.
Newsweek Jun 4, 1984 p. 62

Alcoholism. New victims, new treatments.
Time Apr 22, 1974 p. 75

ALDA, ALAN

Alan Alda talks about work, love and friendship. The most admired man in America is a feminist.
Ms. Jun 1981 p. 46

ALEXANDER THE GREAT

Alexander the Great: Conqueror. Greece part VI.
Life May 3, 1963 p. 62

ALGERIA - POLITICS AND GOVERNMENT

Algeria's Ben Bella. Another Castro?
Newsweek Aug 13, 1962 p. 34

Algeria: Birth of a nation. Premier Benkhedda.
Time Mar 16, 1962 p. 22

Three-way war in Algeria. Terrorist Salan.
Time Jan 26, 1962 p. 22

France's de Gaulle: The final crisis?
Newsweek Feb 8, 1960 p. 23

ALI, MUHAMMAD

'The Greatest' is gone. Muhammad Ali.
Time Feb 27, 1978 p. 72

Norman Mailer on the fight. 9 pages of action color.
Life Mar 19, 1971 p. 18

The $5,000,000 fighters. Frazer. Ali.
Time Mar 8, 1971 p. 63

Battle of the champs. Backstage with Ali and Frazier.
Life   Mar 5, 1971   p. 40

Return of the champ. Muhammad Ali.
Newsweek   Nov 9, 1970   p. 56

Look out—he's back. A different Muhammad Ali returns to the ring.
Life   Oct 23, 1970   p. 44

Cassius Clay.
Life   Mar 6, 1964   p. 34

Cassius Marcellus Clay.
Time   Mar 22, 1963   p. 78

ALIENS, ILLEGAL

Closing the door? The angry debate over illegal immigration. Crossing the Rio Grande.
Newsweek   Jun 25, 1984   p. 18

Proposed immigration reform and control legislation.
Congressional Digest   Aug 1983   p. 195

Invasion from Mexico. It just keeps growing.
U.S. News   Mar 7, 1983   p. 37

Proposed sanctions against employers of illegal aliens.
Congressional Digest   Oct 1981   p. 225

Illegal aliens. Invasion out of control?
U.S. News   Jan 29, 1979   p. 38

Time bomb in Mexico. Why there'll be no end to the invasion by "illegals."
U.S. News   Jul 4, 1977   p. 27

Border crisis. Illegal aliens out of control?
U.S. News   Apr 25, 1977   p. 33

ALLEGHENY INTERNATIONAL INC.

Trouble! Robert Buckley, CEO of Allegheny International, runs a very ailing company. It lost $109 million last year, it is mired in debt, and its stock is near a 1-year low.
Business Week   Aug 11, 1986   p. 56

ALLEN, GEORGE

Pro football's red-hot Redskins. Coach George Allen.
Newsweek   Nov 1, 1971   p. 54

ALLEN, WOODY

A comic genius. Woody Allen comes of age.
Time   Apr 30, 1979   p. 62

Woody.
Newsweek   Apr 24, 1978   p. 62

Everything you always wanted to know about Woody Allen.
Time   Jul 3, 1972   p. 58

My secret life with Bogart by Woody Allen.
Life   Mar 21, 1969   p. 64

ALLENDE, SALVADOR

Chile under the gun.
Newsweek   Sep 24, 1973   p. 42

After the fall. Allende.
Time   Sep 24, 1973   p. 35

Marxist threat in the Americas. Chile's Salvador Allende.
Time   Oct 19, 1970   p. 23

ALLERGIES

Allergies. New drugs and more tests are giving sufferers more way to spell relief.
U.S. News   Feb 20, 1989   p. 68

Allergies: Fighting food intolerance.
USA Today   Oct 1988   p. 1

Pollen. Breath of life and sneezes.
National Geographic   Oct 1984   p. 490

Allergies. New discoveries, new relief.
Newsweek   Aug 23, 1982   p. 40

ALLIED CORP.

Allied after Bendix: R&D is the key.
Business Week   Dec 12, 1983   p. 76

ALPHAND, NICOLE

Washington hostesses. Nicole Alphand.
Time   Nov 22, 1963   p. 21

ALSOP, JOSEPH

Those Washington columnists.
Newsweek   Dec 18, 1961   p. 65

ALTERNATIVE MEDICINE

The new age of alternative medicine.
Why biofeedback and other offbeat
treatments are catching on.
Time   Nov 4, 1991   p. 68

Wonder cures? New respect for fringe
medicine. Acupuncture. Hypnosis.
Biofeedback.
U.S. News   Sep 23, 1991   p. 68

Spiritual healing hits the suburbs.
Psychology Today   Jan 1989   p. 57

Breakthrough: The chemistry of
self-healing.
Omni   Mar 1988   p. 36

Acupuncture: Pinning hopes on Chinese
medicine.
USA Today   Feb 1988   p. 1

Hypnosis. From theater to therapy.
Medical uses.
Psychology Today   Jan 1986   p. 22

The use of hypnosis to cure mental ills.
Life   Mar 7, 1960   p. 106

ALTMAN, ROBERT

Epic of Opry Land.
Newsweek   Jun 30, 1975   p. 46

ALZHEIMER'S DISEASE

Alzheimer's. New advances in the battle
against a terrifying disease.
U.S. News   Aug 12, 1991   p. 40

All about Alzheimer's. What doctors
know. How families cope.
Newsweek   Dec 18, 1989   p. 54

Alzheimer's disease: Myths fuel anxiety.
USA Today   Oct 1989   p. 1

The agony of Alzheimer's disease.
Newsweek   Dec 3, 1984   p. 56

AM INTERNATIONAL

AM International. When technology was
not enough.
Business Week   Jan 25, 1982   p. 62

AMAX INC.

Can coal save Pierre Gousseland? Mired
in debt and losing money, Amax's CEO is
still trying to grow the company by
buying coal.
Business Week   Oct 18, 1982   p. 104

AMAZON

Torching the Amazon. Can the rain forest
be saved?
Time   Sep 18, 1989   p. 76

AMBASSADORS

See DIPLOMATS

AMERICA - ANTIQUITIES

America before Columbus. The untold
story.
U.S. News   Jul 8, 1991   p. 22

AMERICA'S CUP RACE

Going for it. America's Cup skipper
Dennis Conner.
Time   Feb 9, 1987   p. 42

America's Cup: Ultimate in sailing.
Skipper Bus Mosbacher.
Time   Aug 18, 1967   p. 64

America's Cup 1964. Constellation and
American Eagle.
Newsweek   Sep 14, 1964   p. 50

America's Cup: Racing again off Newport.
Newsweek   Aug 6, 1962   p. 45

AMERICAN AIRLINES, INC.

American rediscovers itself.
Business Week   Aug 23, 1982   p. 66

**AMERICAN BROADCASTING COMPANY,
INC.**

Big media, big money. The ABC
takeover. The next targets.
Newsweek   Apr 1, 1985   p. 52

AMERICAN CAN COMPANY

Comeback kid. Jerry Tsai, a new CEO of
American Can, is transforming the
old-line manufacturer into a financial
services giant. He's come a long way
from his gunslinging days on Wall Street
in the 1960s.
Business Week   Aug 18, 1986   p. 72

The new shape of America. A
cross-country look. The four-day work
week. Our public lands up for grabs. The
good life in new towns. What makes us
laugh. The un-radical young.
Life   Jan 8, 1971   p. 2

The troubled American. Special report on
the white majority.
Newsweek   Oct 6, 1969   p. 28

AMERICANS IN FOREIGN COUNTRIES
Americans abroad.
Newsweek   Nov 28, 1966 p. 43

AMERICANS WITH DISABILITIES ACT
Americans with Disabilities Act of 1989.
Congressional Digest Dec 1989   p. 289

AMIN DADA, IDI
Idi Amin's reign of terror.
Newsweek   Mar 7, 1977   p. 28

The wild man of Africa. Uganda's Idi
Amin.
Time   Mar 7, 1977   p. 19

AMNESTY
Amnesty for the war exiles?
Newsweek   Jan 17, 1972   p. 19

AMUSEMENT PARKS
Amusement parks of the future.
Omni   Nov 1990   p. 42

Safari in new-type U.S. fun spot.
Life   Aug 1, 1960   p. 26

ANASTASIA, GRAND DUCHESS OF RUSSIA
The case of a new Anastasia. Is a lady
from Chicago the czar's daughter?
Life   Oct 18, 1963   p. 104

ANCHORAGE (ALASKA)
Hello Anchorage, good-bye dream.
National Geographic Mar 1988   p. 364

ANDERS, WILLIAM
Men of the year. Anders, Borman and
Lovell.
Time   Jan 3, 1969   p. 9

ANDERSON, JACK
Jack Anderson, supersnoop. Washington:
Affluence & influence.
Time   Apr 3, 1972   p. 40

ANDERSON, JOHN
Could he be president?
U.S.News   Aug 11, 1980 p. 25

The Anderson factor. Wild card in the
game.
Newsweek   Jun 9, 1980   p. 28

ANDERSON, TERRY
The smile of freedom. Terry Anderson's
terrible ordeal. The inside story of the
hostage release.
Time   Dec 16, 1991 p. 16

ANDRETTI, MARIO
The speed game. Champion driver Mario
Andretti.
Newsweek   May 29, 1967 p. 64

ANDREWS, JULIE
Julie Andrews.
Time   Dec 23, 1966 p. 53

ANDROPOV, YURI
The succession. Filling a vacuum, again.
Yuri Andropov 1914-1984.
Time   Feb 20, 1984 p. 14

Men of the year. Ronald Reagan. Yuri
Andropov.
Time   Jan 2, 1984   p. 16

Andropov. A year of failure.
U.S. News   Nov 14, 1983 p. 39

The four faces of Andropov.
Psychology Today   May 1983   p. 28

The new boss. A spymaster's rise to
power. Will Moscow get tougher? How
Reagan should respond. Soviet Party
Chief Yuri Andropov.
Newsweek   Nov 22, 1982 p. 28

After Brezhnev. Andropov takes
command.
Time   Nov 22, 1982 p. 10

Russia after Brezhnev.
U.S. News   Nov 22, 1982 p. 22

ANGER
Anger. Should we keep it in or let it
loose?
Psychology Today   Nov 1982   p. 25

ANGKOR, KAMPUCHEA

The temples of Angkor. Will they survive?
National Geographic May 1982   p. 548

ANGLICAN CHURCH

See CHURCH OF ENGLAND

ANGOLA

Angola. Detente under the gun.
Newsweek   Jan 19, 1976   p. 20

ANGOLA AND THE UNITED STATES

U.S. policy toward Angola.
Congressional Digest Apr 1986   p. 99

ANHEUSER-BUSCH, INC.

Anheuser-Busch. The king of beers still rules.
Business Week   Jul 12, 1982   p. 50

ANIMAL BEHAVIOR

Dark secrets of the chimps.
Discover   Nov 1987   p. 66

The science of power.
Omni   Jul 1985   p. 68

ANIMAL COMMUNICATION

Elephant talk.
National Geographic Aug 1989   p. 264

Interspecies communication. The experiment begins.
Omni   Dec 1986   p. 52

Women who talk to animals.
Ms.   Dec 1981   p. 41

ANIMAL EXPERIMENTATION

The battle over animal rights. A question of suffering and science.
Newsweek   Dec 26, 1988   p. 50

Saving lab animals. How computers cut down the killing.
Discover   Sep 1983   p. 76

ANIMAL INTELLIGENCE

How smart are animals? They know more than you think.
Newsweek   May 23, 1988   p. 52

The intelligence revolution. Is IQ dead? Radical new definitions of intellect threaten the conventional tests.
Discover   Oct 1985   p. 25

ANIMALS

Animal oddities.
Omni   Sep 1988   p. 42

ANIMALS - TRAINING

Lords of the ring. Charisma, control, and tradition. Gunther Gebel-Williams.
Psychology Today Oct 1983   p. 26

ANIMALS AND CIVILIZATION

How animals tamed people. What science tells up about the bonds between man and beast.
U.S. News   Mar 20, 1989   p. 74

ANN-MARGRET

Ann-Margret. After 10 years, big success for the 'Sex Kitten.'
Life   Aug 6, 1971   p. 30

Ann-Margret's spin to movie stardom.
Life   Jan 11, 1963   p. 60

ANNE, PRINCESS OF GREAT BRITAIN

Princess Anne at 21.
Life   Aug 20, 1971   p. 30

ANTARCTICA

Antarctica. Is any place safe from mankind?
Time   Jan 15, 1990   p. 56

ANTELOPE

African antelope.
Life   Dec 5, 1969   p. 74

ANTHROPOCENTRISM

The all-creating eye. According to a radical tenet of physics, the universe exists only because it has been, is being, and will be observed.
Discover   May 1987   p. 90

ANTHROPOLOGY

Argument over a woman. Science searches for the real Eve.
Discover   Aug 1990   p. 52

ANTI-BALLISTIC MISSILE TREATY, 1972

The ABM Treaty controversy.
Congressional Digest Nov 1987   p. 257

ANTI-DEPRESSANTS

Prozac. A breakthrough drug for depression.
Newsweek   Mar 26, 1990   p. 38

ANTI-NUCLEAR MOVEMENT

Thinking the unthinkable. Rising fears about nuclear war.
Time   Mar 29, 1982   p. 10

ANTI-NUCLEAR MOVEMENT - CATHOLIC CHURCH

God and the bomb. Catholic bishops debate nuclear morality.
Time   Nov 29, 1982   p. 68

ANTI-NUCLEAR MOVEMENT - EUROPE

Battle over the missiles. Europe's anti-nuclear protests.
Newsweek   Oct 24, 1983   p. 36

Europe's fear. And a bold U.S. proposal.
Time   Nov 30, 1981   p. 36

ANTI-NUCLEAR MOVEMENT - UNITED STATES

Nuclear freeze crusade. Gaining or waning?
U.S. News   Apr 25, 1983   p. 18

The nuclear freeze proposal.
Congressional Digest Aug 1982   p. 195

The nuclear nightmare. The growing outcry over the bomb. How can the arms be halted?
Newsweek   Apr 26, 1982   p. 20

ANTI-SEMITISM - EASTERN EUROPE

The long shadow. New fears of anti-Semitism in Eastern Europe and the Soviet Union.
Newsweek   May 7, 1990   p. 34

ANTI-SEMITISM - SOVIET UNION

The long shadow. New fears of anti-Semitism in Eastern Europe and the Soviet Union.
Newsweek   May 7, 1990   p. 34

ANTI-WAR MOVEMENTS

See VIETNAM WAR, 1957-1975 - PROTESTS AND DEMONSTRATIONS

ANTIMATTER

Strange matter. Is there a parallel material world?
Discover   Nov 1989   p. 62

ANXIETY

Guilt and anxiety.
Time   Mar 31, 1961   p. 44

APARTHEID

South Africa's civil war. The making of a bloodbath.
Newsweek   Jun 23, 1986   p. 34

South Africa. What can be done?
Newsweek   Sep 16, 1985   p. 16

Can South Africa avoid race war?
U.S. News   Aug 26, 1985   p. 20

Can South Africa save itself? Black rage - and signs of white reforms.
Newsweek   Aug 19, 1985   p. 14

South Africa. Black rage, white repression. A challenge to U.S. policy.
Time   Aug 5, 1985   p. 24

South Africa. The defiant white tribe.
Time   Nov 21, 1977   p. 50

South Africa: The delusions of apartheid.
Time   Aug 26, 1966   p. 18

APES

The threatened orangutan. Vanishing wildlife.
Life   Mar 28, 1969   p. 82

APOLLO PROJECT

Apollo 15: The most perilous journey.
Time   Aug 9, 1971   p. 10

On board Apollo 13. The astronauts' own story.
Life   May 1, 1970   p. 24

The saga of Apollo 13.
Newsweek   Apr 27, 1970   p. 21

The return. Astronauts praying after splashdown.
Time   Apr 27, 1970   p. 14

Jim Lovell and Apollo 13.
Life   Apr 24, 1970   p. 28

Apollo 12 on the moon.
Life   Dec 12, 1969   p. 34

On the moon. Footprints and
photographs by Neil Armstrong and
Edwin Aldrin.
Life   Aug 8, 1969   p. 18

The moon voyagers and the earthly
beauty that beckons them back by Anne
Morrow Lindbergh.
Life   Feb 28, 1969   p. 14

Schirra and Apollo 7.
Life   Oct 25, 1968   p. 30

Apollo and the moon men.
Newsweek   Dec 21, 1964   p. 61

APOLLO TESTING ACCIDENT
The nation's goodby to astronauts.
Grissom. White. Chaffee.
Life   Feb 10, 1967   p. 20

The Apollo tragedy. Astronauts Grissom,
White and Chaffee.
Newsweek   Feb 6, 1967   p. 25

The three astronauts. Roger Chaffee. Ed
White. Gus Grissom.
Life   Feb 3, 1967   p. 18

Astronauts Grissom, White & Chaffee.
Time   Feb 3, 1967   p. 13

APOLLO-SOYUZ FLIGHT, 1975
The link-up.
Newsweek   Jul 21, 1975   p. 46

Space spectacular. Science, politics &
show biz.
Time   Jul 21, 1975   p. 53

APPLE COMPUTER INC.
Apple computer. New team, new
strategy. With sales stalled and market
share slipping, Apple is making big
changes: Lower prices, new models, and
ultimately a successor to the Macintosh.
Business Week   Oct 15, 1990   p. 86

Apple's comeback. With profits up, John
Scully aims to win more corporate
customers. The key: Versatile new
models of the easy-to-use Macintosh.
Business Week   Jan 19, 1987   p. 84

Apple's dynamic duo and their plan to
take on IBM in the office.
Business Week   Nov 26, 1984   p. 146

AQUINO, CORAZON
Woman of the Year. Philippine President
Corazon Aquino.
Time   Jan 5, 1987   p. 18

The charisma of Cory Aquino. And the
surprising power of Philippine women.
Ms.   Oct 1986   p. 45

Woman of the year. Can she clean up the
mess Marcos left behind? Should he be
allowed to keep his millions?
Newsweek   Mar 10, 1986   p. 18

Can she make it?
U.S. News   Mar 10, 1986   p. 30

Fighting on. Philippine opposition leader
Corazon Aquino.
Time   Feb 24, 1986   p. 28

ARAB COUNTRIES
Arabia's frankincense trail.
National Geographic Oct 1985   p. 474

ARAB-ISRAELI RELATIONS
See ISRAELI-ARAB RELATIONS

ARAB-ISRAELI WARS
See ISRAELI-ARAB WARS, 1967-

ARABS
Target Iraq. Is air power enough? Facing
the chemical-weapons threat.
U.S. News   Aug 20, 1990   p. 18

Arab world. Where troubles for U.S.
never end.
U.S. News   Feb 6, 1984   p. 24

The Arabs: New pride and power.
Newsweek   Feb 18, 1974   p. 40

The Arabs: Oil, power, violence. Libya's
strongman Gaddafi.
Time   Apr 2, 1973   p. 23

The Arabs in the aftermath. Jordan's King
Hussein.
Time   Jul 14, 1967   p. 22

"Keep your tents separate and bring your hearts together." - Arab proverb. Egypt's Nasser.
Time   Mar 29, 1963   p. 22

ARAFAT, YASIR

The Palestinians. Yasser Arafat.
Time   Nov 11, 1974   p. 27

ARANSAS NATIONAL WILDLIFE REFUGE, TEXAS

Where oil and wildlife mix.
National Geographic Feb 1981   p. 145

ARCHAEOLOGY

The search for man's past. Archaeologist Nelson Glueck.
Time   Dec 13, 1963   p. 50

ARCHITECTURE

Super scrapers. How tall will they get?
Discover   Sep 1988   p. 46

U.S. architects. Doing their own thing.
Time   Jan 8, 1979   p. 52

The shape of things to come.
Newsweek   Apr 19, 1971   p. 78

Building for the year 2000.
Time   Aug 2, 1968   p. 39

Architect Minoru Yamasaki.
Time   Jan 18, 1963   p. 54

ARCTIC EXPLORATION

North to the Pole. Six by dogsled.
National Geographic Sep 1986   p. 289

Exploring a 140-year-old ship under Arctic ice.
National Geographic Jul 1983   p. 104

ARCTIC PEOPLES

Peoples of the Arctic.
National Geographic Feb 1983   p. 144

ARCTIC REGIONS

At home with the arctic wolf.
National Geographic May 1987   p. 562

ARGENTINA - ECONOMIC CONDITIONS

Argentina's new hope. President Raúl Alfonsín restores democracy, but will he repay the country's debt?
Business Week   Feb 6, 1984   p. 60

ARGENTINA - POLITICS AND GOVERNMENT

Democracy's failure in Argentina. Arturo Frondizi.
Time   Mar 30, 1962   p. 27

ARMANI, GIORGIO

Giorgio's gorgeous style. Fashion designer Giorgio Armani.
Time   Apr 5, 1982   p. 60

ARMED FORCES - SOVIET UNION

The Soviet empire: Part 1. Soviet military power. How serious a threat?
U.S. News   Mar 13, 1989   p. 18

ARMED FORCES - UNITED STATES

The U.S. military reborn. After the triumph of Desert Storm.
U.S. News   Mar 18, 1991   p. 30

The military's new stars. Smarter and tougher.
U.S. News   Apr 18, 1988   p. 32

Can't anybody here run a war?
U.S. News   Feb 27, 1984   p. 35

Ready for action - or are they?
U.S. News   Feb 14, 1983   p. 23

Who'll fight for America? The manpower crisis.
Time   Jun 9, 1980   p. 24

How ready to fight?
U.S.News   May 12, 1980   p. 30

Our armed forces. Ready - or not?
U.S. News   Oct 10, 1977   p. 35

The military goes mod. Admiral Zumwalt.
Time   Dec 21, 1970   p. 16

The military under attack.
Time   Apr 11, 1969   p. 20

ARMED FORCES - UNITED STATES - DEMOBILIZATION

After the Cold War. Do we need an army? Of course. But its size and mission are about to change.
U.S. News   Dec 11, 1989   p. 22

ARMS CONTROL

The future of the bomb. Will Bush's plan work? Can we trust the Soviets? What is Saddam hiding?
Newsweek   Oct 7, 1991   p. 18

Defusing the nuclear threat. What Bush did NOT give up. What Gorbachev stands to gain.
Time   Oct 7, 1991   p. 18

The intermediate-range and shorter-range missiles treaty.
Congressional Digest Apr 1988   p. 97

Behind the smiles. Reagan and Gorbachev: A new era? Kissinger: The dangers ahead.
Newsweek   Dec 21, 1987   p. 14

The long road to Washington. Mikhail Gorbachev.
Time   Dec 14, 1987   p. 16

Are we safer now? After the summit: The U.S.-Soviet military balance. A memorandum for the President by Richard Perle.
U.S. News   Dec 14, 1987   p. 22

The ABM Treaty controversy.
Congressional Digest Nov 1987   p. 257

Finally, an arms deal that can work. But not without some risks.
Newsweek   Apr 27, 1987   p. 20

Back on track? Arms control. What Reagan and Gorbachev want from their mini-summit.
U.S. News   Oct 13, 1986   p. 14

Adhering to the SALT II agreements.
Congressional Digest Oct 1986   p. 226

Arms race. Any way to muzzle it?
U.S. News   Mar 18, 1985   p. 22

Arms control at the crossroads.
USA Today   Jan 1985   p. 10

Talking again. Arms control at the crossroads. The fallout on campaign '84.
Newsweek   Oct 1, 1984   p. 22

Nuclear war. Can we reduce the risk?
Newsweek   Dec 5, 1983   p. 44

Soviet walkout. A turning point for arms control. Behind the scenes: An exclusive report. Aftermath of "The day after."
Time   Dec 5, 1983   p. 12

Arms control. Making the wrong moves?
Time   Apr 18, 1983   p. 16

Arms control. Now or never?
Newsweek   Jan 31, 1983   p. 14

The bomb. The next twenty years.
Newsweek   Aug 9, 1965   p. 52

Threshing out the treaty. With Harriman: Behind the scenes in Moscow.
Life   Aug 9, 1963   p. 28

A truce in the Cold War?
Newsweek   Aug 5, 1963   p. 15

Beyond the nuclear agreement.
Time   Aug 2, 1963   p. 15

Bertrand Russell.
Newsweek   Aug 20, 1962   p. 55

Fallout from Russia. The argument over testing.
Time   Nov 10, 1961   p. 21

Khrushchev.
Time   Sep 8, 1961   p. 26

Arms control. Last chance? Sputtering fuse: Test-ban start again.
Newsweek   Mar 20, 1961   p. 35

ARMS DEALERS

Those shadowy arms traders. Adnan Khashoggi's high life and flashy deals.
Time   Jan 19, 1987   p. 26

Arming the world. What are the limits?
Time   Oct 26, 1981   p. 28

Guns for everyone. The world arms trade.
Time   Mar 3, 1975   p. 34

ARMS RACE

War and peace. Psychology at the summit.
Psychology Today   Jun 1988   p. 27

Arms race. Any way to muzzle it?
U.S. News   Mar 18, 1985   p. 22

Is U.S. really No. 2?
U.S. News   Jan 10, 1983   p. 16

The nuclear arms race. The MX muddle.
Reagan's new strategy. Limited war: How
it might happen.
Newsweek   Oct 5, 1981   p. 32

The new arms race. Defense Secretary
Schlesinger.
Time   Feb 11, 1974   p. 15

Missiles vs. missiles. $30 billion decision.
Newsweek   Mar 27, 1967   p. 44

The Pacific tests.
Newsweek   May 7, 1962   p. 26

U.S. nuclear testing. The shots heard
round the world.
Time   May 4, 1962   p. 18

Arms & diplomacy. Re-examing U.S.
military might.
Time   Apr 7, 1961   p. 20

How safe are we now? Berlin - The U.N. -
Ike's task.
Newsweek   May 30, 1960 p. 21

See Also NUCLEAR WEAPONS

ARMS SALES
Arms for sale. After the war, business as
usual?
Newsweek   Apr 8, 1991   p. 22

ARMSTRONG, LOUIS (INTERVIEW)
Louis Armstrong. 'I never did want to be
no Big Star.'
Life   Apr 15, 1966 p. 92

ARMSTRONG-JONES, ANTONY
Margaret and Tony at Windsor Lodge.
Life   Mar 14, 1960 p. 91

ARMY - UNITED STATES
After the Cold War. Do we need an
army? Of course. But its size and mission
are about to change.
U.S. News   Dec 11, 1989   p. 22

The new army. With new punch.
U.S. News   Sep 20, 1982   p. 59

Bill Mauldin's Willie and Joe look at the
new army.
Life   Feb 5, 1971   p. 20

The case of the Green Berets.
Newsweek   Aug 25, 1969   p. 26

"The battlefield is a lonely place."
General Johnson. Army Chief of Staff.
Time   Dec 10, 1965   p. 30

The growing U.S. Army in Germany -
around the world.
Time   Oct 13, 1961   p. 20

ARNAULT, BERNARD
Mr. Luxury. Dior, Vuitton, Hennessy,
Moët. Name a glamorous French product
and Bernard Arnault probably makes
it—or wants it. Can he manage it all?
Business Week   Jul 30, 1990   p. 48

ARSON
Firestarters. Why are middle-class
children setting their worlds on fire?
Psychology Today   Jan 1985   p. 22

ART
Art or obscenity?
Newsweek   Jul 2, 1990   p. 46

Art imitates life. The revival of realism.
Newsweek   Jun 7, 1982   p. 64

The flowering of U.S. folk art.
Life   Jun 1980   p. 112

Art in New York.
Newsweek   Jan 4, 1965   p. 54

ART, AMERICAN
C.M. Russell. Cowboy artist.
National Geographic Jan 1986   p. 60

ART AND CHILDREN
How kids draw. From scribbles to art.
Psychology Today   Aug 1986   p. 24

ART - MUSEUMS
New look for museums. The
Metropolitan's Thomas Hoving.
Newsweek   Apr 1, 1968   p. 54

ART - PRICES
Art and money. Who's winning and
who's losing as prices go through the roof.
Time   Nov 27, 1989   p. 60

Art for money's sake. On the block: The Warhol collection. The booming art market.
Newsweek   Apr 18, 1988   p. 60

Going. . .going. . .gone! The art and antique boom.
Time   Dec 31, 1979   p. 46

The art market.
Time   Nov 24, 1961   p. 52

ART, ROCOCO

Golden cherub in a spectacular German church.
Life   Mar 31, 1961   p. 48

ARTHRITIS

Arthritis. 37 million Americans, young and old, suffer from the disease. There's still no cure, but new treatments offer hope.
Newsweek   Mar 20, 1989   p. 64

ARTIFICIAL INSEMINATION

Whose baby am I? High-tech conceptions: Multiple parents, multiple problems.
Psychology Today   Dec 1984   p. 20

ARTIFICIAL INTELLIGENCE

Six-legged revolution. A tiny robot with the brains of an ant is rocking the world of artificial intelligence.
Discover   Mar 1991   p. 42

Artificial intelligence. It's here.
Business Week   Jul 9, 1984   p. 54

Machines that think. They're brewing a revolution.
U.S. News   Dec 5, 1983   p. 59

User friendly. Objects, foods and tools that make living a whole lot easier.
Psychology Today   Dec 1983   p. 23

Getting computers to understand English. Yale's Roger Schank enters the marketplace.
Psychology Today   Apr 1983   p. 28

Artificial intelligence. The second computer age begins.
Business Week   Mar 8, 1982   p. 66

ARTS

Young talent on the rise.
U.S. News   Aug 20, 1979   p. 39

The culture boom.
U.S. News   Aug 8, 1977   p. 50

Young genius on the rise in the U.S.
U.S. News   May 19, 1975   p. 56

The arts in America.
Newsweek   Dec 24, 1973   p. 34

ARTS - FEDERAL AID

Federal funding of the arts.
Congressional Digest Jan 1991   p. 2

ASHE, ARTHUR

The icy elegance of Arthur Ashe. He topped the tennis world.
Life   Sep 20, 1968   p. 30

ASIA AND THE UNITED STATES

Pacific Rim. America's new frontier.
U.S. News   Aug 20, 1984   p. 45

Where U.S. stands after Vietnam debacle.
U.S. News   Apr 14, 1975   p. 27

President Johnson.
Time   Nov 4, 1966   p. 25

The U.S. in Asia.
Newsweek   Oct 31, 1966   p. 30

Far East fiasco. China's Mao: Will he rule the Pacific?
Newsweek   Jun 27, 1960   p. 23

ASIAN AMERICANS

Those Asian-American whiz kids.
Time   Aug 31, 1987   p. 42

Asian-Americans. Are they making the grade?
U.S. News   Apr 2, 1984   p. 41

ASPIRIN

Miracle drug. Aspirin.
Business Week   Aug 29, 1988   p. 56

What you should know about heart attacks. The aspirin breakthrough. The latest on cholesterol, diet and exercise.
Newsweek   Feb 8, 1988   p. 50

ASSAD, HAFEZ

Master of terror. Syria's President Assad.
U.S. News   Nov 10, 1986   p. 26

ASSASSINATION ATTEMPTS

The plot to kill the Pope. The Bulgarian connection. Was the KGB behind it? [Pope John Paul II]
Newsweek   Jan 3, 1983   p. 22

Again. [Pope John Paul II]
Newsweek   May 25, 1981 p. 22

Terrorist's target. "Why did they do it?" - John Paul II
Time   May 25, 1981 p. 10

A crime that shocked the world. [Pope John Paul II]
U.S. News   May 25, 1981 p. 20

Reagan's close call. The shooting and the surgery. Case history of a gunman. Who's in control. Can the risk be cut?
Newsweek   Apr 13, 1981 p. 25

Moment of madness. What happened - and why. Can it never be stopped? [Ronald Reagan]
Time   Apr 13, 1981 p. 18

What impact? [Ronald Reagan]
U.S. News   Apr 13, 1981 p. 22

"It didn't go off." 'Squeaky' Fromme after capture. [Gerald Ford]
Newsweek   Sep 15, 1975 p. 16

The girl who almost killed Ford. [Gerald Ford]
Time   Sep 15, 1975 p. 8

The Wallace shooting. Cornelia Wallace embraces her husband. [George Wallace]
Life   May 26, 1972 p. 4

Protecting the President.
Time   Oct 6, 1975 p. 6

ASSASSINATIONS

J.F.K.'s assassination: Who was the real target. Twenty-five years later, a new book argues Oswald was actually out to get John Connally.
Time   Nov 28, 1988 p. 30

India's crisis. After Indira.
Newsweek   Nov 12, 1984 p. 42

"If I die today, every drop of my blood will invigorate the nations." Indira Gandhi 1917 - 1984.
Time   Nov 12, 1984 p. 42

'Act of infamy.' The Sadat assassination.
Newsweek   Oct 19, 1981 p. 25

Mideast turmoil. Anwar Sadat - 1918-1981.
Time   Oct 19, 1981 p. 12

Now the shock waves. [Ansar Sadat]
U.S News   Oct 19, 1981 p. 24

The assassins. [Lee Harvey Oswald and James Earl Ray]
Newsweek   Mar 24, 1969 p. 28

Robert F. Kennedy. 1925-1968.
Newsweek   Jun 17, 1968 p. 20

Senator Robert F. Kennedy.
Life   Jun 14, 1968 p. 32

Robert Kennedy.
Time   Jun 14, 1968 p. 15

America's farewell in anger and grief. [Martin Luther King, Jr.]
Life   Apr 19, 1968 p. 28

Martin Luther King, Jr., 1929-1968.
Newsweek   Apr 15, 1968 p. 26

Martin Luther King. 1929 - 1968. Week of shock.
Life   Apr 12, 1968 p. 74

A matter of reasonable doubt. Did Oswald act alone? Amid controversy over the Warren Report Governor Connally examines for LIFE the Kennedy assassination film frame by frame.
Life   Nov 25, 1966 p. 38

Death of Malcolm X and the resulting vengeful gang war.
Life   Mar 5, 1965 p. 26

The assassination. The Warren Commission report. [John F. Kennedy]
Newsweek   Oct 5, 1964 p. 32

The Warren report. How the commission pieced together the evidence. Told by one of its members.
Life   Oct 2, 1964 p. 40

The Warren Commission: No conspiracy, domestic or foreign. Lee Harvey Oswald.
Time   Oct 2, 1964   p. 45

Lee Oswald with the weapons he used to kill President Kennedy and Officer Tippit.
Life   Feb 21, 1964   p. 68

The Warren Commission. Probing Kennedy's death.
Time   Feb 14, 1964   p. 16

John Fitzgerald Kennedy. 1917 - 1963.
Newsweek   Dec 2, 1963   p. 20

President John F. Kennedy. 1917-1963.
Life   Nov 29, 1963   p. 22

President Johnson.
Time   Nov 29, 1963   p. 21

ASSEMBLY LINE

Bored on the job. Industry contends with apathy and anger on the assembly line.
Life   Sep 1, 1972   p. 30

ASTHMA

Asthma: How serious is it and who is at risk?
USA Today   Feb 1990   p. 1

ASTROLOGY

Astrology in the White House. Excerpts from Don Regan's explosive memoirs.
Time   May 16, 1988   p. 24

Astrology and the new cult of the occult.
Time   Mar 21, 1969   p. 69

ASTRONAUTS

New Apollo team and its skipper Wally Schirra.
Life   May 19, 1967   p. 32

The nation's goodby to astronauts. Grissom. White. Chaffee.
Life   Feb 10, 1967   p. 20

The Apollo tragedy. Astronauts Grissom, White and Chaffee.
Newsweek   Feb 6, 1967   p. 25

The three astronauts. Roger Chaffee. Ed White. Gus Grissom.
Life   Feb 3, 1967   p. 18

Astronauts Grissom, White & Chaffee.
Time   Feb 3, 1967   p. 13

The astronauts' Gemini's journey by Gus Grisson and John Young.
Life   Apr 2, 1965   p. 34

The new astronauts. They go head-over-heels into training.
Life   Sep 27, 1963   p. 30

Dawn of the spaceman. The most fascinating story: A special space and atom section.
Newsweek   Jul 11, 1960   p. 55

ASTRONOMY

Heavens! Black holes, quasars, starquakes: Astronomers launch a new age of discovery.
Newsweek   Jun 3, 1991   p. 46

Star crossed. The Hubble telescope. NASA's $1.5 billion blunder.
Newsweek   Jul 9, 1990   p. 48

When the universe was new. A journey to the beginning of time. The Hubble space telescope: Launching astronomy's new golden age.
U.S. News   Mar 26, 1990   p. 52

When galaxies collide. The splendid violence of creation.
Discover   Feb 1990   p. 50

The case of the cosmic rays. No one knows just where they come from or even what they are.
Discover   Sep 1989   p. 52

Chasing the Big Bang. The orbiting space telescope will soon give us our first good look at cosmic creation.
Discover   Jul 1989   p. 68

Unraveling the universe. If you like black holes, you'll love cosmic strings.
Discover   Apr 1988   p. 60

Bang! A star explodes, providing new clues to the nature of the universe.
Time   Mar 24, 1987   p. 60

What can be seen of the universe is like foam on the surface of the ocean, snow on mountaintops. Beyond lies the shadow universe–invisible, unknown, unimaginably immense.
Discover   May 1985   p. 12

Mission for the U-2. Hunting comet dust.
Discover　　　　　Oct 1983　　　p. 74

Eclipse! Unraveling the sun's mysteries.
Discover　　　　　Aug 1983　　　p. 12

A telescope in space. New eye on the
universe.
Discover　　　　　Apr 1983　　　p. 29

Black holes. Violence at the edge of the
universe.
Discover　　　　　Dec 1982　　　p. 22

Is anyone out there?
Discover　　　　　Mar 1982　　　p. 20

The comet is coming.
Discover　　　　　Dec 1981　　　p. 20

Probing the heavens. Any real value?
U.S. News　　　　Nov 16, 1981 p. 76

Stars. Where life begins.
Time　　　　　　Dec 27, 1976 p. 29

Exploring the edge of the universe.
Astronomer Maarten Schmidt.
Time　　　　　　Mar 11, 1966 p. 80

Life and death of the universe.
Astrophysicist Fred Hoyle.
Newsweek　　　　May 25, 1964 p. 63

AT&T
　　See AMERICAN TELEPHONE &
　　TELEGRAPH

ATHLETES
　　Faster. Farther. Higher. What science
　　reveals about the body's ultimate limits.
　　U.S. News　　　　Sep 19, 1988 p. 50

　　Values & violence in sports. The morality
　　of bone crushing.
　　Psychology Today　Oct 1985　　　p. 22

　　The games of summer. Playing to win in
　　politics and sports.
　　Psychology Today　Jul 1984　　　p. 18

ATKINSON, RICK
　　Exclusive book excerpt. West Point Story.
　　The class of '66, from Vietnam to the New
　　Army.
　　U.S. News　　　　Oct 9, 1989　　p. 44

ATLANTIC CITY (NEW JERSEY)
　　Boardwalk of broken dreams.
　　Time　　　　　　Sep 25, 1989 p. 64

ATLANTIC COAST
　　America's beleaguered coast.
　　Life　　　　　　Jul 1980　　　p. 70

ATM
　　See AUTOMATED TELLER MACHINES

ATOMIC BOMBS
　　See NUCLEAR WEAPONS

ATTICA STATE PRISON - RIOT, 1971
　　The Attica tragedy.
　　Newsweek　　　　Sep 27, 1971 p. 22

　　The bitter lessons of Attica.
　　Time　　　　　　Sep 27, 1971 p. 18

ATTORNEYS
　　See LAWYERS

AUDUBON, JOHN JAMES
　　John James Audubon and the birds of
　　North America.
　　USA Today　　　Sep 1985　　　p. 26

AUSTIN (TEXAS)
　　Austin. Deep in the heart of Texans.
　　National Geographic Jun 1990　　　p. 50

AUSTRALIA
　　Northwest Australia. The land & the sea.
　　National Geographic Jan 1991　　　p. 2

　　Australia. A bicentennial down under.
　　National Geographic Feb 1988　　　p. 155

　　The land where the Murray flows.
　　National Geographic Aug 1985　　　p. 252

　　Australia on the march.
　　Newsweek　　　　Feb 21, 1966 p. 42

　　Australia. Things are looking up down
　　under. Prime Minister Menzies.
　　Time　　　　　　Apr 4, 1960　　p. 20

AUSTRALIAN ABORIGINES
　　Australia. A bicentennial down under.
　　National Geographic Feb 1988　　　p. 155

AUTOMATED TELLER MACHINES

Electronic banking.
Business Week   Jan 18, 1982   p. 70

AUTOMATION

High tech to the rescue. Can automation
save American industry?
Business Week   Jun 16, 1986   p. 100

The speedup in automation. Spreading
through the factory. Changing 45 million
jobs.
Business Week   Aug 3, 1981   p. 58

The challenge of automation.
Newsweek   Jan 25, 1965   p. 73

AUTOMOBILE DEALERS

The super-dealers. They're changing the
way auto makers sell cars—and the way
you buy them.
Business Week   Jun 2, 1986   p. 60

AUTOMOBILE INDUSTRY

Honda. Is it an American car? Most
Hondas sold in America are made in
America. But where do their parts really
come from?
Business Week   Nov 18, 1991   p. 104

The greening of Detroit. With
environmentalists and regulators on their
tails, auto makers are scrambling to
develop cleaner machines.
Business Week   Apr 8, 1991   p. 54

Auto quality. Just as Detroit is catching
up, the very concept of quality is
changing. It's not just fewer defects
anymore.
Business Week   Oct 22, 1990   p. 84

Shaking up Detroit. How Japanese auto
plants in the U.S. are changing the Big
Three.
Business Week   Aug 14, 1989   p. 74

Stalled! Can Detroit rev up sales? The Big
Three are trying to create new marketing
strategies to reverse a slump.
Business Week   Jun 12, 1989   p. 78

The auto glut. Too much production
capacity around the world will mean
more plant closings—and perhaps even a
price war in the U.S.
Business Week   Mar 7, 1988   p. 54

Chrysler's next act. Sure, the company's
big comeback turned Lee Iacocca into a
hero. But now Chrysler needs a new
strategy—and Iacocca has plenty of ideas.
Business Week   Nov 3, 1986   p. 66

Toyota's fast lane. Japan's biggest
company is out to overtake GM.
Business Week   Nov 4, 1985   p. 42

Can Detroit cope? With imports about to
soar, the U.S. auto industry will shrink.
But there's some good news, too.
Business Week   Apr 22, 1985   p. 78

Showdown in Detroit. Auto talks will
shape the industry—and the UAW.
Business Week   Sep 10, 1984   p. 102

The vanishing all-American small car.
Costs push Detroit into foreign
partnerships.
Business Week   Mar 12, 1984   p. 88

Detroit's merry-go-round. U.S. auto
makers still haven't shown they can
compete.
Business Week   Sep 12, 1983   p. 72

Are U.S. cars really getting better?
U.S. News   Aug 29, 1983   p. 56

Proposed automobile "domestic content"
legislation.
Congressional Digest Feb 1983   p. 34

U.S. auto makers reshape for world
competition.
Business Week   Jun 21, 1982   p. 82

Can Detroit ever come back?
U.S. News   Mar 8, 1982   p. 45

Why Detroit still can't get going.
Business Week   Nov 9, 1981   p. 106

Mitsubishi. A Japanese giant's plans for
growth in the U.S.
Business Week   Jul 20, 1981   p. 128

Detroit thinks small. Will it pay off?
U.S.News   Sep 29, 1980   p. 56

Detroit's uphill battle. GM's Murphy.
Ford's Caldwell. Chrysler's Iacocca.
Time   Sep 8, 1980   p. 46

Detroit fights back.
U.S.News   Jun 9, 1980   p. 32

AUTOMOBILES, EXPERIMENTAL

The greening of Detroit. With
environmentalists and regulators on their
tails, auto makers are scrambling to
develop cleaner machines.
Business Week   Apr 8, 1991   p. 54

AVEDON, RICHARD

The Avedon look.
Newsweek   Oct 16, 1978   p. 58

AWACS

See AIRBORNE WARNING AND
CONTROL SYSTEM

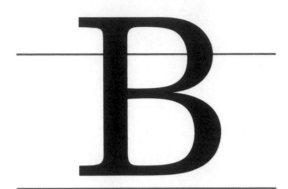

BABIES

See INFANTS

BABY BOOM GENERATION

Those aging baby boomers...and how you sell to them.
Business Week   May 20, 1991   p. 106

The baby boomers turn 40.
Time   May 19, 1986   p. 22

The year of the Yuppie.
Newsweek   Dec 31, 1984   p. 14

Here come the baby-boomers.
U.S. News   Nov 5, 1984   p. 68

Baby boomers push for power.
Business Week   Jul 2, 1984   p. 52

BABY M CASE

Mothers for hire. The battle for Baby M. Surrogate mother Mary Beth Whitehead.
Newsweek   Jan 19, 1987   p. 44

BACALL, LAUREN

Telling all. Memoirs of the stars. Lauren Bacall.
Newsweek   Jan 15, 1979   p. 50

Bacall hits Broadway with song and dance.
Life   Apr 3, 1970   p. 54

BACH, JOHANN SEBASTIAN

Almighty Bach. The world celebrates a composer for all seasons.
Newsweek   Dec 24, 1984   p. 54

Music from the fifth evangelist. Johann Sebastian Bach.
Time   Dec 27, 1968   p. 35

BACH, RICHARD

Getting away from it all with Jonathan Livingston Seagull.
Time   Nov 13, 1972   p. 60

BACHARACH, BURT

The music man 1970. Burt Bacharach.
Newsweek   Jun 22, 1970   p. 50

BACKACHES

That aching back. Latest word on the oldest agony.
Time   Jul 14, 1980   p. 30

BAEZ, JOAN

Folk singer Joan Baez.
Time   Nov 23, 1962   p. 54

BAGWELL, PAUL

Michigan candidate Paul Bagwell.
Time   Oct 24, 1960   p. 29

BAHAMAS

The Bahamas. Boom times and buccaneering.
National Geographic Sep 1982   p. 364

BAILEY, F. LEE

Patty in court. Defense attorney F. Lee Bailey.
Time   Feb 16, 1976   p. 46

The defender. Defense attorney F. Lee Bailey.
Newsweek   Apr 17, 1967   p. 35

BAILEY, PEARL

Well, hello Pearl! As the latest Dolly, Pearl Bailey leads a smash Broadway love-in.
Life   Dec 8, 1967   p. 128

BAKER, ANITA

Anita Baker does it her way.
Ms.   Jun 1989   p. 42

BAKER, BOBBY

"A gentleman with innumerable friendships and connections." Bobby Baker.
Time   Mar 6, 1964   p. 17

Capital buzzes over stories of misconduct in high places. The Bobby Baker bombshell.
Life   Nov 8, 1963   p. 32

BAKER, CARROLL

Carroll Baker: Baby doll grows up.
Life   Nov 28, 1960   p. 41

BAKER, JAMES

The velvet hammer. Secretary of State James Baker is a gentleman who hates to lose.
Time   Feb 13, 1989   p. 26

Jim Baker's treasury. Tax reform gets a new champion.
Business Week   May 13, 1985   p. 110

BAKER, RUSSELL

The good humor man. Columnist Russell Baker.
Time   Jun 4, 1979   p. 48

BAKKE, ALLAN, CASE

After Bakke. No quotas - but race can count.
Newsweek   Jul 10, 1978   p. 19

What Bakke means. Quotas: No. Race: Yes.
Time   Jul 10, 1978   p. 8

Impact of Bakke decision. Allan Bakke and family.
U.S. News   Jul 10, 1978   p. 14

The furor over 'reverse discrimination.'
Newsweek   Sep 26, 1977   p. 26

BAKKER, JIM

God & money. Greed, secrecy and scandal: An inside look at Jim and Tammy Bakker's bankrupt empire.
Time   Aug 3, 1987   p. 48

Heaven can wait while the holy war heats up.
Newsweek   Jun 8, 1987   p. 58

BALANCE OF TRADE

America's hidden problem. The big trade deficit is slashing growth and exporting jobs. Does anyone care?
Business Week   Aug 29, 1983   p. 66

See INTERNATIONAL TRADE

BALANCED BUDGET - CONSTITUTIONAL AMENDMENT

Balanced budget constitutional amendment.
Congressional Digest Nov 1989   p. 257

BALANCHINE, GEORGE

George Balanchine: 'Ballet is woman...'
Newsweek   May 4, 1964   p. 51

BALDRIGE, LETITIA

New American manners. Social arbiter Letitia Baldrige.
Time   Nov 27, 1978   p. 64

BALDWIN, JAMES

Birmingham and beyond: The Negro's push for equality.
Time   May 17, 1963   p. 23

BALEWA, ABUBAKAR TAFAWA

Nigeria's Prime Minister Balewa.
Time   Dec 5, 1960   p. 20

BALIN, INA

Ina Balin: An early look at a star-to-be.
Life   Jul 18, 1960   p. 107

BALL, LUCILLE

Lucy is back! A favorite warms up for her big TV return.
Life   Jan 5, 1962   p. 74

BALLARD, ROBERT

The man who found the *Titanic*.
Discover   Jan 1987   p. 50

BALLET

U.S. ballet soars. Gelsey Kirkland.
Time   May 1, 1978   p. 82

Sugar plum Christmas. The Nutcracker.
Newsweek   Dec 27, 1976   p. 40

Ballet at its best. Baryshnikov and Kirkland.
Newsweek   May 19, 1975   p. 62

Two arts, two visions: The grace of ballet.
The tumult of Hendrix.
Life   Oct 3, 1969   p. 42

Joffrey Ballet's "Astarte."
Time   Mar 15, 1968 p. 44

BALLOON ASCENSIONS
Flight of the Eagle.
Newsweek   Aug 28, 1978 p. 52

BALTIC SEA REGION
The Baltic.
National Geographic May 1989   p. 602

BAND (MUSICAL GROUP)
The new sound of country rock. The
Band.
Time   Jan 12, 1970 p. 42

BANGLADESH
India-Pakistan War. Who's to blame?
Newsweek   Dec 20, 1971 p. 34

The bloody birth of Bangladesh.
Time   Dec 20, 1971 p. 20

The battle for Bengal. India attacks.
Newsweek   Dec 6, 1971   p. 30

Conflict in Asia: India v. Pakistan.
Time   Dec 6, 1971   p. 28

Bengal: The murder of a people.
Newsweek   Aug 2, 1971   p. 26

Pakistan's agony.
Time   Aug 2, 1971   p. 24

BANK OF CREDIT AND COMMERCE INTERNATIONAL
The world's sleaziest bank. How B.C.C.I.
became a one-stop shopping center for
criminals and spies — and how the U.S. is
trying to cover up its involvement.
Time   Jul 29, 1991   p. 42

BANKAMERICA
BankAmerica and Citicorp. The new
banking forces new strategies.
Business Week   Jul 13, 1981   p. 56

BANKS AND BANKING
The future of banking. Can banks hold off
their challengers? Consolidation: Will it
work? The 100 leading banks in the U.S.
Business Week   Apr 22, 1991 p. 72

Can your bank stay afloat? How the
real-estate crash threatens financial
institutions. The best ways to buy and sell
a house in a down market.
U.S. News   Nov 12, 1990 p. 62

Banks. Is big trouble brewing?
Commercial banks aren't about to go the
way of the S&Ls. But many are plagued
by shaky loans and weak profits. That's
bad news for borrowers, financial markets,
and the economy.
Business Week   Jul 16, 1990   p. 146

Can you bank on your banker? The latest
S & L crisis. How feds back up banks.
Banking's dramatic changes.
U.S. News   May 27, 1985 p. 58

America's banks. Awash in troubles.
Time   Dec 3, 1984   p. 48

What's really behind the banking turmoil.
Business Week   Oct 29, 1984 p. 100

How safe is your money?
U.S. News   Jul 9, 1984   p. 51

Bankers as brokers. What's behind the
rush into a riskier business.
Business Week   Apr 11, 1983 p. 70

Bankers. Everybody's favorite target.
U.S. News   Apr 11, 1983 p. 27

Banking's squeeze. High-interest-rate
gridlock. The search for special niches.
Bank scoreboard: The top 200 banks.
Business Week   Apr 12, 1982 p. 67

Electronic banking.
Business Week   Jan 18, 1982 p. 70

BankAmerica and Citicorp. The new
banking forces new strategies.
Business Week   Jul 13, 1981   p. 56

Wholesale banking. The new hard sell.
Business Week   Apr 13, 1981 p. 82

What to do with $14 billion. Bank of
America's Rudolph A. Peterson.
Newsweek   Nov 4, 1963   p. 83

BANKS AND BANKING, INTERNATIONAL
Worry at the world's banks. Problem
loans. Growth instead of judgment.
OPEC's surpluses disappear.
Business Week   Sep 6, 1982   p. 80

BAY OF PIGS INVASION, 1961

Raw untold truth by men who fought Bay of Pigs. Heartbreaking price they paid for U.S. miscalculations.
Life   May 10, 1963   p. 20

Struggle for Cuba.
Newsweek   May 1, 1961   p. 23

The Cuban disaster.
Time   Apr 28, 1961   p. 19

BEATLES (MUSICAL GROUP)

The Beatles. 20 years ago, they invaded America. Did we love 'em? Yeah, yeah, yeah!
Life   Feb 1984   p. 58

The days in the lives of the Beatles. They call it their authentic biography.
Life   Sep 13, 1968   p. 86

The Beatles / Their new incarnation.
Time   Sep 22, 1967   p. 60

The Beatles. They're here again and what a ruckus!
Life   Aug 28, 1964   p. 58

Bugs about Beatles.
Newsweek   Feb 24, 1964   p. 54

BEATTY, WARREN

Warren & Dustin. A new song and dance act hits the road.
Life   May 1987   p. 63

Mister Hollywood. Warren Beatty.
Time   Jul 3, 1978   p. 70

BEES

Killer bees. Stinging sensation on the Texas border.
USA Today   Jun 1991   p. 1

BEGGARS AND BEGGING

To give or not to give? Begging in America.
Time   Sep 5, 1988   p. 68

BEGIN, MENACHEM

Roadblock to peace? Israel's Menachem Begin.
Newsweek   Sep 14, 1981   p. 36

Israel: Day of the hawks. Menahem Begin.
Newsweek   May 30, 1977   p. 32

Israel. Trouble in the promised land. Menachem Begin.
Time   May 30, 1977   p. 22

BEGIN, MENACHEM (INTERVIEW)

Carter's breakthrough.
Time   Oct 2, 1978   p. 8

BEHAVIOR (PSYCHOLOGY)

The science of power.
Omni   Jul 1985   p. 68

BEIRUT

See LEBANON

BEIRUT AIRPLANE HIJACKING, 1985

Striking back. What Reagan might do.
Newsweek   Jul 8, 1985   p. 16

What price for freedom? Dealing for American lives.
U.S. News   Jul 8, 1985   p. 20

Reagan's hostage crisis. Revenge or restraint?
U.S. News   Jul 1, 1985   p. 18

Terror on flight 847.
Newsweek   Jun 24, 1985   p. 18

Hijack terror.
Time   Jun 24, 1985   p. 18

Mideast terror strikes Americans.
U.S. News   Jun 24, 1985   p. 9

BELAUNDE, FERANDO

A Latin American architect of hope. Peru's President Belaúnde.
Time   Mar 12, 1965   p. 32

BELLOW, SAUL

Bellow's gift.
Newsweek   Sep 1, 1975   p. 32

BELMONDO, JEAN-PAUL

Belmondo. The new-style movie hero sexy, crazy and cool.
Life   Nov 11, 1966   p. 111

BELUSHI, JOHN

College humor comes back. John Belushi.
Newsweek   Oct 23, 1978   p. 88

BENCH, JOHNNY

Baseball's best catcher. Cincinnati's
Johnny Bench.
Time   Jul 10, 1972   p. 54

BENEDICT, GAMBLE

The elopers: Gamble and Andrei.
Life   Apr 18, 1960   p. 19

BENEFITS

See EMPLOYEE BENEFITS

BENKHEDDA, BENYOUSSEF

Algeria: Birth of a nation. Premier
Benkhedda.
Time   Mar 16, 1962   p. 22

BENNETT, MICHAEL

Broadway's new kick. Donna McKechnie
in "A Chorus Line."
Newsweek   Dec 1, 1975   p. 66

BENNETT, WILLIAM

The drug warrior. He's ambitious,
abrasive and tough. Can he make a
difference?
Newsweek   Apr 10, 1989   p. 20

BENTON, THOMAS HART

Thomas Hart Benton: Bad boy of the art
world.
USA Today   Nov 1989   p. 32

BENTSEN, LLOYD

The odd couple. Gary Wills: Searching
for Dukakis' soul.
Time   Jul 25, 1988   p. 16

BERENSON, MARISA

Queen of 'The Scene.' Marisa Berenson.
Newsweek   Aug 27, 1973   p. 53

BERG, PAUL

Scientist of the year. Biochemist Paul
Berg.
Discover   Jan 1981   p. 72

BERGEN, CANDICE

Activist actress Candice Bergen.
Life   Jul 24, 1970   p. 40

BERGMAN, INGMAR

Movie director Ingmar Bergman.
Time   Mar 14, 1960   p. 60

BERGMAN, INGRID

Ingrid Bergman ends her exile.
Life   Oct 13, 1967   p. 63

BERKOWITZ, DAVID

The sick world of Son of Sam.
Newsweek   Aug 22, 1977   p. 16

BERLIN CRISIS, 1961

Our report from Berlin. Torn families.
Escapes to freedom. Heartbreak at the
barbed wire.
Life   Aug 25, 1961   p. 28

East Germany's Ulbricht.
Time   Aug 25, 1961   p. 20

'Any dangerous spot is tenable if brave
men will make it so.'
Life   Aug 4, 1961   p. 34

BERLIN (EAST GERMANY)

Berlin thriller: Escape by tunnel.
Life   Oct 16, 1964   p. 57

BERLIN (GERMANY)

Two Berlins.
National Geographic Jan 1982 p. 2

BERLIN WALL

The wall. 1961-1989.
Newsweek   Nov 20, 1989   p. 24

Freedom!
Time   Nov 20, 1989   p. 24

Berlin thriller: Escape by tunnel.
Life   Oct 16, 1964   p. 57

The wall.
Time   Aug 31, 1962   p. 20

From Gettysburg. Ike's stand on Berlin.
Life   Sep 8, 1961   p. 42

Barbed wire and bayonets. Berlin report.
Newsweek   Aug 28, 1961   p. 15

East Germany's Ulbricht.
Time   Aug 25, 1961   p. 20

"We intend to have a wider choice than
humiliation or all-out nuclear action" -
John F. Kennedy.
Newsweek   Aug 7, 1961   p. 13

Berlin: Kennedy acts.
Newsweek   Jul 31, 1961   p. 13

BERNSTEIN, LEONARD

New showcase for the arts. Lincoln
Center. Leonard Bernstein.
Newsweek   Sep 24, 1962   p. 53

BERRIGAN, DANIEL

Rebel priests: The curious case of the
Berrigans.
Time   Jan 25, 1971   p. 12

BERRIGAN, PHILIP

Rebel priests: The curious case of the
Berrigans.
Time   Jan 25, 1971   p. 12

BERTOLUCCI, BERNARDO

The hottest movie. Director Bernardo
Bertolucci.
Newsweek   Feb 12, 1973   p. 54

BETANCOURT, ROMULO

Latin America. The real builders.
Venezuela's President Betancourt.
Time   Feb 8, 1960   p. 34

BETTING

See GAMBLING

**BHOPAL POISONOUS GAS DISASTER,
    INDIA, 1984**

Union Carbide fights for its life.
Business Week   Dec 24, 1984   p. 52

Can it happen here? Poison gas victims in
India.
Newsweek   Dec 17, 1984   p. 26

India's disaster. The night of death. A
global worry.
Time   Dec 17, 1984   p. 20

BIAFRA

See NIGERIA

BIBLE

The Bible's last secrets. Deciphering the
mysteries of the Dead Sea Scrolls.
U.S. News   Oct 7, 1991   p. 64

Who wrote the Bible? The surprising new
theories.
U.S. News   Dec 10, 1990   p. 61

The Bible in America. How one book
unites us, divides us, and still defines us.
Newsweek   Dec 27, 1982   p. 44

How true is the Bible?
Time   Dec 30, 1974   p. 34

The Bible.
Life   Dec 25, 1964   p. 6

**BICENTENNIAL CELEBRATION - UNITED
    STATES**

It was quite a birthday party.
U.S. News   Jul 12, 1976   p. 12

Birthday issues. The promised land.
America's new immigrants. The big 200th
bash.
Time   Jul 5, 1976   p. 8

Our America. A self-portrait at 200.
Newsweek   Jul 4, 1976   p. 12

Here comes '76! America's 200 years in
pictures.
U.S. News   Jan 12, 1976   p. 31

Bicentennial summer.
Newsweek   Jul 14, 1975   p. 28

BING, RUDOLF

Grander days for grand opera. Rudolf
Bing.
Time   Sep 23, 1966   p. 46

The new Met. Rudolf Bing.
Newsweek   Sep 19, 1966   p. 70

BINGHAM, SALLIE

The woman who overturned an empire.
Sallie Bingham.
Ms.   Jun 1986   p. 44

BIOFEEDBACK

Wonder cures? New respect for fringe
medicine. Acupuncture. Hypnosis.
Biofeedback.
U.S. News   Sep 23, 1991   p. 68

BIOLOGICAL RHYTHMS

Body time: Living clocks that make us
tick.
Omni   Sep 1984   p. 48

BIOTECHNOLOGY

Biotech superstar. Wall Street loves
Genentech. The reason: It's on the way to
becoming a major pharmaceutical
company.
Business Week   Apr 14, 1986 p. 68

Biotech comes of age.
Business Week   Jan 23, 1984 p. 84

Spawning new forms of life. Now the
payoff starts.
U.S. News   Mar 28, 1983 p. 48

BIRD, LARRY

Simply the best. Boston's Larry Bird.
Edmonton's Wayne Gretzky.
Time   Mar 18, 1985 p. 50

BIRDS

John James Audubon and the birds of
North America.
USA Today   Sep 1985 p. 26

BIRMINGHAM (ALABAMA)

Bombing in Birmingham.
Newsweek   Sep 30, 1963 p. 20

BIRTH

Back to birth. 6 ways to return to the
womb.
Omni   Aug 1989 p. 34

BIRTH CONTROL

Kids and contraceptives. A moral
dilemma: How to prevent teen pregnancy
- and AIDS.
Newsweek   Feb 16, 1987 p. 54

The new pill: Should you take it?
Ms.   Oct 1985 p. 35

The moment of conception. When sperm
meets egg.
Discover   Oct 1982 p. 32

Crusade against too many people. A
thoughtful new student cause.
Life   Apr 17, 1970 p. 32

The pill.
Time   Apr 7, 1967 p. 78

BIRTH CONTROL - CATHOLIC CHURCH

Rebellion in the Catholic Church.
Time   Nov 22, 1968 p. 42

Birth control. The pill and the church.
Newsweek   Jul 6, 1964 p. 51

BIRTH DEFECTS

Birth defects. Every parent's nightmare.
The father remembers the color of his
son's face when he was born, the color of
dusk. His little chest was quivering with
effort to draw air that would not come.
Newsweek   Mar 16, 1987 p. 56

BIRTH RATE

Are we having enough babies? A
controversial new book, *The Birth Dearth*,
by Ben Wattenberg argues that Americans
must have more children - or face
dangerous consequences.
U.S. News   Jun 22, 1987 p. 56

BISSET, JACQUELINE

A beauty named Bisset.
Newsweek   Jul 11, 1977 p. 68

BLACK ACTORS AND ACTRESSES

New star Leslie Uggams: The Negro in
show business.
Newsweek   Jul 17, 1967 p. 63

BLACK ATHLETES

The angry Black athlete.
Newsweek   Jul 15, 1968 p. 56

BLACK ENTERTAINERS

Greatest Negro stars team up.
Life   Feb 4, 1966 p. 70

BLACK HOLES

Black holes. Violence at the edge of the
universe.
Discover   Dec 1982 p. 22

BLACK, HUGO

That activist Supreme Court. Justice
Black.
Time   Oct 9, 1964 p. 48

BLACK MEN

Brothers. A vivid portrait of Black men in
America.
Newsweek   Mar 23, 1987 p. 54

BLACK PANTHERS

The Panthers and the law.
Newsweek   Feb 23, 1970 p. 26

"We stand for human liberty." "We must be prepared to suffer...even die." "The Federal government encourages these agitators."
Newsweek   Jun 5, 1961   p. 18

See Also CIVIL RIGHTS MOVEMENT

BLACKS - ECONOMIC CONDITIONS
The black middle class. Plenty of gains, but progress is slowing.
Business Week   Mar 14, 1988   p. 62

Middle-class Blacks. Making it in America.
Time   Jun 17, 1974   p. 19

The cry that will be heard. The Negro and the cities.
Life   Mar 8, 1968   p. 48

The Negro in America. What must be done.
Newsweek   Nov 20, 1967   p. 32

The Black mood. A Newsweek survey.
Newsweek   Aug 21, 1967   p. 18

"You've got to give us some victories." Urban League's Whitney Young.
Time   Aug 11, 1967   p. 12

Battlefield, U.S.A.
Newsweek   Aug 7, 1967   p. 18

Twelfth Street, Detroit.
Time   Aug 4, 1967   p. 13

BLACKS - EDUCATION
The school crisis.
Newsweek   Sep 25, 1967   p. 71

BLACKS - EMPLOYMENT
Young Blacks out of work. Time bomb for U.S.
U.S. News   Dec 5, 1977   p. 22

Target: Negro jobs.
Newsweek   Jul 1, 1968   p. 21

BLACKS - HISTORY
The search for a Black past.
Life   Nov 22, 1968   p. 90

BLACKS - INTEGRATION
Black & white in America. Race and the troubled state of integration.
U.S. News   Jul 22, 1991   p. 18

Black & white. How integrated is America?
Newsweek   Mar 7, 1988   p. 18

Retreat from integration.
Time   Mar 9, 1970   p. 9

The sound and the fury. Oxford, Mississippi.
Newsweek   Oct 15, 1962   p. 23

BLACKS - PROTESTS AND DEMONSTRATIONS
The road from Selma.
Newsweek   Apr 5, 1965   p. 23

The savage season begins. Civil rights face-off at Selma. Alabama troopers await marching Negroes in Selma.
Life   Mar 19, 1965   p. 30

Spectacle of the march.
Life   Sep 6, 1963   p. 20

The march on Washington.
Newsweek   Sep 2, 1963   p. 17

'We owe them - and we owe ourselves - a better country...' - President Kennedy. Alabama's Vivian Malone.
Newsweek   Jun 24, 1963   p. 29

Birmingham and beyond: The Negro's push for equality.
Time   May 17, 1963   p. 23

"We stand for human liberty." "We must be prepared to suffer...even die." "The Federal government encourages these agitators."
Newsweek   Jun 5, 1961   p. 18

BLACKS AND JEWS
Black vs. Jew. A tragic confrontation.
Time   Jan 31, 1969   p. 55

BLACKS IN MOTION PICTURES
Black movies. Renaissance or ripoff?
Newsweek   Oct 23, 1972   p. 74

BLACKS IN POLITICS
Seeking votes and clout. A new black drive for political power. Jesse Jackson.
Time   Aug 22, 1983   p. 20

Race and politics. Chicago's ugly election. Campaign '84: New black power at the polls.
Newsweek   Apr 11, 1983   p. 18

The new Black politics. The House caucus.
Newsweek   Jun 7, 1971   p. 30

The Black mayors. How are they doing?
Newsweek   Aug 3, 1970   p. 16

Negro election victories. Cleveland's Mayor Stokes.
Time   Nov 17, 1967   p. 23

BLOOD FLOW
Electric man. Dr. Björn Nordenström claims to have found in the human body a heretofore unknown universe of electrical activity that's the very foundation of the healing process and is as critical to well-being as the flow of blood.
Discover   Apr 1986   p. 22

BLOUGH, ROGER
U.S. Steel's Roger Blough. A strong voice for business.
Newsweek   Jan 22, 1962   p. 69

BLUE COLLAR WORKERS
See WORK FORCE

BLUE, VIDA
New zip in the old game. Vida Blue.
Time   Aug 23, 1971   p. 40

BLUES MUSIC
Janis Joplin. Rebirth of the blues.
Newsweek   May 26, 1969   p. 82

BLUMENTHAL, WERNER (INTERVIEW)
Inflation. How you are being robbed.
U.S. News   Apr 24, 1978   p. 18

BOAT PEOPLE
See REFUGEES, INDOCHINESE

BOCUSE, PAUL
Food. The new wave.
Newsweek   Aug 11, 1975   p. 50

BODY, HUMAN
Faster. Farther. Higher. What science reveals about the body's ultimate limits.
U.S. News   Sep 19, 1988   p. 50

Part II: The human body. How your body converts food to fuel.
Life   Dec 7, 1962   p. 78

The human body.
Life   Oct 26, 1962   p. 76

BODY IMAGE
You and your body image.
Psychology Today   Jul 1985   p. 22

BOEING COMPANY
Flying high. $4 billion for the cruise missile. Boeing boss T.A. Wilson.
Time   Apr 7, 1980   p. 52

BOESKY, IVAN
After the fall. How the insider-trading scandal will change Wall Street. Ivan Boesky.
Business Week   Dec 1, 1986   p. 28

Wall St. scam. Making millions with your money. Investor "Ivan the Terrible" Boesky.
Time   Dec 1, 1986   p. 48

BOISE CASCADE CORP.
Survival in the basic industries. How four companies hope to avoid disaster: Firestone. Kennecott. Inland Steel. Boise Cascade.
Business Week   Apr 26, 1982   p. 74

BOMB SHELTERS
New facts you must know about fallout: The drive for mass shelters.
Life   Jan 12, 1962   p. 34

Shelters for survival?
Newsweek   Nov 6, 1961   p. 19

Shelters. How soon - how big - how safe.
Time   Oct 20, 1961   p. 21

How you can survive fallout. 97 out of 100 people can be saved. Detailed plans for building shelters. And a letter to you from President Kennedy.
Life   Sep 15, 1961   p. 95

BOMBECK, ERMA

How Erma copes. Working the house for laughs. "Housework, if you do it right, can kill you." "Why take pride in cooking, when they don't take pride in eating." "Guilt is the gift that keeps on giving."
Time   Jul 2, 1984   p. 56

BORG, BJORN

The incredible tennis machine. Sweden's Bjorn Borg.
Time   Jun 30, 1980   p. 54

Tennis, everyone! Sweden's Björn Borg.
Newsweek   Jul 1, 1974   p. 44

BORK, ROBERT

Bork. How a young socialist became a conservative and one of history's most controversial Supreme Court nominees.
Time   Sep 21, 1987   p. 12

Where Bork stands. The battle over the future of the Supreme Court.
Newsweek   Sep 14, 1987   p. 22

Judging Bork. Will he change America?
U.S. News   Sep 14, 1987   p. 18

BORMAN, FRANK

Men of the year. Anders, Borman and Lovell.
Time   Jan 3, 1969   p. 9

BOSTON MURDER HOAX, 1990

The Boston murder. Unraveling a grisly hoax. Race, anger and a divided city.
Newsweek   Jan 22, 1990   p. 16

A murder in Boston. How a bizarre case inflamed racial tensions and raised troubling questions about politicians, the police and the press.
Time   Jan 22, 1990   p. 10

BOTSWANA

Botswana. A gathering of waters and wildlife.
National Geographic Dec 1990   p. 5

BOTTI, JOHN

Mafia on trial. Crime boss John Botti.
Time   Sep 29, 1986   p. 16

BOULEZ, PIERRE

New maestro, new beat. New York Philharmonic's Pierre Boulez.
Newsweek   Oct 11, 1971   p. 86

BOWIE, DAVID

Dancing to the music. David Bowie rockets onward.
Time   Jul 18, 1983   p. 54

BOXING

Why the fascination with boxing? Heavyweight Mike Tyson.
Time   Jun 27, 1988   p. 66

The fight of his life. Sugar Ray Leonard takes on Roberto Duran.
Newsweek   Jun 23, 1980   p. 48

Norman Mailer on the fight. 9 pages of action color.
Life   Mar 19, 1971   p. 18

Battle of the champs. Backstage with Ali and Frazier.
Life   Mar 5, 1971   p. 40

BRADY, NICHOLAS

The quiet crusader. Nick Brady's new agenda for business. The Treasury Secretary wants us to stop focusing on the short term. And he has some plans that could change life for both managers and investors.
Business Week   Sep 18, 1989   p. 80

BRAIN

Rebuilding the brain. Birds have an amazing power: unlike us, they can grow new brain cells. Can we learn their secret?
Discover   Jun 1990   p. 48

Chaos and its role in the brain.
Omni   Feb 1990   p. 42

The restless brain. New images of the mind in motion.
Discover   Mar 1989   p. 58

The brain's natural high. A pleasurable chemistry.
Psychology Today   Jul 1988   p. 28

How the brain really works. The new science of memory, thought and emotion.
U.S. News   Jun 27, 1988   p. 48

The emotional brain.
Psychology Today   Feb 1988   p. 34

Brain power. Sex differences. Beliefs and emotions. Left-handedness.
Psychology Today   Nov 1985   p. 28

Brain foods: Diets that sharpen the mind.
Omni   May 1985   p. 36

In the mind's eye. How we visualize.
Psychology Today   May 1985   p. 22

Secrets of the brain. New views of the mind, mental illness, and human nature.
Discover   May 1984   p. 34

Superiority of the female brain.
Omni   Aug 1983   p. 26

How the brain works. The human computer.
Newsweek   Feb 7, 1983   p. 40

Mysteries of the mind.
Omni   Oct 1982   p. 28

Inside the brain.
Time   Jan 14, 1974   p. 50

Chemistry of madness. The brain: Part IV. How drugs and disease affect your mind.
Life   Nov 26, 1971   p. 66

The brain. Part II. The amazing cells that command our bodies.
Life   Oct 22, 1971   p. 42

The brain. A new series. Miracles and mysteries on a tantalizing scientific frontier.
Life   Oct 1, 1971   p. 42

Probing the brain.
Newsweek   Jun 21, 1971   p. 60

BRANDO, MARLON

Sex and death in Paris. Marlon Brando in "Last Tango."
Time   Jan 22, 1973   p. 51

Brando as 'The Godfather.'
Newsweek   Mar 13, 1972   p. 56

The godfather. Brando plays a Mafia chieftain.
Life   Mar 10, 1972   p. 40

Marlon Brando: Actor, director and producer.
Life   Apr 4, 1960   p. 105

BRANDT, WILLY

Man of the year. Willy Brandt.
Time   Jan 4, 1971   p. 6

New leaders for Germany. Socialist Willy Brandt.
Time   Oct 10, 1969   p. 24

BRAZELTON, T. BERRY

Working parents. How to give your kids what they need. By Dr. T. Berry Brazelton.
Newsweek   Feb 13, 1989   p. 66

BRAZIL

Report from Punta del Este: Will Latin America become a success? Brazil's President Costa E Silva.
Time   Apr 21, 1967   p. 29

Goulart's Brazil: Another New Frontier?
Newsweek   Mar 11, 1963   p. 48

Flavio's rescue: Americans bring him from Rio slum to be cured.
Life   Jul 21, 1961   p. 24

BRAZIL AND THE UNITED STATES

Brazil's President Quadros.
Time   Jun 30, 1961   p. 23

BREAK DANCING

Breaking out! Dancing the summer away.
Newsweek   Jul 2, 1984   p. 46

BREAST CANCER

One American woman in ten will get breast cancer. Why—and what can be done?
Time   Jan 14, 1991   p. 48

How to beat breast cancer. What your doctor may not be telling you. Ways men can help.
U.S. News   Jul 11, 1988   p. 52

Breast cancer. Too many radical mastectomies?
Discover   Sep 1981   p. 24

BREWING INDUSTRY

Anheuser-Busch. The king of beers still rules.
Business Week   Jul 12, 1982   p. 50

BREWSTER, KINGMAN

Universities in ferment.
Newsweek   Jun 15, 1970   p. 66

The Ivy League: Is it still the best? Yale's Kingman Brewster.
Newsweek   Nov 23, 1964   p. 65

BREZHNEV, LEONID

Russia after Brezhnev.
U.S. News   Nov 22, 1982   p. 22

Brezhnev's final days. The succession struggle. Communism in crisis.
Newsweek   Apr 12, 1982   p. 30

Brezhnev comes courting. Leonid Brezhnev.
Time   Jun 25, 1973   p. 26

Take-over in the Kremlin. Russia's new leader Leonid Brezhnev.
Life   Oct 23, 1964   p. 30

BREZHNEV, LEONID (INTERVIEW)

America and Russia. Where we stand. Brezhnev: An exclusive interview.
Time   Jan 22, 1979   p. 10

BRIBERY

The payoff scandals.
Newsweek   Feb 23, 1976   p. 26

The big payoff. Lockheed scandal: Graft around the globe.
Time   Feb 23, 1976   p. 28

BRICKER, WILLIAM

The downfall of a CEO. Bill Bricker had big dreams for Diamond Shamrock—and spent freely on an executive lifestyle to match. But as one deal after another failed to pay off, losses mounted, the stock plunged, and Boone Pickens launched a takeover bid.
Business Week   Feb 16, 1987   p. 76

BRINKLEY, DAVID M.

TV's Huntley and Brinkley: One is solemn, the other twinkly.
Newsweek   Mar 13, 1961   p. 53

BROADCAST JOURNALISM

The broadcasting fairness doctrine.
Congressional Digest Oct 1987   p. 227

BROADCASTING

Broadcast deregulation.
Congressional Digest Apr 1984   p. 99

BROKERAGE INDUSTRY

Not since the heyday of J.P. Morgan has Wall Street been buying so many corporations. The major firms are more owners than investors—actually overseeing the companies they buy, from setting overall strategy to picking top managers.
Business Week   Jun 20, 1988   p. 116

BROKERS

The penny stock scam. The epidemic is spreading.
Business Week   Jan 23, 1989   p. 74

Should you believe your broker? In the wake of the crash, Wall Street has a credibility gap. Here's how it's trying to win back investors.
Business Week   Nov 23, 1987   p. 92

Bankers as brokers. What's behind the rush into a riskier business.
Business Week   Apr 11, 1983   p. 70

Managing the new financial supermarkets.
Business Week   Dec 20, 1982   p. 50

BRONFMAN, EDGAR JR.

Seagram's maverick boss. There was a time when Edgar Bronfman Jr. showed little interest in the family business. Now he's running it—and creating a very different company.
Business Week   Dec 18, 1989   p. 90

BRONFMAN, SAMUEL

Kidnapped - Samuel Bronfman II.
Newsweek   Aug 25, 1975   p. 14

BRONZE AGE

Oldest known shipwreck.
National Geographic Dec 1987   p. 693

BROOKE, EDWARD W.

U.S. Senator Edward Brooke.
Time   Feb 17, 1967   p. 20

BROOKLYN BRIDGE (NEW YORK)

A century old, the wonderful Brooklyn Bridge.
National Geographic May 1983 p. 565

BROOKLYN (NEW YORK) - SOCIAL CONDITIONS

A Christmas story. What Sister Geraldine would have visitors understand is that it is not a matter of how much she gives to the people of Sunset Park but how much she gets back. The gift is their lives...
Time Dec 30, 1985 p. 18

BROOKS, MEL

The mad, mad world of Mel Brooks.
Newsweek Feb 17, 1975 p. 54

BROWN, EDMUND G. "PAT"

Nixon. Brown. Biggest state's biggest battle.
Newsweek Oct 29, 1962 p. 19

BROWN, JERRY

The pop politics of Jerry Brown.
Newsweek Apr 23, 1979 p. 24

BROWN, JIM

Cleveland's Jimmy Brown.
Time Nov 26, 1965 p. 80

BRYANT, ANITA

Battle over gay rights. Anita Bryant vs. the homosexuals.
Newsweek Jun 6, 1977 p. 16

BRYANT, LOUISE

Did Diane Keaton give us the real Louise Bryant? What "Reds" didn't tell you.
Ms. Apr 1982 p. 43

BRYANT, PAUL "BEAR"

Supercoach. Alabama's Bear Bryant.
Time Sep 29, 1980 p. 70

BRZEZINSKI, ZBIGNIEW

A new cold war? Carter adviser Brzezinski.
Newsweek Jun 12, 1978 p. 26

BRZEZINSKI, ZBIGNIEW (INTERVIEW)

The new U.S. challenge to Russia. Exclusive interview with Zbigniew Brzezinski.
U.S. News May 30, 1977 p. 35

BUCHER, LLOYD M.

The cruel dilemmas of duty. Bucher of the *Pueblo*.
Life Feb 7, 1969 p. 14

Who is to blame? The Pueblo's Captain: Lloyd M. Bucher.
Newsweek Feb 3, 1969 p. 24

BUCHWALD, ART

Art Buchwald's Washington.
Newsweek Jun 7, 1965 p. 47

BUCKLEY, ROBERT

Trouble! Robert Buckley, CEO of Allegheny International, runs a very ailing company. It lost $109 million last year, it is mired in debt, and its stock is near a 1-year low.
Business Week Aug 11, 1986 p. 56

BUCKLEY, WILLIAM F.

William Buckley / Conservatism can be fun.
Time Nov 3, 1967 p. 70

BUCKLEY, WILLIAM F. (FAMILY)

The Buckleys: A gifted American family.
Life Dec 18, 1970 p. 34

BUDDHISM

Buddhism: Religion and politics.
Time Dec 11, 1964 p. 38

BUDGET - BUSH ADMINISTRATION

Bush league. The President stumbles, Congress bumbles. Boooo!
Newsweek Oct 22, 1990 p. 20

High anxiety. Looming recession, government paralysis and the threat of war are giving Americans a case of the jitters.
Time Oct 15, 1990 p. 30

Tax fight. What kind of new taxes? How big? Who pays? The political price for Bush. The battle lines in Congress.
Business Week Jul 9, 1990 p. 24

BUDGET - CARTER ADMINISTRATION

Guns vs. butter. Battle of the year.
U.S. News Jan 22, 1979 p. 16

Carter and your money. Can he lift the economy?
Newsweek Jan 30, 1978 p. 22

BUDGET - FORD ADMINISTRATION

$350 billion budget. Spur to recovery.
U.S. News   Feb 10, 1975   p. 17

BUDGET - REAGAN ADMINISTRATION

Cuts. The federal budget of the U.S. How the budget will affect you.
U.S. News   Feb 17, 1986   p. 20

The big battle begins.
U.S. News   Feb 11, 1985   p. 24

Drowning in debt. Impact of another $180 billion deficit.
U.S. News   Feb 13, 1984   p. 18

Reagan's good-times budget. An election-year bet on a strong economy.
Business Week   Jan 30, 1984   p. 70

The budget battle begins. Reagan's plan to deal with big deficits. What Congress will do.
Business Week   Feb 7, 1983   p. 88

Guns vs. butter. How to cut defense spending. How to save Social Security.
Business Week   Nov 29, 1982   p. 68

The budget brawl.
Time   Apr 26, 1982   p. 10

The screw tightens.
U.S. News   Feb 15, 1982   p. 16

Now the squeeze really starts.
U.S. News   Oct 5, 1981   p. 22

Reaganomics. Making it work.
Time   Sep 21, 1981   p. 38

The war against Reagan's budget.
U.S. News   Mar 16, 1981   p. 20

The ax falls. Reagan's plan for a "new beginning."
Time   Mar 2, 1981   p. 10

Cut, clash, chop. Budget Director David Stockman.
Newsweek   Feb 16, 1981   p. 20

BUDGET - UNITED STATES

Budget reconciliation act of 1990.
Congressional Digest Dec 1990   p. 291

Balanced budget constitutional amendment.
Congressional Digest Nov 1989   p. 257

Proposed balanced-budget constitutional amendment.
Congressional Digest Oct 1982   p. 195

How the U.S. will spend $413 billion in one year.
U.S. News   Sep 27, 1976   p. 58

BULLFIGHTS

Hemingway: 'The Dangerous Summer,' part I.
Life   Sep 5, 1960   p. 77

BUNDY, MCGEORGE

The crucial choice. U.S. foreign policy in action. McGeorge Bundy.
Time   Jun 25, 1965   p. 26

JFK's McGeorge Bundy. Cool head for the Cold War.
Newsweek   Mar 4, 1963   p. 20

BUNTING, MARY

Girls in college: They have scarcely begun to use their brains.
Time   Nov 3, 1961   p. 68

BUREAUCRACY

How good...how bad. Bureaucrats.
U.S. News   Jun 11, 1979   p. 51

The great American bureaucratic junketing machine.
U.S. News   Dec 18, 1978   p. 56

The bureaucracy explosion. Key campaign issue.
U.S. News   Aug 16, 1976   p. 22

Message from home: Curb the bureaucrats!
U.S. News   Nov 10, 1975   p. 39

Washington's bureaucrats. "Real rulers of America."
U.S. News   Nov 4, 1974   p. 38

BURGER, WARREN E.

The Supreme Court. Warren Burger. Next Chief Justice.
Time   May 30, 1969   p. 16

BUSH, GEORGE - RELATIONS WITH CONGRESS

Bush league. The President stumbles, Congress bumbles. Boooo!
Newsweek   Oct 22, 1990   p. 20

BUSINESS

Stock market killings. College dropout Bill Gates made $750 million last year. Now he's America's youngest billionaire.
U.S. News   Jul 6, 1987   p. 48

America's competitive drive. Are we losing it?
U.S. News   Feb 2, 1987   p. 18

Managing America's business. What makes a top executive?
Psychology Today   Feb 1983   p. 26

Commerce Secretary Hodges: Pro or anti business?
Newsweek   Jul 24, 1961   p. 60

See Also CORPORATIONS

BUSINESS MANAGEMENT

CEO disease. You know the symptoms. The boss doesn't seem to understand the business anymore. Decisions come slowly—only to be abruptly changed. Yes-men are everywhere.
Business Week   Apr 1, 1991   p. 52

Farewell, fast track. Motivating people in difficult times.
Business Week   Dec 10, 1990   p. 192

The best companies for women. How to make your company woman-friendly.
Business Week   Aug 6, 1990   p. 48

Surprise! Some of America's best-run organizations are nonprofits. Here's what Corporate America can learn from them. How Frances Hesselbein showed the way at the Girl Scouts.
Business Week   Mar 26, 1990   p. 66

King customer. Forget market share. Stop worrying about your competitors. The companies that are succeeding now put their customers first.
Business Week   Mar 12, 1990   p. 88

Go team! The payoff from worker participation. When workers are included in decision-making, quality can improve and productivity often goes up. So why won't labor and management cooperate more?
Business Week   Jul 10, 1989   p. 56

Corporate boards. Some directors are finally taking charge, but they could all be more effective. Here's how.
Business Week   Jul 3, 1989   p. 66

Is your company too big?
Business Week   Mar 27, 1989   p. 84

Middle managers. Are they an endangered species? In their own words, six executives describe the frustrations, hopes and fears of life in today's corporation.
Business Week   Sep 12, 1988   p. 80

Lean & mean. America's most competitive companies.
Business Week   Oct 5, 1987   p. 78

Corporate renewal. How America's best companies get better. An exclusive excerpt from a new book by Robert H. Waterman Jr., co-author of *In Search of Excellence*.
Business Week   Sep 14, 1987   p. 98

Quality. To compete, U.S. companies must boost product quality. That means big changes in design, manufacturing— and management thinking.
Business Week   Jun 8, 1987   p. 130

Corporate control. Shareholders vs. managers.
Business Week   May 18, 1987   p. 102

Business fads. What's in. What's out.
Business Week   Jan 20, 1986   p. 52

Oops! First published just two years ago, *In Search of Excellence* quickly became a best-seller. Its appeal was obvious.
Business Week   Nov 5, 1984   p. 76

The new breed of strategic planner.
Business Week   Sep 17, 1984   p. 62

BUSINESS SCHOOLS

The best B-schools. All new ranking.
Business Week   Oct 29, 1990   p. 52

Class reunion. The Harvard business
school class of 1970 was different to begin
with. Here's how the group turned out.
Business Week Jun 18, 1990 p. 160

The best B-schools. Our new ranking of
the top 20 will surprise you.
Business Week Nov 28, 1988 p. 76

The Harvard B-school. Remaking an
institution. Dean John H. McArthur.
Business Week Mar 24, 1986 p. 54

The money chase. What business schools
are doing to us.
Time May 4, 1981 p. 58

BUSING FOR SCHOOL INTEGRATION

Curtailing the role of the Justice
Department in school busing.
Congressional Digest Feb 1981 p. 33

Busing battle.
Time Sep 22, 1975 p. 7

Trouble in schools. Will it get worse?
U.S. News Sep 22, 1975 p. 15

Boston school violence. Turning point in
busing?
U.S. News Oct 28, 1974 p. 22

The battle over busing.
Time Nov 15, 1971 p. 57

BYRD, HARRY

Congress & Kennedy: Defiance.
Time Aug 17, 1962 p. 11

BYRD, ROBERT

Congress. Bold & balky. Senate Majority
Leader Robert Byrd.
Time Jan 23, 1978 p. 8

BYRNE, DAVID

Rock's renaissance man. Singer,
composer, lyricist, guitarist, film director,
writer, actor, video artist, designer,
photographer, David Byrne.
Time Oct 27, 1986 p. 78

BYZANTINE EMPIRE

Byzantine Empire. Rome of the East.
National Geographic Dec 1983 p. 709

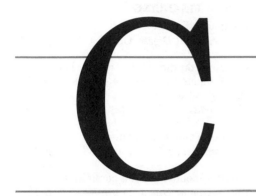

CABBAGE PATCH KIDS

What a doll! The Cabbage Patch craze.
Marketing a Christmas fad.
Newsweek   Dec 12, 1983   p. 78

CABINET - CARTER ADMINISTRATION

Carter's juggling act.
Newsweek   Jul 30, 1979   p. 22

Now what?
Time   Jul 30, 1979   p. 10

Carter's cabinet. How it rates.
U.S. News   Oct 16, 1978   p. 20

What you can expect from Carter's
cabinet.
U.S. News   Jan 10, 1977   p. 16

CABINET - FORD ADMINISTRATION

Ford's big shuffle.
Newsweek   Nov 17, 1975   p. 24

CABINET - REAGAN ADMINISTRATION

The big shake-up. What it means for the
nation.
U.S. News   Jan 21, 1985   p. 22

Rating Reagan's cabinet.
U.S. News   Jul 27, 1981   p. 14

Who are these people - and what do they
stand for?
U.S. News   Jan 19, 1981   p. 18

CABLE TELEVISION

See TELEVISION, CABLE

CAESAR, SID

Sid Caesar. The many faces of comedy.
Newsweek   Nov 26, 1962   p. 51

CALCIUM (MINERAL SUPPLEMENTS)

Calcium. To ward off everything from
osteoporosis to cancer, Americans are
buying millions of dollars worth of
calcium and other mineral supplements.
Do these 'miracle' minerals work?
Newsweek   Jan 27, 1986   p. 48

CALDWELL, SARAH

Music's wonder woman. Sarah Caldwell.
Time   Nov 10, 1975   p. 52

CALIFORNIA

California. The endangered dream.
Time   Nov 18, 1991   p. 32

California. American dream. American
nightmare.
Newsweek   Jul 31, 1989   p. 22

California: Here it comes!
Time   Nov 7, 1969   p. 60

Special issue. The call of California. Its
splendor, its excitement. Why people go,
go and go there.
Life   Oct 19, 1962   p. 12

Number one state. California.
Newsweek   Sep 10, 1962   p. 28

CALLEY, WILLIAM

The killings at Song My. Accused: Lt.
William L. Calley, Jr.
Newsweek   Dec 8, 1969   p. 33

The massacre. Where does the guilt lie?
Lieut. William Calley, Jr.
Time   Dec 5, 1969   p. 23

CAMARENA, ENRIQUE, MURDER

Death of a narc. U.S. drug agent "Kiki"
Camarena's mission was to hunt down
Mexico's drug barons. This is the story of
how they got him.
Time   Nov 7, 1988   p. 84

Crisis across the borders.
U.S. News   Dec 13, 1976   p. 48

Canada in crisis.
Newsweek   Nov 2, 1970   p. 41

Canada's Pearson.
Time   Apr 19, 1963   p. 33

Canada's Diefenbaker. Decline and fall.
Newsweek   Feb 18, 1963   p. 33

CANADA AND THE UNITED STATES

Our troubled neighbors - dangers for U.S.
U.S. News   Mar 9, 1981   p. 35

The Kennedys in Canada.
Life   May 26, 1961   p. 16

CANALS

The Patowmack Canal. Waterway that
led to the Constitution.
National Geographic Jun 1987   p. 716

CANCER

One American woman in ten will get
breast cancer. Why—and what can be
done?
Time   Jan 14, 1991   p. 48

How to beat breast cancer. What your
doctor may not be telling you. Ways men
can help.
U.S. News   Jul 11, 1988   p. 52

The new war on cancer. Biotechnology is
starting to revolutionize treatment. And
industry, not government, is leading the
way.
Business Week   Sep 22, 1986   p. 60

Danger in the sun. A good tan may be
hazardous to your health.
Newsweek   Jun 9, 1986   p. 60

Danger from tea and red wine.
USA Today   Feb 1986   p. 1

Cancer and interleukin-2. The search for a
cure.
Newsweek   Dec 16, 1985   p. 60

Cancer: A progress report.
Newsweek   Nov 2, 1981   p. 94

Breast cancer. Too many radical
mastectomies?
Discover   Sep 1981   p. 24

Interferon. The IF drug for cancer.
Time   Mar 31, 1980   p. 60

What causes cancer?
Newsweek   Jan 26, 1976   p. 62

Toward control of cancer. Immunologist
Robert Good.
Time   Mar 19, 1973   p. 64

War against cancer. A progress report.
Newsweek   Feb 22, 1971   p. 84

A surgeon pits his skill against cancer.
Life   Jan 20, 1961   p. 70

CANCER PATIENTS

Gilda Radner's answer to cancer. Healing
the body with mind and heart.
Life   Mar 1988   p. 74

Living with cancer. The disease that will
strike one in three Americans.
Newsweek   Apr 8, 1985   p. 64

Cancer. Children are winning their battle
against it.
Life   Dec 1980   p. 128

CANION, ROD

Who's afraid of IBM? Not Compaq
Computer. It's challenging Big Blue's new
PC line. So far, so good. But IBM is not
your ordinary Goliath. Rod Canion.
Compaq President and CEO.
Business Week   Jun 29, 1987   p. 68

CANNES FILM FESTIVAL

Natalie Wood at Cannes film festival.
Life   Jun 15, 1962   p. 84

CAPE KENNEDY (FLORIDA)

The moon voyagers and the earthly
beauty that beckons them back by Anne
Morrow Lindbergh.
Life   Feb 28, 1969   p. 14

CAPITAL PUNISHMENT

1990 omnibus crime bill.
Congressional Digest Nov 1990   p. 258

The Bush court. A move to the right.
What it means for: Abortion, the death
penalty, civil rights.
Newsweek   Jul 30, 1990   p. 14

To die or not to die. Minutes away from execution on a prison gurney, J.D. Autry won a dramatic reprieve. An account of his life, his crimes and the continuing battle over the death penalty.
Newsweek   Oct 17, 1983   p. 43

The death penalty. The chair is bolted to the floor near the back of a 12-ft. by 18-ft. room. You sit on a seat of cracked rubber secured by rows of copper tacks. Your ankles are strapped...
Time   Jan 24, 1983   p. 28

Death wish. Convict Gary Gilmore.
Newsweek   Nov 29, 1976   p. 26

Caryl Chessman.
Time   Mar 21, 1960   p. 16

CAPITALISM

Capitalism in China.
Business Week   Jan 14, 1985   p. 52

The church and capitalism. The Catholic Bishops' report on the U.S. economy, out next week, will cause a furor.
Business Week   Nov 12, 1984   p. 104

Is capitalism working?
Time   Apr 21, 1980   p. 40

Can capitalism survive? Don't count me out, folks! Adam Smith.
Time   Jul 14, 1975   p. 52

CAPITALISTS

The Rothschilds today.
Time   Dec 20, 1963   p. 70

Making money work. A Texas technique.
Time   Jun 16, 1961   p. 80

CAPLIN, MORTIMER

Tax time: Sharp pencils, sharper machines.
Newsweek   Apr 16, 1962   p. 87

CAPOTE, TRUMAN

'In Cold Blood.' Truman Capote's hot book.
Newsweek   Jan 24, 1966   p. 59

CAPRIATI, JENNIFER

The 8th grade wonder. Tennis superstar Jennifer Capriati.
Newsweek   May 14, 1990   p. 58

CARBOHYDRATES

How food affects mood. The carbohydrate connection.
Psychology Today   Apr 1988   p. 30

CAREW, ROD

Baseball's best hitter. Rod Carew
Time   Jul 18, 1977   p. 52

CARIBBEAN REGION

The Reagan "Caribbean Basin Initiative."
Congressional Digest Mar 1983   p. 69

Powder keg at our doorstep.
U.S.News   May 19, 1980   p. 21

CARLSON, PAUL

Congo martyr. Photographs, eyewitness reports of the massacre.
Life   Dec 4, 1964   p. 32

CAROLINE, PRINCESS OF MONACO

Caroline. Monaco's very model of a modern princess.
Life   Apr 1986   p. 76

CARON, LESLIE

Leslie Caron.
Life   Jun 30, 1961   p. 97

CARPENTER, SCOTT

Astronaut Carpenter.
Newsweek   Jun 4, 1962   p. 19

By Rene Carpenter. 55 minutes that lasted forever.
Life   Jun 1, 1962   p. 26

New hero for orbit. The loner who found himself.
Life   May 18, 1962   p. 32

CARSON, JOHNNY

Johnny Carson. The lonesome hero of middle America.
Life   Jan 23, 1970   p. 50

Humor in the night. Johnny Carson.
Time   May 19, 1967   p. 104

CARSWELL, HAROLD

The seat Nixon can't fill.
Newsweek   Apr 20, 1970   p. 35

The Carswell defeat. Nixon's embattled
White House.
Time   Apr 20, 1970   p. 8

CARTER, BILLY

The case of the President's brother.
Newsweek   Aug 4, 1980   p. 14

Coping with Billy.
Time   Aug 4, 1980   p. 12

Brother Billy.
Newsweek   Nov 14, 1977   p. 32

CARTER, JIMMY

The Carter Presidency.
Time   Aug 18, 1980   p. 10

The rebellious Democrats.
Newsweek   Aug 11, 1980   p. 18

Rescue mission in Washington.
Newsweek   May 12, 1980   p. 26

Taking charge. "An assault will be
repelled by any means necessary..."
Time   Feb 4, 1980   p. 12

Carter and Kennedy head for a
showdown.
Life   Nov 1979   p. 28

Now what?
Time   Jul 30, 1979   p. 10

At the crossroads.
Time   Jul 23, 1979   p. 20

The energy crisis. A program for the '80s.
Newsweek   Jul 16, 1979   p. 19

The politics of austerity.
Newsweek   Jan 29, 1979   p. 20

Born again!
Newsweek   Oct 2, 1978   p. 22

Carter's breakthrough.
Time   Oct 2, 1978   p. 8

After the summit.
Time   Sep 25, 1978   p. 8

Carter's 18 months. What went wrong?
U.S. News   Jul 24, 1978   p. 17

Carter and the Jews.
Newsweek   Mar 20, 1978   p. 23

The mess in foreign policy.
U.S. News   Jan 23, 1978   p. 27

The Carter impact.
U.S. News   Jan 16, 1978   p. 21

Picking up the pieces.
Newsweek   Oct 3, 1977   p. 22

The Lance affair. What damage to Carter?
Newsweek   Sep 19, 1977   p. 24

The Lance affair. What it cost Carter.
Time   Sep 19, 1977   p. 6

The Lance report. Is he home free?
Newsweek   Aug 29, 1977   p. 16

Carter's foreign policy. Jimmy in the
lion's den.
Time   Aug 8, 1977   p. 8

Uncle Jimmy wants you. But will
America enlist?
Time   May 2, 1977   p. 10

His first big test.
Time   Apr 25, 1977   p. 8

The Carters move in. It's a new
Washington.
Time   Feb 7, 1977   p. 17

Guide to the new government. The
festivities. The power brokers. The major
problems. A talk with Rosalynn.
Newsweek   Jan 24, 1977   p. 16

A new era begins.
U.S. News   Jan 24, 1977   p. 16

Man of the year. Jimmy Carter.
Time   Jan 3, 1977   p. 10

Picking the new team.
Newsweek   Dec 13, 1976   p. 20

Taking charge.
Newsweek   Nov 22, 1976   p. 24

The new look. Election special.
Newsweek   Nov 15, 1976   p. 23

"What I'll do." Special election section.
Time   Nov 15, 1976   p. 12

What Carter will do as President.
U.S. News   Nov 15, 1976   p. 14

CASH, JOHNNY

Johnny Cash. The rough-cut king of country music. Johnny Cash sings of trains, prisons and hard times.
Life   Nov 21, 1969   p. 44

CASSIDY, DAVID

David Cassidy. Teenland's heartthrob.
Life   Oct 29, 1971   p. 70

CASTANEDA, CARLOS

Carlos Castaneda: Magic and reality.
Time   Mar 5, 1973   p. 36

CASTRO, FIDEL

Reagan's goal: Cutting Castro down to size.
U.S. News   Apr 6, 1981   p. 20

Castro. Russia's cat's-paw.
U.S. News   Jun 12, 1978   p. 20

Castro and the Reds: Their real goal.
Newsweek   Sep 5, 1960   p. 42

CATERPILLAR TRACTOR CO.

Caterpillar. Sticking to basics to stay competitive.
Business Week   May 4, 1981   p. 74

CATHOLIC CHURCH

John Paul. How he's changing the Church.
Newsweek   Sep 21, 1987   p. 22

The Pope's foot soldiers. Keeping the faith: Two American priests in a changing church. Catholic priests Raymond Dlugos and Brian Frawley.
U.S. News   Sep 21, 1987   p. 58

The Catholics. A church in crisis.
Newsweek   Dec 9, 1985   p. 66

Discord in the church. The Pope takes a tough line. A radical theology challenges Rome. Women demand a new role.
Time   Feb 4, 1985   p. 50

After Paul VI. Choosing a new Pope.
Newsweek   Aug 21, 1978   p. 48

In search of a Pope.
Time   Aug 21, 1978   p. 62

The Jesuits. Catholicism's troubled front line.
Time   Apr 23, 1973   p. 40

The Pope's unruly flock. A spirit of change shakes the church.
Life   Mar 20, 1970   p. 22

Rebellion in the Catholic Church.
Time   Nov 22, 1968   p. 42

Catholicism's epic venture. The Council ends: its conflicts and achievements.
Life   Dec 17, 1965   p. 22

Pope Paul.
Time   Sep 24, 1965   p. 62

John XXIII: The last picture.
Time   Jun 7, 1963   p. 41

The Vatican Council. Reunion and reform.
Newsweek   Dec 17, 1962   p. 54

The condition of Catholicism. Pope John.
Time   Oct 5, 1962   p. 80

CATHOLIC CHURCH - CLERGY

The Catholic exodus: Why priests and nuns are quitting.
Time   Feb 23, 1970   p. 51

The nun: Going modern.
Newsweek   Dec 25, 1967   p. 45

CATHOLIC CHURCH - UNITED STATES

U.S. Catholics. A feisty flock awaits the Pope.
Time   Sep 7, 1987   p. 46

Taking on American Catholics. The Pope cracks down.
U.S. News   Nov 17, 1986   p. 64

The church and capitalism. The Catholic Bishops' report on the U.S. economy, out next week, will cause a furor.
Business Week   Nov 12, 1984   p. 104

U.S. Catholicism. A church divided.
Time   May 24, 1976   p. 78

Has the Church lost its soul? A survey of U.S. Catholics.
Newsweek   Oct 4, 1971   p. 80

How U.S. Catholics view their church.
Newsweek   Mar 20, 1967   p. 68

Catholicism in the U.S. A surge of
renewal. Boston's Cardinal Cushing.
Time   Aug 21, 1964   p. 35

Catholicism in America.
Newsweek   Oct 14, 1963   p. 66

U.S. Catholics & the state. John Courtney
Murray, S.J.
Time   Dec 12, 1960   p. 64

CATS

Cats. Love 'em! Hate 'em!
Time   Dec 7, 1981   p. 72

CAUTHEN, STEVE

A born winner. Jockey Steve Cauthen.
Time   May 29, 1978   p. 56

CAVES

Charting the splendors of Lechuguilla
Cave.
National Geographic Mar 1991   p. 34

CAVETT, DICK

Wit in the night.
Time   Jun 7, 1971   p. 80

Dick Cavett. Offstage with the brightest
face on screen.
Life   Oct 30, 1970   p. 36

CBS

See COLUMBIA BROADCASTING
SYSTEM, INC.

CEAUSESCU, NICOLAE

The last days of a dictator. A violent end
to a year of revolution. Romania.
Newsweek   Jan 8, 1990   p. 16

CELLS

Secrets of the human cell.
Newsweek   Aug 20, 1979   p. 48

CELLULAR PHONES

Cellular phones. The high-risk empire of
Craig McCaw. He runs America's biggest
cellular phone company. Now all he has
to do is turn a profit.
Business Week   Dec 5, 1988   p. 140

Hello anywhere. Here's the lowdown on
cellular phones.
Business Week   Sep 21, 1987   p. 84

CENSORSHIP

Art or obscenity?
Newsweek   Jul 2, 1990   p. 46

Science and censorship.
Omni   Feb 1987   p. 42

Sex busters.
Time   Jul 21, 1986   p. 12

CENSUS

Portrait of America. The hidden
revolution at home and on the job.
Newsweek   Jan 17, 1983   p. 20

Your color?. . .Your money? . . .Your age -
really? . . .The nosey census of '60.
Newsweek   Mar 21, 1960   p. 45

CENTRAL AMERICA

Is Central America going Communist?
U.S. News   Dec 21, 1981   p. 20

Powder keg at our doorstep.
U.S.News   May 19, 1980   p. 21

**CENTRAL AMERICA AND THE UNITED
STATES**

Policy collision. Mining Nicaragua's
harbors.
Time   Apr 23, 1984   p. 16

In Central America why distrust of U.S.
runs deep.
U.S. News   Oct 17, 1983   p. 36

U.S. Central American policy.
Congressional Digest Oct 1983   p. 225

Central America. The big stick approach.
"We don't want war, but..." Maneuvering
the military. Uproar over covert aid.
Time   Aug 8, 1983   p. 18

Gunboat diplomacy. Reagan gets tougher
with Nicaragua.
Newsweek   Aug 1, 1983   p. 12

Next stop-Central America?
U.S. News   Jul 11, 1983   p. 20

The first casualty. Central America. The death of an adviser in El Salvador. The battle for Nicaragua. Reagan's White Paper.
Newsweek   Jun 6, 1983   p. 20

Central America. Harsh facts, hard choices. "A vital interest, a moral duty."
Time   May 9, 1983   p. 20

The peril grows. Central America's agony. A U.S. dilemma.
Time   Mar 22, 1982   p. 18

The fire next door. Reagan's no-win situation. What can be salvaged. A U.S. poll: Doubts and distrust.
Newsweek   Mar 1, 1982   p. 16

The flag waves in Castro's backyard.
Life   Mar 29, 1963   p. 26

CENTRAL INTELLIGENCE AGENCY

The new spy wars. Is the CIA ready?
U.S. News   Jun 3, 1991   p. 22

The Intelligence Oversight Act.
Congressional Digest Dec 1988   p. 289

Webster's CIA. An exclusive interview with the new director. Cleaning up Casey's mess.
Newsweek   Oct 12, 1987   p. 24

The secret wars of the CIA by Bob Woodward. Exclusive book excerpts.
Newsweek   Oct 5, 1987   p. 44

The CIA. Running strong or running wild?
U.S. News   Jun 16, 1986   p. 24

Inside CIA. What's really going on.
U.S. News   Jun 25, 1984   p. 27

The secret warriors. The CIA is back in business.
Newsweek   Oct 10, 1983   p. 38

Is worst over for CIA?
U.S. News   May 7, 1979   p. 26

The CIA: How badly hurt?
Newsweek   Feb 6, 1978   p. 18

Mission impossible?
Time   Feb 6, 1978   p. 10

CIA murder plots. Weighing the damage to U.S.
U.S. News   Dec 1, 1975   p. 13

CIA: Who's watching whom?
Newsweek   Jun 23, 1975   p. 16

The CIA. Has it gone too far? Director William E. Colby.
Time   Sep 30, 1974   p. 17

The new espionage. CIA chief Richard Helms.
Newsweek   Nov 22, 1971   p. 28

The CIA and the students.
Time   Feb 24, 1967   p. 13

C.I.A. - How super the sleuths? Director Allen Dulles: Triumphs and disasters.
Newsweek   May 8, 1961   p. 29

CERF, BENNETT

Books by the billion. Bennett Cerf.
Time   Dec 16, 1966   p. 100

CHAGALL, MARC

Chagall. Self-portrait.
Time   Jul 30, 1965   p. 42

CHALLENGER (SPACE SHUTTLE) EXPLOSION

What went wrong? The future of space flight. Tom Wolfe on life at the edge.
Newsweek   Feb 10, 1986   p. 26

Space shuttle Challenger. January 28, 1986.
Time   Feb 10, 1986   p. 20

Challengers. January 28, 1986. 11:39.13 A.M.
U.S. News   Feb 10, 1986   p. 14

CHAMBERLAIN, WILT

The greatest one-on-one match in sports. Kareem vs. Wilt.
Life   Mar 24, 1972   p. 58

CHANDLER, BUFF

Building the pavilions of culture. Los Angeles' Buff Chandler.
Time   Dec 18, 1964   p. 46

CHANDLER, OTIS

How to build a publishing empire.
California's Otis Chandler.
Newsweek   Jan 2, 1967   p. 41

CHANEL, GABRIELLE

Hepburn returns to Broadway. Kate and
Coco.
Newsweek   Nov 10, 1969 p. 75

CHANG, NIEM

When China went mad. An
extraordinary memoir of the Cultural
Revolution.
Time   Jun 8, 1987   p. 42

CHAOS (SCIENCE)

Chaos and its role in the brain.
Omni   Feb 1990   p. 42

How God plays dice with the universe.
Omni   May 1983   p. 84

CHAPLIN, CHARLIE

Hello Charlie. Back in the U.S. after 20
years, Chaplin and his wife Oona stand in
front of a welcoming poster.
Life   Apr 21, 1972 p. 86

Chaplin at 77.
Newsweek   Jun 6, 1966   p. 90

Charlie Chaplin directs Sophia.
Life   Apr 1, 1966   p. 80

CHAPLIN, GERALDINE

Charlie Chaplin's daughter. A hit in her
stage debut.
Life   Jan 31, 1964 p. 75

CHARLES, PRINCE OF WALES

Charles the bedeviled. Good guy or
wimp?
Life   Sep 1987   p. 32

Here they come! Charles and Diana.
Time   Nov 11, 1985 p. 56

A royal welcome. Charles and Diana in
America. Her jewels. Inside their
embassy quarters. Their nation's
priceless art treasures.
Life   Nov 1985   p. 29

Royal wedding.
Newsweek   Aug 3, 1981   p. 34

Three cheers!
Time   Aug 3, 1981   p. 20

The man who will be King. Britain's
Prince Charles.
Time   May 15, 1978 p. 32

Prince Charles: Pomp and
circumspection.
Newsweek   Jul 14, 1969   p. 26

Is Prince Charles necessary?
Time   Jun 27, 1969   p. 27

CHARTERHOUSE J. ROTHSCHILD

London's new financial whiz.
Business Week   Apr 23, 1984   p. 64

CHARTRES CATHEDRAL

Queen of cathedrals.
Life   Dec 15, 1961   p. 52

CHASE MANHATTAN CORP.

Agony at Chase. The once-mighty bank of
the Rockefellers is in deep trouble. Can
incoming CEO Tom Labrecque keep
Chase Manhattan independent?
Business Week   Oct 8, 1990   p. 32

Chase's battle to catch up. Searching for
its role in banking's new world.
Business Week   Apr 9, 1984   p. 74

CHAVEZ, CESAR

The grapes of wrath, 1969.
Mexican-Americans on the march.   Cesar
Chavez.
Time   Jul 4, 1969   p. 16

CHECCHI, AL

The fly boys. Finance aces Gary Wilson
and Al Checchi won Northwest Airlines.
Now what? More deals, of course.
Business Week   Mar 5, 1990   p. 54

CHEEVER, JOHN

A great American novel. John Cheever's
'Falconer.'
Newsweek   Mar 14, 1977 p. 61

Author John Cheever.
Time   Mar 27, 1964 p. 66

CHEMICAL AND BIOLOGICAL WARFARE

Biochemical war: The new shape of death.
Omni   Feb 1991   p. 42

Are we ready for this?
Time   Sep 3, 1990   p. 24

Chemical warfare. The fight against 'The Winds of Death.' A showdown with Kaddafi.
Newsweek   Jan 16, 1989   p. 16

CHENEY, DICK

Ready for war. Pentagon partners Dick Cheney and Colin Powell have the troops in place. Now they're waiting for the word.
Time   Nov 12, 1990   p. 24

CHER

The case for Cher.
Ms.   Jul 1988   p. 52

Cher. Movie star, video vamp - and all business.
Newsweek   Nov 30, 1987   p. 66

Cher. Glad rags to riches.
Time   Mar 17, 1975   p. 56

CHERNENKO, KONSTANTIN

The Kremlin's new master. What he might do. His view of the world. The generation dilemma. Konstantin Chernenko.
Time   Feb 27, 1984   p. 28

CHERNOBYL NUCLEAR ACCIDENT, 1986

The victims of Chernobyl. A personal account by the American doctor who helped them.
Life   Aug 1986   p. 20

The Chernobyl syndrome. How the meltdown happened. The Kremlin cover-up. The fall-out: What are the risks?
Newsweek   May 12, 1986   p. 20

Meltdown. Chernobyl reactor.
Time   May 12, 1986   p. 38

Nightmare in Russia. How reckless are the Soviets? Fallout for nuclear power? Can it happen here? Damaged Chernobyl plant.
U.S. News   May 12, 1986   p. 18

CHESS

Bobby's next move?
Newsweek   Jul 31, 1972   p. 42

The big chess battle: Knight-Errant v. King. Spassky. Fischer.
Time   Jul 31, 1972   p. 32

CHESSMAN, CARYL

Caryl Chessman.
Time   Mar 21, 1960   p. 16

CHEVALIER, MAURICE

Chevalier and Crosby: Two old pros in songfest.
Life   Mar 10, 1961   p. 77

CHIANG CHING

See MAO ZEDONG, MME.

CHICAGO (ILLINOIS)

Race and politics. Chicago's ugly election. Campaign '84: New black power at the polls.
Newsweek   Apr 11, 1983   p. 18

How to run a city. Chicago's Mayor Richard J. Daley.
Newsweek   Apr 5, 1971   p. 80

Chicago: The new facade. The next election. Mayor Daley.
Time   Mar 15, 1963   p. 24

CHICAGO SEVEN TRIAL

See TRIALS (CONSPIRACY)

CHICHESTER, SIR FRANCIS

Around the world in the 'Gipsy Moth.' One man's stirring conquest of the sea. Sir Francis Chichester's own story and pictures.
Life   Jun 9, 1967   p. 28

CHILD ABUSE

A tale of abuse. The horrifying Steinberg trial. The psychology of violent relationships.
Newsweek   Dec 12, 1988   p. 56

Mothers on the run. The child-abuse crisis. Thousands of fearful women now flee their husbands by going underground - often in violation of the law.
U.S. News   Jun 13, 1988   p. 22

The nightmare of the sexually abused child.
USA Today   Nov 1985   p. 54

Sexual abuse. The growing outcry over
child molesting.
Newsweek   May 14, 1984   p. 30

See Also FAMILY VIOLENCE

CHILD CARE

Child care.
Congressional Digest Feb 1990   p. 33

Child care legislation.
Congressional Digest Nov 1988   p. 258

A revolutionary new idea in child-care.
Psychology Today   Dec 1987   p. 32

Who's bringing up baby? With both Mom
and Dad at work, the big problem is
finding quality child care.
Time   Jun 22, 1987   p. 54

Whose job is child care? Nationwide
guide. Corporate solutions. Photo tour of
day-care centers.
Ms.   Mar 1987   p. 32

Day care. Who's minding the children?
Newsweek   Sep 10, 1984   p. 14

CHILD, JULIA

What's cooking. Julia Child.
Time   Nov 25, 1966   p. 74

CHILD PSYCHOLOGY

Children under stress. Are we pushing
our kids too hard?
U.S. News   Oct 27, 1986   p. 58

America's forgotten children. Psychiatrist
Robert Coles.
Time   Feb 14, 1972   p. 36

CHILD REARING

Working parents. How to give your kids
what they need. By Dr. T. Berry
Brazelton.
Newsweek   Feb 13, 1989   p. 66

When to have your baby. The trade-offs
of early or late motherhood.
Ms.   Dec 1986   p. 37

Bringing up superbaby. Parents are
pushing their kids to learn earlier than
ever. Does it help or hurt?
Newsweek   Mar 28, 1983   p. 62

Bringing up baby. Is Dr. Spock to blame?
Newsweek   Sep 23, 1968   p. 68

Today's parents: Trapped in a
child-centered world?
Newsweek   Nov 28, 1960   p. 53

CHILDBIRTH

Unforgettable moments of pregnancy and
birth.
Life   Jul 22, 1966   p. 48

CHILDLESSNESS

No baby on board. Not since the
Depression have so many couples
decided not to have kids.
Newsweek   Sep 1, 1986   p. 68

CHILDREN

Do we care about our kids? The sorry
plight of America's most disadvantaged
minority: Its children.
Time   Oct 8, 1990   p. 40

How kids learn.
Newsweek   Apr 17, 1989   p. 50

Save the children. Too many problems,
too little help.
U.S. News   Nov 7, 1988   p. 34

Through the eyes of children. Growing
up in America today.
Time   Aug 8, 1988   p. 32

How kids draw. From scribbles to art.
Psychology Today   Aug 1986   p. 24

The child's view of God.
Psychology Today   Dec 1985   p. 22

Do Americans secretly hate children?
From the explosive new book by Letty
Cottin Pogrebin.
Ms.   Nov 1983   p. 47

Our neglected kids.
U.S. News   Aug 9, 1982   p. 54

The child's world. Christmas 1973.
Time   Dec 24, 1973   p. 60

The middle age child 6 to 12. A special
section. Articles and advice about the
problems and joys of learning to live in
the outside world.
Life   Oct 20, 1972   p. 42

Children. The child's world. Christmas in the Wyeth family. Creativity: a gift that isn't lost. New facts on infant learning. How big a family? Magic and games. Adopting a son.
Life   Dec 17, 1971   p. 6

CHILDREN - DISEASES

Lead and your kids. Disturbing new evidence about the threat to their health. How to protect them.
Newsweek   Jul 15, 1991   p. 42

CHILDREN AND WAR

Child warriors. Burma's Tin Hle is only 13 years old. In war zones around the world, kids like him are fighting — and dying.
Time   Jun 18, 1990   p. 30

Beirut under siege. Send in the Marines? Children of war revisited.
Time   Jul 19, 1982   p. 10

Children of war. Out of the horror, amazing strength.
Time   Jan 11, 1982   p. 32

CHILDREN, EMOTIONALLY DISTURBED

The troubled child.
Newsweek   Apr 8, 1974   p. 52

CHILDREN, GIFTED

Amazing families. Why gifted parents produce gifted children.
U.S. News   Dec 12, 1988   p. 78

Gifted & talented. Nurturing a national treasure.
Psychology Today   Jun 1984   p. 28

CHILDREN OF ALCOHOLICS

Alcohol and the family. Growing up with alcoholic parents can leave scars for life.
Newsweek   Jan 18, 1988   p. 62

CHILDREN OF DIVORCED PARENTS

Children of divorce.
Newsweek   Feb 11, 1980   p. 58

CHILDREN, TERMINALLY ILL

Paul Newman's dream. A caring camp for ailing kids.
Life   Sep 1988   p. 24

CHILE

Chile under the gun.
Newsweek   Sep 24, 1973   p. 42

After the fall. Allende.
Time   Sep 24, 1973   p. 35

Marxist threat in the Americas. Chile's Salvador Allende.
Time   Oct 19, 1970   p. 23

CHINA

A day in the life of China.
Time   Oct 2, 1989   p. 30

China now. 10 years after Mao.
U.S. News   Sep 8, 1986   p. 26

Deng Xiaoping
Time   Jan 6, 1986   p. 24

Banishing Mao's ghost. Theodore H. White on China.
Time   Sep 26, 1983   p. 30

The new China.
Newsweek   Feb 5, 1979   p. 32

Man of the year. Teng Hsiao-p'ing. Visions of a new China.
Time   Jan 1, 1979   p. 12

Where China is headed.
U.S. News   Nov 14, 1977   p. 33

After Mao.
Newsweek   Sep 20, 1976   p. 30

After Mao.
Time   Sep 20, 1976   p. 26

China: Friend or foe? Chou's successor: Teng Hsiao-ping.
Time   Jan 19, 1976   p. 24

China. Looking beyond Mao.
Time   Feb 3, 1975   p. 22

The China Nixon will see.
Newsweek   Feb 21, 1972   p. 34

The Chinese are coming.
Time   Nov 8, 1971   p. 26

Inside China. 21 pages of color, an eyewitness report, a talk with Mao.
Life   Apr 30, 1971   p. 22

China: A whole new game. First color
photos. Yanks in Peking.
Time   Apr 26, 1971   p. 25

China: How big the threat?
Newsweek   Mar 7, 1966   p. 35

Red China.
Newsweek   Mar 15, 1965   p. 36

Red China: A paper dragon?
Newsweek   Nov 25, 1963   p. 44

Red China: The arrogant outcast.
Time   Sep 13, 1963   p. 30

Red China today.
Newsweek   Sep 3, 1962   p. 28

**CHINA - CULTURAL REVOLUTION,
1966-1969**

When China went mad. An
extraordinary memoir of the Cultural
Revolution.
Time   Jun 8, 1987   p. 42

In the hands of the Red Guard torture and
degradation. The most important man to
escape from China writes his story.
Life   Jun 2, 1967   p. 22

CHINA - ECONOMIC CONDITIONS

Inside China. Exclusive: The first
interviews with China's leaders since
Tiananmen Square.
U.S. News   Mar 12, 1990   p. 40

Communism in turmoil. Special reports
on China and the Soviet Union.
Business Week   Jun 5, 1989   p. 34

Sichuan. China changes course.
National Geographic Sep 1985   p. 280

Capitalism in China.
Business Week   Jan 14, 1985   p. 52

Behind the China debate: Hunger and
hate.
Time   Dec 1, 1961   p. 18

CHINA - FOREIGN RELATIONS

China joins the world.
Newsweek   Nov 8, 1971   p. 22

CHINA - HISTORY

China. Behind Mao's Red rule. The 100
violent years.
Life   Sep 23, 1966   p. 61

CHINA - NUCLEAR WEAPONS

The bomb; the overthrow; the squeaker;
the scandal.
Time   Oct 23, 1964   p. 19

CHINA - POLITICS AND GOVERNMENT

Inside China. Exclusive: The first
interviews with China's leaders since
Tiananmen Square.
U.S. News   Mar 12, 1990   p. 40

China. The great leap backward.
Business Week   Jun 19, 1989   p. 28

China. What went wrong. The
Communist Party has lost its moral
authority to govern.
U.S. News   Jun 5, 1989   p. 20

Upheaval in China.
Newsweek   May 29, 1989   p. 14

China in turmoil.
Time   May 29, 1989   p. 36

China. Moving away from Marx. Leader
Deng Xiaoping.
Time   Sep 23, 1985   p. 42

The struggle for China.
Newsweek   Jan 30, 1967   p. 32

China. Crisis in Mao's purge.
Life   Jan 20, 1967   p. 26

China in chaos. Chairman Mao.
Time   Jan 13, 1967   p. 20

The Chinese nightmare. Defense
Minister Lin Piao.
Time   Sep 9, 1966   p. 28

Mao and China.
Newsweek   Aug 8, 1966   p. 36

CHINA - SOCIAL CONDITIONS
China. Future shock.
Omni   Sep 1985   p. 36

CHINA - SOCIAL LIFE AND CUSTOMS
Faces of an unexpected China.
Life   Oct 1980   p. 104

The relevance of faith & myth in twentieth century life. Bishop Pike.
Time   Nov 11, 1966   p. 56

Christian renewal.
Time   Dec 25, 1964   p. 45

"The goal of human life is not death, but resurrection." Theologian Karl Barth.
Time   Apr 20, 1962   p. 59

"The second reformation."
Time   Dec 8, 1961   p. 76

We have seen His star...
Newsweek   Dec 26, 1960   p. 11

CHRISTIE, JULIE

The multiple excitements of Julie Christie. The brillant young Oscar winner.
Life   Apr 29, 1966   p. 61

Julie Christie. New darling of the movies.
Newsweek   Dec 20, 1965   p. 88

CHRISTMAS

Joys of Christmas.
Life   Dec 15, 1972   p. 12

CHRISTMAS BUSINESS

U.S. shopping surge. Trendy Bloomingdale's.
Time   Dec 1, 1975   p. 74

Christmas shopping.
Time   Dec 15, 1961   p. 56

CHRONIC FATIGUE SYNDROME

Chronic fatigue syndrome. A debilitating disease afflicts millions — and the cause is still a mystery.
Newsweek   Nov 12, 1990   p. 62

CHRYSLER CORP.

Chrysler's next act. Sure, the company's big comeback turned Lee Iacocca into a hero. But now Chrysler needs a new strategy—and Iacocca has plenty of ideas.
Business Week   Nov 3, 1986   p. 66

Detroit's comeback kid. Chrysler Chairman Lee Iacocca.
Time   Mar 21, 1983   p. 50

Can Chrysler keep its comeback rolling?
Business Week   Feb 14, 1983   p. 132

Can Chrysler be saved?
Newsweek   Aug 13, 1979   p. 52

CHURCH AND STATE

One nation, under God. Has the separation of church and state gone too far?
Time   Dec 9, 1991   p. 60

When church and state collide.
U.S. News   Mar 5, 1984   p. 42

CHURCH OF ENGLAND

The Anglican communion. Worldly. Worldwide. Catholic and Protestant.
Time   Aug 16, 1963   p. 58

CHURCHES

Golden cherub in a spectacular German church.
Life   Mar 31, 1961   p. 48

CHURCHILL, SIR WINSTON L.

Churchill's funeral.
Life   Feb 5, 1965   p. 26

Churchill, 1874-1965.
Newsweek   Feb 1, 1965   p. 38

CIA

See CENTRAL INTELLIGENCE AGENCY

CIGARETTE SMOKING

See SMOKING

CIRCUS

Lords of the ring. Charisma, control, and tradition. Gunther Gebel-Williams.
Psychology Today   Oct 1983   p. 26

CITICORP

John Reed's Citicorp. The bank's performance is lackluster. But Reed, 47, has a long-term plan: Build reserves to guard against market shocks and gear up for a growth surge in the 1990s.
Business Week   Dec 8, 1986   p. 90

The new shape of banking. Citicorp changed an industry. Now, after the Continental shock, banking will change again—even at Citicorp.
Business Week   Jun 18, 1984   p. 104

BankAmerica and Citicorp. The new banking forces new strategies.
Business Week   Jul 13, 1981   p. 56

CITIES AND TOWNS

America's new boom towns. Hot cities that may surprise you.
U.S. News   Nov 13, 1989   p. 54

Hot cities. America's best places to live and work. Providence. St. Paul. Orlando. Ft. Worth. Sacramento. Columbus.
Newsweek   Feb 6, 1989   p. 42

In search of Eden. '88 stress index. 286 best & worst cities for families.
Psychology Today   Nov 1988   p. 52

Bringing the city back to life.
Time   Nov 23, 1987   p. 72

The small town boom.
Newsweek   Jul 6, 1981   p. 26

Are all big cities doomed?
U.S. News   Apr 5, 1976   p. 49

The sick, sick cities.
Newsweek   Mar 17, 1969   p. 40

The embattled cities. Urbanologist Pat Moynihan.
Time   Jul 28, 1967   p. 10

First Negro in the cabinet. Trying to save the cities. Secretary Weaver.
Time   Mar 4, 1966   p. 29

The U.S. city. Its greatness is at stake.
Life   Dec 24, 1965   p. 6

Urban renewal. Remaking the American city.
Time   Nov 6, 1964   p. 60

Smalltown, U.S.A.
Newsweek   Jul 8, 1963   p. 18

Cities of the '60s. Big, bad and popular.
Time   Mar 23, 1962   p. 16

CITY GOVERNMENT
See MUNICIPAL GOVERNMENT

CIVIL DEFENSE

Shelters for survival?
Newsweek   Nov 6, 1961   p. 19

Shelters. How soon - how big - how safe.
Time   Oct 20, 1961   p. 21

CIVIL RIGHTS

The Civil Rights Act of 1990 [draft].
Congressional Digest Aug 1990   p. 196

The Bush court. A move to the right. What it means for: Abortion, the death penalty, civil rights.
Newsweek   Jul 30, 1990   p. 14

Pending civil rights legislation.
Congressional Digest Jan 1985   p. 1

"Rights" explosion splintering America?
U.S. News   Oct 31, 1977   p. 29

Moral policeman to the world?
U.S. News   Mar 14, 1977   p. 17

The law and dissent. Federal Judge Frank Johnson.
Time   May 12, 1967   p. 72

See Also BLACKS - CIVIL RIGHTS

CIVIL RIGHTS MOVEMENT

He had a dream. Coretta King's moving account of life with her martyred husband.
Life   Sep 12, 1969   p. 54

Which way for the Negro now? Martin Luther King. Floyd McKissick. Roy Wilkins. Stokeley Carmichael. Whitney Young.
Newsweek   May 15, 1967   p. 27

Black and white. A major survey of U.S. racial attitudes today.
Newsweek   Aug 22, 1966   p. 20

The road from Selma.
Newsweek   Apr 5, 1965   p. 23

Martin Luther King.
Time   Mar 19, 1965   p. 23

The Civil Rights Bill. Product of principle and compromise.
Time   Jun 19, 1964   p. 15

Spectacle of the march.
Life   Sep 6, 1963   p. 20

Birmingham and beyond: The Negro's push for equality.
Time   May 17, 1963   p. 23

The South and the freedom riders.
Time   Jun 2, 1961   p. 14

CIVIL WAR

See UNITED STATES - HISTORY - CIVIL WAR

CLANCY, TOM

Tom Clancy, best seller. Master of the techno-thriller.
Newsweek   Aug 8, 1988   p. 60

CLARK, JIM

The quickest man on wheels. Champion driver Jim Clark.
Time   Jul 9, 1965   p. 78

CLARK, JOE

Is getting tough the answer? School prinicpal Joe Clark says yes - and critics are up in arms.
Time   Feb 1, 1988   p. 52

CLASS REUNIONS

Class reunions. Why do we go back?
Psychology Today   Jun 1986   p. 22

CLAY, CASSIUS

See ALI, MUHAMMAD

CLEAN AIR ACT

Clean Air Act.
Congressional Digest Mar 1990   p. 65

The Clean Air Act.
Congressional Digest Feb 1989   p. 35

CLEMENS, SAMUEL

See TWAIN, MARK

CLIMATE

Climate: Blame it on *El Niño*.
USA Today   Jun 1990   p. 1

Climate: Worldwide weather threatens millions.
USA Today   Apr 1989   p. 1

The heat is on. How the Earth's climate is changing. Why the ozone hole is growing.
Time   Oct 19, 1987   p. 58

Monsoons. Life breath of half the world.
National Geographic Dec 1984   p. 712

El Niño. Global weather disaster.
National Geographic Feb 1984   p. 144

Is Mother Nature going berserk?
U.S. News   Feb 22, 1982   p. 66

The broiling summer of '80.
Life   Sep 1980   p. 22

The big freeze.
Time   Jan 31, 1977   p. 22

CLONES (BIOLOGY)

Human cloning: The miracle that's about to happen.
Omni   Oct 1988   p. 58

CLOSE, GLENN

Move over, Meryl. Glenn's got it!
Ms.   Nov 1989   p. 46

CLOWNS

An architect runs away to join the circus as a clown.
Life   Feb 20, 1970   p. 62

COAL INDUSTRY

CSX: Railroading for fun and profit. Coal and deregulation make earnings soar.
Business Week   Nov 30, 1981   p. 80

COASTAL CHANGES

Where's the beach? America's vanishing coastline.
Time   Aug 10, 1987   p. 38

COCA-COLA COMPANY

Coke's man on the spot. Coca-Cola Chairman Roberto C. Goizueta.
Business Week   Jul 29, 1985   p. 56

Coke's big market blitz. New products, new prices, new distribution.
Business Week   May 30, 1983   p. 58

COCAINE

Cocaine Inc. The new drug kings. Cold-blooded and efficient, Colombia's Cali cartel has cornered the market. Can these men be stopped?
Time   Jul 1, 1991   p. 28

Can the children be saved? One block's battle against drugs and despair.
Newsweek   Sep 11, 1989   p. 16

'I am a coke addict.' What happens when nice guys get hooked.
Life   Oct 1986   p. 38

Kids and cocaine. An epidemic strikes middle America.
Newsweek   Mar 17, 1986   p. 58

This amount of cocaine can make you feel that you're brilliant, tireless, masterful, invulnerable, and that you're going to live forever. It can also kill you.
Discover   Mar 1985   p. 16

Cocaine. The evil empire. The explosive Latin connection. Colombia's drug lords. U.S. agents: Targets for terror.
Newsweek   Feb 25, 1985   p. 14

Cocaine wars. South America's bloody business.
Time   Feb 25, 1985   p. 26

The history of cocaine. 1884-1984: From Freud to De Lorean.
Life   May 1984   p. 57

Fighting cocaine's grip. Millions of users. Billions of dollars.
Time   Apr 11, 1983   p. 22

High on cocaine. A drug with status - and menace.
Time   Jul 6, 1981   p. 56

COLBY, WILLIAM E.

The CIA. Has it gone too far? Director William E. Colby.
Time   Sep 30, 1974   p. 17

COLD FUSION

The race for fusion. The scientific debate. Why the stakes are so high.
Newsweek   May 8, 1989   p. 48

Fusion or illusion? How two obscure chemists stirred excitement - and outrage - in the scientific world.
Time   May 8, 1989   p. 72

COLES, ROBERT

America's forgotten children. Psychiatrist Robert Coles.
Time   Feb 14, 1972   p. 36

COLLEGE ATHLETES

The exploitation of college athletes: Will they ever receive a proper education?
USA Today   Nov 1990   p. 24

The price of victory. College sports vs. education. When the cheering stops, are big-time college athletes adequately prepared for the real world? Not often enough...
U.S. News   Jan 8, 1990   p. 44

The college trap. Student athletes earn millions for schools, but are they getting an education?
Time   Apr 3, 1989   p. 54

The shame of college sports.
Newsweek   Sep 22, 1980   p. 54

COLLEGE EDUCATION

Who needs college?
Newsweek   Apr 26, 1976   p. 60

COLLEGE GRADUATES

Job market: Outlook good for college graduates.
USA Today   Apr 1988   p. 1

Jobs! Jobs! Jobs! Introducing a new career magazine for People.
Ms.   Sep 1982   p. 57

Now where are the jobs? The graduate, 1971.
Time   May 24, 1971   p. 49

COLLEGE STUDENTS

Real life on campus. Mother/daughter classmates.
Ms.   Sep 1981   p. 45

Co-ed dorms. An intimate revolution on campus.
Life   Nov 20, 1970   p. 32

Can you trust anyone under 30? The graduate 1968.
Time   Jun 7, 1968   p. 78

Campus '65. The college generation looks at itself – a Newsweek survey.
Newsweek   Mar 22, 1965   p. 43

COLLEGE STUDENTS - SEXUAL BEHAVIOR

Morals on the campus.
Newsweek   Apr 6, 1964   p. 52

COLLEGE TEACHERS

See COLLEGES AND UNIVERSITIES - FACULTY

COLLEGES AND UNIVERSITIES

America's best colleges. How top experts rate 455 schools. The best buys in four-year colleges.
U.S. News   Sep 30, 1991   p. 77

Thought police. Watch what you say. There's a 'Politically Correct' way to talk about race, sex and ideas. Is this the new enlightenment – or the new McCarthyism?
Newsweek   Dec 24, 1990   p. 48

America's best colleges. Exclusive rankings of 405 universities and colleges. Teaching versus research: New priorities on campus.
U.S. News   Oct 15, 1990   p. 104

America's best colleges.
U.S. News   Oct 16, 1989   p. 53

America's best colleges. Exclusive ratings. The 125 top schools.
U.S. News   Oct 10, 1988   p. 2

America's best colleges. Expert advice on getting and paying for college. SAT scores, school by school.
U.S. News   Oct 26, 1987   p. 48

Death of the university.
USA Today   Sep 1987   p. 32

The best colleges in America. How to pick one. How to pay for it. How to get the most out of it. Poll of 788 college presidents on the top schools. Education Secretary William Bennett on the lure of learning.
U.S. News   Nov 25, 1985   p. 46

Rating the colleges. Exclusive national survey.
U.S. News   Nov 28, 1983   p. 41

U.S. colleges. Life and death struggle.
U.S. News   May 29, 1978   p. 64

Universities in ferment.
Newsweek   Jun 15, 1970   p. 66

Megaversity: How good?
Newsweek   Feb 26, 1968   p. 78

Rise of the public universities: Quality as well as quantity. New York's Chancellor Samuel B. Gould.
Time   Jan 12, 1968   p. 43

The precarious future of the private college.
Time   Jun 23, 1967   p. 78

The Ivy League: Is it still the best? Yale's Kingman Brewster.
Newsweek   Nov 23, 1964   p. 65

University of California's Clark Kerr.
Time   Oct 17, 1960   p. 58

See Also EDUCATION, HIGHER

COLLEGES AND UNIVERSITIES - FACULTY

Marxism in U.S. classrooms.
U.S. News   Jan 25, 1982   p. 42

COLLEGES AND UNIVERSITIES - GRADUATE SCHOOLS

America's best graduate schools. Business. Law. Medicine. Engineering.
U.S. News   Apr 29, 1991   p. 62

America's best graduate schools. Business. Law. Medicine. Engineering.
U.S. News   Mar 19, 1990   p. 46

COLLEGES AND UNIVERSITIES - RESEARCH

Science under siege. Tight money, blunders and scandal plague America's researchers.
Time   Aug 26, 1991   p. 44

COLLINS, JOAN

Joan Collins. Dynasty's bad girl as you've never seen her before.
Life   Oct 1985   p. 61

COLLINS, JUDY

Singer Judy Collins. Gentle voice amid the strife.
Life   May 2, 1969   p. 40

COLOR PERCEPTION

How we see color. New clues from the brain.
Discover   Dec 1988   p. 52

COLORADO RIVER

The Colorado. The West's lifeline is now America's most endangered river.
Time   Jul 22, 1991   p. 20

COLUMBIA BROADCASTING SYSTEM, INC.

The man who captured CBS. Loews'
Laurence Tisch takes over.
Time   Sep 22, 1986   p. 68

Civil war at CBS. The struggle for the soul
of a legendary network.
Newsweek   Sep 15, 1986   p. 20

COLUMBIA, SOUTH CAROLINA

The South. Into a new century.
Newsweek   May 3, 1965   p. 26

COLUMBIA (SPACE SHUTTLE)

Columbia closes a circle.
National Geographic Oct 1981   p. 474

'We're in space to stay.'
Newsweek   Apr 27, 1981   p. 22

Right on! Winging into a new era.
Time   Apr 27, 1981   p. 16

Comeback in space.
U.S. News   Feb 23, 1981   p. 58

Aiming high in '81. Space shuttle
Columbia.
Time   Jan 12, 1981   p. 8

COLUMBUS, CHRISTOPHER

Discovery! The 500th anniversary of
Columbus' voyage to the New World is
provoking controversy amidst
celebration.
USA Today   Nov 1991   p. 48

America before Columbus. The untold
story.
U.S. News   Jul 8, 1991   p. 22

Our search for the true Columbus landfall.
National Geographic Nov 1986   p. 566

COLUMNISTS

See JOURNALISTS

COMANECI, NADIA

Nadia. The strange and terrible story of
the Olympic angel who won our hearts at
the 1976 Games—and went to hell in
Ceausescu's Romania.
Life   Mar 1990   p. 24

A star is born.
Newsweek   Aug 2, 1976   p. 60

COMETS

Did comets kill the dinosaurs? A new
theory about mass extinctions.
Time   May 6, 1985   p. 72

Riding comets to the stars.
Omni   Jun 1984   p. 54

Mission for the U-2. Hunting comet dust.
Discover   Oct 1983   p. 74

COMIC BOOKS, STRIPS, ETC.

Inside Doonesbury's brain. Garry
Trudeau finally talks.
Newsweek   Oct 15, 1990   p. 60

He's 50! [Superman]
Time   Mar 14, 1988   p. 66

Doonesbury is back! Mike and J.J. are
married—and other exciting surprises.
Life   Oct 1984   p. 55

Doonesbury. Politics in the funny papers.
Time   Feb 9, 1976   p. 57

Charlie Brown and Snoopy. Winners at
last. The great 'Peanuts' craze.
Life   Mar 17, 1967   p. 74

Comment in the comics. The world
according to Peanuts.
Time   Apr 9, 1965   p. 80

COMMON MARKET

See EUROPEAN ECONOMIC
COMMUNITY

COMMUNAL LIVING

Breaking away. Coming of age in fanatical
groups.
Psychology Today   Aug 1984   p. 20

COMMUNES

The youth communes. New way of living
confronts the U.S.
Life   Jul 18, 1969   p. 16

COMMUNICATION

Reach out and touch someone. When
you should.
Psychology Today   Mar 1988   p. 30

Loving & living. There's a rhythm to
everything you do.
Psychology Today   Nov 1987   p. 36

COMMUNICATION SATELLITES

The communications explosion. Early
bird - and after.
Time   May 14, 1965   p. 84

Leo D. Welch. Chairman,
Communications Satellite Corp.
Newsweek   Mar 16, 1964   p. 85

COMMUNISM

In the Kremlin, Communism's last stand.
Gorbachev's desperate new bid to save
his party — and his revolution.
U.S. News   Feb 19, 1990   p. 30

The collapse of Communism. Is the
Soviet Union next?
U.S. News   Jan 15, 1990   p. 31

Communist meltdown. The crumbling
Iron Curtain. The Soviet economy in
ruins.
U.S. News   Nov 20, 1989   p. 20

Collapse of Communism. In China,
Poland and the Soviet Union, the people
defy their leaders.
U.S. News   Jun 19, 1989   p. 18

Communism in turmoil. Special reports
on China and the Soviet Union.
Business Week   Jun 5, 1989   p. 34

Communism. The great economic failure.
U.S. News   Mar 1, 1982   p. 33

Is Central America going Communist?
U.S. News   Dec 21, 1981   p. 20

Twilight of Communism?
U.S.News   Dec 22, 1980   p. 27

Russia's 60 years of Communism.
Success or failure?
U.S. News   Oct 24, 1977   p. 42

In the next decade - Breakup of
communist world?
U.S. News   Aug 9, 1976   p. 24

Communist summit: Trying to pick up
the pieces.
Time   Jun 13, 1969   p. 24

How Russia survived Marxism: Soviet
life today.
Time   Nov 10, 1967   p. 32

Post Khrushchev Communism. China's
Chou En-Lai greeted by Russia's Kosygin.
Time   Nov 13, 1964   p. 44

Marx: How Communism has changed.
Newsweek   Apr 27, 1964   p. 47

The Communist split. Lenin.
Time   Apr 24, 1964   p. 26

K vs. Mao. How wide the split?
Newsweek   Mar 26, 1962   p. 32

Reds step up the pace.
Life   Nov 10, 1961   p. 30

Party Congress: How Russia is ruled.
Newsweek   Oct 23, 1961   p. 29

Communism. Red gods, leaders,
puppets.
Life   Oct 20, 1961   p. 107

COMMUNIST COUNTRIES

Crackup.
Newsweek   Sep 9, 1991   p. 18

The end of the empire.
U.S. News   Sep 9, 1991   p. 20

People of the year. Standing up for
freedom. 1989. Changing the course of
history.
Newsweek   Dec 25, 1989   p. 18

Can he ride the tiger? With Eastern
Europe out of control and his economy in
ruins, Gorbachev faces his toughest test.
Newsweek   Dec 4, 1989   p. 34

Communist meltdown. The crumbling
Iron Curtain. The Soviet economy in
ruins.
U.S. News   Nov 20, 1989   p. 20

The big break. Moscow lets Eastern
Europe go its own way.
Time   Nov 6, 1989   p. 40

The party's over. Communism crumbles
in Poland.
Newsweek   Aug 28, 1989   p. 16

Revolt against Communism. China.
Poland. USSR.
Time   Jun 19, 1989   p. 10

Collapse of Communism. In China,
Poland and the Soviet Union, the people
defy their leaders.
U.S. News   Jun 19, 1989   p. 18

The Soviet Union: Part 3. Revolution and
ruin. Hope and anger in a collapsing
empire.
U.S. News   Apr 3, 1989   p. 34

The Red Bloc in crisis.
Newsweek   Apr 8, 1968   p. 52

Eastern Europe. Life under a relaxed
Communism.
Time   Mar 18, 1966   p. 34

The new Rumania. The satellites look
west.
Newsweek   Aug 10, 1964   p. 31

Marx: How Communism has changed.
Newsweek   Apr 27, 1964   p. 47

COMMUNIST COUNTRIES - ECONOMIC POLICY

The Marxist world. Lure of capitalism.
U.S. News   Feb 4, 1985   p. 36

COMMUNIST PARTIES

Russia in trouble.
Newsweek   Jun 16, 1969   p. 38

Communist summit: Trying to pick up
the pieces.
Time   Jun 13, 1969   p. 24

COMMUNIST PARTY - ITALY

Italy. The Red threat.
Time   Jun 14, 1976   p. 20

COMMUTING

Gridlock.
Time   Sep 12, 1988   p. 52

The agony of the commuter.
Newsweek   Jan 18, 1971   p. 44

The agony of getting anywhere.
Newsweek   Jan 9, 1967   p. 43

Getting to work. The trials of U.S.
commuters.
Time   Jan 18, 1960   p. 74

COMPAQ COMPUTER CORP.

Who's afraid of IBM? Not Compaq
Computer. It's challenging Big Blue's new
PC line. So far, so good. But IBM is not
your ordinary Goliath. Rod Canion.
Compaq President and CEO.
Business Week   Jun 29, 1987   p. 68

COMPETITIVENESS

Can America still compete? With its new
Saturn, GM bets the answer is yes.
Time   Oct 29, 1990   p. 74

Lean & mean. America's most
competitive companies.
Business Week   Oct 5, 1987   p. 78

America's competitive drive. Are we
losing it?
U.S. News   Feb 2, 1987   p. 18

Competing. For winners, the name of the
game is cooperation. Parenting. To rear
children successfully, train mom and dad.
Managing. Meet your new corporate
coach—the computer.
Psychology Today   Sep 1986   p. 22

COMPREHENSIVE EDUCATION AND TRAINING ACT

Controversy over the CETA program.
Congressional Digest Apr 1981   p. 99

COMPUTER CHIPS

Super chips. This experimental silicon
chip is about to start a revolution in
electronics.
Business Week   Jun 10, 1985   p. 82

The chip. Electronic mini-marvel that is
changing your life.
National Geographic Oct 1982   p. 421

COMPUTER CRIMES

Compucop: Putting the byte on crime.
Omni   Aug 1990   p. 34

Is your computer secure? Hackers,
viruses, and other threats.
Business Week   Aug 1, 1988   p. 64

Computer capers. Trespassing in the
Information Age - pranks or sabotage?
Newsweek   Sep 5, 1983   p. 42

Crime by computer.
Omni   Mar 1983   p. 52

Computer crime. The spreading danger to business.
Business Week   Apr 20, 1981   p. 86

COMPUTER INDUSTRY

Laptops take off. Laptops are the fastest growing computer market by far. The Japanese are ahead—with Compaq, Tandy and Zenith in hot pursuit. Can IBM and Apple catch up?
Business Week   Mar 18, 1991   p. 118

The genius. Seymour Cray invented the supercomputer. Now he's struggling to come up with a radically different machine that could once again revolutionize computer technology.
Business Week   Apr 30, 1990   p. 80

IBM. A bold move in mainframes. IBM has launched the most ambitious software project in its history. The goal: Make mainframes the heart of computer networks. Will this restore Big Blue's growth?
Business Week   May 29, 1989   p. 72

Computers. Is the industry maturing?
Business Week   Mar 6, 1989   p. 68

Intel. The next revolution. When Intel invented the computer-on-a-chip 17 years ago, it opened the era of personal computers. In 1989 Intel will take the next step: A chip so powerful it will become the heart of even the biggest computer.
Business Week   Sep 26, 1988   p. 74

Computers. The industry's new look. The mainframe era is fading as powerful micros take over many jobs. The implications are profound—for buyers and sellers.
Business Week   Nov 30, 1987   p. 112

Computers: When will the slump end?
Business Week   Apr 21, 1986   p. 58

The computer slump. Why now? How long?
Business Week   Jun 24, 1985   p. 74

Apple's dynamic duo and their plan to take on IBM in the office.
Business Week   Nov 26, 1984   p. 146

Computer shock. A wild proliferation hits the office – confusing buyers, sellers, and managers.
Business Week   Aug 8, 1983   p. 46

Moving away from mainframes. The large computer makers' strategy for survival.
Business Week   Feb 15, 1982   p. 78

COMPUTER INDUSTRY - HEALTH ASPECTS

A new American nightmare? Medical exposé. For seven years, their work was breaking down their immune system—so says their doctor now. They have a high-tech disease with no name.
Ms.   Mar 1986   p. 35

COMPUTER INDUSTRY - JAPAN

Computers. Japan comes on strong. From laptops to supercomputers, Japan is pushing into America. Will it succeed—as it did in cars and electronics?
Business Week   Oct 23, 1989   p. 104

COMPUTER INDUSTRY - STANDARDS

Computer confusion. Industry standards were supposed to make things easier. Instead, buyers now face so many choices they're more baffled than ever. The result? They're spending less on computers than they might.
Business Week   Jun 10, 1991   p. 72

COMPUTER NETWORKS

Rethinking the computer. How those mainframes on a chip are changing the way we use computers.
Business Week   Nov 26, 1990   p. 116

Software. How the game is changing. Networks of computers are altering the way businesses work. So software companies need new products, new ways to sell them, and a new service mentality.
Business Week   Jun 4, 1990   p. 102

COMPUTER SOFTWARE

Software made simple. It's called object-oriented programming–a way to make computers a lot easier to use. Here's what it can do for you.
Business Week   Sep 30, 1991   p. 92

Computer software. The magic inside the machine.
Time   Apr 16, 1984   p. 56

Software. The new driving force.
Business Week   Feb 27, 1984   p. 74

COMPUTER STORES

Computer stores. Tantalizing opportunity selling computers to consumers.
Business Week   Sep 28, 1981   p. 76

COMPUTER VIRUSES

Computer viruses.
Time   Sep 26, 1988   p. 62

COMPUTERS

Computers of the future.
Time   Mar 28, 1988   p. 54

User friendly. Objects, foods and tools that make living a whole lot easier.
Psychology Today   Dec 1983   p. 23

Saving lab animals. How computers cut down the killing.
Discover   Sep 1983   p. 76

Super computers. The high-stakes race to build a machine that thinks. Can the U.S. beat Japan?
Newsweek   Jul 4, 1983   p. 58

Getting computers to understand English. Yale's Roger Schank enters the marketplace.
Psychology Today   Apr 1983   p. 28

Managing America's business. What makes a top executive?
Psychology Today   Feb 1983   p. 26

Using bacteria to make computers.
Discover   May 1982   p. 76

Machines that think. Hello, I am your friend Chip. I'm getting smarter all the time. Soon, I will be everywhere. And by my instant calculations society will never be the same.
Newsweek   Jun 30, 1980   p. 50

The computer society.
Time   Feb 20, 1978   p. 44

The computer in society.
Time   Apr 2, 1965   p. 84

The 'think machine' - smarter and smarter.
Newsweek   Oct 24, 1960   p. 85

COMPUTERS - BANKING USE

Electronic banking.
Business Week   Jan 18, 1982   p. 70

COMPUTERS - MEDICAL USE

Medicine's new vision.
National Geographic Jan 1987   p. 2

Computers that can film insanity.
Omni   Jan 1984   p. 84

Computer surgery.
Discover   May 1983   p. 86

COMPUTERS - MUSICAL USE

Bach to the future: Computer music grows up.
Omni   Mar 1991   p. 42

COMPUTERS - PSYCHOLOGICAL ASPECTS

Robopsychology and computers: Love at first byte.
Omni   Nov 1988   p. 42

COMPUTERS AND CHILDREN

Computer education. School work & home work.
Psychology Today   Sep 1984   p. 22

Computer generation. A new breed of whiz kids.
Time   May 3, 1982   p. 50

COMPUTERS, GOVERNMENT USE OF

Uncle Sam's computer has got you.
U.S. News   Apr 10, 1978   p. 44

COMPUTERS IN MOTION PICTURES

Computerizing the movies.
Discover   Aug 1984   p. 76

COMPUTERS, PERSONAL

Personal computers. The coming decade. On the 10th anniversary of IBM's PC, the industry is in turmoil. Will IBM and Apple, working together, still dominate? What technology will be hot? How will we use PCs in the year 2000.
Business Week   Aug 12, 1991   p. 58

Home computers. Will they sell this time?
Business Week   Sep 10, 1990   p. 64

Apple's comeback. With profits up, John
Scully aims to win more corporate
customers. The key: Versatile new
models of the easy-to-use Macintosh.
Business Week   Jan 19, 1987   p. 84

IBM vs. the clones. From Taiwan to
Texas, companies are turning out
low-priced versions of IBM's personal
computer. What will IBM do?
Business Week   Jul 28, 1986   p. 62

Personal computers and the winner
is...IBM.
Business Week   Oct 3, 1983   p. 76

Computer shock. A wild proliferation hits
the office – confusing buyers, sellers, and
managers.
Business Week   Aug 8, 1983   p. 46

Machine of the year. The computer
moves in.
Time   Jan 3, 1983   p. 12

Zap! The coming shakeout in personal
computers.
Business Week   Nov 22, 1982   p. 72

Home is where the computer is.
Newsweek   Feb 22, 1982   p. 50

The home information revolution.
Window on the world.
Business Week   Jun 29, 1981   p. 74

CONCORDE AIRLINER

See AIRPLANES, SUPERSONIC

CONGO

See ZAIRE

CONGRESS

The untouchables. America's voters said
no to politics as usual. So why are 96% of
these people going back to Washington?
Time   Nov 19, 1990 p. 30

Bush league. The President stumbles,
Congress bumbles. Boooo!
Newsweek   Oct 22, 1990   p. 20

Congress on the auction block. How can
we eliminate the sale of our legislators to
the highest bidder?
USA Today   May 1990   p. 10

Congress. It doesn't work. Let's fix it.
Business Week   Apr 16, 1990   p. 54

How Congress really works. Jim Wright
and the new capitol culture.
Newsweek   Apr 24, 1989   p. 26

Controversy over the legislative veto.
Congressional Digest Dec 1983   p. 290

The budget brawl.
Time   Apr 26, 1982   p. 10

Explosion of new laws. How they affect
you.
U.S. News   Oct 23, 1978   p. 23

Congress. Bold & balky. Senate Majority
Leader Robert Byrd.
Time   Jan 23, 1978   p. 8

Our junket-happy congress. What secret
records disclose.
U.S. News   Jun 27, 1977   p. 19

Message from home: Curb the
bureaucrats!
U.S. News   Nov 10, 1975   p. 39

Crisis in Congress.
Time   Jan 15, 1973   p. 12

New Congress v. Nixon.
Time   Feb 1, 1971   p. 12

Congress: Consensus or conflict? The
Senators Kennedy.
Newsweek   Jan 17, 1966   p. 17

The new Congress: Democratic and busy.
Time   Jan 15, 1965   p. 16

Walter Lippman: A critique of Congress.
Newsweek   Jan 20, 1964   p. 18

Kennedy & Congress. What price victory?
Speaker Rayburn.
Time   Feb 10, 1961   p. 11

CONNALLY, JOHN

J.F.K.'s assassination: Who was the real
target. Twenty-five years later, a new
book argues Oswald was actually out to
get John Connally.
Time   Nov 28, 1988 p. 30

Hot on the trail. G.O.P. candidate John
Connally.
Time　　　　Sep 10, 1979　p. 12

Nixon's No. 2 man? Treasury Secretary
John Connally.
Newsweek　　　Aug 9, 1971　p. 16

Texas: Where myth & reality merge.
Governor Connally.
Time　　　　Jan 17, 1964　p. 16

CONNER, DENNIS

Going for it. America's Cup skipper
Dennis Conner.
Time　　　　Feb 9, 1987　p. 42

CONNORS, JIMMY

Storming the courts. Jimmy Connors.
Time　　　　Apr 28, 1975　p. 46

CONSERVATION

The natural world of Aldo Leopold.
National Geographic Nov 1981　　p. 682

Special issue. Our splendid outdoors.
The land we love and enjoy...and the
fight to save it.
Life　　　　Dec 22, 1961　p. 22

CONSERVATION CORPS, AMERICAN

The proposed American Conservation
Corps.
Congressional Digest May 1983　　p. 131

CONSERVATISM

End of the permissive society? Jail for
drunk drivers! Bring back the death
penalty! Raise school standards.
Tougher sentences for criminals. Outlaw
drug paraphernalia! Stamp out
pornography.
U.S. News　　　Jun 28, 1982　p. 45

Is America turning right?
Newsweek　　　Nov 7, 1977　p. 34

William Buckley / Conservatism can be
fun.
Time　　　　Nov 3, 1967　p. 70

Thunder on the right. The conservatives.
The radicals. The fanatic fringe.
Newsweek　　　Dec 4, 1961　p. 18

Conservatism. On the campus. In U.S.
politics. In the nation. Arizona's Barry
Goldwater: Leader of the right.
Newsweek　　　Apr 10, 1961　p. 28

CONSTANTINE II

Greece: The palace coup. King
Constantine.
Time　　　　Apr 28, 1967　p. 28

CONSTITUTION - UNITED STATES

We the people.
Time　　　　Jul 6, 1987　p. 20

Genius of the people. A special report
celebrating the Constitution.
Newsweek　　　May 25, 1987　p. 44

We did it! The miracle at Philadelphia,
1787. The U.S. Constitution at 200. How it
shapes our lives today.
U.S. News　　　Apr 27, 1987　p. 24

Attorney General Edwin Meese:
Interpreting the Constitution.
USA Today　　　Sep 1986　　p. 36

CONSTITUTIONAL CONVENTION, 1787

We did it! The miracle at Philadelphia,
1787. The U.S. Constitution at 200. How it
shapes our lives today.
U.S. News　　　Apr 27, 1987　p. 24

CONSUMER PROTECTION

Product liability legislation.
Congressional Digest Jan 1987　　p. 3

A consumer's best friend. Bess Myerson
on the prowl for stores that cheat us.
Life　　　　Jul 16, 1971　p. 22

The consumer revolt. Ralph Nader.
Time　　　　Dec 12, 1969　p. 89

CONTINENTAL TELEPHONE

Continental Telephone. Taking on the
giants in telecommunications.
Business Week　　Feb 9, 1981　p. 50

CONTRACEPTIVES

See BIRTH CONTROL

CONTRAS (NICARAGUA)

Contra aid.
Congressional Digest Mar 1988　　p. 67

Conglomerates: The new business giants.
President Harold S. Geneen.
Time   Sep 8, 1967   p. 86

The technology industry. How a whiz kid
makes it pay. Litton's "Tex" Thornton.
Time   Oct 4, 1963   p. 104

CORPORATIONS - ACQUISITIONS AND MERGERS

The age of consolidation. Mergers and
strategic alliances are again reshaping
American business. Will the U.S.
economy really become more
competitive?
Business Week   Oct 14, 1991   p. 86

The best and worst deals of the 1980s.
What we learned from all those mergers,
acquisitions, LBOs, and takeovers. Paul
Reichmann.
Business Week   Jan 15, 1990   p. 52

Corporate merger legislation.
Congressional Digest Mar 1989   p. 67

A game of greed. This man could pocket
$100 million from the largest corporate
takeover in history. Has the buyout craze
gone too far? RJR Nabisco's Ross
Johnson.
Time   Dec 5, 1988   p. 66

Merger mania. Why it just won't stop.
Most mergers don't work. But the current
crop may fare better.
Business Week   Mar 21, 1988   p. 122

Deal mania. The restructuring of
Corporate America. Is it good or bad?
Managing in the takeover era. The power
shift to Wall Street. Investing in the
merger game.
Business Week   Nov 24, 1986   p. 74

Raider or manager? With the crisis over
at TWA, Carl Icahn is after USX. Critics
say he wants a fast buck. He says he'll
revitalize the company.
Business Week   Oct 27, 1986   p. 98

Merger tango.
Time   Dec 23, 1985   p. 42

New? Improved? The brand-name
mergers.
Business Week   Oct 21, 1985   p. 108

What are mergers doing to America?
Your job. What happens after the sale.
Your money. How to profit from
takeovers. Your town. Will it boom or
bust?
U.S. News   Jul 22, 1985   p. 48

Do mergers really work? No, not very
often. And that raises even more
questions about the current merger
mania.
Business Week   Jun 3, 1985   p. 88

The raiders. How takeover fears distort
corporate behavior. Why the game may
change. Are takeovers good for the
economy? Where the raiders get their
money.
Business Week   Mar 4, 1985   p. 80

Asset redeployment. Everything is for
sale now.
Business Week   Aug 24, 1981   p. 68

Is big business getting too big?
Newsweek   Jul 27, 1981   p. 50

Takeovers in high gear. Threat or boon to
U.S. business?
Time   Mar 7, 1969   p. 75

Jim Ling the merger king.
Newsweek   Oct 9, 1967   p. 71

CORPORATIONS - CORRUPT PRACTICES

Corporate crime. The untold story.
U.S. News   Sep 6, 1982   p. 25

The payoff scandals.
Time   Feb 23, 1976   p. 26

The big payoff. Lockheed scandal: Graft
around the globe.
Time   Feb 23, 1976   p. 28

CORPORATIONS - DIRECTORS

Corporate boards. Some directors are
finally taking charge, but they could all be
more effective. Here's how.
Business Week   Jul 3, 1989   p. 66

The corporate elite. Chief executives of
the *Business Week* top 1000. A directory.
Business Week   Oct 23, 1987   p. 99

A job nobody wants. Joined any boards lately? The trouble can outweigh the honor—which is why the outside director may become an endangered species.
Business Week   Sep 8, 1986   p. 56

CORPORATIONS - DIVESTITURE

Splitting up. It's the opposite of merger mania. Companies divesting assets, spinning off divisions, even liquidating themselves. The trick is knowing when it makes sense.
Business Week   Jul 1, 1985   p. 52

CORPORATIONS - FINANCE

The perilous hunt for corporate financing.
Business Week   Mar 1, 1982   p. 44

CORPORATIONS, INTERNATIONAL

The stateless corporation. The multinational of the 1970s is obsolete. Global companies must be more than just a bunch of overseas subsidiaries that execute decisions made at headquarters.
Business Week   May 14, 1990   p. 98

Global companies. Too big to handle?
Newsweek   Nov 20, 1972   p. 96

COSBY, BILL

Cosby, Inc. Funny, famous, fifty - and really rich.
Time   Sep 28, 1987   p. 56

Cosby. He's No. 1.
Newsweek   Sep 2, 1985   p. 50

Cosby! America's funniest father.
Life   Jun 1985   p. 34

COSELL, HOWARD

This is Howard Cosell...
Newsweek   Oct 2, 1972   p. 54

COSMETIC INDUSTRY

The beauty business.
Newsweek   Jun 3, 1968   p. 80

COSMETIC SURGERY

Plastic surgery. Who should, who shouldn't. A guide to the procedures.
U.S. News   May 1, 1989   p. 68

Quest for beauty. The cosmetic surgery craze.
Psychology Today   May 1988   p. 28

COSMIC RAYS

The case of the cosmic rays. No one knows just where they come from or even what they are.
Discover   Sep 1989   p. 52

COSMOLOGY

Master of the universe. One scientist's courageous voyage to the frontiers of the cosmos. Physicist Stephen Hawking.
Newsweek   Jun 13, 1988   p. 56

How the universe began. Looking beyond the Big Bang.
Discover   Jun 1983   p. 92

COST OF LIVING

Food prices. How much higher?
U.S. News   Feb 18, 1974   p. 41

The meat furor.
Newsweek   Apr 9, 1973   p. 73

Food prices: The big beef.
Time   Apr 9, 1973   p. 11

The high cost of eating.
Newsweek   Mar 5, 1973   p. 52

COSTNER, KEVIN

Kevin Costner. The new American hero - smart, sexy and on a roll.
Time   Jun 26, 1989   p. 76

COUNTERCULTURE

Happenings. The worldwide underground of the arts creates the other culture.
Life   Feb 17, 1967   p. 86

COUNTERFEITS AND COUNTERFEITING

Counterfeit goods. It's not just Gucci handbags or Cartier watches that are illegally copied. Hundreds of fake products are now sold around the world, from pharmaceuticals and computers to auto parts and military hardware.
Business Week   Dec 16, 1985   p. 64

COUNTRY MUSIC

Country music. Songs of love, loyalty & doubt. Merle Haggard.
Time   May 6, 1974   p. 51

The country music craze.
Newsweek   Jun 18, 1973   p. 65

COURTS

Controversy over Federal criminal
sentencing policy.
Congressional Digest Jun 1984 p. 163

Efforts in the Congress to curtail the
Federal Courts.
Congressional Digest May 1982 p. 131

How to break logjam in courts. Exclusive
inverview with Chief Justice Burger.
U.S. News Dec 19, 1977 p. 21

Too much law?
Newsweek Jan 10, 1977 p. 42

COUSTEAU, JACQUES YVES

Skindiving. Poetry, pleasure & self.
Jacques Cousteau.
Time Mar 28, 1960 p. 66

COUVE DE MURVILLE, M.

The siren's song. French diplomacy from
Richelieu to de Gaulle. Foreign Minister
Couve de Murville.
Time Feb 7, 1964 p. 26

COVERT MILITARY OPERATIONS

See MILITARY OPERATIONS, COVERT

COX, ARCHIBALD

The tapes crisis. Archibald Cox.
Newsweek Oct 29, 1973 p. 22

Nixon on the brink.
Time Oct 29, 1973 p. 12

CRACK (COCAINE)

The men who created crack. The history
of the drug plaguing America's cities.
U.S. News Aug 19, 1991 p. 44

Crack kids. Their mothers used drugs,
and now it's the children who suffer.
Time May 13, 1991 p. 56

Growing up in East Harlem.
National Geographic May 1990 p. 52

Crack. Hour by hour. The junkies, the
jailer, the pimps and the tiniest addicts.
Newsweek Nov 28, 1988 p. 64

Crack and crime. The drug crisis.
Newsweek Jun 16, 1986 p. 15

CRAY, SEYMOUR

The genius. Seymour Cray invented the
supercomputer. Now he's struggling to
come up with a radically different
machine that could once again
revolutionize computer technology.
Business Week Apr 30, 1990 p. 80

CREATION

The all-creating eye. According to a
radical tenet of physics, the universe
exists only because it has been, is being,
and will be observed.
Discover May 1987 p. 90

CREATIONISM

The creation. Religion's search for a
common ground with science.
U.S. News Dec 23, 1991 p. 56

Science and censorship.
Omni Feb 1987 p. 42

Darwin on trial. Creationism vs.
evolution in Little Rock.
Discover Feb 1982 p. 14

CREATIVITY

Creativity. The source, the secrets, the
exercises.
Omni Apr 1989 p. 16

Are you creative? The latest research
suggests people can be taught to be more
creative. Many companies are applying
the new techniques—with surprisingly
good results.
Business Week Sep 30, 1985 p. 80

Breakthroughs of the mind–how they
occur.
Psychology Today Jul 1981 p. 64

CREDIT

Is nothing private? Computers know
more about you than you realize—and
now anyone can tap in.
Business Week Sep 4, 1989 p. 74

The credit tumble.
Newsweek Mar 31, 1980 p. 52

CREDIT CARDS

Credit: Don't get swamped this holiday
season.
USA Today Dec 1989 p. 1

The U.S. takes off on credit cards.
Life   Mar 27, 1970   p. 48

CRIME

Cops under fire. They are outmanned, outgunned, second-guessed — and their lives are tougher than ever.
U.S. News   Dec 3, 1990   p. 32

Corporate crime. The untold story.
U.S. News   Sep 6, 1982   p. 25

Our losing battle against crime.
U.S. News   Oct 12, 1981   p. 39

The epidemic of violent crime.
Newsweek   Mar 23, 1981   p. 46

The curse of violent crime.
Time   Mar 23, 1981   p. 16

Fear stalks the streets.
U.S.News   Oct 27, 1980   p. 58

Crime. Why - and what to do.
Time   Jun 30, 1975   p. 10

The losing battle against crime in America.
U.S. News   Dec 16, 1974   p. 30

Living with crime.
Newsweek   Dec 18, 1972   p. 31

The cities lock up. Fear of crime creates a life-style behind steel.
Life   Nov 19, 1971   p. 26

Cops v. crime: Ready for a hot summer.
Time   Jul 13, 1970   p. 34

Investigative report: St. Louis. The mayor, the mob, and the lawyer.
Life   May 29, 1970   p. 40

Law and order. Volatile campaign issue. Security alert for Democratic Convention.
Life   Aug 23, 1968   p. 14

Crime in the streets.
Newsweek   Aug 16, 1965   p. 20

CRIME PREVENTION

Crime. How *not* to become a victim.
USA Today   Aug 1991   p. 1

Street crime. People fight back.
U.S. News   Apr 15, 1985   p. 42

The people's war against crime.
U.S. News   Jul 13, 1981   p. 53

Spiraling crime. How to protect yourself.
U.S. News   Nov 24, 1975   p. 83

War on crime by fed-up citizens.
U.S. News   Sep 29, 1975   p. 19

What it takes to stop rampant crime.
U.S. News   Jun 10, 1974   p. 37

CRIME, VICTIMS OF

Victims of rape. Should their names be kept secret? Privacy, the media and the Kennedy case.
Newsweek   Apr 29, 1991   p. 26

Victims of crime. Why the cops and courts are failing. The emotional and psychological trauma. One victim's story.
U.S. News   Jul 31, 1989   p. 16

CRIMINAL JUSTICE, ADMINISTRATION OF

1990 omnibus crime bill.
Congressional Digest Nov 1990   p. 258

Controversy over Federal criminal sentencing policy.
Congressional Digest Jun 1984   p. 163

"Revolving door" justice: Why criminals go free.
U.S. News   May 10, 1976   p. 36

What it takes to stop rampant crime.
U.S. News   Jun 10, 1974   p. 37

CRIMINAL PROCEDURE

Moving the Constitution into the police station. Danny Escobedo.
Time   Apr 29, 1966   p. 52

CRO-MAGNON MAN

The way we were. Our Ice Age heritage: Language, art, fashion, and the family.
Newsweek   Nov 10, 1986   p. 62

CRONKITE, WALTER

The private life of Walter Cronkite.
Life   Nov 1980   p. 132

Walter Cronkite. A visit with a nice guy.
Life   Mar 26, 1971   p. 50

The electronic front page. Walter
Cronkite.
Time   Oct 14, 1966   p. 66

The TV news battle. Walter Cronkite of
CBS.
Newsweek   Sep 23, 1963   p. 62

CROSBY, BING
Chevalier and Crosby: Two old pros in
songfest.
Life   Mar 10, 1961   p. 77

CROWN, LESTER
The Crown family empire. Henry Crown
built one of America's largest fortunes.
Beyond vast real estate holdings, he and
his secretive family own a quarter of
General Dynamics, the No. 2 defense
contractor, plus blocks of stock. . .
Business Week   Mar 31, 1986   p. 50

CRUISE, TOM
Cruise control. Hollywood's top gun gets
serious in a bold new movie about Viet
Nam.
Time   Dec 25, 1989   p. 74

Paul Newman & Tom Cruise. A private
visit with the new hustler and the old pro.
Life   Nov 1986   p. 72

CRUSADES
Retracing the First Crusade.
National Geographic Sep 1989   p. 326

CRYONICS
Cold storage. Cryonics: The chilling truth.
Discover   Feb 1988   p. 52

CRYSTAL, BILLY
The genius of Billy Crystal. How a great
comic does it.
Life   Apr 1990   p. 90

CUBA
Inside Castro's Cuba. A penetrating
report in pictures.
Life   Mar 15, 1963   p. 28

Communism's western beachhead.
Cuba's Che Guevara.
Time   Aug 8, 1960   p. 36

CUBA - POLITICS AND GOVERNMENT
Cuba: The decaying revolution.
Time   Oct 8, 1965   p. 36

Cuba: Chaos in the economy. Conflict
among the Reds. Communist chief Blas
Roca.
Time   Apr 27, 1962   p. 33

CUBA AND THE UNITED STATES
Reagan's goal: Cutting Castro down to
size.
U.S. News   Apr 6, 1981   p. 20

Castro. Russia's cat's-paw.
U.S. News   Jun 12, 1978   p. 20

If U.S. does business with Castro -
U.S. News   Sep 8, 1975   p. 17

Showdown. 'The cost of freedom is
always high...'
Newsweek   Nov 5, 1962   p. 27

Castro's Cuba. How U.S. voters feel.
Newsweek   Oct 22, 1962   p. 21

The Monroe Doctrine and Communist
Cuba.
Time   Sep 21, 1962   p. 17

Struggle for Cuba.
Newsweek   May 1, 1961   p. 23

The Cuban disaster.
Time   Apr 28, 1961   p. 19

Castro and Cuba. Can they survive?
Crisis on our doorstep.
Newsweek   Jan 16, 1961   p. 15

Castro and the Reds: Their real goal.
Newsweek   Sep 5, 1960   p. 42

CUBAN MISSILE CRISIS, 1962
What happened in the Kremlin?
Newsweek   Nov 12, 1962   p. 21

Dealing with the deadly crisis. The U.S.
and its people withstand the nuclear
threat.
Life   Nov 9, 1962   p. 36

After Khrushchev's retreat.
Time   Nov 9, 1962   p. 26

Showdown. 'The cost of freedom is
always high...'
Newsweek   Nov 5, 1962   p. 27

The danger-filled week of decision. Cuba.
Life   Nov 2, 1962   p. 34

Showdown on Cuba. The evidence that
led to action.
Time   Nov 2, 1962   p. 15

CUBANS IN THE UNITED STATES

The Cuban influx. Can Carter control it?
Newsweek   May 26, 1980   p. 22

Cuban extremists in U.S. A growing terror
threat.
U.S. News   Dec 6, 1976   p. 29

CULTS

Scientology. The cult of greed. How the
growing Dianetics empire squeezes
millions from believers worldwide.
Time   May 6, 1991   p. 50

Breaking away. Coming of age in fanatical
groups.
Psychology Today   Aug 1984   p. 20

America's cults. Gaining ground again.
U.S. News   Jul 5, 1982   p. 37

Children of a Hare Krishna commune.
Life   Apr 1980   p. 44

The cult of death.
Time   Dec 4, 1978   p. 38

Cult of death.
Time   Dec 4, 1978   p. 16

CULTURAL LITERACY

What Americans should know (and
don't).
U.S. News   Sep 28, 1987   p. 86

CUMMINS ENGINE CO.

Mr. Rust Belt. Henry Schacht of
Cummins Engine did everything right: He
invested for the long term, defended
market share, and beat back the Japanese.
So where are the profits?
Business Week   Oct 17, 1988   p. 72

CUOMO, MARIO

What to make of Mario. New York
governor Cuomo.
Time   Jun 2, 1986   p. 28

Is Mario Cuomo for real? A profile: The
governor, the Italian-American, the
Catholic, the candidate.
Newsweek   Mar 24, 1986   p. 22

CUSHING, RICHARD JAMES, CARDINAL

Catholicism in the U.S. A surge of
renewal. Boston's Cardinal Cushing.
Time   Aug 21, 1964   p. 35

CUSTOMER SERVICE

King customer. Forget market share.
Stop worrying about your competitors.
The companies that are succeeding now
put their customers first.
Business Week   Mar 12, 1990   p. 88

Why is service so bad? The hapless
American consumer.
Time   Feb 2, 1987   p. 48

CYPRESS SEMICONDUCTOR CORP.

The bad boy of Silicon Valley. The
offbeat management ideas of Cypress
Semiconductor's T.J. Rodgers.
Business Week   Dec 9, 1991   p. 64

CYPRUS - POLITICS AND GOVERNMENT

Makarios of Cyprus.
Newsweek   Mar 2, 1964   p. 34

Cyprus. Turks with shotguns guard a
road against Greeks.
Life   Feb 28, 1964   p. 24

CZECHOSLOVAKIA - POLITICS AND GOVERNMENT

The birth of freedom. A picture album of
one of the 20th century's great moments
by the photographers of Czechoslovakia.
Life   Feb 1990   p. 26

The Red Bloc in crisis.
Newsweek   Apr 8, 1968   p. 52

Self-determination for Czechoslovakia.
Party boss Dubcek.
Time   Apr 5, 1968   p. 26

CZECHOSLOVAKIA - RUSSIAN INVASION, 1968

The Czech crisis.
Newsweek   Sep 2, 1968   p. 10

Czechoslovakia. Death of the bright
young freedom.
Life   Aug 30, 1968   p. 14

Invasion.
Time   Aug 30, 1968   p. 22

CZECHOSLOVAKIA AND THE SOVIET UNION

Defying the Kremlin. Czechoslovakia's Alexander Dubcek.
Newsweek   Jul 29, 1968   p. 32

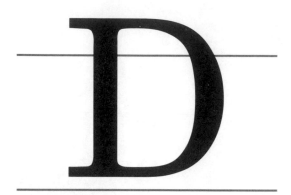

D

D-DAY INVASION, 1944

The men who hit the beaches.
Remembering D-Day, 1944.
Newsweek   Jun 11, 1984   p. 18

D-Day. Forty years after the great
crusade.
Time   May 28, 1984 p. 10

DALEY, RICHARD

How to run a city. Chicago's Mayor
Richard J. Daley.
Newsweek   Apr 5, 1971   p. 80

Chicago: The new facade. The next
election. Mayor Daley.
Time   Mar 15, 1963 p. 24

DANILOFF-ZAKHAROV ESPIONAGE CASE, 1986

Next move? Superpower chess game.
Journalist Nicholas Daniloff.
U.S. News   Sep 22, 1986   p. 14

Frame-up. The Daniloff arrest in Moscow.
The threat to superpower relations.
Working the Kremlin: journalists beware.
Exclusive: Ruth Daniloff's Diary of
anguish. The KGB's new muscle.
U.S. News   Sep 15, 1986   p. 14

DARMAN, RICHARD

The trillion dollar man. Budget Director
Dick Darman wants to do more than cut
the deficit. He wants to reshape America.
And he's not kidding.
Business Week   Mar 13, 1989   p. 100

DATE RAPE

See RAPE

DATING (SOCIAL CUSTOMS)

How millions are finding love in the
classifieds.
Ms.   Aug 1983   p. 39

DAVID-WEILL, MICHEL

The last emperor. Wall Street's Michel
David-Weill. An inside look at how he
rules the private world of Lazard Frères.
Business Week   May 30, 1988 p. 64

DAVIS, ANGELA

Angela Davis. Black revolutionary.
Newsweek   Oct 26, 1970   p. 18

The making of a fugitive. Wanted by the
FBI: Angela Davis.
Life   Sep 11, 1970   p. 20

DAWKINS, PETER

Captain Pete Dawkins keeps on winning.
Army's All-America Rhodes Scholar, now
in Vietnam.
Life   Apr 8, 1966   p. 91

DAY CARE

See CHILD CARE

DAY, DORIS

Box office bonanza. Sunny Doris Day in a
shivery role.
Life   Oct 10, 1960   p. 136

DE BENEDETTI, CARLO

The dealmaker. Carlo De Benedetti leads
an extraordinary double life—CEO of
Olivetti and international entrepreneur.
So why is he worried?
Business Week   Aug 24, 1987 p. 42

DE GAULLE, CHARLES

Showdown in France.
Newsweek   Jun 10, 1968   p. 38

France: Beyond the deluge. Charles de
Gaulle.
Time   May 31, 1968 p. 20

France's fading hero. Charles de Gaulle.
Newsweek   Aug 28, 1967 p. 30

De Gaulle's bold power play—what it
does to us. Like it or not, it's a changed
Europe.
Life   Jul 8, 1966   p. 18

De Gaulle in Russia.
Newsweek   Jul 4, 1966   p. 34

Omnis Europa in unam partem? De
Gaulle.
Time   Jul 1, 1966   p. 20

De Gaulle: Once and future king.
Newsweek   Dec 13, 1965 p. 41

Charles de Gaulle enters Mexico City with
President López Mateos.
Life   Mar 27, 1964 p. 24

De Gaulle's France: A return to greatness?
Newsweek   Feb 10, 1964 p. 40

The perils of grandeur. De Gaulle.
Time   Feb 8, 1963   p. 22

De Gaulle. Apres moi...?
Newsweek   Jan 28, 1963 p. 25

De Gaulle. Mission to America.
Newsweek   Apr 25, 1960 p. 39

France's de Gaulle: The final crisis?
Newsweek   Feb 8, 1960   p. 23

DE LOREAN, JOHN

The bottom line...busted. De Lorean's
shattered dream.
Time   Nov 1, 1982   p. 30

DE VOSJOLI, THYRAUD

The French spy scandal. The former
chief of French Intelligence in the U.S.
reveals the fantastic story of Soviet
espionage that penetrated De Gaulle's
official family.
Life   Apr 26, 1968 p. 30

DEAD SEA SCROLLS

The Bible's last secrets. Deciphering the
mysteries of the Dead Sea Scrolls.
U.S. News   Oct 7, 1991   p. 64

DEAN, JOHN

Dean vs. Nixon.
Newsweek   Jul 9, 1973   p. 12

The accuser. John Dean.
Newsweek   Jul 2, 1973   p. 13

Dean talks.
Time   Jul 2, 1973   p. 12

DEAN WITTER REYNOLDS INC.

The peril in financial services.
Business Week   Aug 20, 1984 p. 52

DEATH

Choosing death. More doctors are
helping the very sick die gently.
Newsweek   Aug 26, 1991 p. 40

New dimensions in death [near-death
experiences].
Omni   Feb 1982   p. 58

Living with dying.
Newsweek   May 1, 1978   p. 52

DEATH PENALTY
See CAPITAL PUNISHMENT

DEAVER, MICHAEL

Who's this man calling? Influence
peddling in Washington. Lobbyist
Michael Deaver.
Time   Mar 3, 1986   p. 26

DEBAKEY, MICHAEL

A bitter feud. Two great surgeons at war
over the human heart. Dr. Denton
Cooley. Dr. Michael DeBakey.
Life   Apr 10, 1970 p. 62

Toward an artificial heart. Surgeon
Michael DeBakey.
Time   May 28, 1965 p. 46

DEBATEGATE CASE

Feeling the heat. The 'debategate' plot
thickens. Who's telling the truth - and will
heads roll?
Newsweek   Jul 18, 1983 p. 14

DEBT

Storm clouds over the recovery.
America's troubled economy. Why too
much debt threatens your pocketbook
and the nation's economy.
U.S. News   May 6, 1991 p. 52

The debt bomb. The worldwide peril of
go-go lending.
Time   Jan 10, 1983 p. 42

The great American debtor.
Newsweek   Jan 8, 1962   p. 54

DEBT, CORPORATE

The debt binge. Have takeovers gone too far? A new wave of merger and LBO proposals, using billions in borrowed money, is hitting the food industry. This comes when corporate debt is already at record levels—which some see as a healthy phenomenon. . .
Business Week   Nov 7, 1988   p. 138

Debt's new dangers. Forcing companies into a survival strategy. Making lenders more wary.
Business Week   Jul 26, 1982   p. 44

DECISION MAKING

The science of decision making. How we make up our minds, and why we're so often wrong.
Discover   Jun 1985   p. 22

DEFECTORS, POLITICAL

The mind of a defector. Did Yurchenko fool the CIA? Storm over a Soviet sailor. Vitaly Yurchenko on his way home.
Newsweek   Nov 18, 1985   p. 34

A defector's story. The highest-ranking Soviet diplomat to break with Moscow since World War II describes the Kremlin's inner workings.
Time   Feb 11, 1985   p. 48

DEFENSE CONTRACTS

The defense scandal. The impact on the industry. The 'Beltway Bandits.' Where the probe is headed. How to reform the system.
Business Week   Jul 4, 1988   p. 28

DEFENSE POLICY - KENNEDY ADMINISTRATION

Weapons & diplomacy. Cuba, Canada and Europe. Secretary McNamara.
Time   Feb 15, 1963   p. 22

DEFENSE POLICY - REAGAN ADMINISTRATION

U.S. defense policy. The right direction?
U.S. News   Nov 23, 1981   p. 24

DEFENSE SPENDING

Who pays for peace? A shrinking defense budget will benefit America. But right now, there's a lot of pain in many companies and communities—with more to come.
Business Week   Jul 2, 1990   p. 64

The peace economy. How defense cuts will pay off for America.
Business Week   Dec 11, 1989   p. 50

The defense budget: Spending more, getting less?
USA Today   Nov 1988   p. 12

Defending America. How to cut the Pentagon's budget - and keep the nation strong.
Newsweek   Dec 20, 1982   p. 22

DEFENSE SPENDING - BUSH ADMINISTRATION

Shrinking the military. Weapons, missions and manpower: What to keep, what to cut.
U.S. News   Oct 14, 1991   p. 24

Scaling down defense. How to really cut military costs.
Time   Feb 12, 1990   p. 16

How to survive on $300 billion a year. Bush's defense dilemma.
Newsweek   Jan 23, 1989   p. 12

DEFENSE SPENDING - CARTER ADMINISTRATION

What price power? Expanding America's arsenal.
Time   Oct 29, 1979   p. 24

DEFENSE SPENDING - REAGAN ADMINISTRATION

Defense spending. How much is enough?
Newsweek   Feb 11, 1985   p. 18

A trillion for defense. Do we get our money's worth?
U.S. News   Sep 17, 1984   p. 24

How much is enough? Special report on defense.
U.S. News   Jun 13, 1983   p. 33

Defending defense. Budget battles and star wars.
Time   Apr 4, 1983   p. 8

U.S. defense spending. Are billions being wasted?
Time   Mar 7, 1983   p. 12

Guns vs. butter. How to cut defense spending. How to save Social Security.
Business Week   Nov 29, 1982 p. 68

How to spend a trillion. Defense Secretary Caspar Weinberger.
Time   Jul 27, 1981   p. 6

Reagan's defense buildup. Does it make sense? Can we afford it?
Newsweek   Jun 8, 1981   p. 28

Billions down the Pentagon drain.
U.S. News   Apr 27, 1981 p. 25

DEFENSES, NATIONAL
See UNITED STATES - DEFENSES

DEFICIT FINANCING
Drowning in debt. Impact of another $180 billion deficit.
U.S. News   Feb 13, 1984 p. 18

DELTA AIR LINES, INC.
Delta. The world's most profitable airline.
Business Week   Aug 31, 1981 p. 68

DEMOCRACY
Is democracy dying? Verdict of 8 leading world scholars.
U.S. News   Mar 8, 1976   p. 50

See Also PRO-DEMOCRACY MOVEMENT

DEMOCRATIC NATIONAL CONVENTION, 1960
The demonstration for Jack Kennedy.
Life   Jul 25, 1960   p. 18

DEMOCRATIC NATIONAL CONVENTION, 1964
The Humphreys.
Newsweek   Sep 7, 1964   p. 16

The big show in color.
Life   Sep 4, 1964   p. 20

President Johnson.
Newsweek   Aug 31, 1964 p. 15

DEMOCRATIC NATIONAL CONVENTION, 1968
Corruption of Chicago police. Where discipline broke down. Walker report discloses the police rioted at the Democratic convention.
Life   Dec 6, 1968   p. 34

Battle of Chicago.
Newsweek   Sep 9, 1968   p. 24

The winners. But what a week. Humphrey and Muskie stand before the Democratic convention in Chicago.
Life   Sep 6, 1968   p. 18

The Democrats after Chicago.
Time   Sep 6, 1968   p. 15

DEMOCRATIC NATIONAL CONVENTION, 1972
Convention portraits by Norman Mailer.
Life   Jul 28, 1972   p. 26

Target: Nixon and Agnew.
Newsweek   Jul 24, 1972   p. 16

In quest of a second miracle. The Democratic ticket.
Time   Jul 24, 1972   p. 18

Five showdown days with the McGoverns in the victory suite.
Life   Jul 21, 1972   p. 6

New wave hits Miami.
Newsweek   Jul 17, 1972   p. 14

DEMOCRATIC NATIONAL CONVENTION, 1976
Coming on strong.
Newsweek   Jul 26, 1976   p. 16

The Democrats reborn.
Time   Jul 26, 1976   p. 8

Inside convention city.
Time   Jul 19, 1976   p. 14

DEMOCRATIC NATIONAL CONVENTION, 1980
Now for the hard part.
Newsweek   Aug 25, 1980 p. 18

Running tough. "A choice between two futures."
Time   Aug 25, 1980 p. 8

DEPARTMENT OF HEALTH AND HUMAN SERVICES

How to spend $182 billion.
Time Jun 12, 1978 p. 24

Battle plan for the home front. "Our theme is pragmatism." HEW Secretary Robert Finch.
Time May 2, 1969 p. 10

DEPARTMENT OF HEALTH, EDUCATION AND WELFARE

Battle plan for the home front. "Our theme is pragmatism." HEW Secretary Robert Finch.
Time May 2, 1969 p. 10

DEPARTMENT OF HOUSING AND URBAN DEVELOPMENT - SCANDAL

The HUD scandal. Anatomy of a ripoff.
Newsweek Aug 7, 1989 p. 16

DEPARTMENT OF JUSTICE

Bleak days at Justice Department.
U.S. News Feb 6, 1978 p. 23

The Attorney General speaks out: Gun control, illegal aliens, marijuana laws, rising crime, death penalty.
U.S. News Jun 30, 1975 p. 30

DEPARTMENT OF TREASURY

The quiet crusader. Nick Brady's new agenda for business. The Treasury Secretary wants us to stop focusing on the short term. And he has some plans that could change life for both managers and investors.
Business Week Sep 18, 1989 p. 80

DEPRESSION (FINANCIAL), 1929-1939

Crash of '29. Have we learned anything?
U.S. News Oct 29, 1979 p. 32

What a depression is really like. Scenes from the 1930s.
U.S. News Nov 11, 1974 p. 36

DEPRESSION (MENTAL)

Prozac. A breakthrough drug for depression.
Newsweek Mar 26, 1990 p. 38

Beating depression. New treatments bring success.
U.S. News Mar 5, 1990 p. 48

When mental illness hits home. What we know about depression and schizophrenia. How families cope with their ordeal.
U.S. News Apr 24, 1989 p. 54

Boomer blues. Generation of too great expectations.
Psychology Today Oct 1988 p. 50

Cheer up! There's good news about depression.
Ms. Dec 1987 p. 48

Depression. The bad news: It's striking more young adults. The good news: Almost all can be helped.
Newsweek May 4, 1987 p. 48

Depression: Holiday blues. Fact and fiction.
USA Today Dec 1984 p. 1

New hope for the depressed.
U.S. News Jan 24, 1983 p. 39

Coping with depression.
Newsweek Jan 8, 1973 p. 51

DEREGULATION

Is deregulation working?
Business Week Dec 22, 1986 p. 50

Deregulating America. American business is undergoing its first redirection in 50 years.
Business Week Nov 28, 1983 p. 80

Deregulation. A fast start for the Reagan strategy.
Business Week Mar 9, 1981 p. 62

DESERTS

A new vista in the American West. Opening up the desert for living.
Life Mar 23, 1962 p. 62

DESIGN, INDUSTRIAL

Rebel with a cause. How Hartmut Esslinger is shaking up the world of industrial design.
Business Week Dec 3, 1990 p. 130

Smart design. Quality is the new style.
Business Week Apr 11, 1988 p. 102

DETECTIVE AND MYSTERY STORIES

The big thrill. Mystery writers are making a killing. 'Glitz' author Elmore Leonard.
Newsweek   Apr 22, 1985   p. 58

The art of murder. Detective novelist Ross Macdonald.
Newsweek   Mar 22, 1971   p. 101

DEVALUATION OF CURRENCY

See MONEY - INTERNATIONAL ASPECTS

DEVELOPING COUNTRIES

The survival summit. What the South will ask for. What the North should do.
Newsweek   Oct 26, 1981   p. 36

Third World. Uncle Sam's new stand.
U.S. News   Oct 26, 1981   p. 20

Third World. Cockpit of turmoil.
U.S. News   Jun 25, 1979   p. 51

DIAMOND SHAMROCK CORP.

The downfall of a CEO. Bill Bricker had big dreams for Diamond Shamrock—and spent freely on an executive lifestyle to match. But as one deal after another failed to pay off, losses mounted, the stock plunged, and Boone Pickens launched a takeover bid.
Business Week   Feb 16, 1987   p. 76

DIANA, PRINCESS OF WALES

Here they come! Charles and Diana.
Time   Nov 11, 1985   p. 56

A royal welcome. Charles and Diana in America. Her jewels. Inside their embassy quarters. Their nation's priceless art treasures.
Life   Nov 1985   p. 29

Guess who's coming to dinner. Princess Diana.
Newsweek   Oct 28, 1985   p. 66

Diana and the newest star in the royal family.
Life   Dec 1984   p. 154

Royalty vs. the press.
Time   Feb 28, 1983   p. 52

A sleek, stylish Princess Di is back and stealing the scene.
Life   Dec 1982   p. 51

Royal wedding.
Newsweek   Aug 3, 1981   p. 34

Three cheers!
Time   Aug 3, 1981   p. 20

The prince's charmer. Lady Diana is wowing Britain.
Time   Apr 20, 1981   p. 64

DIEFENBAKER, GEORGE

Canada's Diefenbaker. Decline and fall.
Newsweek   Feb 18, 1963   p. 33

DIEM, NGO DINH

See NGO DINH DIEM

DIET

See NUTRITION

DIETING

Getting slim. How to find the right diet.
U.S. News   May 14, 1990   p. 56

Liquid diets. Are they safe? How they work.
Newsweek   Apr 30, 1990   p. 52

The mindset that makes diets work.
Psychology Today   Jun 1989   p. 31

The dangerous diet pills. How millions of women are risking their health with 'fat doctors.'
Life   Jan 26, 1968   p. 22

See Also REDUCING

See REDUCING

DIGESTIVE SYSTEM

Part II: The human body. How your body converts food to fuel.
Life   Dec 7, 1962   p. 78

DIGITAL EQUIPMENT CORP.

What next for Digital? The hot computer company has cooled off. So why isn't DEC's Ken Olsen worried?
Business Week   May 16, 1988   p. 88

A new strategy for the no. 2 in computers. Will DEC's massive overhaul pay off?
Business Week   May 2, 1983   p. 66

Disney World opens.
Life   Oct 15, 1971   p. 44

DISSENTERS
Moscow trials - testing Carter.
Newsweek   Jul 24, 1978   p. 18

Detente. The trial of Anatoli
Shcharansky.
Time   Jul 24, 1978   p. 24

The dissidents. Challenge to Moscow.
Time   Feb 21, 1977   p. 20

DIVORCE
Divorce: Victims of no-fault divorce.
USA Today   Dec 1986   p. 1

Divorce. How the game is played now.
U.S. News   Nov 21, 1983   p. 39

Splitting up the family. The courts are
changing the rules of divorce and child
custody - and often making things worse.
Newsweek   Jan 10, 1983   p. 42

The divorced woman.
Newsweek   Feb 13, 1967   p. 64

See Also CHILDREN OF DIVORCED
PARENTS

DLUGOS, RAYMOND
The Pope's foot soldiers. Keeping the
faith: Two American priests in a changing
church. Catholic priests Raymond
Dlugos and Brian Frawley.
U.S. News   Sep 21, 1987   p. 58

DNA
See GENETIC ENGINEERING

DNA FINGERPRINTS
DNA fingerprints. New witness for the
prosecution.
Discover   Jun 1988   p. 44

DOCTORS
See PHYSICIANS

DOG SLEDS AND SLEDDING
North to the Pole. Six by dogsled.
National Geographic Sep 1986   p. 289

DOGS
Dogs you never saw before.
Life   Jan 1979   p. 42

DOLLAR
See MONEY

DOLPHINS
Dolphins that talk.
Omni   Jun 1989   p. 26

DOMINGO, PLACIDO
King of the opera. Tenor Placido
Domingo.
Newsweek   Mar 8, 1982   p. 56

**DOMINICAN REPUBLIC AND THE UNITED
STATES**
Trying to prevent another Cuba.
Time   May 7, 1965   p. 28

DONAHUE, PHIL
The talk of TV. Phil Donahue.
Newsweek   Oct 29, 1979   p. 76

DONNER, FRED G.
The world's biggest manufacturer.
General Motors Chairman Frederic G.
Donner.
Time   May 18, 1962   p. 85

DOONESBURY (COMIC STRIP)
Inside Doonesbury's brain. Garry
Trudeau finally talks.
Newsweek   Oct 15, 1990   p. 60

Doonesbury. Politics in the funny papers.
Time   Feb 9, 1976   p. 57

DOUGLAS-HOME, SIR ALEC
Britain's Harold Wilson. Will Labor win?
Newsweek   Sep 28, 1964   p. 44

Britain's Lord Home.
Time   Oct 25, 1963   p. 31

DOWN, LESLEY-ANNE
Lesley-Anne Down—sexy, saucy and
talented.
Life   Mar 1979   p. 115

DRAFT, MILITARY
See MILITARY SERVICE,
COMPULSORY

DREAMS
Dreams. How to have them. How to read
them. How to control them.
Omni   Nov 1989   p. 42

Guided dreams. Using your power to control your dreams.
Psychology Today   Oct 1989   p. 27

Dreams. New lessons from the theater of the mind.
Newsweek   Aug 14, 1989 p. 40

Dreaming. A startling new analysis from the man who brought you DNA.
Psychology Today   Nov 1983   p. 22

DREXEL BURNHAM LAMBERT INC.

After Drexel. Now, Drexel is on the ropes, junk-bond king Michael Milken is under indictment, and the junk market is in turmoil. The impact will be felt for years to come.
Business Week   Feb 26, 1990 p. 36

Predator's fall. The collapse of Drexel Burnham, the house that junk built, is only the latest of Wall Street's woes. So where are the tears?
Time   Feb 26, 1990 p. 46

Power on Wall Street. There's a new relationship between Wall Street and Corporate America—largely because of the work of one man: Drexel Burnham's Mike Milken.
Business Week   Jul 7, 1986   p. 56

DRINKING OF ALCOHOLIC BEVERAGES

Drinking: Americans' attitudes toward alcohol.
USA Today   Apr 1991   p. 1

DRINKING WATER

Is your water safe? The dangerous state of drinking water in America.
U.S. News   Jul 29, 1991   p. 48

DROUGHTS

The big dry.
Time   Jul 4, 1988   p. 12

Africa's stricken Sahel.
National Geographic Aug 1987   p. 140

Somalia's hour of need.
National Geographic Jun 1981   p. 748

Drought. Will history repeat?
U.S. News   Apr 4, 1977   p. 46

DRUG ABUSE

The deadly dilemma. What finally will stop drugs' threat to the American way of life. A special section of solutions.
USA Today   Jul 1990   p. 15

A family guide. How you can beat drugs. Prevention, treatment and community action.
U.S. News   Sep 11, 1989   p. 69

Addictive personalities. Who gets hooked on drugs and alcohol - and why. Kitty Dukakis: Her private struggle.
Time   Feb 20, 1989   p. 52

Crack. Hour by hour. The junkies, the jailer, the pimps and the tiniest addicts.
Newsweek   Nov 28, 1988 p. 64

'I am a coke addict.' What happens when nice guys get hooked.
Life   Oct 1986   p. 38

Drugs. The enemy within.
Time   Sep 15, 1986   p. 58

"Saying No!" The nation's new campaign against users. A poll on drug testing, enforcement and privacy. An exclusive interview with President Reagan.
Newsweek   Aug 11, 1986 p. 14

Beyond crack: The growing peril of designer drugs.
Discover   Aug 1986   p. 24

Killer drugs. New facts, new enemies.
U.S. News   Jul 28, 1986   p. 48

This amount of cocaine can make you feel that you're brilliant, tireless, masterful, invulnerable, and that you're going to live forever. It can also kill you.
Discover   Mar 1985   p. 16

Getting straight. How Americans are breaking the grip of drugs and alcohol.
Newsweek   Jun 4, 1984   p. 62

How drugs sap the nation's strength.
U.S. News   May 16, 1983 p. 55

Violent showdown over drugs between father and son. [Richie]
Life   May 5, 1972   p. 82

The heroin plague.
Newsweek   Jul 5, 1971   p. 27

Heroin hits the young.
Time   Mar 16, 1970   p. 16

LSD and the mind drugs.
Newsweek   May 9, 1966   p. 59

See Also COCAINE, HEROIN,
MARIJUANA

DRUG ENFORCEMENT ADMINISTRATION

The drug warrior. He's ambitious,
abrasive and tough. Can he make a
difference?
Newsweek   Apr 10, 1989 p. 20

DRUG TESTING

Reagan administration drug testing
program.
Congressional Digest May 1987   p. 131

DRUG TRAFFICKING

Cocaine Inc. The new drug kings.
Cold-blooded and efficient, Colombia's
Cali cartel has cornered the market. Can
these men be stopped?
Time   Jul 1, 1991   p. 28

The dirty 300. How Colombia's drug
rings operate in America.
Newsweek   Nov 13, 1989 p. 36

Death of a narc. U.S. drug agent "Kiki"
Camarena's mission was to hunt down
Mexico's drug barons. This is the story of
how they got him.
Time   Nov 7, 1988   p. 84

The drug thugs. Panama's Noriega
proves they're a law unto themselves.
Time   Mar 7, 1988   p. 26

Drugs, money and death. The sordid
story of Panama's outlaw dictator. Gen.
Manuel Antonio Noriega.
Newsweek   Feb 15, 1988   p. 32

Drugs. Terror and politics. The deadly
new alliance.
U.S. News   May 4, 1987   p. 30

The return of the French connection.
How drug agents broke up the $225
million heroin deal of the decade.
Newsweek   Apr 13, 1987   p. 56

Controversy over omnibus drug
legislation.
Congressional Digest Nov 1986   p. 259

The U.S. campaign against international
narcotics trafficking: A cure worse than the
disease.
USA Today   Nov 1986   p. 14

Cocaine. The evil empire. The explosive
Latin connection. Colombia's drug lords.
U.S. agents: Targets for terror.
Newsweek   Feb 25, 1985   p. 14

Cocaine wars. South America's bloody
business.
Time   Feb 25, 1985   p. 26

The Colombian connection. Billions in
pot & coke.
Time   Jan 29, 1979   p. 22

The global war on heroin.
Time   Sep 4, 1972   p. 22

500 Americans in foreign jails for
smuggling dope.
Life   Jun 26, 1970   p. 28

DRUGS - LAWS AND REGULATIONS

Should drugs be made legal?
Time   May 30, 1988 p. 12

Controversy over omnibus drug
legislation.
Congressional Digest Nov 1986   p. 259

DRUGS AND ARTISTS

LSD art. New experience that bombards
the senses.
Life   Sep 9, 1966   p. 60

DRUGS AND CRIME

The lonely war. In drug-infested
neighborhoods, across America, angry
citizens like Detroit's Rantine McKesson
are fighting back.
Time   Sep 11, 1989 p. 12

Murder zones. America is full of its own
Beiruts, where drug lords reign and no
cops tread.
U.S. News   Apr 10, 1989 p. 20

Inside America's biggest drug bust. A
blow by blow account of how the Feds hit
the Sicilian Mafia, based on
unprecedented access to agents working
the case.
U.S. News   Apr 11, 1988 p. 18

The drug gangs. Waging war in America's cities.
Newsweek   Mar 28, 1988   p. 20

Crack and crime. The drug crisis.
Newsweek   Jun 16, 1986   p. 15

DRUGS AND EMPLOYMENT

Privacy. Should companies test employees for drug use? Or screen job applicants for diseases? Or give lie detector tests? Or eavesdrop on office phone calls? All this is now happening.
Business Week   Mar 28, 1988   p. 61

Drugs on the job.
Time   Mar 17, 1986   p. 52

Drugs on the job.
Newsweek   Aug 22, 1983   p. 52

DRUGS AND GANGS

The drug gangs. Waging war in America's cities.
Newsweek   Mar 28, 1988   p. 20

DRUGS AND INFANTS

Crack kids. Their mothers used drugs, and now it's the children who suffer.
Time   May 13, 1991   p. 56

DRUGS AND YOUTH

Can the children be saved? One block's battle against drugs and despair.
Newsweek   Sep 11, 1989   p. 16

Kids who sell crack. Call him Frog. He says he rakes in $200 a week selling "rock" in East L.A. He brags that he uses his drug money to rent a Nissan Z on weekends - but at 4 ft. 10 in. he has trouble seeing over the dashboard...
Time   May 9, 1988   p. 20

Kids and cocaine. An epidemic strikes middle America.
Newsweek   Mar 17, 1986   p. 58

Heroin hits the young.
Time   Mar 16, 1970   p. 16

Drugs and the young.
Time   Sep 26, 1969   p. 68

The hippies. Philosophy of a subculture.
Time   Jul 7, 1967   p. 18

DRUGS (PHARMACEUTICAL)

Halcion. It's the most widely prescribed sleeping pill in the world. But is it safe?
Newsweek   Aug 19, 1991   p. 44

The race for miracle drugs. Custom cures—from colds to cancers.
Business Week   Jul 22, 1985   p. 92

DRUNK DRIVING

The war on drunk driving. Getting tough with the killers of 26,000 Americans a year.
Newsweek   Sep 13, 1982   p. 34

DU PONT CORPORATION

The modern alchemists. Du Pont's Copeland.
Time   Nov 27, 1964   p. 94

DUBCEK, ALEXANDER

Self-determination for Czechoslovakia. Party boss Dubcek.
Time   Apr 5, 1968   p. 26

DUKAKIS, MICHAEL

The Duke and the Democrats. Michael Dukakis' nomination symbolizes the change in the party—from liberal to pragmatic. But will that be enough to win? Or to govern?
Business Week   Jul 25, 1988   p. 22

Dukakis. By the people who know him best.
Newsweek   Jul 25, 1988   p. 24

The odd couple. Gary Wills: Searching for Dukakis' soul.
Time   Jul 25, 1988   p. 16

Dukakis. How good a president? He's cool, shrewd and still trying to prove he's tough.
U.S. News   Jul 25, 1988   p. 12

The Duke. Can he unite the Democrats?
Time   May 2, 1988   p. 20

DUNAWAY, FAYE

Bonnie fashion's new darling. Faye Dunaway in a '30s revival.
Life   Jan 12, 1968   p. 69

DUONG VAN MINH

Military coup in Viet Nam. General
Duong Van Minh.
Time   Nov 8, 1963   p. 28

DURAN, ROBERTO

The fight of his life. Sugar Ray Leonard
takes on Roberto Duran.
Newsweek   Jun 23, 1980   p. 48

DYLAN, BOB

Dylan's back.
Newsweek   Jan 14, 1974   p. 46

EAGLETON, THOMAS

The Eagleton affair.
Time   Aug 7, 1972   p. 11

The Eagleton crisis.
Newsweek   Aug 7, 1972   p. 12

EARTH

The struggle to save our planet.
Discover   Apr 1990   p. 36

Planet of the year. Endangered earth.
Time   Jan 2, 1989   p. 24

Planet earth. How it works. How to fix it.
U.S. News   Oct 31, 1988   p. 56

How the earth will look in 250 million
years.
Discover   Nov 1982   p. 20

Highest photos of earth taken by man.
Growing clutter of space trash. Progress
toward space law.
Life   Aug 5, 1966   p. 24

New portrait of our planet. What IGY
taught us.
Life   Nov 7, 1960   p. 74

EARTH - PHOTOGRAPHS FROM SPACE

Our planet. Breathtaking views from
space by those who have been there.
Life   Nov 1988   p. 189

EARTHQUAKE PREDICTION

Forecast: Earthquake.
Time   Sep 1, 1975   p. 36

EARTHQUAKES

The next quake. Science's startling new
view of the turbulent forces inside the
earth.
U.S. News   Oct 30, 1989   p. 28

Earthquake! There is a 50% to 90% chance
that a major quake will devastate Los
Angeles in the next 50 years. It could
happen in the year 2036. It could happen
next week.
Discover   Jul 1986   p. 52

EARTHQUAKES - ALASKA, 1964

Earthquake in Alaska.
Life   Apr 10, 1964   p. 26

EARTHQUAKES - ARMENIA, 1988

The agony.
Newsweek   Dec 19, 1988   p. 16

EARTHQUAKES - IRAN, 1962

Report and photos from Iran. Amid the
rubble of a mighty quake. Then from the
U.S., a helping hand.
Life   Sep 21, 1962   p. 26

EARTHQUAKES - MEXICO, 1985

Mexico's killer quake.
Time   Sep 30, 1985   p. 34

Mexico. The killer quake. The frantic
rescue. The risk in the U.S.
Newsweek   Sep 30, 1985   p. 16

EARTHQUAKES - SAN FRANCISCO (CALIFORNIA), 1989

The next quake. Science's startling new
view of the turbulent forces inside the
earth.
U.S. News   Oct 30, 1989   p. 28

San Francisco. October 17, 1989.
Time   Oct 30, 1989   p. 30

Bracing for the big one. The lessons of
San Francisco.
Newsweek   Oct 30, 1989   p. 22

EASTER

Easter in Jerusalem. Jarring contrast of
piety and tourism on Via Dolorosa.
Life   Mar 24, 1967   p. 50

Rebuilding America. It will cost trillions.
U.S.News   Sep 22, 1980   p. 56

Goodbye to our good life?
U.S.News   Aug 4, 1980   p. 45

Economy out of control.
U.S.News   Mar 24, 1980   p. 20

U.S. economy in '80s. Can we meet the challenge?
U.S.News   Jan 21, 1980   p. 57

The squeeze of '79. Tighter money. Higher prices. Wall Street woes.
Time   Oct 22, 1979   p. 8

ABC's of how our economy works.
U.S. News   May 1, 1978   p. 41

Midyear '75 business outlook. How strong a recovery? Can inflation be stopped? Any cure for high unemployment? What's ahead in profits? Why business has a black eye.
U.S. News   Jul 14, 1975   p. 15

Jobs... Prices... Profits... What next?
U.S. News   Feb 3, 1975   p. 14

Christmas '74: Let nothing you dismay.
Newsweek   Dec 30, 1974   p. 12

Recession's greetings. P.S. There's some good news too.
Time   Dec 9, 1974   p. 28

How bad a slump?
Newsweek   Dec 2, 1974   p. 68

Special report. Squeeze on America's middle class.
U.S. News   Oct 14, 1974   p. 42

Special economic report. What to do?
Newsweek   Sep 30, 1974   p. 62

A sick economy. What's to be done - Ford's strategy takes shape. Runaway prices. Battered stock market. Inflated government. Troubled banks. Ailing trade.
U.S. News   Sep 9, 1974   p. 13

Economy. The big headache.
Time   Sep 9, 1974   p. 22

The cheaper dollar. Impact on prices & jobs. George Shultz.
Time   Feb 26, 1973   p. 79

The battle of the buck. Worth 73 cents.
Time   Dec 14, 1970   p. 82

Can inflation be stopped? The economy in 1970.
Newsweek   Jan 12, 1970   p. 49

Will there be a recession?
Time   Dec 19, 1969   p. 66

Defending the dollar. The federal reserve's William McChesney Martin.
Newsweek   Dec 4, 1967   p. 68

Tax hike. Medicare. Education. Poverty. Space. War. Urban renewal. Highways.
Newsweek   Aug 14, 1967   p. 65

The U.S. economy, 1967. Concern and confidence. Bank of America's Rudolph Peterson.
Time   Dec 30, 1966   p. 47

How much inflation?
Newsweek   Sep 5, 1966   p. 69

The economy: What's ahead? Presidential adviser Gardner Ackley.
Newsweek   Jul 18, 1966   p. 67

What's good for the economy . . . General Motors President Roche.
Time   May 20, 1966   p. 100

Gross national product. $700 billion plus.
Newsweek   Jan 10, 1966   p. 49

The consumer economy. Macy's Jack Straus.
Time   Jan 8, 1965   p. 58

The rising U.S. economy.
Time   May 31, 1963   p. 73

Key to the economy: The mighty U.S. consumer.
Newsweek   Jul 30, 1962   p. 63

The bite on the middle class. What recovery?
Newsweek   Nov 4, 1991   p. 18

Financing the 90s. Too much debt. Too many bad loans. Too much unneeded real estate. The excesses of the 1980s have damaged many of our financial institutions and corporations.
Business Week   Nov 4, 1991   p. 112

A strong recovery. Yes, it's possible.
Business Week   Jul 1, 1991   p. 48

Storm clouds over the recovery. America's troubled economy. Why too much debt threatens your pocketbook and the nation's economy.
U.S. News   May 6, 1991   p. 52

High anxiety. Looming recession, government paralysis and the threat of war are giving Americans a case of the jitters.
Time   Oct 15, 1990   p. 30

Are we in recession? No. Unemployment is still low and the economy is still growing, however slowly. Yes. The usual numbers are highly suspect. Besides, the old definition just doesn't apply in today's economy.
Business Week   Aug 13, 1990   p. 28

The economy: Old get richer while young get poorer.
USA Today   Aug 1988   p. 1

Into the storm: America confronts the 1990s.
USA Today   May 1988   p. 16

The crash: Was just the beginning. The worst is yet to come. Was a necessary correction for excesses in the market and the economy. Didn't matter at all.
Business Week   Apr 18, 1988   p. 55

Wake up, America! The stock market may recover somewhat, but the message underlying the crash remains largely unheeded. We have spent too much, borrowed too much and imported too much. We have lived beyond, relying on foreigners to finance. . .
Business Week   Nov 16, 1987   p. 158

Starting over. Damage control on Wall Street. How companies and consumers are responding. Reforming the casino society. Mutual fund update. The right economic policies.
Business Week   Nov 9, 1987   p. 31

Where to invest. Stocks are still the best bet. Picking the big winners. The best mutual funds. The hottest foreign stock markets. New ways to profit from bonds. The investment stars. Playing inflation hedges.
Business Week   Jul 6, 1987   p. 56

How worried should you be? The end of the bull market? Nah, just a correction...I think. A recession? You're kidding, aren't you? Hey, fellas. Don't start a trade war. Mr. Volcker, stop the dollar's fall. But not by raising interest rates. How? I dunno.
Business Week   May 11, 1987   p. 40

Can America compete? The U.S. economy has been sluggish for years, despite lots of fiscal and monetary stimulus. Now, faced with the urgent need to reduce its budget and trade deficits, America may well see its enviable standard of living decline.
Business Week   Apr 20, 1987   p. 44

Will he stay? Paul Volcker's term at the Federal Reserve has four months to go. Suddenly reappointment looks much more likely.
Business Week   Mar 30, 1987   p. 76

America's deflation belt. Oil, agriculture, and mining are all depressed industries. Their troubles are hurting a wide swath of the country—and restraining what would otherwise be a robust expansion.
Business Week   Jun 9, 1986   p. 52

The casino society. No, it's not Las Vegas or Atlantic City. It's the U.S. financial system.
Business Week   Sep 16, 1985   p. 78

Economic slowdown. How bad? How long?
Business Week   Dec 10, 1984   p. 114

Dollar fever infects the world. A $100 billion GNP loss for the U.S. A huge capital outflow from Europe.
Business Week   Jun 27, 1983   p. 90

How strong a recovery? Growth could be surprisingly good. But everyone is wary of unemployment and deficits.
Business Week   Jan 31, 1983   p. 88

The fed's plan for economic recovery. Is Chairman Paul Volcker aiming too low?
Business Week   Dec 13, 1982   p. 90

The built-in deficit. How federal spending outpaces revenues. The trouble is Congress. What the deficits are doing to the economy.
Business Week   Aug 16, 1982   p. 84

Here comes the recovery. But how strong? And how long?
Business Week   May 10, 1982   p. 140

America's restructured economy. Five separate segments. Dangerous regional disparities. Growth industries for the 1980s. Needed: New fiscal policies.
Business Week   Jun 1, 1981   p. 55

Inflation, recession and a frantic bear market.
Life   Jun 5, 1970   p. 28

The dollar squeeze. High taxes and high prices make everybody feel poor.
Life   Aug 15, 1969   p. 18

ECONOMIC CONDITIONS - WORLD

Super dollar. Reshaping the world economy. How long will it last? New strategy for U.S. multinationals. America's top importers.
Business Week   Oct 8, 1984   p. 164

Poor vs. rich. A global struggle.
U.S. News   Jul 31, 1978   p. 55

Toward a world market. The year in business.
Time   Dec 28, 1962   p. 50

The dollar in danger?
Newsweek   Dec 5, 1960   p. 48

ECONOMIC FORECASTING

Where to invest in 1992. Stocks. Funds. Bonds.
Business Week   Dec 30, 1991   p. 59

Where to invest now. The top 50 small stocks. The top 65 mutual funds. How to afford retirement.
U.S. News   Jul 15, 1991   p. 50

Industry outlook 1991. What's ahead for America's 24 key industries.
Business Week   Jan 14, 1991   p. 61

The new America. The nation's changing demography—and what it means. Six key trends of the 1990s. Economic prospects for the year 2000.
Business Week   Sep 25, 1989   p. 90

Industry outlook. 1989. What's ahead for America's 24 key industries.
Business Week   Jan 9, 1989   p. 64

Where to put your money now.
U.S. News   Dec 5, 1988   p. 75

Where to invest now. Stocks-bonds-mutual funds. 10 top brokers tell you where to put your money.
U.S. News   Jun 6, 1988   p. 56

1986 industry outlook. What's ahead for America's 25 key industries—from high tech to banking.
Business Week   Jan 13, 1986   p. 55

Where to invest in 1986. The hottest stocks. Trouble ahead in real estate. Bonds are booming.
Business Week   Dec 30, 1985   p. 72

Investment outlook 1985.
Business Week   Dec 31, 1984   p. 61

Industry outlooks 1984.
Business Week   Jan 9, 1984   p. 51

Investment outlook 84.
Business Week   Dec 26, 1983   p. 47

1983 industry outlooks. How the experts see 16 major industries faring.
Business Week   Jan 17, 1983   p. 57

Where do we go from here? How strong a recovery. Lasting scars of recession. Next for the stock market. Job outlook for college grads.
U.S. News   Dec 13, 1982   p. 24

The big money questions. Will interest rates drop? When will buying spree start? Where to invest now? What will new budget look like?
U.S. News   May 31, 1982   p. 24

Investment outlook 1982.
Business Week   Jan 4, 1982   p. 75

Investment outlook 82.
Business Week   Dec 28, 1981   p. 75

Industry outlooks 1981. A multi-tiered economy. Growing. Information. Oil. Solid. Chemicals. Machinery. Paper. Ailing. Autos. Food. Steel.
Business Week   Jan 12, 1981   p. 51

Midyear outlook. When will business bounce back? How much will inflation slow? How steep a drop in profits? What's ahead for stock market? Where to put your money now?
U.S.News   Jul 14, 1980   p. 20

A look into '77. Special section - Business.
U.S. News   Oct 11, 1976   p. 54

ECONOMIC POLICY - BUSH ADMINISTRATION

High anxiety. The elusive recovery worries consumers, business—and now the stock market.
Business Week   Dec 2, 1991   p. 28

ECONOMIC POLICY - CARTER ADMINISTRATION

Carter vs. inflation. The President's demand: "Discipline ... discipline ... discipline."
Time   Mar 24, 1980   p. 8

To the rescue!
Time   Nov 13, 1978   p. 18

Saving the dollar. But risking a recession.
Newsweek   Nov 13, 1978   p. 40

Carter's inflation fighter. A no-win job?
U.S. News   Nov 6, 1978   p. 17

Inflation fighters. Can they win?
Newsweek   Nov 6, 1978   p. 30

Inflation. Where do we go from here?
U.S. News   Oct 2, 1978   p. 30

Can the dollar be saved?
U.S. News   Mar 13, 1978   p. 41

Carter's pep pill for business.
U.S. News   Jan 30, 1978   p. 16

Trying to build confidence. Treasury Secretary Blumenthal.
Time   Jan 30, 1978   p. 12

Carter and your money. Can he lift the economy?
Newsweek   Jan 30, 1978   p. 22

Economy '78. A new look?
Newsweek   Jan 9, 1978   p. 48

ECONOMIC POLICY - FORD ADMINISTRATION

How far is down?
Newsweek   Feb 24, 1975   p. 58

Doctoring the economy. What will work?
Time   Jan 27, 1975   p. 13

Trying to turn it around.
Time   Jan 20, 1975   p. 9

Can Ford win with - Higher taxes. Easier credit. No controls.
U.S. News   Oct 21, 1974   p. 19

Trying to fight back. Inflation. Recession. Oil.
Time   Oct 14, 1974   p. 25

ECONOMIC POLICY - JOHNSON ADMINISTRATION

Business in 1965: The Keynesian influence on the expansionist economy. John Maynard Keynes.
Time   Dec 31, 1965   p. 64

ECONOMIC POLICY - KENNEDY ADMINISTRATION

The market & economic policy. White House adviser Walter Heller.
Time   Jun 8, 1962   p. 19

Kennedy's economic planners. White House economist Walter W. Heller.
Time   Mar 3, 1961   p. 18

Douglas Dillon: Republican in the Cabinet and his job.
Newsweek   Jan 30, 1961   p. 27

ECONOMIC POLICY - NIXON ADMINISTRATION

The economic issue. '1972 will be a very good year.' Richard Nixon.
Newsweek   Jan 31, 1972   p. 62

The impact of Phase II.
Time   Oct 18, 1971   p. 10

Living with controls.
Newsweek   Oct 18, 1971   p. 26

Nixon's economic gamble.
Time   Aug 30, 1971   p. 4

Your new dollar. Nixon's recovery plan.
Newsweek   Aug 30, 1971   p. 10

ECONOMIC POLICY - REAGAN ADMINISTRATION

Now the hard part. The budget deficit:
Will it be cut at last? Tax reform: How
much will survive?
Business Week   Feb 11, 1985   p. 102

Chapter two. Reagan's mandate. The
new look in Congress. Labor's lost clout.
The coming fight over taxes and
spending. The prospect for arms control.
Business Week   Nov 19, 1984   p. 36

The recovery cheers the GOP. Amid
prosperity the gender gap haunts Reagan.
Business Week   Sep 3, 1984   p. 74

Investment outlook 84.
Business Week   Dec 26, 1983   p. 47

The unfinished agenda. Reagan's goals:
Sustaining economic growth. Protecting
the big buildup in defense. Shifting to a
more pragmatic foreign policy.
Business Week   Oct 31, 1983   p. 106

How strong a recovery? Growth could be
surprisingly good. But everyone is wary
of unemployment and deficits.
Business Week   Jan 31, 1983   p. 88

The search for a new policy. How to get
the economy growing again.
Business Week   Nov 8, 1982   p. 108

Reagan stands firm on Reaganomics. At
the summit.
Business Week   Jun 7, 1982   p. 100

Reagan's big gamble. Defying the deficits.
Can he pass the bucks to the states?
Newsweek   Feb 8, 1982   p. 24

The new money game. How you can play
it. Where it leads the economy.
Newsweek   Oct 12, 1981   p. 68

Reaganomics. Making it work.
Time   Sep 21, 1981   p. 38

Reaganomics. The confidence gap. Wall
Street votes no. The black-hole budget.
The interest-rate squeeze.
Newsweek   Sep 21, 1981   p. 26

Smile, please. How the tax cut helps you.
Will it hurt the economy? The battered
Democrats.
Newsweek   Aug 10, 1981   p. 16

The war against Reagan's budget.
U.S. News   Mar 16, 1981   p. 20

The Reagan revolution. Impact on
business taxes... jobs. Investors. Cities.
Farmers.
U.S. News   Mar 2, 1981   p. 18

Reagan's New Deal.
Newsweek   Mar 2, 1981   p. 22

Reagan starts rolling.
U.S. News   Feb 2, 1981   p. 16

Reagan's biggest challenge. Mending the
economy.
Time   Jan 19, 1981   p. 60

How to get America back on track.
Reagan's brain trust tells what's ahead.
U.S.News   Nov 24, 1980   p. 48

ECONOMICS

Heading off hard times. What the experts
think should be done. How to invest for
the long term by Jane Bryant Quinn.
Newsweek   Nov 9, 1987   p. 24

How to get the country moving again.
Advice from six Nobel prize economists.
Milton Friedman. Paul Samuelson.
George Stigler. Lawrence Klein. Kenneth
Arrow. James Tobin.
U.S. News   Jan 31, 1983   p. 66

How to bring back prosperity.
U.S. News   Apr 5, 1982   p. 35

Prosperity without inflation. Interviews
with four Nobel Prize winners.
U.S.News   Dec 15, 1980   p. 50

Rx for reviving America.
U.S.News   Jun 23, 1980   p. 48

The topsy-turvy economy. New ideas to
set it right.
Time   Aug 27, 1979   p. 24

ABC's of how our economy works.
U.S. News   May 1, 1978   p. 41

EDUCATION

The flight from public schools. Five leading alternatives: Parochial. For-profit schools. Prep. Afrocentric. Home education.
U.S. News   Dec 9, 1991   p. 66

The 10 best schools in the world. And what we can learn from them.
Newsweek   Dec 2, 1991   p. 50

Choice in schools.
Congressional Digest Dec 1991   p. 290

Can this man save our schools? Education Secretary Lamar Alexander.
Time   Sep 16, 1991   p. 54

Making kids smarter. How magnet education is giving children the edge they need.
U.S. News   May 27, 1991   p. 58

Human capital. The decline of America's work force. The nation's ability to compete is threatened by inadequate investment in our most important resource: people.
Business Week   Sep 19, 1988   p. 100

Yes, our schools can be saved. The story of a school that's getting better.
Newsweek   May 2, 1988   p. 54

Is getting tough the answer? School prinicpal Joe Clark says yes - and critics are up in arms.
Time   Feb 1, 1988   p. 52

U.S. vs. Japan. Is your child getting a first-class education? He is.
U.S. News   Jan 19, 1987   p. 58

Education and the future mind. 77 schools of the future. The power of a newborn brain. Seymour Papert and the teaching turtle.
Omni   Oct 1985   p. 28

What makes great schools great.
U.S. News   Aug 27, 1984   p. 46

Shaping up. America's schools are getting better.
Time   Oct 10, 1983   p. 58

Back to school - and back to basics.
U.S. News   Sep 19, 1983   p. 50

Saving our schools. A scathing report demands better teachers and tougher standards.
Newsweek   May 9, 1983   p. 50

Signs of hope for our schools.
U.S. News   Sep 7, 1981   p. 50

Why public schools are flunking. Part one of a special report.
Newsweek   Apr 20, 1981   p. 62

Kids, teachers and parents: "Give us better schools."
U.S. News   Sep 10, 1979   p. 31

Quest for better schools.
U.S. News   Sep 11, 1978   p. 50

Big city schools. Can they be saved?
Newsweek   Sep 12, 1977   p. 62

Why Johnny can't write.
Newsweek   Dec 8, 1975   p. 58

Crisis in the schools.
U.S. News   Sep 1, 1975   p. 42

"Education is too important to be left solely to the educators." Commissioner Keppel.
Time   Oct 15, 1965   p. 60

The plight of the urban schools.
Newsweek   Sep 16, 1963   p. 55

EDUCATION - FEDERAL AID

Tuition tax credits.
Congressional Digest Jan 1984   p. 3

EDUCATION - MULTICULTURAL

Who are we? American kids are getting a new—and divisive—view of Thomas Jefferson, Thanksgiving and the Fourth of July.
Time   Jul 8, 1991   p. 12

EDUCATION, BILINGUAL

Controversy over bilingual education.
Congressional Digest Mar 1987   p. 68

EDUCATION, ELEMENTARY

The new grade school. Learning can be fun.
Newsweek   May 3, 1971   p. 60

The Eisenhower years in the White House. The President's chair: Mightiest seat in the world.
Newsweek   Nov 14, 1960   p. 30

On the road: Salesman K and salesman Ike.
Newsweek   Feb 29, 1960   p. 27

Man of the year. Dwight D. Eisenhower.
Time   Jan 4, 1960   p. 11

EISENHOWER, JULIE (NIXON)

Julie. The David Eisenhowers.
Newsweek   Oct 14, 1974   p. 39

EISENSTAEDT, ALFRED

A great photographer's finest pictures. *The Face of Our Time* by Alfred Eisenstaedt.
Life   Sep 16, 1966   p. 110

EISNER, MICHAEL

Why is this mouse smiling? Because Michael Eisner's magic has transformed Disney into a $3 billion kingdom.
Time   Apr 25, 1988   p. 66

Disney's magic. It's back! Corporate profits are surging as Chairman Michael Eisner launches new theme parks and broadens the company's role in movies and television.
Business Week   Mar 9, 1987   p. 62

EL NIÑO (OCEAN CURRENT)

Climate: Blame it on *El Niño*.
USA Today   Jun 1990   p. 1

El Niño. Global weather disaster.
National Geographic Feb 1984   p. 144

EL SALVADOR AND THE UNITED STATES

El Salvador. The death squads. Can they be stopped?
Newsweek   Jan 16, 1984   p. 24

Sounding the alarm. El Salvador. Washington's hard sell for more aid. The Pope's mission for peace.
Newsweek   Mar 14, 1983   p. 16

El Salvador. Can it be saved?
U.S. News   Mar 29, 1982   p. 18

Storm over El Salvador.
Newsweek   Mar 16, 1981   p. 34

ELDERLY

See OLDER AMERICANS

ELECTION LAWS

Extension of the Voting Rights Act.
Congressional Digest Dec 1981   p. 291

ELECTIONS

Impact of '74 election - Inflation. Taxes. White House. Business. Jobs. Congress.
U.S. News   Nov 18, 1974   p. 19

ELECTIONS - GERMANY (WEST)

New leaders for Germany. Socialist Willy Brandt.
Time   Oct 10, 1969   p. 24

ELECTIONS - GREAT BRITAIN, 1979

Britain's fighting lady. Prime Minister Margaret Thatcher.
Time   May 14, 1979   p. 30

Britain turns right. Margaret Thatcher.
Newsweek   May 14, 1979   p. 50

ELECTIONS - PANAMA, 1989

Politics, Panama-style. Noriega bludgeons his opposition, and the U.S. turns up the heat.
Time   May 22, 1989   p. 40

ELECTIONS - PHILIPPINES, 1986

Now for the hard part.
Time   Mar 10, 1986   p. 14

Fighting on. Philippine opposition leader Corazon Aquino.
Time   Feb 24, 1986   p. 28

Election mess. What the U.S. can do.
Newsweek   Feb 17, 1986   p. 14

What's at stake. The Philippine election. Challenger Aquino. President Marcos.
Time   Feb 3, 1986   p. 26

ELECTIONS - UNITED STATES

See Also PRESIDENTIAL ELECTIONS

ELECTIONS - UNITED STATES, 1970

New faces of 1970.
Time   Nov 16, 1970   p. 16

The Democrats shape up.
Newsweek   Nov 16, 1970   p. 30

ELECTIONS - UNITED STATES, 1974

Now what?
Time   Nov 18, 1974   p. 8

ELECTIONS - UNITED STATES, 1978

Election impact on - Business outlook.
Carter strategy. Temper of congress.
More tax cuts. War on inflation. Labor's
goals.
U.S. News   Nov 20, 1978   p. 19

Big winners. Adding up the results.
Mood: Cautious, restless, quirky. Taxing
& spending: Stop! Stop! Stop! The
senate: A huge freshman class. Parties:
Are they collapsing?
Time   Nov 20, 1978   p. 16

Elections '78. The tax slashers.
Time   Oct 23, 1978   p. 12

ELECTIONS - UNITED STATES, 1982

Election impact. A troublesome congress.
Reagan's hard choices. Business outlook
now. Tax cuts in danger. The '84 race.
U.S. News   Nov 15, 1982   p. 18

America's message. Keep on course - but
trim the sails.
Time   Nov 15, 1982   p. 10

What course now?
Newsweek   Nov 15, 1982   p. 34

As politics heat up - Preview of '82
election. Voters who hold the key. Are
Parties falling apart?
U.S. News   Oct 11, 1982   p. 41

ELECTIONS - UNITED STATES, 1984

Political mania takes over.
U.S. News   Jul 16, 1984   p. 71

ELECTIONS - UNITED STATES, 1988

Basic campaign issues of the 1988
elections.
Congressional Digest Oct 1988   p. 225

ELECTIONS - UNITED STATES, 1990

The untouchables. America's voters said
no to politics as usual. So why are 96% of
these people going back to Washington?
Time   Nov 19, 1990   p. 30

Throw the bums out! Government is
paralyzed, and voters are angry. Is there
any way out of the political mess?
U.S. News   Oct 22, 1990   p. 28

ELECTRIC POWER FAILURES

Blackout '77. Once more, with looting.
Time   Jul 25, 1977   p. 12

Blackout!
Newsweek   Jul 25, 1977   p. 16

The big blackout.
Newsweek   Nov 22, 1965   p. 27

The biggest blackout.
Time   Nov 19, 1965   p. 36

5:28 P.M., Nov. 9th. The lights went out.
Life   Nov 19, 1965   p. 36

ELECTRIC UTILITIES

Are utilities obsolete? A troubled system
faces radical change.
Business Week   May 21, 1984   p. 116

ELECTRONIC INDUSTRY

The future of Silicon Valley. Do we need
a high-tech industrial policy?
Business Week   Feb 5, 1990   p. 54

Has the Orient totally conquered U.S.
electronics? Seven companies say no.
USA Today   Jan 1989   p. 16

**ELECTRONIC OFFICE MACHINE
INDUSTRY**

The portable executive. How faxes, PCs,
laptops, cellular phones, voice mail, and
all the rest are changing our work life.
Special report on office automation.
Business Week   Oct 10, 1988   p. 102

ELECTRONIC WARFARE

The new era of invisible warfare. The
Pentagon reveals the B-2 Stealth bomber.
Is it a wonder weapon or a costly waste?
U.S. News   Nov 28, 1988   p. 20

ELECTRONICS - MILITARY USE

Killer electronic weaponry. Fighting in
Lebanon and the Falklands opens a new
era in weapons.
Business Week   Sep 20, 1982   p. 74

ELECTRONICS IN CRIMINAL INVESTIGATIONS, ESPIONAGE, ETC.

The big snoop. Electronic snooping. Insidious invasions of privacy. In business. In the home. By law enforcers. By the underworld. By anyone who's out to get you.
Life   May 20, 1966   p. 38

ELEPHANTS

Elephants. Out of time, out of space.
National Geographic May 1991   p. 2

The ivory trail. From Africa to Asia, a story of greed and slaughter.
Time   Oct 16, 1989   p. 66

Elephant talk.
National Geographic Aug 1989   p. 264

ELITE

Our new elite. For better or for worse?
U.S.News   Feb 25, 1980   p. 65

ELIZABETH II, QUEEN OF GREAT BRITAIN

Queen for our day. Elizabeth II and her jubilee.
Newsweek   Jun 13, 1977   p. 29

Grandest tour: Elizabeth in India.
Life   Feb 3, 1961   p. 38

ELLIS ISLAND (NEW YORK)

How we came to America. Ellis Island reopens—and brings our history back to life.
Life   Sep 1990   p. 26

ELLSBERG, DANIEL

The war exposés: Battle over the right to know. Daniel Ellsberg.
Time   Jul 5, 1971   p. 6

EMBARGO - SOVIET UNION

Grain as a weapon. Who wins. Who loses.
Time   Jan 21, 1980   p. 12

EMBRYOLOGY

The first pictures ever of how life begins.
Life   Aug 1990   p. 26

Whose baby am I? High-tech conceptions: Multiple parents, multiple problems.
Psychology Today   Dec 1984   p. 20

The moment of conception. When sperm meets egg.
Discover   Oct 1982   p. 32

How life begins. Biology's new frontier.
Newsweek   Jan 11, 1982   p. 38

EMERSON ELECTRIC

High profits from low tech. But Emerson Electric must change its winning formula.
Business Week   Apr 4, 1983   p. 58

EMOTIONALLY DISTURBED CHILDREN

See CHILDREN, EMOTIONALLY DISTURBED

EMOTIONS

Where emotions come from. Unlocking the biological secrets of joy, fear, anger and despair.
U.S. News   Jun 24, 1991   p. 54

Jealousy. That very human emotion.
Psychology Today   Sep 1985   p. 22

This baby is: Surprised, interested, joyful.
Psychology Today   Aug 1983   p. 14

Anger. Should we keep it in or let it loose?
Psychology Today   Nov 1982   p. 25

Links between mood and memory.
Psychology Today   Jun 1981   p. 60

Coding the faces of emotion.
Psychology Today   Feb 1981   p. 42

EMPLOYEE BENEFITS

The Family and Medical Leave Act.
Congressional Digest Apr 1991   p. 98

Ouch! The squeeze on your health plan. Skyrocketing costs are forcing companies to change medical benefits. Here's what it means for you.
Business Week   Nov 20, 1989 p. 110

Can you afford to get sick? The battle over health benefits.
Newsweek   Jan 30, 1989   p. 44

Family and medical leave policy.
Congressional Digest May 1988   p. 129

Benefits shock. How to protect yourself from cuts in health care and other benefits.
U.S. News   Mar 28, 1988   p. 57

EMPLOYEE DISMISSAL

How safe is your job? The warning signals. How to cope.
Newsweek　　　　Nov 5, 1990　　p. 44

You're fired! Starting over: A survival guide.
U.S. News　　　　Mar 23, 1987　p. 50

EMPLOYEE MORALE

The end of corporate loyalty? Thousands of managers are losing their jobs as corporations cut costs. The emotional cost is high. And even for those who remain, things will never be the same.
Business Week　　　Aug 4, 1986　　p. 42

EMPLOYEE RIGHTS

Beyond unions. It's no secret that labor unions are losing power. But that doesn't mean companies will ride roughshod over workers.
Business Week　　　Jul 8, 1985　　p. 72

EMPLOYEE STOCK OWNERSHIP PLANS

Employee ownership. The rush to ESOPs. Is it good for you? Or your company?
Business Week　　　May 15, 1989　p. 116

Revolution or ripoff? They're called ESOPs—for Employee Stock Ownership Plans—and they're starting to sweep Corporate America.
Business Week　　　Apr 15, 1985　p. 94

EMPLOYMENT

See JOBS

EMPLOYMENT TESTS

Can you pass the job test? From lie detectors to genetic screening.
Newsweek　　　　May 5, 1986　　p. 46

New tests to find the right person for the job.
Psychology Today　　Jan 1981　　　p. 34

END OF THE WORLD

Armageddon. The end is nigh (again).
Omni　　　　　Jan 1990　　　p. 42

ENDANGERED SPECIES

Who gives a hoot? The timber industry says that saving this spotted owl will cost 30,000 jobs. It isn't that simple.
Time　　　　　Jun 25, 1990　p. 56

A personal vision of vanishing wildlife.
National Geographic Apr 1990　　　p. 84

Endangered species. Can they be saved?
U.S. News　　　　Oct 2, 1989　　p. 52

Rare zoo babies. Breeding endangered animals in captivity.
Life　　　　　Jun 1982　　　p. 42

Wildlife in danger.
Newsweek　　　　Jan 6, 1975　　p. 36

ENDORPHIN

The brain's natural high. A pleasurable chemistry.
Psychology Today　　Jul 1988　　　p. 28

ENDOWMENTS

Foundations. The American way of giving.
Newsweek　　　　Mar 14, 1966　p. 87

ENERGY

Energy: Find it! Save it! Use it!
Omni　　　　　May 1991　　p. 34

Energy. Special report.
Newsweek　　　　Apr 18, 1977　p. 70

ENERGY CONSERVATION

Conservation power. The payoff in energy efficiency.
Business Week　　　Sep 16, 1991　p. 86

Energy conservation. Spawning a billion-dollar business.
Business Week　　　Apr 6, 1981　　p. 58

ENERGY CRISIS

Energy. Impact. How Carter's plan would hit your pocketbook. OPEC. Ways to foil the oil cartel. Autos. Changes ahead for motorists.
U.S. News　　　　Apr 9, 1979　　p. 19

Energy crunch: Real or phony? William Simon.
Time　　　　　Jan 21, 1974　p. 22

The big car: End of the affair.
Time　　　　　Dec 31, 1973　p. 18

The coldest winter.
Newsweek　　　　Dec 31, 1973　p. 6

The big freeze. Nixon's energy cuts.
Time   Dec 3, 1973   p. 29

How bad a slump?
Newsweek   Dec 3, 1973   p. 86

The oil squeeze. Saudi Arabia's King Feisal.
Time   Nov 19, 1973   p. 88

Running out of everything.
Newsweek   Nov 19, 1973   p. 109

Arab oil squeeze.
Newsweek   Sep 17, 1973   p. 33

The energy crisis.
Newsweek   Jan 22, 1973   p. 52

ENERGY POLICY

The energy crisis. A program for the '80s.
Newsweek   Jul 16, 1979   p. 19

The energy mess. Rebellious truckers. Insatiable OPEC.
Time   Jul 2, 1979   p. 14

The energy tangle.
Newsweek   Apr 16, 1979   p. 22

ENERGY POLICY - BUSH ADMINISTRATION

National Energy Policy.
Congressional Digest May 1991   p. 130

ENERGY POLICY - CARTER ADMINISTRATION

Tightening the belt on energy. Can it be done?
U.S. News   Jul 30, 1979   p. 19

Energy. Will Americans pay the price?
U.S. News   May 2, 1977   p. 13

Uncle Jimmy wants you. But will America enlist?
Time   May 2, 1977   p. 10

Carter up close. What price energy?
Newsweek   May 2, 1977   p. 32

His first big test.
Time   Apr 25, 1977   p. 8

Mr. Energy. Tackling a superproblem. James Schlesinger.
Time   Apr 4, 1977   p. 58

ENERGY RESOURCES

Rocky mountain high. Soaring prospects for the '80s.
Time   Dec 15, 1980   p. 28

Fuels for America's future.
U.S. News   Aug 13, 1979   p. 32

ENGINEERING

Mammoth machines for 2001.
Omni   Sep 1983   p. 80

ENGLISH LANGUAGE

The English language. Out to conquer the world.
U.S. News   Feb 18, 1985   p. 49

Why Johnny can't write.
Newsweek   Dec 8, 1975   p. 58

ENGLISH LANGUAGE - ERRORS

Slips of the tongue. Oops, did I say that?
Psychology Today Feb 1987   p. 24

ENTERTAINMENT INDUSTRY

Picking the hits. All it takes is intuition, experience and guts.
Psychology Today Jul 1986   p. 22

ENTREPRENEURS

The new entrepreneurs. Lots of startups give America an edge in product development. Big corporations try to imitate the entrepreneurial spirit.
Business Week   Apr 18, 1983   p. 78

Striking it rich. America's risk takers.
Time   Feb 15, 1982   p. 36

ENVIRONMENT

The war for the West. Fighting for the soul of America's mythic land.
Newsweek   Sep 30, 1991   p. 18

Earth to women: "Help!"
Ms.   Sep 1991   p. 20

Doomed. The last 10 paradises on earth.
Omni   Sep 1990   p. 34

The miracle of trees. They give us shade, beauty, the air we breathe. If we let them, they could even save our environment.
Life   May 1990   p. 26

Life on the Mississippi. Huck's river faces all of the nation's environmental problems.
Newsweek   Apr 16, 1990   p. 66

Predictions: Doomsday warnings are dangerous.
USA Today   Apr 1990   p. 1

The struggle to save our planet.
Discover   Apr 1990   p. 36

Buried alive. The garbage glut: An environmental crisis reaches our doorstop.
Newsweek   Nov 27, 1989 p. 66

Alaska's oil spill. The disaster that wasn't. Why the environment will recover. Should Exxon continue the cleanup?
U.S. News   Sep 18, 1989 p. 60

Torching the Amazon. Can the rain forest be saved?
Time   Sep 18, 1989 p. 76

The Alaska spill. What Exxon leaves behind. Is the damage permanent? Cutting through the hype, hysteria and confusion.
Newsweek   Sep 18, 1989 p. 50

Save the planet. A 16-page activist's primer to healing an ailing earth.
Omni   Sep 1989   p. 34

Cleaning up our mess. What works, what doesn't and what we must do to reclaim our air, land and water.
Newsweek   Jul 24, 1989 p. 26

Alaska. The battle for America's last frontier.
Time   Apr 17, 1989 p. 56

Planet of the year. Endangered earth.
Time   Jan 2, 1989   p. 24

As we begin our second century, the *Geographic* asks: Can man save this fragile earth?
National Geographic Dec 1988   p. 765

The heat is on. How the Earth's climate is changing. Why the ozone hole is growing.
Time   Oct 19, 1987 p. 58

The environmental Superfund controversy.
Congressional Digest Jun 1986   p. 163

The big cleanup. The environmental crisis '72.
Newsweek   Jun 12, 1972 p. 36

Environment: Nixon's new issue. Ecologist Barry Commoner. The emerging science of survival.
Time   Feb 2, 1970   p. 56

The ravaged environment.
Newsweek   Jan 26, 1970 p. 30

ENVIRONMENT - EASTERN EUROPE

East Europe's dark dawn.
National Geographic Jun 1991   p. 36

ENVIRONMENTAL POLICY - BUSH ADMINISTRATION

National policy: An environment agenda for Bush.
USA Today   Aug 1989   p. 1

ENVIRONMENTAL PROTECTION AGENCY

Cleaning up the mess. The toxic-waste threat to America's health. Chaos at the EPA.
Newsweek   Mar 7, 1983   p. 16

ENVY

Envy. Will it turn <u>you</u> upside-down in the '90s?
Psychology Today   Dec 1989   p. 46

ERHARD, LUDWIG

Germany & the defense of Europe. Ludwig Erhard.
Time   Nov 1, 1963   p. 30

A new German era. Ludwig Erhard.
Newsweek   Oct 7, 1963   p. 52

ERIKSON, ERIK

The quest for identity. Psychoanalyst Erik. H. Erikson.
Newsweek   Dec 21, 1970 p. 84

ERIKSON, ERIK (INTERVIEW)

The father of the "Identity Crisis" talks about Gandhi, wonder, sex, and a new identity for the human species.
Psychology Today   Jun 1983   p. 22

ERVIN, SAM

Showdown over secrecy. Senate v. White House. Watergate prober Sam Ervin.
Time   Apr 16, 1973   p. 10

ESCOBEDO RULING

Moving the Constitution into the police station. Danny Escobedo.
Time   Apr 29, 1966   p. 52

ESKIMOS

Greenland's 500-year-old mummies.
National Geographic Feb 1985   p. 191

Hunting the Greenland narwhal.
National Geographic Apr 1984   p. 520

ESPIONAGE

Betrayal. "This was the most scandalous fact of all: that the security of Moscow station and the protection of many of America's most important global secrets depended on the integrity of a single young Marine...
Time   Feb 20, 1989   p. 50

To catch a spy. Inside a top-secret U.S. agency: A case study of sloppy security. How one spy milked the files at six intelligence agencies. The KGB in Washington: Spotting weaknesses and exploiting them.
U.S. News   Jun 1, 1987   p. 20

Spy scandals. Marine Corps woes. High-tech surveillance. Assessing the damage.
Time   Apr 20, 1987   p. 14

How Soviets steal America's high-tech secrets. And how U.S. fights back.
U.S. News   Aug 12, 1985   p. 30

The spy scandal grows. "There are very serious losses." -Caspar Weinberger.
Time   Jun 17, 1985   p. 18

A family of spies. How much did they tell Moscow? The epidemic of Soviet espionage.
Newsweek   Jun 10, 1985   p. 32

The great superpower spy war. KGB vs. CIA.
U.S. News   Oct 29, 1984   p. 38

The KGB in America.
Newsweek   Nov 23, 1981   p. 50

Eavesdropping on the world's secrets.
U.S. News   Jun 26, 1978   p. 45

The new espionage. CIA chief Richard Helms.
Newsweek   Nov 22, 1971   p. 28

The new spy.
Time   Oct 11, 1971   p. 41

The French spy scandal. The former chief of French Intelligence in the U.S. reveals the fantastic story of Soviet espionage that penetrated De Gaulle's official family.
Life   Apr 26, 1968   p. 30

ESPIONAGE, INDUSTRIAL

How Soviets steal America's high-tech secrets. And how U.S. fights back.
U.S. News   Aug 12, 1985   p. 30

ESSLINGER, HARTMUT

Rebel with a cause. How Hartmut Esslinger is shaking up the world of industrial design.
Business Week   Dec 3, 1990   p. 130

ESTES, BILLIE SOL

Farm trouble. Behind the Billie Sol mess. Agriculture Secretary Orville Freeman.
Newsweek   May 28, 1962   p. 25

The Billie Sol Estes scandal.
Time   May 25, 1962   p. 24

ESTONIA - NATIONALISM

The Baltic nations. Estonia, Latvia, and Lithuania struggle toward independence.
National Geographic Nov 1990   p. 2

ESTROGEN

Dangerous liaisons. Women & estrogen. The story they want you to swallow.
Ms.   Apr 1989   p. 38

ETHICS

Gloria Steinem: Answers to the ethics crisis.
Ms.   Sep 1987   p. 57

What ever happened to ethics? Assaulted by sleaze, scandals and hypocrisy, America searches for its moral bearings.
Time   May 25, 1987   p. 14

Greed on Wall Street. A $12 million stock scandal stuns the financial world - and raises questions about the values of a new generation of America's best and brightest who are making millions doing deals.
Newsweek   May 26, 1986   p. 44

PT's survey report on cheating, lying and guilt.
Psychology Today   Nov 1981   p. 34

Capitol capers.
Newsweek   Jun 14, 1976   p. 18

The big payoff. Lockheed scandal: Graft around the globe.
Time   Feb 23, 1976   p. 28

The payoff scandals.
Newsweek   Feb 23, 1976   p. 26

ETHIOPIA
Famine. Why are Ethiopians starving again? What should the world do - and not do?
Time   Dec 21, 1987   p. 34

ETHNIC GROUPS
America's changing colors. What will the U.S. be like when whites are no longer the majority?
Time   Apr 9, 1990   p. 28

Splintered America. Peril or promise.
U.S.News   Jul 7, 1980   p. 33

ETIQUETTE
Mind your manners! The new concern with civility.
Time   Nov 5, 1984   p. 62

New American manners. Social arbiter Letitia Baldrige.
Time   Nov 27, 1978   p. 64

ETOSHA NATIONAL PARK, NAMIBIA
Family life of lions.
National Geographic Dec 1982   p. 800

EUROPE
The man who conquered Communism. "The New Europe" by Vaclav Havel, playwright-president of Czechoslovakia.
U.S. News   Feb 26, 1990   p. 28

The decline of Europe.
Newsweek   Apr 9, 1984   p. 44

Europe. America's new rival.
Time   Mar 12, 1973   p. 33

EUROPE - DEFENSES
Germany & the defense of Europe. Ludwig Erhard.
Time   Nov 1, 1963   p. 30

EUROPE - ECONOMIC CONDITIONS
Europe's economic malaise. Widening the split with the U.S.
Business Week   Dec 7, 1981   p. 74

EUROPE - POLITICS
Europe 1964: de Gaulle the defiant.
Newsweek   Nov 30, 1964   p. 40

EUROPE AND THE UNITED STATES
Tomorrow's Europe - friend or foe?
U.S. News   Jun 11, 1984   p. 29

Will Europe follow Carter?
U.S. News   May 16, 1977   p. 19

Time for pullback in Europe?
U.S. News   Apr 1, 1974   p. 15

EUROPEAN ECONOMIC COMMUNITY
The battle for Europe. The world's largest market is up for grabs. While the Europeans and Americans are losing ground, the Japanese are coming on strong.
Business Week   Jun 3, 1991   p. 44

Reshaping Europe. 1992 and beyond. The fight for one market. How U.S. giants will play. The new world of finance. Are small companies in danger?
Business Week   Dec 12, 1988   p. 48

The decline of Europe.
Newsweek   Apr 9, 1984   p. 44

Kennedy or de Gaulle. Whose grand design?
Newsweek   Feb 11, 1963   p. 17

The perils of grandeur. De Gaulle.
Time   Feb 8, 1963   p. 22

De Gaulle. Apres moi...?
Newsweek   Jan 28, 1963   p. 25

The Eurocrats. Common Market's Walter Hallstein.
Newsweek   Jan 7, 1963   p. 26

Toward a world market. The year in business.
Time   Dec 28, 1962   p. 50

Britain & the Common Market. A historic decision for Europe.
Time   Jul 13, 1962   p. 29

New strength for the West. Europe unites in the Common Market.
Time   Oct 6, 1961   p. 28

EUTHANASIA
The right to die.
Time   Mar 19, 1990   p. 62

A right to die?
Newsweek   Nov 3, 1975   p. 58

EVANGELICALISM
The Evangelicals. New empire of faith.
Time   Dec 26, 1977   p. 52

Born again! Evangelicals.
Newsweek   Oct 25, 1976   p. 68

EVERS, MEDGAR W.
A martyr—and the Negro presses on.
Life   Jun 28, 1963   p. 34

EVOLUTION
Early man. The radical new view of where we came from.
U.S. News   Sep 16, 1991   p. 53

Argument over a woman. Science searches for the real Eve.
Discover   Aug 1990   p. 52

The great leap forward. Why we succeeded and Neanderthal failed.
Discover   May 1989   p. 50

The search for Adam & Eve. Scientists explore a controversial theory about man's origins.
Newsweek   Jan 11, 1988   p. 46

What were dinosaurs really like?
Discover   Mar 1987   p. 51

An extraordinary 2.5 million-year-old skull found in Kenya has overturned all previous notions of the course of early hominid evolution. We no longer know who gave rise to whom — perhaps not even how, or when, we came into being.
Discover   Sep 1986   p. 86

Future universe. The evolution of life over the next one hundred billion years.
Omni   Aug 1986   p. 36

The ape in your past. He is a lot closer than you think.
Discover   Jul 1983   p. 22

Mysteries of evolution. Paleontologist Stephan Jay Gould.
Newsweek   Mar 29, 1982   p. 44

EVOLUTION - STUDY AND TEACHING
Science and censorship.
Omni   Feb 1987   p. 42

Darwin on trial. Creationism vs. evolution in Little Rock.
Discover   Feb 1982   p. 14

EVTUSHENKO, EVGENY
Russia's new generation. Soviet poet Evtushenko.
Time   Apr 13, 1962   p. 28

EXCELLENCE
The best of America. The year's most outstanding people, places, products, and ideas.
U.S. News   Jul 9, 1990   p. 43

EXECUTIVE APPOINTMENTS - CARTER ADMINISTRATION
The great talent hunt.
Time   Dec 20, 1976   p. 8

Picking the new team.
Newsweek   Dec 13, 1976   p. 20

Taking charge.
Newsweek   Nov 22, 1976   p. 24

EXECUTIVE APPOINTMENTS - FORD ADMINISTRATION
White House shakeup - Meaning for defense, foreign policy, '76 elections.
U.S. News   Nov 17, 1975   p. 16

Ford's big shuffle.
Newsweek   Nov 17, 1975   p. 24

EXECUTIVE APPOINTMENTS - KENNEDY ADMINISTRATION
Kennedy's men. The face of the new administration. Secretary of State: Dean Rusk.
Time   Dec 26, 1960   p. 8

EXECUTIVE APPOINTMENTS - NIXON ADMINISTRATION

Nixon's palace guard. Kissinger, Mitchell, Haldeman, Ehrlichman.
Time   Jun 8, 1970   p. 15

Changing the guard.
Newsweek   Dec 23, 1968   p. 16

The new administration. William Rogers: Nixon's Secretary of State.
Time   Dec 20, 1968   p. 10

EXECUTIVE APPOINTMENTS - REAGAN ADMINISTRATION

Starting over. New White House Chief of Staff Howard Baker. CIA nominee William Webster. National Security Adviser Frank Carlucci.
Time   Mar 16, 1987   p. 18

EXECUTIVE POWER - UNITED STATES

The War Powers Act and the Persian Gulf.
Congressional Digest Dec 1987   p. 289

EXECUTIVE SEARCH CONSULTANTS

The new headhunters. Meet Tom Neff. He's filling million-dollar jobs—and shaking up his industry.
Business Week   Feb 6, 1989   p. 64

EXECUTIVES

Tough times, tough bosses. The new breed of CEO in Corporate America.
Business Week   Nov 25, 1991   p. 174

I'm worried about my job! A career survival kit for the '90s.
Business Week   Oct 7, 1991   p. 943

The executive suite. Why women can't, won't, don't want to make it to the top.
U.S. News   Jun 17, 1991   p. 40

CEO disease. You know the symptoms. The boss doesn't seem to understand the business anymore. Decisions come slowly—only to be abruptly changed. Yes-men are everywhere.
Business Week   Apr 1, 1991   p. 52

Farewell, fast track. Motivating people in difficult times.
Business Week   Dec 10, 1990   p. 192

The new headhunters. Meet Tom Neff. He's filling million-dollar jobs—and shaking up his industry.
Business Week   Feb 6, 1989   p. 64

The corporate elite. Chief executives of the *Business Week* top 1000. A directory.
Business Week   Oct 21, 1988   p. 71

Middle managers. Are they an endangered species? In their own words, six executives describe the frustrations, hopes and fears of life in today's corporation.
Business Week   Sep 12, 1988   p. 80

The corporate elite. Chief executives of the *Business Week* top 1000. A directory.
Business Week   Oct 23, 1987   p. 99

Fast-track kids. A new generation is rising in the ranks of Corporate America. Here are some of the best and the brightest—their attitudes, goals, and problems—and how they'll reshape big business.
Business Week   Nov 10, 1986   p. 90

Business celebrities.
Business Week   Jun 23, 1986   p. 100

Neurotic companies.
Psychology Today   Oct 1984   p. 26

Turnover at the top. Why executives lose their jobs so quickly.
Business Week   Dec 19, 1983   p. 104

Managing America's business. What makes a top executive?
Psychology Today   Feb 1983   p. 26

EXECUTIVES - RELOCATION

America's new immobile society.
Business Week   Jul 27, 1981   p. 58

EXECUTIVES - SALARIES, PENSIONS, ETC.

Are CEOs paid too much?
Business Week   May 6, 1991   p. 90

Executive pay. Who made the most and are they worth it? 1989 top ten CEOs.
Business Week   May 7, 1990   p. 56

Executive pay. Who made the most and are they worth it? 1988 top ten.
Business Week   May 1, 1989   p. 46

The Alaska spill. What Exxon leaves
behind. Is the damage permanent?
Cutting through the hype, hysteria and
confusion.
Newsweek   Sep 18, 1989   p. 50

Fateful voyage. What really happened
aboard the Exxon Valdez. Captain Joseph
Hazelwood.
Time   Jul 24, 1989   p. 42

Alaska. The battle for America's last
frontier.
Time   Apr 17, 1989   p. 56

FACE

Coding the faces of emotion.
Psychology Today   Feb 1981   p. 42

FAIRCHILD, JOHN

The man behind the midi mania. John
Fairchild of "Women's Wear Daily."
Time   Sep 14, 1970   p. 35

FAIRCHILD, SHERMAN

Those glamour stocks. New ideas & new
millionaires. Fairchild Industries'
Sherman Fairchild.
Time   Jul 25, 1960   p. 62

FAIRS

State fairs. Bigger and brassier than ever.
U.S. News   Sep 5, 1977   p. 43

See Also WORLD'S FAIR

FAISAL, KING OF SAUDI ARABIA

Man of the Year. King Faisal.
Time   Jan 6, 1975   p. 8

FALKLAND ISLANDS WAR, 1982

The spoils of war. Carving up Lebanon.
Surrender at Stanley. U.S. frustrations.
Time   Jun 28, 1982   p. 8

An extraordinary week. Furies in the
Falklands. A Pope comes to Britain.
Reagan girds for Europe.
Time   Jun 7, 1982   p. 6

The British go in.
Newsweek   May 31, 1982   p. 18

D-day in the Falklands.
Time   May 31, 1982   p. 24

Are big ships doomed? The Falklands
fallout.
Newsweek   May 17, 1982   p. 28

Explosive Falklands. Naval war in the
missile age. Striving to shape a truce.
Time   May 17, 1982   p. 12

The war is on.
Newsweek   May 10, 1982   p. 28

The British attack.
Time   May 10, 1982   p. 18

The empire strikes back. The Falklands
crisis.
Newsweek   Apr 19, 1982   p. 40

Battle stations. Showdown in the South
Atlantic.
Time   Apr 19, 1982   p. 26

FAMILY

Breakup of the family. Single-parent
households, soaring divorce rates,
childless couples, and alternative
lifestyles are fragmenting the traditional
family.
USA Today   May 1991   p. 50

How will we survive the 1990s?
Introducing a yearlong series on the
American family.
Life   Apr 1991   p. 26

Working parents. How to give your kids
what they need. By Dr. T. Berry
Brazelton.
Newsweek   Feb 13, 1989   p. 66

Amazing families. Why gifted parents
produce gifted children.
U.S. News   Dec 12, 1988   p. 78

Tracking the dream. The American
family in focus.
Ms.   Mar 1988   p. 36

The blended family. What used to be
called a stepfamily is a new norm.
Ms.   Feb 1985   p. 33

Two-career couples. How they do it. The commuting alternative, the social life squeeze & other trade-offs.
Ms.   Jun 1984   p. 39

The American family. Bent - but not broken.
U.S.News   Jun 16, 1980   p. 48

Saving the family.
Newsweek   May 15, 1978   p. 63

The American family. Can it survive today's shocks?
U.S. News   Oct 27, 1975   p. 30

The broken family.
Newsweek   Mar 12, 1973   p. 47

The U.S. family: "Help!"
Time   Dec 28, 1970   p. 34

See Also SINGLE PARENT FAMILIES

FAMILY AND MEDICAL LEAVE
The Family and Medical Leave Act.
Congressional Digest Apr 1991   p. 98

FAMILY VIOLENCE
A tale of abuse. The horrifying Steinberg trial. The psychology of violent relationships.
Newsweek   Dec 12, 1988   p. 56

Mothers on the run. The child-abuse crisis. Thousand of fearful women now flee their husbands by going underground - often in violation of the law.
U.S. News   Jun 13, 1988   p. 22

Private violence. Child abuse. Wife beating. Rape.
Time   Sep 5, 1983   p. 18

FAMINES
Famine. Why are Ethiopians starving again? What should the world do - and not do?
Time   Dec 21, 1987   p. 34

We are the children. The new wave of sympathy and aid may come too late to save Africa's lost generation.
Newsweek   Jun 3, 1985   p. 28

Famine. Africa's nightmare. The world reaches out.
Newsweek   Nov 26, 1984   p. 50

FANTASY
Mind-trippers. Fantasy addicts speak out.
Omni   Jun 1988   p. 64

The power of daydreams.
Psychology Today Oct 1987   p. 36

FARMERS AND FARMING
Farmers up in arms.
U.S. News   Mar 11, 1985   p. 22

Bitter harvest. America's angry farmers. The fight over subsidies.
Newsweek   Feb 18, 1985   p. 52

Going broke. Tangled policies. Failing farms.
Time   Feb 18, 1985   p. 18

Why the recovery may skip the farm belt.
Business Week   Mar 21, 1983   p. 106

The new U.S. farmer.
Time   Nov 6, 1978   p. 92

Food prices: The big beef.
Time   Apr 9, 1973   p. 11

See Also AGRICULTURE

FARRELL, EILEEN
What makes a prima donna? Eileen Farrell of the Met.
Newsweek   Feb 13, 1961   p. 63

FARROW, MIA
The young actors. Stars and anti-stars. Dustin Hoffman and Mia Farrow.
Time   Feb 7, 1969   p. 50

Mia. The gifted, wide-eyed sprite who is Mrs. Sinatra.
Life   May 5, 1967   p. 75

FASHION
Hurrah for the bra. It's 100 years old this month.
Life   Jun 1989   p. 88

Ms. Fashion. Liz Claiborne built a billion-dollar empire by designing smart clothing for professional women. Hit by the fashion slump, she's now trying to bounce back.
Business Week   Jan 16, 1989   p. 64

Who would wear this stuff? The fashion revolt.
Newsweek   Dec 5, 1988   p. 60

The heat is on. Fashion goes feminine - and Ungaro leads the way.
Newsweek   Apr 4, 1988   p. 54

Selling that sporty look. Polo's Ralph Lauren.
Time   Sep 1, 1986   p. 54

You're so vain. Men are primping, preening - and spending millions to look good.
Newsweek   Apr 14, 1986   p. 48

The fashion statement. Dressing for effect.
Psychology Today   Apr 1986   p. 20

Bathing beauties.
Life   Feb 1986   p. 72

Brooke bares the new swimsuits.
Life   Feb 1985   p. 81

Giorgio's gorgeous style. Fashion designer Giorgio Armani.
Time   Apr 5, 1982   p. 60

Lingerie to show off in public.
Life   Feb 1979   p. 72

Fashion '78. Soft and sexy. Designer Calvin Klein.
Newsweek   May 8, 1978   p. 80

American chic in fashion.
Time   Mar 22, 1976   p. 62

Fall fashions. Ease and elegance designed by Halston.
Newsweek   Aug 21, 1972   p. 48

The new China look.
Life   Dec 10, 1971   p. 59

Fashion '71. Anything goes.
Newsweek   Mar 29, 1971   p. 68

Male plumage. He-men return to elegance.
Life   Sep 25, 1970   p. 42

The man behind the midi mania. John Fairchild of "Women's Wear Daily."
Time   Sep 14, 1970   p. 35

The midi muscles in.
Life   Aug 21, 1970   p. 22

Midi vs. mini.
Newsweek   Mar 16, 1970   p. 70

The great hemline hassle.
Life   Mar 13, 1970   p. 38

That young New York look.
Life   Aug 22, 1969   p. 32

Male plumage '68.
Newsweek   Nov 25, 1968   p. 70

Sweden's wild style. New fashion find—the land of blondes.
Life   Sep 27, 1968   p. 88

Bonnie fashion's new darling. Faye Dunaway in a '30s revival.
Life   Jan 12, 1968   p. 69

The miniskirt is here to stay (until spring, anyway). Designer Rudi Gernreich.
Time   Dec 1, 1967   p. 70

Acapulco. Bold and bare. The shape of tans to come at the top jet resort.
Life   Jan 27, 1967   p. 48

Face it! Revolution in male clothes.
Life   May 13, 1966   p. 82

New fashions from Paris.
Life   Aug 30, 1963   p. 77

The rites of fashion.
Newsweek   Aug 12, 1963   p. 48

Jean Seberg. Stars pick their Paris spring favorites.
Life   Mar 8, 1963   p. 82

Elsa Martinelli in a toga to shed before going to bed.
Life   Jul 27, 1962   p. 63

Explosion in style. The bold Italian look that changed fashion.
Life   Dec 1, 1961   p. 66

Sensational clothes by America's Norell
stir up style storm.
Life   Sep 26, 1960   p. 22

FAST FOOD RESTAURANTS

The fun of American food.
Time   Aug 26, 1985   p. 54

FATHERS

Are men discovering the joys of
fatherhood?
Ms.   Feb 1982   p. 41

FATHERS AND SONS

Fathers and sons: The search for reunion.
Psychology Today   Jun 1982   p. 22

FAULKNER, WILLIAM,

Faulkner's Mississippi.
National Geographic Mar 1989   p. 313

The South: View from within. William
Faulkner.
Time   Jul 17, 1964   p. 44

FBI

See FEDERAL BUREAU OF
INVESTIGATION

FEAR

Nuclear fear. Growing up scared...of not
growing up.
Psychology Today   Apr 1984   p. 18

FEDERAL BUREAU OF INVESTIGATION

The truth about Hoover.
Time   Dec 22, 1975   p. 14

The FBI in politics. L. Patrick Gray III.
Time   Mar 26, 1973   p. 17

Hoover's FBI. Time for a change?
Newsweek   May 10, 1971   p. 28

Emperor of the FBI. The 47-year reign of
J. Edgar Hoover.
Life   Apr 9, 1971   p. 39

J. Edgar Hoover and the FBI.
Newsweek   Dec 7, 1964   p. 21

**FEDERAL COMMUNICATIONS
  COMMISSION**

Has the FCC gone too far? Chairman
Mark Fowler pushes deregulation of
telecommunications and broadcasting.
Business Week   Aug 5, 1985   p. 48

FEDERAL DEFICIT

Budget reconciliation act of 1990.
Congressional Digest Dec 1990   p. 291

Wake up, America! The stock market
may recover somewhat, but the message
underlying the crash remains largely
unheeded. We have spent too much,
borrowed too much and imported too
much. We have lived beyond, relying on
foreigners to finance. . .
Business Week   Nov 16, 1987   p. 158

How to cut the deficit. An in-depth look at
spending: For defense, the elderly, the
poor, agriculture, state and local aid, the
bureaucracy. And the right way to raise
taxes. What can be done about big
deficits? Plenty.
Business Week   Mar 26, 1984   p. 49

Controversy over the Federal budget
deficit.
Congressional Digest Feb 1984   p. 33

Guns vs. butter. How to cut defense
spending. How to save Social Security.
Business Week   Nov 29, 1982   p. 68

The built-in deficit. How federal spending
outpaces revenues. The trouble is
Congress. What the deficits are doing to
the economy.
Business Week   Aug 16, 1982   p. 84

FEDERAL EXPRESS

Mr. Smith goes global. Founder Fred
Smith loves high-risk deals. His latest:
Going deep in debt to buy Flying Tiger
and expand overseas.
Business Week   Feb 13, 1989   p. 66

FEDERAL RESERVE BOARD

The fed's plan for economic recovery. Is
Chairman Paul Volcker aiming too low?
Business Week   Dec 13, 1982   p. 90

FEDERAL RESERVE SYSTEM

Shock treatment for inflation.
Newsweek   Oct 22, 1979   p. 36

The squeeze of '79. Tighter money.
Higher prices. Wall Street woes.
Time   Oct 22, 1979   p. 8

Economy '78. A new look?
Newsweek   Jan 9, 1978   p. 48

FINLEY, CHARLES

Baseball's super showman. Oakland's
Charlie Finley.
Time Aug 18, 1975 p. 42

FINNEY, ALBERT

Albert Finney in 'Luther.' The new prince
of players.
Newsweek Oct 28, 1963 p. 56

FIRESTONE TIRE & RUBBER CO.

Survival in the basic industries. How four
companies hope to avoid disaster:
Firestone. Kennecott. Inland Steel. Boise
Cascade.
Business Week Apr 26, 1982 p. 74

FIREWORKS

The new science of fireworks.
Discover Jul 1982 p. 24

FIRST LADIES

See WIVES OF THE PRESIDENTS

FISCHER, BOBBY

Bobby's next move?
Newsweek Jul 31, 1972 p. 42

The deadly gamesman. Bobby Fischer is
one match away from the world chess
championship.
Life Nov 12, 1971 p. 50

FISHING

Salty excitement of ocean fishing.
Life Apr 7, 1961 p. 80

FITNESS

See EXERCISE

FLAG BURNING

Flag desecration legislation.
Congressional Digest Aug 1989 p. 193

FLAGS - UNITED STATES

Fight over the flag: Patriots and put-ons.
Time Jul 6, 1970 p. 8

FLEMING, IAN

Alias James Bond. The real story of Ian
Fleming.
Life Oct 7, 1966 p. 102

FLEMING, PEGGY

Olympic charmer. Peggy Fleming.
Life Feb 23, 1968 p. 52

FLOODS

Deluge and havoc in the Northwest.
Life Jan 8, 1965 p. 20

FLOODS - ITALY

Heroic job of rescuing a great heritage. A
mission of restoration after Italy's
devastating floods.
Life Dec 16, 1966 p. 28

FLORENCE (ITALY)

Heroic job of rescuing a great heritage. A
mission of restoration after Italy's
devastating floods.
Life Dec 16, 1966 p. 28

FLORIDA

Florida watershed.
National Geographic Jul 1990 p. 89

Man and manatee.
National Geographic Sep 1984 p. 400

Paradise lost? South Florida.
Time Nov 23, 1981 p. 22

FLU (DISEASE)

Best ways to fight that cold.
U.S. News Jan 29, 1990 p. 54

Respiratory system: What do we know
about colds?
USA Today Dec 1988 p. 1

Respiratory disease: Was Grandma right?
USA Today Oct 1985 p. 1

Man vs. virus. Fighting the flu.
Newsweek Jan 20, 1969 p. 62

Tricky viruses on the loose. (A special
medicine report on the ever-changing
menace.)
Newsweek Jan 25, 1960 p. 51

FOLKLORE - UNITED STATES

American folklore, part III: The rich
treasury of colonial tales.
Life Jan 25, 1960 p. 50

FONDA, HENRY

Jane, Henry, and Peter: The flying
Fondas.
Time Feb 16, 1970 p. 58

Pittsburgh's front four. Half a ton of trouble.
Time   Dec 8, 1975   p. 62

Building for the Super Bowl. Miami coach Don Shula.
Time   Dec 11, 1972   p. 91

The running backs.
Newsweek   Dec 4, 1972   p. 76

Pro football's game plan: Back to the attack.
Time   Oct 16, 1972   p. 46

Rough, tough pros. A gallery of Sunday heroes without their masks or pads.
Life   Oct 6, 1972   p. 76

Super Bowl.
Time   Jan 17, 1972   p. 42

Suicide squad. Pro football's most violent men.
Life   Dec 3, 1971   p. 32

Pro football's red-hot Redskins. Coach George Allen.
Newsweek   Nov 1, 1971   p. 54

Trials of a rookie.
Newsweek   Oct 5, 1970   p. 58

Pro football '69. Namath of the Jets.
Newsweek   Sep 15, 1969   p. 29

My Colts. Verses and reverses by Ogden Nash.
Life   Dec 13, 1968   p. 75

Controlled violence of the pros.
Life   Oct 14, 1966   p. 76

Battle of the pros for the college stars.
Life   Dec 10, 1965   p. 36

The sport of the '60s. Green Bay coach Vince Lombardi.
Time   Dec 21, 1962   p. 56

Under fire with the pros. Battle cry: Get the quarterback.
Life   Nov 17, 1961   p. 148

Sunday's hero. The pro.
Newsweek   Oct 30, 1961   p. 43

Kickoff by the Colts before capacity house.
Life   Dec 5, 1960   p. 113

FORD, BETTY

Free spirit in the White House.
Newsweek   Dec 29, 1975   p. 19

Betty Ford's folksy White House.
U.S. News   Dec 30, 1974   p. 12

The operation. Betty Ford.
Newsweek   Oct 7, 1974   p. 30

FORD, BETTY (INTERVIEW)

Betty vs. Rosalynn. Life on the campaign trail.
U.S. News   Oct 18, 1976   p. 22

FORD, CRISTINA

Chistina Ford. Rich, impish and almost Americanized.
Life   Jun 4, 1971   p. 46

FORD, EILEEN

Hunting down the world's loveliest girls.
Life   Nov 13, 1970   p. 63

FORD, GERALD

How good a President?
Newsweek   Oct 18, 1976   p. 30

Ford's plan to beat the odds.
U.S. News   Aug 30, 1976   p. 12

Ford in trouble.
Newsweek   Dec 22, 1975   p. 20

China to Ford: Protect us from Russia.
U.S. News   Dec 15, 1975   p. 13

Can he stop Ford?
Newsweek   Nov 24, 1975   p. 30

If Reagan runs against Ford.
U.S. News   Oct 20, 1975   p. 14

At ease in the White House. Ford's first year.
Time   Jul 28, 1975   p. 7

What Ford wants in Europe.
U.S. News   Jun 2, 1975   p. 17

Ford. How he rates now. Kennedy. Democrats' choice after all?
U.S. News   Apr 28, 1975   p. 25

A day in the life of the President.
U.S. News   Feb 24, 1975   p. 12

The Mustang. Newest breed out of
Detroit. Ford's Lee Iacocca.
Newsweek   Apr 20, 1964   p. 97

Ford's Lee Iacocca.
Time   Apr 17, 1964   p. 92

FORECASTING

What's ahead. 24 predictions for the new
year. Money. Election '92. Health.
Business.
U.S. News   Dec 30, 1991   p. 36

The 90's. A survival guide. Issues,
people and predictions for the age of
anxiety.
Newsweek   Dec 31, 1990   p. 14

Outlook 1991. What's ahead. 24
predictions for the new year.
U.S. News   Dec 31, 1990   p. 43

What's ahead. Politics. Exclusive:
George Bush on the '90s. Economy.
America's place in a global race.
Environment. A new national security
issue. Society. How we will live and
work. People. Future movers...
U.S. News   Jan 1, 1990   p. 21

What's ahead. Politics. Exclusive:
George Bush on the '90s. Economy.
America's place in a global race.
Environment. A new national security
issue. Society. How we will live and
work. People. Future movers...
U.S. News   Dec 25, 1989   p. 21

Trends and predictions for the year 2000
and beyond.
Omni   Oct 1989   p. 66

America enters the new world. Politics.
What to expect from the Bush Presidency.
Economy. Is America losing control of its
destiny? Environment. How to keep the
earth from destroying itself. Health...
U.S. News   Dec 26, 1988   p. 20

2001. It's only 13 years away. What will
life really be like?
Discover   Nov 1988   p. 25

Outlook '88. What's ahead. Politics:
What the candidates aren't telling us.
Economy: Getting ready for the crunch.
Money: Where to invest in the new year.
Health: New ways to stop heart attacks.
U.S. News   Dec 28, 1987   p. 24

14 great minds predict the future.
Omni   Jan 1987   p. 36

Outlook 87. What's ahead. Reagan: Can
he make a comeback? World: Trouble
spots for the U.S. Money: Hot picks for
the new year. Health: Breakthroughs on
the horizon.
U.S. News   Dec 29, 1986   p. 17

A rekindled spirit. Outlook '86. Business.
More growth ahead. Nation. The can-do
mood in the states. World. U.S. takes the
lead. Money. Where to invest now.
U.S. News   Dec 30, 1985   p. 20

Outlook '85. Reagan. Changes in the
wind. Money. Where to invest now.
Business. More good times ahead.
World. New demands on U.S.
U.S. News   Dec 31, 1984   p. 20

Outlook '84. Business. Will it boom?
Reagan. Second term a cinch? Money.
Where to invest now? President's size-up
of the world.
U.S. News   Dec 26, 1983   p. 24

Living without inflation. Where prices are
headed. Places to put your money. Tips
for consumers. Rent or buy a home.
Impact on your career.
U.S. News   Jul 18, 1983   p. 14

What the next 50 years will bring.
U.S. News   May 9, 1983   p. 66

Outlook '83. Business: How fast a
pickup? Reagan: Can he tame congress?
Money: Where to invest now? World:
Next crisis spots?
U.S. News   Dec 27, 1982   p. 18

Outlook '82. Recession. When will it end?
Reagan. Will he change course? World.
Next hot spots for U.S.? Money. Where to
invest now?
U.S. News   Dec 28, 1981   p. 20

Outlook '81. Reagan. Can he turn U.S.
around? Business. How fast a recovery?
World. New muscle for America. Money.
Where to invest now.
U.S.News   Dec 29, 1980   p. 18

What next 20 years hold for you.
U.S.News   Dec 1, 1980   p. 51

Outlook '80. Recession. How deep, how long? Elections. Another term for Carter? World. More trouble brewing? Money. Where to put it now?
U.S. News   Dec 31, 1979   p. 20

Outlook '79. Top questions of the year. Business. Recession for sure? Carter. Can he tame congress? Money. Where to invest now? Mideast. Never-ending problem?
U.S. News   Dec 25, 1978   p. 20

Outlook '78. Key questions of the year. Carter. Will he change course? Business. Can we avoid recession? Peace. Mideast solution soon? Money. Where to put it now?
U.S. News   Dec 26, 1977   p. 16

Outlook '77. Top questions of the year.
U.S. News   Dec 27, 1976   p. 12

America's third century. A look ahead.
U.S. News   Jul 5, 1976   p. 37

Outlook '76. Year of big decisions. Recovery: Sturdy or frail? Will Ford hold the White House? How far can Russia push? President vs. Congress - endless feud? Where should you invest now?
U.S. News   Jan 5, 1976   p. 11

What kind of future for America?
U.S. News   Jul 7, 1975   p. 44

Into a new era. How your life will change. 1975...2000.
U.S. News   Mar 3, 1975   p. 32

Merry Christmas. Plus signs in America's future.
U.S. News   Dec 23, 1974   p. 11

'74. Special report on a crucial year. Can a recession be avoided? Real peace abroad? An end to fuel crisis? What's in store for Nixon. Any good news for investors?
U.S. News   Jan 7, 1974   p. 11

The U.S. economy, 1967. Concern and confidence. Bank of America's Rudolph Peterson.
Time   Dec 30, 1966   p. 47

Q and A '61.
Newsweek   Dec 12, 1960   p. 23

FOREIGN INVESTMENTS
See INVESTMENTS, FOREIGN

FOREIGN POLICY - BUSH ADMINISTRATION
Waiting for Washington. The U.S. dithers while Moscow woos Europe. Soviet Foreign Minister Shevardnadze says he's eager to talk.
Time   May 15, 1989   p. 22

FOREIGN POLICY - CARTER ADMINISTRATION
It's Carter's turn to cope with Russia.
U.S.News   Feb 4, 1980   p. 16

America's lonely role.
U.S.News   Jan 28, 1980   p. 21

Carter's juggling act. China. SALT. NATO. Russia. Mid-East. OPEC. Iran.
U.S. News   Jan 8, 1979   p. 13

Tug of war over foreign policy.
U.S. News   Jun 19, 1978   p. 37

The mess in foreign policy.
U.S. News   Jan 23, 1978   p. 27

The Carter impact.
U.S. News   Jan 16, 1978   p. 21

Carter's foreign policy. Jimmy in the lion's den.
Time   Aug 8, 1977   p. 8

FOREIGN POLICY - JOHNSON ADMINISTRATION
American foreign policy. Drift or design.
Newsweek   May 17, 1965   p. 27

FOREIGN POLICY - KENNEDY ADMINISTRATION
Secretary Rusk. New policies for old problems?
Newsweek   Jul 9, 1962   p. 21

New tempo in foreign policy. Kennedy's man Rusk.
Newsweek   Feb 6, 1961   p. 19

FOREIGN POLICY - NIXON ADMINISTRATION
In search of a foreign policy.
Newsweek   Dec 14, 1970   p. 28

FRANCE - FOREIGN RELATIONS

Charles de Gaulle enters Mexico City with President López Mateos.
Life   Mar 27, 1964   p. 24

The siren's song. French diplomacy from Richelieu to de Gaulle. Foreign Minister Couve de Murville.
Time   Feb 7, 1964   p. 26

The perils of grandeur. De Gaulle.
Time   Feb 8, 1963   p. 22

FRANCE - POLITICS AND GOVERNMENT

France's new look. Socialist President François Mitterrand.
Time   Jun 29, 1981   p. 26

France after de Gaulle. Candidate Pompidou.
Newsweek   May 12, 1969   p. 41

France after de Gaulle. Georges Pompidou.
Time   May 9, 1969   p. 30

France: Beyond the deluge. Charles de Gaulle.
Time   May 31, 1968   p. 20

France's fading hero. Charles de Gaulle.
Newsweek   Aug 28, 1967   p. 30

De Gaulle: Once and future king.
Newsweek   Dec 13, 1965   p. 41

De Gaulle's triumph.
Time   Dec 7, 1962   p. 21

FRANCE - RIOTS

Showdown in France.
Newsweek   Jun 10, 1968   p. 38

French revolution 1968.
Newsweek   May 27, 1968   p. 44

FRANCE AND THE SOVIET UNION

De Gaulle in Russia.
Newsweek   Jul 4, 1966   p. 34

Omnis Europa in unam parten? De Gaulle.
Time   Jul 1, 1966   p. 20

FRANCE AND THE UNITED STATES

Kennedy or de Gaulle. Whose grand design?
Newsweek   Feb 11, 1963   p. 17

Kennedy in Paris.
Life   Jun 9, 1961   p. 42

President Kennedy.
Time   Jun 9, 1961   p. 9

De Gaulle. Mission to America.
Newsweek   Apr 25, 1960   p. 39

FRANCO, FRANCISCO

Franco's last hurrah?
Newsweek   Oct 13, 1975   p. 41

Spain looks to the future. General Franco.
Time   Jan 21, 1966   p. 26

Franco's Spain today.
Newsweek   Jul 2, 1962   p. 25

FRANK, BARNEY

Barney Frank's story. A congressman talks about his double life. A Newsweek poll on homosexuality and politics.
Newsweek   Sep 25, 1989   p. 14

FRANKENSTEIN

Happy 150th, dear Frankenstein. Strange revelations about how Mrs. Percy Bysshe Shelley created the monster.
Life   Mar 15, 1968   p. 74

FRANKLIN, ARETHA

The sound of soul. Singer Aretha Franklin.
Time   Jun 28, 1968   p. 62

FRAUD

The great national rip-off.
U.S. News   Jul 3, 1978   p. 27

How people cheat Uncle Sam out of billions.
U.S. News   Jul 11, 1977   p. 16

FRAWLEY, BRIAN

The Pope's foot soldiers. Keeping the faith: Two American priests in a changing church. Catholic priests Raymond Dlugos and Brian Frawley.
U.S. News   Sep 21, 1987   p. 58

FRAZIER, JOE

Norman Mailer on the fight. 9 pages of action color.
Life   Mar 19, 1971   p. 18

The $5,000,000 fighters. Frazer. Ali.
Time   Mar 8, 1971   p. 63

Battle of the champs. Backstage with Ali and Frazier.
Life   Mar 5, 1971   p. 40

FREEDOM OF INFORMATION

Controversy over the Freedom of Information Act.
Congressional Digest Feb 1982   p. 35

FREEDOM RIDERS

See BLACKS - PROTESTS AND DEMONSTRATIONS

FREEMAN, ORVILLE

Agriculture Secretary Freeman.
Time   Apr 5, 1963   p. 21

Farm trouble. Behind the Billie Sol mess. Agriculture Secretary Orville Freeman.
Newsweek   May 28, 1962 p. 25

FREUD, SIGMUND

The hidden Freud. His secret life. His theories under attack.
Newsweek   Nov 30, 1981 p. 64

FRIEDLAND, GERALD

The AIDS doctor. Gerald Friedland has treated nearly 300 men and women with AIDS. More than 200 are dead. The rest are dying. This is the story of his caring and his struggle.
Newsweek   Jul 21, 1986   p. 38

FRIENDSHIP

Love and friendship. Take a good friend, add passion, fascination and, sometimes, grief: Voilà, you have a lover.
Psychology Today   Feb 1985   p. 22

FROMME, LYNETTE

"It didn't go off." 'Squeaky' Fromme after capture.
Newsweek   Sep 15, 1975 p. 16

The girl who almost killed Ford.
Time   Sep 15, 1975 p. 8

FRONDIZI, ARTURO

Democracy's failure in Argentina. Arturo Frondizi.
Time   Mar 30, 1962 p. 27

FRONTIER AND PIONEER LIFE

The old West. The new view of frontier life.
U.S. News   May 21, 1990 p. 56

Oregon Trail. The itch to move west.
National Geographic Aug 1986   p. 147

FROST, ROBERT

America's ageless poet Robert Frost. Seven poems from his wonderful new book.
Life   Mar 30, 1962 p. 60

FUEL - CONSERVATION

The cooling of America. Cold wave hits. Fuel prices up.
Time   Dec 24, 1979 p. 48

FULBRIGHT, WILLIAM

U.S. foreign policy: How to relate self-interest and the preservation of freedom. Senator Fulbright.
Time   Jan 22, 1965 p. 14

FULLER, R. BUCKMINSTER

Buckminster Fuller.
Time   Jan 10, 1964 p. 46

FUNDAMENTALISM

Thunder on the right. The growth of Fundamentalism.
Time   Sep 2, 1985   p. 48

FURSTENBERG, DIANE VON

Rags & riches. Dress designer Diane von Fustenberg.
Newsweek   Mar 22, 1976 p. 52

FUSION

See NUCLEAR FUSION

FUSION, COLD

See COLD FUSION

FUTURE

See FORECASTING

G

GABLE, CLARK
Gable's last film.
Life Jan 13, 1961 p. 53

GABLE, JOHN CLARK
Mrs. Clark Gable and son, John Clark.
Life Apr 14, 1961 p. 99

GADDAFI
See QADDAFI, MUAMMAR AL-

GAGARIN, YURI
The voyage of Yuri Gagarin.
Newsweek Apr 24, 1961 p. 22

Man in space. Russia's Yuri Gagarin.
Time Apr 21, 1961 p. 46

GALAXIES
When galaxies collide. The splendid violence of creation.
Discover Feb 1990 p. 50

GALBRAITH, JOHN KENNETH
John Kenneth Galbraith. The all-purpose critic.
Time Feb 16, 1968 p. 24

GALLEONS
Track of the Manila galleons.
National Geographic Sep 1990 p. 5

GAMBLING
Boardwalk of broken dreams.
Time Sep 25, 1989 p. 64

You bet your life. Pete Rose and the great American obsession.
Time Jul 10, 1989 p. 16

Winning the derby: High-tech formulas that really work.
Omni May 1989 p. 42

Gambling fever. Is it good for us?
Business Week Apr 24, 1989 p. 112

Gambling rage. Out of control?
U.S. News May 30, 1983 p. 27

Playing for high emotional stakes: The chronic gambler's game.
Psychology Today Sep 1982 p. 50

Gambling goes legit.
Time Dec 6, 1976 p. 54

The gambling explosion.
Newsweek Apr 10, 1972 p. 46

Sports gambling madness.
Newsweek Jun 6, 1960 p. 75

GANDHI, INDIRA
Indira's iron fist.
Newsweek Jul 7, 1975 p. 22

Prime Minister Indira Gandhi.
Newsweek Apr 4, 1966 p. 36

Troubled India in a woman's hands. Indira Gandhi
Time Jan 28, 1966 p. 24

GANDHI, INDIRA - ASSASSINATION
India's crisis. After Indira.
Newsweek Nov 12, 1984 p. 42

"If I die today, every drop of my blood will invigorate the nations." Indira Gandhi 1917 - 1984.
Time Nov 12, 1984 p. 42

GANGS
The drug gangs. Waging war in America's cities.
Newsweek Mar 28, 1988 p. 20

The new face of organized crime. Asians, Jamaicans and other ethnic gangs are giving the Mafia a run for its money.
U.S. News   Jan 18, 1988   p. 29

GARDENING

Paradise found. America returns to the garden.
Time   Jun 20, 1988   p. 62

The joy (and also the tedium, rage and sheer hard work) of gardening.
Newsweek   Jul 26, 1982   p. 50

The green thumb means business.
Newsweek   Apr 11, 1960   p. 100

GARDNER, ERLE STANLEY

Erle Stanley Gardner. 'Mr. Mystery': After 100 books, Perry Mason wins again.
Newsweek   Jan 18, 1960   p. 53

GARDNER, JOHN W.

Can the Great Society be built and managed? H.E.W. Secretary Gardner.
Time   Jan 20, 1967   p. 16

Building the Great Society. HEW's John W. Gardner.
Newsweek   Feb 28, 1966   p. 22

GARR, TERI

Something about Teri Garr.
Ms.   Mar 1983   p. 39

GASOLINE PRICES

Good news! Cheap oil! Bad news! Cheap oil!
Time   Apr 14, 1986   p. 62

A long, dry summer?
Newsweek   May 21, 1979   p. 24

Energy: Higher prices close in on motorists, home-owners, air travelers, manufacturers.
U.S. News   Sep 15, 1975   p. 11

GASOLINE SUPPLY

Hostage to oil. Why the Gulf showdown is driving up prices. How costs would soar in a war with Iraq.
U.S. News   Oct 8, 1990   p. 56

A long, dry summer?
Newsweek   May 21, 1979   p. 24

The gas crisis.
Newsweek   Feb 7, 1977   p. 14

Energy crunch: Real or phony? William Simon.
Time   Jan 21, 1974   p. 22

Gas shortage - Fact or fiction?
U.S. News   Jan 14, 1974   p. 13

See Also PETROLEUM SUPPLY

GATES, BILL

The whiz kid. At 31, Bill Gates has built Microsoft into a software powerhouse. Now IBM is introducing a new generation of personal computers that rely on Microsoft's two latest programs. No wonder Gates is smiling.
Business Week   Apr 13, 1987   p. 68

GATES, ROBERT

The new spy wars. Is the CIA ready?
U.S. News   Jun 3, 1991   p. 22

GAY MEN AND WOMEN

The future of gay America. Militants versus the mainstream. Testing the limits of tolerance.
Newsweek   Mar 12, 1990   p. 90

Growing up gay. The society's dilemma. One family's crisis.
Newsweek   Jan 13, 1986   p. 50

Gay America. Sex, politics and the impact of AIDS.
Newsweek   Aug 8, 1983   p. 30

See Also HOMOSEXUALITY

GAY RIGHTS

Battle over gay rights. Anita Bryant vs. the homosexuals.
Newsweek   Jun 6, 1977   p. 16

"I am a homosexual." The gay drive for acceptance.
Time   Sep 8, 1975   p. 32

GEBEL-WILLIAMS, GUNTHER

Lords of the ring. Charisma, control, and tradition. Gunther Gebel-Williams.
Psychology Today   Oct 1983   p. 26

GEMINI 4

Back to Earth - Where the trouble is.
Newsweek   Jun 21, 1965   p. 22

The space walk.
Life   Jun 18, 1965   p. 26

The flight of the Gemini 4.
Newsweek   Jun 14, 1965   p. 30

The McDivitt-White flight. Ed White &
Jim McDivitt.
Time   Jun 11, 1965   p. 24

GEMINI 5

Astronaut Conrad at start of flight. The
anatomy of the Gemini 5 spacecraft.
Life   Sep 3, 1965   p. 60

GENEALOGY

Everybody's search for roots.
Newsweek   Jul 4, 1977   p. 26

GENEEN, HAROLD S.

Conglomerates: The new business giants.
President Harold S. Geneen.
Time   Sep 8, 1967   p. 86

GENENTECH INC.

Biotech superstar. Wall Street loves
Genentech. The reason: It's on the way to
becoming a major pharmaceutical
company.
Business Week   Apr 14, 1986   p. 68

GENERAL DYNAMICS CORP.

General Dynamics under fire.
Business Week   Mar 25, 1985   p. 70

General Dynamics. Striking it rich on
defense. But can he shuck the habit of
unexpected losses?
Business Week   May 3, 1982   p. 102

GENERAL ELECTRIC CO.

GE's Jack Welch. How good a manager is
he?
Business Week   Dec 14, 1987   p. 92

The dynamo. Jack Welch is often
described in three words: tough, tough,
and tough. He's determined to transform
GE. So far, so good.
Business Week   Jun 30, 1986   p. 62

General Electric. The financial wizards
switch back to technology.
Business Week   Mar 16, 1981   p. 110

GENERAL ELECTRIC CREDIT CORP.

General Electric credit. From financing
home appliances to an aggressive source
of funds for industry.
Business Week   Aug 30, 1982   p. 54

GENERAL MOTORS CORP.

Here comes GM's Saturn. It's more than a
car. It's GM's hope for reinventing itself.
Business Week   Apr 9, 1990   p. 56

GM faces reality. A decline in market
share is forcing it to shrink. Now
president Robert Stempel has to make the
strategy work.
Business Week   May 9, 1988   p. 114

GM. What went wrong. In the late 1970s,
General Motors executives mapped out a
$40 billion strategy to redesign every car
and to overhaul or replace every factory.
The goal: Fight imports—and leave Ford
and Chrysler in the dust. So far, the
strategy has failed.
Business Week   Mar 16, 1987   p. 102

Ross Perot's crusade. "Revitalizing
General Motors is like teaching an
elephant to tap dance. You find the
sensitive spots and start poking."
Business Week   Oct 6, 1986   p. 60

GM moves into a new era. It picks many
partners to help change strategy.
Business Week   Jul 16, 1984   p. 48

GM challenges the Japanese. Chevrolet's
new 'J' car.
Newsweek   May 11, 1981   p. 56

What's good for the economy . . . General
Motors President Roche.
Time   May 20, 1966   p. 100

Hot year for General Motors.
Newsweek   Feb 25, 1963   p. 67

The world's biggest manufacturer.
General Motors Chairman Frederic G.
Donner.
Time   May 18, 1962   p. 85

GENERATION GAP

How to educate your parents.
Time   Aug 17, 1970   p. 35

The generation gap.
Life   May 17, 1968   p. 81

GENETIC ENGINEERING

Genetic miracles. How a medical revolution is saving lives–and raising fears.
U.S. News   Nov 4, 1991   p. 64

Ending genetic disease. The new molecular surgery.
Discover   Mar 1990   p. 60

The gene doctors. It seems incredible, but hereditary diseases may soon be cured by manipulating human genes.
Business Week   Nov 18, 1985 p. 76

The gene doctors. Unlocking the mysteries of cancer, heart disease and genetic defects.
Newsweek   Mar 5, 1984   p. 64

Tampering with human embryos?
Omni   Mar 1982   p. 52

Shaping life in the lab. The boom in genetic engineering.
Time   Mar 9, 1981   p. 50

Weaving new life in the lab. Magnified 50,000 times in this photograph, a man-made gene enters a cell.
Life   May 1980   p. 48

DNA's new miracles. How science is retooling genes.
Newsweek   Mar 17, 1980 p. 62

The DNA furor. Tinkering with life.
Time   Apr 18, 1977 p. 32

The genetics: Man into Superman.
Time   Apr 19, 1971 p. 33

Science and sex. When new methods of human reproduction become available—can traditional family life survive? Will marital infidelity increase? Will children and parents still love each other?
Life   Jun 13, 1969 p. 37

Exploring the secrets of life. Model of DNA molecule.
Newsweek   May 13, 1963 p. 63

GENETIC MAPPING

Solving the mysteries of heredity. The drive to map human genes could revolutionize medicine but also raises troubling ethical questions.
Time   Mar 20, 1989 p. 62

GENETIC RESEARCH

The genetic age. Science is establishing the link between genes and disease, opening a new era in medicine. But what about the legal, ethical, and social consequences.
Business Week   May 28, 1990 p. 68

The search for Adam & Eve. Scientists explore a controversial theory about man's origins.
Newsweek   Jan 11, 1988 p. 46

Predicting diseases. New genetic clues to heart disease, cancer, AIDS and other killers could save your life.
U.S. News   May 25, 1987 p. 64

Scientists close in on the secret of life.
Life   Oct 4, 1963   p. 70

Exploring the secrets of life. Model of DNA molecule.
Newsweek   May 13, 1963 p. 63

GENETIC RESEARCH - ETHICAL ASPECTS

Would you want to know how and when you're going to die?
Discover   Jun 1987   p. 26

GENIUS

The billion-dollar search for a new Einstein.
Omni   Nov 1982   p. 78

GENOCIDE

Proposed ratification of the Genocide Treaty.
Congressional Digest Dec 1984   p. 289

GEOLOGY

New portrait of our planet. What IGY taught us.
Life   Nov 7, 1960   p. 74

GERE, RICHARD

Richard Gere. A different American hero?
Ms.   Feb 1986   p. 41

GLENN, JOHN

My own story of the orbit by John Glenn. The moment I learned I might burn up. What I saw in space and on earth below. Why I said 'go' for the third orbit. Overwhelming impact of sudden acclaim.
Life   Mar 9, 1962   p. 20

John Glenn: One machine that worked without flaw.
Newsweek   Mar 5, 1962   p. 19

The space race is a go. Spaceman Glenn.
Time   Mar 2, 1962   p. 11

Ordeal of a spaceman.
Newsweek   Feb 5, 1962   p. 15

Making of a brave man. John Glenn's personal album.
Life   Feb 2, 1962   p. 22

Exclusive on men picked for space. Astronaut first team. Glenn, Grissom, Shepard.
Life   Mar 3, 1961   p. 24

GLENN, JOHN (FAMILY)

The Glenn story nobody saw. At home with Annie and the kids while John orbited the earth.
Life   Mar 2, 1962   p. 20

GLUECK, NELSON

The search for man's past. Archaeologist Nelson Glueck.
Time   Dec 13, 1963   p. 50

GOD

Who is God?
Life   Dec 1990   p. 47

The child's view of God.
Psychology Today   Dec 1985   p. 22

Is God dead?
Time   Apr 8, 1966   p. 82

GOETZ, BERNHARD, SUBWAY SHOOTING CASE

The Goetz case. New charges in the subway shooting. Rising fear of violent crime. Public anger at the justice system.
Time   Apr 8, 1985   p. 28

GOIZUETA, ROBERT C.

Coke's man on the spot. Coca-Cola Chairman Roberto C. Goizueta.
Business Week   Jul 29, 1985   p. 56

GOLD

Proposals for a gold-based monetary system.
Congressional Digest Jun 1982   p. 163

A return to the gold standard. Why Reagan might try it. How it would be done. How it might work.
Business Week   Sep 21, 1981   p. 114

GOLD AS AN INVESTMENT

The gold rush of '79. And the economic mess behind it.
Newsweek   Oct 1, 1979   p. 48

"Gold rush." Why the slow start?
U.S. News   Jan 13, 1975   p. 9

The new gold rush.
Newsweek   Dec 16, 1974   p. 78

GOLD MINES AND MINING

The great gold scandal. A billion-dollar giveaway is ravaging the American West.
U.S. News   Oct 28, 1991   p. 44

GOLDBERG, ARTHUR

Labor & the new frontier.
Time   Sep 22, 1961   p. 21

Can a labor man run labor? Goldberg's real challenge.
Newsweek   Mar 6, 1961   p. 35

GOLDWATER, BARRY

'A choice - not an echo.'
Newsweek   Jul 27, 1964   p. 18

The Goldwater convention.
Life   Jul 24, 1964   p. 20

Can Goldwater be stopped?
Newsweek   Jun 15, 1964   p. 23

Barry Goldwater.
Time   Jun 12, 1964   p. 31

Ike and the GOP race.
Newsweek   May 18, 1964   p. 27

Candidate-watching in the G.O.P. Can they find a winner? Barry Goldwater.
Time   Jun 14, 1963   p. 26

Goldwater in '64?
Newsweek   May 20, 1963   p. 28

Barry Goldwater.
Time   Jun 23, 1961   p. 12

Conservatism. On the campus. In U.S. politics. In the nation. Arizona's Barry Goldwater: Leader of the right.
Newsweek   Apr 10, 1961   p. 28

GOLDWATER, BARRY (INTERVIEW)

Barry Goldwater speaks his mind on Richard Nixon.
U.S. News   Feb 11, 1974   p. 38

GONE WITH THE WIND (BOOK) - SEQUEL

Here it is at last—the sequel to *Gone with the Wind*. Rhett and Scarlett: The love story continues.
Life   Sep 1991   p. 64

At last—the sequel to *Gone With the Wind*.
Life   May 1988   p. 26

GOOD AND EVIL

Evil. Does it exist — or do bad things just happen?
Time   Jun 10, 1991   p. 48

GOODEN, DWIGHT

Doctor K. Baseball's hottest pitcher. Dwight Gooden of the Mets.
Time   Apr 7, 1986   p. 52

GORBACHEV, MIKHAIL

Gorbachev says he'll fight on, but he's already a man without a country.
Time   Dec 23, 1991   p. 18

The second Russian Revolution.
Newsweek   Sep 2, 1991   p. 18

The Russian Revolution. August 1991.
Time   Sep 2, 1991   p. 18

The odd couple. How George Bush has become a true believer in Mikhail Gorbachev.
U.S. News   Jul 1, 1991   p. 24

Russia's maverick. Boris Yeltsin, the bad boy of Soviet politics, battles Gorbachev in a crucial vote this week.
Time   Mar 25, 1991   p. 26

Falling star. After the summit: The growing danger for Gorbachev back in the U.S.S.R.
U.S. News   Jun 11, 1990   p. 24

Why Gorbachev is failing.
Newsweek   Jun 4, 1990   p. 16

In the eye of the storm. With his country in a perilous passage, Gorbachev defines his course and answers his critics.
Time   Jun 4, 1990   p. 24

Man of the decade. Mikhail Gorbachev.
Time   Jan 1, 1990   p. 42

Can he ride the tiger? With Eastern Europe out of control and his economy in ruins, Gorbachev faces his toughest test.
Newsweek   Dec 4, 1989   p. 34

Man of the year. Mikhail Sergeyevich Gorbachev.
Time   Jan 4, 1988   p. 16

A new revolution. Can Gorbachev save a failing system?
U.S. News   Oct 19, 1987   p. 30

Margaret Thatcher on dealing with Gorbachev.
Life   Oct 1987   p. 32

Gorbachev's revolution. Can he make it work? Is the Cold War fading?
Time   Jul 27, 1987   p. 28

Gorbachev's gamble. Opening a closed society. How far will he go? Sakharov on his struggle.
Newsweek   Jan 5, 1987   p. 12

Gorbachev's Russia. Can he revive the Soviet economy? Why it's lagging in high tech. Summit prospects—and a special BW poll. The outlook for U.S.-Soviet trade.
Business Week   Nov 11, 1985 p. 82

Gorbachev: "The situation in the world today is highly complex, very tense. I would even go so far as to say it is explosive."
Time   Sep 9, 1985   p. 16

Moscow's new generation. Mikhail
Gorbachev
Newsweek   Mar 25, 1985   p. 22

Moscow's new boss. Younger, smoother
and probably formidable. Mikhail
Gorbachev.
Time   Mar 25, 1985   p. 14

Gorbachev's Kremlin. What now?
U.S. News   Mar 25, 1985   p. 22

**GORBACHEV, MIKHAIL - VISIT TO THE
UNITED STATES, 1987**

Moscow on the Potomac. Is Gorbachev
playing a winning hand?
U.S. News   Dec 21, 1987   p. 20

Gorbachev in America. How the Soviets
see us.
Newsweek   Dec 14, 1987   p. 18

Over to you, George. Gorbachev's newest
peace offensive challenges the U.S. to
respond.
Time   Dec 19, 1988   p. 16

How to respond to Gorbachev.
U.S. News   Dec 19, 1988   p. 16

GORBACHEV, MIKHAIL (INTERVIEW)

His game plan. A talk with Gorbachev.
Newsweek   May 30, 1988 p. 20

GORBACHEV, RAISA

Raisa. A new image for the Soviet
Union's overworked, underappreciated
women.
Time   Jun 6, 1988   p. 28

GOSSIP

Gossip. Where does it come from — and
why does America love it?
Time   Mar 5, 1990   p. 46

Gossip!
Newsweek   May 24, 1976 p. 56

GOTTI, JOHN

Mafia on trial. Crime boss John Gotti.
Time   Sep 29, 1986   p. 16

GOULART, JOAO

Goulart's Brazil: Another New Frontier?
Newsweek   Mar 11, 1963   p. 48

GOULD, ELLIOTT

Star for an uptight age. Elliott Gould.
Time   Sep 7, 1970   p. 35

GOULD INC.

Bill Ylvisaker bets his company on
electronics.
Business Week   Nov 2, 1981

GOULD, SAM

Rise of the public universities: Quality as
well as quantity. New York's Chancellor
Samuel B. Gould.
Time   Jan 12, 1968   p. 43

GOULD, STEPHEN JAY

Mysteries of evolution. Paleontologist
Stephan Jay Gould.
Newsweek   Mar 29, 1982   p. 44

GOVERNMENT BONDS

Trouble in the government bond markets.
Business Week   May 28, 1984 p. 112

GOVERNMENT INVESTIGATIONS

"A city without guts." Why Washington
is losing the war on waste. J. Peter Grace,
Chairman of the President's survey.
U.S. News   Jul 25, 1983   p. 53

"A gentleman with innumerable
friendships and connections." Bobby
Baker.
Time   Mar 6, 1964   p. 17

GOVERNMENT PUBLICITY

The great American bureaucratic
propaganda machine.
U.S. News   Aug 27, 1979 p. 43

GOVERNMENT SPENDING POLICY

J. Peter Grace: Government waste—a
danger to our freedoms?
USA Today   May 1986   p. 10

GRACE, J. PETER

J. Peter Grace. Building a new company
Wall Street ignors.
Business Week   Oct 5, 1981   p. 80

GRACE, J. PETER (INTERVIEW)

"A city without guts." Why Washington
is losing the war on waste. J. Peter Grace,
Chairman of the President's survey.
U.S. News   Jul 25, 1983   p. 53

GRACE, PRINCESS OF MONACO

The last fairy tale. Princess Grace,
1929-1982.
Newsweek   Sep 27, 1982   p. 36

The Kelly princess beguiling Erin.
Life   Jun 23, 1961   p. 39

GRAHAM, BILLY

The President's preacher. Billy Graham
and the surging Southern Baptists.
Newsweek   Jul 20, 1970   p. 50

Billy Graham in Africa.
Life   Mar 21, 1960   p. 28

GRANDMA MOSES

Happy 100th birthday, Grandma Moses.
Life   Sep 19, 1960   p. 104

GRANDPARENTS

Grandparents. The silent saviors.
Protecting millions of children from
troubled parents, drugs and abuse.
U.S. News   Dec 16, 1991   p. 80

GRASS, GUNTER

Novelist between the generations. A man
who can speak to the young. Germany's
Gunter Grass.
Time   Apr 13, 1970   p. 68

GRASSO, ELLA

Women in politics. Ella Grasso for
Governor.
Newsweek   Nov 4, 1974   p. 20

GRAVITY

Gravity's revenge. The end of the solar
system?
Discover   May 1990   p. 54

The fifth force: A new look at the realities
of antigravity.
Omni   Mar 1987   p. 36

GRAY, BOWMAN

R. J. Reynolds' Bowman Gray.
Time   Apr 11, 1960   p. 104

GREAT BRITAIN - ECONOMIC
CONDITIONS

What hath Thatcher wrought? Four years
of restrictive economic policies. Is it too
late to save British industry?
Business Week   Jun 6, 1983   p. 44

Embattled Britain. Prime Minister
Thatcher.
Time   Feb 16, 1981   p. 28

Devaluation. Britain's Harold Wilson.
Can Labor last?
Newsweek   Nov 27, 1967   p. 73

Britain's money crisis. Causes &
consequences.
Time   Nov 24, 1967   p. 29

Britain & the Common Market. A historic
decision for Europe.
Time   Jul 13, 1962   p. 29

GREAT BRITAIN - POLITICS AND
GOVERNMENT

The iron lady falls. A greengrocer's
daughter who bent a nation to her will.
Newsweek   Dec 3, 1990   p. 28

The lady bows out. What Maggie
Thatcher's departure means for the U.S.
and Europe.
Time   Dec 3, 1990   p. 60

Maggie by a mile. What it means. What
she'll do. British Prime Minister Margaret
Thatcher.
Time   Jun 20, 1983   p. 28

Is Maggie losing the new battle of Britain?
Prime Minister Margaret Thatcher.
U.S. News   Dec 24, 1979   p. 27

The winner. Prime Minister Heath.
Newsweek   Jun 29, 1970   p. 30

Upset in Britain. The Tories take over.
Prime Minister Edward Heath.
Time   Jun 29, 1970   p. 16

The surprising socialist. Britain's Harold
Wilson.
Time   Apr 30, 1965   p. 35

The bomb; the overthrow; the squeaker;
the scandal.
Time   Oct 23, 1964   p. 19

Britain's Harold Wilson. Will Labor win?
Newsweek   Sep 28, 1964   p. 44

Britain's Lord Home.
Time   Oct 25, 1963   p. 31

What Labor offers England. Britain's
Harold Wilson.
Time　　　　　　　Oct 11, 1963　　p. 34

Britain's Harold Wilson. The next Prime
Minister?
Newsweek　　　　　Apr 15, 1963　p. 42

GREAT BRITAIN - SOCIAL CONDITIONS

Britain's troubled mood.
Time　　　　　　　Jan 25, 1963　　p. 18

GREECE

Greece: How the colonels run the
country.
Newsweek　　　　　Jan 19, 1970　p. 31

GREECE - POLITICS AND GOVERNMENT

Greece: The palace coup. King
Constantine.
Time　　　　　　　Apr 28, 1967　p. 28

GREECE, ANCIENT

Greece: Final installment. Her art lives
on.
Life　　　　　　　Jul 19, 1963　　p. 52

Alexander the Great: Conqueror. Greece
part VI.
Life　　　　　　　May 3, 1963　　p. 62

Greece part V: The two wars of destiny.
Life　　　　　　　Apr 5, 1963　　p. 78

Greece: Part III. Soaring thought, stark
drama.
Life　　　　　　　Feb 8, 1963　　p. 60

Greece part II. Myths, gods, heroes.
Life　　　　　　　Jan 18, 1963　　p. 52

The miracle of Greece. Burst of genius
that opened the way to our modern
world.
Life　　　　　　　Jan 4, 1963　　p. 28

GREED

The 80's are over. Greed goes out of style.
Newsweek　　　　　Jan 4, 1988　　p. 40

GREENHOUSE EFFECT

Earth on ice. A bold attack on global
warming.
Discover　　　　　Apr 1991　　p. 54

Global warming: Catastrophe looms as sea
levels rise.
USA Today　　　　Jun 1989　　p. 1

The greenhouse effect. This summer was
merely a warm-up.
Discover　　　　　Oct 1988　　p. 50

The greenhouse effect. Danger: More hot
summers ahead.
Newsweek　　　　　Jul 11, 1988　p. 18

The heat is on. How the Earth's climate is
changing. Why the ozone hole is
growing.
Time　　　　　　　Oct 19, 1987　p. 58

America in 2035? New York and other
coastal cities are permanently flooded.
Grain won't grow in the nation's
breadbasket, and everything west of the
Rockies is a desert.
Discover　　　　　Jan 1986　　p. 28

See Also OZONE

GREENLAND

Greenland's 500-year-old mummies.
National Geographic Feb 1985　　p. 191

Hunting the Greenland narwhal.
National Geographic Apr 1984　　p. 520

GREENSPAN, ALAN

Inside the Fed. In two years as chairman
of the Federal Reserve, Alan Greenspan
has done a very good job. Here's a close
look at how this politically savvy
number-cruncher runs the Fed's very
private world.
Business Week　　Jul 31, 1989　p. 58

Chairman Greenspan. How federal
reserve policy will change. Profile of a
consummate conservative. Paul
Volcker's legacy.
Business Week　　Jun 15, 1987　p. 26

The new Mr. Dollar. Fed nominee Alan
Greenspan.
Time　　　　　　　Jun 15, 1987　p. 46

GREER, GERMAINE

Saucy feminist that even men like.
Germaine Greer.
Life　　　　　　　May 7, 1971　　p. 30

GRENADA-AMERICAN INVASION, 1983

Americans at war.
Newsweek   Nov 7, 1983   p. 52

Worth the price? Tough moves, hard questions. Rescue in Grenada. Sacrifice in Beirut.
Time   Nov 7, 1983   p. 22

Agonizing decisions. What next in Grenada? Why stay in Lebanon? How to defuse critics.
U.S. News   Nov 7, 1983   p. 24

GRETSKY, WAYNE

Simply the best. Boston's Larry Bird. Edmonton's Wayne Gretzky.
Time   Mar 18, 1985   p. 50

GRIFFITH, MELANIE

Starting over. Melanie Griffith & Don Johnson tell their love story.
Life   Apr 1989   p. 50

GRISSOM, VIRGIL

Exclusive on men picked for space. Astronaut first team. Glenn, Grissom, Shepard.
Life   Mar 3, 1961   p. 24

GRIZZLY BEARS

Can grizzlies and people coexist?
Life   Aug 1984   p. 38

GROMYKO, ANDREI

Moscow's hard line. What it means. Reagan's new response. Foreign Minister Andrei Gromyko.
Time   Jun 25, 1984   p. 22

GROSS, CALVIN

The man with 1,000,000 children. New York City's Superintendent Calvin Gross.
Time   Nov 15, 1963   p. 86

GUATEMALA - ANTIQUITIES

Río Azul. Lost city of the Maya.
National Geographic Apr 1986   p. 420

GUATEMALA - POLITICS AND GOVERNMENT

Guatemala. A fragile democracy.
National Geographic Jun 1988   p. 768

GUEVARA, ERNESTO "CHE"

Communism's western beachhead. Cuba's Che Guevara.
Time   Aug 8, 1960   p. 36

GUIDEBOOKS

The supertourist: Temple Fielding.
Time   Jun 6, 1969   p. 79

GUIDED MISSILES - DEFENSES

The great missile debate.
Time   Mar 14, 1969   p. 22

The chilling facts behind the decision to build the anti ballistic missile.
Life   Sep 29, 1967   p. 28

GULF OF TONKIN INCIDENT

See VIETNAM WAR, 1957-1975 - GULF OF TONKIN INCIDENT

GULF OIL CORP.

Why Gulf fell. What's behind the biggest corporate takeover.
Business Week   Mar 19, 1984   p. 76

Restructuring big oil. The fight over Gulf is just the start.
Business Week   Nov 14, 1983   p. 138

GUN CONTROL

The Brady Handgun Violence Prevention Act.
Congressional Digest Jun 1991   p. 162

1990 omnibus crime bill.
Congressional Digest Nov 1990   p. 258

The gun control controversy.
Congressional Digest May 1986   p. 130

Guns are out of control.
Life   Apr 1982   p. 30

A question of guns.
Newsweek   Jun 24, 1968   p. 81

GUNS IN THE UNITED STATES

Who is the NRA? A look at America's embattled gun lobby.
Time   Jan 29, 1990   p. 16

Death by gun. America's toll in one typical week: 464. The faces behind the statistics. A 28-page portfolio.
Time   Jul 17, 1989   p. 30

Guns. Americans and firearms: The attraction, the debate.
U.S. News   May 8, 1989   p. 20

Armed America. More guns, more shootings, more massacres.
Time   Feb 6, 1989   p. 20

Machine gun U.S.A. Nearly 500,000 automatic weapons are now in the hands of collectors - and criminals.
Newsweek   Oct 14, 1985   p. 46

The gun in America.
Time   Jun 21, 1968   p. 13

GUTHRIE, ARLO

Alice's restaurant's kids. Folk singer Arlo Guthrie.
Newsweek   Sep 29, 1969   p. 101

HAGGARD, MERLE

Country music. Songs of love, loyalty & doubt. Merle Haggard.
Time   May 6, 1974   p. 51

HAIG, ALEXANDER

Drawing the line in Central America. Haig looks back. On foreign policy. On Reagan's men.
Time   Apr 2, 1984   p. 40

Why Haig quit.
Newsweek   Jul 5, 1982   p. 18

Foreign policy shakeup. Out goes Haig. In comes Schultz.
Time   Jul 5, 1982   p. 8

Who's in charge here? Secretary of State Alexander Haig.
Newsweek   Apr 6, 1981   p. 26

Taking command. The world according to Haig.
Time   Mar 16, 1981   p. 12

HAITIANS IN THE UNITED STATES

The Haitians. Refugees or prisoners?
Newsweek   Feb 1, 1982   p. 24

HALDEMAN, H. R.

The best of the book. Haldeman talks. How the Russians almost A-bombed China. The Nixon nobody saw - an insider's candid view. How Nixon set off the Watergate break-in. Secrets of the 18 1/2 minute gap...
Newsweek   Feb 27, 1978   p. 41

Nixon's palace guard. Presidential aide Haldeman.
Newsweek   Mar 19, 1973   p. 24

HALL, ARSENIO

Arsenio. TV's hip host grabs the post-Carson generation.
Time   Nov 13, 1989   p. 92

HALL, JIM

Racing to the top. Jim Hall and the Chaparral.
Newsweek   Feb 7, 1966   p. 48

HALLEY'S COMET

Skywatch. Halley's comet swings by.
Time   Dec 16, 1985   p. 60

The comet is coming. Halley's marvel gives scientists and stargazers a once-in-a-lifetime thrill.
Newsweek   Sep 9, 1985   p. 74

Comets: Pioneer will observe Halley's Comet.
USA Today   Jun 1985   p. 1

The comet is coming.
Discover   Dec 1981   p. 20

HALLOWEEN

A halloween salute to specters and spooks.
Life   Oct 31, 1960   p. 52

HALLSTEIN, WALTER

The Eurocrats. Common Market's Walter Hallstein.
Newsweek   Jan 7, 1963   p. 26

HALLUCINATIONS AND ILLUSIONS

The science of illusions and the mysteries of perception.
Omni   Apr 1985   p. 52

HALLUCINOGENIC DRUGS

Getting high at Harvard.
Omni   Jul 1982   p. 68

HATCH ACT OF 1939 - AMENDMENTS
Proposed Federal employees' political
activities legislation.
Congressional Digest Jan 1988   p. 3

HATCHER, RICHARD
Negro election victories. Cleveland's
Mayor Stokes.
Time   Nov 17, 1967   p. 23

HATE GROUPS
A special report. Women in the Klan,
Aryan Nation, skinheads. Why?
Ms.   Mar 1991   p. 20

HAVEL, VACLAV
The man who conquered Communism.
"The New Europe" by Vaclav Havel,
playwright-president of Czechoslovakia.
U.S. News   Feb 26, 1990   p. 28

HAWAII
Holiday in Hawaii: An enchanting
extravaganza.
USA Today   Mar 1985   p. 42

Aloha! Sun and fun islands.
Newsweek   Jan 2, 1978   p. 30

Hawaii. 50th state. Vigor and languor on
flowing tropical isles.
Life   Oct 8, 1965   p. 84

HAWKING, STEPHEN
Master of the universe. One scientist's
courageous voyage to the frontiers of the
cosmos. Physicist Stephen Hawking.
Newsweek   Jun 13, 1988   p. 56

HAWN, GOLDIE
Solid Goldie. Comedienne Goldie Hawn.
Newsweek   Jan 12, 1981   p. 52

HAYNSWORTH, CLEMENT
Why Haynsworth lost.
Newsweek   Dec 1, 1969   p. 21

HAZARDOUS WASTES
The environmental Superfund
controversy.
Congressional Digest Jun 1986   p. 163

Toxic wastes. The poisoning of America
'85.
Time   Oct 14, 1985   p. 76

Storing up trouble. Hazardous waste.
National Geographic Mar 1985   p. 318

Cleaning up the mess. The toxic-waste
threat to America's health. Chaos at the
EPA.
Newsweek   Mar 7, 1983   p. 16

The poisoning of America. Those toxic
chemical wastes.
Time   Sep 22, 1980   p. 58

HEADACHES
Headaches. New way to cope with the
pain.
Newsweek   Dec 7, 1987   p. 76

Those splitting headaches - How near a
cure?
Newsweek   May 16, 1960 p. 106

HEALTH
Best ways to stay healthy. Exercise and
your heart. A live-longer diet. Surgery
without knives.
U.S. News   May 20, 1991 p. 68

The sleep gap. Too much to do, too little
rest.
Time   Dec 17, 1990   p. 78

Best ways to stay healthy. The ten most
important new developments. Plus the
A-to-Z health almanac.
U.S. News   Jun 18, 1990   p. 54

Body & soul. Scientists discover the links
between the brain and your health.
Newsweek   Nov 7, 1988   p. 88

Defending your health. How to ward off
the 5 top killers.
U.S. News   Aug 17, 1987   p. 56

The truth about Americans' health.
USA Today   May 1987   p. 54

The beauty of health.
Ms.   Apr 1987   p. 39

The beauty of health.
Ms.   May 1986   p. 43

The beauty of health.
Ms.   May 1985   p. 57

The beauty of health.
Ms.   May 1984   p. 51

The beauty of health. How do you know you're healthy?
Ms.   May 1983   p. 51

America's health crusade. How we stay well. What we believe about sickness and aging. Why health has become a national obsession.
Psychology Today   Oct 1982   p. 28

The fitness craze. America shapes up.
Time   Nov 2, 1981   p. 94

HEALTH CARE
See MEDICAL CARE

HEARST, PATRICIA, CASE

Guilty!
Newsweek   Mar 29, 1976 p. 23

Patty's defense.
Newsweek   Mar 1, 1976   p. 20

Patty in court. Defense attorney F. Lee Bailey.
Time   Feb 16, 1976 p. 46

Patty on trial.
Newsweek   Feb 2, 1976   p. 24

The story of Patty Hearst.
Newsweek   Sep 29, 1975 p. 20

Apprehended. Patricia Hearst, alias Tania.
Time   Sep 29, 1975 p. 11

Patty Hearst. After the shoot-out.
Newsweek   May 27, 1974 p. 18

The saga of Patty Hearst.
Newsweek   Apr 29, 1974 p. 20

Patty Hearst.
Time   Apr 29, 1974 p. 11

Terror and repression. The hostage. The exile.
Newsweek   Feb 25, 1974 p. 18

HEART - DISEASES

How to reverse heart disease. A tough new program to combat America's No. 1 killer.
U.S. News   Aug 6, 1990   p. 54

"Good" cholesterol. Encouraging news for your heart.
Time   Dec 12, 1988 p. 62

Cholesterol. And now the bad news...
Time   Mar 26, 1984 p. 56

America's $39 billion heart business.
U.S. News   Mar 15, 1982 p. 53

A bitter feud. Two great surgeons at war over the human heart. Dr. Denton Cooley. Dr. Michael DeBakey.
Life   Apr 10, 1970 p. 62

The corridors of the heart. Views never seen before filmed inside the arteries.
Life   Jan 19, 1968 p. 22

Heart and diet.
Newsweek   Feb 8, 1965   p. 53

HEART, ARTIFICIAL

Bill Schroeder's artificial heart. The inside story of a medical experiment. The patient with his surgeon, William DeVries.
Life   May 1985   p. 33

Replacing the heart.
Discover   Feb 1983   p. 13

Man makes a heart. The bold new world of cardiac medicine. Jarvik-7 artificial heart.
Newsweek   Dec 13, 1982 p. 70

The artificial heart is here. Exclusive pictures of Dr. Cooley's historic heart surgery.
Life   Sep 1981   p. 28

Toward an artificial heart. Surgeon Michael DeBakey.
Time   May 28, 1965 p. 46

HEART ATTACKS

What you should know about heart attacks. The aspirin breakthrough. The latest on cholesterol, diet and exercise.
Newsweek   Feb 8, 1988   p. 50

How to prevent heart attacks. New research, new techniques.
Discover   Mar 1984   p. 19

Heart attacks. New insights, new
treatments.
Time   Jun 1, 1981   p. 52

Heart attack. Curbing the killer.
Newsweek   May 1, 1972   p. 73

HEART TRANSPLANTATION

See TRANSPLANTATION OF ORGANS,
TISSUES, ETC.

HEATH, EDWARD

The winner. Prime Minister Heath.
Newsweek   Jun 29, 1970   p. 30

Upset in Britain. The Tories take over.
Prime Minister Edward Heath.
Time   Jun 29, 1970   p. 16

HEFNER, HUGH

The pursuit of hedonism. Playboy's
Hugh Hefner.
Time   Mar 3, 1967   p. 76

HELICOPTERS

Space age copters. The next generation.
Discover   May 1988   p. 48

HELL

The rekindling of hell. Religion in the
'90s. Record numbers of Americans now
believe in a netherworld–and in a wide
variety of after-death punishments.
U.S. News   Mar 25, 1991   p. 56

HELLER, WALTER W.

Kennedy's economic planners. White
House economist Walter W. Heller.
Time   Mar 3, 1961   p. 18

HELMS, JESSE

To the right, march! Conservative
Senator Jesse Helms.
Time   Sep 14, 1981   p. 24

HELMSLEY, LEONA

Rhymes with rich. Hotel queen Leona
Helmsley battles the tax man.
Newsweek   Aug 21, 1989   p. 48

HEMINGWAY, ERNEST

The call of danger. In pictures, a great
writer's fascination with bravery and
death.
Life   Jul 14, 1961   p. 59

Hemingway: 'The Dangerous Summer,'
part I.
Life   Sep 5, 1960   p. 77

HEMINGWAY, MARGAUX

The new beauties. Margaux Hemingway
Time   Jun 16, 1975   p. 34

HENDRIX, JIMMY

Two arts, two visions: The grace of ballet.
The tumult of Hendrix.
Life   Oct 3, 1969   p. 42

HENSON, JIM

The Muppets say goodbye to their best
friend. Jim Henson.
Life   Jul 1990   p. 92

HEPBURN, KATHARINE

Kate. A rare talk with the invincible
Hepburn. And exclusive excerpt from her
new memoir.
Newsweek   Aug 31, 1987   p. 48

Katharine Hepburn. The freedom that
comes with age.
Ms.   Jan 1982   p. 45

Hepburn returns to Broadway. Kate and
Coco.
Newsweek   Nov 10, 1969   p. 75

The comeback of Kate. For Hepburn, a
burst of movies—and a new career as
singing star of musical comedy.
Life   Jan 5, 1968   p. 60

HEREDITY

Solving the mysteries of heredity. The
drive to map human genes could
revolutionize medicine but also raises
troubling ethical questions.
Time   Mar 20, 1989   p. 62

The gene factor. How heredity shapes
personality.
U.S. News   Apr 13, 1987   p. 58

HEROES AND HEROINES

Garrison Keillor's Fourth of July. Plus:
America's unsung heroes.
Newsweek   Jul 4, 1988   p. 30

A celebration of heroes. Past and present.
Newsweek   Jul 6, 1987   p. 52

Where have all our heroes gone?
USA Today   Jan 1986   p. 20

Heroes are back. Young Americans tell why.
U.S. News   Apr 22, 1985   p. 44

Where have all the heroes gone?
Newsweek   Aug 6, 1979   p. 44

HEROIN
The return of the French connection. How drug agents broke up the $225 million heroin deal of the decade.
Newsweek   Apr 13, 1987   p. 56

The global war on heroin.
Time   Sep 4, 1972   p. 22

The heroin plague.
Newsweek   Jul 5, 1971   p. 27

HERPES
Herpes. Today's scarlet letter.
Time   Aug 2, 1982   p. 62

HERTZ, GUSTAV CRANE
Secret struggle to free Gus Hertz from the Vietcong. Heartbreaking effort to get back kidnaped U.S. official—if he is still alive.
Life   Jul 21, 1967   p. 22

HESBURGH, THEODORE
"Where are the Catholic intellectuals?" Notre Dame's President Hesburgh.
Time   Feb 9, 1962   p. 48

HESSELBEIN, FRANCES
Surprise! Some of America's best-run organizations are nonprofits. Here's what Corporate America can learn from them. How Frances Hesselbein showed the way at the Girl Scouts.
Business Week   Mar 26, 1990   p. 66

HEWLETT-PACKARD CO.
Can John Young redesign Hewlett-Packard.
Business Week   Dec 6, 1982   p. 72

HEYERDAHL, THOR
Lost empires of the Americas. New finds reveal our ancient past. Inca Emperor Pachacuti.
U.S. News   Apr 2, 1990   p. 46

HIBERNATION, HUMAN
Human hibernation: Cure for aging and obesity?
Omni   Mar 1984   p. 68

HICKS, LOUISE DAY
Backlash in Boston. Mayoral candidate Louise Day Hicks.
Newsweek   Nov 6, 1967   p. 29

HIGH BLOOD PRESSURE
See HYPERTENSION

HIGH DEFINITION TELEVISION
Super television. High stakes in high-definition TV.
Business Week   Jan 30, 1989   p. 56

HIGH SCHOOLS
High schools in trouble. A tale of three cities.
Time   Nov 14, 1977   p. 62

What's wrong with the high schools?
Newsweek   Feb 16, 1970   p. 65

Collision course in the high schools. How much should students decide policy? Would more blacks be harmful to your school? What do older people least understand? How much dissent should schools permit?
Life   May 16, 1969   p. 22

HIJACKING, AIRPLANE
Striking back. What Reagan might do.
Newsweek   Jul 8, 1985   p. 16

What price for freedom? Dealing for American lives.
U.S. News   Jul 8, 1985   p. 20

America under the gun. The struggle against terrorism.
Time   Jul 1, 1985   p. 8

Reagan's hostage crisis. Revenge or restraint?
U.S. News   Jul 1, 1985   p. 18

Terror on flight 847.
Newsweek   Jun 24, 1985   p. 18

Hijack terror.
Time   Jun 24, 1985   p. 18

Mideast terror strikes Americans.
U.S. News   Jun 24, 1985   p. 9

War on terrorism.
Newsweek   Oct 31, 1977   p. 48

War on terrorism.
Time   Oct 28, 1977   p. 28

Skyjacking. The get-tough policy could
make it even worse. Escape route for a
skyjacker—the rear hatch on a Braniff jet.
Airline has now sealed hatches on its
727s.
Life   Aug 11, 1972   p. 26

The hijack war.
Newsweek   Sep 21, 1970   p. 20

Pirates in the sky.
Time   Sep 21, 1970   p. 18

HIJACKING, SHIP
Hijack fallout.
Time   Oct 28, 1985   p. 22

Getting even. How Reagan did it. Will
justice be done? The risks ahead.
Newsweek   Oct 21, 1985   p. 20

Turning the tables. The U.S. strikes back
at terrorism.
Time   Oct 21, 1985   p. 22

Will Americans still be terrorist targets?
'We want...justice done.'
U.S. News   Oct 21, 1985   p. 24

HILL, ANITA
Anita Hill: 'I had to tell the truth.'
Clarence Thomas: 'It is a high-tech
lynching.'
Newsweek   Oct 21, 1991   p. 24

Sex, lies & politics. America's watershed
debate on sexual harassment.
Time   Oct 21, 1991   p. 34

Sex and justice. The Thomas affair. The
furor over sexual harassment.
U.S. News   Oct 21, 1991   p. 32

HILL, PHIL
Phil Hill: First world champion from the
U.S.?
Newsweek   Jul 17, 1961   p. 55

HILLS, CARLA
Trade warrior. Carla Hills has one of the
toughest jobs in Washington this year:
Negotiate trade policy with Japan and
Europe without succumbing to
protectionist pressure.
Business Week   Jan 22, 1990   p. 50

HILTON, CONRAD
Innkeeper to the world. Conrad Hilton.
Time   Jul 19, 1963   p. 66

HIMALAYA, ASIA
Tracking the snow leopard.
National Geographic Jun 1986   p. 793

HINCKLEY, JOHN, JR.
The insanity defense. Should it be
abolished? John Hinckley, Jr.
Newsweek   May 24, 1982   p. 56

HIPPIES
Trouble in Hippieland.
Newsweek   Oct 30, 1967   p. 84

The hippies. Philosophy of a subculture.
Time   Jul 7, 1967   p. 18

HIROSHIMA (JAPAN) - BOMBING, 1945
On the 40th anniversary of Hiroshima,
say hi to the bomb makers.
Discover   Aug 1985   p. 24

HISPANIC AMERICANS
Magnifico! Hispanic culture breaks out of
the barrio. Actor Edward James Olmos.
Time   Jul 11, 1988   p. 46

Hispanics make their move.
U.S. News   Aug 24, 1981   p. 60

Hispanic Americans. Soon: The biggest
minority.
Time   Oct 16, 1978   p. 48

HISTORY
History's hidden turning points. How
Paul made Christianity. Who says
Columbus discovered America? Who
killed chastity–and why.
U.S. News   Apr 22, 1991   p. 52

HISTORY, TEACHING OF

Who are we? American kids are getting a new—and divisive—view of Thomas Jefferson, Thanksgiving and the Fourth of July.
Time   Jul 8, 1991   p. 12

HITLER, ADOLF

Hitler's war against the world.
U.S. News   Aug 28, 1989   p. 32

HITLER, ADOLF - FORGERIES

Forgery. Uncovering the Hitler hoax.
Newsweek   May 16, 1983 p. 56

Forgery. Hitler's diaries join the long list of famous frauds.
Time   May 16, 1983 p. 36

Hitler's secret diaries. Are they genuine? How they could rewrite history. Hitler and the Jews.
Newsweek   May 2, 1983   p. 50

HO CHI MINH

New era in North Viet Nam. Ho Chi Minh.
Time   Sep 12, 1969   p. 22

Viet Nam: The intransigent North. Ho Chi Minh.
Time   Jul 16, 1965   p. 24

HOCKEY, PROFESSIONAL

Hockey. War on ice.
Time   Feb 24, 1975   p. 48

HODGES, LUTHER

Commerce Secretary Hodges: Pro or anti business?
Newsweek   Jul 24, 1961   p. 60

HOFFA, JIMMY

The Hoffa case.
Newsweek   Aug 18, 1975 p. 14

Hoffa of the teamsters: Driving for more power.
Newsweek   Jul 10, 1961   p. 57

HOFFMAN, DUSTIN

Warren & Dustin. A new song and dance act hits the road.
Life   May 1987   p. 63

A choice of heroes. Dusty and the Duke.
Life   Jul 11, 1969   p. 36

The young actors. Stars and anti-stars. Dustin Hoffman and Mia Farrow.
Time   Feb 7, 1969   p. 50

HOLLYWOOD (CALIFORNIA)

Hollywood: Legend and reality.
USA Today   Jul 1987   p. 44

HOLMES, LARRY

Heavyweight hits! Boxing scores one-two punch at the box office. Gerry Cooney fighting champ Larry Holmes in Las Vegas. Sylvester Stallone fighting his own legacy in Hollywood.
Time   Jun 14, 1982   p. 54

HOLOCAUST

See JEWS - PERSECUTIONS

HOLOGRAPHY

The laser: "A splendid light" for man's use.
National Geographic Mar 1984   p. 335

HOME EQUITY LOANS

Home equity. The hot new way to borrow. Should you do it? Will it spur the economy? How dangerous is it?
Business Week   Feb 9, 1987   p. 64

HOME SHOPPING

Home shopping. Retailing on TV is exploding—and now Sears has jumped in. But is it just a fad?
Business Week   Dec 15, 1986 p. 62

HOME, WILLIAM DOUGLAS

See DOUGLAS-HOME, SIR ALEC

HOMELESS

Homelessness in America: A mental health problem?
USA Today   Mar 1988   p. 26

Finally, hope for the homeless. Five approaches that work.
U.S. News   Feb 29, 1988 p. 24

Abandoned. They are America's castoffs-turned away from mental institutions and into the streets. Who will care for them?
Newsweek   Jan 6, 1986   p. 14

Homeless in America.
Newsweek   Jan 2, 1984   p. 20

HOMOCIDE

See MURDER

HOMOSEXUALITY

The future of gay America. Militants versus the mainstream. Testing the limits of tolerance.
Newsweek   Mar 12, 1990   p. 90

Growing up gay. The society's dilemma. One family's crisis.
Newsweek   Jan 13, 1986   p. 50

Gay America. Sex, politics and the impact of AIDS.
Newsweek   Aug 8, 1983   p. 30

How gay is gay? Homosexuality in America.
Time   Apr 23, 1979   p. 72

The homosexual in America.
Time   Oct 31, 1969   p. 56

See Also GAY MEN AND WOMEN

HONDA MOTOR CO.

Honda. Is it an American car? Most Hondas sold in America are made in America. But where do their parts really come from?
Business Week   Nov 18, 1991   p. 104

The Americanization of Honda.
Business Week   Apr 25, 1988   p. 90

HONESTY

Lying in America. Public concern over honesty and standards of behavior has reached the highest level since Watergate.
U.S. News   Feb 23, 1987   p. 54

HONG KONG

Hong Kong. Countdown to 1997. Plight of the boat people.
National Geographic Feb 1991   p. 103

The future of Hong Kong. Can Michael Sandberg's Hongkong & Shanghai Bank live with 'Red Capitalism'?
Business Week   Mar 5, 1984   p. 50

Hong Kong under the gun.
Newsweek   Jul 31, 1967   p. 30

Hong Kong.
Time   Nov 21, 1960   p. 28

HOOVER, J. EDGAR

The truth about Hoover.
Time   Dec 22, 1975   p. 14

Hoover's FBI. Time for a change?
Newsweek   May 10, 1971   p. 28

Emperor of the FBI. The 47-year reign of J. Edgar Hoover.
Life   Apr 9, 1971   p. 39

J. Edgar Hoover and the FBI.
Newsweek   Dec 7, 1964   p. 21

HOPE, BOB

Bob Hope: On the road with an American institution.
Life   Jan 29, 1971   p. 48

Christmas in Viet Nam. Bob Hope.
Time   Dec 22, 1967   p. 58

Bob Hope at the merry peak of his career.
Life   May 11, 1962   p. 92

HOPPER, DENNIS

The Easy Rider makes a wild new movie. Actor-director Dennis Hopper.
Life   Jun 19, 1970   p. 48

HORMONES

Hormones. How they affect behavior, growth, sex and health.
Newsweek   Jan 12, 1987   p. 50

HORMONES, SEX

Sex hormones: Discovering and harnessing new powers in the human brain.
Omni   Aug 1985   p. 62

HORNE, LENA

Lena Horne!
Ms.   Aug 1981   p. 43

HORNUNG, PAUL

Sunday's hero. The pro.
Newsweek   Oct 30, 1961   p. 43

HOROWITZ, VLADIMIR

Triumph in Moscow. Pianist Vladimir Horowitz.
Time   May 5, 1986   p. 56

HORSE RACING

Winning the derby: High-tech formulas
that really work.
Omni   May 1989   p. 42

Superhorse. Secretariat.
Newsweek   Jun 11, 1973   p. 62

Super horse. Secretariat.
Time   Jun 11, 1973   p. 85

HOSPITALS

America's best hospitals. Exclusive
rankings. How to find care in 15
specialties from AIDS to urology.
U.S. News   Aug 5, 1991   p. 36

America's best hospitals. Exclusive
ratings. A national guide that helps you
choose.
U.S. News   Apr 30, 1990   p. 51

Life and death: Scenes from a hospital
emergency ward.
USA Today   Jul 1989   p. 41

Inside our hospitals.
U.S. News   Mar 5, 1979   p. 33

Our sick hospitals.
Newsweek   Jul 11, 1966   p. 57

HOSPITALS - EMERGENCY CARE

Emergency! Overwhelmed and
understaffed, medicine's front lines are
collapsing across America.
Time   May 28, 1990   p. 58

HOSTAGES - IRAQ

Will it be war?
Newsweek   Aug 27, 1990   p. 18

HOSTAGES - LEBANON

The smile of freedom. Terry Anderson's
terrible ordeal. The inside story of the
hostage release.
Time   Dec 16, 1991   p. 16

Why now? Who's next? Hostages. John
McCarthy's release may signal that the
kidnappers are ready to cut a deal.
Time   Aug 19, 1991   p. 26

The hostage agony. A Time poll: Talk,
don't shoot. No ransom. Israel went too
far.
Time   Aug 14, 1989   p. 14

Hostage to terror. What the U.S. can do.
U.S. News   Feb 9, 1987   p. 24

See Also IRAN HOSTAGE CRISIS,
1979-1981

HOT AIR BALLOONS

High time in a balloon.
Life   Jul 6, 1962   p. 51

HOTELS, MOTELS, ETC.

Renaissance on Broadway.
USA Today   Mar 1987   p. 34

The man with 300,000 beds. Innkeeper
Kemmons Wilson.
Time   Jun 12, 1972   p. 77

Innkeeper to the world. Conrad Hilton.
Time   Jul 19, 1963   p. 66

HOUGHTON, JAMES R.

Class act. How Corning's Jamie Houghton
is reinventing an American corporation.
Business Week May 13, 1991 p. 68

HOUSING

Housing's storm. The squeeze on
builders, lenders and buyers.
Business Week Sep 7, 1981   p. 60

HOUSING - CONSTRUCTION

Homebuilding's new look.
Business Week Nov 7, 1983   p. 92

HOUSING - COSTS

What your home is worth. The 25 top
housing markets. The outlook for prices
this year. Strategies for buyers and sellers.
U.S. News   Apr 1, 1991   p. 56

Can your bank stay afloat? How the
real-estate crash threatens financial
institutions. The best ways to buy and sell
a house in a down market.
U.S. News   Nov 12, 1990   p. 62

The real estate bust. "How to survive" by
Jane Bryant Quinn.
Newsweek   Oct 1, 1990   p. 46

What is your home worth now? The 25
top housing markets.
U.S. News   Apr 9, 1990   p. 51

What's your home worth? The decision to buy or rent. When to move, when to improve. The latest financing wrinkles.
U.S. News   Apr 17, 1989   p. 66

Sky-high housing. Building up, prices up.
Time   Sep 12, 1977   p. 50

HOVING, THOMAS

New look for museums. The Metropolitan's Thomas Hoving.
Newsweek   Apr 1, 1968   p. 54

HOYLE, FRED

Life and death of the universe. Astrophysicist Fred Hoyle.
Newsweek   May 25, 1964   p. 63

HUBBLE SPACE TELESCOPE

Star crossed. The Hubble telescope. NASA's $1.5 billion blunder.
Newsweek   Jul 9, 1990   p. 48

When the universe was new. A journey to the beginning of time. The Hubble space telescope: Launching astronomy's new golden age.
U.S. News   Mar 26, 1990   p. 52

Chasing the Big Bang. The orbiting space telescope will soon give us our first good look at cosmic creation.
Discover   Jul 1989   p. 68

Astronomy: Seeing the edge of the universe.
USA Today   Jun 1986   p. 1

Seeing beyond the stars. A preview of America's biggest year in space.
Life   Dec 1985   p. 29

HUD

See DEPARTMENT OF HOUSING AND URBAN DEVELOPMENT

HUDSON, ROCK

Easygoing Rock in another hit.
Life   Feb 16, 1962   p. 65

HUGHES, HOWARD

Howard Hughes. A psychological autopsy.
Psychology Today   May 1986   p. 22

Howard Hughes. Exclusive: His secret life.
Time   Dec 13, 1976   p. 22

The secret world of Howard Hughes.
Newsweek   Apr 19, 1976   p. 24

The Hughes legacy. Scramble for the billions.
Time   Apr 19, 1976   p. 20

Nina. The singing baroness in the Hughes affair. Nina van Pallandt traveled with Clifford Irving.
Life   Feb 11, 1972   p. 30

The Hughes affair. Clifford Irving says Howard Hughes looks like this—but did he ever see him?
Life   Feb 4, 1972   p. 32

The Hughes mystery.
Time   Jan 24, 1972   p. 10

The Howard Hughes puzzle.
Newsweek   Jan 15, 1968   p. 25

HULL, BOBBY

Chicago's Bobby Hull. Fastest shot in the fastest game.
Time   Mar 1, 1968   p. 54

HUMAN RELATIONSHIPS

Creating trust and intimacy in the age of divorce.
Psychology Today   May 1989   p. 27

HUMOR

Is nothing sacred? The low art of parody - spoofing for fun and profit.
Newsweek   Apr 25, 1983   p. 64

College humor comes back. John Belushi.
Newsweek   Oct 23, 1978   p. 88

HUMPHREY, HUBERT H.

Humphrey. The happy warrior.
Newsweek   Jan 23, 1978   p. 16

The Democrats after Chicago.
Time   Sep 6, 1968   p. 15

H • H • H.
Time   May 3, 1968   p. 15

Can he stop Bobby? Vice President Humphrey.
Newsweek   Apr 29, 1968   p. 23

The activated Vice President. Hubert Humphrey.
Time   Apr 1, 1966   p. 21

The Humphreys.
Newsweek   Sep 7, 1964   p. 16

Johnson & Humphrey.
Time   Sep 4, 1964   p. 20

The new Hubert Humphrey. LBJ's civil rights whip.
Newsweek   Apr 13, 1964   p. 26

Hubert and Jack in Wisconsin.
Life   Mar 28, 1960   p. 22

Humphrey and Kennedy. Wisconsin - who'll tumble?
Newsweek   Mar 28, 1960   p. 29

Humphrey for President.
Time   Feb 1, 1960   p. 13

HUNGER
Running out of food?
Newsweek   Nov 11, 1974   p. 56

Starving children of Biafra War.
Life   Jul 12, 1968   p. 20

World hunger. 10,000 deaths every day.
Newsweek   Jun 17, 1963   p. 43

HUNT, NELSON AND BUNKER
The billion dollar gambler. Silver king Bunker Hunt.
Newsweek   Apr 7, 1980   p. 54

HUNTING
Should hunting be banned? Animal-rights activists war on blood sports.
U.S. News   Feb 5, 1990   p. 30

HUNTINGTON'S DISEASE
Would you want to know how and when you're going to die?
Discover   Jun 1987   p. 26

HUNTLEY, CHET
TV's Huntley and Brinkley: One is solemn, the other twinkly.
Newsweek   Mar 13, 1961   p. 53

HURD, GALE ANNE
Madame Blockbuster. Hollywood producer Gale Anne Hurd teeters on the abyss.
Ms.   Sep 1989   p. 66

HURRICANES
In the eye of a mighty storm.
Life   Sep 22, 1961   p. 30

HUSSEIN, KING OF JORDAN
The Arabs in the aftermath. Jordan's King Hussein.
Time   Jul 14, 1967   p. 22

HUSSEIN, SADDAM
Saddam Hussein. The real target?
U.S. News   Feb 18, 1991   p. 20

Saddam's endgame. More than just a madman.
Newsweek   Jan 7, 1991   p. 14

Baghdad's bully. Can he be stopped? The war of the future. Oil shocks ahead.
Newsweek   Aug 13, 1990   p. 16

The most dangerous man in the world. Saddam Hussein, President of Iraq.
U.S. News   Jun 4, 1990   p. 38

HUTTON, LAUREN
The '74 model. Lauren Hutton.
Newsweek   Aug 26, 1974   p. 52

HYDROGEN BOMB
Space bomb in color. Eerie spectacle in Pacific sky.
Life   Jul 20, 1962   p. 26

HYPERSPACE
Life in the fourth dimension.
Omni   May 1987   p. 52

HYPERTENSION
Hypertension. Conquering the quiet killer.
Time   Jan 13, 1975   p. 60

HYPNOTISM
Wonder cures? New respect for fringe medicine. Acupuncture. Hypnosis. Biofeedback.
U.S. News   Sep 23, 1991   p. 68

Hypnosis. From theater to therapy.
Medical uses.
Psychology Today   Jan 1986   p. 22

The use of hypnosis to cure mental ills.
Life   Mar 7, 1960   p. 106

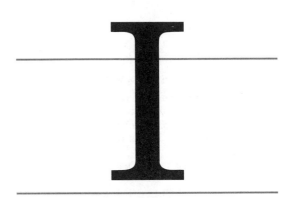

IACOCCA, LEE

Chrysler's next act. Sure, the company's big comeback turned Lee Iacocca into a hero. But now Chrysler needs a new strategy—and Iacocca has plenty of ideas.
Business Week   Nov 3, 1986   p. 66

At home and on the road with Iacocca.
Life   Jun 1986   p. 34

"I gotta tell ya." America loves listening to Lee. Chrysler's Iacocca.
Time   Apr 1, 1985   p. 30

Iacocca. An American legend tells his own story.
Newsweek   Oct 8, 1984   p. 50

Detroit's comeback kid. Chrysler Chairman Lee Iacocca.
Time   Mar 21, 1983   p. 50

The Mustang. Newest breed out of Detroit. Ford's Lee Iacocca.
Newsweek   Apr 20, 1964   p. 97

Ford's Lee Iacocca.
Time   Apr 17, 1964   p. 92

IBM

See INTERNATIONAL BUSINESS MACHINES CORPORATION

IBN BATTULA, MOHAMMED

Prince of travelers. Ibn Battula.
National Geographic Dec 1991   p. 2

ICAHN, CARL

Raider or manager? With the crisis over at TWA, Carl Icahn is after USX. Critics say he wants a fast buck. He says he'll revitalize the company.
Business Week   Oct 27, 1986   p. 98

ICE AGE

The way we were. Our Ice Age heritage: Language, art, fashion, and the family.
Newsweek   Nov 10, 1986   p. 62

ICE CREAM

Ice cream. Getting your licks.
Time   Aug 10, 1981   p. 52

ICELAND

Iceland. Life under the glaciers.
National Geographic Feb 1987   p. 184

IDENTITY (PSYCHOLOGY)

Personal mythology. Are you Venus, Apollo...in the story you live by?
Psychology Today   Dec 1988   p. 42

ILLEGAL ALIENS

See ALIENS, ILLEGAL

IMMIGRANTS IN THE UNITED STATES

'Only in America.'
U.S. News   Jul 7, 1986   p. 25

Immigrants. The changing face of America.
Time   Jul 8, 1985   p. 24

"English sometimes spoken here." Our big cities go ethnic.
U.S. News   Mar 21, 1983   p. 49

The new immigrants.
Newsweek   Jul 7, 1980   p. 26

America. Still the promised land.
U.S. News   Jul 9, 1979   p. 26

New faces. How they're changing U.S.
U.S. News   Feb 20, 1978   p. 28

The smart taxpayer's guide. Money saving strategies for 1987. How to avoid an IRS audit.
U.S. News   Mar 2, 1987   p. 50

Making tax reform work for you. Smart strategies for families, homeowners, investors, employees, entrepreneurs. 10 ways to save money this year.
U.S. News   Oct 6, 1986   p. 46

Tax reform at last! A simpler system—will it spur growth? Which industries come out on top. Personal investing: How it changes. For the future, more reforms.
Business Week   Sep 1, 1986   p. 54

Breakthrough. Tax reform.
Time   Aug 25, 1986   p. 12

86 ways to save on your '85 taxes.
U.S. News   Mar 3, 1986   p. 50

Reagan's tax package. What's in it for you.
Time   Jun 10, 1985   p. 14

The tax bite. How painful?
U.S. News   Feb 25, 1985   p. 20

Your income tax. Standing up to the IRS. Last-minute tax tips. Tax changes on the way. What happens to your return now.
U.S. News   Mar 26, 1984   p. 36

ABC's of your income tax. What's wrong with the system. Billions the IRS never gets. The games people play. What happens to your return now.
U.S. News   Apr 18, 1983   p. 39

Income taxes. New crackdown by IRS? Interview with top tax man. Underground economy: $100 billion in lost taxes. What happens to your return now.
U.S. News   Apr 19, 1982   p. 43

Smile, please. How the tax cut helps you. Will it hurt the economy? The battered Democrats.
Newsweek   Aug 10, 1981   p. 16

Income taxes. What happens to your return now. How tough will IRS get? Interview with new chief. Tax cuts you can expect in '81.
U.S. News   Apr 20, 1981   p. 38

Income taxes. Myth of IRS efficiency. How the honest bear the burden. Now that Uncle Sam has your return.
U.S.News   Apr 21, 1980   p. 39

Burned up over taxes.
Newsweek   Apr 10, 1978   p. 70

Taxes. How to ease the squeeze.
Newsweek   Feb 24, 1969   p. 65

Tax hike. Medicare. Education. Poverty. Space. War. Urban renewal. Highways.
Newsweek   Aug 14, 1967   p. 65

Taxes: All those deductions, loopholes, credits, etc.
Time   Feb 1, 1963   p. 12

Will your taxes be cut? Congressman Wilbur Mills.
Time   Jan 11, 1963   p. 19

Tax time: Sharp pencils, sharper machines.
Newsweek   Apr 16, 1962   p. 87

INDIA

India by rail. Pakistan to Bangladesh.
National Geographic Jun 1984   p. 696

The bloody birth of Bangladesh.
Time   Dec 20, 1971   p. 20

Pakistan's agony.
Time   Aug 2, 1971   p. 24

Prime Minister Indira Gandhi.
Newsweek   Apr 4, 1966   p. 36

Troubled India in a woman's hands. Indira Gandhi
Time   Jan 28, 1966   p. 24

Shastri's last journey.
Life   Jan 21, 1966   p. 20

India without Nehru.
Time   Aug 13, 1965   p. 18

Shastri of India.
Newsweek   Jun 29, 1964   p. 38

India's Nehru. Reveille for the neutrals.
Newsweek   Dec 3, 1962   p. 37

India's lost illusions. Nehru.
Time   Nov 30, 1962   p. 23

War in India.
Life   Nov 16, 1962   p. 46

INDIA - HISTORY

When the Moguls ruled.
National Geographic Apr 1985   p. 463

INDIA - POLITICS AND GOVERNMENT

India's crisis. After Indira.
Newsweek   Nov 12, 1984   p. 42

"If I die today, every drop of my blood
will invigorate the nation." Indira Gandhi
1917 - 1984.
Time   Nov 12, 1984   p. 42

Indira's iron fist.
Newsweek   Jul 7, 1975   p. 22

Elections in India. Krishna Menon.
Time   Feb 2, 1962   p. 16

INDIA AND PAKISTAN

War over Kashmir.
Newsweek   Sep 20, 1965   p. 33

Shock of a new war. Pakistani–Indian
hatreds.
Life   Sep 17, 1965   p. 40

New war in Asia. Pakistan's Ayub v.
India's Shastri.
Time   Sep 17, 1965   p. 44

INDIA-PAKISTAN WAR, 1971

India-Pakistan War. Who's to blame?
Newsweek   Dec 20, 1971   p. 34

The battle for Bengal. India attacks.
Newsweek   Dec 6, 1971   p. 30

Conflict in Asia: India v. Pakistan.
Time   Dec 6, 1971   p. 28

Bengal: The murder of a people.
Newsweek   Aug 2, 1971   p. 26

INDIANS OF NORTH AMERICA

1491. America before Columbus.
National Geographic Oct 1991   p. 4

Peoples of the Arctic.
National Geographic Feb 1983   p. 144

Our Indian heritage.
Life   Jul 2, 1971   p. 38

The American Indian: Goodbye to Tonto.
Time   Feb 9, 1970   p. 14

Return of the Red man.
Life   Dec 1, 1967   p. 52

INDIANS OF NORTH AMERICA - POTTERY

Pueblo pottery.
National Geographic Nov 1982   p. 593

INDIVIDUALISM

Personal mythology. Are you Venus,
Apollo...in the story you live by?
Psychology Today   Dec 1988   p. 42

The struggle to be an individual. Modern
society's growing challenge.
Life   Apr 21, 1967   p. 60

The individual in America.
Time   May 10, 1963   p. 20

INDONESIA

Indonesia: The land the Communists lost.
General Suharto.
Time   Jul 15, 1966   p. 22

The other Asian crisis. Indonesia's
Sukarno.
Newsweek   Feb 15, 1965   p. 40

INDUSTRIAL DESIGN

'I can't work this thing!' From VCRs and
telephones to copiers and microwaves,
poorly designed machines cluttered with
unwanted features are driving consumers
crazy. Whatever happened to
user-friendly?
Business Week   Apr 29, 1991   p. 58

INDUSTRIAL MANAGEMENT

Survival in the basic industries. How four
companies hope to avoid disaster:
Firestone. Kennecott. Inland Steel. Boise
Cascade.
Business Week   Apr 26, 1982   p. 74

The coming industrial miracle.
U.S. News   Nov 30, 1981   p. 52

INDUSTRIAL RELATIONS

The new industrial relations. Moving
away from the old adversarial
relationship. More worker involvement
in shop-floor decisions. Improved job
satisfaction with improved productivity.
Business Week   May 11, 1981   p. 84

Shock treatment for inflation.
Newsweek   Oct 22, 1979   p. 36

Rocketing inflation. How much worse?
Who's hit hardest? Any way to cope?
U.S. News   Oct 1, 1979   p. 43

Runaway inflation. Can Carter corral it?
U.S. News   Mar 12, 1979   p. 71

Saving the dollar. But risking a recession.
Newsweek   Nov 13, 1978   p. 40

Inflation fighters. Can they win?
Newsweek   Nov 6, 1978   p. 30

Carter's inflation fighter. A no-win job?
U.S. News   Nov 6, 1978   p. 17

Inflation. Where do we go from here?
U.S. News   Oct 2, 1978   p. 30

The inflation fighter. Federal Reserve
Chairman G. William Miller.
Time   Jul 17, 1978   p. 58

Inflation.
Newsweek   May 29, 1978   p. 68

Inflation. How you are being robbed.
U.S. News   Apr 24, 1978   p. 18

Can the dollar be saved?
U.S. News   Mar 13, 1978   p. 41

Inflation. Why can't this headache be
cured?
U.S. News   Aug 22, 1977   p. 15

Can Ford win with - Higher taxes. Easier
credit. No controls.
U.S. News   Oct 21, 1974   p. 19

Trying to fight back. Inflation. Recession.
Oil.
Time   Oct 14, 1974   p. 25

Inflation. How did it get out of hand? Can
you protect yourself? What's the cure?
U.S. News   Jun 17, 1974   p. 28

World inflation.
Time   Apr 8, 1974   p. 72

The big squeeze.
Newsweek   Mar 4, 1974   p. 58

"Cruelest tax." Inflation's bite - Any relief
in sight?
U.S. News   Jan 28, 1974   p. 15

Nixon's other crisis.
Time   Jun 18, 1973   p. 26

Battle of the economy: Stand pat or do
something?
Time   Aug 16, 1971   p. 64

Your dollar problem. How some
Americans beat inflation.
Life   Feb 13, 1970   p. 20

How much inflation?
Newsweek   Sep 5, 1966   p. 69

INFLUENZA
See FLU (DISEASE)

INFORMATION SERVICES
The information business. Lots of
companies find it alluring. But only a few
are making money. When will the big
payoff come?
Business Week   Aug 25, 1986   p. 82

The home information revolution.
Window on the world.
Business Week   Jun 29, 1981   p. 74

INFORMATION TECHNOLOGY
Information power. Many smart
companies are now using new
information technologies to gain a
strategic edge in everything from product
development to marketing. Are you?
Business Week   Oct 14, 1985   p. 108

INHERITANCE
The new way to get rich. Never before
have so many people stood to inherit so
much money.
U.S. News   May 7, 1990   p. 26

INNOVATIONS
The innovators. 25 Americans on the
cutting edge. Science. Technology.
Medicine. Business. Education. Fun and
games. Design. The arts. Filmmaker
Spike Lee.
Newsweek   Oct 2, 1989   p. 4

Special issue. One hundred of the most important young men and women in the United States. The take-over generation. Its breakthrough in government, science, space, business, education, religion and the arts.
Life   Sep 14, 1962   p. 4

See Also TECHNOLOGICAL INNOVATIONS

INSANE, CRIMINALLY

Turned loose too soon? Criminally insane.
U.S. News   Jun 27, 1983   p. 52

INSANITY DEFENSE

The insanity defense. Should it be abolished? John Hinckley, Jr.
Newsweek   May 24, 1982 p. 56

INSECT CONTROL

The bugs are coming.
Time   Jul 12, 1976   p. 38

INSIDER TRADING

See STOCK MARKET - INSIDER TRADING

INSURANCE COMPANIES - FINANCE

Insurance. An industry under siege. Consumers, politicians, and even corporate executives are all fighting mad. The outlook: A smaller, less profitable industry.
Business Week   Aug 21, 1989 p. 72

INSURANCE, HEALTH

Federal catastrophic health insurance.
Congressional Digest Apr 1987   p. 97

Teddy comes on strong. The battle over health care.
Newsweek   May 28, 1979 p. 26

Medical costs. Seeking the cure.
Time   May 28, 1979 p. 60

INSURANCE, LIABILITY

Sorry, America, your insurance has been canceled.
Time   Mar 24, 1986 p. 16

INSURANCE, LIFE

Are you really insured? Is your pension money at risk? What about that policy you bought? Just how bad will this get? What you can do to protect yourself.
Business Week   Aug 5, 1991   p. 42

Upheaval in life insurance. Can new products bolster a lagging industry?
Business Week   Jun 25, 1984   p. 58

The changing life insurers. New high-yield products mean high-risk investments.
Business Week   Sep 14, 1981   p. 66

INSURANCE, MALPRACTICE

Malpractice: Doctors in revolt.
Newsweek   Jun 9, 1975   p. 58

INTEGRATION, RACIAL

See BLACKS - INTEGRATION

INTEL CORP.

Intel. The next revolution. When Intel invented the computer-on-a-chip 17 years ago, it opened the era of personal computers. In 1989 Intel will take the next step: A chip so powerful it will become the heart of even the biggest computer.
Business Week   Sep 26, 1988   p. 74

INTELLIGENCE

The intelligence revolution. Is IQ dead? Radical new definitions of intellect threaten the conventional tests.
Discover   Oct 1985   p. 25

IQ: Are the Japanese really smarter?
Discover   Sep 1982   p. 18

INTERACTIVE VIDEO

TV 2000—the future of interactive television.
Omni   Jun 1990   p. 55

INTEREST RATES

The outlook for interest rates. They'll fall now but rise next year. If deficits stay big, the fed will tighten.
Business Week   Sep 26, 1983   p. 136

A break in interest rates. How it affects you. Wall Street's wildest week.
Newsweek   Aug 30, 1982   p. 16

Interest rate anguish. Federal Reserve Chairman Paul Volcker.
Time   Mar 8, 1982   p. 74

INTERNAL REVENUE SERVICE

Auditing the IRS.
Business Week   Apr 16, 1984 p. 84

Income taxes. What happens to your return now. How tough will IRS get? Interview with new chief. Tax cuts you can expect in '81.
U.S. News   Apr 20, 1981   p. 38

Income taxes. Myth of IRS efficiency. How the honest bear the burden. Now that Uncle Sam has your return.
U.S.News   Apr 21, 1980   p. 39

INTERNATIONAL BUSINESS MACHINES CORPORATION

The new IBM. Is it new enough?
Business Week   Dec 16, 1991 p. 112

IBM. What's wrong? What's next?
Business Week   Jun 17, 1991 p. 24

IBM. A bold move in mainframes. IBM has launched the most ambitious software project in its history. The goal: Make mainframes the heart of computer networks. Will this restore Big Blue's growth?
Business Week   May 29, 1989 p. 72

IBM. Big changes at Big Blue. Just as John Akers became chairman three years ago, the computer giant went into its worst profit slide ever. Now his plan to rejuvenate the company is in place. Will it work?
Business Week   Feb 15, 1988 p. 92

IBM fights back. Big Blue is hurting. Earnings are off, the stock is down, and customers are straying. What will IBM do? A lot.
Business Week   Nov 17, 1986 p. 152

IBM vs. the clones. From Taiwan to Texas, companies are turning out low-priced versions of IBM's personal computer. What will IBM do?
Business Week   Jul 28, 1986   p. 62

IBM. Led by a new CEO, it aims to top $185 billion in sales by 1994—making it the world's biggest company. That requires new moves in communications and software. It won't be easy.
Business Week   Feb 18, 1985 p. 84

The colossus that works. Big is bountiful at IBM.
Time   Jul 11, 1983   p. 44

No. 1's awesome strategy. How IBM will get bigger and stronger in the 1980s.
Business Week   Jun 8, 1981   p. 84

INTERNATIONAL BUSINESSES

The year in business. U.S. industry's global reach.
Time   Dec 29, 1967   p. 56

INTERNATIONAL GEOPHYSICAL YEAR

New portrait of our planet. What IGY taught us.
Life   Nov 7, 1960   p. 74

INTERNATIONAL HARVESTER CO.

Harvester's tough boss.
Business Week   Aug 15, 1983 p. 80

International Harvester. Can it survive when the banks move in?
Business Week   Jun 22, 1981 p. 66

INTERNATIONAL TELEPHONE AND TELEGRAPH

ITT's big gamble. Can it win in U.S. telecommunications?
Business Week   Oct 22, 1984 p. 114

The ITT affair: Politics and justice. Acting Attorney General Richard G. Kleindienst.
Newsweek   Mar 20, 1972 p. 24

INTERNATIONAL TRADE

Can you compete? The global economy. Foreign competition is fundamentally changing America's role in the world—altering the very way we work and how well we live. All of us will be affected.
Business Week   Dec 17, 1990 p. 60

The U.S. vs. Japan vs. Germany. Will America lose out in the new global boom?
U.S. News   Jul 16, 1990   p. 22

Trade. Will we ever close the gap? The limits of the cheap dollar. How Washington will respond. The new protectionism. How much can small companies help?
Business Week   Feb 27, 1989   p. 86

U.S. foreign trade policy.
Congressional Digest Jun 1987   p. 163

The new trade strategy. Will it help U.S. companies compete? Will it stem the protectionism tide? Can the U.S. still afford free trade?
Business Week   Oct 7, 1985   p. 90

The Yankee trader. Death of a salesman?
U.S. News   Apr 8, 1985   p. 64

New restrictions on world trade. Bartering goods and protecting jobs. Governments link imports to exports.
Business Week   Jul 19, 1982   p. 118

Can the world head off a trade war?
U.S. News   Apr 23, 1979   p. 43

World trade: Can the U.S. compete?
Newsweek   Apr 24, 1972   p. 63

INTERNATIONAL TRADE WITH CHINA

The U.S.-China Act of 1991.
Congressional Digest Oct 1991   p. 225

INTERNATIONAL TRADE WITH JAPAN

How to beat the Japanese.
U.S. News   Aug 24, 1987   p. 38

Trade wars. The U.S. gets tough with Japan.
Time   Apr 13, 1987   p. 28

Can Detroit cope? With imports about to soar, the U.S. auto industry will shrink. But there's some good news, too.
Business Week   Apr 22, 1985   p. 78

Collision course. Can the U.S. avert a trade war with Japan?
Business Week   Apr 8, 1985   p. 50

INTERNATIONAL TRADE WITH MEXICO

Mexico. A new economic era. A rush to free trade will reshuffle jobs and factories — creating a new North American economy.
Business Week   Nov 12, 1990   p. 102

INTERPERSONAL RELATIONS

Breaking up. Deception & cover-up in failing relationships.
Psychology Today   Jul 1987   p. 36

INTERRACIAL MARRIAGES

Tackling a taboo. Spike Lee's take on interracial romance. Mixed couples on love and prejudice.
Newsweek   Jun 10, 1991   p. 44

Mr. & Mrs. Guy Smith / An interracial wedding.
Time   Sep 29, 1967   p. 28

INTUITION

The experienced brain. When to trust your intuition.
Psychology Today   Sep 1989   p. 35

INVENTIONS

New products.
Time   Sep 19, 1960   p. 94

INVESTMENT ADVISORS

Why money managers don't do better. They can't even outperform the S&P 500.
Business Week   Feb 4, 1985   p. 58

Will money managers wreck the economy?
Business Week   Aug 13, 1984   p. 86

INVESTMENT BANKING

Not since the heyday of J.P. Morgan has Wall Street been buying so many corporations. The major firms are more owners than investors—actually overseeing the companies they buy, from setting overall strategy to picking top managers.
Business Week   Jun 20, 1988   p. 116

The traders take charge. How the big investment banks are changing.
Business Week   Feb 20, 1984   p. 58

INVESTMENTS

Where to invest in 1992. Stocks. Funds. Bonds.
Business Week   Dec 30, 1991   p. 59

Where to invest. With the recovery coming. Stocks. Mutual funds. Muni bonds. Real estate. Futures.
Business Week   Jun 24, 1991   p. 70

The best mutual funds. Getting the most reward for the least risk. Our annual ratings. To help you find the right fund.
Business Week   Feb 18, 1991   p. 76

Where to invest in 1991. Stocks. Bonds. Funds.
Business Week   Jan 7, 1991   p. 71

The 200 best stocks and mutual funds. How to rebuild a battered portfolio. Where to put your money now. What's ahead for investors.
U.S. News   Dec 17, 1990   p. 79

How to prosper in hard times. The smart investor's guide.
U.S. News   Sep 24, 1990   p. 80

How to build your fortune. Retirement: A guide for late starters. Investing: Where you should put your money now. Saving: Ways to sock away more. Checklist: How you compare with others.
U.S. News   Jul 30, 1990   p. 46

Where to invest. Midyear outlook. Stocks. Mutual funds. Bonds. Junk bonds. Money funds. Futures.
Business Week   Jun 25, 1990   p. 72

Mutual funds. Winning back the small investor. The battle for your 401(k) money. Which family of funds does best.
Business Week   Jun 11, 1990   p. 56

The best mutual funds. Our annual ratings. To help you find the right fund. Getting the most reward for the least risk.
Business Week   Feb 19, 1990   p. 70

Where to invest in 1990. Stocks. Bonds. Funds.
Business Week   Jan 1, 1990   p. 73

Best places for your money. Stocks. Bonds. Real estate. Collectibles.
U.S. News   Dec 4, 1989   p. 66

Investing for the 1990s. Where to look for the new growth stocks. Rebuilding. Trade. Environment. Computers. Banking. The age wave.
Business Week   Oct 16, 1989   p. 91

Building your fortune. Savings. Inheritance. Investments. Insurance.
U.S. News   Jul 17, 1989   p. 50

Where to invest. Special midyear outlook. Stocks get stronger. Booming bonds. The hottest mutual funds. Commodities take a hit. First-half stars.
Business Week   Jun 26, 1989   p. 92

The best mutual funds. Our annual ratings. To help you find the right fund. Getting the best return for the least risk.
Business Week   Feb 20, 1989   p. 80

Where to invest in 1989. Stocks. Bonds. Mutual funds.
Business Week   Jan 2, 1989   p. 92

The best mutual funds. Who did well despite the crash. Reducing risk in the year ahead. A new roster of long-term leaders.
Business Week   Feb 22, 1988   p. 62

Where to invest in 1988. Stocks after the crash. Where the best values are now. The sturdiest mutual funds. Shock-proofing your portfolio. Picking the right bonds. How to find good yields with low risk.
Business Week   Jan 4, 1988   p. 95

Should you believe your broker? In the wake of the crash, Wall Street has a credibility gap. Here's how it's trying to win back investors.
Business Week   Nov 23, 1987   p. 92

Heading off hard times. What the experts think should be done. How to invest for the long term by Jane Bryant Quinn.
Newsweek   Nov 9, 1987   p. 24

How to ride out the bear market. Best strategies for investors. Where interest rates are heading.
U.S. News   Nov 9, 1987   p. 24

After the crash. Robert Samuelson: The specter of depression. Jane Bryant Quinn: Keeping your money safe.
Newsweek   Nov 2, 1987   p. 14

After the fall. How to protect your money now. Is a recession coming?
U.S. News   Nov 2, 1987   p. 18

Is the party over? A jolt for Wall Street's whiz kids. How to play it safe, by Jane Bryant Quinn.
Newsweek   Oct 26, 1987   p. 50

The Bull market. Time to get out? The experts pick the best buys now. How to protect your winnings.
U.S. News   Aug 31, 1987   p. 56

How to measure your financial health. Saving: 12 ways to build a fortune. Retirement: What to do now to quit early. Real estate: How to make your home pay off. Investing: Risk-taking strategies that work.
U.S. News   Jun 8, 1987   p. 52

How you can play the global money game. Risks and rewards in volatile markets. Should you buy foreign stocks? An investor's guide: The smart moves now. The best overseas mutual funds.
U.S. News   May 11, 1987 p. 49

The best mutual funds. Who's ahead in this year's rally. Winners and losers in 1986. The leaders over the past ten years.
Business Week   Feb 23, 1987   p. 64

The mutual fund jungle. Your money. Choosing a fund: The do's and don'ts. Picking winners: The top forty.
U.S. News   Feb 16, 1987   p. 52

Where to invest in 1987. The hottest stocks. Picking winners in a volatile market. Playing the global market. Where to look for hidden values. The dazzle in bonds. How to reach for higher yields.
Business Week   Jan 5, 1987   p. 53

Taking care of your money. How to invest, save and earn more under tax reform.
U.S. News   Nov 24, 1986 p. 56

Make your money grow. Stocks, beating the Dow. Real estate, bargains for buyers. Savings, where to stash your cash. Mutual funds, new ways to win big.
U.S. News   Jun 9, 1986   p. 53

The best mutual funds. Introducing new annual ratings to help you pick the right fund.
Business Week   Feb 24, 1986   p. 54

Where to invest in 1986. The hottest stocks. Trouble ahead in real estate. Bonds are booming.
Business Week   Dec 30, 1985   p. 72

Taking care of your money. Personal investing. The experts' smart-money advice on stocks, bonds, IRA's, shelters, real estate, CD's - and more. Plus: How the rich stay that way.
U.S. News   Jun 10, 1985 p. 56

Investment outlook 1985.
Business Week   Dec 31, 1984   p. 61

How to make your money grow. Mutual funds. Real estate. Bonds. Stocks.
U.S. News   Jun 4, 1984   p. 38

Investment outlook 84.
Business Week   Dec 26, 1983   p. 47

The savings revolution. Everybody wants your money!
Time   Jun 8, 1981   p. 58

Best ways to beat inflation.
U.S. News   Nov 21, 1977 p. 48

INVESTMENTS, FOREIGN

The selling of America. An international game of economic conquest.
USA Today   Mar 1989   p. 12

The selling of America. Foreign investors buy, buy, buy.
Time   Sep 14, 1987   p. 52

The buying of America.
Newsweek   Nov 27, 1978   p. 78

High stakes – U.S. investment in Europe.
Newsweek   Mar 8, 1965   p. 67

Japan invades Hollywood. Sony's $3.4 billion deal for Columbia. Five ways to meet the challenge on trade, takeovers and technology.
Newsweek   Oct 9, 1989   p. 62

Japan moves in. Tokyo Inc.'s bold thrust into the American heartland.
U.S. News   May 9, 1988   p. 43

Japan in America.
Business Week   Jul 14, 1986   p. 44

IOWA

Iowa. A profile of the feisty folks who have an outsized say in picking the next President.
Time   Jan 25, 1988   p. 10

Heading for a showdown. Anti-American mob in Teheran.
Newsweek   Dec 3, 1979   p. 44

Attacking America. Fury in Iran. Rescue in Pakistan.
Time   Dec 3, 1979   p. 24

U.S. builds for a showdown.
U.S. News   Dec 3, 1979   p. 25

The test of wills.
Time   Nov 26, 1979   p. 20

Test of U.S. resolve.
U.S. News   Nov 26, 1979   p. 29

Blackmailing the U.S. "America is the great Satan" - Ayatullah Khomeini.
Time   Nov 19, 1979   p. 14

IRAN HOSTAGE RESCUE ATTEMPT, 1980

The Iran rescue mission. The untold story. The Pentagon's man in Teheran. Richard J. Meadows.
Newsweek   Jul 12, 1982   p. 16

Rescue mission in Washington.
Newsweek   May 12, 1980   p. 26

Fiasco in Iran.
Newsweek   May 5, 1980   p. 24

Debacle in the desert. Bulletin: An attempt to rescue the American hostages in Iran was aborted Friday when eight crew members of U.S. aircraft were killed...President Carter "accepts full responsibility..."
Time   May 5, 1980   p. 12

IRAN-CONTRA AFFAIR

"Reagan knew everything." Ollie North tells his story.
Time   Oct 28, 1991   p. 36

Television's blinding power. How it shapes our views.
U.S. News   Jul 27, 1987   p. 14

Ollie takes the Hill. The fall guy becomes a folk hero.
Newsweek   Jul 20, 1987   p. 12

"I was authorized to do everything that I did" -Oliver North.
Time   Jul 20, 1987   p. 12

How Ollie stormed the Hill. A TV triumph turns the tables on his critics. Who really gave the orders.
U.S. News   Jul 20, 1987   p. 18

Oliver North, star witness. Plus Gore Vidal and Pat Buchanan on the hearings.
Newsweek   Jul 13, 1987   p. 14

Front and center. Lieut. Colonel Oliver North.
Time   Jul 13, 1987   p. 22

Ollie's private world. Out of the shadows.
U.S. News   Jul 13, 1987   p. 20

The Secord story. A close-up look at the first witness in the Iran-Contra TV hearings. Will he link Reagan to the conspiracy?
Newsweek   May 11, 1987 p. 16

The big sting. New information on the Iran affair points to a grand deception, conceived by Ayatolla Khomeini and his men, that entrapped the Americans, the Israelis, the middlemen and even the Soviets.
U.S. News   Mar 30, 1987   p. 18

Reagan's failure. Can he recover?
Newsweek   Mar 9, 1987   p. 16

Can he recover?
Time   Mar 9, 1987   p. 20

The teflon is gone. A question of competence. Can Howard Baker rebuild a shattered Presidency. How Nancy Reagan defends her man.
U.S. News   Mar 9, 1987   p. 14

Coverup. To protect the President, NSC staffers say Don Regan ordered them to conceal the early approval of arms sales to Iran by Ronald Reagan. This week the Tower Commission will tell how the president changed his story.
Newsweek   Mar 2, 1987   p. 20

The pressure builds. McFarlane's suicide attempt. The NSC's computer secret. Turmoil in the White House.
Newsweek   Feb 23, 1987   p. 18

Probing the mess. Fresh money trails. The CIA role. An interview with Casey.
Time   Dec 22, 1986   p. 14

Reagan's role. His secret message to Iran. His green light to the CIA. His attempt to contain the damage.
Newsweek   Dec 15, 1986   p. 26

America's shadow network. Behind the secret deals with Iran and the Contras.
U.S. News   Dec 15, 1986   p. 22

Who knew? The looming shake-up. Plus: John Ehrlichman on a White House under siege.
Newsweek   Dec 8, 1986   p. 32

How far does it go? Reagan lashes out. "There is a bitter bile in my throat."
Time   Dec 8, 1986   p. 16

Who else knew? Reagan's damaged presidency.
U.S. News   Dec 8, 1986   p. 16

His biggest blunder. The Iran mess. Exclusive: How Reagan's 'cowboys' got out of control.
Newsweek   Dec 1, 1986   p. 26

The Iran connection. Reagan's secret strategy.
Newsweek   Nov 17, 1986   p. 46

Reagan's secret dealings with Iran.
Time   Nov 17, 1986   p. 12

IRANIAN AIR DOWNING, 1988

Why it happened. The Gulf tragedy. Time to talk with Iran by Henry Kissinger.
Newsweek   Jul 18, 1988   p. 18

IRANIAN-IRAQI WAR, 1979-1988

Iran on the march. "This is a war between Islam and blasphemy." - Ayatullah Khomeini.
Time   Jul 26, 1982   p. 18

The Gulf. Will it explode?
Time   Oct 27, 1980   p. 34

The Gulf War: Rising risks.
Newsweek   Oct 20, 1980   p. 40

War in the oil fields.
Newsweek   Oct 6, 1980   p. 28

War in the Gulf.
Time   Oct 6, 1980   p. 34

IRAQ

Desert warriors. How the Gulf is testing the new U.S military. The diplomatic moves to contain Saddam Hussein.
U.S. News   Sep 10, 1990   p. 26

The vise tightens. Pressure mounts against Iraq. How well will it work—and how soon? The crisis strains some traditional alliances. And the markets stay worried.
Business Week   Aug 27, 1990   p. 22

The most dangerous man in the world. Saddam Hussein, President of Iraq.
U.S. News   Jun 4, 1990   p. 38

A dangerous nuclear game. Israel's raid: The inside story. Impact on the Mideast. U.S. policy dilemma. The rush to build the bomb: Can it be halted?
Newsweek   Jun 22, 1981   p. 20

Attack - and fallout. The target: Iraq's reactor.
Time   Jun 22, 1981   p. 24

IRAQ - DEFENSES

Saddam's bomb. The secrets of Iraq's nuclear weapons program.
U.S. News   Nov 25, 1991   p. 34

IRAQ - POLITICS AND GOVERNMENT

'Why won't he help us?' Exodus of the Kurds. Bush's dilemma.
Newsweek   Apr 15, 1991   p. 22

Saddam's latest victims. Can Bush avoid a human tragedy?
Time   Apr 15, 1991   p. 18

Saddam's revenge. Iraq's killing fields: Should the U.S. stop the slaughter?
U.S. News   Apr 15, 1991   p. 26

Revolt in Iraq. Bush keeps the pressure on.
Newsweek   Mar 25, 1991   p. 16

IRELAND

Ireland. Its long travail.
National Geographic Apr 1981   p. 432

Ireland. New spirit in the Ould Sod.
Time   Jul 12, 1963   p. 28

IRISH AMERICANS

Irish in America: Smiling-eyed beauty
Sheila Finn.
Life   Mar 17, 1961   p. 113

IRISH UNIFICATION QUESTION

Bleeding Ireland.
Newsweek   Apr 3, 1972   p. 32

Ireland: The tactics of terror.
Time   Jan 10, 1972   p. 30

IRS

See INTERNAL REVENUE SERVICE

IRVING, CLIFFORD

Con man of the year. Clifford Irving by
Elmyr de Hory.
Time   Feb 21, 1972   p. 12

Nina. The singing baroness in the Hughes
affair. Nina van Pallandt traveled with
Clifford Irving.
Life   Feb 11, 1972   p. 30

The Hughes affair. Clifford Irving says
Howard Hughes looks like this—but did
he ever see him?
Life   Feb 4, 1972   p. 32

IRVING, JOHN

Wrestling life into fable. Garp creator
John Irving strikes again.
Time   Aug 31, 1981   p. 46

ISLAM

Islam in ferment.
U.S. News   Dec 10, 1979   p. 27

Islam. The militant revival.
Time   Apr 16, 1979   p. 40

ISRAEL

A house divided. Israel's war with the
Palestinians and with itself.
U.S. News   Apr 4, 1988   p. 28

Troubled Israel. Military tensions.
Chaotic economy. Election showdown.
Time   May 18, 1981   p. 32

ISRAEL - HISTORY

Israel. 40 years of achievement. 40 years
of conflict.
Time   Apr 4, 1988   p. 36

ISRAEL - POLITICS AND GOVERNMENT

What next for Israel? Prime Minister
Yitzhak Shamir. Opposition leader
Shimon Peres.
Time   Jul 9, 1984   p. 28

Middle East: Toward the brink. Israel's
Golda Meir.
Time   Sep 19, 1969   p. 28

ISRAEL AND LEBANON

Israel strikes back.
Newsweek   Mar 27, 1978   p. 26

Peace: The chances now.
Time   Mar 27, 1978   p. 24

ISRAEL AND THE UNITED STATES

Begin digs in. A defiant "No" to Reagan's
peace plan.
Time   Sep 20, 1982   p. 24

Roadblock to peace? Israel's Menachem
Begin.
Newsweek   Sep 14, 1981   p. 36

The U.S. and Israel. Feeling the strain.
Newsweek   Oct 17, 1977   p. 26

Pushing toward Geneva. "The legitimate
rights of the Palestinian people must be
recognized." "We shall not negotiate for a
Palestinian state."
Time   Oct 17, 1977   p. 25

American Jews and Israel.
Time   Mar 10, 1975   p. 14

ISRAELI-ARAB RELATIONS

Israel. 40 years of achievement. 40 years
of conflict.
Time   Apr 4, 1988   p. 36

A house divided. Israel's war with the
Palestinians and with itself.
U.S. News   Apr 4, 1988   p. 28

Israel in torment. After the massacre: Can
Begin survive? The anguish of American
Jews.
Newsweek   Oct 4, 1982   p. 20

Deathtrap. Can the PLO survive? The
U.S. evacuation plan.
Newsweek   Jul 19, 1982   p. 14

A dangerous nuclear game. Israel's raid: The inside story. Impact on the Mideast. U.S. policy dilemma. The rush to build the bomb: Can it be halted?
Newsweek   Jun 22, 1981   p. 20

Attack - and fallout. The target: Iraq's reactor.
Time   Jun 22, 1981   p. 24

The Mideast in agony. Special report: How Israel got the bomb.
Time   Apr 12, 1976   p. 30

Mid-East massacres.
Time   May 27, 1974   p. 24

Facing the Middle East. When to use or not use power.
Time   Oct 5, 1970   p. 10

Showdown in Jordan. The Arab guerrillas.
Time   Sep 28, 1970   p. 16

Can the Mideast truce work?
Newsweek   Aug 17, 1970   p. 19

Middle East: Push for peace.
Time   Aug 10, 1970   p. 14

Israel and her enemies.
Time   Jun 22, 1970   p. 22

Palestinian Arabs: new pride and unity.
Life   Jun 12, 1970   p. 26

Russia in the Mideast.
Newsweek   Jun 1, 1970   p. 37

Deadlock in the Middle East. Egypt's Nasser.
Time   May 16, 1969   p. 29

The Arab commandos. Defiant new force in the Middle East.
Time   Dec 13, 1968   p. 29

Israel: The struggle to survive.
Time   Jun 9, 1967   p. 38

The Arabs vs. Israel.
Newsweek   Jun 5, 1967   p. 40

ISRAELI-ARAB WARS, 1967-

The guns of terror. The secret wars of the Middle East: No boundaries, no rules.
U.S. News   May 2, 1988   p. 30

Carter and the Jews.
Newsweek   Mar 20, 1978   p. 23

Man of the year. Anwar Sadat.
Time   Jan 2, 1978   p. 10

Pushing toward Geneva. "The legitimate rights of the Palestinian people must be recognized." "We shall not negotiate for a Palestinian state."
Time   Oct 17, 1977   p. 25

Israel: Day of the hawks. Menahem Begin.
Newsweek   May 30, 1977 p. 32

Israel. Trouble in the promised land. Menachem Begin.
Time   May 30, 1977 p. 22

The Mideast in agony. Special report: How Israel got the bomb.
Time   Apr 12, 1976   p. 30

Mid-East. Is peace at hand?
Time   Aug 25, 1975   p. 18

The Mideast erupts.
Newsweek   Oct 15, 1973   p. 38

War in the Middle East.
Time   Oct 15, 1973   p. 30

Wrap-up of the astounding war.
Life   Jun 23, 1967   p. 20

Victory in the desert. Israeli Defense Minister Moshe Dayan.
Newsweek   Jun 19, 1967   p. 24

Mideast unhinged—the Israeli onslaught.
Life   Jun 16, 1967   p. 26

How Israel won the war.
Time   Jun 16, 1967   p. 22

ISRAELI-ARAB WARS, 1967-PEACE AND MEDIATION

Deal with China. Deadlock with Israel.
Time   Dec 25, 1978   p. 16

Peace: The chances now.
Time   Mar 27, 1978   p. 24

Israel besieged. Premier Yitzhat Rabin.
Time   Dec 2, 1974   p. 43

Mideast miracle. Henry Kissinger.
Time   Jun 10, 1974   p. 34

ISRAELI-EGYPTIAN TREATY, 1979

Giving peace a chance. How Carter did it.
What's the cost? Will it work?
Newsweek   Mar 26, 1979   p. 28

Mideast peace. Its risks and rewards.
Time   Mar 26, 1979   p. 12

Carter's quest for peace.
Newsweek   Mar 19, 1979   p. 20

Carter's bold mission.
Time   Mar 19, 1979   p. 14

Carter's fateful move.
U.S. News   Mar 19, 1979   p. 20

ITALY - ANTIQUITIES

The dead do tell tales at Vesuvius.
National Geographic May 1984   p. 557

ITALY - INDUSTRIES

Italy: Industrialists as heroes. Fiat's
Giovanni Agnelli.
Time   Jan 17, 1969   p. 58

ITT

See INTERNATIONAL TELEPHONE
AND TELEGRAPH

IVORY TRADING

The ivory trail. From Africa to Asia, a
story of greed and slaughter.
Time   Oct 16, 1989   p. 66

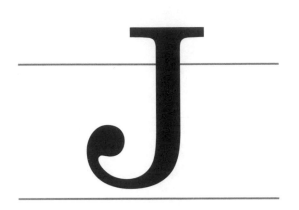

J

J.P. MORGAN & CO., INC.

Remaking J.P. Morgan. How it became the most profitable big bank in America.
Business Week   Dec 23, 1991   p. 64

JACKSON, HENRY "SCOOP"

Scoop out front. Democrat Henry Jackson.
Time   Feb 17, 1975   p. 11

JACKSON, JESSE

Can he win? The Democratic battle.
Newsweek   Apr 11, 1988   p. 22

Jesse!?
Time   Apr 11, 1988   p. 12

The power broker. What Jesse Jackson wants.
Newsweek   Mar 21, 1988   p. 18

Jesse Jackson. The man who would be king.
U.S. News   Nov 16, 1987   p. 34

What Jesse wants.
Newsweek   May 7, 1984   p. 40

The Jackson factor. Black pride, white concerns.
Time   May 7, 1984   p. 30

What makes Jesse run? Presidential candidate Jesse Jackson.
Newsweek   Nov 14, 1983   p. 50

Seeking votes and clout. A new black drive for political power. Jesse Jackson.
Time   Aug 22, 1983   p. 20

JACKSON, MICHAEL

Michael on stage & off. An exclusive 12-page photo album of the musical tour of the decade.
Life   Sep 1984   p. 87

The tour. The hype, the hysteria. Michael Jackson in Kansas City.
Newsweek   Jul 16, 1984   p. 64

Michael Jackson. Why he's a thriller. Inside his world.
Time   Mar 19, 1984   p. 54

JACKSON, REGGIE

One-man wild bunch. Oakland's Reggie Jackson.
Time   Jun 3, 1974   p. 62

JADE

Jade. Stone of heaven.
National Geographic Sep 1987   p. 282

JAGGER, MICK

The Stones are rolling again. Mick Jagger, Stones' leader.
Life   Jul 14, 1972   p. 30

JAPAN

Special edition: Japan 2000.
Omni   Jun 1985   p. 66

Japan. A nation in search of itself.
Time   Aug 1, 1983   p. 18

How Japan does it. The world's toughest competitor.
Time   Mar 30, 1981   p. 54

It's a tougher world for Japan.
Time   Oct 4, 1971   p. 34

Japan. Salesman to the world. Expo '70 in color.
Newsweek   Mar 9, 1970   p. 64

Japan shows off at Expo '70.
Time   Mar 2, 1970   p. 20

Island of stability in Asia. Japan's Premier Sato.
Time   Feb 10, 1967   p. 24

Special issue. Japan.
Life   Sep 11, 1964   p. 10

JAPAN - DEFENSES

Rearming Japan. Why the U.S. wants a
big buildup. The dangers of sharing
American technology.
Business Week   Mar 14, 1983   p. 106

JAPAN - ECONOMIC CONDITIONS

Hidden Japan. How the system really
works.
Business Week   Aug 26, 1991   p. 34

Japan. Can it cope? Suddenly, a series of
shocks is buffeting the mighty Japanese
economy. Japan has proved remarkably
adaptable to adversity in the past. This
time, it may be harder.
Business Week   Apr 23, 1990   p. 46

The Tokyo stock market and how it
affects you.
Business Week   Feb 12, 1990   p. 74

Japan. Remaking a nation. The new
export: Money. The power shift after
Nakasone. The rising service economy.
The coming social changes.
Business Week   Jul 13, 1987   p. 48

Will Japan really change? The rising yen
means Japan may not be able to live off
exports much longer. But will the nation
be able to remake its economy and
change social values?
Business Week   May 12, 1986 p. 46

Japan: Asia's first consumer market.
Industrialist Matsushita.
Time   Feb 23, 1962   p. 93

JAPAN - ECONOMIC POLICY

Japan's strategy for the '80s. To dominate
information processing requires
dominating semiconductors.
Business Week   Dec 14, 1981   p. 39

JAPAN - SOCIAL CONDITIONS

Japan. Remaking a nation. The new
export: Money. The power shift after
Nakasone. The rising service economy.
The coming social changes.
Business Week   Jul 13, 1987   p. 48

JAPAN - TECHNOLOGY

Japan's high-tech challenge.
Newsweek   Aug 9, 1982   p. 48

JAPAN AND THE UNITED STATES

Honda. Is it an American car? Most
Hondas sold in America are made in
America. But where do their parts really
come from?
Business Week   Nov 18, 1991   p. 104

The U.S. vs. Japan vs. Germany. Will
America lose out in the new global boom?
U.S. News   Jul 16, 1990   p. 22

What Japan thinks of us. A nation of
crybabies?
Newsweek   Apr 2, 1990   p. 18

The future of Silicon Valley. Do we need
a high-tech industrial policy?
Business Week   Feb 5, 1990   p. 54

Rethinking Japan. At a time of political
crisis in Japan, America's challenge is to
restore economic balance without
destroying our broader relationship.
Business Week   Aug 7, 1989   p. 44

Has the Orient totally conquered U.S.
electronics? Seven companies say no.
USA Today   Jan 1989   p. 16

Japan's influence in America. Its clout in
Washington. Its role at U.S. universities.
Its philanthropy and image-building.
Business Week   Jul 11, 1988   p. 64

Japan on Wall Street. Tokyo brokers
already dominate the government bond
market—and they're moving up fast in
corporate finance, stocks, and real estate.
Business Week   Sep 7, 1987   p. 82

How to beat the Japanese.
U.S. News   Aug 24, 1987   p. 38

Quality. To compete, U.S. companies
must boost product quality. That means
big changes in design, manufacturing—
and management thinking.
Business Week   Jun 8, 1987   p. 130

Quality. To compete, U.S. companies
must boost product quality. That means
big changes in design, manufacturing—
and management thinking.
Business Week   Jun 8, 1987   p. 130

Trade wars. The U.S. gets tough with
Japan.
Time   Apr 13, 1987   p. 28

Japan in America.
Business Week   Jul 14, 1986   p. 44

U.S. vs. Japan. Can American workers
win the battle?
U.S. News   Sep 2, 1985   p. 40

Fighting back. How some companies are
fending off Japanese competition—and
why others aren't trying.
Business Week   Aug 26, 1985   p. 62

Collision course. Can the U.S. avert a
trade war with Japan?
Business Week   Apr 8, 1985   p. 50

Rearming Japan. Why the U.S. wants a
big buildup. The dangers of sharing
American technology.
Business Week   Mar 14, 1983   p. 106

IQ: Are the Japanese really smarter?
Discover   Sep 1982   p. 18

High-technology gateway. Foreigners
demand a piece of NTT's $3 billion
market.
Business Week   Aug 9, 1982   p. 40

How to cope with Japan's business
invasion.
Time   May 10, 1971   p. 84

Japan: Cold War cockpit. U.S.
Ambassador Douglas MacArthur II.
Time   Jun 27, 1960   p. 10

Japan's Kishi.
Time   Jan 25, 1960   p. 24

JAPANESE
Your next boss may be Japanese.
Hundreds of thousands are already
working for Japan Inc.
Newsweek   Feb 2, 1987   p. 42

JARUZELSKI, WOJCIECH
Poland's ordeal. The darkness descends.
General Jaruzelski.
Time   Dec 28, 1981   p. 8

JAVITS, JACOB
Senator Jacob Javits.
Time   Jun 24, 1966   p. 25

JAWORSKI, LEON
Charging Nixon's men. Special
prosecutor Leon Jaworski.
Time   Mar 11, 1974   p. 11

JAZZ MUSIC
The new jazz age.
Time   Oct 22, 1990   p. 64

Jazz comes back!
Newsweek   Aug 8, 1977   p. 50

Jazz: Bebop and beyond. Jazzman
Thelonious Monk.
Time   Feb 28, 1964   p. 84

JEALOUSY
Jealousy. That very human emotion.
Psychology Today   Sep 1985   p. 22

JELLYFISH
The sea wasp, or box jelly—insubstantial,
toothless, and so diaphanous it barely
casts a shadow—is the most poisonous
sea creature known to man.
Discover   Aug 1987   p. 42

JENKINS, THOMAS
The war comes home. Lance Cpl.
Thomas Jenkins, 21, killed in action in
Saudi Arabia. A small town mourns its
first casualty.
Time   Feb 18, 1991   p. 14

JENKINS, WALTER - SCANDAL
The bomb; the overthrow; the squeaker;
the scandal.
Time   Oct 23, 1964   p. 19

JERUSALEM
Jerusalem. In the eye of the storm -
protest and prayer.
Time   Apr 12, 1982   p. 26

Easter in Jerusalem. Jarring contrast of
piety and tourism on Via Dolorosa.
Life   Mar 24, 1967   p. 50

JESUITS
The Jesuits. Catholicism's troubled front
line.
Time   Apr 23, 1973   p. 40

Jobs of the future. High tech. Where the best careers are. Executives. Who will be tomorrow's bosses? Schools. How they will train the new workers.
U.S. News   Dec 23, 1985   p. 40

Wanted! 20 million new jobs by 1990.
U.S. News   Sep 5, 1983   p. 22

Jobs. A million that will never come back.
U.S. News   Sep 13, 1982   p. 53

Jobs! Jobs! Jobs! Introducing a new career magazine for People.
Ms.   Sep 1982   p. 57

Where tomorrow's jobs will be.
U.S. News   Nov 13, 1978   p. 47

Challenge to U.S. 72,000 new jobs needed every week.
U.S. News   Jun 28, 1976   p. 20

Now where are the jobs? The graduate, 1971.
Time   May 24, 1971   p. 49

JOBS, STEVE

Steve Jobs. Can he do it again? The inside story of how his new company, Next, developed an innovative computer for universities.
Business Week   Oct 24, 1988   p. 74

Mr. Chips. Steve Jobs puts the 'wow' back in computers.
Newsweek   Oct 24, 1988   p. 46

Apple's dynamic duo and their plan to take on IBM in the office.
Business Week   Nov 26, 1984   p. 146

JOHN, ELTON

Rock's Captain Fantastic. Elton John.
Time   Jul 7, 1975   p. 36

JOHN F. KENNEDY CENTER FOR THE PERFORMING ARTS

JFK's memorial.
Newsweek   Sep 20, 1971   p. 22

Washington super ball. Gala party at the JFK Center.
Life   Jun 11, 1971   p. 26

JOHN PAUL I, POPE

The 34 days of John Paul I.
Newsweek   Oct 9, 1978   p. 70

The church in shock. John Paul I. 1912-1978.
Time   Oct 9, 1978   p. 68

Pope John Paul I.
Newsweek   Sep 4, 1978   p. 40

The new Pope. John Paul I.
Time   Sep 4, 1978   p. 60

JOHN PAUL II, POPE

John Paul. How he's changing the Church.
Newsweek   Sep 21, 1987   p. 22

Why forgive? The Pope pardons the gunman.
Time   Jan 9, 1984   p. 26

A Pope on the move.
U.S. News   Oct 8, 1979   p. 21

A Polish Pope. John Paul II
Newsweek   Oct 30, 1978   p. 78

John Paul II.
Time   Oct 30, 1978   p. 84

JOHN PAUL II, POPE - ASSASSINATION ATTEMPT

The plot to kill the Pope. The Bulgarian connection. Was the KGB behind it?
Newsweek   Jan 3, 1983   p. 22

Again.
Newsweek   May 25, 1981 p. 22

Terrorist's target. "Why did they do it?" - John Paul II
Time   May 25, 1981 p. 10

A crime that shocked the world.
U.S. News   May 25, 1981 p. 20

JOHN PAUL II, POPE - VISIT TO CENTRAL AMERICA, 1983

"To share the pain." The Pope in Central America.
Time   Mar 14, 1983 p. 34

JOHN PAUL II, POPE - VISIT TO GREAT BRITAIN, 1982

An extraordinary week. Furies in the Falklands. A Pope comes to Britain. Reagan girds for Europe.
Time   Jun 7, 1982   p. 6

JOHN PAUL II, POPE - VISIT TO POLAND, 1979

Triumphal return. The Pope in Poland.
Time   Jun 18, 1979   p. 26

JOHN PAUL II, POPE - VISIT TO POLAND, 1983

Prayer and defiance. The Pope's challenge to Warsaw.
Newsweek   Jun 27, 1983   p. 38

Homecoming. The return of the Polish Pope.
Time   Jun 27, 1983   p. 28

Mission to Poland. The Pope's dramatic pilgrimage.
Newsweek   Jun 20, 1983   p. 36

JOHN PAUL II, POPE - VISIT TO THE UNITED STATES, 1979

John Paul's triumph.
Newsweek   Oct 15, 1979   p. 38

John Paul, superstar. Special: An album of his journey.
Time   Oct 15, 1979   p. 12

The Pope's historic visit.
Newsweek   Oct 8, 1979   p. 36

The Pope is coming our way. An exuberant John Paul II.
Life   Sep 1979   p. 45

JOHN XXIII, POPE

An artist's memoir of the saintly Pope John. The story of a remarkable friendship.
Life   Oct 11, 1968   p. 52

Great princes of the church: Among them, the next Pope.
Life   Jun 14, 1963   p. 26

Pope John XXIII.
Newsweek   Jun 10, 1963   p. 42

Pope John XXIII.
Life   Jun 7, 1963   p. 78

John XXIII: The last picture.
Time   Jun 7, 1963   p. 41

Man of the year. John XXIII.
Time   Jan 4, 1963   p. 50

Pope John XXIII. As Catholic prelates assemble in Rome, the moving story of a humble man.
Life   Oct 12, 1962   p. 74

The condition of Catholicism. Pope John.
Time   Oct 5, 1962   p. 80

JOHNS, JASPER

Super artist. Jasper Johns.
Newsweek   Oct 24, 1977   p. 66

JOHNSON, DON

Starting over. Melanie Griffith & Don Johnson tell their love story.
Life   Apr 1989   p. 50

JOHNSON, FRANK

The law and dissent. Federal Judge Frank Johnson.
Time   May 12, 1967   p. 72

JOHNSON & JOHNSON

Changing a corporate culture. Can J&J move from band-aids to high tech?
Business Week   May 14, 1984   p. 130

JOHNSON, KEITH

"The battlefield is a lonely place." General Johnson. Army Chief of Staff.
Time   Dec 10, 1965   p. 30

JOHNSON, LADY BIRD

Lady Bird Johnson writes about her private world.
Life   Aug 13, 1965   p. 56

The First Lady.
Newsweek   Dec 28, 1964   p. 11

Lady Bird Johnson.
Time   Aug 28, 1964   p. 20

JOHNSON, LUCI BAINES

Luci's wedding.
Life   Aug 19, 1966   p. 20

White House wedding.
Newsweek   Aug 15, 1966   p. 17

Getting married in public. Pat & Luci.
Time   Aug 5, 1966   p. 19

The Johnson girls.
Newsweek   May 23, 1966   p. 36

Luci Baines Johnson. Teen-ager in the White House.
Life   May 15, 1964   p. 90

JOHNSON, LYNDA

The Johnson girls.
Newsweek   May 23, 1966   p. 36

JOHNSON, LYNDON B.

L.B.J. back home.
Life   May 21, 1971   p. 44

Johnson and the Kennedys. Why LBJ was really picked. How the Kennedys managed him. LBJs feud with Bobby.
Life   Aug 7, 1970   p. 44

President Johnson.
Time   Apr 12, 1968   p. 22

Man of the year. L.B.J. as Lear.
Time   Jan 5, 1968   p. 13

LBJ in trouble.
Newsweek   Sep 4, 1967   p. 17

President Johnson.
Time   Nov 4, 1966   p. 25

The President's operation.
Newsweek   Oct 18, 1965   p. 65

War and the Great Society. How the people feel about Johnson. President Johnson.
Time   Aug 6, 1965   p. 18

The politics of power.
Newsweek   Aug 2, 1965   p. 18

Man of the year. President Johnson.
Time   Jan 1, 1965   p. 14

Election extra.
Time   Nov 4, 1964   p. 5

President Johnson.
Newsweek   Aug 31, 1964   p. 15

The complex and extraordinary man who is the President. In two articles, an intimate and revealing portrait.
Life   Aug 14, 1964   p. 24

The whirlwind President. At garden press conference.
Time   May 1, 1964   p. 17

President Johnson at his White House desk.
Life   Dec 13, 1963   p. 26

President Johnson.
Newsweek   Dec 9, 1963   p. 19

President Johnson.
Time   Nov 29, 1963   p. 21

Veep-to-be. The ambassador or the senator?
Newsweek   Oct 31, 1960   p. 23

Johnson of Texas. Can he swing the South?
Newsweek   Aug 15, 1960   p. 18

Democrats in Los Angeles. Battle in the stretch. Lyndon Johnson.
Time   Jul 18, 1960   p. 9

Lyndon Baines Johnson.
Time   Apr 25, 1960   p. 20

The decisive hours of Lyndon Johnson.
Newsweek   Mar 14, 1960   p. 28

JOHNSON, LYNDON B. (FAMILY)

A rare photo for the President's album. In Luci's hospital room the proud grandfather meets Patrick Lyndon Nugent.
Life   Jul 7, 1967   p. 47

JOHNSON, LYNDON B. - INAUGURATION

Inaugural spectacle.
Life   Jan 29, 1965   p. 24

JOHNSON, LYNDON B. - PETS

Her and him. The President's dogs on the lawn of their house.
Life   Jun 19, 1964   p. 68

JOHNSON, LYNDON B. - RELATIONS WITH CONGRESS

LBJ's problem Congress. Republican leaders Ford and Dirksen.
Newsweek   Jan 23, 1967   p. 22

JOHNSON, LYNDON B. - STAFF

The power in the Pentagon. Defense Secretary McNamara with Joint Chief of Staff.
Newsweek   Dec 6, 1965   p. 30

American foreign policy. Drift or design.
Newsweek   May 17, 1965   p. 27

Inside the White House.
Newsweek   Mar 1, 1965   p. 27

JOHNSON, LYNDON B. - STATE OF THE UNION MESSAGE

The state of LBJ.
Newsweek   Jan 29, 1968   p. 16

The state of the Union. President Johnson.
Newsweek   Jan 11, 1965   p. 15

JOHNSON, LYNDON B. - VISIT TO ASIA, 1966

The President's trip.
Life   Nov 4, 1966   p. 24

JOHNSON, MAGIC

'Even me'—Magic Johnson.
Newsweek   Nov 18, 1991   p. 58

JOHNSON, NED

Fidelity fights back. Can Ned Johnson revive the giant of the mutual fund industry?
Business Week   Apr 17, 1989   p. 68

JOHNSON, RAFER

The Olympics. U.S. decathlon star Rafer Johnson.
Time   Aug 29, 1960   p. 52

JOHNSON, SONIA

The woman who talked back to God. Sonia Johnson's own story: "*From Housewife to Heretic.*"
Ms.   Nov 1981   p. 51

JOINT VENTURES

Odd couples. Strategic alliances, joint ventures...whatever you call them, these corporate combinations are growing fast. They can work wonders. But more often they don't. Here's why.
Business Week   Jul 21, 1986   p. 100

JONATHAN LIVINGSTON SEAGULL (FICTIONAL CHARACTER)

Getting away from it all with Jonathan Livingston Seagull.
Time   Nov 13, 1972   p. 60

JONES, JAMES EARL

New star on Broadway. James Earl Jones.
Newsweek   Oct 21, 1968   p. 66

JONES, JIM

The cult of death.
Newsweek   Dec 4, 1978   p. 38

Cult of death.
Time   Dec 4, 1978   p. 16

JONES, TOM

The aerospace industry.
Time   Oct 27, 1961   p. 89

JONESTOWN, GUYANA, MASS DEATHS, 1978

The cult of death.
Newsweek   Dec 4, 1978   p. 38

Cult of death.
Time   Dec 4, 1978   p. 16

JOPLIN, JANIS

Janis Joplin. Rebirth of the blues.
Newsweek   May 26, 1969   p. 82

JORDAN

Explosion in Jordan.
Newsweek   Sep 28, 1970   p. 35

Showdown in Jordan. The Arab guerrillas.
Time   Sep 28, 1970   p. 16

JORDAN, WILLIAM HAMILTON

The President's boys. Jody Powell. Hamilton Jordan.
Time   Jun 6, 1977   p. 26

JOURNALISTIC ETHICS

Poison Pen. Kitty vs. Nancy. The boom in trash biography.
Newsweek   Apr 22, 1991   p. 52

Is she that bad? What's true–and not true–in Kitty Kelley's slasher biography of Nancy Reagan.
Time   Apr 22, 1991   p. 64

JOURNALISTS

Those Washington columnists.
Newsweek   Dec 18, 1961   p. 65

JOYNER-KERSEE, JACKIE

Gold rush! The magnificent Joyners take Seoul by storm.
Ms.   Oct 1988   p. 30

JUAN CARLOS I, KING OF SPAIN

Spain after Franco.
Time   Nov 3, 1975   p. 25

Prince Juan Carlos weds his princess.
Life   May 25, 1962 p. 26

JUDGES

Judging the judges. An outsize job - and getting bigger.
Time   Aug 20, 1979   p. 48

The power of our judges – Are they going too far?
U.S. News   Jan 19, 1976   p. 29

Why courts are in trouble.
U.S. News   Mar 31, 1975   p. 28

JUNK BONDS

After Drexel. Now, Drexel is on the ropes, junk-bond king Michael Milken is under indictment, and the junk market is in turmoil. The impact will be felt for years to come.
Business Week   Feb 26, 1990   p. 36

Crunch time! No recession. Lower interest rates. So why are so many highly leveraged companies suddenly in trouble?
Business Week   Sep 11, 1989   p. 84

JURY

You the jury. Can you trust an eyewitness? Hypnosis: How reliable is it? Law and language.
Psychology Today   Feb 1984   p. 22

We, the jury. That irksome, boring, vital, rewarding experience.
Time   Sep 28, 1981   p. 44

JUSTICE

Justice on trial.
Newsweek   Mar 8, 1971   p. 16

JUSTICE, ADMINISTRATION OF

Justice under Reagan. New agenda: Ed Meese pushes his program. New judges: An enduring impact. New crackdown: More criminals behind bars longer.
U.S. News   Oct 14, 1985   p. 58

American justice. ABC's of how it really works.
U.S. News   Nov 1, 1982   p. 35

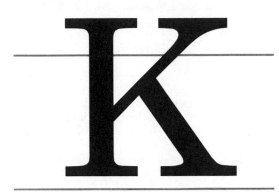

KADDAFI
See QADDAFI, MUAMMAR AL-

KAPPEL, FRED
The world's biggest company. A.T. & T. chairman Kappel.
Time   May 29, 1964   p. 74

KAYE, DANNY
Danny Kaye: The entertainer.
Newsweek   Dec 23, 1963   p. 43

KEATING, KEN
Keating vs. Kennedy.
Newsweek   Oct 12, 1964   p. 35

KEATON, DIANE
The Keaton charm. Diane Keaton.
Newsweek   Feb 15, 1982   p. 54

Diane Keaton. Annie Hall meets Mr. Goodbar.
Time   Sep 26, 1977   p. 68

KEILLOR, GARRISON
Garrison Keillor's Fourth of July. Plus: America's unsung heroes.
Newsweek   Jul 4, 1988   p. 30

Heartland humor. Let's hear it for Lake Wobegon. Author and radio bard Garrison Keillor.
Time   Nov 4, 1985   p. 68

KELLEY, KITTY
Poison Pen. Kitty vs. Nancy. The boom in trash biography.
Newsweek   Apr 22, 1991   p. 52

Is she that bad? What's true–and not true–in Kitty Kelley's slasher biography of Nancy Reagan.
Time   Apr 22, 1991   p. 64

KELLY, GRACE
See GRACE, PRINCESS OF MONACO

KEMPER, JOHN M.
Excellence & intensity in U.S. prep schools. Andover's John M. Kemper.
Time   Oct 26, 1962   p. 76

KENNECOTT CORP.
Survival in the basic industries. How four companies hope to avoid disaster: Firestone. Kennecott. Inland Steel. Boise Cascade.
Business Week   Apr 26, 1982   p. 74

KENNEDY, CAROLINE
On her pony Macaroni: The fun of being Caroline Kennedy.
Life   Sep 7, 1962   p. 32

Caroline in the White House.
Newsweek   May 15, 1961   p. 65

KENNEDY CENTER
See JOHN F. KENNEDY CENTER FOR THE PERFORMING ARTS

KENNEDY, EDWARD M.
The Kennedy challenge.
Time   Nov 5, 1979   p. 14

Carter and Kennedy head for a showdown.
Life   Nov 1979   p. 28

Teddy chips away.
Newsweek   Sep 24, 1979   p. 28

Why Kennedy legend lives on.
U.S. News   Jul 23, 1979   p. 29

Teddy comes on strong. The battle over health care.
Newsweek   May 28, 1979   p. 26

Ready for Teddy?
Newsweek   Jun 2, 1975   p. 19

Ford. How he rates now. Kennedy.
Democrats' choice after all?
U.S. News   Apr 28, 1975   p. 25

Could he win in '72? Ted Kennedy.
Time   Nov 29, 1971   p. 16

The fateful turn for Ted Kennedy. Grave
questions about his midnight car accident.
Life   Aug 1, 1969   p. 16

Teddy cracks the whip.
Newsweek   Jan 13, 1969   p. 13

The Democrats regroup. Senator Edward
Kennedy.
Time   Jan 10, 1969   p. 13

Can Teddy stay out? Senator Edward M.
Kennedy.
Newsweek   Aug 5, 1968   p. 13

Congress: Consensus or conflict? The
Senators Kennedy.
Newsweek   Jan 17, 1966   p. 17

As Congress opens: Ted Kennedy's
recovery. Wearing brace, the Senator
takes swimming pool therapy for his back.
Life   Jan 15, 1965   p. 28

Teddy Kennedy.
Time   Sep 28, 1962   p. 14

The Senate seat scramble in
Massachusetts. Head-on collision of three
political clans. Eddie McCormick. Teddie
Kennedy. George Lodge.
Life   Jun 29, 1962   p. 59

**KENNEDY, EDWARD M. -
ACCIDENT, 1969**

The Kennedy debacle: A girl dead, a
career in jeopardy. Edward Kennedy
after funeral.
Time   Aug 1, 1969   p. 11

'Should I resign?' Senator Kennedy.
Newsweek   Aug 4, 1969   p. 22

KENNEDY, ETHEL

Ethel Kennedy.
Time   Apr 25, 1969   p. 46

KENNEDY, GERALD

The Methodist church. A concern for
religious relevance. Bishop Gerald
Kennedy.
Time   May 8, 1964   p. 74

KENNEDY, JACQUELINE

See ONASSIS, JACQUELINE KENNEDY

KENNEDY, JOHN F.

25 years later. JFK's vision and what has
come of it.
U.S. News   Oct 24, 1988   p. 30

What JFK meant to us. 30 Americans
reflect on the man, the myth, the legacy.
Newsweek   Nov 28, 1983   p. 60

J.F.K. How good a President was he?
Time   Nov 14, 1983   p. 58

Johnson and the Kennedys. Why LBJ
was really picked. How the Kennedys
managed him. LBJs feud with Bobby.
Life   Aug 7, 1970   p. 44

A Thousand Days. The historian resumes
his Kennedy narrative. Part 4: Life in the
White House. How 'White Housitis'
affected J.F.K., his family and his friends.
Life   Nov 5, 1965   p. 84

A Thousand Days. First portrait of
Kennedy by a member of his team.
Life   Jul 16, 1965   p. 28

Jacqueline Kennedy. She writes about
her husband's mementos—the ones he
liked most.
Life   May 29, 1964   p. 32

Mrs. Kennedy, Caroline, and John Jr. wait
to join procession to capitol [funeral of
John F. Kennedy].
Life   Dec 6, 1963   p. 38

Walter Lippmann on Kennedy.
Newsweek   Jan 21, 1963   p. 24

Kennedy and his critics.
Newsweek   Jul 16, 1962   p. 15

Man of the year. John F. Kennedy.
Time   Jan 5, 1962   p. 9

'Any dangerous spot is tenable if brave
men will make it so.'
Life   Aug 4, 1961   p. 34

Kennedy in Paris.
Life   Jun 9, 1961   p. 42

The Kennedys in Canada.
Life   May 26, 1961   p. 16

The inauguration of John Fitzgerald
Kennedy.
Time   Jan 27, 1961   p. 8

"New Frontier" - special section.
Newsweek   Jan 23, 1961   p. 15

The Kennedys and their son at
christening.
Life   Dec 19, 1960   p. 29

The victorious young Kennedys.
Life   Nov 21, 1960   p. 32

Candidate Kennedy.
Time   Nov 7, 1960   p. 26

The Kennedy strategy. Campaign
manager Bobby Kennedy.
Time   Oct 10, 1960   p. 21

The demonstration for Jack Kennedy.
Life   Jul 25, 1960   p. 18

Democrats in Los Angeles. Battle in the
stretch. Lyndon Johnson.
Time   Jul 18, 1960   p. 9

The Kennedy family.
Time   Jul 11, 1960   p. 19

Can anybody stop Kennedy? The experts
answer - A 50-state listening post.
Newsweek   Jul 4, 1960   p. 18

Hubert and Jack in Wisconsin.
Life   Mar 28, 1960   p. 22

Humphrey and Kennedy. Wisconsin -
who'll tumble?
Newsweek   Mar 28, 1960   p. 29

KENNEDY, JOHN F. - ASSASSINATION

JFK. Why we still care. A new movie
about the assassination reopens an old
controversy.
Life   Dec 1991   p. 34

J.F.K.'s assassination: Who was the real
target. Twenty-five years later, a new
book argues Oswald was actually out to
get John Connally.
Time   Nov 28, 1988   p. 30

The Kennedy assassination: 4 days that
stopped America.
Life   Nov 1983   p. 48

Why Kennedy went to Texas. A
contribution to history. Governor
Connally sets the record straight on the
fateful visit.
Life   Nov 24, 1967   p. 86

A matter of reasonable doubt. Did
Oswald act alone? Amid controversy
over the Warren Report Governor
Connally examines for LIFE the Kennedy
assassination film frame by frame.
Life   Nov 25, 1966   p. 38

The assassination. The Warren
Commission report.
Newsweek   Oct 5, 1964   p. 32

The Warren report. How the commission
pieced together the evidence. Told by
one of its members.
Life   Oct 2, 1964   p. 40

The Warren Commission: No conspiracy,
domestic or foreign. Lee Harvey Oswald.
Time   Oct 2, 1964   p. 45

Lee Oswald with the weapons he used to
kill President Kennedy and Officer Tippit.
Life   Feb 21, 1964   p. 68

The Warren Commission. Probing
Kennedy's death.
Time   Feb 14, 1964   p. 16

President Johnson.
Newsweek   Dec 9, 1963   p. 19

John Fitzgerald Kennedy. 1917 - 1963.
Newsweek   Dec 2, 1963   p. 20

President John F. Kennedy. 1917-1963.
Life   Nov 29, 1963   p. 22

President Johnson.
Time   Nov 29, 1963   p. 21

KENNEDY, ROSE

An intimate visit with Rose Kennedy at 80.
Life   Jul 17, 1970   p. 20

KENNEDY, TED

See KENNEDY, EDWARD M.

KENT STATE UNIVERSITY - RIOT (MAY 4, 1970)

Nixon's home front.
Newsweek   May 18, 1970 p. 26

Protest!
Time   May 18, 1970 p. 6

Crisis for Nixon.
Life   May 15, 1970 p. 28

KENYA

Kenya's Kenyatta. From Mau Mau to statehood.
Newsweek   Dec 16, 1963   p. 36

Kenya's Tom Mboya.
Time   Mar 7, 1960   p. 22

KENYATTA, JOMO

Kenya's Kenyatta. From Mau Mau to statehood.
Newsweek   Dec 16, 1963   p. 36

KEPPEL, FRANK

"Education is too important to be left solely to the educators." Commissioner Keppel.
Time   Oct 15, 1965   p. 60

KERR, CLARK

University of California's Clark Kerr.
Time   Oct 17, 1960   p. 58

KERR, JEAN

Playwright Jean Kerr.
Time   Apr 14, 1961   p. 82

KEYNES, JOHN MAYNARD

Business in 1965: The Keynesian influence on the expansionist economy. John Maynard Keynes.
Time   Dec 31, 1965   p. 64

KEYS, ANCEL

Diet & health.
Time   Jan 13, 1961   p. 48

KGB

The KGB today. Andropov's eyes on the world.
Time   Feb 14, 1983   p. 30

The KGB in America.
Newsweek   Nov 23, 1981   p. 50

KHANH, NGUYEN

See NGUYEN KHANH

KHMER ROUGE

The temples of Angkor. Will they survive?
National Geographic May 1982   p. 548

KHOMEINI, RUHOLLAH

'Satanic' fury. Putting a price on the head of Salman Rushdie.
Newsweek   Feb 27, 1989   p. 34

The Ayatullah orders a hit. He causes an uproar by sentencing author Salman Rushdie to death for his book *The Satanic Verses*.
Time   Feb 27, 1989   p. 28

Man of the year. Ayatullah Khomeini.
Time   Jan 7, 1980   p. 8

Iran: Anarchy and exodus.
Time   Feb 26, 1979   p. 26

Iran's mystery man. Ayatollah Khomeini.
Newsweek   Feb 12, 1979   p. 42

Iran: Now the power play. Ayatullah Khomeini.
Time   Feb 12, 1979   p. 32

KHRUSHCHEV, NIKITA S.

Khrushchev remembers World War II. The great battles. His fear of execution. Stalin's cowardice.
Life   Dec 4, 1970   p. 48

Khrushchev remembers. An extraordinary first-person story begins this week. Part I: The terror of life with Stalin.
Life   Nov 27, 1970   p. 30

Brezhnev. Shake-up in the Kremlin.
Newsweek   Oct 26, 1964   p. 45

Khrushchev at the crossroads.
Newsweek   Jul 22, 1963   p. 29

Shooting to kill. The Soviets destroy an airliner.
Time   Sep 12, 1983   p. 10

Trigger-happy Soviets. A jolt to relations with U.S.
U.S. News   Sep 12, 1983   p. 22

KOREAN WAR, 1950-1953

The forgotten war. 40 years after Korea.
U.S. News   Jun 25, 1990   p. 30

KOSYGIN, ALEKSEI

Premier Kosygin. A candid and chilling talk with Life's editors. Vietnam. The Mideast. State of the Soviet Union.
Life   Feb 2, 1968   p. 21

Take-over in the Kremlin. Russia's new leader Leonid Brezhnev.
Life   Oct 23, 1964   p. 30

KOUFAX, SANDY

The mostest pitcher: Most wins, most shutouts, most strike-outs. The Dodgers' Sandy Koufax.
Life   Aug 2, 1963   p. 54

KRAVIS, HENRY

King Henry. Is KKR's Henry Kravis headed for a fall?
Business Week   Nov 14, 1988   p. 124

KRISHNA MENON, V. K.

Elections in India. Krishna Menon.
Time   Feb 2, 1962   p. 16

KU KLUX KLAN

Courtroom pictures of the Klan murder trial.
Life   May 21, 1965   p. 32

KUBRICK, STANLEY

Kubrick's grandest gamble. Marisa Berenson in "Barry Lyndon."
Time   Dec 15, 1975   p. 72

From '2001' to 'A Clockwork Orange.' The startling vision of Stanley Kubrick.
Newsweek   Jan 3, 1972   p. 28

KURDS

'Why won't he help us?' Exodus of the Kurds. Bush's dilemma.
Newsweek   Apr 15, 1991   p. 22

Saddam's latest victims. Can Bush avoid a human tragedy?
Time   Apr 15, 1991   p. 18

Saddam's revenge. Iraq's killing fields: Should the U.S. stop the slaughter?
U.S. News   Apr 15, 1991   p. 26

KUWAIT

Was it worth it? The mess in Kuwait. Saddam's staying power. A rocky road to Mideast peace.
Time   Aug 5, 1991   p. 32

What is Kuwait? And is it worth dying for?
Time   Dec 24, 1990   p. 26

KUWAIT-IRAQI INVASION, 1990 - AMERICAN INVOLVEMENT

What is Kuwait? And is it worth dying for?
Time   Dec 24, 1990   p. 26

With the cavalry. Desert Shield exclusive. And with the families back home.
U.S. News   Dec 24, 1990   p. 28

"This will not be another Vietnam." A deadline for diplomacy. And a plan for all-out war.
Newsweek   Dec 10, 1990   p. 24

What war would be like.
Time   Dec 10, 1990   p. 26

Should we fight? Americans take sides. "Why We Must Break Saddam's Stranglehold" by President Bush.
Newsweek   Nov 26, 1990   p. 26

Letters in the sand. In millions of letters our soldiers tell their story.
Newsweek   Nov 19, 1990   p. 22

Ready for war. Pentagon partners Dick Cheney and Colin Powell have the troops in place. Now they're waiting for the word.
Time   Nov 12, 1990   p. 24

The case against war. The case for war. The Gulf Crisis. How will Bush decide?
Newsweek   Oct 29, 1990   p. 22

Top guns. What America's military commanders think about waging war.
U.S. News   Oct 1, 1990   p. 28

Under the gun. Saudi anxieties. Bush's resolve. The quick-strike option.
Time   Sep 24, 1990   p. 32

Women warriors. Sharing the danger.
Newsweek   Sep 10, 1990   p. 14

Desert warriors. How the Gulf is testing the new U.S military. The diplomatic moves to contain Saddam Hussein.
U.S. News   Sep 10, 1990   p. 26

Horror show. Saddam's prisoners of war.
Newsweek   Sep 3, 1990   p. 15

Are we ready for this?
Time   Sep 3, 1990   p. 24

Talk of war. Saddam's foreign pawns. Bush's massive buildup. Diplomacy's last chance.
Time   Aug 27, 1990   p. 14

Showdown. Can Bush make Saddam blink?
Time   Aug 20, 1990   p. 18

Target Iraq. Is air power enough? Facing the chemical-weapons threat.
U.S. News   Aug 20, 1990   p. 18

What America can do about Iraq. The military options. The new oil crisis.
U.S. News   Aug 13, 1990   p. 20

KUWAIT-IRAQI INVASION, 1990-1991

The path to war. 'We'll win, but why rush?'
Newsweek   Jan 21, 1991   p. 14

January 15. Deadline for war.
Time   Jan 21, 1991   p. 22

Showdown. The Gulf crisis. Last-ditch diplomacy. What war won't solve.
U.S. News   Jan 21, 1991   p. 18

Saddam's endgame. More than just a madman.
Newsweek   Jan 7, 1991   p. 14

The Moscow connection. On the day before the Iraqi invasion, the Kremlin got a CIA alert that the attack was imminent... The inside story of secret diplomacy between the superpowers.
Newsweek   Sep 17, 1990   p. 20

Playing cat and mouse. Saddam sends mixed signals while Bush holds firm. Does diplomacy stand a chance?
Time   Sep 10, 1990   p. 20

Flash point. With Iraq holding Westerners hostage, the Mideast crisis escalates.
Business Week   Sep 3, 1990   p. 26

Will it be war?
Newsweek   Aug 27, 1990   p. 18

Drawing the line.
Newsweek   Aug 20, 1990   p. 18

Baghdad's bully. Can he be stopped? The war of the future. Oil shocks ahead.
Newsweek   Aug 13, 1990   p. 16

Iraq on the march.
Time   Aug 13, 1990   p. 16

KWAN, NANCY

Nancy Kwan: A new star as Suzie Wong.
Life   Oct 24, 1960   p. 55

KY, NGUYEN CAO

See NGUYEN CAO KY

LABOR

A revolution in work rules. New job flexibility boosts productivity.
Business Week   May 16, 1983   p. 100

New breed of workers. Prosperous. Restless. Demanding.
U.S. News   Sep 3, 1979   p. 35

Blue collar power.
Time   Nov 9, 1970   p. 68

LABOR CONTRACTS - COAL INDUSTRY

Coal. Will the deal stick?
Newsweek   Mar 6, 1978   p. 22

LABOR PRODUCTIVITY

The productivity paradox. Can America compete? American manufacturers have boosted productivity for several years now, largely by closing old plants and laying off workers. But the U.S. still lags behind Japan and other countries in productivity growth.
Business Week   Jun 6, 1988   p. 100

Can America compete? The U.S. economy has been sluggish for years, despite lots of fiscal and monetary stimulus. Now, faced with the urgent need to reduce its budget and trade deficits, America may well see its enviable standard of living decline.
Business Week   Apr 20, 1987   p. 44

The revival of productivity.
Business Week   Feb 13, 1984   p. 92

The productivity crisis. Can America renew its economic promise?
Newsweek   Sep 8, 1980   p. 50

LABOR SUPPLY

Help wanted. The coming labor shortage.
Business Week   Aug 10, 1987   p. 48

LABOR UNIONS

Striker replacement legislation.
Congressional Digest Nov 1991   p. 259

Beyond unions. It's no secret that labor unions are losing power. But that doesn't mean companies will ride roughshod over workers.
Business Week   Jul 8, 1985   p. 72

Why unions are running scared.
U.S. News   Sep 10, 1984   p. 62

Concessionary bargaining. Will the new cooperation last?
Business Week   Jun 14, 1982   p. 66

Labor seeks less. Trouble in the economy blunts the union's demands.
Business Week   Dec 21, 1981   p. 82

Unions on the run.
U.S. News   Sep 14, 1981   p. 61

Union corruption. Worse than ever.
U.S.News   Sep 8, 1980   p. 33

Fight over the freeze. AFL-CIO's George Meany.
Newsweek   Sep 6, 1971   p. 46

Labor in the freeze.
Time   Sep 6, 1971   p. 9

Strike fever and the public interest. Planes grounded, people stranded. Distinguished newspaper killed. Labor leaders in a dilemma. Rampant new militancy.
Life   Aug 26, 1966   p. 24

The great featherbedding fight.
Time   Jul 26, 1963   p. 13

Is labor's only weapon a monkey wrench?
Time   Mar 1, 1963   p. 13

Labor & the new frontier.
Time   Sep 22, 1961   p. 21

"I shall continue to be disatisfied..." -
Walter Reuther, Auto Workers' Chief.
Newsweek   Sep 4, 1961   p. 51

Hoffa of the teamsters: Driving for more
power.
Newsweek   Jul 10, 1961   p. 57

LABRECQUE, THOMAS

Agony at Chase. The once-mighty bank of
the Rockefellers is in deep trouble. Can
incoming CEO Tom Labrecque keep
Chase Manhattan independent?
Business Week   Oct 8, 1990   p. 32

LAETRILE

Laetrile and cancer. Should the drug be
banned?
Newsweek   Jun 27, 1977   p. 48

LAIRD, MELVIN R.

Shaking up the Pentagon. Defense
Secretary Laird.
Time   Aug 29, 1969   p. 13

LAKONIA (SHIP)

Fire at sea. Exclusive pictures of the
Lakonia Disaster.
Life   Jan 3, 1964   p. 10

LANCE, THOMAS BERTRAM

The Lance affair. What damage to Carter?
Newsweek   Sep 19, 1977   p. 24

The Lance affair. What it cost Carter.
Time   Sep 19, 1977   p. 6

The Lance report. Is he home free?
Newsweek   Aug 29, 1977   p. 16

LAND, EDWIN

A genius and his magic camera. Dr.
Edwin Land of Polaroid demonstrates his
new invention.
Life   Oct 27, 1972   p. 42

LANDON, MICHAEL

'If I'm gonna die, death's gonna have to
fight to get me.' Facing the battle of his
life, Michael Landon, in an exclusive
interview, talks about hope, fear, family
and the power of love.
Life   Jun 1991   p. 24

LANDSBURY, ANGELA

Auntie Mame's newest exploit a musical
smash.
Life   Jun 17, 1966   p. 88

LANGUAGE AND LANGUAGES

Thought police. Watch what you say.
There's a 'Politically Correct' way to talk
about race, sex and ideas. Is this the new
enlightenment – or the new
McCarthyism?
Newsweek   Dec 24, 1990   p. 48

The roots of language. How modern
speech evolved from a single, ancient
source.
U.S. News   Nov 5, 1990   p. 60

LAOS AND THE UNITED STATES

The U.S. & Laos. In the jungle of
neutralism. General Kong Le.
Time   Jun 26, 1964   p. 24

Laos: Test of U.S. intentions.
Time   Mar 17, 1961   p. 20

LARAGH, JOHN

Hypertension. Conquering the quiet killer.
Time   Jan 13, 1975   p. 60

LASERS

The laser: "A splendid light" for man's
use.
National Geographic Mar 1984   p. 335

LASERS - MEDICAL USE

Laser medicine. Healing with light.
Life   May 1982   p. 129

Lasers in surgery: The light that heals.
Discover   Jul 1981   p. 14

LASSER, LOUISE

TV's new craze. Mary Hartman.
Newsweek   May 3, 1976   p. 54

LAST SUPPER IN ART

The Last Supper. Restoration reveals
Leonardo's masterpiece
National Geographic Nov 1983   p. 664

**LATIN AMERICA - POLITICS AND
GOVERNMENT**

Latin America: The promise and the
threat. Venezuela's President Leoni.
Newsweek   Mar 30, 1964   p. 34

The crisis in our hemisphere. Part I:
Exclusive photo report shows how Castro
and the Communists are working to seize
Latin America.
Life   Jun 2, 1961   p. 81

LATIN AMERICA AND THE UNITED STATES

Latin America: The promise and the
threat. Venezuela's President Leoni.
Newsweek   Mar 30, 1964   p. 34

The U.S. & Latin America. State
Department's Thomas Mann.
Time   Jan 31, 1964   p. 15

The crisis in our hemisphere. Part I:
Exclusive photo report shows how Castro
and the Communists are working to seize
Latin America.
Life   Jun 2, 1961   p. 81

LATVIA - NATIONALISM

The Baltic nations. Estonia, Latvia, and
Lithuania struggle toward independence.
National Geographic Nov 1990   p. 2

LAUPER, CYNDI

Cyndi Lauper. Is she still having fun?
Ms.   Aug 1988   p. 57

LAUREN, RALPH

Selling that sporty look. Polo's Ralph
Lauren.
Time   Sep 1, 1986   p. 54

LAWSUITS

How to alleviate the glut of lawsuits.
USA Today   Jul 1988   p. 30

What damage claims cost you. Liability
lawsuits out of control?
U.S. News   Jan 27, 1986   p. 35

"See you in court." Our suing society.
U.S. News   Dec 20, 1982   p. 58

Why everybody is suing everybody.
U.S. News   Dec 4, 1978   p. 50

LAWYERS

Glut of doctors. Glut of lawyers. Good or
bad?
U.S. News   Dec 19, 1983   p. 62

Why lawyers are in the doghouse.
U.S. News   May 11, 1981   p. 38

Those lawyers!
Time   Apr 10, 1978   p. 56

Complaints about lawyers. Are they
justified? Interview with a law school
dean.
U.S. News   Jul 21, 1975   p. 46

America's lawyers - "A sick profession?"
U.S. News   Mar 25, 1974   p. 23

LAWYERS - WASHINGTON, D.C.

Washington's lawyers. Rise of the power
brokers.
U.S.News   Mar 10, 1980   p. 52

LAZARD FRERES & CO.

The last emperor. Wall Street's Michel
David-Weill. An inside look at how he
rules the private world of Lazard Frères.
Business Week   May 30, 1988   p. 64

LE CARRE, JOHN

An old spy's new game. John le Carré
comes in from the cold with 'Russia
House.'
Newsweek   Jun 5, 1989   p. 52

Master of the spy story. John le Carré
strikes again.
Time   Oct 3, 1977   p. 58

LE CORBUSIER

Architect Le Corbusier.
Time   May 5, 1961   p. 60

LEACHMAN, CLORIS

TV's fall season.
Newsweek   Sep 8, 1975   p. 44

LEAD POISONING

Lead and your kids. Disturbing new
evidence about the threat to their health.
How to protect them.
Newsweek   Jul 15, 1991   p. 42

LEADERSHIP

Is government dead? Unwilling to lead,
politicians are letting America slip into
paralysis.
Time   Oct 23, 1989   p. 28

The new American establishment.
U.S. News   Feb 8, 1988   p. 37

Who's in charge? The crash on Wall Street spotlights America's leadership crisis.
Time   Nov 9, 1987   p. 18

Leadership in America. 50 faces for the future.
Time   Aug 6, 1979   p. 24

Leadership in America. Special section: 200 rising leaders.
Time   Jul 15, 1974   p. 21

Special issue. One hundred of the most important young men and women in the United States. The take-over generation. Its breakthrough in government, science, space, business, education, religion and the arts.
Life   Sep 14, 1962   p. 4

LEADERSHIP (SURVEY)

Who runs America? Hidden influences on the elite. The price of power. Leaders rate their peers. Tomorrow's stars under 40.
U.S. News   May 20, 1985 p. 54

Who runs America.
U.S. News   May 14, 1984 p. 38

Who runs America.
U.S. News   May 23, 1983 p. 38

Who runs America.
U.S. News   May 10, 1982 p. 34

Who runs America.
U.S. News   May 18, 1981 p. 38

Who runs America.
U.S.News   Apr 14, 1980 p. 34

Who runs America.
U.S. News   Apr 16, 1979 p. 32

Who runs America.
U.S. News   Apr 17, 1978 p. 30

Who runs America.
U.S. News   Apr 18, 1977 p. 28

Who runs America?
U.S. News   Apr 19, 1976 p. 24

Who runs America?
U.S. News   Apr 21, 1975 p. 28

Who runs America?
U.S. News   Apr 22, 1974   p. 30

LEAKEY, RICHARD

How man became man. Anthropologist Richard Leakey with Homo habilis.
Time   Nov 7, 1977   p. 64

LEARNING, PSYCHOLOGY OF

Speed learning. Memory fitness tips. How to be the best and brightest at everything.
Omni   Apr 1990   p. 66

How kids learn.
Newsweek   Apr 17, 1989 p. 50

Education and the future mind. 77 schools of the future. The power of a newborn brain. Seymour Papert and the teaching turtle.
Omni   Oct 1985   p. 28

Early learning right in the crib. Astonishing discoveries in infant aptitudes.
Life   Mar 31, 1967   p. 40

LEBANON

Israel in torment. After the massacre: Can Begin survive? The anguish of American Jews.
Newsweek   Oct 4, 1982   p. 20

Israeli strike. New test for U.S.
U.S. News   Jun 21, 1982   p. 14

LEBANON - HOSTAGES

See HOSTAGES - LEBANON

LEBANON - ISRAELI INVASION, 1982

Destroying Beirut. Israel tightens the noose.
Time   Aug 16, 1982   p. 10

Deathtrap. Can the PLO survive? The U.S. evacuation plan.
Newsweek   Jul 19, 1982   p. 14

Beirut under siege. Send in the Marines? Children of war revisited.
Time   Jul 19, 1982   p. 10

What next?
U.S. News   Jul 19, 1982   p. 18

LEONARD, ELMORE

The big thrill. Mystery writers are making a killing. 'Glitz' author Elmore Leonard.
Newsweek   Apr 22, 1985   p. 58

LEONARD, SUGAR RAY

The fight of his life. Sugar Ray Leonard takes on Roberto Duran.
Newsweek   Jun 23, 1980   p. 48

LEONARDO DA VINCI

The Last Supper. Restoration reveals Leonardo's masterpiece
National Geographic Nov 1983   p. 664

Lost notebooks of Leonardo da Vinci. The cache of drawings in which the master set down his ideas and visions.
Life   Mar 3, 1967   p. 24

LEOPARDS

Tracking the snow leopard.
National Geographic Jun 1986   p. 793

The great cats of Africa. A spectacular new series photographed in the wild.
Life   Jan 6, 1967   p. 36

LEOPOLD, ALDO

The natural world of Aldo Leopold.
National Geographic Nov 1981   p. 682

LERNER, ALAN JAY

The rough road to Broadway. Lerner & Loewe.
Time   Nov 14, 1960   p. 64

LETTERMAN, DAVID

Staying up late with Letterman.
Newsweek   Feb 3, 1986   p. 46

LEVERAGED BUYOUTS

RJR. Nervous about debt? Not Lou Gerstner, who runs the biggest LBO of all.
Business Week   Oct 2, 1989   p. 72

King Henry. Is KKR's Henry Kravis headed for a fall?
Business Week   Nov 14, 1988   p. 124

The bashful billionaire. Robert Bass is shy—except when it comes to making big deals.
Business Week   Oct 3, 1988   p. 96

Not since the heyday of J.P. Morgan has Wall Street been buying so many corporations. The major firms are more owners than investors—actually overseeing the companies they buy, from setting overall strategy to picking top managers.
Business Week   Jun 20, 1988   p. 116

LEVI, EDWARD H. (INTERVIEW)

The Attorney General speaks out: Gun control, illegal aliens, marijuana laws, rising crime, death penalty.
U.S. News   Jun 30, 1975   p. 30

LEVINE, JAMES

Making opera grand. James Levine: America's top maestro.
Time   Jan 17, 1983   p. 52

LIBEL AND SLANDER

Sharon vs. Time. An absence of malice.
Newsweek   Feb 4, 1985   p. 52

LIBYAN-AMERICAN CONFLICT, 1986

Shooting to kill. Did the U.S. go too far - or not far enough? The terrorists strike back. The new threat to air travel.
Newsweek   Apr 28, 1986   p. 16

Hitting home. Tripoli under attack.
Time   Apr 28, 1986   p. 16

America's new war. Can it be won? At what price.
U.S. News   Apr 28, 1986   p. 20

Target Gaddafi.
Time   Apr 21, 1986   p. 18

'America is our target.' Inside the terror network. Reagan takes on Kaddafi.
Newsweek   Apr 7, 1986   p. 20

LIBYAN-AMERICAN CONFLICT, 1989

Chemical warfare. The fight against 'The Winds of Death.' A showdown with Kaddafi.
Newsweek   Jan 16, 1989   p. 16

LIE DETECTORS AND DETECTION

The truth about lie detectors.
Discover   Mar 1986   p. 24

LIEDTKE, HUGH

Mr. Pennzoil. Hugh Liedtke built his company with some controversial deals. Now he wants to grow bigger—with Texaco's money.
Business Week   Jan 27, 1986   p. 88

LIFE (BIOLOGY) - ORIGIN

Asimov on the origins of life.
Omni   Nov 1983   p. 56

LIFE ON OTHER PLANETS

The search for extraterrestrial intelligence: How much do scientists (and the government) really know?
Omni   Dec 1990   p. 42

Alien worlds. The search heats up.
Discover   Oct 1987   p. 66

Extraterrestrial life: New hope in our own solar system.
Omni   Aug 1984   p. 44

Life in space. The search begins.
Discover   Mar 1983   p. 29

Is anyone out there?
Discover   Mar 1982   p. 20

Seeking other worlds. Astronomer Carl Sagan.
Newsweek   Aug 15, 1977   p. 46

Looking for life out there.
Time   Dec 13, 1971   p. 50

Life in outer space? The search begins. The big 'dishes' seek the answer.
Newsweek   Feb 22, 1960   p. 68

LIFE (PERIODICAL)

25 years of Life. Special double issue.
Life   Dec 26, 1960   p. 14

LIFESTYLES

Men now. Seeking the enriched life.
Ms.   Oct 1987   p. 48

Presto! The convenience industry. Too busy to cook, clean, get the car fixed, or do other chores? Lots of people are. So these new service companies are booming.
Business Week   Apr 27, 1987   p. 86

Can men have it all? It's time to ask.
Ms.   Sep 1986   p. 33

Lifestyles: More Americans living alone—and liking it.
USA Today   Aug 1985   p. 1

Lifestyle of the '80s. Anything goes!
U.S. News   Aug 1, 1983   p. 45

LIGHTNING

Bolts from the blue. A new view of a quirky killer.
Discover   Dec 1990   p. 50

LINCOLN, ABRAHAM

Lincoln. The President who gave meaning, honor and purpose to the Civil War speaks to us still.
Life   Feb 1991   p. 22

Rare photographs, new-found facts tell the incredible story of what happened to Lincoln's body.
Life   Feb 15, 1963   p. 83

LINDSAY, JOHN V.

A switch in time? John V. Lindsay.
Newsweek   Aug 23, 1971   p. 15

Lindsay and the fight for New York.
Newsweek   Nov 3, 1969   p. 27

The Lindsay style. Cool mayor in a pressure cooker. John Vliet Lindsay, Mayor of New York.
Life   May 24, 1968   p. 74

Lindsay wins New York. New look for the GOP?
Newsweek   Nov 15, 1965   p. 31

Stunning victory of a loner. John Lindsay.
Life   Nov 12, 1965   p. 42

The new mayor of New York: "To make our great city once again the empire city of the world." Republican John Lindsay.
Time   Nov 12, 1965   p. 28

GOP hope: Lindsay of New York.
Newsweek   May 31, 1965   p. 23

Young G.O.P. star makes a big move. Congressman John Lindsay runs for Mayor of New York.
Life   May 28, 1965   p. 32

LONGEVITY

Longevity: Exclusive report on youth
pills. Laser face-lifts. Born-again genes.
Souls on ice. Artificial skin. Surrogate
brains.
Omni   Oct 1986   p. 6

LOONS

Cry of the loon.
National Geographic Apr 1989   p. 510

LOPEZ PORTILLO, JOSE - VISIT TO THE UNITED STATES, 1979

Mexico: An angry neighbor. President
José López Portillo.
Time   Oct 8, 1979   p. 50

LOREN, SOPHIA

With Sophia Loren in her new villa.
Life   Sep 18, 1964   p. 80

Sophia Loren.
Time   Apr 6, 1962   p. 78

Lovely ways and wiles of a captivating
woman. Sophia Loren.
Life   Aug 11, 1961   p. 50

Tiger-eyed temptress, Sophia Loren.
Life   Nov 14, 1960   p. 129

LORENZO, FRANK

The high flier. Frank Lorenzo's bid for
Eastern Air Lines is the latest and most
daring move in the restructuring of the
airline industry. Will it work?
Business Week   Mar 10, 1986 p. 104

LOS ANGELES (CALIFORNIA)

Los Angeles. America's uneasy new
melting pot.
Time   Jun 13, 1983   p. 18

Mayor Yorty.
Time   Sep 2, 1966   p. 14

Los Angeles traffic reflects civic boom.
Life   Jun 20, 1960   p. 74

LOUDON, JOHN H.

John H. Loudon of Royal Dutch Shell.
Time   May 9, 1960   p. 92

LOVE

Love and friendship. Take a good friend,
add passion, fascination and, sometimes,
grief: Voilà, you have a lover.
Psychology Today   Feb 1985   p. 22

LOVELL, JAMES

Jim Lovell and Apollo 13.
Life   Apr 24, 1970   p. 28

Men of the year. Anders, Borman and
Lovell.
Time   Jan 3, 1969   p. 9

LOWELL, ROBERT

Poetry in an age of prose. Robert Lowell.
Time   Jun 2, 1967   p. 67

LOYALTY

The end of corporate loyalty? Thousands
of managers are losing their jobs as
corporations cut costs. The emotional cost
is high. And even for those who remain,
things will never be the same.
Business Week   Aug 4, 1986   p. 42

LSD

LSD and the mind drugs.
Newsweek   May 9, 1966   p. 59

LSD. The exploding threat of the mind
drug that got out of control. Turmoil in a
capsule. One dose of LSD is enough to set
off a mental riot of vivid colors and
insights—or of terror and convulsions.
Life   Mar 25, 1966   p. 28

LUCAS, GEORGE

Father of the Jedi. 'Star Wars' genius
George Lucas strikes again.
Life   Jun 1983   p. 84

Star Wars III. Return of the Jedi. George
Lucas & friends wrap it all up.
Time   May 23, 1983 p. 62

LUCE, CLAIRE BOOTH (INTERVIEW)

What's happening to America's values. A
conversation with Claire Booth Luce.
U.S. News   Jun 24, 1974   p. 52

LUCE, HENRY R.

Henry R. Luce. 1898 - 1967.
Newsweek   Mar 13, 1967   p. 68

Henry R. Luce.
Time   Mar 10, 1967   p. 26

LUMBER INDUSTRY

Who gives a hoot? The timber industry says that saving this spotted owl will cost 30,000 jobs. It isn't that simple.
Time   Jun 25, 1990   p. 56

LUSITANIA (SHIP)

Lusitania. New evidence on the 'unprovoked' sinking that dragged us toward war.
Life   Oct 13, 1972   p. 58

LUTHER, MARTIN

Martin Luther.
Time   Mar 24, 1967   p. 70

LYING

Lying in America. Public concern over honesty and standards of behavior has reached the highest level since Watergate.
U.S. News   Feb 23, 1987   p. 54

LYME DISEASE

Lyme disease. A tiny tick is spreading a mysterious illness in 43 states. How to protect yourself this summer.
Newsweek   May 22, 1989   p. 66

LYNCH, DAVID

David Lynch. The wild-at-art genius behind *Twin Peaks*.
Time   Oct 1, 1990   p. 84

LYSERGIC ACID DIETHYLAMIDE

See LSD

MA SITSON

In the hands of the Red Guard torture and degradation. The most important man to escape from China writes his story.
Life   Jun 2, 1967   p. 22

MACARTHUR, DOUGLAS II

General Douglas MacArthur. 1880-1964.
Life   Apr 17, 1964   p. 28

The old soldier looks back. Beginning a new series by Douglas MacArthur.
Life   Jan 10, 1964   p. 46

Japan: Cold War cockpit. U.S. Ambassador Douglas MacArthur II.
Time   Jun 27, 1960   p. 10

MACDONALD, ROSS

The art of murder. Detective novelist Ross Macdonald.
Newsweek   Mar 22, 1971   p. 101

MACGRAW, ALI

The return to romance. Ali MacGraw.
Time   Jan 11, 1971   p. 40

MACLAINE, SHIRLEY

Getting her kicks at 50. Shirley MacLaine.
Time   May 14, 1984   p. 60

Show biz in politics. Shirley MacLaine.
Newsweek   Sep 25, 1972   p. 34

Dual role for Shirley.
Life   Feb 17, 1961   p. 91

MACY'S

See RH MACY AND CO.

MADONNA

That fabulous couple. Madonna and the camera.
Life   Dec 1986   p. 50

Madonna. Why she's hot.
Time   May 27, 1985   p. 74

MADRID HURTADO, MIGUEL DE LA (INTERVIEW)

Mexico's crisis. "We are in an emergency." New President Miguel de la Madrid.
Time   Dec 20, 1982   p. 30

MAFIA

See ORGANIZED CRIME

MAGNET SCHOOLS

Making kids smarter. How magnet education is giving children the edge they need.
U.S. News   May 27, 1991   p. 58

MAIL-ORDER BUSINESS

Hey. Don't miss our really interesting story on the junk mail explosion!
Time   Nov 26, 1990   p. 62

Catalogues. Delivering the gala goods.
Time   Nov 8, 1982   p. 72

MAILER, NORMAN

Monroe meets Mailer.
Time   Jul 16, 1973   p. 60

The world of Norman Mailer.
Newsweek   Dec 9, 1968   p. 84

MAKARIOS II, ARCHBISHOP

Makarios of Cyprus.
Newsweek   Mar 2, 1964   p. 34

MALAYSIA

A new nation in Asia. Malaysia's Abdul Rahman.
Time   Apr 12, 1963   p. 43

MALCOLM X - ASSASSINATION

Death of Malcolm X and the resulting vengeful gang war.
Life   Mar 5, 1965   p. 26

MALINOVSKY, RODION

Russia's new hard line. Soviet Defense Minister Malinovsky.
Time   May 30, 1960 p. 16

MALONE, JOHN C.

The king of cable. TCI President John Malone is fast becoming the most powerful man in the television industry. And a lot of poeple don't like it.
Business Week   Oct 26, 1987   p. 88

MALPRACTICE INSURANCE

See INSURANCE, MALPRACTICE

MAN

The peopling of the earth.
National Geographic Oct 1988   p. 434

MAN - INFLUENCE ON NATURE

As we begin our second century, the *Geographic* asks: Can man save this fragile earth?
National Geographic Dec 1988   p. 765

MAN - ORIGIN

Early man. The radical new view of where we came from.
U.S. News   Sep 16, 1991   p. 53

The first humans. Science's new view of who we were and the way we lived.
U.S. News   Feb 27, 1989   p. 52

The search for Adam & Eve. Scientists explore a controversial theory about man's origins.
Newsweek   Jan 11, 1988   p. 46

The search for early man. Holographic image of Africa's Taung child, one to two million years old.
National Geographic Nov 1985   p. 560

How man became man. Anthropologist Richard Leakey with Homo habilis.
Time   Nov 7, 1977   p. 64

MAN, PREHISTORIC

The great leap forward. Why we succeeded and Neanderthal failed.
Discover   May 1989   p. 50

The way we were. Our Ice Age heritage: Language, art, fashion, and the family.
Newsweek   Nov 10, 1986   p. 62

MANAGEMENT

21st century executive. Four key traits for managers of the future. Rupert Murdoch: On the importance of being tough.
U.S. News   Mar 7, 1988   p. 48

Neurotic companies.
Psychology Today   Oct 1984   p. 26

The intolerable boss. Dealing with your Mr. Dithers. Don't get mad...get smarter.
Psychology Today   Jan 1984   p. 44

A new era for management. The shrinking of middle management. Computer-run offices and factories. A disenchanted middle class.
Business Week   Apr 25, 1983   p. 50

Europe's new managers. Going global with a U.S. style.
Business Week   May 24, 1982 p. 116

MANATEES

Man and manatee.
National Geographic Sep 1984   p. 400

MANCHESTER, WILLIAM

Privacy vs. history. Jacqueline Kennedy and "The Death of a President."
Newsweek   Dec 26, 1966   p. 39

MANDELA, NELSON

A hero in America. Nelson Mandela.
Time   Jul 2, 1990   p. 14

Free! Breakthrough in South Africa.
Newsweek   Feb 19, 1990   p. 36

Mandela: Free at last? After 27 years, a changing South Africa prepares to release its most famous political prisoner.
Time   Feb 5, 1990   p. 26

MANILA (PHILIPPINES) - HISTORY

Track of the Manila galleons.
National Geographic Sep 1990   p. 5

MANN, THOMAS C.

The U.S. & Latin America. State Department's Thomas Mann.
Time   Jan 31, 1964   p. 15

MANNED SPACE FLIGHT

See SPACE FLIGHT

MANSFIELD, MICHAEL J.

Can Democrats control a Democratic
senate? Majority leader Mansfield.
Time   Mar 20, 1964   p. 22

MANSON, CHARLES

The love and terror cult. The man who
was their leader. The charge of multiple
murder. The dark edge of hippie life.
Life   Dec 19, 1969   p. 20

MANTLE, MICKEY

Mantle's misery. He faces physical pain
and a fading career. Mickey Mantle at 33.
in his 15th year with the New York
Yankess.
Life   Jul 30, 1965   p. 46

MANUFACTURING INDUSTRIES

Manufacturing: The key to growth. 1988
industry outlook.
Business Week   Jan 11, 1988   p. 69

The hollow corporation. A new kind of
company is evolving in the U.S.—
manufacturing companies that do little
manufacturing. Instead, they import
components or products from low-wage
countries, slap their own names on them,
and sell them in America.
Business Week   Mar 3, 1986   p. 56

MANZU, GIACOMO

An artist's memoir of the saintly Pope
John. The story of a remarkable
friendship.
Life   Oct 11, 1968   p. 52

MAO ZEDONG

Mao's wife tells her story. From actress to
empress.
Time   Mar 21, 1977   p. 42

After Mao.
Newsweek   Sep 20, 1976   p. 30

After Mao.
Time   Sep 20, 1976   p. 26

The struggle for China.
Newsweek   Jan 30, 1967   p. 32

China in chaos. Chairman Mao.
Time   Jan 13, 1967   p. 20

Mao and China.
Newsweek   Aug 8, 1966   p. 36

Far East fiasco. China's Mao: Will he rule
the Pacific?
Newsweek   Jun 27, 1960   p. 23

MAO ZEDONG, MME.

Mao's wife tells her story. From actress to
empress.
Time   Mar 21, 1977   p. 42

MARCOS, FERDINAND

Two decades of independence in Asia.
Philippine President Marcos.
Time   Oct 21, 1966   p. 38

**MARGARET, PRINCESS OF GREAT
BRITAIN**

Bridal procession leaves the Abbey.
Life   May 16, 1960 p. 28

Margaret and Tony at Windsor Lodge.
Life   Mar 14, 1960 p. 91

Memorable night at the White House.
Life   Dec 3, 1965   p. 32

MARICHAL, JUAN

The best right arm in baseball. Juan
Marichal.
Time   Jun 10, 1966   p. 88

MARIJUANA

Guns, grass and money. America's
billion-dollar marijuana crop.
Newsweek   Oct 25, 1982   p. 36

Marijuana: Bad news and good.
Discover   Aug 1981   p. 14

Marijuana: Time to change the law?
Newsweek   Sep 7, 1970   p. 20

Marijuana. At least 12 million Americans
have now tried it. Are penalties too
severe? Should it be legalized?
Life   Oct 31, 1969   p. 26

Drugs and the young.
Time   Sep 26, 1969   p. 68

Marijuana. The pot problem.
Newsweek   Jul 24, 1967   p. 46

MARINE ANIMALS

Suruga Bay. In the shadow of Mount Fuji.
National Geographic Oct 1990 p. 2

MARINE CORPS

Comeback of the marines.
U.S. News Jan 12, 1981 p. 57

MARINE POLLUTION

Troubled waters. Can anything be done
to clean up the mess in the oceans? Yes.
Do we have the will to do it? We'd better.
Business Week Oct 12, 1987 p. 88

MARINER 2

Venus: What Mariner saw.
Time Mar 8, 1963 p. 76

MARINER 4

Mariner to Mars.
Newsweek Jul 26, 1965 p. 54

Taking the measure of Mars.
Time Jul 23, 1965 p. 36

MARKETING

Value marketing. It's the way to sell in
the 90's.
Business Week Nov 11, 1991 p. 132

Stalking the new consumer. Call it micro
marketing. In today's fractured world,
companies are finding novel ways to
reach the elusive consumer. Even Procter
& Gamble, king of mass marketers, is
changing its ways.
Business Week Aug 28, 1989 p. 54

Sports marketing. Hire a famous athlete,
sponsor a sporting event. It's the hot new
way to promote your products. Here's
why.
Business Week Aug 31, 1987 p. 48

Home shopping. Retailing on TV is
exploding—and now Sears has jumped
in. But is it just a fad?
Business Week Dec 15, 1986 p. 62

Marketing. The new priority. The mass
market has splintered, so companies are
targeting products.
Business Week Nov 21, 1983 p. 96

MARRIAGE

Marriage: Surviving the first year.
USA Today Dec 1987 p. 1

How to stay married. The divorce rate
drops as couples try harder to stay
together.
Newsweek Aug 24, 1987 p. 52

Relationships: How to avoid "rerun" of
failed first marriage.
USA Today Apr 1987 p. 1

The marriage crunch. If you're a single
woman, here are your chances of getting
married.
Newsweek Jun 2, 1986 p. 54

Staying in love. Secrets of marriages that
last. Major new study of trust and
intimacy. Still surprising each other:
Personal stories. What about sex?
Ms. Jun 1985 p. 41

Why marriages last.
Psychology Today Jun 1985 p. 22

Marriage. It's back in style!
U.S. News Jun 20, 1983 p. 44

Play in marriage–more than fun and
games.
Psychology Today Feb 1982 p. 32

Marrying late: Why women finally say
"yes."
Ms. Mar 1981 p. 47

Fighting the housewife blues.
Time Mar 14, 1977 p. 62

The marriage experiments. Unmarried
parents in a Boston suburb. Collective
family in a big house in Berkeley.
Work-sharing contract in New York.
Frontier partnership in Idaho.
Life Apr 28, 1972 p. 42

See Also INTERRACIAL MARRIAGE

MARS (PLANET)

Our next home. Mars: Bringing a dead
world to life.
Life May 1991 p. 24

Mars. The myths and mysteries.
Omni Mar 1985 p. 26

Mariner to Mars.
Newsweek Jul 26, 1965 p. 54

Taking the measure of Mars.
Time Jul 23, 1965 p. 36

MARSALIS, WYNTON

The new jazz age.
Time   Oct 22, 1990   p. 64

MARTIN, STEVE

Steve Martin: He's off the wall.
Time   Aug 24, 1987   p. 50

Comedy's new face. Steve Martin is one
wild and crazy guy.
Newsweek   Apr 3, 1978   p. 60

MARTINS, PETER

Prince of the city. Peter Martins of the
New York City Ballet.
Newsweek   Dec 26, 1983   p. 56

MARXISM

Marxism in U.S. classrooms.
U.S. News   Jan 25, 1982   p. 42

MARY, MOTHER OF JESUS

The search for Mary. Was the most
revered woman in history God's
handmaid — or the first feminist?
Time   Dec 30, 1991   p. 62

MASS MEDIA

Accusing the press. What are its sins?
Time   Dec 12, 1983   p. 76

MASS MEDIA AND YOUTH

Do you know what your children are
listening to?
U.S. News   Oct 28, 1985   p. 46

MASS TRANSIT

Mass transit: The expensive dream.
Business Week   Aug 27, 1984   p. 62

**MASSACHUSETTS INSTITUTE OF
TECHNOLOGY**

M.I.T. at 100: A race with the future.
Newsweek   Apr 3, 1961   p. 57

**MASTER OF BUSINESS ADMINISTRATION
DEGREE**

The money chase. What business schools
are doing to us.
Time   May 4, 1981   p. 58

MATERIALISM

The simple life. Rejecting the rat race,
Americans get back to basics.
Time   Apr 8, 1991   p. 58

MATERIALS RESEARCH

The new alchemy. Call it the Materials
Age. By combining atoms in novel ways,
scientists are creating materials that open
up bold possibilities.
Business Week   Jul 29, 1991   p. 48

MATSUSHITA, KONOSUKE

Japan: Asia's first consumer market.
Industrialist Matsushita.
Time   Feb 23, 1962   p. 93

MATTER

Strange matter. Is there a parallel material
world?
Discover   Nov 1989   p. 62

MAULDIN, WILLIAM

Cartoonist Bill Mauldin.
Time   Jul 21, 1961   p. 50

**MAX HEADROOM (FICTIONAL
CHARACTER)**

Mad about Max. The making of a video
cult. Max Headroom.
Newsweek   Apr 20, 1987   p. 58

MAX, PETER

Peter Max: Portrait of the artist as a very
rich man.
Life   Sep 5, 1969   p. 34

MAY, PETER

The new aces of low tech. Nelson Peltz
and Peter May think there's still big
money in running a basic industry. With
this old-fashioned idea—and new-fangled
junk bonds—they have built a $4 billion
empire.
Business Week   Sep 15, 1986   p. 132

MAYAGUEZ INCIDENT, 1975

The rescue.
Newsweek   May 26, 1975   p. 16

Ford draws the line.
Time   May 26, 1975   p. 9

MAYAS

La Ruta Maya.
National Geographic Oct 1989   p. 424

Río Azul. Lost city of the Maya.
National Geographic Apr 1986   p. 420

MAYAS - ART

Maya art discovered in cave.
National Geographic Aug 1981   p. 220

MAYORS

America's mayors. The politics of
survival. Ed Koch of New York.
Time   Jun 15, 1981   p. 22

MBA

See MASTER OF BUSINESS
ADMINISTRATION DEGREE

MBOYA, TOM

Kenya's Tom Mboya.
Time   Mar 7, 1960   p. 22

MCARTHUR, JOHN

The Harvard B-school. Remaking an
institution. Dean John H. McArthur.
Business Week   Mar 24, 1986 p. 54

MCAULIFFE, CHRISTA

Seeing beyond the stars. A preview of
America's biggest year in space.
Life   Dec 1985   p. 29

MCCARTHY, EUGENE

Voyage of the loner.
Life   Jun 7, 1968   p. 34

Three's a crowd. The Johnson -
Kennedy - McCarthy fight. Eugene
McCarthy.
Time   Mar 22, 1968 p. 12

MCCARTNEY, PAUL

McCartney comes back.
Time   May 31, 1976 p. 40

Paul McCartney. The ex-Beatle tells his
story.
Life   Apr 16, 1971 p. 52

Paul is still with us. The case of the
'missing' Beatle. Paul and his family last
week in Scotland.
Life   Nov 7, 1969   p. 103

MCCAW, CRAIG

Cellular phones. The high-risk empire of
Craig McCaw. He runs America's biggest
cellular phone company. Now all he has
to do is turn a profit.
Business Week   Dec 5, 1988   p. 140

MCCOLL, HUGH

Super banker. Hugh McColl is going after
his biggest deal yet. It would make his
NCNB the nation's second-largest bank
and change the face of banking in the U.S.
Business Week   Jul 15, 1991   p. 116

MCCORMACK, EDWARD

The Senate seat scramble in
Massachusetts. Head-on collision of three
political clans. Eddie McCormick. Teddie
Kennedy. George Lodge.
Life   Jun 29, 1962   p. 59

MCCORMACK, JOHN

Head of the House. The other man from
Massachusetts. Speaker McCormack.
Time   Jan 19, 1962   p. 16

McCormack of Massachusetts. The new
Congress.
Newsweek   Jan 15, 1962   p. 15

MCDONALD'S CORP.

McRisky. McDonald's faces a growth
crisis. So CEO Mike Quinlan is changing
its tried-and-true recipe.
Business Week   Oct 21, 1991   p. 114

McWorld? McDonald's is raising Golden
Arches from Berlin to Bangkok. But can
the company export its unique
management style.
Business Week   Oct 13, 1986   p. 78

The hamburger empire. McDonald's.
Time   Sep 17, 1973   p. 84

MCDONNELL, JAMES

The industrial conquest of the sky.
Aerospaceman James McDonnell.
Time   Mar 31, 1967   p. 79

MCENROE, JOHN

The champ you love to hate. John
McEnroe.
Newsweek   Sep 7, 1981   p. 50

MCFARLANE, ROBERT

The pressure builds. McFarlane's suicide
attempt. The NSC's computer secret.
Turmoil in the White House.
Newsweek   Feb 23, 1987   p. 18

MCGINLEY, PHYLLIS

"I rise to defend /The quite possible She."
Phyllis McGinley.
Time   Jun 18, 1965   p. 74

MCGOVERN, ELEANOR

The other campaigners. Pat Nixon.
Eleanor McGovern.
Time   Oct 9, 1972   p. 14

MCGOVERN, GEORGE

George McGovern talks. An outspoken
self-portrait.
Life   Jul 7, 1972   p. 30

Can he put the party together? George
and Eleanor McGovern.
Newsweek   Jun 19, 1972   p. 22

Here comes the prairie populist. Senator
George McGovern.
Time   May 8, 1972   p. 16

MCGOWAN, WILLIAM

The long-distance warrior. Bill
McGowan's MCI broke AT&T's phone
monopoly. That was the easy part. Now
he has to compete.
Business Week   Feb 17, 1986   p. 86

MCKONE, JOHN

Return of the airmen. Gambit in the Cold
War.
Time   Feb 3, 1961   p. 10

MCLAIN, DENNY

The year of the pitcher. Denny McLain.
Time   Sep 13, 1968   p. 76

MCLUHAN, MARSHALL

The message of Marshall McLuhan.
Newsweek   Mar 6, 1967   p. 53

MCNAMARA, ROBERT S.

McNamara. Why is he leaving?
Newsweek   Dec 11, 1967   p. 25

The power in the Pentagon. Defense
Secretary McNamara with Joint Chief of
Staff.
Newsweek   Dec 6, 1965   p. 30

Weapons & diplomacy. Cuba, Canada
and Europe. Secretary McNamara.
Time   Feb 15, 1963   p. 22

Defense Secretary McNamara.
Newsweek   Mar 12, 1962   p. 26

Ford's McNamara: Wanted on the New
Frontier.
Newsweek   Dec 19, 1960   p. 20

MCNEALY, SCOTT

High noon for Sun. Can it stay ahead in
workstations? In only seven years, Scott
McNealy built Sun Microsystems into a
$1.8 billion company. But rising
competition and the strains of rapid
growth may soon produce its first
quarterly loss.
Business Week   Jul 24, 1989   p. 70

MCQUEEN, STEVE

Steve McQueen. Problem kid becomes a
star.
Life   Jul 12, 1963   p. 62

MEAT

The meat furor.
Newsweek   Apr 9, 1973   p. 73

Sky-high meat prices. Outrage at the
checkout counter. Who gets all that
money for beef. How a family copes with
food bills.
Life   Apr 14, 1972   p. 32

MECHAM, EVAN

Raising hell in Arizona. The women who
whipped Governor Mecham.
Ms.   Jun 1988   p. 44

MEDICAL CARE

America's best hospitals. Exclusive
rankings. How to find care in 15
specialties from AIDS to urology.
U.S. News   Aug 5, 1991   p. 36

Health care for the 21st century. Despite
great medical advances, will nightmarish
costs and ethical concerns threaten our
well-being?
USA Today   Sep 1990   p. 50

Emergency! Overwhelmed and
understaffed, medicine's front lines are
collapsing across America.
Time   May 28, 1990   p. 58

America's best hospitals. Exclusive
ratings. A national guide that helps you
choose.
U.S. News   Apr 30, 1990   p. 51

How doctors decide who shall live and
who shall die.
U.S. News   Jan 22, 1990   p. 50

Life and death: Scenes from a hospital
emergency ward.
USA Today   Jul 1989   p. 41

Health care: Medical care revolution.
USA Today   Feb 1987   p. 1

The revolution in medicine. A special
report on how money, machines, and
politics are changing America's doctors -
and the way they treat you.
Newsweek   Jan 26, 1987   p. 40

How good is your health care?
Revolution in the hospitals - for better or
worse.
U.S. News   Apr 14, 1986   p. 60

Crisis in the operating room.
U.S. News   May 15, 1978   p. 39

Health care in America. Progress–and
problems.
U.S. News   Jun 16, 1975   p. 50

What's wrong with U.S. medicine.
Time   Feb 21, 1969   p. 53

See Also ALTERNATIVE MEDICINE

MEDICAL CARE - FRAUD

Billions of Medicaid ripoffs. Can anyone
stop it?
U.S. News   Mar 22, 1976   p. 18

Doctors and the Rx scandal. How some
M.D.s short-cut ethics and profit from
their own prescriptions.
Life   Jun 24, 1966   p. 86

**MEDICAL CARE - INTERNATIONAL
  ASPECTS**

The power to heal. From ancient arts to
modern medicine. A photo portfolio.
Newsweek   Sep 24, 1990   p. 38

MEDICAL CARE, COST OF

10 ways to cure the health care mess.
Time   Nov 25, 1991   p. 34

Aging: Controlling health care costs.
USA Today   Oct 1990   p. 1

Ouch! The squeeze on your health plan.
Skyrocketing costs are forcing companies
to change medical benefits. Here's what it
means for you.
Business Week   Nov 20, 1989   p. 110

Can you afford to get sick? The battle
over health benefits.
Newsweek   Jan 30, 1989   p. 44

Are cost cuts crippling health care?
Discover   May 1986   p. 24

Corporate Rx for medical costs. Changing
how the health care industry works.
Business Week   Oct 15, 1984   p. 138

Soaring hospital costs. The brewing
revolt. Room, $190 a day. Surgeon,
$3,500. Anesthesia, $600. Blood, $85 a
pint. Intensive care, $490 a day.
Operating room, $2,790. Drugs, $1,190.
X-rays, $720.
U.S. News   Aug 22, 1983   p. 39

Upheaval in health care. Here come
government cost controls.
Business Week   Jul 25, 1983   p. 44

America's $39 billion heart business.
U.S. News   Mar 15, 1982   p. 53

The spiraling costs of health care. Rx:
Competition.
Business Week   Feb 8, 1982   p. 58

Medical costs. Seeking the cure.
Time   May 28, 1979   p. 60

Inside our hospitals.
U.S. News   Mar 5, 1979   p. 33

Uproar over medical bills.
U.S. News   Mar 28, 1977   p. 35

Higher cost of better medicine. How
should it be paid for?
Time   Jul 7, 1961   p. 56

MEDICAL CARE INDUSTRY

Medicine and profits. Unhealthy mixture?
U.S. News   Aug 17, 1981   p. 50

MEDICAL ETHICS

The gift of life. Little Marissa was born to provide lifesaving bone marrow to her big sister Anissa. This is a story of miracles and moral dilemmas.
Time   Jun 17, 1991   p. 54

Doctor's dilemma. Treat or let die?
U.S. News   Dec 6, 1982   p. 53

When doctors play God. The ethics of life-and-death decisions.
Newsweek   Aug 31, 1981   p. 48

Doctors and the Rx scandal. How some M.D.s short-cut ethics and profit from their own prescriptions.
Life   Jun 24, 1966   p. 86

MEDICAL TECHNOLOGY

Medicine's new vision.
National Geographic Jan 1987   p. 2

Medicine's new triumphs. Surgery that melts, cuts and vaporizes. Solving secrets of the brain. Surviving burns with synthetic skin. Artificial parts replacing flesh and bone.
U.S. News   Nov 11, 1985   p. 46

Medical miracles. But how to pay the bill?
Time   Dec 10, 1984   p. 70

Computers that can film insanity.
Omni   Jan 1984   p. 84

Laser medicine. Healing with light.
Life   May 1982   p. 129

The new medicine.
Newsweek   Apr 24, 1967   p. 60

Control of life. Profound and astonishing biological revolution. Audacious experiments promise decades of added life, superbabies with improved minds and bodies, and even a kind of immortality.
Life   Sep 10, 1965   p. 59

MEDICAL TESTING

Warning: Medical tests may be hazardous to your health.
U.S. News   Nov 23, 1987   p. 60

MEDICARE

Our sick hospitals.
Newsweek   Jul 11, 1966   p. 57

Medicare: Who should pay the bill?
Newsweek   Apr 2, 1962   p. 51

MEDICINE, ALTERNATIVE

See ALTERNATIVE MEDICINE

MEESE, EDWIN

Under fire. Attorney General-Designate Edwin Meese III.
Newsweek   Apr 2, 1984   p. 22

MEHTA, ZUBIN

Macho Maestro. Conductor Zubin Mehta.
Newsweek   Dec 18, 1978   p. 72

Conductor Zubin Mehta. The baton is passed to youth.
Time   Jan 19, 1968   p. 76

MEIR, GOLDA

Middle East: Toward the brink. Israel's Golda Meir.
Time   Sep 19, 1969   p. 28

MEMORY

Molecules of memory. Decoding the brain's electric language.
Discover   Dec 1989   p. 46

Memory. New insights into how we remember and why we forget.
Newsweek   Sep 29, 1986   p. 48

Memory. How it works, how to improve it.
Discover   Nov 1983   p. 18

Links between mood and memory.
Psychology Today   Jun 1981   p. 60

MEN

What do men really want? Drums, sweat and tears. Now they have a movement of their own.
Newsweek   Jun 24, 1991   p. 46

Men now. Seeking the enriched life.
Ms.   Oct 1987   p. 48

The sexes: Where are the sensitive men?
USA Today   Aug 1987   p. 1

Can men have it all? It's time to ask.
Ms.   Sep 1986   p. 33

Richard Gere. A different American hero?
Ms.   Feb 1986   p. 41

Straight from the heart. Men talk about sex, intimacy, class, competition, friendship, fathers, and how close can we get?
Ms.   Sep 1985   p. 33

The American male. 'New and improved...' Beyond macho - The search for self. The future of fatherhood. Women: The view from the majority.
U.S. News   Jun 3, 1985   p. 44

What men haven't said to women. About change, love, work, sex, "wimps"...
Ms.   Aug 1984   p. 41

What do men want?
Ms.   Oct 1982   p. 35

How men are changing.
Newsweek   Jan 16, 1978   p. 52

MENON, VENGALIL KRISHNAN KRISHNA
See KRISHNA MENON, V.K.

MENTAL ILLNESS
When mental illness hits home. What we know about depression and schizophrenia. How families cope with their ordeal.
U.S. News   Apr 24, 1989   p. 54

Homelessness in America: A mental health problem?
USA Today   Mar 1988   p. 26

Secrets of the brain. New views of the mind, mental illness, and human nature.
Discover   May 1984   p. 34

MENTALLY HANDICAPPED
A special kind of hero. A TV actor with Down syndrome steals America's heart.
Life   Nov 1989   p. 70

MENZIES, ROBERT GORDON
Australia. Things are looking up down under. Prime Minister Menzies.
Time   Apr 4, 1960   p. 20

MERCENARY SOLDIERS
Have guns, will travel. The secret world of America's new mercenaries.
Newsweek   Nov 3, 1986   p. 32

MERCK & CO.
The miracle company. Roy Vagelos has made Merck a superstar in drugs—and on Wall Street. Only six companies have a higher market value. What's his formula?
Business Week   Oct 19, 1987   p. 84

MERCOURI, MELINA
Melina Mercouri. The 'Never on Sunday' girl comes to Broadway.
Life   Dec 2, 1966   p. 51

MEREDITH, JAMES
The Meredith March.
Newsweek   Jun 20, 1966   p. 27

The sound and the fury. Oxford, Mississippi.
Newsweek   Oct 15, 1962   p. 23

MERGERS, CORPORATE
See CORPORATIONS - ACQUISITIONS AND MERGERS

MERRICK, DAVID
Broadway's David Merrick.
Time   Mar 25, 1966   p. 52

MERRILL, DINA
Dina Merrill: Actress, socialite, springtime model.
Life   Jan 11, 1960   p. 56

MERRILL LYNCH & CO., INC.
Merrill Lynch's big dilemma. Its strong broker system is now a costly handicap in a deregulated world.
Business Week   Jan 16, 1984   p. 60

MEVACOR (MEDICATION)
The miracle company. Roy Vagelos has made Merck a superstar in drugs—and on Wall Street. Only six companies have a higher market value. What's his formula?
Business Week   Oct 19, 1987   p. 84

MEXICANS IN THE UNITED STATES
The disappearing border. Will the Mexican migration create a new nation?
U.S. News   Aug 19, 1985   p. 30

MEXICO
Why Pemex can't pay Mexico's bills.
Business Week   Feb 28, 1983   p. 58

Mexico's crisis. "We are in an emergency." New President Miguel de la Madrid.
Time   Dec 20, 1982   p. 30

Powder keg at our doorstep.
U.S.News   May 19, 1980   p. 21

Time bomb in Mexico. Why there'll be no end to the invasion by "illegals."
U.S. News   Jul 4, 1977   p. 27

Crisis across the borders.
U.S. News   Dec 13, 1976   p. 48

MEXICO - ECONOMIC CONDITIONS

Will Mexico make it? The IMF sees a turnaround—but harder tests loom.
Business Week   Oct 1, 1984   p. 74

MEXICO AND THE UNITED STATES

Mexico. A new economic era. A rush to free trade will reshuffle jobs and factories — creating a new North American economy.
Business Week   Nov 12, 1990   p. 102

Our troubled neighbors - dangers for U.S.
U.S. News   Mar 9, 1981   p. 35

Mexico: An angry neighbor. President José López Portillo.
Time   Oct 8, 1979   p. 50

MEXICO CITY (MEXICO)

Mexico City. The population curse.
Time   Aug 6, 1984   p. 24

Mexico City. An alarming giant.
National Geographic Aug 1984   p. 138

MEYERSON, BESS

Undone by love? Bess Myerson.
Ms.   Sep 1988   p. 40

MIAMI (FLORIDA)

Miami. America's Casablanca.
Newsweek   Jan 25, 1988   p. 22

MICHELANGELO BUONARROTI, 1475-1564

The Sistine restoration. A renaisance for Michelangelo.
National Geographic Dec 1989   p. 688

MICRO MARKETING

Stalking the new consumer. Call it micro marketing. In today's fractured world, companies are finding novel ways to reach the elusive consumer. Even Procter & Gamble, king of mass marketers, is changing its ways.
Business Week   Aug 28, 1989   p. 54

MICROMECHANICS

Nanotechnology. Molecular machines that mimic life.
Omni   Nov 1986   p. 56

Micromachines: The technology of tininess.
Omni   Dec 1982   p. 58

MICROSOFT CORP.

The whiz kid. At 31, Bill Gates has built Microsoft into a software powerhouse. Now IBM is introducing a new generation of personal computers that rely on Microsoft's two latest programs. No wonder Gates is smiling.
Business Week   Apr 13, 1987   p. 68

MIDDLE AGE

Middle age: Dating doesn't get easier after 50.
USA Today   Aug 1986   p. 1

Middle Age. The best of times?
U.S. News   Oct 25, 1982   p. 67

The pleasures & perils of middle age.
Time   Jul 29, 1966   p. 50

MIDDLE CLASS

The bite on the middle class. What recovery?
Newsweek   Nov 4, 1991   p. 18

Keeping up is hard to do. The middle-class struggle to hold on.
U.S. News   Aug 18, 1986   p. 36

America's middle class. Angry, frustrated and losing ground.
U.S. News   Mar 30, 1981   p. 39

Special report. Squeeze on America's middle class.
U.S. News   Oct 14, 1974   p. 42

Man and woman of the year. The middle Americans.
Time   Jan 5, 1970   p. 10

MIDDLE EAST

Mideast: If Kissinger fails–
U.S. News Mar 17, 1975 p. 14

The Middle East riddle.
Time May 17, 1971 p. 23

The Mideast after Nasser.
Newsweek Oct 12, 1970 p. 31

The Arab world after Nasser.
Time Oct 12, 1970 p. 20

Facing the Middle East. When to use or
not use power.
Time Oct 5, 1970 p. 10

Explosion in Jordan.
Newsweek Sep 28, 1970 p. 35

Israel and her enemies.
Time Jun 22, 1970 p. 22

The Mideast: Slow boil. Nasser of the
U.A.R.
Newsweek Sep 11, 1967 p. 34

MIDDLE EAST - HISTORY

Beginning a series on the Middle East.
The roots of bitterness. The 100
convulsive years behind the trouble
today.
Life Oct 6, 1967 p. 52

MIDDLE EAST - POLITICS AND
GOVERNMENT

Danger! Highly explosive. A talk with
Israel's Premier.
Newsweek Feb 17, 1969 p. 43

MIDDLE EAST - STRATEGIC ASPECTS

Defending the oil fields. The U.S. military
buildup.
Newsweek Jul 14, 1980 p. 30

MIDDLE EAST AND THE UNITED STATES

About face. Why Arafat said the magic
words. How the U.S. changed course.
What next in the Middle East.
Time Dec 26, 1988 p. 18

Reagan's retreat. The price of failure.
Newsweek Feb 27, 1984 p. 14

Arab world. Where troubles for U.S.
never end.
U.S. News Feb 6, 1984 p. 24

Collision course over the PLO.
Newsweek Sep 3, 1979 p. 18

The Andrew Young affair.
Newsweek Aug 27, 1979 p. 14

MIDDLE WESTERN STATES

America's deflation belt. Oil, agriculture,
and mining are all depressed industries.
Their troubles are hurting a wide swath of
the country—and restraining what would
otherwise be a robust expansion.
Business Week Jun 9, 1986 p. 52

MIDLER, BETTE

Good lawdy, Miss Bawdy! Bette gets
serious.
Ms. Mar 1989 p. 52

You Bette! Midler strikes again in
Outrageous Fortune.
Time Mar 2, 1987 p. 64

Is the best Bette still to come?
Ms. Dec 1983 p. 41

Here comes Bette! The divine Miss
Midler.
Newsweek Dec 17, 1973 p. 62

MIGRATION, INTERNAL

Americans on the move.
Time Mar 15, 1976 p. 54

"Okies" of the '70s. Mass migration in
search of jobs.
U.S. News Mar 24, 1975 p. 16

MILITARY ASSISTANCE, CUBAN-AFRICA

Castro. Russia's cat's-paw.
U.S. News Jun 12, 1978 p. 20

Cubans in Africa. Moscow tests Carter.
Newsweek Mar 13, 1978 p. 36

MILITARY LAW

Military justice on trial.
Newsweek Aug 31, 1970 p. 18

MILITARY OPERATIONS, COVERT

Secret warriors. Inside the covert military
operations of the Reagan era. Exclusive:
Oliver North's private notebooks.
U.S. News Mar 21, 1988 p. 24

MILITARY PERSONNEL

The top brass. Can they fight a modern war?
Newsweek   Jul 9, 1984   p. 32

MILITARY SERVICE, COMPULSORY

The draft—who beats it and how. What's wrong with the law. Attitudes on the campus. Dodging techniques, legal and otherwise. Pro football's magical immunity.
Life   Dec 9, 1966   p. 40

Viet Nam & the class of '66.
Time   Jun 3, 1966   p. 21

The draft. Welcome to the United States Army.
Newsweek   Apr 11, 1966   p. 30

The draft.
Life   Aug 20, 1965   p. 22

MILITARY-INDUSTRIAL COMPLEX

Who pays for peace? A shrinking defense budget will benefit America. But right now, there's a lot of pain in many companies and communities—with more to come.
Business Week   Jul 2, 1990   p. 64

The defense scandal. The impact on the industry. The 'Beltway Bandits.' Where the probe is headed. How to reform the system.
Business Week   Jul 4, 1988   p. 28

The military industrial complex.
Newsweek   Jun 9, 1969   p. 74

MILKEN, MIKE

Power on Wall Street. There's a new relationship between Wall Street and Corporate America—largely because of the work of one man: Drexel Burnham's Mike Milken.
Business Week   Jul 7, 1986   p. 56

MILLER, ARTHUR

'After the Fall.' Playwright Arthur Miller.
Newsweek   Feb 3, 1964   p. 49

MILLER, G. WILLIAM

The inflation fighter. Federal Reserve Chairman G. William Miller.
Time   Jul 17, 1978   p. 58

MILLER, JOHNNY

Golf's new golden boy.
Newsweek   Feb 3, 1975   p. 44

MILLETT, KATE

The politics of sex. Kate Millett of women's lib.
Time   Aug 31, 1970   p. 16

MILLIKEN & CO.

Roger Milliken. Running textiles' premier performer.
Business Week   Jan 19, 1981   p. 62

MILLIONAIRES

How ordinary people get rich. A million millionaires. Who they are - how they did it.
U.S. News   Jan 13, 1986   p. 43

America's invisible millionaires. A spectacular boom.
U.S. News   Mar 17, 1980   p. 34

Today's "poor" millionaires.
U.S. News   Aug 14, 1978   p. 38

Millionaires under 40.
Time   Dec 3, 1965   p. 88

MILLS, HAYLEY

Hayley Mills, a pert and perfect Pollyanna.
Life   Jun 13, 1960   p. 12

MILLS, WILBUR

Taxes. To cut or not to cut? Rep. Wilbur Mills. Chairman, Ways and Means.
Newsweek   Jan 14, 1963   p. 14

Will your taxes be cut? Congressman Wilbur Mills.
Time   Jan 11, 1963   p. 19

MIMIEUX, YVETTE

Yvette Mimieux learns to surf for Dr. Kildare.
Life   Oct 25, 1963   p. 119

Yvette Mimieux: Warmly wistful starlet.
Life   May 9, 1960   p. 85

MIND

Unlocking the unconscious. New evidence of Freud's inner world.
Discover   Feb 1985   p. 12

Mysteries of the mind.
Omni　　　　　Oct 1982　　　p. 28

Breakthroughs of the mind–how they
occur.
Psychology Today　　Jul 1981　　　p. 64

MINELLI, LIZA

Liza Minnelli in 'Cabaret.' A star is born.
Newsweek　　　Feb 28, 1972　p. 82

The new Miss Show Biz. Liza Minnelli.
Time　　　　　Feb 28, 1972　p. 65

**MINES AND MINERAL RESOURCES -
UNITED STATES**

The great gold scandal. A billion-dollar
giveaway is ravaging the American West.
U.S. News　　　Oct 28, 1991　　p. 44

Controversy over wilderness area
minerals policy.
Congressional Digest　Dec 1982　　p. 289

MINIMUM WAGE

Minimum wage controversy.
Congressional Digest　May 1989　　p. 131

Raising the minimum wage.
Congressional Digest　Aug 1987　　p. 193

The proposed subminimum wage for
youth.
Congressional Digest　Apr 1985　　p. 99

MINING INDUSTRY

The death of mining.
Business Week　　Dec 17, 1984　p. 64

MINNESOTA

The good life in Minnesota. Gov.
Wendell Anderson.
Time　　　　　Aug 13, 1973　p. 24

MINNESOTA MINING & MFG. CO.

Masters of innovation. How 3M keeps
new products coming.
Business Week　　Apr 10, 1989　p. 58

MINOW, NEWTON

Minow of the FCC: Television and the
public interest.
Newsweek　　　Sep 11, 1961　p. 61

MIRACLES

Do you believe in miracles? If you do,
you're not alone. From a vision of the
Virgin Mary on a hillside in Yugoslavia to
the face of Christ on a billboard in
Georgia, signs of a divine presence are
touching millions.
Life　　　　　Jul 1991　　　p. 38

MISCARRIAGES

Miscarriages. As many as 1 in 3
pregnancies fails. Doctors are just
beginning to understand why.
Newsweek　　　Aug 15, 1988　p. 46

MISS PIGGY (MUPPET)

Secrets of Miss Piggy's backstage life.
Life　　　　　Aug 1980　　　p. 54

MISSING CHILDREN

Stolen children. What can be done about
child abduction.
Newsweek　　　Mar 19, 1984　p. 78

MISSIONARIES, CHRISTIAN

The new missionary.
Time　　　　　Dec 27, 1982　p. 50

The missionary's new mission.
Newsweek　　　Dec 30, 1963　p. 36

Christian missionaries. From St. Paul to
1960.
Time　　　　　Apr 18, 1960　p. 64

MISSISSIPPI

Faulkner's Mississippi.
National Geographic　Mar 1989　　p. 313

MISSISSIPPI - RACE RELATIONS

Mississippi. Summer, 1964.
Newsweek　　　Jul 13, 1964　　p. 18

MITCHELL, JOHN

Indicted. John Mitchell.
Newsweek　　　May 21, 1973　p. 16

Mr. Law-and-Order. Attorney General
John Mitchell.
Newsweek　　　Sep 8, 1969　　p. 29

MITCHELL, JONI

Rock women. Pride and passion. Joni
Mitchell.
Time　　　　　Dec 16, 1974　p. 63

MITCHELL, MARTHA

The wives of Washington. Martha Mitchell.
Time   Nov 30, 1970   p. 31

Martha Mitchell. Talkative as ever, she finds Washington tough going.
Life   Oct 2, 1970   p. 37

MITSUBISHI GROUP COMPANIES

Mighty Mitsubishi. Japan's largest industrial group is on the move around the world and it's bringing the unique *keiretsu* system to America.
Business Week   Sep 24, 1990   p. 98

Mitsubishi. A Japanese giant's plans for growth in the U.S.
Business Week   Jul 20, 1981   p. 128

MITTERRAND, FRANCOIS

Can Mitterrand remake France's economy?
Business Week   Jan 10, 1983   p. 44

France's new look. Socialist President François Mitterrand.
Time   Jun 29, 1981   p. 26

MIXED MARRIAGES

See INTERRACIAL MARRIAGES

MOBIL CORP.

Mobil's costly Saudi strategy.
Business Week   Oct 17, 1983   p. 76

MODELS, FASHION

The '80s look.
Time   Feb 9, 1981   p. 82

Hunting down the world's loveliest girls.
Life   Nov 13, 1970   p. 63

Black models take center stage.
Life   Oct 17, 1969   p. 34

MOGUL EMPIRE

When the Moguls ruled.
National Geographic Apr 1985   p. 463

MOHAMMED REZA PAHLEVI, SHAH OF IRAN

Center of the storm. Iran's deposed Shah.
Time   Dec 10, 1979   p. 24

Showdown for the Shah.
Newsweek   Nov 20, 1978   p. 58

Iran in turmoil. The Shah.
Time   Sep 18, 1978   p. 32

The emperor of oil. The Shah of Iran.
Time   Nov 4, 1974   p. 28

Iran: Struggle for stability.
Time   Sep 12, 1960   p. 31

MONACO - ROYAL FAMILY

After Grace, Monaco's royal family recovers. An exclusive visit plus a talk with Prince Rainer.
Life   Mar 1983   p. 22

MONDALE, WALTER

Peace and war. Exclusive interviews on where they stand.
U.S. News   Oct 22, 1984   p. 29

Now it's a race.
Time   Mar 12, 1984   p. 16

Can anyone stop Fritz? Democratic candidate Walter Mondale.
Newsweek   Jan 9, 1984   p. 26

MONETARY POLICY

Proposals for a gold-based monetary system.
Congressional Digest Jun 1982   p. 163

MONETARY POLICY - UNITED STATES

A return to the gold standard. Why Reagan might try it. How it would be done. How it might work.
Business Week   Sep 21, 1981   p. 114

MONEY - INTERNATIONAL ASPECTS

The future of money: One world—one economy.
Omni   Jun 1991   p. 50

The lords of money. Should the world monetary system be overhauled? Treasury Secretary Baker thinks so—and wants finance ministers to back him at next month's economic summit.
Business Week   Apr 28, 1986   p. 72

Super dollar. Has it peaked?
U.S. News   Dec 3, 1984   p. 53

Super dollar. Reshaping the world economy. How long will it last? New strategy for U.S. multinationals. America's top importers.
Business Week   Oct 8, 1984   p. 164

Dollar fever infects the world. A $100 billion GNP loss for the U.S. A huge capital outflow from Europe.
Business Week   Jun 27, 1983   p. 90

A return to the gold standard. Why Reagan might try it. How it would be done. How it might work.
Business Week   Sep 21, 1981   p. 114

The money crisis.
Newsweek   Dec 2, 1968   p. 68

World money crisis.
Time   Nov 29, 1968   p. 19

The future of money.
Time   Mar 29, 1968   p. 80

The world's need for money. Should the dollar be almighty? The Secretary of the Treasury Fowler.
Time   Sep 10, 1965   p. 84

MONEY LAUNDERING

The world's sleaziest bank. How B.C.C.I. became a one-stop shopping center for criminals and spies — and how the U.S. is trying to cover up its involvement.
Time   Jul 29, 1991   p. 42

Money laundering. The trillion-dollar shell game.
Time   Dec 18, 1989   p. 50

Money laundering. How it works. What can be done.
Business Week   Mar 18, 1985   p. 74

MONK, THELONIOUS

Jazz: Bebop and beyond. Jazzman Thelonious Monk.
Time   Feb 28, 1964   p. 84

MONKEYS

Snow monkeys of Japan.
Life   Jan 30, 1970   p. 36

MONNET, JEAN

New strength for the West. Europe unites in the Common Market.
Time   Oct 6, 1961   p. 28

MONROE DOCTRINE

The Monroe Doctrine and Communist Cuba.
Time   Sep 21, 1962   p. 17

MONROE, MARILYN

Marilyn Monroe. If she had lived, who would she be today?
Ms.   Aug 1986   p. 40

The unseen Marilyn. Never published photographs—20 years after her death.
Life   Aug 1982   p. 52

Monroe meets Mailer.
Time   Jul 16, 1973   p. 60

Remember Marilyn. A photographic exhibit recalls the allure of a tragic star.
Life   Sep 8, 1972   p. 71

What really killed Marilyn.
Life   Aug 7, 1964   p. 68

Memories of Marilyn.
Life   Aug 17, 1962   p. 32

Marilyn Monroe. A skinny-dip you'll never see on the screen.
Life   Jun 22, 1962   p. 87

Marilyn's co-star: Yves Montand, idol of France.
Life   Aug 15, 1960   p. 63

MONSOONS

Monsoons. Life breath of half the world.
National Geographic Dec 1984   p. 712

MONTANA, JOE

Superdreams.
Time   Jan 25, 1982   p. 62

MONTAND, YVES

Marilyn's co-star: Yves Montand, idol of France.
Life   Aug 15, 1960   p. 63

MONTEREY BAY (CALIFORNIA)

Between Monterey tides.
National Geographic Feb 1990   p. 2

MOON

Apollo 12 on the moon.
Life   Dec 12, 1969   p. 34

Barnstorming the moon.
Life   Jun 6, 1969   p. 30

The true color of the moon. The latest lunar report from Surveyor.
Life   Jul 1, 1966   p. 62

MOORE, MARY TYLER

TV's funny girls. Mary Tyler Moore.
Valerie Harper.
Time   Oct 28, 1974   p. 58

MOORE, PAUL

The church faces life.
Newsweek   Dec 25, 1972   p. 55

MOORE, SARA JANE

Can the risk be cut?
Newsweek   Oct 6, 1975   p. 18

MORALE, NATIONAL

Is the malaise real? Nation's mood in
autumn.
U.S. News   Nov 12, 1979   p. 25

To lift the nation's spirit.
Newsweek   Jul 23, 1979   p. 20

MORALITY

Morality test. Do you cut corners on your
taxes? Is gambling immoral? Are
Americans too sexually permissive? Is
lying ever justified? Does it pay to be
moral?
U.S. News   Dec 9, 1985   p. 52

See Also ETHICS

MOREAU, JEANNE

Jeanne Moreau.
Time   Mar 5, 1965   p. 78

MORGAN, MARABEL

Fighting the housewife blues.
Time   Mar 14, 1977   p. 62

MORMONS

The woman who talked back to God.
Sonia Johnson's own story: *"From
Housewife to Heretic."*
Ms.   Nov 1981   p. 51

MORO, ALDO, KIDNAPPING

Italy's agony.
Newsweek   May 22, 1978   p. 30

MORRISON, TONI

Black magic. Novelist Toni Morrison.
Newsweek   Mar 30, 1981   p. 52

MORSE, ROBERT

Broadway's Robert Morse: Hottest ticket
in town.
Newsweek   Nov 27, 1961   p. 37

MOSTEL, ZERO

Zero Mostel. Broadway's brightest star.
Newsweek   Oct 19, 1964   p. 94

MOTHER TERESA

See TERESA, MOTHER

MOTHERS

Single mothers. Trying to measure up to
Supermom.
Ms.   Apr 1981   p. 47

MOTHERS AND SONS

Sons & mothers. The making of powerful
men.
Psychology Today   Mar 1983   p. 32

MOTHERS - EMPLOYMENT

See WORKING MOTHERS

**MOTION PICTURE ACTORS AND
ACTRESSES**

The stars celebrate Hollywood.
Life   Apr 1987   p. 130

Celebrating the movies. Hollywood's
most powerful women.
Life   May 1986   p. 41

The male idols. Hollywood's new sex
symbols.
Newsweek   May 23, 1983   p. 48

A new breed of actor.
Newsweek   Dec 7, 1981   p. 90

Mania for Marilyn. And Joan. And Lana.
And Shirley.
Life   Oct 1981   p. 136

Whatever became of Mary Astor and
other lost stars?
Life   Feb 1980   p. 89

Hollywood's whiz kids.
Time   Aug 13, 1979   p. 64

The new actresses. Sissy Spacek.
Newsweek   Feb 14, 1977   p. 56

The young actors. Stars and anti-stars.
Dustin Hoffman and Mia Farrow.
Time   Feb 7, 1969   p. 50

Faye Dunaway. The new American
beauties.
Newsweek   Mar 4, 1968   p. 42

New star Leslie Uggams: The Negro in
show business.
Newsweek   Jul 17, 1967   p. 63

The new beauties. Lovely young film
stars of Europe.
Life   Jan 28, 1966   p. 40

MOTION PICTURE INDUSTRY

How TV is revolutionizing Hollywood.
The challenge of pay TV. The fear of
video piracy.
Business Week   Feb 21, 1983   p. 78

Inside Hollywood. High stakes! Fast
bucks! Shady deals!
Newsweek   Feb 13, 1978   p. 70

The new Hollywood. Francis Ford
Coppola and the 'Godfathers.'
Newsweek   Nov 25, 1974   p. 70

MOTION PICTURE PRODUCERS AND DIRECTORS

Cinema as an international art.
Time   Sep 20, 1963   p. 78

MOTION PICTURES

The twisted truth of 'JFK.' Why Oliver
Stone's new movie can't be trusted.
Newsweek   Dec 23, 1991   p. 46

JFK. Why we still care. A new movie
about the assassination reopens an old
controversy.
Life   Dec 1991   p. 34

Star Trek VI: An exclusive look at the film,
the family, and future of starship
Enterprise by director Nicholas Meyer.
Omni   Dec 1991   p. 52

Why Thelma & Louise strikes a nerve.
Time   Jun 24, 1991   p. 52

Tackling a taboo. Spike Lee's take on
interracial romance. Mixed couples on
love and prejudice.
Newsweek   Jun 10, 1991   p. 44

Godfather III. After 16 years, an offer no
moviegoer can refuse.
Life   Nov 1990   p. 50

Hot tickets. Hollywood's high-stakes
summer. Madonna and Warren Beatty
go for broke in 'Dick Tracy'.
Newsweek   Jun 25, 1990   p. 44

Mississippi Burning. A new movie's
searing view of racism stirs a debate over
fact vs. fiction.
Time   Jan 9, 1989   p. 56

Love those gorillas! The jungle diaries of
Sigourney Weaver.
Life   Oct 1988   p. 3

Hanks hits it big. The dazzling actor
scores again in "Punchline."
Newsweek   Sep 26, 1988   p. 56

Who was Jesus? A startling new movie
raises an age-old question.
Time   Aug 15, 1988   p. 34

Who is Roger Rabbit? Spielberg and
Disney take a $45 million gamble.
Newsweek   Jun 27, 1988   p. 54

'Broadcast News.' Hollywood scores with
love and laughs. Albert Brooks, Holly
Hunter and William Hurt.
Newsweek   Dec 28, 1987   p. 44

The thriller is back. In *Fatal Attraction*,
stars Glenn Close and Michael Douglas
live a nightmare of the late 1980s.
Time   Nov 16, 1987   p. 72

'The Untouchables.' Mob hit. Robert
DeNiro as Al Capone.
Newsweek   Jun 22, 1987   p. 62

Future films. 7 great directors sneak
preview their own movies for 2001 A.D.
Omni   Jun 1987   p. 44

Platoon. Vietnam as it really was.
Time   Jan 26, 1987   p. 54

Horrors! The summer's scariest movie.
Sigourney Weaver and she-monster in
Aliens.
Time   Jul 28, 1986   p. 54

Showing the flag. Rocky, Rambo, and the return of the American hero. Sylvester Stallone.
Newsweek   Dec 23, 1985   p. 58

The Color Purple becomes a movie. Whoopi & Alice & Quincy.
Ms.   Dec 1985   p. 66

An old master's new triumph. David Lean directs "A Passage to India."
Time   Dec 31, 1984   p. 54

Arthur C. Clarke's "2010". The film and beyond.
Omni   Dec 1984   p. 76

Indiana Jones returns. And Kate Capshaw lands him in the new 'Raiders' movie sequel.
Life   Jun 1984   p. 88

Star Wars III. Return of the Jedi. George Lucas & friends wrap it all up.
Time   May 23, 1983   p. 62

Golden oldies. Hepburn and Fonda in "On Golden Pond."
Time   Nov 16, 1981   p. 112

Cliffhanger classic. 'Raiders of the Lost Ark.'
Newsweek   Jun 15, 1981   p. 58

Secretary as hero!
Ms.   Jan 1981   p. 43

The empire strikes back. Star Wars. Archvillain Darth Vader.
Time   May 19, 1980   p. 66

Hollywood's scary summer.
Newsweek   Jun 18, 1979   p. 54

'Apocalypse Now.' Francis Coppola's long-awaited movie about Vietnam.
Life   Jun 1979   p. 110

Superman to the rescue!
Newsweek   Jan 1, 1979   p. 46

The UFO's are coming! Hollywood's 'Close Encounters.'
Newsweek   Nov 21, 1977   p. 88

Diane Keaton. Annie Hall meets Mr. Goodbar.
Time   Sep 26, 1977   p. 68

DeNiro: A star for the '70s. In 'New York, New York.'
Newsweek   May 16, 1977   p. 80

Here comes King Kong.
Time   Oct 25, 1976   p. 64

Watergate on film. Hoffman & Redford in "All the President's Men."
Time   Mar 29, 1976   p. 54

Kubrick's grandest gamble. Marisa Berenson in "Barry Lyndon."
Time   Dec 15, 1975   p. 72

Epic of Opry Land.
Newsweek   Jun 30, 1975   p. 46

Super shark. "Jaws" on film and other summer thrillers.
Time   Jun 23, 1975   p. 42

The Great Gatsby supersell. Robert Redford & Mia Farrow.
Time   Mar 18, 1974   p. 82

The hottest movie. Director Bernardo Bertolucci.
Newsweek   Feb 12, 1973   p. 54

Sex and death in Paris. Marlon Brando in "Last Tango."
Time   Jan 22, 1973   p. 51

The return to romance. Ali MacGraw.
Time   Jan 11, 1971   p. 40

The new movies.
Newsweek   Dec 7, 1970   p. 62

"Catch 22" on film. Director Mike Nichols. War as horror-comedy.
Time   Jun 15, 1970   p. 66

Alice's restaurant's kids. Folk singer Arlo Guthrie.
Newsweek   Sep 29, 1969   p. 101

From laugh-in to scare-in. Movie career for Rowan and Martin.
Life   May 23, 1969   p. 54

'Husbands' on the run. Peter Falk, Ben Gazzara and John Cassavetes make a movie.
Life   May 9, 1969   p. 53

Streisand's Dolly. The $20 million film
that cannot be released.
Life   Feb 14, 1969   p. 58

Director and star. The Newmans triumph
with *Rachel, Rachel.*
Life   Oct 18, 1968   p. 46

The new cinema: Violence...sex...art...
Bonnie and Clyde.
Time   Dec 8, 1967   p. 66

Nightmare revisited. 'In Cold Blood' is
filmed on scene of the crime.
Life   May 12, 1967   p. 98

In the children's classic Rex Harrison as
Dr. Dolittle.
Life   Sep 30, 1966   p. 122

Liz in a shocker. Her movie shatters the
rules of censorship. Liz Taylor in 'Who's
Afraid of Virginia Woolf?'
Life   Jun 10, 1966   p. 87

Charlie Chaplin directs Sophia.
Life   Apr 1, 1966   p. 80

James Bond in 'Thunderball.' Wildest
007 movie yet.
Life   Jan 7, 1966   p. 79

Julie Andrews. A hit again in her new
movie *Sound of Music.*
Life   Mar 12, 1965   p. 52

Peter O'Toole as 'Lord Jim'. His
off-camera misadventures on location in
the Far East.
Life   Jan 22, 1965   p. 85

A matter for James Bond. Shirley Eaton,
gilded victim in *Goldfinger,* funniest and
money-makingest of the 007 movies.
Life   Nov 6, 1964   p. 116

Carroll Baker with Masai warriors on
location in Kenya.
Life   Jul 17, 1964   p. 76

The movies.
Life   Dec 20, 1963   p. 14

Shirley MacLaine as Irma La Douce.
Life   Jun 21, 1963   p. 62

Cleopatra. Most talked-about movie ever
made.
Life   Apr 19, 1963   p. 72

Elizabeth Taylor: Cleopatra's fortunes.
Newsweek   Mar 25, 1963   p. 63

Alfred Hitchcock: His horror film 'The
Birds.'
Life   Feb 1, 1963   p. 68

Three epic movies including Marlon
Brando in 'Mutiny on the Bounty.'
Life   Dec 14, 1962   p. 112

Shirley MacLaine. Tortured role in a
daring movie.
Life   Feb 23, 1962   p. 88

Jill Haworth and Sal Mineo in 'Exodus.'
Life   Dec 12, 1960   p. 70

Box office bonanza. Sunny Doris Day in a
shivery role.
Life   Oct 10, 1960   p. 136

Her hair cropped, Silvana Mangano acts
collaborator role.
Life   Apr 11, 1960   p. 75

MOTION PICTURES - SPECIAL EFFECTS
Computerizing the movies.
Discover   Aug 1984   p. 76

MOTOROLA INC.
Competing with Japan. How Motorola
does it.
Business Week   Nov 13, 1989   p. 108

Motorola's new strategy. Adding
computers to its base in electronics.
Business Week   Mar 29, 1982   p. 128

MOUNT EVEREST (CHINA AND NEPAL)
Mass conquest of mighty Everest.
Life   Sep 20, 1963   p. 68

**MOUNT ST. HELENS, WASHINGTON
(STATE)**
Mount St. Helens. Rumblings and
renewal 5 years after the blast.
Life   Sep 1985   p. 20

Mount St. Helens. Mountain with a death
wish.
National Geographic Jan 1981   p. 3

The big bang.
Newsweek   Jun 2, 1980   p. 22

The big blowup.
Time   Jun 2, 1980   p. 26

MYTHOLOGY, GREEK
Greece part II. Myths, gods, heroes.
Life   Jan 18, 1963   p. 52

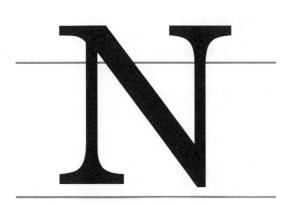

N

NABISCO COMPANY
See RJR NABISCO, INC.

NABOKOV, VLADIMIR
The novel is alive and living in Antiterra. Vladimir Nabokov.
Time   May 23, 1969   p. 81

Lolita's creator: Vladimir Nabokov.
Newsweek   Jun 25, 1962   p. 51

NADER, RALPH
The consumer revolt. Ralph Nader.
Time   Dec 12, 1969   p. 89

Consumer crusader. Ralph Nader.
Newsweek   Jan 22, 1968   p. 65

NAIPAUL, V.S.
The storyteller's art. V.S. Naipaul's tales of a troubled world.
Newsweek   Nov 16, 1981   p. 104

NAMATH, JOE
Namath. The juicy rewards of a painful life.
Life   Nov 3, 1972   p. 36

Pro football's game plan: Back to the attack.
Time   Oct 16, 1972   p. 46

Pro football '69. Namath of the Jets.
Newsweek   Sep 15, 1969   p. 29

Behind the Namath affair. A question of the bad company he keeps.
Life   Jun 20, 1969   p. 22

NAMIBIA
Namibia. Nearly a nation?
National Geographic Jun 1982   p. 755

NANOTECHNOLOGY
Nanotechnology. Molecular machines that mimic life.
Omni   Nov 1986   p. 56

NAPOLEON
Napoleon.
National Geographic Feb 1982   p. 142

NASA
See NATIONAL AERONAUTICS AND SPACE ADMINISTRATION

NASSER, GAMAL ABDEL
The Mideast after Nasser.
Newsweek   Oct 12, 1970   p. 31

The Arab world after Nasser.
Time   Oct 12, 1970   p. 20

The Mideast after Nasser.
Life   Oct 9, 1970   p. 28

Deadlock in the Middle East. Egypt's Nasser.
Time   May 16, 1969   p. 29

"Keep your tents separate and bring your hearts together." - Arab proverb. Egypt's Nasser.
Time   Mar 29, 1963   p. 22

NATIONAL AERONAUTICS AND SPACE ADMINISTRATION
Star crossed. The Hubble telescope. NASA's $1.5 billion blunder.
Newsweek   Jul 9, 1990   p. 48

The future: Disaster and indecision could cost U.S. entire generation of space scientists.
USA Today   Jun 1987   p. 1

Fixing NASA.
Time   Jun 9, 1986   p. 14

Space: NASA's next steps toward the stars.
Omni   Jan 1986   p. 78

Here comes Skylab. Ten years after the moon walk.
Time   Jul 16, 1979   p. 20

New adventures in space.
U.S. News   Jul 16, 1979   p. 33

NATIONAL BROADCASTING COMPANY

Cool cops. Hot show. NBC's Miami Vice.
Time   Sep 16, 1985   p. 60

NATIONAL GALLERY OF ART (WASHINGTON, D.C.)

Celebration! The National Gallery of Art's 50th anniversary.
USA Today   Jul 1991   p. 22

NATIONAL GEOGRAPHIC SOCIETY

100 years. Reporting on "the world and all that is in it."
National Geographic Sep 1988   p. 270

Great photographs from the National Geographic Society's Centennial.
USA Today   Sep 1988   p. 36

One hundred years of increasing and diffusing geographic knowledge.
National Geographic Jan 1988   p. 8

NATIONAL GUARD

Red Arrow division gets the call. Back to duty.
Life   Nov 3, 1961   p. 40

NATIONAL PARKS AND RESERVES

Can we save our parks? The stuggle between man and beast.
Newsweek   Jul 28, 1986   p. 48

National parks in peril. Montana's glacier wilderness and others are facing ruin.
Life   Jul 1983   p. 106

Watt's land rush. Digging up the last frontier? Interior Secretary James Watt.
Newsweek   Jun 29, 1981   p. 22

NATIONAL RIFLE ASSOCIATION

Who is the NRA? A look at America's embattled gun lobby.
Time   Jan 29, 1990   p. 16

NATIONAL SECURITY AGENCY

Eavesdropping on the world's secrets.
U.S. News   Jun 26, 1978   p. 45

NATIONAL SERVICE

National service.
Congressional Digest May 1990   p. 131

America needs you. The push for voluntary national service.
U.S. News   Feb 13, 1989   p. 20

NATIONALISM

From Africa to Viet Nam: New policies in a changing world.
Time   Mar 13, 1964   p. 30

NATIVE AMERICANS

America before Columbus. The untold story.
U.S. News   Jul 8, 1991   p. 22

NATIVE PEOPLES

Lost tribes, lost knowledge. When native cultures disappear, so does a trove of scientific and medical wisdom.
Time   Sep 23, 1991   p. 46

NATURAL DISASTERS

Is Mother Nature going berserk?
U.S. News   Feb 22, 1982   p. 66

NATURAL GAS INDUSTRY

Gas pipeliners. Priced into a no-growth future. Massacre in the marketplace.
Business Week   Aug 2, 1982   p. 44

NAVRATILOVA, MARTINA

A style of her own. Martina Navratilova.
Newsweek   Sep 6, 1982   p. 44

NAVY - SOVIET UNION

Russia's navy: A new challenge at sea.
Time   Feb 23, 1968   p. 23

NAVY - UNITED STATES

Tough new Navy. 600 ships, an aggressive strategy and a strong top gun. Secretary of the Navy, John F. Lehman, Jr.
U.S. News   Aug 4, 1986   p. 28

The U.S. Navy in the Western Pacific: The view from the mid-1980's.
USA Today   May 1985   p. 10

Attack on the Navy.
Time   May 8, 1978   p. 14

U.S. Navy in distress.
U.S. News   Mar 6, 1978   p. 24

NBC

See NATIONAL BROADCASTNG
COMPANY

NCNB CORP.

Super banker. Hugh McColl is going after
his biggest deal yet. It would make his
NCNB the nation's second-largest bank
and change the face of banking in the U.S.
Business Week   Jul 15, 1991   p. 116

NDEBELE TRIBESPEOPLE

Dilemma of independence for South
Africa's Ndebele.
National Geographic Feb 1986   p. 260

NEFF, TOM

The new headhunters. Meet Tom Neff.
He's filling million-dollar jobs—and
shaking up his industry.
Business Week   Feb 6, 1989   p. 64

NEHRU, JAWAHARLAL

The cremation of Nehru [funeral and
memorial service].
Life   Jun 5, 1964   p. 32

India's lost illusions. Nehru.
Time   Nov 30, 1962   p. 23

Nehru in America: "For us, peace is a
passion."
Newsweek   Nov 20, 1961   p. 37

NELSON, WILLIE

Willie Nelson. Where C&W's top star
hides away with his family.
Life   Aug 1983   p. 76

King of country music. Willie Nelson.
Newsweek   Aug 14, 1978   p. 52

NEPTUNE (PLANET)

The blue planet. A close encounter with
Neptune.
Newsweek   Sep 4, 1989   p. 50

NEUTRON BOMBS

Furor over the neutron bomb.
Newsweek   Apr 17, 1978   p. 34

NEW AGE MOVEMENT

Om....The New Age. Starring Shirley
MacLaine, faith healers, channelers, space
travelers and crystals galore.
Time   Dec 7, 1987   p. 62

16 ways to control your mind. Test your
psychic abilities.
Omni   Oct 1987   p. 14

NEW DEAL LEGISLATION

The New Deal. FDR's disputed legacy.
Time   Feb 1, 1982   p. 20

NEW YORK (CITY)

The rotting of the Big Apple.
Time   Sep 17, 1990   p. 36

Washington vs. New York. Why they
hate each other. Why America hates
them both.
Newsweek   Jun 20, 1988   p. 16

The New York colossus. The city's surge
to world financial supremacy.
Business Week   Jul 23, 1984   p. 98

Blackout!
Newsweek   Jul 25, 1977   p. 16

Blackout '77. Once more, with looting.
Time   Jul 25, 1977   p. 12

Ford and New York.
Newsweek   Nov 10, 1975   p. 18

Brother, can you spare $4 billion?
Time   Oct 20, 1975   p. 9

New York's last gasp?
Newsweek   Aug 4, 1975   p. 18

New York: The breakdown of a city.
Time   Nov 1, 1968   p. 20

5:28 P.M., Nov. 9th. The lights went out.
Life   Nov 19, 1965   p. 36

Art in New York.
Newsweek   Jan 4, 1965   p. 54

The man with 1,000,000 children. New
York City's Superintendent Calvin Gross.
Time   Nov 15, 1963   p. 86

New York, N.Y. Can anyone run it?
Newsweek   Nov 13, 1961   p. 26

U.S. policy toward Nicaragua.
Congressional Digest Nov 1984   p. 259

America's secret war. Target: Nicaragua.
Newsweek   Nov 8, 1982   p. 42

Taking aim at Nicaragua. The
propaganda blitz. What U.S. intelligence
shows. How real a threat?
Newsweek   Mar 22, 1982 p. 20

NICHOLS, MIKE
"Catch 22" on film. Director Mike Nichols.
War as horror-comedy.
Time   Jun 15, 1970 p. 66

Mike Nichols. Lighting up Broadway.
Newsweek   Nov 14, 1966 p. 95

NICHOLSON, JACK
Jack Nicholson. The star with the killer
smile.
Time   Aug 12, 1974 p. 44

The new movies.
Newsweek   Dec 7, 1970   p. 62

NICKLAUS, JACK
U.S. Open champ Jack Nicklaus.
Time   Jun 29, 1962 p. 38

NIGER - NATIVE PEOPLES
Niger's Wodaabe: "People of the taboo."
National Geographic Oct 1983   p. 483

NIGERIA
Africa's woes. Coups, conflict and
corruption.
Time   Jan 16, 1984 p. 24

Biafra: End of a rebellion.
Time   Jan 26, 1970 p. 18

Biafra's agony. Colonel Ojukwu.
Time   Aug 23, 1968 p. 20

Starving children of Biafra War.
Life   Jul 12, 1968 p. 20

Nigeria's Prime Minister Balewa.
Time   Dec 5, 1960   p. 20

NINETEEN HUNDRED AND EIGHTIES
Financing the 90s. Too much debt. Too
many bad loans. Too much unneeded
real estate. The excesses of the 1980s have
damaged many of our financial
institutions and corporations.
Business Week   Nov 4, 1991   p. 112

The eight big ideas of the eighties.
Discover   Oct 1989   p. 30

The 80's are over. Greed goes out of style.
Newsweek   Jan 4, 1988   p. 40

Ten years that shook America...now, the
'80s.
Newsweek   Nov 19, 1979 p. 84

Challenges of the '80s.
U.S. News   Oct 15, 1979 p. 45

NINETEEN HUNDRED AND EIGHTY
The year in pictures.
Life   Jan 1981   p. 7

Pictures of '80.
Newsweek   Dec 29, 1980 p. 28

NINETEEN HUNDRED AND EIGHTY-EIGHT
88 the year in pictures.
Life   Jan 1989   p. 8

NINETEEN HUNDRED AND EIGHTY-FIVE
The year in pictures 85.
Life   Jan 1986   p. 6

NINETEEN HUNDRED AND EIGHTY-FOUR
The year in science.
Discover   Jan 1985   p. 60

84. The year in pictures.
Life   Jan 1985   p. 6

NINETEEN HUNDRED AND EIGHTY-NINE
1989. The top 45 science stories.
Discover   Jan 1990   p. 14

The year 89 in pictures.
Life   Jan 1990   p. 8

NINETEEN HUNDRED AND EIGHTY-ONE
Looking back at '81.
Newsweek   Jan 4, 1982   p. 26

The year in science. Saturn fly-by.
Animal tests. Shuttle flight. Medfly crisis.
Discover   Jan 1982   p. 66

The year in pictures.
Life   Jan 1982   p. 8

NINETEEN HUNDRED AND EIGHTY-SEVEN

1988. The year in science. The top 35 science stories.
Discover   Jan 1989   p. 18

1987. The top 35 science stories.
Discover   Jan 1988   p. 23

1987. The year in pictures.
Life   Jan 1988   p. 3

NINETEEN HUNDRED AND EIGHTY-SIX

The year in pictures 86.
Life   Jan 1987   p. 8

A letter to the year 2086. "Do you see starlight? So do we. Smell the fire? We do too. Draw close. Let us tell each other a story."
Time   Dec 29, 1986   p. 24

NINETEEN HUNDRED AND EIGHTY-THREE

The year in science.
Discover   Jan 1984   p. 58

'83. The year in pictures.
Life   Jan 1984   p. 8

NINETEEN HUNDRED AND EIGHTY-TWO

The year in science. Scientist of the year. [Robert Weinberg]
Discover   Jan 1983   p. 62

The year in pictures.
Life   Jan 1983   p. 8

NINETEEN HUNDRED AND FIFTIES

The fifties. Re-living it up. Why America loves the food, the fashion, the fun.
Life   Aug 1985   p. 77

The 50s. Wacky revival of hula hoops. Ducktails. Sock hops. Marilyn Monroe look. Rock 'n' roll. Elvis himself.
Life   Jun 16, 1972   p. 38

NINETEEN HUNDRED AND FORTY

Defying Hitler. World War II. 1940. America on the eve of war. The air battle for Britain.
U.S. News   Aug 27, 1990   p. 44

NINETEEN HUNDRED AND NINETIES

The 90's. A survival guide. Issues, people and predictions for the age of anxiety.
Newsweek   Dec 31, 1990   p. 14

NINETEEN HUNDRED AND NINETY

1990. The top 50 science stories.
Discover   Jan 1991   p. 24

The year in pictures 1990.
Life   Jan 1991   p. 6

The best of '90. Yes, Bart, even you made the list.
Time   Dec 31, 1990   p. 40

NINETEEN HUNDRED AND SEVENTIES

The 70's. Special issue. The decade in pictures.
Life   Dec 1979   p. 4

Ten years that shook America...now, the '80s.
Newsweek   Nov 19, 1979   p. 84

Into the '70s.
Life   Jan 9, 1970   p. 40

NINETEEN HUNDRED AND SEVENTY-ONE

The year in pictures.
Life   Dec 31, 1971   p. 2

NINETEEN HUNDRED AND SEVENTY-SEVEN

Pictures of '77.
Newsweek   Dec 26, 1977   p. 16

NINETEEN HUNDRED AND SEVENTY-SIX

Pictures of '76.
Newsweek   Jan 3, 1977   p. 12

NINETEEN HUNDRED AND SEVENTY-TWO

The year in pictures 1972.
Life   Dec 29, 1972   p. 3

NINETEEN HUNDRED AND SIXTIES

Will we ever get over the '60s?
Newsweek   Sep 5, 1988   p. 14

Good-bye to the '60s.
Newsweek   Dec 29, 1969   p. 12

Nixon's China odyssey.
Time   Mar 6, 1972   p. 10

The young Nixon. His career as an actor.
The steady girl he didn't marry. Breaking
into the dean's office. Poker champ of
Green Island atoll.
Life   Nov 6, 1970   p. 54

Bebe Rebozo. President Nixon's best
friend.
Life   Jul 31, 1970   p. 18

Nixon in trouble.
Newsweek   Oct 13, 1969   p. 30

The war: Nixon's big test.
Newsweek   Mar 31, 1969   p. 20

Winter White House. Nixon warms up
for Europe on Key Biscayne.
Life   Feb 21, 1969   p. 26

President and Mrs. Richard M. Nixon.
Newsweek   Jan 27, 1969   p. 17

Can Nixon unite the nation?
Newsweek   Nov 18, 1968   p. 38

The Nixon era begins.
Life   Nov 15, 1968   p. 36

The election. Richard Nixon.
Time   Nov 15, 1968   p. 22

How Nixon won. The President-Elect.
Newsweek   Nov 11, 1968   p. 31

The GOP ticket.
Newsweek   Aug 19, 1968   p. 18

The G.O.P. ticket.
Time   Aug 16, 1968   p. 10

Can the GOP come back? Nixon on the
road.
Newsweek   Oct 10, 1966   p. 30

Nixon. Brown. Biggest state's biggest
battle.
Newsweek   Oct 29, 1962   p. 19

The stories I kept to myself by Richard
Nixon. Great crises in my career. Part I:
The famous fund.
Life   Mar 16, 1962   p. 94

Nixon for governor.
Newsweek   Oct 9, 1961   p. 24

Candidate Nixon.
Time   Oct 31, 1960   p. 13

Balloons soar as the Nixons begin
campaign.
Life   Aug 8, 1960   p. 16

Republicans: Platform for the '60s.
Rockefeller & Nixon.
Time   Aug 1, 1960   p. 9

NIXON, RICHARD M. (FAMILY)
Julie. The David Eisenhowers.
Newsweek   Oct 14, 1974   p. 39

NIXON, RICHARD M. - HEALTH
How sick is Nixon?
Newsweek   Sep 23, 1974   p. 30

NIXON, RICHARD M. - IMPEACHMENT
Impeachment. The formal charges.
Outlook in the House. Nixon's defense
strategy. What the people say. A lesson
from history - Trial of Andrew Johnson.
U.S. News   Aug 12, 1974   p. 15

The impeachment vote.
Newsweek   Aug 5, 1974   p. 18

Nixon. The case for and against.
U.S. News   Aug 5, 1974   p. 11

How good a case?
Newsweek   Jul 29, 1974   p. 16

The G.O.P.'s moment of truth.
Time   Jul 29, 1974   p. 6

The evidence.
Newsweek   Jul 22, 1974   p. 14

Impeachment crisis - key decisions at
hand.
U.S. News   Jul 22, 1974   p. 15

The Nixon crisis. Where will it lead?
U.S. News   May 27, 1974   p. 17

Will he resign?
Newsweek   May 20, 1974   p. 22

All about impeachment.
Newsweek   Mar 25, 1974   p. 28

"I know what I meant."
Newsweek   Mar 18, 1974   p. 22

NONPROFIT INSTITUTIONS

Surprise! Some of America's best-run organizations are nonprofits. Here's what Corporate America can learn from them. How Frances Hesselbein showed the way at the Girl Scouts.
Business Week　　　Mar 26, 1990　p. 66

NORDENSTROM, BJORN

Electric man. Dr. Björn Nordenström claims to have found in the human body a heretofore unknown universe of electrical activity that's the very foundation of the healing process and is as critical to well-being as the flow of blood.
Discover　　　Apr 1986　　p. 22

NORELL, NORMAN

Sensational clothes by America's Norell stir up style storm.
Life　　　Sep 26, 1960　p. 22

NORIEGA, MANUEL

The Noriega files. His treacherous links with the drug cartel, Castro, Bush and the CIA. Excerpts from a new book by Frederick Kempe.
Newsweek　　　Jan 15, 1990　p. 14

Drugs, money and death. The sordid story of Panama's outlaw dictator. Gen. Manuel Antonio Noriega.
Newsweek　　　Feb 15, 1988　p. 32

NORODOM SIHANOUK

The U.S. & Southeast Asia. How to cope with never-never land. Cambodia's Prince Sihanouk.
Time　　　Apr 3, 1964　　p. 32

NORTH ATLANTIC TREATY ORGANIZATION

Controversy over NATO cost-sharing.
Congressional Digest Aug 1984　　p. 193

New U.S. foreign policy. Can the alliance be saved?
Business Week　　　Feb 22, 1982　p. 60

NORTH DAKOTA

North Dakota. Tough times on the prairie.
National Geographic Mar 1987　　p. 320

NORTH, OLIVER

"Reagan knew everything." Ollie North tells his story.
Time　　　Oct 28, 1991　p. 36

The other Oliver North.
Life　　　Aug 1987　　p. 12

Ollie takes the Hill. The fall guy becomes a folk hero.
Newsweek　　　Jul 20, 1987　p. 12

"I was authorized to do everything that I did" -Oliver North.
Time　　　Jul 20, 1987　p. 12

How Ollie stormed the Hill. A TV triumph turns the tables on his critics. Who really gave the orders.
U.S. News　　　Jul 20, 1987　p. 18

Oliver North, star witness. Plus Gore Vidal and Pat Buchanan on the hearings.
Newsweek　　　Jul 13, 1987　p. 14

Front and center. Lieut. Colonel Oliver North.
Time　　　Jul 13, 1987　p. 22

Ollie's private world. Out of the shadows.
U.S. News　　　Jul 13, 1987　p. 20

Probing the mess. Fresh money trails. The CIA role. An interview with Casey.
Time　　　Dec 22, 1986　p. 14

NORTH POLE

North to the Pole. Six by dogsled.
National Geographic Sep 1986　　p. 289

NORTHEASTERN STATES

The North fights back.
U.S. News　　　Jun 15, 1981　p. 27

NORTHROP CORP.

Northrop. Look who's heading for no. 1 in defense.
Business Week　　　Apr 19, 1982　p. 70

NOSTALGIA

101 things worth saving.
Life　　　Oct 1989　　p. 50

The fifties. Re-living it up. Why America loves the food, the fashion, the fun.
Life　　　Aug 1985　　p. 77

The great nostalgia kick.
U.S. News   Mar 22, 1982   p. 57

Mania for Marilyn. And Joan. And Lana.
And Shirley.
Life   Oct 1981   p. 136

Yearning for the fifties. The good old
days.
Newsweek   Oct 16, 1972   p. 78

The 50s. Wacky revival of hula hoops.
Ducktails. Sock hops. Marilyn Monroe
look. Rock 'n' roll. Elvis himself.
Life   Jun 16, 1972   p. 38

Everybody's just wild about nostalgia.
Life   Feb 19, 1971   p. 40

Nostalgia. The vogue for the old.
Newsweek   Dec 28, 1970   p. 34

NUCLEAR ENERGY
See NUCLEAR POWER PLANTS

NUCLEAR FREEZE MOVEMENT
See ANTI-NUCLEAR MOVEMENT

NUCLEAR FUSION
Fusion in a bottle. Miracle or mistake? A
scientific detective story.
Business Week   May 8, 1989   p. 100

The race for fusion. The scientific debate.
Why the stakes are so high.
Newsweek   May 8, 1989   p. 48

Fusion: Tapping the cosmic furnace.
Omni   Jan 1981   p. 38

NUCLEAR POWER PLANTS
Nuclear power. Do we have a choice?
Time   Apr 29, 1991   p. 54

Nuclear renaissance. Reactors are back
and reactions are good.
Omni   May 1988   p. 40

Nuclear power. Bombing out?
Time   Feb 13, 1984   p. 34

Judgment day for nuclear power. Is
public confidence gone forever? Are the
newest plants safe to open? Can the
problem of toxic wastes be solved?
Life   May 1979   p. 22

How safe is nuclear energy?
Newsweek   Apr 12, 1976   p. 70

NUCLEAR POWER PLANTS - ACCIDENTS
The victims of Chernobyl. A personal
account by the American doctor who
helped them.
Life   Aug 1986   p. 20

The Chernobyl syndrome. How the
meltdown happened. The Kremlin
cover-up. The fall-out: What are the risks?
Newsweek   May 12, 1986   p. 20

Meltdown. Chernobyl reactor.
Time   May 12, 1986   p. 38

Nightmare in Russia. How reckless are
the Soviets? Fallout for nuclear power?
Can it happen here? Damaged Chernobyl
plant.
U.S. News   May 12, 1986   p. 18

Nuclear accident.
Newsweek   Apr 9, 1979   p. 24

Nuclear nightmare.
Time   Apr 9, 1979   p. 8

NUCLEAR PROPULSION
A-power: Things to come.
Newsweek   Sep 19, 1960   p. 69

NUCLEAR SUBMARINES
Deep down patrol on a Polaris sub.
Exclusive photos of our no.1 weapon.
Life   Mar 22, 1963   p. 22

NUCLEAR TEST BAN
See ARMS CONTROL

NUCLEAR WARFARE
America's doomsday project. The U.S.
has a secret survival plan in the event of
nuclear war, but would it work? Critics
have doubts.
U.S. News   Aug 7, 1989   p. 26

War and peace. Psychology at the
summit.
Psychology Today   Jun 1988   p. 27

Nuclear fear. Growing up scared...of not
growing up.
Psychology Today   Apr 1984   p. 18

NUCLEAR WEAPONS

On the 40th anniversary of Hiroshima, say hi to the bomb makers.
Discover   Aug 1985   p. 24

Zero hour. Forty years of the Atomic Age.
Newsweek   Jul 29, 1985   p. 28

The Atomic Age. "My God, what have we done?" Captian Robert Lewis co-pilot of the Enola Gay. Hiroshima. August 6, 1945.
Time   Jul 29, 1985   p. 32

Who has the bomb. The nuclear threat is spreading.
Time   Jun 3, 1985   p. 36

Nuclear war. Can we reduce the risk?
Newsweek   Dec 5, 1983   p. 44

Nuclear poker. The stakes get higher and higher.
Time   Jan 31, 1983   p. 10

The nuclear arms race. The MX muddle. Reagan's new strategy. Limited war: How it might happen.
Newsweek   Oct 5, 1981   p. 32

Furor over the neutron bomb.
Newsweek   Apr 17, 1978   p. 34

Missiles vs. missiles. $30 billion decision.
Newsweek   Mar 27, 1967   p. 44

The bomb. The next twenty years.
Newsweek   Aug 9, 1965   p. 52

As the test ban approaches: The size & condition of the U.S. atomic arsenal.
Time   Aug 23, 1963   p. 11

Beyond the nuclear agreement.
Time   Aug 2, 1963   p. 15

Space bomb in color. Eerie spectacle in Pacific sky.
Life   Jul 20, 1962   p. 26

The Pacific tests.
Newsweek   May 7, 1962   p. 26

U.S. nuclear testing. The shots heard round the world.
Time   May 4, 1962   p. 18

For war - the atom - for peace. Seaborg of the AEC: A scientist in command.
Newsweek   Oct 16, 1961   p. 63

Khrushchev.
Time   Sep 8, 1961   p. 26

See Also ARMS CONTROL

NUCLEAR WEAPONS - IRAQ

Saddam's bomb. The secrets of Iraq's nuclear weapons program.
U.S. News   Nov 25, 1991   p. 34

NUNS

See CATHOLIC CHURCH - CLERGY

NUREYEV, RUDOLF

Nureyev: The new Nijinsky.
Newsweek   Apr 19, 1965   p. 88

Rudolf Nureyev.
Time   Apr 16, 1965   p. 48

NUTRITION

Fed up! Is there anything left we can eat?
Newsweek   May 27, 1991   p. 46

Best ways to stay healthy. Exercise and your heart. A live-longer diet. Surgery without knives.
U.S. News   May 20, 1991   p. 68

Can corn flakes cure cancer? Of course not. But health claims for food are becoming ridiculous. Here's what you should know.
Business Week   Oct 9, 1989   p. 114

The truth about designer diets. Can eating the right foods really prevent heart attacks, cancer, pain - even old age?
U.S. News   Feb 15, 1988   p. 73

Diet wars. The new science of nutrition. Good for you? Bad for you? How to know what's right for you.
U.S. News   Jan 20, 1986   p. 62

Brain foods: Diets that sharpen the mind.
Omni   May 1985   p. 36

The vitamin diet that makes you young.
Omni   Apr 1982   p. 68

Profiles in eating.
Psychology Today   Oct 1981   p. 51

Diet crazes.
Newsweek   Dec 19, 1977   p. 66

Are you eating right?
U.S. News   Nov 28, 1977   p. 39

Eating may not be good for you.
Time   Dec 18, 1972   p. 68

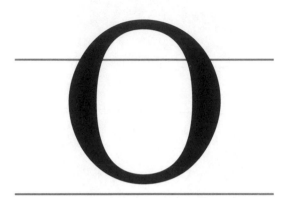

OATES, JOYCE CAROL

Love and violence: A vision of America.
Novelist Joyce Carol Oates.
Newsweek   Dec 11, 1972   p. 72

OBRIEN, LAWRENCE

White House & Congress. Power,
patronage, and persuasion.
Time   Sep 1, 1961   p. 10

OBSCENITY (LAW)

Art or obscenity?
Newsweek   Jul 2, 1990   p. 46

Dirty words. America's foul-mouthed
pop culture.
Time   May 7, 1990   p. 92

OCCULT

The real ghostbusters. Scientists examine
the occult.
Omni   Aug 1988   p. 34

Scientific investigation: UFO's, Loch Ness,
and parapsychology.
USA Today   Jun 1988   p. 1

The occult revival. Satan returns.
Time   Jun 19, 1972   p. 62

See Also PARAPSYCHOLOGY

OCCUPATIONAL HEALTH AND SAFETY

Occupational health controversy.
Congressional Digest Apr 1989   p. 98

OCCUPATIONS
See JOBS

OCEAN MINING

Law of the Sea Treaty.
Congressional Digest Jan 1983   p. 2

OCEANOGRAPHIC SUBMERSIBLES

Voyages to the bottom of the sea. Alvin
exploring the Titanic.
Time   Aug 11, 1986   p. 48

OCEANOGRAPHY

Secrets of the sea. New light on the
mysteries of the deep. Scientists vs.
salvagers: The fight over shipwrecks.
U.S. News   Aug 21, 1989   p. 48

Mysteries of the deep. Robots probe the
Titanic. Amphibious man: The next step
in human evolution. Underwater comets.
Whale suicides.
Omni   Jul 1986   p. 14

Sea probe. Man moves into a rich new
realm.
Life   Oct 4, 1968   p. 64

The sea. Special double issue.
Life   Dec 21, 1962   p. 16

The big dive: Seven miles down to sea's
deepest pit.
Life   Feb 15, 1960   p. 110

OCONNOR, SANDRA DAY

The battle over abortion. The Court
confronts Roe vs. Wade. Justice
O'Connor's key role. Sandra Day
O'Connor.
Newsweek   May 1, 1989   p. 28

Justice - at last. Reagan nominee Sandra
O'Connor.
Time   Jul 20, 1981   p. 8

OFFICE BUILDINGS

End of the office boom. Developers face
financial ruin. Bankers are left holding the
bag.
Business Week   Oct 4, 1982   p. 94

OHARA, JOHN

The world of John O'Hara.
Newsweek   Jun 3, 1963   p. 53

OIL INDUSTRY

See PETROLEUM INDUSTRY

OIL WELL DRILLING

Controversy over wilderness area minerals policy.
Congressional Digest Dec 1982   p. 289

OKEEFFE, GEORGIA

Stark visions of a pioneer painter. Georgia O'Keeffe in New Mexico.
Life   Mar 1, 1968   p. 40

OLD AGE

The American family. Who's taking care of our parents?
Newsweek   May 6, 1985   p. 60

Old age. How to help our parents.
Time   Jun 2, 1975   p. 44

Growing old in America. The unwanted generation.
Time   Aug 3, 1970   p. 49

OLDER AMERICANS

Aging: Controlling health care costs.
USA Today   Oct 1990   p. 1

And now for the fun years. Americans are living longer and enjoying it more - but who will foot the bill?
Time   Feb 22, 1988   p. 66

Dynamic elderly. Busier, healthier, happier.
U.S. News   Jul 2, 1984   p. 48

Living longer, living better. Growing old without thinking old. How America treats the elderly.
Newsweek   Nov 1, 1982   p. 56

Life begins at 55.
U.S.News   Sep 1, 1980   p. 50

Growing old in America. The unwanted generation.
Time   Aug 3, 1970   p. 49

OLMOS, EDWARD JAMES

Magnifico! Hispanic culture breaks out of the barrio. Actor Edward James Olmos.
Time   Jul 11, 1988   p. 46

OLMSTEAD, FREEMAN

Return of the airmen. Gambit in the Cold War.
Time   Feb 3, 1961   p. 10

OLSEN, KENNETH

What next for Digital? The hot computer company has cooled off. So why isn't DEC's Ken Olsen worried?
Business Week   May 16, 1988   p. 88

OLSON, JAMES E.

AT&T. The making of a comeback. An inside look at Chairman Jim Olson's management strategy.
Business Week   Jan 18, 1988   p. 56

OLYMPIC ATHLETES

Here they come. The Olympians.
Life   Feb 1988   p. 76

OLYMPIC GAMES, 1960

U.S.A. gymnasts frolic in Rome's Stadio dei Marmi.
Life   Sep 12, 1960   p. 16

The Olympics: Sports summit at Rome.
Newsweek   Aug 29, 1960   p. 77

The Olympics. U.S. decathlon star Rafer Johnson.
Time   Aug 29, 1960   p. 52

U.S. record-breakers head for Olympics.
Life   Aug 22, 1960   p. 92

OLYMPIC GAMES, 1964

America's great swimmer Don Schollander. First U.S. athlete since Jesse Owens to win four Olympic gold medals.
Life   Oct 30, 1964   p. 74

Star U.S. Olympic swimmer Donna de Varona.
Life   Oct 9, 1964   p. 102

OLYMPIC GAMES, 1972

The haywire Olympics. Can they be fixed by '76?
Life   Sep 22, 1972   p. 28

The Olympic tragedy. Israel buries its dead.
Newsweek   Sep 18, 1972   p. 24

Murder in Munich.
Time   Sep 18, 1972   p. 22

OLYMPIC GAMES (WINTER), 1988

Winter wonders. Debi Thomas. Can America's sweetheart dethrone East Germany's Katarina Witt? Super-Z. Will Primin Zurbriggen zip and zap them all? The battling Brians. Orser of Canada vs. Boitano of the U.S.
Time   Feb 15, 1988   p. 40

Here they come. The Olympians.
Life   Feb 1988   p. 76

ONASSIS, CHRISTINA

Christina Onassis. Poor little rich girl.
Newsweek   Jul 28, 1975   p. 56

ONASSIS, JACQUELINE KENNEDY

Happy birthday Jackie. Her 60 years in photographs.
Life   Jul 1989   p. 72

Jackie vs. the Jackie watcher. Silly courtroom battle.
Life   Mar 31, 1972   p. 64

Jackie-watching.
Life   Feb 12, 1971   p. 32

Jackie's wedding.
Life   Nov 1, 1968   p. 18

Jackie Onassis.
Newsweek   Oct 28, 1968   p. 38

Jackie's marriage.
Time   Oct 25, 1968   p. 19

Jackie in Cambodia.
Life   Nov 17, 1967   p. 97

Privacy vs. history. Jacqueline Kennedy and "The Death of a President."
Newsweek   Dec 26, 1966   p. 39

Jackie in Spain.
Life   May 6, 1966   p. 78

Jacqueline Kennedy. Looking ahead.
Newsweek   Jan 6, 1964   p. 15

Charming album of Jackie growing up. Her secret is out—and here's a story of the First Lady as a child herself.
Life   Apr 26, 1963   p. 26

The new White House.
Newsweek   Sep 17, 1962   p. 71

Jacqueline Kennedy.
Newsweek   Jan 1, 1962   p. 31

The First Lady. She tells her plans for the White House.
Life   Sep 1, 1961   p. 54

Kennedy in Paris.
Life   Jun 9, 1961   p. 42

Jacqueline Kennedy.
Time   Jan 20, 1961   p. 18

The First-Lady-to-be: 'Pat' Nixon or 'Jackie' Kennedy.
Newsweek   Oct 17, 1960   p. 31

ONEAL, TATUM

Tatum! The Hollywood kid.
Newsweek   Feb 9, 1976   p. 48

ONEILL, THOMAS P.

"Tip" and his Democrats. Where now? Thomas P. O'Neill, Jr., Speaker of the House.
U.S. News   Nov 26, 1984   p. 28

The impeachment Congress. House leader 'Tip' O'Neill.
Time   Feb 4, 1974   p. 14

OPEC

See ORGANIZATION OF PETROLEUM EXPORTING COUNTRIES

OPERA

Grander days for grand opera. Rudolf Bing.
Time   Sep 23, 1966   p. 46

The new Met. Rudolf Bing.
Newsweek   Sep 19, 1966   p. 70

Soprano Leontyne Price.
Time   Mar 10, 1961   p. 58

What makes a prima donna? Eileen Farrell of the Met.
Newsweek   Feb 13, 1961   p. 63

ORCHESTRAS

New maestro, new beat. New York Philharmonic's Pierre Boulez.
Newsweek   Oct 11, 1971   p. 86

America's great orchestras. Cleveland conductor George Szell.
Time   Feb 22, 1963   p. 58

Special issue. Our splendid outdoors.
The land we love and enjoy...and the
fight to save it.
Life   Dec 22, 1961   p. 22

OUTER-SPACE EXPLORATION

Record jump starts nineteen miles up.
Life   Aug 29, 1960   p. 20

OWLS

Who gives a hoot? The timber industry
says that saving this spotted owl will cost
30,000 jobs. It isn't that simple.
Time   Jun 25, 1990   p. 56

OZONE

The sky is falling. A deadly hole in the
ozone layer.
Omni   Aug 1987   p. 36

See Also GREENHOUSE EFFECT

Israel's blitz.
Time   Jun 21, 1982   p. 14

Israeli strike. New test for U.S.
U.S. News   Jun 21, 1982   p. 14

Collision course over the PLO.
Newsweek   Sep 3, 1979   p. 18

PALESTINIAN ARABS

A long, bloody search for nationhood.
The Palestinians.
Time   Jul 23, 1990   p. 30

The Palestinians. Where do they go from here?
Newsweek   Aug 16, 1982   p. 10

The Palestinians. Key to a Mideast peace.
Time   Apr 14, 1980   p. 40

The Palestinians. Yasser Arafat.
Time   Nov 11, 1974   p. 27

PALMER, ARNOLD

Arnold Palmer: Perfection under pressure.
Newsweek   Jun 18, 1962   p. 53

Arnold Palmer.
Time   May 2, 1960   p. 54

PAN AMERICAN FLIGHT 103 DISASTER, 1988

Explosion in the sky. Tragedy and terror on Pan Am 103. How families cope with sudden loss.
Newsweek   Jan 2, 1989   p. 14

PANAMA

Politics, Panama-style. Noriega bludgeons his opposition, and the U.S. turns up the heat.
Time   May 22, 1989   p. 40

PANAMA AND THE UNITED STATES

Amateur hour. The U.S. vs. Noriega. Step by step: Did Bush go too far or not far enough?
Newsweek   Oct 16, 1989   p. 26

Panama. A doomed treaty?
U.S. News   Sep 19, 1977   p. 18

Getting out of the canal (slowly).
Time   Aug 22, 1977   p. 8

Panama City: At Canal Zone border rioters hoist flag above a flaming car.
Life   Jan 24, 1964   p. 22

PANAMA-AMERICAN INVASION, 1989-1990

When tyrants fall. Rumania. A firing squad for Ceausescu. Panama. End of the line for Noriega?
Time   Jan 8, 1990   p. 26

Target: Noriega. Bush's invasion. How high a price? How long a stay?
Newsweek   Jan 1, 1990   p. 12

PANDAS

Secrets of the giant panda.
National Geographic Mar 1986   p. 284

Pandas in the wild.
National Geographic Dec 1981   p. 735

PANIC DISORDER

Why panic? The biological roots.
Psychology Today   Apr 1985   p. 26

PAPER AIRPLANES

World's most mysterious paper airplane: Cutout model inside.
Omni   Apr 1984   p. 64

PAPERBACK BOOKS

The godfather of the paperback boom. Author Mario Puzo.
Time   Aug 28, 1978   p. 68

PAPP, JOSEPH

New life in the American theater. Producer Joseph Papp.
Newsweek   Jul 3, 1972   p. 52

PAPUA NEW GUINEA

Papua New Guinea. Nation in the making.
National Geographic Aug 1982   p. 143

PARAMOUNT (MOTION PICTURE CO.)

Goodby to the glory days. Hollywood puts its past up for sale.
Life   Feb 27, 1970   p. 38

PARAPSYCHOLOGY

The new science of imagination.
Omni   Nov 1987   p. 126

16 ways to control your mind. Test your psychic abilities.
Omni   Oct 1987   p. 14

China's psychic children
Omni   Jan 1985   p. 62

The psychics.
Time   Mar 4, 1974   p. 65

See Also OCCULT

PARENT AND CHILD
Our neglected kids.
U.S. News   Aug 9, 1982   p. 54

Who's raising the kids?
Newsweek   Sep 22, 1975   p. 48

How to educate your parents.
Time   Aug 17, 1970   p. 35

Today's parents: Trapped in a child-centered world?
Newsweek   Nov 28, 1960   p. 53

PARENTING
See CHILD REARING

PARSCEGHIAN, ARA
The fighting Irish fight again. Notre Dame coach Parsceghian.
Time   Nov 20, 1964   p. 84

PARTICIPATORY MANAGEMENT
Go team! The payoff from worker participation. When workers are included in decision-making, quality can improve and productivity often goes up. So why won't labor and management cooperate more?
Business Week   Jul 10, 1989   p. 56

PARTICLES (NUCLEAR PHYSICS)
Beyond Einstein. The fastest thing in the universe (and why physicists hate it).
Discover   Feb 1989   p. 56

PATOWMACK CANAL (MARYLAND)
The Patowmack Canal. Waterway that led to the Constitution.
National Geographic Jun 1987   p. 716

PAUL VI, POPE
Pope Paul.
Time   Sep 24, 1965   p. 62

Paul VI. The missionary Pope.
Newsweek   Dec 14, 1964   p. 52

The new Pope: the spectacle and the man.
Life   Jul 5, 1963   p. 22

The new Pope.
Newsweek   Jul 1, 1963   p. 42

Pope Paul VI.
Time   Jun 28, 1963   p. 40

PAUL VI, POPE - VISIT TO THE HOLY LAND, 1964
The Pope's pilgrimage.
Life   Jan 17, 1964   p. 18

PAUL VI, POPE - VISIT TO THE UNITED STATES, 1965
Pope Paul VI in America.
Life   Oct 15, 1965   p. 40

PAULEY, JANE
Our loss, her dream. How Jane Pauley got what she wanted—time for her kids, prime time for herself.
Life   Dec 1989   p. 46

PAVAROTTI, LUCIANO
Bravo Pavarotti! Opera's golden tenor.
Time   Sep 24, 1979   p. 60

Prince of the tenors. Luciano Pavarotti
Newsweek   Mar 15, 1976   p. 56

PEACE CORPS
The Peace Corps. A U.S. ideal abroad. Sargent Shriver.
Time   Jul 5, 1963   p. 18

Peace Corps in action: Ira Gwin.
Newsweek   Dec 25, 1961   p. 12

PEANUTS (COMIC STRIP)
Charlie Brown and Snoopy. Winners at last. The great 'Peanuts' craze.
Life   Mar 17, 1967   p. 74

Comment in the comics. The world according to Peanuts.
Time   Apr 9, 1965   p. 80

PEARL HARBOR, ATTACK ON, 1941
Day of infamy. December 7, 1941. Pearl Harbor.
Time   Dec 2, 1991   p. 30

Pearl Harbor. America fights back.
U.S. News Dec 2, 1991 p. 30

Remembering Pearl Harbor.
Newsweek Nov 25, 1991 p. 30

Pearl Harbor. 1941 - 1966. Where are they now? Where were they then?
Newsweek Dec 12, 1966 p. 36

PEARSON, LESTER

Canada's Pearson.
Time Apr 19, 1963 p. 33

PELTZ, NELSON

The new aces of low tech. Nelson Peltz and Peter May think there's still big money in running a basic industry. With this old-fashioned idea—and new-fangled junk bonds—they have built a $4 billion empire.
Business Week Sep 15, 1986 p. 132

PENGUINS

Protecting the wild penguins of Patagonia.
Life Apr 1984 p. 60

PENNZOIL COMPANY

Mr. Pennzoil. Hugh Liedtke built his company with some controversial deals. Now he wants to grow bigger—with Texaco's money.
Business Week Jan 27, 1986 p. 88

PENSIONS

Pension power. The nation's pension funds have $2.6 trillion of capital—and everyone is suddenly battling over it. The real question: Will the money be there when you need it?
Business Week Nov 6, 1989 p. 154

PENTAGON

See DEPARTMENT OF DEFENSE

PENTAGON PAPERS

Victory for the press.
Newsweek Jul 12, 1971 p. 16

The war exposés: Battle over the right to know. Daniel Ellsberg.
Time Jul 5, 1971 p. 6

The secret history of Vietnam.
Newsweek Jun 28, 1971 p. 12

Pentagon Papers: The secret war.
Time Jun 28, 1971 p. 11

PENTAGON PROCUREMENT SCANDAL

The great weapons scandal. How 'Pentagate' weakens our military strength.
U.S. News Jul 4, 1988 p. 16

PEOPLE EXPRESS INC.

Up, up and away? Donald Burr's People Express became a $1 billion company in just five years—and a model of 'humane management.' Now, People is in the throes of change.
Business Week Nov 25, 1985 p. 80

PEOPLES TEMPLE (CULT)

The cult of death.
Newsweek Dec 4, 1978 p. 38

Cult of death.
Time Dec 4, 1978 p. 16

PEPPER, CLAUDE

Spokesman for the elderly. "They deserve much - and need much." Congressman Claude Pepper.
Time Apr 25, 1983 p. 20

PERCY, CHARLES

The Midwestern battleground. Illinois Republican Percy.
Time Sep 18, 1964 p. 33

PERCY, SHARON

The Percy-Rockefeller wedding.
Life Apr 14, 1967 p. 85

PEREIRA, WILLIAM

Vistas for the future. Planner William Pereira.
Time Sep 6, 1963 p. 68

PERLMAN, ITZHAK

Top fiddle. Violinist Itzhak Perlman.
Newsweek Apr 14, 1980 p. 62

PERON, JUAN

Democrary's failure in Argentina. Arturo Frondizi.
Time Mar 30, 1962 p. 27

PEROT, H. ROSS

Super patriot Ross Perot. How he'll make his next billion.
U.S. News Jun 20, 1988 p. 24

Ross Perot's crusade. "Revitalizing
General Motors is like teaching an
elephant to tap dance. You find the
sensitive spots and start poking."
Business Week   Oct 6, 1986   p. 60

PERSIAN GULF WAR, 1991

Was it worth it? The mess in Kuwait.
Saddam's staying power. A rocky road to
Mideast peace.
Time   Aug 5, 1991   p. 32

After the storm. The Persian Gulf.
National Geographic Aug 1991   p. 2

Secret warriors. Behind Iraqi lines. How
SEALS and Scud-hunters helped win the
war.
Newsweek   Jun 17, 1991   p. 20

The reluctant warrior. Doubts and
divisions on the road to war. Gen. Colin
Powell.
Newsweek   May 13, 1991   p. 18

The secret history of the war.
Newsweek   Mar 18, 1991   p. 28

A moment to savor. And the lessons of
victory. Inside Kuwait: Anger and chaos.
Time   Mar 18, 1991   p. 18

The U.S. military reborn. After the
triumph of Desert Storm.
U.S. News   Mar 18, 1991   p. 30

Winning the peace.
Business Week   Mar 11, 1991   p. 24

Victory! And what comes next.
Newsweek   Mar 11, 1991   p. 16

Kuwait City. Feb. 27, 1991.
Time   Mar 11, 1991   p. 20

Knockout.
U.S. News   Mar 11, 1991   p. 10

Bush's battle plan. Target: Total victory.
Newsweek   Mar 4, 1991   p. 14

Into Kuwait! Tightening the noose
around Saddam. The inside story of
Soviet diplomacy.
Time   Mar 4, 1991   p. 18

The last act.
U.S. News   Mar 4, 1991   p. 24

Persian Gulf policy.
Congressional Digest Mar 1991   p. 67

In time of war.
Life   Mar 1991   p. 4

Saddam on the ropes.
Newsweek   Feb 25, 1991   p. 14

Beginning of the end. The ground war:
How it will be fought. Inside Iraq: Photos
of the bombing.
Time   Feb 25, 1991   p. 16

Saddam's desperate hours. Facing a
crushing military defeat, Iraq's dictator
hopes a political offensive will save his
skin.
U.S. News   Feb 25, 1991   p. 22

The new science of war. High-tech
hardware: How many lives can it save?
Countdown to a ground strike.
Newsweek   Feb 18, 1991   p. 38

The war comes home. Lance Cpl.
Thomas Jenkins, 21, killed in action in
Saudi Arabia. A small town mourns its
first casualty.
Time   Feb 18, 1991   p. 14

Saddam Hussein. The real target?
U.S. News   Feb 18, 1991   p. 20

Heat of battle. The showdown in the
sand.
Newsweek   Feb 11, 1991   p. 16

Saddam's weird war.
Time   Feb 11, 1991   p. 20

War power. Inside the air war. Our man
in charge.
U.S. News   Feb 11, 1991   p. 20

Managing the war. The new role of
military managers. Colin L. Powell.
Chairman, Joint Chiefs of Staff.
Business Week   Feb 4, 1991   p. 34

Hard days ahead. A brutal war on the
ground? The POWs: Torture and
torment. Saddam's environmental terror.
Newsweek   Feb 4, 1991   p. 20

Stalking Saddam.
Time   Feb 4, 1991   p. 16

The coming ground war. Operation Desert Storm.
U.S. News   Feb 4, 1991   p. 24

War.
Business Week   Jan 28, 1991   p. 26

America at war.
Newsweek   Jan 28, 1991   p. 12

War in the Gulf.
Time   Jan 28, 1991   p. 14

America at war. Operation Desert Storm.
U.S. News   Jan 28, 1991   p. 20

Showdown. The Gulf crisis. Last-ditch diplomacy. What war won't solve.
U.S. News   Jan 21, 1991   p. 18

Desert warfare. If diplomacy fails. How a war would be fought in the air and on the ground.
U.S. News   Jan 14, 1991   p. 20

Oil war. Bush leads the world against Iraq.
Business Week   Aug 20, 1990   p. 22

PERSONAL COMPUTERS
See COMPUTERS

PERU
A Latin American architect of hope. Peru's President Belaúnde.
Time   Mar 12, 1965   p. 32

PETERSON, RUDY
What to do with $14 billion. Bank of America's Rudolph A. Peterson.
Newsweek   Nov 4, 1963   p. 83

PETROLEOS MEXICANOS
Why Pemex can't pay Mexico's bills.
Business Week   Feb 28, 1983   p. 58

PETROLEUM - ALASKA
The great oil hunt. Alaska's North Slope.
Newsweek   Sep 22, 1969   p. 80

PETROLEUM - ARCTIC REGIONS
Arctic oil and gas. Why everybody is rushing to spend prodigious sums. Finding energy in the world's worst weather.
Business Week   Jan 24, 1983   p. 52

PETROLEUM - INTERNATIONAL ASPECTS
Hostage to oil. Why the Gulf showdown is driving up prices. How costs would soar in a war with Iraq.
U.S. News   Oct 8, 1990   p. 56

The oil game.
Time   May 7, 1979   p. 70

PETROLEUM - MEXICO
Why Pemex can't pay Mexico's bills.
Business Week   Feb 28, 1983   p. 58

PETROLEUM INDUSTRY
The takeover game. Corporate raider T. Boone Pickens.
Time   Mar 4, 1985   p. 52

Restructuring big oil. The fight over Gulf is just the start.
Business Week   Nov 14, 1983   p. 138

Oil-field suppliers. The crash after a boom. An uncertain future.
Business Week   Sep 27, 1982   p. 66

A breather for oil prices. Why consuming countries are in control for now.
Business Week   May 25, 1981   p. 104

Oil profits running wild?
U.S. News   Nov 5, 1979   p. 24

John H. Loudon of Royal Dutch Shell.
Time   May 9, 1960   p. 92

PETROLEUM PIPELINES
At last. Alaska's oil flows south.
U.S. News   Jun 20, 1977   p. 35

Alaska: Last chance for the last frontier.
Time   Jul 27, 1970   p. 44

PETROLEUM PRICES
The new world of oil. How the economy might look by 1990. Plowing up the oil patch. Smart plays for investors. Europe and Japan are sitting pretty.
Business Week   Feb 10, 1986   p. 78

How cheaper oil will boost the world economy.
Business Week   Mar 7, 1983   p. 92

The leverage of lower oil prices.
Business Week   Mar 22, 1982   p. 66

Over a barrel.
Newsweek   Jul 9, 1979   p. 18

The world over a barrel. OPEC's
tightening oil squeeze.
Time   Jul 9, 1979   p. 12

How high a price?
Newsweek   Jan 7, 1974   p. 18

PETROLEUM SUPPLY

West African oil. At last, an alternative to
the Mideast.
Business Week   Aug 10, 1981   p. 52

A long, dry summer?
Newsweek   May 21, 1979   p. 24

The coming oil crunch.
Newsweek   Feb 19, 1979   p. 20

The oil squeeze. Saudi Arabia's King
Feisal.
Time   Nov 19, 1973   p. 88

Arab oil squeeze.
Newsweek   Sep 17, 1973   p. 33

See Also GASOLINE SUPPLY

PETS

How animals tamed people. What
science tells up about the bonds between
man and beast.
U.S. News   Mar 20, 1989   p. 74

The American pet.
Time   Dec 23, 1974   p. 58

PFEIFFER, MICHELLE

Scene stealer. Michelle Pfeiffer takes big
risks for the right roles.
Newsweek   Nov 6, 1989   p. 64

PHILANTHROPY

See ENDOWMENTS

**PHILIP, CONSORT OF ELIZABETH II,
QUEEN OF GREAT BRITAIN**

Prince Philip describes a violent world
ahead.
U.S. News   Nov 22, 1976   p. 40

PHILIP MORRIS CO.

Beyond Marlboro country. The decline in
smoking means Philip Morris must make
diversification work. Can it?
Business Week   Aug 8, 1988   p. 54

PHILIPPINES

The Philippines. Another Iran? America
tries to back away from Marcos.
Newsweek   Nov 4, 1985   p. 30

Two decades of independence in Asia.
Philippine President Marcos.
Time   Oct 21, 1966   p. 38

**PHILIPPINES - POLITICS AND
GOVERNMENT**

The charisma of Cory Aquino. And the
surprising power of Philippine women.
Ms.   Oct 1986   p. 45

Woman of the year. Can she clean up the
mess Marcos left behind? Should he be
allowed to keep his millions.
Newsweek   Mar 10, 1986   p. 18

Now for the hard part.
Time   Mar 10, 1986   p. 14

Can she make it?
U.S. News   Mar 10, 1986   p. 30

Showdown. The last act in Manila.
Newsweek   Mar 3, 1986   p. 30

Fighting on. Philippine opposition leader
Corazon Aquino.
Time   Feb 24, 1986   p. 28

Election mess. What the U.S. can do.
Newsweek   Feb 17, 1986   p. 14

What's at stake. The Philippine election.
Challenger Aquino. President Marcos.
Time   Feb 3, 1986   p. 26

PHILIPS INDUSTRIES

Philips' high-tech crusade. Snubbed by
Europe, it links up with AT&T.
Business Week   Jul 18, 1983   p. 152

Philips. An electronics giant rearms to
fight Japan.
Business Week   Mar 30, 1981   p. 86

PHOBIAS

Phobias. New drugs and therapies are helping people conquer their fears.
Newsweek   Apr 23, 1984   p. 66

PHOENIX (ARIZONA)

Rising Phoenix: 'Miracle' in Arizona.
Newsweek   Jan 4, 1960   p. 45

PHOTOGRAPHY

Photography.
Newsweek   Oct 21, 1974   p. 64

30th anniversary. Photography.
Life   Dec 23, 1966   p. 6

PHOTOJOURNALISM

The year in pictures 1990.
Life   Jan 1991   p. 6

The ycar 89 in pictures.
Life   Jan 1990   p. 8

A day in the life of China.
Time   Oct 2, 1989   p. 30

88 the year in pictures.
Life   Jan 1989   p. 8

Great photographs from the National Geographic Society's Centennial.
USA Today   Sep 1988   p. 36

1987. The year in pictures.
Life   Jan 1988   p. 3

A day in the life of the Soviet Union. A 38-page portrait of the changing superpower.
Time   Oct 26, 1987   p. 54

The year in pictures 86.
Life   Jan 1987   p. 8

A day in the life of America. A picture portfolio by the world's best photographer.
Newsweek   Oct 27, 1986   p. 43

The year in pictures 85.
Life   Jan 1986   p. 6

The photojournalist.
USA Today   Jul 1985   p. 46

84. The year in pictures.
Life   Jan 1985   p. 6

'83. The year in pictures.
Life   Jan 1984   p. 8

The year in pictures.
Life   Jan 1983   p. 8

Looking back at '81.
Newsweek   Jan 4, 1982   p. 26

The year in pictures.
Life   Jan 1982   p. 8

The year in pictures.
Life   Jan 1981   p. 7

Pictures of '80.
Newsweek   Dec 29, 1980   p. 28

The 70's. Special issue. The decade in pictures.
Life   Dec 1979   p. 4

Pictures of '77.
Newsweek   Dec 26, 1977   p. 16

Pictures of '76.
Newsweek   Jan 3, 1977   p. 12

The year in pictures 1972.
Life   Dec 29, 1972   p. 3

The year in pictures.
Life   Dec 31, 1971   p. 2

Picture contest winners.
Life   Jul 9, 1971   p. 35

Prizewinning pictures. Life's photography contest.
Life   Dec 25, 1970   p. 14

The incredible year '68.
Life   Jan 10, 1969   p. 20

PHYSICAL FITNESS

Best ways to stay healthy. The ten most important new developments. Plus the A-to-Z health almanac.
U.S. News   Jun 18, 1990   p. 54

Staying fit for life! How Grete Waitz is getting better.
Ms.   Aug 1985   p. 28

America's fitness binge.
U.S. News   May 3, 1982   p. 58

The fitness craze. America shapes up.
Time   Nov 2, 1981   p. 94

The fitness mania.
U.S. News   Feb 27, 1978   p. 37

Keeping fit.
Newsweek   May 23, 1977   p. 78

See EXERCISE

PHYSICIANS
How doctors decide who shall live and
who shall die.
U.S. News   Jan 22, 1990   p. 50

Doctors and patients. Image vs. reality.
Time   Jul 31, 1989   p. 48

Glut of doctors. Glut of lawyers. Good or
bad?
U.S. News   Dec 19, 1983   p. 62

Crisis in the operating room.
U.S. News   May 15, 1978   p. 39

America's doctors. A profession in
trouble.
U.S. News   Oct 17, 1977   p. 50

PHYSICIANS AND PATIENTS
Physicians & patients. The delicate
imbalance.
Psychology Today   Nov 1986   p. 22

How good is your doctor?
Newsweek   Dec 23, 1974   p. 46

PHYSICS
The new theory of everything. A
physicist tackles the ultimate cosmic
riddle.
Discover   Aug 1991   p. 54

The theory of everything. It's called
superstrings, and it's a theory of our
universe.
Discover   Nov 1986   p. 34

Einstein's dream. Have scientists created
the ultimate theory?
Discover   Dec 1983   p. 44

Mysteries of the universe. Frontiers in
physics.
Newsweek   Mar 12, 1979   p. 46

PICASSO, PABLO
Picasso. The show of shows.
Time   May 26, 1980   p. 70

Picasso.
Life   Dec 27, 1968   p. 10

PICKENS, T. BOONE
The takeover game. Corporate raider T.
Boone Pickens.
Time   Mar 4, 1985   p. 52

Why Gulf fell. What's behind the biggest
corporate takeover.
Business Week   Mar 19, 1984   p. 76

PIKE, JAMES
The relevance of faith & myth in twentieth
century life. Bishop Pike.
Time   Nov 11, 1966   p. 56

PIPELINES
See PETROLEUM PIPELINES

PITTSBURGH (PENNSYLVANIA)
Pittsburgh. Innovative American city.
USA Today   Mar 1986   p. 22

PLANETS
The secrets of Venus. Earth's sister planet
helps us understand our own world.
U.S. News   May 13, 1991   p. 60

The planets: Between fire and ice.
National Geographic Jan 1985   p. 4

PLANETS - EXPLORATION
Remapping the heavens. From our space
probes a new picture atlas of the planets.
Life   Jun 1981   p. 75

Probing the planets. Man's closest look at
Saturn.
Newsweek   Sep 10, 1979   p. 40

See Also SPECIFIC PLANETS

PLASTIC SURGERY
See COSMETIC SURGERY

PLAYBOY ENTERPRISES, INC.
Playboy. The party's over.
Newsweek   Aug 4, 1986   p. 50

The pursuit of hedonism. Playboy's
Hugh Hefner.
Time   Mar 3, 1967   p. 76

POLITICAL CANDIDATES, 1962

U.S. politics: The next two years.
Republican George Romney.
Time   Nov 16, 1962   p. 20

Nixon. Brown. Biggest state's biggest
battle.
Newsweek   Oct 29, 1962   p. 19

Politics 1962. The campaign in full cry.
Pennsylvania's William Scranton.
Time   Oct 19, 1962   p. 19

The Senate seat scramble in
Massachusetts. Head-on collision of three
political clans. Eddie McCormick. Teddie
Kennedy. George Lodge.
Life   Jun 29, 1962   p. 59

G.O.P. dark horse. George Romney. The
great game of politics.
Newsweek   Feb 19, 1962   p. 23

POLITICAL CANDIDATES, 1964

The year of the split ticket.
Time   Oct 30, 1964   p. 30

Senate races: California & others. Pierre
Salinger.
Time   Oct 16, 1964   p. 34

The Midwestern battleground. Illinois
Republican Percy.
Time   Sep 18, 1964   p. 33

POLITICAL CANDIDATES, 1966

The new GOP galaxy.
Newsweek   Nov 21, 1966   p. 31

Republican resurgence.
Time   Nov 18, 1966   p. 23

California's governorship race. Ronald
Reagan.
Time   Oct 7, 1966   p. 31

Campaign '66. How much of the way
with LBJ?
Newsweek   Sep 26, 1966   p. 25

Politics '66. GOP challenger Ronald
Reagan.
Newsweek   Mar 28, 1966   p. 27

POLITICAL CANDIDATES, 1967

Backlash in Boston. Mayoral candidate
Louise Day Hicks.
Newsweek   Nov 6, 1967   p. 29

POLITICAL CANDIDATES, 1970

Battle for the Senate.
Time   Oct 26, 1970   p. 18

POLITICAL CANDIDATES, 1974

New faces, key races.
Time   Oct 21, 1974   p. 26

Politics heats up. Preview of '74
campaign. Now that Ted Kennedy is out -
Rockefeller's wealth. The facts about
political polls.
U.S. News   Oct 7, 1974   p. 20

POLITICAL CANDIDATES, 1978

Politics heats up. Preview of '78 voting.
Carter: Help or hindrance? Tax revolt at
the polls. Labor takes aim at its enemies.
U.S. News   Oct 9, 1978   p. 24

POLITICAL CANDIDATES, 1984

Political mania takes over.
U.S. News   Jul 16, 1984   p. 71

Fluke or real threat?
U.S. News   Mar 12, 1984   p. 20

POLITICAL CARTOONS AND CARICATURES

The art of politics.
Newsweek   Oct 13, 1980   p. 74

POLITICAL CONVENTIONS

The games of summer. Playing to win in
politics and sports.
Psychology Today   Jul 1984   p. 18

POLITICAL PRISONERS

The forgotten. The world's prisoners of
conscience suffer harsh jail terms, torture
and ruined lives. Does America still care
about human rights?
Newsweek   Feb 14, 1983   p. 40

POLITICS

ABC's of the great game of politics.
U.S. News   Oct 8, 1984   p. 65

POLLEN

Pollen. Breath of life and sneezes.
National Geographic Oct 1984   p. 490

POLLS

See PUBLIC OPINION POLLS

POLLUTION

Life on the Mississippi. Huck's river faces all of the nation's environmental problems.
Newsweek   Apr 16, 1990   p. 66

Buried alive. The garbage glut: An environmental crisis reaches our doorstop.
Newsweek   Nov 27, 1989   p. 66

Cleaning up our mess. What works, what doesn't and what we must do to reclaim our air, land and water.
Newsweek   Jul 24, 1989   p. 26

Cleaner air and water. Can we afford 690 billion dollars?
U.S. News   Feb 28, 1983   p. 27

A clean America. Will people pay the price?
U.S. News   Feb 7, 1977   p. 40

The ravaged environment.
Newsweek   Jan 26, 1970   p. 30

POLLUTION - EASTERN EUROPE

East Europe's dark dawn.
National Geographic Jun 1991   p. 36

POLLUTION, AIR

Clean Air Act.
Congressional Digest Mar 1990   p. 65

Dirty air. The losing battle to clean up the atmosphere. What pollution does to your health.
U.S. News   Jun 12, 1989   p. 48

The Clean Air Act.
Congressional Digest Feb 1989   p. 35

Controversy over the Clean Air Act.
Congressional Digest Jan 1982   p. 3

The polluted air. Los Angeles at 3:30 P.M.
Time   Jan 27, 1967   p. 48

POLLUTION, MARINE

Don't go near the water. Our polluted oceans.
Newsweek   Aug 1, 1988   p. 42

Our filthy seas.
Time   Aug 1, 1988   p. 44

POLLUTION, RADIOACTIVE

The nuclear scandal.
Time   Oct 31, 1988   p. 60

POLLUTION, WATER

Future scope of the Clean Water Act.
Congressional Digest Dec 1985   p. 290

POMPIDOU, GEORGES

France after de Gaulle. Candidate Pompidou.
Newsweek   May 12, 1969   p. 41

France after de Gaulle. Georges Pompidou.
Time   May 9, 1969   p. 30

POOR

Exposé: Who creates the poor.
Ms.   Nov 1990   p. 32

See POVERTY

POPES (CATHOLIC CHURCH)

See SPECIFIC NAMES, e.g., JOHN PAUL II, POPE

POPES - ELECTION

After Paul VI. Choosing a new Pope.
Newsweek   Aug 21, 1978   p. 48

In search of a Pope.
Time   Aug 21, 1978   p. 62

Great princes of the church: Among them, the next Pope.
Life   Jun 14, 1963   p. 26

POPULAR CULTURE

See UNITED STATES - POPULAR CULTURE

POPULATION - UNITED STATES

End of youth culture. Changes it will bring.
U.S. News   Oct 3, 1977   p. 54

The graying of America.
Newsweek   Feb 28, 1977   p. 50

The baby riddle. What will happen to American life if each family has one child? Or two? Or three?
Life   May 19, 1972 p. 46

Your color?. . .Your money? . . .Your age -
really? . . .The nosey census of '60.
Newsweek   Mar 21, 1960   p. 45

POPULATION - WORLD

Mexico City. The population curse.
Time   Aug 6, 1984   p. 24

Too many babies? World population
crisis.
Newsweek   Jul 23, 1962   p. 27

That population explosion.
Time   Jan 11, 1960   p. 19

PORK BARREL LEGISLATION

The $75 billion pork barrel ripoff.
U.S. News   May 2, 1983   p. 18

PORNOGRAPHY

Sex busters.
Time   Jul 21, 1986   p. 12

Is one woman's sexuality another
woman's pornography? It's the question
behind the newest legal battle facing the
country.
Ms.   Apr 1985   p. 37

The war against pornography. Feminists,
free speech and the law.
Newsweek   Mar 18, 1985   p. 58

The porno plague.
Time   Apr 5, 1976   p. 58

In an era of sexuality, growing concern
about pornography.
Life   Aug 28, 1970   p. 18

PORTER, SYLVIA

Business columnist Sylvia Porter.
Time   Nov 28, 1960   p. 46

PORTUGAL

Red threat in Portugal. Lisbon's troika.
Time   Aug 11, 1975   p. 22

PORUMBEANU, ANDREI

The elopers: Gamble and Andrei.
Life   Apr 18, 1960   p. 19

POSTAL SERVICE

The day the mail stopped.
Newsweek   Mar 30, 1970   p. 14

Postal breakdown: A national crisis.
Time   Mar 30, 1970   p. 11

The U.S. mail mess.
Life   Nov 28, 1969   p. 24

POSTERS

The big poster hang-up—walls and walls
of expendable art.
Life   Sep 1, 1967   p. 36

POVERTY

The hidden poor. There are 9 million of
them, mostly white and working. And
their ranks could soon grow.
U.S. News   Jan 11, 1988   p. 18

Broken lives. America's underclass.
U.S. News   Mar 17, 1986   p. 18

Poverty trap. No way out?
U.S. News   Aug 16, 1982   p. 31

Reagan's America. And the poor get
poorer.
Newsweek   Apr 5, 1982   p. 16

The Underclass. Minority within a
minority.
Time   Aug 29, 1977   p. 14

America's forgotten children. Psychiatrist
Robert Coles.
Time   Feb 14, 1972   p. 36

Poverty in America: Its cause and extent.
Time   May 17, 1968   p. 24

Crossfire in the war on poverty. Sargent
Shriver.
Time   May 13, 1966   p. 25

The war on poverty.
Newsweek   Sep 13, 1965   p. 22

Poverty, U.S.A.
Newsweek   Feb 17, 1964   p. 19

POWELL, ADAM CLAYTON

Must Adam leave Eden? Congressman
Adam Clayton Powell.
Newsweek   Jan 16, 1967   p. 24

POWELL, COLIN

The reluctant warrior. Doubts and
divisions on the road to war. Gen. Colin
Powell.
Newsweek   May 13, 1991   p. 18

The U.S. military reborn. After the
triumph of Desert Storm.
U.S. News   Mar 18, 1991   p. 30

Managing the war. The new role of
military managers. Colin L. Powell.
Chairman, Joint Chiefs of Staff.
Business Week   Feb 4, 1991   p. 34

Ready for war. Pentagon partners Dick
Cheney and Colin Powell have the troops
in place. Now they're waiting for the
word.
Time   Nov 12, 1990   p. 24

POWELL, JOSEPH "JODY"

The President's boys. Jody Powell.
Hamilton Jordan.
Time   Jun 6, 1977   p. 26

POWER

The waiting game. Power has its
privilege.
Psychology Today   Apr 1987   p. 24

Women and power. The drives. The
hang-ups. The joys. The price.
Ms.   Dec 1982   p. 39

POWER FAILURES
See ELECTRIC POWER FAILURES

POWER RESOURCES

Are utilities obsolete? A troubled system
faces radical change.
Business Week   May 21, 1984   p. 116

POWERS, FRANCIS GARY

The Cold War gets hotter. The high-flying
U-2 & the cloudy summit. Pilot Francis
Powers.
Time   May 16, 1960   p. 15

PREDICTING
See FORECASTING

PREGNANCY

Giving birth in America. Whose fetus is it
anyway? The pregnant woman's Bill of
Rights. Birth stories.
Ms.   Sep 1984   p. 45

The new baby bloom.
Time   Feb 22, 1982   p. 52

Emotional influences on the unborn child.
Psychology Today   May 1981   p. 49

Unforgettable moments of pregnancy and
birth.
Life   Jul 22, 1966   p. 48

German measles and pregnancy. Current
U.S. epidemic will damage up to 20,000
babies.
Life   Jun 4, 1965   p. 24

Drama of life before birth. Unprecedented
photographic feat in color.
Life   Apr 30, 1965   p. 54

PREMATURE INFANTS
See INFANTS, PREMATURE

PRESIDENTIAL AIDES
See SPECIFIC PRESIDENTS - STAFF, e.g.,
REAGAN, RONALD - STAFF

PRESIDENTIAL CAMPAIGN ISSUES, 1964

The nuclear issue.
Time   Sep 25, 1964   p. 15

PRESIDENTIAL CAMPAIGN ISSUES, 1972

A spectrum of views on the real issues of
'72. Daniel P. Moynihan. Mary
McCarthy. Richard Goodwin. Kevin P.
Phillips. Gloria Steinem. Richard J.
Whalen. Imamu Amiri Baraka. George
W. Ball.
Newsweek   Jul 10, 1972   p. 21

PRESIDENTIAL CAMPAIGN ISSUES, 1976

Voting your pocketbook. Are things as
good as Ford says? Or as bad as Carter
says?
Time   Nov 1, 1976   p. 18

Head-to-head on the issues. Exclusive
interviews with the candidates - before the
TV debates.
U.S. News   Sep 13, 1976   p. 19

What Carter would do as President.
U.S. News   Jul 26, 1976   p. 17

Where Reagan stands. Interview on the
issues.
U.S. News   May 31, 1976   p. 20

What Carter believes. Interview on the
issues.
U.S. News   May 24, 1976   p. 18

PRESIDENTIAL CAMPAIGN ISSUES, 1988

Mr. President. How he did it. The policy choices he will face. His starting lineup. Coping with Congress. What now for the Democrats?
Business Week   Nov 21, 1988   p. 32

PRESIDENTIAL CAMPAIGNS

Is this any way to elect a president? Adventures in campaignland.
Newsweek   Feb 1, 1988   p. 18

PRESIDENTIAL CAMPAIGNS, 1960

The Kennedy strategy. Campaign manager Bobby Kennedy.
Time   Oct 10, 1960   p. 21

Hubert and Jack in Wisconsin.
Life   Mar 28, 1960   p. 22

PRESIDENTIAL CAMPAIGNS, 1964

The new thrust in American politics. Goldwater accepting nomination.
Time   Jul 24, 1964   p. 22

PRESIDENTIAL CAMPAIGNS, 1968

The frustrated voter. Can it happen again? We want Wilkie.
Newsweek   Jul 22, 1968   p. 16

RFK: Up, up and away?
Newsweek   May 20, 1968   p. 34

The stars leap into politics.
Life   May 10, 1968   p. 64

Three's a crowd. The Johnson - Kennedy - McCarthy fight. Eugene McCarthy.
Time   Mar 22, 1968   p. 12

PRESIDENTIAL CAMPAIGNS, 1972

The other campaigners. Pat Nixon. Eleanor McGovern.
Time   Oct 9, 1972   p. 14

The two Americas. Is it still a contest?
Time   Oct 2, 1972   p. 15

Target: Nixon and Agnew.
Newsweek   Jul 24, 1972   p. 16

In quest of a second miracle. The Democratic ticket.
Time   Jul 24, 1972   p. 18

New wave hits Miami.
Newsweek   Jul 17, 1972   p. 14

The battle for the Democratic Party. McGovern's young legions take on the old pros.
Time   Jul 17, 1972   p. 11

PRESIDENTIAL CAMPAIGNS, 1976

Undecided. Why millions wear this button.
U.S. News   Oct 25, 1976   p. 17

Ford's setback.
Time   Oct 18, 1976   p. 10

Campaign kickoff.
Time   Sep 13, 1976   p. 11

The G.O.P. strategy: Give 'em hell.
Time   Aug 30, 1976   p. 6

Reagan's last gamble.
Newsweek   Aug 9, 1976   p. 14

Ford closes in. Behind the Reagan gamble.
Time   Aug 9, 1976   p. 7

The coming of Carter.
Newsweek   Jul 19, 1976   p. 13

How Democrats plan to win.
U.S. News   Jul 19, 1976   p. 16

Carter's game plan.
Newsweek   Jun 21, 1976   p. 14

Our next President (pick one).
Time   Jun 21, 1976   p. 8

Can anyone stop Carter?
Newsweek   May 31, 1976   p. 16

Jolted!
Newsweek   May 17, 1976   p. 22

Republican rumble.
Time   May 17, 1976   p. 9

Carter's sweep.
Newsweek   May 10, 1976   p. 26

Jimmy's breakthrough.
Time   May 10, 1976   p. 10

Round 2 begins.
U.S. News   Apr 12, 1976   p. 19

If Reagan runs against Ford.
U.S. News   Oct 20, 1975   p. 14

New York's Rockefeller. Target '64.
Newsweek   May 14, 1962 p. 31

PRESIDENTIAL CANDIDATES, 1968

The revolt of the right: Wallace and LeMay.
Time   Oct 18, 1968   p. 15

The third party threat. Alabama's George C. Wallace.
Newsweek   Sep 16, 1968   p. 25

The Nixons and the Agnews. Finale at Miami Beach.
Life   Aug 16, 1968   p. 22

The challengers.
Time   Jul 26, 1968   p. 18

Voyage of the loner.
Life   Jun 7, 1968   p. 34

Bobby Kennedy.
Time   May 24, 1968   p. 22

The new GOP race. The Rockefellers.
Newsweek   May 13, 1968   p. 26

Can he stop Bobby? Vice President Humphrey.
Newsweek   Apr 29, 1968   p. 23

The fight to dump LBJ. McCarthy and Kennedy.
Newsweek   Mar 25, 1968   p. 21

...and then there was Nixon. Can Rocky stop him?
Newsweek   Mar 11, 1968   p. 27

The race for the G.O.P. nomination.
Time   Mar 8, 1968   p. 20

Politics '68.
Newsweek   Jan 8, 1968   p. 17

For President. Rockefeller of New York. For Vice President. Reagan of California.
Time   Oct 20, 1967   p. 17

Weighing in for '68.
Time   Apr 14, 1967   p. 27

PRESIDENTIAL CANDIDATES, 1972

Once more with feeling.
Time   Aug 28, 1972   p. 9

The Democrats try again. Sargent Shriver.
Time   Aug 14, 1972   p. 15

The Eagleton crisis.
Newsweek   Aug 7, 1972   p. 12

The Eagleton affair.
Time   Aug 7, 1972   p. 11

George McGovern talks. An outspoken self-portrait.
Life   Jul 7, 1972   p. 30

Can he put the party together? George and Eleanor McGovern.
Newsweek   Jun 19, 1972   p. 22

The new Democratic race.
Newsweek   May 8, 1972   p. 22

Here comes the prairie populist. Senator George McGovern.
Time   May 8, 1972   p. 16

Democrats in disorder. The wild card of politics '72. George Wallace.
Newsweek   Mar 27, 1972   p. 22

Now who's on first?
Time   Mar 27, 1972   p. 22

Who can beat Nixon?
Newsweek   Jan 10, 1972   p. 10

Could he win in '72? Ted Kennedy.
Time   Nov 29, 1971   p. 16

Front runner for '72. Senator Edmund Muskie.
Time   Sep 13, 1971   p. 14

PRESIDENTIAL CANDIDATES, 1976

Who is Jimmy Carter? And why do they love/hate him?
Time   Mar 8, 1976   p. 15

Politics '76. Here they come!
Newsweek   Jan 12, 1976   p. 16

Ronald Reagan. Heating up the G.O.P.
Time   Nov 24, 1975   p. 16

Ready for Teddy?
Newsweek   Jun 2, 1975   p. 19

Ford. How he rates now. Kennedy.
Democrats' choice after all?
U.S. News   Apr 28, 1975   p. 25

Scoop out front. Democrat Henry
Jackson.
Time   Feb 17, 1975   p. 11

PRESIDENTIAL CANDIDATES, 1980

And the winner is...
Newsweek   Nov 3, 1980   p. 27

Now. The choice.
Time   Nov 3, 1980   p. 18

Head to head on the issues. Exclusive
interviews with Carter and Reagan.
U.S.News   Oct 6, 1980   p. 59

Could he be President?
U.S.News   Aug 11, 1980   p. 25

Reagan up close. His character. His
career. His potential.
Newsweek   Jul 21, 1980   p. 24

The Anderson factor. Wild card in the
game.
Newsweek   Jun 9, 1980   p. 28

Reagan. What he stands for.
U.S.News   May 5, 1980   p. 29

Back in the saddle again.
Newsweek   Mar 10, 1980   p. 26

Ronnie's romp! And now the real race is
on.
Time   Mar 10, 1980   p. 12

White House race. Already a circus.
U.S. News   Nov 19, 1979   p. 33

'80 sweepstakes. At the starting gate.
U.S. News   Jun 4, 1979   p. 28

The rush is on.
U.S. News   Feb 13, 1978   p. 24

PRESIDENTIAL CANDIDATES, 1984

Landslide? Interviews with Reagan and
Mondale.
Newsweek   Nov 5, 1984   p. 24

Peace and war. Exclusive interviews on
where they stand.
U.S. News   Oct 22, 1984   p. 29

The recovery cheers the GOP. Amid
prosperity the gender gap haunts Reagan.
Business Week   Sep 3, 1984   p. 74

The Democrats. A party at war with itself.
Business Week   Jul 30, 1984   p. 90

Political mania takes over.
U.S. News   Jul 16, 1984   p. 71

Now, the hard part.
Newsweek   Jun 18, 1984   p. 26

"I am the nominee." Mondale stakes his
claim.
Time   Jun 18, 1984   p. 14

What Jesse wants.
Newsweek   May 7, 1984   p. 40

The Jackson factor. Black pride, white
concerns.
Time   May 7, 1984   p. 30

Hart's charge. Who he is. What he stands
for. His plan to win.
Newsweek   Mar 12, 1984   p. 20

Now it's a race.
Time   Mar 12, 1984   p. 16

The Reagan magic. Can he make it work
again? 1984.
Newsweek   Feb 6, 1984   p. 14

There he goes again.
Time   Feb 6, 1984   p. 16

It's Reagan vs. the field.
U.S. News   Jan 30, 1984   p. 31

Can anyone stop Fritz? Democratic
candidate Walter Mondale.
Newsweek   Jan 9, 1984   p. 26

What makes Jesse run? Presidential
candidate Jesse Jackson.
Newsweek   Nov 14, 1983   p. 50

'The Right Stuff.' Can a movie help make
a president?
Newsweek   Oct 3, 1983   p. 30

PRESIDENTIAL CANDIDATES, 1988

George Bush. Can he bounce back?
Business Week   Aug 22, 1988   p. 26

Bush. High stakes in New Orleans. A revealing interview. Nixon on the race.
Newsweek   Aug 22, 1988   p. 14

In search of stature.
Time   Aug 22, 1988   p. 16

The Duke and the Democrats. Michael Dukakis' nomination symbolizes the change in the party—from liberal to pragmatic. But will that be enough to win? Or to govern?
Business Week   Jul 25, 1988   p. 22

Dukakis. By the people who know him best.
Newsweek   Jul 25, 1988   p. 24

The odd couple. Gary Wills: Searching for Dukakis' soul.
Time   Jul 25, 1988   p. 16

Dukakis. How good a president? He's cool, shrewd and still trying to prove he's tough.
U.S. News   Jul 25, 1988   p. 12

The Duke. Can he unite the Democrats?
Time   May 2, 1988   p. 20

Can he win? The Democratic battle.
Newsweek   Apr 11, 1988   p. 22

Jesse!?
Time   Apr 11, 1988   p. 12

Pat Robertson's amazing race. How he is raising a 'hidden army' to take over the Republican Party.
U.S. News   Feb 22, 1988   p. 14

The grinch who stole Christmas. Will Gary Hart spoil the Democrats' chances?
Time   Dec 28, 1987   p. 14

Fighting the 'wimp' factor. George Bush.
Newsweek   Oct 19, 1987   p. 28

Sex, politics and the press. Gary Hart self-destructs.
Newsweek   May 18, 1987   p. 22

Hart's fall. Sex and politics. Democrats in a quandary. Questions about press ethics.
Time   May 18, 1987   p. 14

Wildcards for the White House.
U.S. News   Jul 14, 1986   p. 20

PRESIDENTIAL CANDIDATES, 1992

No bull. The campaign America needs—but won't get.
Newsweek   Oct 14, 1991   p. 22

PRESIDENTIAL DEBATES, 1960

The TV debates and stormy K. How much influence on the election?
Newsweek   Oct 10, 1960   p. 26

PRESIDENTIAL DEBATES, 1976

Stay tuned. "The Governor has also played a little fast and loose with the facts about vetoes." "Except for avoiding another Watergate, Mr. Ford has not accomplished one single major program."
Newsweek   Oct 4, 1976   p. 22

The character test.
Time   Oct 4, 1976   p. 14

After big debate. The picture now.
U.S. News   Oct 4, 1976   p. 12

The debates.
Newsweek   Sep 27, 1976   p. 24

PRESIDENTIAL DEBATES, 1984

Round two. Who won - and why.
Newsweek   Oct 29, 1984   p. 26

Showdown. Who won, and why.
Time   Oct 29, 1984   p. 22

A real race?
Time   Oct 22, 1984   p. 24

Who won? The debate. A Newsweek poll. How the experts called it.
Newsweek   Oct 15, 1984   p. 30

PRESIDENTIAL DEBATES, 1988

1988, you're no 1960. Myth, memory and the politics of personality.
Time   Oct 24, 1988   p. 18

Hardball. The debate. Dukakis and Bush go on the attack. A Newsweek poll assesses the results.
Newsweek   Oct 3, 1988   p. 22

Battle of the handlers. Dukakis' John Sasso. Bush's James Baker.
Time   Oct 3, 1988   p. 16

PRESIDENTIAL ELECTIONS

Iowa. A profile of the feisty folks who have an outsized say in picking the next President.
Time   Jan 25, 1988   p. 10

ABC's of how a President is chosen.
U.S.News   Feb 18, 1980   p. 45

ABC's of how a President is chosen.
U.S. News   Mar 1, 1976   p. 45

PRESIDENTS - CHILDREN

All the Presidents' children. Their living sons & daughters in exclusive new pictures.
Life   Nov 1984   p. 32

PRESIDENTS - UNITED STATES

What he will do. The President's opportunities and the menaces he faces.
U.S. News   Nov 14, 1988   p. 20

How Reagan decides. An inside look at the presidency. The qualities a president needs.
Time   Dec 13, 1982   p. 12

PRESIDENTS - UNITED STATES - PRESS RELATIONS

Who manages news?
Newsweek   Apr 8, 1963   p. 59

PRESLEY, ELVIS

Thirteen years after the death of Elvis Presley new evidence points to an inescapable conclusion—suicide.
Life   Jun 1990   p. 96

Elvis. Ten years after, the legend grows.
Newsweek   Aug 3, 1987   p. 48

PRESLEY, LISA

Elvis' daughter talks about dad, drugs, mom, and marriage.
Life   Dec 1988   p. 46

PRESS

America's press. Too much power for too few?
U.S. News   Aug 15, 1977   p. 27

America's press under fire.
U.S. News   Aug 2, 1976   p. 20

See Also NEWSPAPER PUBLISHERS AND PUBLISHING

PRESS AND POLITICS

The press: Fair or foul.
Time   Jul 8, 1974   p. 68

Nixon and the media.
Newsweek   Jan 15, 1973   p. 42

PRICE, LEONTYNE

Soprano Leontyne Price.
Time   Mar 10, 1961   p. 58

PRIESTS

See CATHOLIC CHURCH - CLERGY

PRIMATES

Tired of arguing about "natural" inferiority?
Ms.   Nov 1982   p. 41

PRIMERICA

The return of Sandy Weill. He built Shearson but ran into trouble at American Express. Now he's tapping Primerica's money to attempt a big Wall Street comeback.
Business Week   Dec 4, 1989   p. 88

PRINCE PHILIP

See PHILIP, CONSORT OF ELIZABETH II, QUEEN OF GREAT BRITAIN

PRIONS

The amazing prion. It has been hailed as a major breakthrough, perhaps a new form of life. So what is it, where is it, and why doesn't anybody know?
Discover   Dec 1986   p. 28

PRISONS

Inside America's toughest prison.
Newsweek   Oct 6, 1986   p. 46

Bulging prisons. Curbing crime - or wasting lives?
U.S. News   Apr 23, 1984   p. 42

The inmate nation. What are prisons for?
Time   Sep 13, 1982   p. 38

Big change in prisons. Punish - not reform.
U.S. News   Aug 25, 1975   p. 21

The bitter lessons of Attica.
Time   Sep 27, 1971   p. 18

U.S. prisons: Schools for crime.
Time   Jan 18, 1971   p. 48

PRIVACY, RIGHT OF

Somebody's watching. How business,
government and even the folks next door
are tracking your secrets.
Time   Nov 11, 1991   p. 34

Is nothing private? Computers know
more about you than you realize—and
now anyone can tap in.
Business Week   Sep 4, 1989   p. 74

Privacy. Should companies test
employees for drug use? Or screen job
applicants for diseases? Or give lie
detector tests? Or eavesdrop on office
phone calls? All this is now happening.
Business Week   Mar 28, 1988   p. 61

Who is watching you? Report on privacy.
U.S. News   Jul 12, 1982   p. 34

Is privacy dead?
Newsweek   Jul 27, 1970   p. 15

PRO-DEMOCRACY MOVEMENT

The year of Yeltsin. Decade of
democracy.
Newsweek   Dec 30, 1991   p. 18

People of the year. Standing up for
freedom. 1989. Changing the course of
history.
Newsweek   Dec 25, 1989   p. 18

Communist meltdown. The crumbling
Iron Curtain. The Soviet economy in
ruins.
U.S. News   Nov 20, 1989   p. 20

The big break. Moscow lets Eastern
Europe go its own way.
Time   Nov 6, 1989   p. 40

Collapse of Communism. In China,
Poland and the Soviet Union, the people
defy their leaders.
U.S. News   Jun 19, 1989   p. 18

Battle for democracy. The crisis in
Panama. The students in the streets of
Beijing. Eruptions in the Soviet
Republics. Solidarity reborn in Poland.
In dozens of countries around the world,
the rulers and the ruled...
U.S. News   May 22, 1989   p. 28

PRO-DEMOCRACY MOVEMENT - CHINA

Revolt against Communism. China.
Poland. USSR.
Time   Jun 19, 1989   p. 10

People power. Beijing: Defying
dictatorship. Moscow: Demanding
democracy.
Time   Jun 5, 1989   p. 16

Upheaval in China.
Newsweek   May 29, 1989   p. 14

China in turmoil.
Time   May 29, 1989   p. 36

PRO-DEMOCRACY MOVEMENT - EASTERN EUROPE

Can he ride the tiger? With Eastern
Europe out of control and his economy in
ruins, Gorbachev faces his toughest test.
Newsweek   Dec 4, 1989   p. 34

PRO-DEMOCRACY MOVEMENT - GERMANY

The wall. 1961-1989.
Newsweek   Nov 20, 1989   p. 24

Freedom!
Time   Nov 20, 1989   p. 24

PRO-DEMOCRACY MOVEMENT - POLAND

The birth of freedom. A picture album of
one of the 20th century's great moments
by the photographers of Czechoslovakia.
Life   Feb 1990   p. 26

The party's over. Communism crumbles
in Poland.
Newsweek   Aug 28, 1989   p. 16

Revolt against Communism. China.
Poland. USSR.
Time   Jun 19, 1989   p. 10

PRO-DEMOCRACY MOVEMENT - ROMANIA

The last days of a dictator. A violent end
to a year of revolution. Romania.
Newsweek   Jan 8, 1990   p. 16

When tyrants fall. Rumania. A firing
squad for Ceausescu. Panama. End of the
line for Noriega?
Time   Jan 8, 1990   p. 26

Rebels on the campus. Confrontation at
Columbia.
Newsweek   Sep 30, 1968   p. 63

Student protest.
Newsweek   May 6, 1968   p. 40

Martin Luther King, Jr., 1929-1968.
Newsweek   Apr 15, 1968   p. 26

Protest! Protest! Protest! Protest! A week
of antiwar demonstrations.
Time   Oct 27, 1967   p. 23

The demonstrators. Who? Why? How
many?
Newsweek   Nov 1, 1965   p. 25

The road from Selma.
Newsweek   Apr 5, 1965   p. 23

Martin Luther King.
Time   Mar 19, 1965   p. 23

PROZAC
Prozac. A breakthrough drug for
depression.
Newsweek   Mar 26, 1990   p. 38

PRUDENTIAL-BACHE SECURITIES INC.
The mess at Pru-Bache. George Ball is
gone. But he leaves behind a legal and
financial nightmare at the troubled
securities firm.
Business Week   Mar 4, 1991   p. 66

Managing the new financial
supermarkets.
Business Week   Dec 20, 1982   p. 50

PRYOR, RICHARD
Richard Pryor busts loose.
Newsweek   May 3, 1982   p. 48

PSYCHIATRY
Psychiatry's depression.
Time   Apr 2, 1979   p. 74

Neuroses: One psychiatrist's troubled
patients.
Newsweek   May 29, 1961   p. 57

PSYCHIC RESEARCH
See PARAPSYCHOLOGY

PSYCHOANALYSIS
The quest for identity. Psychoanalyst
Erik. H. Erikson.
Newsweek   Dec 21, 1970   p. 84

PSYCHOLOGY
Self deception. A little can help.
Psychology Today   Mar 1987   p. 24

Unlocking the unconscious. New
evidence of Freud's inner world.
Discover   Feb 1985   p. 12

Six Nobel Prize winners envision
psychology tomorrow.
Psychology Today   Dec 1982   p. 21

Self-critics: What they're up to when they
put themselves down.
Psychology Today   Jul 1982   p. 45

Understanding psychological man.
Psychology Today   May 1982   p. 40

Searching for self-fulfillment in a world
turned upside down.
Psychology Today   Apr 1981   p. 35

Psychological traps. How we get into
them, how we can get out of them.
Psychology Today   Mar 1981   p. 52

Getting your head together.
Newsweek   Sep 6, 1976   p. 56

B. F. Skinner says: We can't afford
freedom.
Time   Sep 20, 1971   p. 47

PSYCHOPHARMACOLOGY
Drugs for the mind. Psychiatry's newest
weapons.
Newsweek   Nov 12, 1979   p. 98

PSYCHOTHERAPY
A new series on psychotherapy: Treating
the emotions.
Life   Feb 1982

Putting time limits on therapy–can
deadlines speed a cure?
Psychology Today   Aug 1981   p. 60

New ways to help disturbed minds.
Where will it all lead?
U.S. News   Feb 16, 1976   p. 33

PTL SCANDAL

God & money. Greed, secrecy and scandal: An inside look at Jim and Tammy Bakker's bankrupt empire.
Time   Aug 3, 1987   p. 48

Heaven can wait while the holy war heats up.
Newsweek   Jun 8, 1987   p. 58

Holy wars. Money, sex and power. Evangelists Jim and Tammy Bakker.
Newsweek   Apr 6, 1987   p. 16

PUBLIC EMPLOYEES - POLITICAL ACTIVITY

Proposed Federal employees' political activities legislation.
Congressional Digest Jan 1988   p. 3

PUBLIC LANDS

The great gold scandal. A billion-dollar giveaway is ravaging the American West.
U.S. News   Oct 28, 1991   p. 44

The war for the West. Fighting for the soul of America's mythic land.
Newsweek   Sep 30, 1991   p. 18

Our forests under siege. Do we really have the will to restrict the destruction by timber industry's screaming chainsaws?
USA Today   Mar 1991   p. 17

Battle for the wilderness. The fate of America's pristine land is at stake.
U.S. News   Jul 3, 1989   p. 16

The great outdoors. Stunning secret places. Top spots for bird-watching.
Life   Jul 1987   p. 35

Battle over the wilderness. Uncle Sam owns one-third of the country, and Americans are fighting over every acre.
Newsweek   Jul 25, 1983   p. 22

Controversy over wilderness area minerals policy.
Congressional Digest Dec 1982   p. 289

Going, going...! Land sale of the century.
Time   Aug 23, 1982   p. 16

Watt's land rush. Digging up the last frontier? Interior Secretary James Watt.
Newsweek   Jun 29, 1981   p. 22

PUBLIC OFFICIALS

The great American bureaucratic junketing machine.
U.S. News   Dec 18, 1978   p. 56

Public officials for sale. Now a crackdown.
U.S. News   Feb 28, 1977   p. 36

PUBLIC OPINION

Polls: Critical challenges facing the nation.
USA Today   Dec 1990   p. 1

Are you better off now than you were 4 years ago? Yes. No.
U.S. News   Oct 15, 1984   p. 30

Women in 1984: Political time bomb.
Ms.   Jul 1984   p. 51

We're rallying. America's springtime mood.
U.S. News   Jun 8, 1981   p. 22

Who'll win? Results of 50-state survey.
U.S. News   Nov 1, 1976   p. 20

People speak their minds. '76 nationwide survey.
U.S. News   May 17, 1976 p. 21

Mood of America. "Where do we turn?"
U.S. News   Oct 6, 1975   p. 12

Things have got to get better. Mood of America.
U.S. News   May 5, 1975   p. 10

Mood of America. Prices ... politics ... taxes ... morality.
U.S. News   Sep 30, 1974   p. 20

Springtime mood at grass roots. On - Nixon ... Inflation ... Politics ... Business ... Morale.
U.S. News   May 6, 1974   p. 16

What voters tell Congress about: Impeaching Nixon. Pain of high prices. Fuel fiasco. Next November's elections.
U.S. News   Jan 21, 1974   p. 13

What America really thinks of Nixon.
Newsweek   Aug 28, 1972   p. 16

PUBLIC OPINION POLLS

The polls. Do they count?
Newsweek   Jul 8, 1968   p. 23

QADDAFI, MUAMMAR AL-

Hitting home. Tripoli under attack.
Time   Apr 28, 1986   p. 16

Target Gaddafi.
Time   Apr 21, 1986   p. 18

Kaddafi. The 'flaky' fanatic. The Reagan
plan to stop him.
Newsweek   Jan 20, 1986   p. 14

Libya's hit teams. The specter of
terrorism. Colonel Muammar Gaddafi.
Time   Dec 21, 1981   p. 16

Kaddafi. The most dangerous man in the
world?
Newsweek   Jul 20, 1981   p. 40

QUADROS, JANIO

Brazil's President Quadros.
Time   Jun 30, 1961   p. 23

QUALITY CONTROL

Quality. To compete, U.S. companies
must boost product quality. That means
big changes in design, manufacturing—
and management thinking.
Business Week   Jun 8, 1987   p. 130

Quality. The U.S. drives to catch up. Top
management takes up the challenge. How
key industries are doing.
Business Week   Nov 1, 1982   p. 66

QUALITY OF LIFE

How women are changing the way
America lives. Life stories about home,
work, love, community & commitment.
Ms.   Apr 1, 1986   p. 33

QUANTUM THEORY

Weird science. New experiments confirm
the strange world that Einstein refused to
accept.
Discover   Nov 1, 1990   p. 62

QUAYLE, DAN

The Quayle handicap. Is he a
lightweight—or smarter than you think?
Newsweek   May 20, 1991   p. 20

No joke. This man could be our next
president. A probing look by Garry Wills.
Time   Apr 23, 1990   p. 28

Shaky start. Questions about Quayle.
Can Bush get back on track?
Newsweek   Aug 29, 1988   p. 16

The Quayle factor.
Time   Aug 29, 1988   p. 16

QUEBEC (CANADA)

Powder keg at our doorstep.
U.S.News   May 19, 1980   p. 21

Canada. A house divided. Prime
Minister Trudeau & Quebec Premier
Lévesque.
Time   Feb 13, 1978   p. 32

QUINLAN, KAREN ANNE

A right to die?
Newsweek   Nov 3, 1975   p. 58

QUINLAN, MICHAEL

McRisky. McDonald's faces a growth
crisis. So CEO Mike Quinlan is changing
its tried-and-true recipe.
Business Week   Oct 21, 1991   p. 114

QUINTUPLETS

Stay-at-home father. And the quints he
raised while mom went to work.
Life   Jul 1, 1984   p. 71

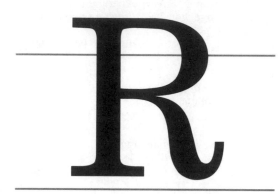

R

R.H. MACY AND CO.

The consumer economy. Macy's Jack Straus.
Time   Jan 8, 1965   p. 58

R.J. INDUSTRIES, INC.

R.J. Reynolds: The consumer is king again.
Business Week   Jun 4, 1984   p. 92

RABIN, YITZHAK

Israel besieged. Premier Yitzhak Rabin.
Time   Dec 2, 1974   p. 43

RACE RELATIONS - UNITED STATES

Black & white in America. Race and the troubled state of integration.
U.S. News   Jul 22, 1991   p. 18

The new politics of race.
Newsweek   May 6, 1991   p. 22

Race and the South. How blacks and whites are remaking the old confederacy.
U.S. News   Jul 23, 1990   p. 22

The Boston murder. Unraveling a grisly hoax. Race, anger and a divided city.
Newsweek   Jan 22, 1990   p. 16

A murder in Boston. How a bizarre case inflamed racial tensions and raised troubling questions about politicians, the police and the press.
Time   Jan 22, 1990   p. 10

Black and white. A major survey of U.S. racial attitudes today.
Newsweek   Aug 22, 1966   p. 20

What the white man thinks of the Negro revolt.
Newsweek   Oct 21, 1963   p. 44

The Negro in America. The first definitive national survey - who he is, what he wants, what he fears, what he hates, how he lives, how he votes, why he is fighting . . . and why now?
Newsweek   Jul 29, 1963   p. 15

See Also BLACKS - INTEGRATION

RACKETEERING

Union corruption. Worse than ever.
U.S.News   Sep 8, 1980   p. 33

RADAR AVOIDANCE SYSTEMS

See ELECTRONIC WARFARE

RADICALS AND RADICALISM

Marxism in U.S. classrooms.
U.S. News   Jan 25, 1982   p. 42

RADIO INDUSTRY

Broadcast deregulation.
Congressional Digest Apr 1984   p. 99

RADIO PROGRAMS

Psychology on the air–here it comes, crazy or not.
Psychology Today   Dec 1981   p. 31

RADIOACTIVE WASTE DISPOSAL

The nuclear scandal.
Time   Oct 31, 1988   p. 60

RADNER, GILDA

Gilda Radner's answer to cancer. Healing the body with mind and heart.
Life   Mar 1988   p. 74

RADZIWILL, LEE

New career for Princess Lee Radziwill.
Life   Jul 14, 1967   p. 52

RAGGHIANTI, MARIE

The woman who stopped the "red-neck mafia." Marie Ragghianti. A new American hero.
Ms.   Jun 1983   p. 43

RAHMAN, ABDUL

A new nation in Asia. Malaysia's Abdul Rahman.
Time   Apr 12, 1963   p. 43

RAILROADS

Federal subsidy of Amtrak.
Congressional Digest Aug 1985   p. 194

India by rail. Pakistan to Bangladesh.
National Geographic Jun 1984   p. 696

CSX: Railroading for fun and profit. Coal and deregulation make earnings soar.
Business Week   Nov 30, 1981 p. 80

Railroads of the future.
Time   Jan 26, 1968 p. 70

Tough times on the railroads.
Time   Aug 11, 1961 p. 57

RAIN FORESTS

Torching the Amazon. Can the rain forest be saved?
Time   Sep 18, 1989 p. 76

Rain forests. Nature's dwindling treasures.
National Geographic Jan 1983   p. 2

RAINWATER, RICHARD

The man behind a $5 billion dynasty. The remarkable saga of how Richard Rainwater helped make the Bass family one of the richest in America—and why he's now going out on his own.
Business Week   Oct 20, 1986 p. 94

RAMSEY, ARTHUR (ARCHBISHOP)

The Anglican communion. Worldly. Worldwide. Catholic and Protestant.
Time   Aug 16, 1963 p. 58

RAP MUSIC

Rap Rage. Yo! Street rhyme has gone big time. But are those sounds out of bounds?
Newsweek   Mar 19, 1990 p. 56

RAPE

What you don't see. Behind the drama at the Smith rape trial.
Newsweek   Dec 16, 1991 p. 18

Date Rape.
Time   Jun 3, 1991   p. 48

Victims of rape. Should their names be kept secret? Privacy, the media and the Kennedy case.
Newsweek   Apr 29, 1991 p. 26

The mind of the rapist. The psychology of sexual violence. New York's grisly 'Jogger' trial. The fear of AIDS.
Newsweek   Jul 23, 1990 p. 46

Rape and the law. A disturbing case focuses attention on how the legal system deals with the most personal of violent crimes.
Newsweek   May 20, 1985 p. 60

Private violence. Child abuse. Wife beating. Rape.
Time   Sep 5, 1983   p. 18

RATHER, DAN

The ambush that failed. CBS gunslinger Dan Rather.
Time   Feb 8, 1988   p. 16

The $8,000,000 man. TV's news explosion.
Time   Feb 25, 1980 p. 64

RAUSCHENBERG, ROBERT

The joy of art. Rauschenberg by Rauschenberg.
Time   Nov 29, 1976 p. 54

RAWL, LARRY

The rebel shaking up Exxon. CEO Lawrence G. Rawl.
Business Week   Jul 18, 1988 p. 104

RAY, DIXY LEE

The Pacific Northwest. Washington Governor Dixy Lee Ray.
Time   Dec 12, 1977 p. 26

RAY, JAMES EARL

Ray's escape.
Newsweek   Jun 20, 1977 p. 22

The escape. James Earl Ray.
Time   Jun 20, 1977   p. 12

The assassins.
Newsweek   Mar 24, 1969   p. 28

The two accused. The psycho-biology of violence.
Life   Jun 21, 1968   p. 24

The accused killer. Ray alias Galt. The revealing story of a mean kid.
Life   May 3, 1968   p. 20

RAYBURN, SAM
Kennedy & Congress. What price victory? Speaker Rayburn.
Time   Feb 10, 1961   p. 11

RCA CORP.
RCA. RCA+. Will it ever be a top performer?
Business Week   Apr 2, 1984   p. 52

RCA: Still another master. Undoing the errors of previous bosses.
Business Week   Aug 17, 1981   p. 80

REAGAN, NANCY
Poison Pen. Kitty vs. Nancy. The boom in trash biography.
Newsweek   Apr 22, 1991   p. 52

Is she that bad? What's true–and not true–in Kitty Kelley's slasher biography of Nancy Reagan.
Time   Apr 22, 1991   p. 64

Nancy Reagan's 'My Turn.' On astrology. On Don Regan. On Raisa. On her kids.
Newsweek   Oct 23, 1989   p. 50

White House co-star. Nancy Reagan's growing role.
Time   Jan 14, 1985   p. 24

Nancy Reagan, First Ranch Lady.
Life   Oct 1983   p. 48

The First Lady's world.
Newsweek   Dec 21, 1981   p. 22

The race for First Lady.
U.S.News   Oct 20, 1980   p. 27

REAGAN, NANCY (INTERVIEW)
Nancy Reagan's role.
U.S. News   Jun 1, 1981   p. 46

REAGAN, RONALD
Reagan. Memoirs: "An American Life."
Time   Nov 5, 1990   p. 60

How Reagan changed America.
Newsweek   Jan 9, 1989   p. 12

What Reagan has meant to America. Behind-the-scenes photos of the president at work and play.
U.S. News   Jan 9, 1989   p. 18

After Reagan. America's agenda for the 1990s.
Business Week   Feb 1, 1988   p. 56

Reagan's failure. Can he recover?
Newsweek   Mar 9, 1987   p. 16

Can he recover?
Time   Mar 9, 1987   p. 20

The teflon is gone. A question of competence. Can Howard Baker rebuild a shattered Presidency. How Nancy Reagan defends her man.
U.S. News   Mar 9, 1987   p. 14

Why is this man so popular?
Time   Jul 7, 1986   p. 12

Chapter two. Reagan's mandate. The new look in Congress. Labor's lost clout. The coming fight over taxes and spending. The prospect for arms control.
Business Week   Nov 19, 1984   p. 36

Reagan's triumph. What it means to America.
Time   Nov 19, 1984   p. 36

Four more years!
U.S. News   Nov 19, 1984   p. 24

After the avalanche.
U.S. News   Nov 12, 1984   p. 22

Peace and war. Exclusive interviews on where they stand.
U.S. News   Oct 22, 1984   p. 29

How good a President?
Newsweek   Aug 27, 1984   p. 28

The Reagan magic. Can he make it work again? 1984.
Newsweek   Feb 6, 1984   p. 14

REAGAN, RONALD - ASSASSINATION ATTEMPT

REAGAN, RONALD - EXECUTIVE APPOINTMENTS

REAGAN, RONALD - HEALTH

Reagan's prognosis. The cancer scare.
How swift a recovery?
Newsweek   Jul 22, 1985   p. 14

Reagan's illness.
Time   Jul 22, 1985   p. 16

REAGAN, RONALD - INAUGURATION

Encore!
Newsweek   Jan 28, 1985   p. 18

The second term. A fresh agenda. A new
lineup.
Time   Jan 28, 1985   p. 20

A day to remember.
Newsweek   Feb 2, 1981   p. 16

REAGAN, RONALD - STAFF

The second term. A fresh agenda. A new
lineup.
Time   Jan 28, 1985   p. 20

Changing the guard. Tackling the deficit -
and arms control. The new White House
Chief of Staff Donald Regan.
Newsweek   Jan 21, 1985   p. 14

Shake-up at the White House. Reagan
gets a tough new Chief of Staff. Donald
Regan.
Time   Jan 21, 1985   p. 10

Making his moves. A shocker for Interior.
A shake-up for the NSC. And a big "Why
not?" for 1984.
Time   Oct 24, 1983   p. 16

The President's men. How the White
House works - and doesn't.
Time   Dec 14, 1981   p. 16

Reagan's big three. Too much power?
U.S. News   Nov 2, 1981   p. 28

REAGAN, RONALD - STATE OF THE UNION
MESSAGE

Can Reagan keep control?
U.S. News   Feb 7, 1983   p. 20

REAGAN, RONALD - VISIT TO WEST
GERMANY, 1985

Reagan in Germany. "Horror cannot
outlast hope."
Time   May 13, 1985   p. 16

Reagan in Germany. Coming to terms
with the past. Eric Sevareid on trusting
the Germans. America's stake in the
Bonn Summit. Concentration camp
survivors today. U.S. power 40 years after
V-E Day.
U.S. News   May 6, 1985   p. 24

Fury over the Reagan trip. The wounds
of war.
Newsweek   Apr 29, 1985   p. 14

May 8, 1945. "Never a greater day." But
Reagan opens old wounds.
Time   Apr 29, 1985   p. 18

REAGAN, RONALD (INTERVIEW)

Going in strong. Exclusive interview with
President Reagan on the Summit, Star
Wars and the Soviets.
U.S. News   Nov 18, 1985   p. 28

How Reagan decides. An inside look at
the presidency. The qualities a President
needs.
Time   Dec 13, 1982   p. 12

Where Reagan stands. Interview on the
issues.
U.S. News   May 31, 1976   p. 20

REAL ESTATE BUSINESS

Can your bank stay afloat? How the
real-estate crash threatens financial
institutions. The best ways to buy and sell
a house in a down market.
U.S. News   Nov 12, 1990   p. 62

The real estate bust. "How to survive" by
Jane Bryant Quinn.
Newsweek   Oct 1, 1990   p. 46

REBOZO, CHARLES G. "BEBE"

Bebe and the $100,000. Charles G.
Rebozo.
Newsweek   Apr 22, 1974   p. 28

Bebe Rebozo. President Nixon's best
friend.
Life   Jul 31, 1970   p. 18

RECESSION

High anxiety. The elusive recovery
worries consumers, business—and now
the stock market.
Business Week   Dec 2, 1991   p. 28

A strong recovery. Yes, it's possible.
Business Week   Jul 1, 1991   p. 48

Riding out the recession. The 'fear' factor.
Newsweek   Jan 14, 1991   p. 32

The new face of recession. No doubt about it, we're in recession. The real estate collapse, the related banking problems, and the very high level of debt make this a finance-led recession.
Business Week   Dec 24, 1990   p. 58

Here comes the recovery. But how strong? And how long?
Business Week   May 10, 1982   p. 140

What it will take to end the recession.
U.S. News   Jan 20, 1975   p. 15

Recession's greetings. P.S. There's some good news too.
Time   Dec 9, 1974   p. 28

How bad a slump?
Newsweek   Dec 2, 1974   p. 68

Is this slump necessary?
Time   Jun 1, 1970   p. 39

Recession.
Newsweek   May 25, 1970   p. 74

RECOMBINANT DNA
See GENETIC ENGINEERING

RECREATION
Our endless pursuit of happiness.
U.S. News   Aug 10, 1981   p. 58

How Americans pursue happiness.
U.S. News   May 23, 1977   p. 60

The endless weekend. A special issue on Americans outdoors.
Life   Sep 3, 1971   p. 8

REDFORD, ROBERT
The all-star. Robert Redford in 'The Natural.'
Newsweek   May 28, 1984   p. 74

The great Redford. Robert Redford in "The Great Gatsby."
Newsweek   Feb 4, 1974   p. 44

New star Robert Redford, a real Sundance Kid.
Life   Feb 6, 1970   p. 38

REDGRAVE, LYNN
Lynn & Vanessa Redgrave.
Time   Mar 17, 1967   p. 80

REDGRAVE, VANESSA
The Vanessa Redgrave controversy.
Newsweek   Sep 29, 1980   p. 52

Lynn & Vanessa Redgrave.
Time   Mar 17, 1967   p. 80

REDUCING
Getting slim. How to find the right diet.
U.S. News   May 14, 1990   p. 56

Liquid diets. Are they safe? How they work.
Newsweek   Apr 30, 1990   p. 52

Slimming down. What works. What won't. What's new.
Time   Jan 20, 1986   p. 54

Diet crazes.
Newsweek   Dec 19, 1977   p. 66

See Also DIETING

REED, JOHN
John Reed's Citicorp. The bank's performance is lackluster. But Reed, 47, has a long-term plan: Build reserves to guard against market shocks and gear up for a growth surge in the 1990s.
Business Week   Dec 8, 1986   p. 90

REFUGEES
Hong Kong. Countdown to 1997. Plight of the boat people.
National Geographic Feb 1991   p. 103

The new refugees. Should America take them in?
U.S. News   Oct 23, 1989   p. 84

Refugees. Stung by a backlash.
U.S.News   Oct 13, 1980   p. 60

REFUGEES, CAMBODIAN
Starvation. Deathwatch in Cambodia.
Time   Nov 12, 1979   p. 42

Preachers in politics.
U.S. News   Sep 24, 1979   p. 37

The President's preacher. Billy Graham
and the surging Southern Baptists.
Newsweek   Jul 20, 1970   p. 50

U.S. Catholics & the state. John Courtney
Murray, S.J.
Time   Dec 12, 1960   p. 64

RELIGION AND SOCIAL PROBLEMS

The church and capitalism. The Catholic
Bishops' report on the U.S. economy, out
next week, will cause a furor.
Business Week   Nov 12, 1984   p. 104

Messengers of love and hope. Living
saints. Mother Teresa.
Time   Dec 29, 1975   p. 47

RELIGION IN PUBLIC SCHOOLS

One nation, under God. Has the
separation of church and state gone too
far?
Time   Dec 9, 1991   p. 60

The school prayer controversy.
Congressional Digest May 1984   p. 131

REMICK, LEE

The offstage charms of Lee Remick.
Life   Jun 6, 1960   p. 100

REPORTERS AND REPORTING

Sex, politics and the press. Gary Hart
self-destructs.
Newsweek   May 18, 1987   p. 22

Hart's fall. Sex and politics. Democrats in
a quandary. Questions about press
ethics.
Time   May 18, 1987   p. 14

Private lives. How much are we entitled
to know about public figures? The
self-destruction of Gary Hart.
U.S. News   May 18, 1987   p. 18

America's news industry. Responsible -
or reckless?
U.S. News   Apr 29, 1974   p. 32

REPRODUCTION

Sperm wars. The battle for conception.
Discover   Jul 1991   p. 48

The first pictures ever of how life begins.
Life   Aug 1990   p. 26

The future of mothers. The dilemmas of
the new birth technologies.
Ms.   May 1988   p. 70

New birth technologies. Male pregnancy.
Prenatal learning. Ideal sperm donor.
Choices in childbirth. Man-made womb.
Omni   Dec 1985   p. 24

The moment of conception. When sperm
meets egg.
Discover   Oct 1982   p. 32

Science and sex. When new methods of
human reproduction become
available—can traditional family life
survive? Will marital infidelity increase?
Will children and parents still love each
other?
Life   Jun 13, 1969   p. 37

REPUBLICAN NATIONAL CONVENTION,

Balloons soar as the Nixons begin
campaign.
Life   Aug 8, 1960   p. 16

REPUBLICAN NATIONAL CONVENTION, 1964

'A choice - not an echo.'
Newsweek   Jul 27, 1964   p. 18

The Goldwater convention.
Life   Jul 24, 1964   p. 20

The new thrust in American politics.
Goldwater accepting nomination.
Time   Jul 24, 1964   p. 22

Scranton for President. Goldwater for
President. GOP convention.
Newsweek   Jul 20, 1964   p. 16

REPUBLICAN NATIONAL CONVENTION, 1968

The GOP ticket.
Newsweek   Aug 19, 1968   p. 18

The Nixons and the Agnews. Finale at
Miami Beach.
Life   Aug 16, 1968   p. 22

The G.O.P. ticket.
Time   Aug 16, 1968   p. 10

The GOP in Miami.
Newsweek   Aug 12, 1968   p. 14

Republicans: The men and the issues.
Time   Aug 9, 1968   p. 16

REPUBLICAN NATIONAL CONVENTION, 1972

The Spiro of '76?
Newsweek   Sep 4, 1972   p. 27

REPUBLICAN NATIONAL CONVENTION, 1976

The underdogs.
Newsweek   Aug 30, 1976   p. 16

The G.O.P. strategy: Give 'em hell.
Time   Aug 30, 1976   p. 6

Ford's plan to beat the odds.
U.S. News   Aug 30, 1976   p. 12

High noon.
Newsweek   Aug 23, 1976   p. 18

The plight of the G.O.P. Looking beyond Kansas City.
Time   Aug 23, 1976   p. 10

REPUBLICAN NATIONAL CONVENTION, 1980

Photo finish. How the Ford deal fizzled.
Newsweek   Jul 28, 1980   p. 14

Getting it together. Exclusive: Inside the Ford drama.
Time   Jul 28, 1980   p. 10

Feeling super in Detroit.
Time   Jul 21, 1980   p. 6

REPUBLICAN NATIONAL CONVENTION, 1984

Republican encore. Coronation in Dallas.
Time   Aug 27, 1984   p. 8

REPUBLICAN NATIONAL CONVENTION, 1988

The keys to election '88. The Quayle affair. The cutting issues. The swing voters.
U.S. News   Aug 29, 1988   p. 22

REPUBLICAN PARTY

Losing ground. GOP losses in Congress, statehouse setbacks, and internal party strife are eroding George Bush's authority—and his ability to lead the nation.
Business Week   Nov 19, 1990   p. 42

The recovery cheers the GOP. Amid prosperity the gender gap haunts Reagan.
Business Week   Sep 3, 1984   p. 74

A dying party? 5 Republican leaders speak out.
U.S. News   Aug 29, 1977   p. 22

The Republicans. Can they pull together?
U.S. News   Aug 23, 1976   p. 12

The new GOP galaxy.
Newsweek   Nov 21, 1966   p. 31

The GOP: A trunkful of troubles.
Newsweek   Nov 16, 1964   p. 25

RESEARCH

Science under siege. Tight money, blunders and scandal plague America's researchers.
Time   Aug 26, 1991   p. 44

RESNICK, PAT

Secretary as hero!
Ms.   Jan 1981   p. 43

RESORTS

See SUMMER RESORTS

RESTON, JAMES "SCOTTY"

Those Washington columnists.
Newsweek   Dec 18, 1961   p. 65

Washington columnist Scotty Reston.
Time   Feb 15, 1960   p. 74

RETAIL TRADE

The power retailers. The best-run stores: Will their formula work in a season of worries?
Business Week   Dec 21, 1987   p. 86

RETIREMENT

Retirement. Tips to help you build your nest egg. Mapping out a new career after retirement. A work sheet to chart your savings.
U.S. News   Aug 14, 1989   p. 55

Controversy over mandatory retirement policy.
Congressional Digest Nov 1982   p. 259

Can you afford to retire? The Social Security crisis. Turmoil in pension plans.
Newsweek   Jun 1, 1981   p. 24

Will inflation tarnish your golden years?
U.S. News   Feb 26, 1979   p. 55

Revolt of the old. The battle over forced retirement.
Time   Oct 10, 1977   p. 18

RETIREMENT COMMUNITIES

The retirement city. A new way of life for the old.
Time   Aug 3, 1962   p. 46

REUTHER, WALTER

"I shall continue to be disatisfied..." - Walter Reuther, Auto Workers' Chief.
Newsweek   Sep 4, 1961   p. 51

REVLON, INC.

Cosmetics. Kiss and sell. Revlon's Michel Bergerac.
Time   Dec 11, 1978   p. 86

REVOLUTIONARY WAR

See UNITED STATES - HISTORY - REVOLUTION

REVOLUTIONS

Revolution. What are the causes? How does it start? Can it happen here?
Life   Oct 10, 1969   p. 100

REYNOLDS, BURT

Hollywood's honchos. Burt Reynolds. Clint Eastwood.
Time   Jan 9, 1978   p. 48

RHEAULT, ROBERT

The Green Beret Colonel. Colonel Rheault talks about the end of his career.
Life   Nov 14, 1969 p. 34

The case of the Green Berets.
Newsweek   Aug 25, 1969 p. 26

RHODESIA

See ZIMBABWE

RHYTHMIC GYMNASTICS

A new event for the Olympics—and you. The best gymnastics and dance.
Ms.   Feb 1983   p. 55

RIBICOFF, ABRAHAM

Ribicoff: Health, education - and a welfare state?
Newsweek   Feb 20, 1961 p. 26

RICH

The rich in America. How they made their money. The populist assault on them.
U.S. News   Nov 18, 1991 p. 34

U.S. News 100 super-rich owners of American business.
U.S. News   Jul 21, 1986   p. 36

How ordinary people get rich. A million millionaires. Who they are - how they did it.
U.S. News   Jan 13, 1986   p. 43

The hot new rich.
Time   Jun 13, 1977   p. 72

RIDE, SALLY

Space woman. Sally Ride prepares to make history on shuttle Mission 7. NASA's latest plans for space travel.
Newsweek   Jun 13, 1983   p. 83

Sally Ride, astronaut the world is watching.
Ms.   Jan 1983   p. 45

RIGGS, BOBBY

The happy hustler. Bobby Riggs.
Time   Sep 10, 1973   p. 54

RIGHT AND LEFT (POLITICAL SCIENCE)

The revolt of the right: Wallace and LeMay.
Time   Oct 18, 1968   p. 15

Thunder on the right. The conservatives. The radicals. The fanatic fringe.
Newsweek   Dec 4, 1961   p. 18

RIGHT (POLITICAL SCIENCE)

See CONSERVATISM

RIGHT TO DIE

Choosing death. More doctors are
helping the very sick die gently.
Newsweek   Aug 26, 1991   p. 40

RIGHTER, CARL

Astrology and the new cult of the occult.
Time   Mar 21, 1969   p. 69

RINGWALD, MOLLY

Ain't she sweet. Teen actress Molly
Ringwald.
Time   May 26, 1986   p. 66

RIOTS - BOSTON (MASSACHUSETTS)

Boston school violence. Turning point in
busing?
U.S. News   Oct 28, 1974   p. 22

RIOTS - DETROIT (MICHIGAN)

Battlefield, U.S.A.
Newsweek   Aug 7, 1967   p. 18

Negro revolt: The flames spread.
Life   Aug 4, 1967   p. 16

Twelfth Street, Detroit.
Time   Aug 4, 1967   p. 13

RIOTS - HARLEM (NEW YORK)

Harlem: Hatred in the streets.
Newsweek   Aug 3, 1964   p. 16

Harlem.
Time   Jul 31, 1964   p. 11

RIOTS - KENT STATE UNIVERSITY (OHIO)

Nixon's home front.
Newsweek   May 18, 1970   p. 26

Protest!
Time   May 18, 1970   p. 6

Crisis for Nixon.
Life   May 15, 1970   p. 28

RIOTS - MIAMI (FLORIDA)

Rage in Miami. A warning?
U.S.News   Jun 2, 1980   p. 19

RIOTS - NEWARK (NEW JERSEY)

Newark: The predictable insurrection.
Shooting war in the streets.
Life   Jul 28, 1967   p. 16

Anatomy of a race riot.
Time   Jul 21, 1967   p. 15

RIOTS - OXFORD (MISSISSIPPI)

The sound and the fury. Oxford,
Mississippi.
Newsweek   Oct 15, 1962   p. 23

RIOTS - UNITED STATES

Martin Luther King, Jr., 1929-1968.
Newsweek   Apr 15, 1968   p. 26

RIOTS - WATTS (CALIFORNIA)

Watts still seething. 1965—When the riot
cry was 'Burn, baby, burn!' 1966—Why
the ghetto today is close to flashpoint.
Life   Jul 15, 1966   p. 34

Los Angeles: Why?
Newsweek   Aug 30, 1965   p. 13

Arson and street war—most destructive
riot in U.S. history.
Life   Aug 27, 1965   p. 20

The Los Angeles riot.
Time   Aug 20, 1965   p. 13

RIPLEY, ALEXANDER BRAID

At last—the sequel to *Gone With the Wind*.
Life   May 1988   p. 26

RISK TAKING (PSYCHOLOGY)

The cult of risk taking. Why people go
out on a limb. A special test: Are you a
risk taker?
U.S. News   Jan 26, 1987   p. 60

Wheeeeeeee! Chasing thrills and
adventure.
Time   Aug 29, 1983   p. 52

RITES AND CEREMONIES

The journey of our lives. Birth.
Adolescence. Marriage. Death. A special
issue in pictures celebrating the most
important moments in every lifetime.
Life   Oct 1991   p. 4

RJR NABISCO INC.

RJR. Nervous about debt? Not Lou
Gerstner, who runs the biggest LBO of all.
Business Week   Oct 2, 1989   p. 72

A game of greed. This man could pocket
$100 million from the largest corporate
takeover in history. Has the buyout craze
gone too far? RJR Nabisco's Ross
Johnson.
Time   Dec 5, 1988   p. 66

ROBBERIES AND ASSAULTS
Highwaymen masquerade as cops in the
Great Mail Robbery. Re-enactment of the
crime.
Life   Aug 31, 1962 p. 61

ROBERTSON, OSCAR
Oscar Robertson.
Time   Feb 17, 1961   p. 54

ROBERTSON, PAT
Pat Robertson's amazing race. How he is
raising a 'hidden army' to take over the
Republican Party.
U.S. News   Feb 22, 1988   p. 14

ROBINSON, JAMES
American Express. The failed vision.
Business Week   Mar 19, 1990 p. 108

Do you know me? An intimate portrait of
James Robinson III, CEO of American
Express.
Business Week   Jan 25, 1988   p. 72

American Express: The golden plan. Now
it has to make its financial empire work.
Business Week   Apr 30, 1984   p. 118

ROBOTS
Six-legged revolution. A tiny robot with
the brains of an ant is rocking the world of
artificial intelligence.
Discover   Mar 1991   p. 42

Robo-bugs and the world's smallest
machines.
Omni   May 1990   p. 66

A single machine is challenging our
concepts of intelligence, emotion, and
individuality. It will change the way we
work and the way we live. The machine
is, of course, the robot.
Omni   Apr 1983   p. 26

The 'think machine' - smarter and
smarter.
Newsweek   Oct 24, 1960   p. 85

ROBOTS, INDUSTRIAL
High tech to the rescue. Can automation
save American industry?
Business Week   Jun 16, 1986   p. 100

The robot revolution.
Time   Dec 8, 1980   p. 72

ROCA, BLAS
Cuba: Chaos in the economy. Conflict
among the Reds. Communist chief Blas
Roca.
Time   Apr 27, 1962   p. 33

ROCK MUSIC
Rock rolls on. Aging stars like the Rolling
Stones strut their staying power.
Time   Sep 4, 1989   p. 58

Historic songfest for Africa.
Life   Apr 1985   p. 36

Britain rocks America - again. From the
Beatles to Boy George and beyond.
Newsweek   Jan 23, 1984   p. 50

Rock stars at home with their parents.
The Jackson Five with Mom and Pop.
Life   Sep 24, 1971   p. 46

The new rock: Bittersweet and low.
Time   Mar 1, 1971   p. 45

The future of rock.
Newsweek   Jan 4, 1971   p. 44

The new sound of country rock. The
Band.
Time   Jan 12, 1970   p. 42

The new rock. Music that's hooked the
whole vibrating world.
Life   Jun 28, 1968   p. 51

Rock 'n' roll: Everybody's turned on.
Time   May 21, 1965 p. 84

ROCK VIDEOS
Video rocks! A musical revolution.
Time   Dec 26, 1983   p. 54

ROCKEFELLER, DAVID
David Rockefeller: New era in banking.
Newsweek   Apr 3, 1967   p. 72

Banker David Rockefeller.
Time   Sep 7, 1962   p. 67

ROCKEFELLER, JOHN

The Percy-Rockefeller wedding.
Life   Apr 14, 1967   p. 85

ROCKEFELLER, NELSON

The Ford team.
Newsweek   Sep 2, 1974   p. 14

Nelson Rockefeller.
Time   Sep 2, 1974   p. 14

The new GOP race. The Rockefellers.
Newsweek   May 13, 1968   p. 26

Upset in the West. Rockefeller in Oregon.
Time   May 22, 1964   p. 17

Happy and Rocky. Back in the race.
Newsweek   Aug 26, 1963   p. 20

Rockefellers' honeymoon. Governor and
the new Mrs. Rockefeller.
Life   May 17, 1963   p. 41

Nelson Rockefeller.
Time   Jun 15, 1962   p. 16

New York's Rockefeller. Target '64.
Newsweek   May 14, 1962   p. 31

Republicans: Platform for the '60s.
Rockefeller & Nixon.
Time   Aug 1, 1960   p. 9

The Rockefeller challenge. Will it split the
GOP? A 50-state survey. New York's
Gov. Rockefeller: It's up to Nixon.
Newsweek   Jun 20, 1960   p. 29

ROCKEFELLER, NELSON (FAMILY)

A great American family. The Nelson
Rockefellers.
Life   Jul 11, 1960   p. 81

ROCKEFELLER, NELSON (INTERVIEW)

Rockefeller talks about his job and future.
Exclusive interview with the Vice
President.
U.S. News   Oct 13, 1975   p. 50

ROCKEFELLER, WINTHROP

The transformation of Arkansas.
Governor-elect Winthrop Rockefeller.
Time   Dec 2, 1966   p. 24

ROCKETTES

The Rockettes. Spectacle of their dancing.
How five of them work and live.
Life   Dec 11, 1964   p. 76

RODGERS, T.J.

The bad boy of Silicon Valley. The
offbeat management ideas of Cypress
Semiconductor's T.J. Rodgers.
Business Week   Dec 9, 1991   p. 64

ROHATYN, FELIX

The cities' Mr. Fixit. Felix Rohatyn.
Newsweek   May 4, 1981   p. 26

ROLLING STONES (MUSICAL GROUP)

The Stones are rolling again. Mick Jagger,
Stones' leader.
Life   Jul 14, 1972   p. 30

ROMANIA

The new Rumania. The satellites look
west.
Newsweek   Aug 10, 1964   p. 31

ROMANIA - POLITICS AND GOVERNMENT

The last days of a dictator. A violent end
to a year of revolution. Romania.
Newsweek   Jan 8, 1990   p. 16

When tyrants fall. Rumania. A firing
squad for Ceausescu. Panama. End of the
line for Noriega?
Time   Jan 8, 1990   p. 26

ROME, ANCIENT

The Romans. Part V. The Caesars.
Madmen, statesmen and saints.
Life   Jun 3, 1966   p. 56

The Romans. How a people born to rule
won an empire and forever shaped our
world.
Life   Mar 4, 1966   p. 56

ROMNEY, GEORGE

U.S. politics: The next two years.
Republican George Romney.
Time   Nov 16, 1962   p. 20

G.O.P. dark horse. George Romney. The
great game of politics.
Newsweek   Feb 19, 1962   p. 23

RONSTADT, LINDA

Linda Ronstadt: Torchy rock.
Time   Feb 28, 1977   p. 58

ROONEY, MICKEY

Mickey Rooney lights up Broadway.
Life   Mar 1980   p. 68

ROOSEVELT, FRANKLIN D.

The New Deal. FDR's disputed legacy.
Time   Feb 1, 1982   p. 20

F.D.R.'s secret romance. 'I do not feel I
have peeped and told.'
Life   Sep 2, 1966   p. 60

Democrats backstage. F.D.R. - Present but
not voting.
Newsweek   Jul 18, 1960   p. 28

ROSE, PETE

You bet your life. Pete Rose and the great
American obsession.
Time   Jul 10, 1989   p. 16

Play ball! ...and nobody plays it like Pete.
Cincinnati's wondrous Rose.
Time   Aug 19, 1985   p. 44

ROSELLINI, ISABELLA

Hot faces from Europe. Actress Nastassia
Kinski.
Time   May 2, 1983   p. 44

ROSS, DIANA

Diana Ross. The star shows off home
husband and babies.
Life   Dec 8, 1972   p. 42

ROSS, STEVEN J.

Time Warner. Synergy? Not much.
Strategic alliances? Not yet. Rights
offering? Not so fast. No wonder
shareholders are mad.
Business Week   Jul 22, 1991   p. 70

ROSTROPOVICH, MSTISLAV

The magnificent maestro. Mstislav
Rostropovich.
Time   Oct 24, 1977   p. 82

ROTHSCHILD FAMILY

The Rothschilds today.
Time   Dec 20, 1963   p. 70

ROTHSCHILD, JACOB

London's new financial whiz.
Business Week   Apr 23, 1984   p. 64

ROUSE, JAMES

Cities are fun. Master planner James
Rouse.
Time   Aug 24, 1981   p. 42

ROYALTY

See NOBILITY

RUBELLA

German measles and pregnancy. Current
U.S. epidemic will damage up to 20,000
babies.
Life   Jun 4, 1965   p. 24

RUBINSTEIN, ARTUR

Artur Rubinstein.
Time   Feb 25, 1966   p. 84

RUMANIA

See ROMANIA

RUMSFELD, DONALD H. (INTERVIEW)

How U.S. sizes up Russia now. Two
exclusive interviews. Secretary of
Defense, Donald H. Rumsfeld. Secretary
of State, Henry A. Kissinger.
U.S. News   Mar 15, 1976   p. 24

RUNAWAY ADULTS

Why so many wives are running away.
U.S. News   Feb 23, 1976   p. 24

Dropout wife. A striking current
phenomenon.
Life   Mar 17, 1972   p. 34

RUNAWAYS

The runaway epidemic. AIDS on the
streets.
Psychology Today   Jan 1988   p. 28

Runaway kids.
Life   Nov 3, 1967   p. 18

RUNNING

Running for joy!
Ms.   Jul 1981   p. 47

Jim Ryun. How fast the mile?
Newsweek   Jul 25, 1966   p. 53

RUSHDIE, SALMAN

My life in hiding. Salman Rushdie talks about his death sentence — and defends 'Satanic Verses'.
Newsweek   Feb 12, 1990   p. 46

How Iran's terrorists operate. Are Americans at risk from Khomeini's death threat to Salman Rushdie?
U.S. News   Mar 6, 1989   p. 20

'Satanic' fury. Putting a price on the head of Salman Rushdie.
Newsweek   Feb 27, 1989   p. 34

The Ayatullah orders a hit. He causes an uproar by sentencing author Salman Rushdie to death for his book *The Satanic Verses*.
Time   Feb 27, 1989   p. 28

RUSK, DEAN

The new administration. A promise of continuity & action. Secretary of State Dean Rusk.
Time   Dec 6, 1963   p. 24

Secretary Rusk. New policies for old problems?
Newsweek   Jul 9, 1962   p. 21

New tempo in foreign policy. Kennedy's man Rusk.
Newsweek   Feb 6, 1961   p. 19

Kennedy's men. The face of the new administration. Secretary of State: Dean Rusk.
Time   Dec 26, 1960   p. 8

RUSSELL, BERTRAND

Bertrand Russell.
Newsweek   Aug 20, 1962   p. 55

RUSSELL, CHARLES M.

C.M. Russell. Cowboy artist.
National Geographic Jan 1986   p. 60

RUSSELL, DONALD

Tough times on the railroads.
Time   Aug 11, 1961   p. 57

RUSSELL, RICHARD

Civil rights: The South's stand. Georgia's Senator Richard Russell.
Newsweek   Aug 19, 1963   p. 20

RUSSIA

See SOVIET UNION

RYAN, NOLAN

Fastest arm in the West.
Newsweek   Jun 16, 1975   p. 56

RYUN, JIM

Jim Ryun. How fast the mile?
Newsweek   Jul 25, 1966   p. 53

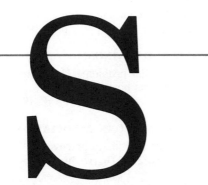

SADAT, ANWAR

Man of the year. Anwar Sadat.
Time   Jan 2, 1978   p. 10

The Mideast. What next?
Newsweek   Dec 5, 1977   p. 24

Mideast. New quest for peace.
Time   Jun 9, 1975   p. 24

SADAT, ANWAR - ASSASSINATION, 1981

'Act of infamy.' The Sadat assassination.
Newsweek   Oct 19, 1981   p. 25

Mideast turmoil. Anwar Sadat - 1918-1981.
Time   Oct 19, 1981   p. 12

Now the shock waves.
U.S. News   Oct 19, 1981   p. 24

SADAT, ANWAR - VISIT TO ISRAEL, 1977

Sadat in Israel.
Newsweek   Nov 28, 1977   p. 36

The 'Sacred Mission.' Egypt's President Sadat.
Time   Nov 28, 1977   p. 28

SAGAN, CARL

The marketing of Dr. Carl Sagan.
Omni   Jun 1982   p. 45

Showman of science. Astronomer Carl Sagan.
Time   Oct 20, 1980   p. 62

Seeking other worlds. Astronomer Carl Sagan.
Newsweek   Aug 15, 1977   p. 46

SAHEL (REGION), AFRICA

Africa's stricken Sahel.
National Geographic Aug 1987   p. 140

SAHL, MORT

Comedian Mort Sahl.
Time   Aug 15, 1960   p. 42

SAKHAROV, ANDREI

Sakharov. Memoirs of a 20th century giant.
Time   May 14, 1990   p. 40

Gorbachev's gamble. Opening a closed society. How far will he go? Sakharov on his struggle.
Newsweek   Jan 5, 1987   p. 12

"My ordeal" by Andrei Sakharov. 'I was seized by KGB men disguised in doctors' white coats. They took me by force to Gorky Regional Hospital, kept me there by force and tormented me for four months...'
U.S. News   Feb 24, 1986   p. 29

SALAN, RAOUL

Three-way war in Algeria. Terrorist Salan.
Time   Jan 26, 1962   p. 22

SALARIES

See WAGES AND SALARIES

SALINGER, J. D.

A private world of love and death.
Time   Sep 15, 1961   p. 84

SALINGER, PIERRE

Senate races: California & others. Pierre Salinger.
Time   Oct 16, 1964   p. 34

SALOMON INC.

The king of Wall Street. An inside look at Salomon Brothers' stunning rise to preeminence—and how it wields its power.
Business Week   Dec 9, 1985   p. 98

SALT IN THE BODY

Salt: A new villain.
Time   Mar 15, 1982   p. 64

SCHWEITZER, ALBERT

The great white wizard. Dr. Schweitzer at 90.
Life   Feb 19, 1965   p. 82

SCIENCE AND LAW

The supreme court of science. Rulings on: Surrogate motherhood. Genetic engineering. Computer privacy. Psychic powers.
Omni   Jan 1988   p. 40

SCIENCE AND SCIENTISTS

A celebration of women in science.
Discover   Dec 1991   p. 36

Science under siege. Tight money, blunders and scandal plague America's researchers.
Time   Aug 26, 1991   p. 44

1990. The top 50 science stories.
Discover   Jan 1991   p. 24

A celebration of the scientist. From the man who rocks the Earth to the woman who spins the stars.
Discover   Oct 1990   p. 40

1989. The top 45 science stories.
Discover   Jan 1990   p. 14

The eight big ideas of the eighties.
Discover   Oct 1989   p. 30

1988. The year in science. The top 35 science stories.
Discover   Jan 1989   p. 18

1987. The top 35 science stories.
Discover   Jan 1988   p. 23

The year in science.
Discover   Jan 1985   p. 60

The year in science.
Discover   Jan 1984   p. 58

The year in science. Scientist of the year. [Robert Weinberg]
Discover   Jan 1983   p. 62

1982's worst scientific achievements.
Omni   Jan 1983   p. 60

The year in science. Saturn fly-by. Animal tests. Shuttle flight. Medfly crisis.
Discover   Jan 1982   p. 66

1982's worst scientific achievements.
Omni   Jan 1982   p. 74

Science. America's struggle to stay ahead.
U.S.News   Sep 15, 1980   p. 52

U.S. scientists. Men of the year.
Time   Jan 2, 1961   p. 40

SCIENCE TALENT SEARCH

What puts the whiz in whiz kids. A revealing look at America's best science students. Nurturing talent: What works and what doesn't.
U.S. News   Mar 14, 1988   p. 48

SCIENTOLOGY

Scientology. The cult of greed. How the growing Dianetics empire squeezes millions from believers worldwide.
Time   May 6, 1991   p. 50

SCOTT, GEORGE C.

An actor's art: Rage beneath the surface. George C. Scott.
Time   Mar 22, 1971   p. 63

SCRANTON, WILLIAM

The Scrantons. A family's uphill fight.
Life   Jun 26, 1964   p. 28

William Scranton: Eleventh hour bid.
Newsweek   Jun 22, 1964   p. 21

GOP's Scranton. Coming up fast.
Newsweek   Jan 27, 1964   p. 19

Politics 1962. The campaign in full cry. Pennsylvania's William Scranton.
Time   Oct 19, 1962   p. 19

SCUBA DIVING

Life under water.
Newsweek   Jul 12, 1976   p. 44

SCULLEY, JOHN

Apple's dynamic duo and their plan to take on IBM in the office.
Business Week   Nov 26, 1984   p. 146

SCULPTURE

Sculptor Tony Smith. Art outgrows the museum.
Time   Oct 13, 1967   p. 80

SEABORG, GLENN T.

For war - the atom - for peace. Seaborg of
the AEC: A scientist in command.
Newsweek   Oct 16, 1961   p. 63

SEAGRAM CO.

Seagram's maverick boss. There was a
time when Edgar Bronfman Jr. showed
little interest in the family business. Now
he's running it—and creating a very
different company.
Business Week   Dec 18, 1989   p. 90

SEALS (ANIMALS)

Seals and their kin.
National Geographic Apr 1987   p. 475

Seals and their kin.
National Geographic Apr 1987   p. 475

SEARS, ROEBUCK AND CO.

Sassy Sears. Toasters and tires...and
Cheryl Tiegs.
Time   Aug 20, 1984   p. 82

The new Sears. Unable to grow retailing,
it turns to financial services.
Business Week   Nov 16, 1981   p. 140

Sears. Santa's biggest helper.
Newsweek   Dec 11, 1961   p. 72

SECORD, RICHARD

The Secord story. A close-up look at the
first witness in the Iran-Contra TV
hearings. Will he link Reagan to the
conspiracy?
Newsweek   May 11, 1987 p. 16

SECRETARIAT (HORSE)

Superhorse. Secretariat.
Newsweek   Jun 11, 1973   p. 62

Super horse. Secretariat.
Time   Jun 11, 1973   p. 85

SELF HELP GROUPS

Afflicted? Addicted? Support groups are
the answer for 15 million Americans.
Newsweek   Feb 5, 1990   p. 50

SELLERS, PETER

Who is this man? The many faces of
Peter Sellers.
Time   Mar 3, 1980   p. 64

SELLING

Super sellers. They have what it takes:
Energy, confidence and the drive to
succeed.
Psychology Today   Mar 1984   p. 36

Hypnotic techniques of the artful
salesman.
Psychology Today   Aug 1982   p. 50

SEMICONDUCTOR INDUSTRY

Chip wars. Japan's stronger
semiconductor threat.
Business Week   May 23, 1983 p. 80

SEMICONDUCTORS

Using bacteria to make computers.
Discover   May 1982   p. 76

SENSES AND SENSATION

Reach out and touch someone. When
you should.
Psychology Today   Mar 1988   p. 30

SERENGETI NATIONAL PARK (TANZANIA)

The Serengeti.
National Geographic May 1986   p. 560

SERIAL MURDERS

The sick world of Son of Sam.
Newsweek   Aug 22, 1977 p. 16

The psychotic & society. Charles
Whitman.
Time   Aug 12, 1966 p. 14

SERVICE

See CUSTOMER SERVICE

SESAME STREET

See TELEVISION AND CHILDREN

SEVENTIES

See NINETEEN HUNDRED AND
SEVENTIES

SEX AND RELIGION

Sex and religion. Churches, the Bible and
the furor over modern sexuality.
U.S. News   Jun 10, 1991   p. 58

SEX AND TELEVISION

Sex and TV.
Newsweek   Feb 20, 1978 p. 54

SEX (BIOLOGY)

The riddle of sex. Why did it evolve?
Why does it persist?
Discover   Feb 1984   p. 24

SEX DIFFERENCES

Sex. The rational, the bizarre and the
uncertain future of gender.
Omni   Oct 1990   p. 80

Men vs. women. The new debate over
sex differences.
U.S. News   Aug 8, 1988   p. 50

The riddle of sex. Why did it evolve?
Why does it persist?
Discover   Feb 1984   p. 24

Tired of arguing about "natural"
inferiority?
Ms.   Nov 1982   p. 41

The sexes. How they differ - and why.
Newsweek   May 18, 1981   p. 72

The sexes and the brain.
Discover   Apr 1981   p. 14

SEX DIFFERENCES (PSYCHOLOGY)

Guns and dolls. Scientists explore the
differences between girls and boys.
Newsweek   May 28, 1990   p. 56

SEX DISCRIMINATION

Battle of the sexes. Men fight back.
U.S.News   Dec 8, 1980   p. 50

SEX EDUCATION

Sex education. What should children
know? When should they know it?
Time   Nov 24, 1986   p. 54

Teenage temptation. Sex & consequences.
Psychology Today   Oct 1986   p. 22

Mother daughter sex-talk...do feminists do
it better?
Ms.   May 1982   p. 41

Sex education for little children. Debate
splits the nation's schools.
Life   Sep 19, 1969   p. 34

SEX IN THE ARTS

The sex explosion.
Time   Jul 11, 1969   p. 61

Sex and the arts.
Newsweek   Apr 14, 1969   p. 67

How far is far enough? Sex in the lively
arts.
Life   Apr 4, 1969   p. 22

SEX THERAPY

The new sex therapy.
Newsweek   Nov 27, 1972   p. 65

SEXUAL BEHAVIOR

Safe sex. What you and your children
should know.
Newsweek   Dec 9, 1991   p. 52

The heat is on. Sex, romance, love & lust
in the '90s.
Ms.   May 1989   p. 39

Sex in the Age of AIDS. Masters &
Johnson. Excerpts from their
controversial new book.
Newsweek   Mar 14, 1988   p. 42

The big chill. How heterosexuals are
coping with AIDS.
Time   Feb 16, 1987   p. 50

Re-making love.
Ms.   Jul 1986   p. 40

The fear of sex. Why habits are changing.
U.S. News   Jun 2, 1986   p. 53

The new 'other woman.' Caught in the
same old trap.
Psychology Today   Feb 1986   p. 22

"Everything else you always wanted to
know about sex. But that we were afraid
you'd never ask."
Discover   Apr 1985   p. 70

Sex in the '80s. The revolution is over.
Time   Apr 9, 1984   p. 74

Sex and love in the '80s. Lust and
romance. Intimacy and control.
Ceremony and abandon.
Ms.   Feb 1984   p. 35

More than you want to know about sex.
Newsweek   Aug 24, 1970   p. 38

Sex education for adults. Researchers
Masters and Johnson.
Time   May 25, 1970   p. 49

Sex in the U.S.: Mores & morality.
Time   Jan 24, 1964   p. 54

SEXUAL HARASSMENT

Anita Hill: 'I had to tell the truth.'
Clarence Thomas: 'It is a high-tech
lynching.'
Newsweek   Oct 21, 1991   p. 24

Sex, lies & politics. America's watershed
debate on sexual harassment.
Time   Oct 21, 1991   p. 34

Sex and justice. The Thomas affair. The
furor over sexual harassment.
U.S. News   Oct 21, 1991   p. 32

SEXUALLY TRANSMITTED DISEASES

Safe sex. What you and your children
should know.
Newsweek   Dec 9, 1991   p. 52

The fear of sex. Why habits are changing.
U.S. News   Jun 2, 1986   p. 53

Herpes. Today's scarlet letter.
Time   Aug 2, 1982   p. 62

VD. The epidemic.
Newsweek   Jan 24, 1972   p. 46

SEYMOUR, JIM

The power of talent & teamwork. Notre
Dame's Seymour and Hanratty.
Time   Oct 28, 1966   p. 50

SHAH OF IRAN

See MOHAMMED REZA PAHLEVI,
SHAH OF IRAN

SHAKESPEARE, WILLIAM, 1564-1616

Burton as Hamlet. Shakespeare: A special
series.
Life   Apr 24, 1964   p. 58

SHAKESPEARE, WILLIAM - DRAMA

Shakespeare. Midsummer night's box
office.
Time   Jul 4, 1960   p. 60

SHARANSKY, NATAN (ANATOLY)

The man who beat the KGB. Exclusive
book excerpt. Natan (Anatoly) Sharansky
spent nine years in Soviet prisons,
sustained by the love of his bride Avital
and a remarkable force of will . FEAR NO
EVIL is his harrowing account...
U.S. News   May 23, 1988   p. 30

Detente. The trial of Anatoli
Shcharansky.
Time   Jul 24, 1978   p. 24

SHARKS

Shark alert! The age-old struggle between
man and shark has become a killing
frenzy. We are slaughtering 100 million
every year, driving them to extinction.
Life   Aug 1991   p. 9

March 3, 1985, was a perfect day for a
picnic at Wiseman's Beach in South
Australia. While her four children built
sand castles, Shirley Ann Durdin, 34,
snorkeled for scallops in six feet of water
150 yards offshore. Suddenly...
Discover   Jul 1985   p. 26

Jawbreaker for sharks.
National Geographic May 1981   p. 664

SHARON, ARIEL

Sharon vs. Time. An absence of malice.
Newsweek   Feb 4, 1985   p. 52

SHASTRI, LAL BAHADUR

Shastri's last journey.
Life   Jan 21, 1966   p. 20

Shastri of India.
Newsweek   Jun 29, 1964   p. 38

SHELLEY, MARY

Happy 150th, dear Frankenstein. Strange
revelations about how Mrs. Percy Bysshe
Shelley created the monster.
Life   Mar 15, 1968   p. 74

SHEPARD, ALAN

Shepard relaxes with his fan mail.
Life   May 19, 1961   p. 24

'AOK!' The U.S. is in space. Success! Al
Shepard is hauled into copter.
Life   May 12, 1961   p. 18

"What a beautiful sight."
Time May 12, 1961 p. 52

Exclusive on men picked for space.
Astronaut first team. Glenn, Grissom,
Shepard.
Life Mar 3, 1961 p. 24

SHEPARD, SAM
True West. Sam Shepard. Leading man,
playwright, maverick.
Newsweek Nov 11, 1985 p. 68

SHEPHERD, CYBILL
Sly and sexy. TV's fun couple.
Moonlighting's Bruce Willis and Cybill
Shepherd.
Newsweek Sep 8, 1986 p. 46

SHEVARDNADZE, EDUARD
Waiting for Washington. The U.S. dithers
while Moscow woos Europe. Soviet
Foreign Minister Shevardnadze says he's
eager to talk.
Time May 15, 1989 p. 22

SHEVCHENKO, ARKADY N.
A defector's story. The highest-ranking
Soviet diplomat to break with Moscow
since World War II describes the
Kremlin's inner workings.
Time Feb 11, 1985 p. 48

SHIELDS, BROOKE
Brooke bares the new swimsuits.
Life Feb 1985 p. 81

Brooke brings back the bikini.
Life Feb 1983 p. 84

Brooke Shields: The most beautiful
conglomerate in the world.
Life Dec 1981 p. 144

SHIPWRECKS
Oldest known shipwreck.
National Geographic Dec 1987 p. 693

The man who found the *Titanic*.
Discover Jan 1987 p. 50

A long last look at *Titanic*.
National Geographic Dec 1986 p. 698

Ghost ships of the War of 1812.
National Geographic Mar 1983 p. 289

SHORE, DINAH
Dinah Shore and her TV glad rags.
Life Feb 1, 1960 p. 73

SHRIMPTON, JEAN
Cover girl Jean Shrimpton.
Newsweek May 10, 1965 p. 67

SHRIVER, SARGENT
The Democrats try again. Sargent
Shriver.
Time Aug 14, 1972 p. 15

Crossfire in the war on poverty. Sargent
Shriver.
Time May 13, 1966 p. 25

The Peace Corps. A U.S. ideal abroad.
Sargent Shriver.
Time Jul 5, 1963 p. 18

SHULA, DON
Building for the Super Bowl. Miami coach
Don Shula.
Time Dec 11, 1972 p. 91

SHULTZ, GEORGE
Why Haig quit.
Newsweek Jul 5, 1982 p. 18

Foreign policy shakeup. Out goes Haig.
In comes Shultz.
Time Jul 5, 1982 p. 8

SHUMAN, CHARLES
The man who wants the government to
get off the farm. Farm Bureau's Charles
Shuman.
Time Sep 3, 1965 p. 22

SIBERIA (SOVIET UNION)
Siberia: In from the cold.
National Geographic Mar 1990 p. 2

SICHUAN PROVINCE (CHINA)
Sichuan. China changes course.
National Geographic Sep 1985 p. 280

SICKNESS
Body & soul. Scientists discover the links
between the brain and your health.
Newsweek Nov 7, 1988 p. 88

SIHANOUK, NORODOM
See NORODOM SIHANOUK

SMELL

Mood altering scents.
Omni   Apr 1986   p. 48

SMITH, FRED

Mr. Smith goes global. Founder Fred
Smith loves high-risk deals. His latest:
Going deep in debt to buy Flying Tiger
and expand overseas.
Business Week   Feb 13, 1989   p. 66

SMITH, MARGARET CHASE

Women in politics. Maine's senate race.
Smith v. Cormier.
Time   Sep 5, 1960   p. 13

SMITH, ROGER

GM. What went wrong. In the late 1970s,
General Motors executives mapped out a
$40 billion strategy to redesign every car
and to overhaul or replace every factory.
The goal: Fight imports—and leave Ford
and Chrysler in the dust. So far, the
strategy has failed.
Business Week   Mar 16, 1987   p. 102

SMITH, WILLIAM KENNEDY

What you don't see. Behind the drama at
the Smith rape trial.
Newsweek   Dec 16, 1991   p. 18

SMOKING

No smoking. The social revolution
sweeping America. How business is
dealing with smoking restrictions. New
ways to kick the habit. The impact on the
tobacco industry.
Business Week   Jul 27, 1987   p. 40

Smoking and health.
Newsweek   Nov 18, 1963   p. 61

SMOKING - LAWS AND REGULATIONS

Butt out! The war over smoking.
Time   Apr 18, 1988   p. 64

SNAKES

Fearsome fascinating world of snakes and
why they scare you.
Life   Mar 1, 1963   p. 37

SNOWMOBILES

Uproar over snowmobiles.
Life   Feb 26, 1971   p. 20

SOAP OPERAS

TV's hottest show. Luke and Laura of
'General Hospital.'
Newsweek   Sep 28, 1981   p. 26

Soap operas. Sex and suffering in the
afternoon.
Time   Jan 12, 1976   p. 6

SOCIAL SECURITY

Controversy over Social Security reform
proposals.
Congressional Digest Apr 1983   p. 99

Who will pay? The Social-Security crisis.
The growing burden on the young. The
mounting worries of the old.
Newsweek   Jan 24, 1983   p. 18

Guns vs. butter. How to cut defense
spending. How to save Social Security.
Business Week   Nov 29, 1982   p. 68

Social Security. What can the nation
afford?
Time   May 24, 1982   p. 16

Controversy over financing Social
Security.
Congressional Digest Aug 1981   p. 195

Can you afford to retire? The Social
Security crisis. Turmoil in pension plans.
Newsweek   Jun 1, 1981   p. 24

Social Security. Will it be there when you
need it?
U.S. News   Apr 30, 1979   p. 24

Social Security. Promising too much to
too many?
U.S. News   Jul 15, 1974   p. 26

SOCIALISM

Socialism.
Time   Mar 13, 1978   p. 24

SOCIETY, UPPER

See UPPER CLASSES

SOCIOBIOLOGY

Why you do what you do. Sociobiology:
A new theory of behavior.
Time   Aug 1, 1977   p. 54

South Africa. Black rage, white repression.
A challenge to U.S. policy.
Time   Aug 5, 1985   p. 24

Apartheid and U.S. policy. How to deal
with South Africa.
Newsweek   Mar 11, 1985   p. 28

SOUTH AMERICA
See LATIN AMERICA

SOUTH VIETNAM
See VIETNAM

SOUTHEAST ASIA
Laos and Vietnam.
Newsweek   Jul 15, 1963   p. 36

SOUTHEAST ASIA AND THE UNITED STATES
The U.S. & Southeast Asia. How to cope
with never-never land. Cambodia's
Prince Sihanouk.
Time   Apr 3, 1964   p. 32

SOUTHERN STATES
Race and the South. How blacks and
whites are remaking the old confederacy.
U.S. News   Jul 23, 1990   p. 22

The South today. Carter country and
beyond.
Time   Sep 27, 1976   p. 28

Dixie whistles a different tune. Georgia
Governor Jimmy Carter.
Time   May 31, 1971   p. 14

The South. Into a new century.
Newsweek   May 3, 1965   p. 26

Tourists at Tennessee natural wonder.
Life   Apr 25, 1960   p. 80

SOVIET UNION
The new U.S.S.R.
Time   Apr 10, 1989   p. 46

The Soviet Union: Part 3. Revolution and
ruin. Hope and anger in a collapsing
empire.
U.S. News   Apr 3, 1989   p. 34

A day in the life of the Soviet Union. A
38-page portrait of the changing
superpower.
Time   Oct 26, 1987   p. 54

A new revolution. Can Gorbachev save a
failing system?
U.S. News   Oct 19, 1987   p. 30

Gorbachev's revolution. Can he make it
work? Is the Cold War fading?
Time   Jul 27, 1987   p. 28

The world according to Gorbachev. After
Iceland.
U.S. News   Oct 20, 1986   p. 14

Moscow's new generation. Mikhail
Gorbachev
Newsweek   Mar 25, 1985   p. 22

Moscow's new boss. Younger, smoother
and probably formidable. Mikhail
Gorbachev.
Time   Mar 25, 1985   p. 14

Inside the U.S.S.R.
Time   Jun 23, 1980   p. 21

Russia's 60 years of Communism.
Success or failure?
U.S. News   Oct 24, 1977   p. 42

Kremlin roulette: New faces coming up?
Time   Mar 29, 1971   p. 27

Shift and surprise in the Soviet Union.
Life   Nov 10, 1967   p. 41

How Russia survived Marxism: Soviet
life today.
Time   Nov 10, 1967   p. 32

Russia after 50 years.
Newsweek   Oct 23, 1967   p. 40

Life in Russia.
Newsweek   May 2, 1966   p. 36

Special issue. In this year of change a
long visit with the Soviet people.
Life   Sep 13, 1963   p. 34

SOVIET UNION - ARMED FORCES
Death of a nation. U.S.S.R. 1917 –
U.S. News   Nov 19, 1990   p. 34

Who rules Russia? In color: The Soviet
military in action.
Time   May 4, 1970   p. 33

SOVIET UNION - POLITICS AND GOVERNMENT

Russia's maverick. Boris Yeltsin, the bad boy of Soviet politics, battles Gorbachev in a crucial vote this week.
Time   Mar 25, 1991   p. 26

Death of a nation. U.S.S.R. 1917 –
U.S. News   Nov 19, 1990   p. 34

The Yeltsin challenge. After the summit.
Newsweek   Jun 11, 1990   p. 14

Falling star. After the summit: The growing danger for Gorbachev back in the U.S.S.R.
U.S. News   Jun 11, 1990   p. 24

Why Gorbachev is failing.
Newsweek   Jun 4, 1990   p. 16

In the eye of the storm. With his country in a perilous passage, Gorbachev defines his course and answers his critics.
Time   Jun 4, 1990   p. 24

Soviet disunion. Growing cries for independence bring Gorbachev's empire to the breaking point.
Time   Mar 12, 1990   p. 26

Starting over. Gorbachev turns his back on Lenin.
Time   Feb 19, 1990   p. 28

In the Kremlin, Communism's last stand. Gorbachev's desperate new bid to save his party — and his revolution.
U.S. News   Feb 19, 1990   p. 30

The collapse of Communism. Is the Soviet Union next?
U.S. News   Jan 15, 1990   p. 31

Gorbachev's gamble. Opening a closed society. How far will he go? Sakharov on his struggle.
Newsweek   Jan 5, 1987   p. 12

Gorbachev's Kremlin. What now?
U.S. News   Mar 25, 1985   p. 22

The Kremlin's new master. What he might do. His view of the world. The generation dilemma. Konstantin Chernenko.
Time   Feb 27, 1984   p. 28

The succession. Filling a vacuum, again. Yuri Andropov 1914-1984.
Time   Feb 20, 1984   p. 14

What next in Russia?
U.S. News   Feb 20, 1984   p. 22

Is military taking over the Kremlin?
U.S. News   Jan 23, 1984   p. 26

How to deal with Moscow. An exclusive report by Henry Kissinger. Andropov's peace offensive. Reagan, the bishops and the freeze.
Newsweek   Nov 29, 1982   p. 26

The new boss. A spymaster's rise to power. Will Moscow get tougher? How Reagan should respond. Soviet Party Chief Yuri Andropov.
Newsweek   Nov 22, 1982   p. 28

After Brezhnev. Andropov takes command.
Time   Nov 22, 1982   p. 10

Russia after Brezhnev.
U.S. News   Nov 22, 1982   p. 22

Brezhnev's final days. The succession struggle. Communism in crisis.
Newsweek   Apr 12, 1982   p. 30

Who rules Russia? In color: The Soviet military in action.
Time   May 4, 1970   p. 33

Brezhnev. Shake-up in the Kremlin.
Newsweek   Oct 26, 1964   p. 45

Take-over in the Kremlin. Russia's new leader Leonid Brezhnev.
Life   Oct 23, 1964   p. 30

The bomb; the overthrow; the squeaker; the scandal.
Time   Oct 23, 1964   p. 19

What happened in the Kremlin?
Newsweek   Nov 12, 1962   p. 21

After Khrushchev's retreat.
Time   Nov 9, 1962   p. 26

Party Congress: How Russia is ruled.
Newsweek   Oct 23, 1961   p. 29

SOVIET UNION AND CHINA

Russia vs. China. Struggle for Asia.
U.S. News   Feb 5, 1979   p. 27

Russia in trouble.
Newsweek   Jun 16, 1969   p. 38

Show of toughness in Moscow.
Life   Nov 20, 1964   p. 42

Post Khrushchev Communism. China's
Chou En-Lai greeted by Russia's Kosygin.
Time   Nov 13, 1964   p. 44

K vs. Mao. How wide the split?
Newsweek   Mar 26, 1962   p. 32

SOVIET UNION AND EASTERN EUROPE

Brezhnev's nightmare. Breakaway in
Europe.
U.S. News   Aug 1, 1977   p. 28

SOVIET UNION AND THE MIDDLE EAST

Russia in the Middle East. Thrust of new
arms and aid.
Life   Nov 29, 1968   p. 22

SOVIET UNION AND THE UNITED STATES

The future of the bomb. Will Bush's plan
work? Can we trust the Soviets? What is
Saddam hiding?
Newsweek   Oct 7, 1991   p. 18

The odd couple. How George Bush has
become a true believer in Mikhail
Gorbachev.
U.S. News   Jul 1, 1991   p. 24

The Moscow connection. On the day
before the Iraqi invasion, the Kremlin got
a CIA alert that the attack was imminent...
The inside story of secret diplomacy
between the superpowers.
Newsweek   Sep 17, 1990   p. 20

After the Cold War. Bush's dilemma:
How to deal with Gorbachev.
Newsweek   May 15, 1989   p. 20

How to respond to Gorbachev.
U.S. News   Dec 19, 1988   p. 16

Moscow on the Potomac. Is Gorbachev
playing a winning hand?
U.S. News   Dec 21, 1987   p. 20

Gorbachev in America. How the Soviets
see us.
Newsweek   Dec 14, 1987   p. 18

Gorbachev's revolution. Can he make it
work? Is the Cold War fading?
Time   Jul 27, 1987   p. 28

Finally, an arms deal that <u>can</u> work. But
not without some risks.
Newsweek   Apr 27, 1987   p. 20

Heavy strains. Washington vs. Moscow.
The superpowers grope for ways to repair
the damage that threatens a second
summit.
U.S. News   Sep 29, 1986   p. 22

Can we deal with Moscow? Beyond the
Daniloff affair.
Newsweek   Sep 22, 1986   p. 20

Thaw at last?
U.S. News   Jan 14, 1985   p. 20

Talking again. Arms control at the
crossroads. The fallout on campaign '84.
Newsweek   Oct 1, 1984   p. 22

Gromyko comes calling. High stakes in
U.S.-Soviet relations.
Time   Oct 1, 1984   p. 12

Moscow's hard line. What it means.
Reagan's new response. Foreign Minister
Andrei Gromyko.
Time   Jun 25, 1984   p. 22

Are the Games dead?
Newsweek   May 21, 1984   p. 18

Olympic turmoil. Why the Soviets said
nyet.
Time   May 21, 1984   p. 14

Olympics. Hostage to big-power politics.
U.S. News   May 21, 1984   p. 24

Pullout in Beirut. Death in Moscow.
Newsweek   Feb 20, 1984   p. 18

How to deal with Moscow. An exclusive
report by Henry Kissinger. Andropov's
peace offensive. Reagan, the bishops and
the freeze.
Newsweek   Nov 29, 1982   p. 26

The great propaganda war.
U.S. News   Jan 11, 1982   p. 27

SPACE FLIGHT - JAPAN

Spaceward ho!
Omni   Jul 1991   p. 12

SPACE FLIGHT - SOVIET UNION

The Soviets in space. Why the U.S.
should worry about Moscow's conquest
of the heavens.
U.S. News   May 16, 1988 p. 48

Moscow takes the lead. An inside look at
the Soviet space program.
Time   Oct 5, 1987   p. 64

Soviets in space. Are they ahead?
National Geographic Oct 1986   p. 420

The Soviets' space station.
Omni   Sep 1986   p. 66

Voskhod versus Gemini. The space race
now.
Newsweek   Mar 29, 1965 p. 52

Outside in space.
Time   Mar 26, 1965 p. 85

Russia's men in space.
Newsweek   Aug 27, 1962 p. 15

Russia's feat: Where it leaves us in the
race the moon.
Life   Aug 24, 1962   p. 20

Russian cosmonauts. Nikolayev &
Popovich.
Time   Aug 24, 1962   p. 14

The voyage of Yuri Gagarin.
Newsweek   Apr 24, 1961 p. 22

19 pages on space. Inside Yuri's capsule.
Celebration in Moscow. Impact on
Washington. U.S. space future.
Life   Apr 21, 1961   p. 20

Man in space. Russia's Yuri Gagarin.
Time   Apr 21, 1961   p. 46

SPACE FLIGHT - UNITED STATES

The blue planet. A close encounter with
Neptune.
Newsweek   Sep 4, 1989   p. 50

Outer space. New missions, new
discoveries.
U.S. News   May 15, 1989 p. 52

Lost in space. How to get America off the
ground.
Newsweek   Aug 17, 1987 p. 34

25th anniversary of American manned
spaceflight.
Omni   May 1986   p. 6

A return to space. Military and industrial
missions. A manned space station by
1991.
Business Week   Jun 20, 1983   p. 50

Highest photos of earth taken by man.
Growing clutter of space trash. Progress
toward space law.
Life   Aug 5, 1966   p. 24

Rendezvous in space.
Newsweek   Dec 27, 1965 p. 42

Rendezvous on the road to the moon.
Time   Dec 24, 1965 p. 32

Most remarkable views of earth ever
recorded. From 100 miles up in Gemini
5. Cooper and Conrad write their stories
of the flight.
Life   Sep 24, 1965 p. 30

Flight director Chris Kraft.
Time   Aug 27, 1965 p. 46

Back to Earth - Where the trouble is.
Newsweek   Jun 21, 1965   p. 22

The space walk.
Life   Jun 18, 1965   p. 26

The flight of the Gemini 4.
Newsweek   Jun 14, 1965   p. 30

The McDivitt-White flight. Ed White &
Jim McDivitt.
Time   Jun 11, 1965   p. 24

The astronauts' Gemini's journey by Gus
Grisson and John Young.
Life   Apr 2, 1965   p. 34

Voskhod versus Gemini. The space race
now.
Newsweek   Mar 29, 1965 p. 52

His flight heralds a fantastic era of
shrinking time. Cooper's trip and
Einstein's theory.
Life   May 24, 1963 p. 28

Stock market killings. College dropout Bill Gates made $750 million last year. Now he's America's youngest billionaire.
U.S. News   Jul 6, 1987   p. 48

Oh, that market. Take your mind off the stock ticker for a moment. The astonishing 4 1/2 -year runup has a deeper meaning: We're seeing a fundamental revaluation of corporate assets. And that may well change the way companies are financed and managed.
Business Week   Feb 2, 1987   p. 58

Is it good for America? High-tech Wall Street.
Time   Nov 10, 1986   p. 64

Those big swings on Wall St. The controversy over program trading.
Business Week   Apr 7, 1986   p. 32

How high is up? The stock market rally is far from over. Here's why.
Business Week   Mar 17, 1986   p. 94

The great bull market of '85. Stocks through the roof. Advice from big investors. Where the values still are. An exclusive survey: What 133 top brokers think.
U.S. News   Dec 16, 1985   p. 26

Cashing in big. The men who make the killings.
Time   Jan 23, 1984   p. 44

Bull market. It's not over yet.
U.S. News   Aug 15, 1983   p. 27

The rebirth of equities. The rally launches a new age for stocks.
Business Week   May 9, 1983   p. 120

Behind the market's wild ride.
Business Week   Oct 25, 1982   p. 98

Wall Street. Olé! The economy. Eh?
Time   Sep 6, 1982   p. 38

Wall Street's bad news bulls.
Newsweek   Dec 1, 1980   p. 64

Shock treatment for inflation.
Newsweek   Oct 22, 1979   p. 36

The big bad bear.
Newsweek   Sep 9, 1974   p. 58

What stock market is saying.
U.S. News   Jul 29, 1974   p. 11

Wall Street in trouble.
Newsweek   Nov 30, 1970   p. 71

Changing Wall Street. Dreyfus Fund's Howard Stein.
Time   Aug 24, 1970   p. 52

Wall Street in a whirl.
Newsweek   Jun 8, 1970   p. 71

Inflation, recession and a frantic bear market.
Life   Jun 5, 1970   p. 28

Wall Street: Hitting bottom?
Newsweek   Sep 12, 1966   p. 74

Wall Street: The nervous market.
Time   Aug 19, 1966   p. 66

The worries of Wall Street
Newsweek   Jun 28, 1965   p. 63

Stocks surge - But where's the public?
Newsweek   Apr 29, 1963   p. 73

Stock market shock waves.
Newsweek   Jun 11, 1962   p. 19

What went wrong in the wild stock market. What it means to the U.S.
Life   Jun 8, 1962   p. 63

Bear v. bull on Wall Street.
Time   Jun 1, 1962   p. 71

New bull market...?
Newsweek   Aug 21, 1961   p. 63

Those glamour stocks. New ideas & new millionaires. Fairchild Industries' Sherman Fairchild.
Time   Jul 25, 1960   p. 62

STOCK MARKET - INSIDER TRADING

The scandal. Wall Street's elite under fire. Arbitrage: The myth of the 'Chinese Wall.' What it means for Corporate America. Washington: Can new rules make a difference?
Business Week   Mar 2, 1987   p. 28

After the fall. How the insider-trading scandal will change Wall Street. Ivan Boesky.
Business Week   Dec 1, 1986   p. 28

Wall St. scam. Making millions with your money. Investor "Ivan the Terrible" Boeskey.
Time   Dec 1, 1986   p. 48

How the stock market is rigged against you. Wall Street's insider trading scandal.
U.S. News   Dec 1, 1986   p. 44

Insider trading. The Wall Street epidemic that Washington can't stop.
Business Week   Apr 29, 1985   p. 78

STOCK MARKET - TOKYO

The Tokyo stock market and how it affects you.
Business Week   Feb 12, 1990   p. 74

STOCK MARKET CRASH, 1929

The crash: Was just the beginning. The worst is yet to come. Was a necessary correction for excesses in the market and the economy. Didn't matter at all.
Business Week   Apr 18, 1988   p. 55

Crash of '29. Have we learned anything?
U.S. News   Oct 29, 1979   p. 32

STOCK MARKET CRASH, 1987

After the crash. Robert Samuelson: The specter of depression. Jane Bryant Quinn: Keeping your money safe.
Newsweek   Nov 2, 1987   p. 14

The crash. After a wild week on Wall Street, the world is different.
Time   Nov 2, 1987   p. 20

After the fall. How to protect your money now. Is a recession coming?
U.S. News   Nov 2, 1987   p. 18

Is the party over? A jolt for Wall Street's whiz kids. How to play it safe, by Jane Bryant Quinn.
Newsweek   Oct 26, 1987   p. 50

STOCKMAN, DAVID

The inside story. David Stockman on the heroes, villains and fatal flaws of the Reagan revolution. Excerpts from his book "The Triumph of Politics."
Newsweek   Apr 21, 1986   p. 38

Cut, clash, chop. Budget Director David Stockman.
Newsweek   Feb 16, 1981   p. 20

STOKES, CARL BURTON

Negro election victories. Cleveland's Mayor Stokes.
Time   Nov 17, 1967   p. 23

STRATEGIC ARMS LIMITATION TALKS

Adhering to the SALT II agreements.
Congressional Digest Oct 1986   p. 226

Now the great debate: Salt II.
Time   May 21, 1979   p. 22

Salt II. Can it end the arms race?
U.S. News   May 21, 1979   p. 21

See Also ARMS CONTROL

STRATEGIC DEFENSE INITIATIVE

No deal. Star Wars sinks the summit.
Time   Oct 20, 1986   p. 19

Star war games. The stakes go up.
Time   Jun 23, 1986   p. 16

Star Wars. Whatever its feasibility or political merits, it's fast becoming our most ambitious scientific undertaking. A special report—Where we are: The state of the technology.
Discover   Sep 1985   p. 28

Star warriors. The people behind the weapons of the future.
Newsweek   Jun 17, 1985   p. 34

Star Wars. What's at stake in Geneva. The scientific challenge.
Time   Mar 11, 1985   p. 12

The "Star Wars" controversy.
Congressional Digest Mar 1985   p. 69

Space-war era. It's already here.
U.S. News   Dec 17, 1984   p. 28

Star Wars. How the U.S.S.R. could destroy the U.S. satellite defense system.
Omni   Jul 1984   p. 42

Star wars. Reagan's new nuclear strategy. Will space be the next battleground?
Newsweek   Apr 4, 1983   p. 16

STRAUSS, FRANZ JOSEPH

West Germany's Franz Joseph Strauss.
Time   Dec 19, 1960   p. 25

STRAUSS, ROBERT S.

Carter's Mr. Fix-It. Robert S. Strauss.
U.S. News   Aug 7, 1978   p. 14

STRAVINSKY, IGOR

Stravinsky at 80.
Newsweek   May 21, 1962   p. 53

STREEP, MERYL

Deep Streep. The secret of Meryl's magic.
Ms.   Dec 1988   p. 68

Meryl Streep. On top—and tough enough
to stay there.
Life   Dec 1987   p. 72

Magic Meryl. Actress Meryl Streep.
Time   Sep 7, 1981   p. 38

Meryl Streep, America's best actress.
Life   Apr 1981   p. 80

A star for the '80s. Meryl Streep.
Newsweek   Jan 7, 1980   p. 52

STREISAND, BARBRA

Streisand. The way she really is.
Life   Dec 1983   p. 116

Barbra Streisand.
Newsweek   Jan 5, 1970   p. 36

Barbra Streisand. The fear-ridden girl
behind the star.
Life   Mar 18, 1966   p. 95

Great new star. Barbra Streisand. Her
success and her precarious love story.
Life   May 22, 1964   p. 51

Barbra Streisand.
Time   Apr 10, 1964   p. 62

STRESS

The rat race. How America is running
itself ragged.
Time   Apr 24, 1989   p. 58

Stress on the job. What you and the boss
can do about it.
Newsweek   Apr 25, 1988   p. 40

Stress. How to map it! How to zap it!
Ms.   May 1987   p. 37

Children under stress. Are we pushing
our kids too hard?
U.S. News   Oct 27, 1986   p. 58

Stress: Effects of unemployment.
USA Today   Feb 1985   p. 1

Stress! Seeking cures for modern
anxieties.
Time   Jun 6, 1983   p. 48

STRIKES

Striker replacement legislation.
Congressional Digest Nov 1991   p. 259

Strike fever and the public interest.
Planes grounded, people stranded.
Distinguished newspaper killed. Labor
leaders in a dilemma. Rampant new
militancy.
Life   Aug 26, 1966   p. 24

STRIKES - AIR TRAFFIC CONTROLLERS

Who controls the air? Reagan's tough
line. The strike's impact. The public's
view: A poll.
Newsweek   Aug 17, 1981   p. 18

Winging it. Coping without controllers.
Time   Aug 17, 1981   p. 14

STRIKES - AIRLINE EMPLOYEES

What the airlines mean to the country.
Time   Jul 22, 1966   p. 80

STRIKES - AUTOMOBILE WORKERS

Walkout in Detroit. UAW's Walter
Reuther.
Newsweek   Sep 18, 1967   p. 71

STRIKES - COAL MINERS

Coal crisis.
Time   Mar 20, 1978   p. 8

Chaos in the coal fields.
U.S. News   Mar 20, 1978   p. 12

Coal. Will the deal stick?
Newsweek   Mar 6, 1978   p. 22

The big raise. Labor & inflation.
Time   Nov 25, 1974   p. 22

Getting ready for Geneva. At the U.N. Reagan on the offensive. At the White House. The prepping of the President.
U.S. News   Nov 4, 1985   p. 26

The Bitburg summit. 'Out of the ashes, hope.'
Newsweek   May 13, 1985   p. 20

Reagan in Germany. Coming to terms with the past. Eric Sevareid on trusting the Germans. America's stake in the Bonn Summit. Concentration camp survivors today. U.S. power 40 years after V-E Day.
U.S. News   May 6, 1985   p. 24

SUMMIT CONFERENCE, 1986

Stalemate. The Iceland summit.
Newsweek   Oct 20, 1986   p. 20

No deal. Star Wars sinks the summit.
Time   Oct 20, 1986   p. 19

The world according to Gorbachev. After Iceland.
U.S. News   Oct 20, 1986   p. 14

Danger at the summit? Plus: What Reagan hopes to get. Gorbachev's game plan.
Newsweek   Oct 13, 1986   p. 24

Getting down to business. Appointment in Iceland.
Time   Oct 13, 1986   p. 26

Heavy strains. Washington vs. Moscow. The superpowers grope for ways to repair the damage that threatens a second summit.
U.S. News   Sep 29, 1986   p. 22

SUMMIT CONFERENCE, 1987

Behind the smiles. Reagan and Gorbachev: A new era? Kissinger: The dangers ahead.
Newsweek   Dec 21, 1987   p. 14

Moscow on the Potomac. Is Gorbachev playing a winning hand?
U.S. News   Dec 21, 1987   p. 20

Gorbachev in America. How the Soviets see us.
Newsweek   Dec 14, 1987   p. 18

The long road to Washington. Mikhail Gorbachev.
Time   Dec 14, 1987   p. 16

Are we safer now? After the summit: The U.S.-Soviet military balance. A memorandum for the President by Richard Perle.
U.S. News   Dec 14, 1987   p. 22

SUMMIT CONFERENCE, 1988

"I never expected to be here." Reagan reflects on his remarkable voyage.
Time   Jun 13, 1988   p. 12

Reagan in Moscow.
Newsweek   Jun 6, 1988   p. 18

SUMMIT CONFERENCE, 1989

Super partners. An ambitious game plan for a new era.
Newsweek   Dec 11, 1989   p. 28

Building a new world.
Time   Dec 11, 1989   p. 34

SUMMIT CONFERENCE, 1990

The Yeltsin challenge. After the summit.
Newsweek   Jun 11, 1990   p. 14

SUN

Great ball of fire. An angry sun stages a spectacular show.
Time   Jul 3, 1989   p. 46

SUN MICROSYSTEMS INC.

High noon for Sun. Can it stay ahead in workstations? In only seven years, Scott McNealy built Sun Microsystems into a $1.8 billion company. But rising competition and the strains of rapid growth may soon produce its first quarterly loss.
Business Week   Jul 24, 1989   p. 70

SUNTAN

Danger in the sun. A good tan may be hazardous to your health.
Newsweek   Jun 9, 1986   p. 60

SUNUNU, JOHN

Bush's bad cop. From taxes to clean air, John Sununu is the power to reckon with.
Time   May 21, 1990 p. 18

SUPER BOWLS

Bad news Bears. Superbowl XX.
Time   Jan 27, 1986   p. 46

Superbowl: Duel of wits.
Newsweek   Jan 25, 1982   p. 62

Superdreams.
Time   Jan 25, 1982   p. 62

A really super bowl.
Newsweek   Jan 22, 1979   p. 58

Super Bowl XII. Broncomania v. Cowboy cool.
Time   Jan 16, 1978   p. 64

Super Bowl. The great American spectacle.
Time   Jan 10, 1977   p. 28

Super Bowl. Scouting report. The pros rate the two teams.
Life   Jan 14, 1972   p. 32

SUPERCONDUCTING SUPERCOLLIDERS

Smash! Colossal colliders are unlocking the secrets of the universe.
Time   Apr 16, 1990   p. 50

Finding God in an atom.
Omni   Feb 1984   p. 40

SUPERCONDUCTORS AND SUPERCONDUCTIVITY

Wiring the future. The superconductivity revolution.
Time   May 11, 1987   p. 64

Super conductors. Every so often a new technology spurs immense change. Now comes superconductivity.
Business Week   Apr 6, 1987   p. 94

SUPERFUND - GOVERNMENT POLICY

The environmental Superfund controversy.
Congressional Digest Jun 1986   p. 163

SUPERMAN (FICTIONAL CHARACTER)

He's 50!
Time   Mar 14, 1988   p. 66

SUPERNATURAL

Scientific investigation: UFO's, Loch Ness, and parapsychology.
USA Today   Jun 1988   p. 1

SUPERSTRING THEORY (PHYSICS)

The new theory of everything. A physicist tackles the ultimate cosmic riddle.
Discover   Aug 1991   p. 54

Unraveling the universe. If you like black holes, you'll love cosmic strings.
Discover   Apr 1988   p. 60

The theory of everything. It's called superstrings, and it's a theory of our universe.
Discover   Nov 1986   p. 34

SUPPLY-SIDE ECONOMICS

After Reagan. America's agenda for the 1990s.
Business Week   Feb 1, 1988   p. 56

SUPREME COURT

How far right? Abortion, crime & quotas: The court that will change America.
Newsweek   Jul 8, 1991   p. 18

Just who is David Souter?
Time   Aug 6, 1990   p. 16

The Bush court. A move to the right. What it means for: Abortion, the death penalty, civil rights.
Newsweek   Jul 30, 1990   p. 14

Reagan's law. By 1989 half of all federal judges will be his appointments. The impact on abortion, civil rights and crime and punishment.
Newsweek   Jun 30, 1986   p. 14

Reagan's Mr. Right. Supreme court justice William Rehnquist.
Time   Jun 30, 1986   p. 24

Reagan's man in court. Chief Justice-designate William Rehnquist.
U.S. News   Jun 30, 1986   p. 16

Decisions, decisions. The high court in transition.
Time   Oct 8, 1984   p. 28

Justice - at last. Reagan nominee Sandra O'Connor.
Time   Jul 20, 1981   p. 8

Inside the Burger court. Special report on the revealing new book by Woodward & Armstrong.
Newsweek   Dec 10, 1979   p. 76

Supreme Court. Trials and tribulations.
U.S. News   Mar 26, 1979   p. 32

The Nixon court. William H. Rehnquist. Lewis F. Powell, Jr.
Time   Nov 1, 1971   p. 14

The seat Nixon can't fill.
Newsweek   Apr 20, 1970   p. 35

The Carswell defeat. Nixon's embattled White House.
Time   Apr 20, 1970   p. 8

The Supreme Court. Warren Burger. Next Chief Justice.
Time   May 30, 1969   p. 16

That activist Supreme Court. Justice Black.
Time   Oct 9, 1964   p. 48

The Warren Court: Ten momentous years.
Newsweek   May 11, 1964   p. 24

Bigger voice for big cities. The Supreme Court decision. Chief Justice Earl Warren.
Newsweek   Apr 9, 1962   p. 29

SURGERY

Computer surgery.
Discover   May 1983   p. 86

Miracles of microsurgery. Sewing people back together. A surgeon who stitches on severed limbs.
Life   Aug 1979   p. 22

Crisis in the operating room.
U.S. News   May 15, 1978   p. 39

If they can operate, you're lucky.
Time   May 3, 1963   p. 44

A surgeon pits his skill against cancer.
Life   Jan 20, 1961   p. 70

SURGERY, COSMETIC

Cosmetic surgery. The quest for new faces and bodies - at a price.
Newsweek   May 27, 1985   p. 64

SURROGATE MOTHERS

Woman as wombs. The multinational birth industry.
Ms.   May 1991   p. 28

Mothers for hire. The battle for Baby M. Surrogate mother Mary Beth Whitehead.
Newsweek   Jan 19, 1987   p. 44

Whose baby am I? High-tech conceptions: Multiple parents, multiple problems.
Psychology Today   Dec 1984   p. 20

SURUGA BAY (JAPAN)

Suruga Bay. In the shadow of Mount Fuji.
National Geographic Oct 1990   p. 2

SWIMMING

America's best swimming holes.
Life   Aug 1981   p. 100

SYMBIONESE LIBERATION ARMY

Patty Hearst. After the shoot-out.
Newsweek   May 27, 1974   p. 18

The saga of Patty Hearst.
Newsweek   Apr 29, 1974   p. 20

Patty Hearst.
Time   Apr 29, 1974   p. 11

SYMINGTON, STUART

Candidate Stu Symington. A second Missouri compromise?
Newsweek   May 9, 1960   p. 30

SYRIA AND THE UNITED STATES

Syria. Clashing with the U.S. Bidding for a bigger role.
Time   Dec 19, 1983   p. 22

SZELL, GEORGE

America's great orchestras. Cleveland conductor George Szell.
Time   Feb 22, 1963   p. 58

TALK SHOWS

Psychology on the air--here it comes, crazy or not.
Psychology Today   Dec 1981   p. 31

TANGANYIKA - POLITICS AND GOVERNMENT

Tanganyika: British commando brings in captured mutineers.
Life   Feb 7, 1964   p. 44

TANZANIA

The Serengeti.
National Geographic May 1986   p. 560

TAX EVASION

Tax cheating. Bad and getting worse.
Time   Mar 28, 1983 p. 26

The underground economy. How 20 million Americans cheat Uncle Sam out of billions in taxes.
U.S. News   Oct 22, 1979   p. 49

How people cheat Uncle Sam out of billions.
U.S. News   Jul 11, 1977   p. 16

TAX REFORM

Capital gains tax.
Congressional Digest Jan 1990   p. 2

Taking care of your money. How to invest, save and earn more under tax reform.
U.S. News   Nov 24, 1986 p. 56

What tax reform means to you. Who pays more, who pays less. New ways to invest your money. Ten hot tax shelters.
Newsweek   Aug 25, 1986 p. 14

The tax reform controversy.
Congressional Digest Feb 1986   p. 35

What tax reform really means. The impact of economic growth. New incentives for investors. The new war between the states. The coming political battle.
Business Week   Jun 17, 1985 p. 128

Tax busters. How the reform plan would help - or hurt. The budget: A freeze or a 'massacre.'
Newsweek   Dec 10, 1984 p. 26

Higher taxes? Who would pay.
U.S. News   Dec 10, 1984 p. 20

President Reagan's tax-reduction proposal.
Congressional Digest Jun 1981   p. 163

Taxes. To cut or not to cut? Rep. Wilbur Mills. Chairman, Ways and Means.
Newsweek   Jan 14, 1963 p. 14

TAX SHELTERS

Tax shelters. How millions of Americans beat the tax man.
Newsweek   Apr 16, 1984 p. 56

TAXATION

Tax fight. What kind of new taxes? How big? Who pays? The political price for Bush. The battle lines in Congress.
Business Week   Jul 9, 1990   p. 24

Tax reform at last! A simpler system—will it spur growth? Which industries come out on top. Personal investing: How it changes. For the future, more reforms.
Business Week   Sep 1, 1986   p. 54

Is a tax hike coming? It seems inevitable. And that may mean new energy levies or perhaps even a European-style value-added tax.
Business Week   Feb 3, 1986   p. 48

Tax squeeze. What it means to you.
U.S. News   Aug 30, 1982   p. 18

Big tax changes ahead: Who's helped most.
U.S. News   Feb 2, 1976   p. 14

The war over taxes. Ford vs. Congress.
U.S. News   Dec 29, 1975   p. 7

Is the U.S. going broke?
Time   Mar 13, 1972   p. 66

TAXATION - CALIFORNIA

Tax revolt!
Newsweek   Jun 19, 1978   p. 20

Tax revolt. California's Howard Jarvis.
Time   Jun 19, 1978   p. 12

TAXES

See INCOME TAX

TAYLOR, ELIZABETH

Liz Taylor at 50. Looking great and on the loose.
Life   Mar 1982   p. 82

Liz Taylor is 40!
Life   Feb 25, 1972   p. 57

Burton analyzes Liz. 'My nagging, scheming, seductive, honest wife.'
Life   Feb 24, 1967   p. 78

Elizabeth Taylor talks about herself.
Life   Dec 18, 1964   p. 74

Blazing new page in the legend of Liz. Richard Burton with Elizabeth Taylor on Cleopatra set.
Life   Apr 13, 1962   p. 32

Liz Taylor. Back at work as Cleopatra.
Life   Oct 6, 1961   p. 93

Elizabeth Taylor: An Oscar at last.
Life   Apr 28, 1961   p. 69

TAYLOR, JAMES

The new rock: Bittersweet and low.
Time   Mar 1, 1971   p. 45

TAYLOR, MAXWELL DAVENPORT

A soldier & the White House.
Time   Jul 28, 1961   p. 9

TEACHERS

Who's teaching our children?
Time   Nov 14, 1988   p. 58

Are we failing our kids? New report on American teachers.
U.S. News   May 26, 1986   p. 52

Why teachers fail. How to make them better.
Newsweek   Sep 24, 1984   p. 64

What's wrong with our teachers?
U.S. News   Mar 14, 1983   p. 37

Help! Teacher can't teach.
Time   Jun 16, 1980   p. 54

Why teachers are under fire.
U.S. News   Dec 12, 1977   p. 50

Great teachers.
Time   May 6, 1966   p. 80

TEAMSTERS UNION

The Hoffa case.
Newsweek   Aug 18, 1975   p. 14

TECHNOLOGICAL INNOVATIONS

Innovation. Has America lost its edge?
Newsweek   Jun 4, 1979   p. 58

See Also INNOVATIONS

TECHNOLOGY

'I can't work this thing!' From VCRs and telephones to copiers and microwaves, poorly designed machines cluttered with unwanted features are driving consumers crazy. Whatever happened to user-friendly?
Business Week   Apr 29, 1991   p. 58

The portable executive. How faxes, PCs, laptops, cellular phones, voice mail, and all the rest are changing our work life. Special report on office automation.
Business Week   Oct 10, 1988   p. 102

Enhance your work life. High-tech exec. Have office, will travel.
Psychology Today   Sep 1988   p. 42

High tech anxiety. Why so many disasters.
U.S. News   May 19, 1986   p. 19

America's high-tech crisis. Why Silicon
Valley is losing its edge.
Business Week   Mar 11, 1985   p. 56

High tech. Blessing or curse?
U.S. News   Jan 16, 1984   p. 38

America rushes to high tech for growth.
But not enough new jobs are there.
Business Week   Mar 28, 1983   p. 84

Technologies for the '80s.
Business Week   Jul 6, 1981   p. 48

New products.
Time   Sep 19, 1960   p. 94

TECHNOLOGY - ECONOMIC ASPECTS

The new economy. Where the jobs will
be. Industry winners & losers. Menace of
protectionism.
Time   May 30, 1983   p. 62

TECHNOLOGY - JAPAN

Japan's high-tech challenge.
Newsweek   Aug 9, 1982   p. 48

TEENAGE PREGNANCY

Teen abortions. The story of one girl's
solitary court battle and why she couldn't
tell her parents.
Ms.   Apr 1988   p. 46

Kids and contraceptives. A moral
dilemma: How to prevent teen
pregnancy - and AIDS.
Newsweek   Feb 16, 1987   p. 54

Children having children. Teen
pregnancy in America.
Time   Dec 9, 1985   p. 78

High school pregnancy.
Life   Apr 2, 1971   p. 34

TEENAGERS

See YOUTH - UNITED STATES

TELECOMMUNICATIONS

Airwave wars. The communications
spectrum is too crowded. So how do we
make room for all those new
technologies?
Business Week   Jul 23, 1990   p. 48

Information power. Many smart
companies are now using new
information technologies to gain a
strategic edge in everything from product
development to marketing. Are you?
Business Week   Oct 14, 1985   p. 108

Has the FCC gone too far? Chairman
Mark Fowler pushes deregulation of
telecommunications and broadcasting.
Business Week   Aug 5, 1985   p. 48

Did it make sense to break up AT&T?
Business Week   Dec 3, 1984   p. 86

What next? A world of communications
wonders.
U.S. News   Apr 9, 1984   p. 59

Telecommunications. The global battle.
An $88 billion market within five years.
Business Week   Oct 24, 1983   p. 126

Changing phone habits. AT&T and its
offspring give customers new choices in
communications.
Business Week   Sep 5, 1983   p. 68

Telecommunications. Everybody's
favorite business. The battle for a piece of
the action.
Business Week   Oct 11, 1982   p. 60

TELEDYNE INC.

A strategy hooked to cash is faltering.
Henry Singleton of Teledyne.
Business Week   May 31, 1982   p. 58

TELEPHONE INDUSTRY

The Baby Bells. They're not just local
phone companies anymore. They're into
real estate, computer stores,
publishing—and want to diversify more.
Should they?
Business Week   Dec 2, 1985   p. 94

TELESCOPES

A telescope in space. New eye on the
universe.
Discover   Apr 1983   p. 29

TELEVANGELISM

See TELEVISION - RELIGIOUS
PROGRAMS

TELEVISION, CABLE

The king of cable. TCI President John Malone is fast becoming the most powerful man in the television industry. And a lot of poeple don't like it.
Business Week   Oct 26, 1987   p. 88

Cable TV. Coming of age.
Newsweek   Aug 24, 1981   p. 44

TELEVISION, CABLE - LAWS AND REGULATIONS

Cable television deregulation.
Congressional Digest Feb 1991   p. 33

TELEVISION IN POLITICS

The ad blitz. Prime time for politics.
Psychology Today   Nov 1984   p. 22

The selling of the candidates 1970.
Newsweek   Oct 19, 1970   p. 34

TELEVISION INDUSTRY

Zapped. The networks under attack.
Time   Oct 17, 1988   p. 56

Has the FCC gone too far? Chairman Mark Fowler pushes deregulation of telecommunications and broadcasting.
Business Week   Aug 5, 1985   p. 48

Who will control TV? And CBS News and 'Dynasty' and 'Today' and Diane Sawyer and Ted Koppel and 'Sportsworld' and 'Hill Street Blues' and, yes, Dan Rather. Special survey. What America thinks of TV.
U.S. News   May 13, 1985 p. 60

A star is born. Capital Cities becomes a media giant overnight by acquiring ABC. But blending two very different corporate cultures will be tough.
Business Week   Apr 1, 1985   p. 74

Big media, big money. The ABC takeover. The next targets.
Newsweek   Apr 1, 1985   p. 52

Broadcast deregulation.
Congressional Digest Apr 1984   p. 99

How TV is revolutionizing Hollywood. The challenge of pay TV. The fear of video piracy.
Business Week   Feb 21, 1983   p. 78

TV: A growth industry again. Plugging in to the electronic home.
Business Week   Feb 23, 1981   p. 88

Chaos in television...and what it takes to be No. 1.
Time   Mar 12, 1979   p. 60

TV's master showman. ABC's Fred Silverman.
Time   Sep 5, 1977   p. 46

TELEVISION PROGRAMS

The Civil War remembered. A stunning TV series sparks old passions and new controversies.
Newsweek   Oct 8, 1990   p. 58

Why America love the Simpsons. TV's twisted new take on the family.
Newsweek   Apr 23, 1990   p. 58

Trash TV. From the lurid to the loud, anything goes. Geraldo Rivera.
Newsweek   Nov 14, 1988 p. 72

Q & A. Nightline's Ted Koppel asks all the right questions.
Newsweek   Jun 15, 1987   p. 50

The women of "L.A. Law." Terry Louise Fisher dreamed up this season's most exciting characters.
Ms.   Jun 1987   p. 38

Mad about Max. The making of a video cult. Max Headroom.
Newsweek   Apr 20, 1987   p. 58

Game shows. America's obsession. TV cashes in. Wheel of Fortune Vanna White.
Newsweek   Feb 9, 1987   p. 62

Cool cops. Hot show. NBC's Miami Vice.
Time   Sep 16, 1985   p. 60

TV's nuclear nightmare. Public service or propaganda? How will it affect children? ABC's 'The Day After.'
Newsweek   Nov 21, 1983 p. 66

Farewell to M*A*S*H. Will prime-time TV ever be as good?
Newsweek   Feb 28, 1983   p. 44

ABC's gigantic gamble. Robert Mitchum in *The Winds of War*.
Time   Feb 7, 1983   p. 70

Can women be buddies–under pressure?
Ms.   Oct 1981   p. 47

TV's hottest show. Luke and Laura of
'General Hospital.'
Newsweek   Sep 28, 1981   p. 26

TV's sunrise serenades.
Time   Dec 1, 1980   p. 62

TV's Dallas. Whodunit?
Time   Aug 11, 1980   p. 60

Son of Star Wars. TV's 'Battlestar
Galactica.'
Newsweek   Sep 11, 1978   p. 58

TV's new pitch. More sex. Less violence.
U.S. News   Sep 12, 1977   p. 20

TV's hot serials.
Newsweek   Sep 5, 1977   p. 52

Why 'Roots' hit home.
Time   Feb 14, 1977   p. 69

TV's new craze. Mary Hartman.
Newsweek   May 3, 1976   p. 54

TV's fall season.
Newsweek   Sep 8, 1975   p. 44

Alistair Cooke - What TV is doing to
America.
U.S. News   Apr 15, 1974   p. 47

TV's year of the cop. Peter Falk as
Columbo.
Time   Nov 26, 1973   p. 117

The new TV season: Toppling old taboos.
Fred Sanford. Cousin Maude. Archie
Bunker.
Time   Sep 25, 1972   p. 48

TV's 'All in the Family.' The Bunkers.
Newsweek   Nov 29, 1971   p. 52

Rowan and Martin.
Time   Oct 11, 1968   p. 50

Mad new world of Batman, Superman
and Marquis de Sade.
Life   Mar 11, 1966   p. 22

Puppets parody flyweight feud, Paar vs.
Sullivan.
Life   Mar 24, 1961   p. 33

TENG, HSIAO-PING
  See DENG XIAOPING

TENNECO INC.
  Tenneco. Growth fuels problems for a
  conglomerate.
  Business Week   Nov 23, 1981   p. 80

TENNESSEE - INDUSTRIES
  Japan moves in. Tokyo Inc.'s bold thrust
  into the American heartland.
  U.S. News   May 9, 1988   p. 43

**TENNESSEE BOARD OF PARDONS AND
  PAROLES**
  The woman who stopped the "red-neck
  mafia." Marie Ragghianti. A new
  American hero.
  Ms.   Jun 1983   p. 43

TENNIS
  Sex & tennis. The new battleground.
  Time   Sep 6, 1976   p. 34

  Tennis, everyone! Sweden's Björn Borg.
  Newsweek   Jul 1, 1974   p. 44

  Tennis: The women take over.
  Newsweek   Jun 26, 1972   p. 56

TERESA, MOTHER
  Messengers of love and hope. Living
  saints. Mother Teresa.
  Time   Dec 29, 1975   p. 47

TERRORISM
  How safe is your food?
  Newsweek   Mar 27, 1989   p. 16

  Is anything safe? How two grapes
  triggered a panic about what we eat.
  Time   Mar 27, 1989   p. 24

  How Iran's terrorists operate. Are
  Americans at risk from Khomeini's death
  threat to Salman Rushdie?
  U.S. News   Mar 6, 1989   p. 20

  Explosion in the sky. Tragedy and terror
  on Pan Am 103. How families cope with
  sudden loss.
  Newsweek   Jan 2, 1989   p. 14

Memo. To: The President. From: G. Gordon Liddy. Subject: Near future potential for massive terrorism on U.S. soil.
Omni   Jan 1989   p. 42

The technology of terrorism. This could be a terrorist's bomb.
Discover   Jun 1986   p. 22

Terrorists. All the world's their stage.
Psychology Today   Mar 1986   p. 18

Will Americans still be terrorist targets? 'We want...justice done.'
U.S. News   Oct 21, 1985   p. 24

Ten ways to fight terrorism. When to retaliate - and how does TV help or hurt?
Newsweek   Jul 1, 1985   p. 14

America under the gun. The struggle against terrorism.
Time   Jul 1, 1985   p. 8

America. Next target for terrorists?
U.S. News   Jan 9, 1984   p. 24

Libya's hit teams. The specter of terrorism. Colonel Nuammar Gaddafi.
Time   Dec 21, 1981   p. 16

Terrorism. Russia's secret weapon?
U.S. News   May 4, 1981   p. 27

Terror gangs. Is anyone safe?
U.S. News   May 22, 1978   p. 30

Seizing hostages. Scourge of the '70s.
Newsweek   Mar 21, 1977   p. 16

Political terror in U.S. What next?
U.S. News   Mar 4, 1974   p. 15

The urban guerrillas.
Time   Nov 2, 1970   p. 19

TERRORISTS

The capture of a terrorist. Fawaz Younis is the first accused terrorist to be arrested overseas and brought to the U.S. for trial. This is the inside story of how American agents tracked him down in the Middle East...
U.S. News   Sep 12, 1988   p. 26

Terror gangs. Is anyone safe?
U.S. News   May 22, 1978   p. 30

TERRORISTS, ARAB

How Iran's terrorists operate. Are Americans at risk from Khomeini's death threat to Salman Rushdie?
U.S. News   Mar 6, 1989   p. 20

'America is our target.' Inside the terror network. Reagan takes on Kaddafi.
Newsweek   Apr 7, 1986   p. 20

TERRORISTS, GERMAN

War on terrorism.
Newsweek   Oct 31, 1977   p. 48

War on terrorism.
Time   Oct 28, 1977   p. 28

TERRORISTS, ITALIAN

Italy's agony.
Newsweek   May 22, 1978   p. 30

TEST TUBE BABIES

See FERTILIZATION IN VITRO, HUMAN

TEXAS

Texas takes a tumble.
U.S. News   Apr 21, 1986   p. 20

Where oil and wildlife mix.
National Geographic Feb 1981   p. 145

Texas! The superstate.
Newsweek   Dec 12, 1977   p. 36

Texas: Where myth & reality merge. Governor Connally.
Time   Jan 17, 1964   p. 16

TEXAS INSTRUMENTS

TI. After the $119 million loss.
Business Week   Sep 19, 1983   p. 56

TEXTILE INDUSTRY

The Textile and Apparel Trade Act.
Congressional Digest Jan 1989   p. 1

Roger Milliken. Running textiles' premier performer.
Business Week   Jan 19, 1981   p. 62

THAILAND

A monarchy fights for freedom. The King and Queen of Thailand.
Time   May 27, 1966   p. 28

Sex, lies & politics. America's watershed debate on sexual harassment.
Time   Oct 21, 1991   p. 34

Sex and justice. The Thomas affair. The furor over sexual harassment.
U.S. News   Oct 21, 1991   p. 32

Judging Thomas. The life and contradictions of the Supreme Court nominee.
Newsweek   Sep 16, 1991   p. 18

THOMAS, DEBI

Winter wonders. Debi Thomas. Can America's sweetheart dethrone East Germany's Katarina Witt? Super-Z. Will Primin Zurbriggen zip and zap them all? The battling Brians. Orser of Canada vs. Boitano of the U.S.
Time   Feb 15, 1988   p. 40

THORTON, CHARLES

The technology industry. How a whiz kid makes it pay. Litton's "Tex" Thornton.
Time   Oct 4, 1963   p. 104

THOUGHT AND THINKING

In the mind's eye. How we visualize.
Psychology Today   May 1985   p. 22

When we think we're thinking–but we're not.
Psychology Today   Apr 1982   p. 60

TIANANMEN SQUARE (CHINA) STUDENT DEMONSTRATION, 1989

Reign of terror. China's crackdown.
Newsweek   Jun 19, 1989   p. 14

Bloodbath.
Newsweek   Jun 12, 1989   p. 24

Massacre in Beijing.
Time   Jun 12, 1989   p. 24

TIEGS, CHERYL

The all-American model. Cheryl Tiegs.
Time   Mar 6, 1978   p. 48

TIGER INTERNATIONAL INC.

Tiger International. Is its grand transportation plan more than a dream?
Business Week   Apr 27, 1981   p. 90

TIGERS

The tiger's kill. Photographed in the jungles of India.
Life   Jun 25, 1965   p. 52

TIME

The rat race. How America is running itself ragged.
Time   Apr 24, 1989   p. 58

One way. In the universes of both Newton and Einstein, time flows backward into the past as readily as it does forward into the future.
Discover   Feb 1987   p. 62

On time. Our perspectives govern our lives.
Psychology Today   Mar 1985   p. 20

TIME INC.

The battle over Time Inc.
Newsweek   Jun 26, 1989   p. 48

Time's Nick & Dick show. How they plan to keep the raiders away. Time Inc. President Nicholas J. Nicholas. Chief Executive J. Richard Munro.
Business Week   Aug 3, 1987   p. 54

Sharon vs. Time. An absence of malice.
Newsweek   Feb 4, 1985   p. 52

TIME TRAVEL

Time travel. A new reality—from the physicist who brought us black holes.
Discover   Jun 1989   p. 58

TIME WARNER INC.

Time Warner. Synergy? Not much. Strategic alliances? Not yet. Rights offering? Not so fast. No wonder shareholders are mad.
Business Week   Jul 22, 1991   p. 70

TIME'S MACHINE OF THE YEAR

Machine of the year. The computer moves in.
Time   Jan 3, 1983   p. 12

TIME'S MAN OF THE DECADE

Man of the decade. Mikhail Gorbachev.
Time   Jan 1, 1990   p. 42

TIME'S MAN/WOMAN OF THE YEAR

Men of the year. The two George Bushes.
Time   Jan 7, 1991   p. 18

Man of the year. Mikhail Sergeyevich Gorbachev.
Time   Jan 4, 1988   p. 16

Woman of the year. Philippine President Corazon Aquino.
Time   Jan 5, 1987   p. 18

Man of the year. Deng Xiaoping.
Time   Jan 6, 1986   p. 24

Man of the year. Peter Ueberroth. The achievement was Olympian.
Time   Jan 7, 1985   p. 20

Men of the year. Ronald Reagan. Yuri Andropov.
Time   Jan 2, 1984   p. 16

Man of the year. Poland's Lech Walesa.
Time   Jan 4, 1982   p. 12

Man of the year. Ronald Reagan.
Time   Jan 5, 1981   p. 10

Man of the year. Ayatullah Khomeini.
Time   Jan 7, 1980   p. 8

Man of the year. Teng Hsiao-p'ing. Visions of a new China.
Time   Jan 1, 1979   p. 12

Man of the year. Anwar Sadat.
Time   Jan 2, 1978   p. 10

Man of the year. Jimmy Carter.
Time   Jan 3, 1977   p. 10

Women of the year.
Time   Jan 5, 1976   p. 6

Man of the Year. King Faisal.
Time   Jan 6, 1975   p. 8

Man of the year. Judge John Sirica.
Time   Jan 7, 1974   p. 8

Men of the year. Triumph and trial. Henry Kissinger. Richard Nixon.
Time   Jan 1, 1973   p. 13

Man of the year. Richard M. Nixon.
Time   Jan 3, 1972   p. 10

Man of the year. Willy Brandt.
Time   Jan 4, 1971   p. 6

Man and woman of the year. The middle Americans.
Time   Jan 5, 1970   p. 10

Men of the year. Anders, Borman and Lovell.
Time   Jan 3, 1969   p. 9

Man of the year. L.B.J. as Lear.
Time   Jan 5, 1968   p. 13

Man of the year. Twenty-five and under.
Time   Jan 6, 1967   p. 18

Man of the year. General Westmoreland.
Time   Jan 7, 1966   p. 15

Man of the year. President Johnson.
Time   Jan 1, 1965   p. 14

Man of the year. Martin Luther King, Jr.
Time   Jan 3, 1964   p. 13

Man of the year. John XXIII.
Time   Jan 4, 1963   p. 50

Man of the year. John F. Kennedy.
Time   Jan 5, 1962   p. 9

U.S. scientists. Men of the year.
Time   Jan 2, 1961   p. 40

Man of the year. Dwight D. Eisenhower.
Time   Jan 4, 1960   p. 11

TIME'S PLANET OF THE YEAR
Planet of the year. Endangered earth.
Time   Jan 2, 1989   p. 24

TISCH, LAURENCE
The man who captured CBS. Loews' Laurence Tisch takes over.
Time   Sep 22, 1986   p. 68

TITANIC (STEAMSHIP)
The man who found the *Titanic*.
Discover   Jan 1987   p. 50

A long last look at *Titanic*.
National Geographic Dec 1986   p. 698

Voyages to the bottom of the sea. Alvin exploring the Titanic.
Time   Aug 11, 1986   p. 48

TOBACCO INDUSTRY

R. J. Reynolds' Bowman Gray.
Time   Apr 11, 1960   p. 104

TOMLIN, LILY

New queen of comedy. Lily Tomlin.
Time   Mar 28, 1977   p. 68

TOMOGRAPHY

Computers that can film insanity.
Omni   Jan 1984   p. 84

TORNADOES

Wind warriors. Taming tornadoes.
Omni   Jun 1986   p. 82

TOUCH

Reach out and touch someone. When
you should.
Psychology Today   Mar 1988   p. 30

TOURIST TRADE

On the go-'60: A Newsweek spotlight on
business.
Newsweek   Jun 13, 1960   p. 81

TOWER COMMISSION REPORT, 1987

Reagan's failure. Can he recover?
Newsweek   Mar 9, 1987   p. 16

The teflon is gone. A question of
competence. Can Howard Baker rebuild a
shattered Presidency. How Nancy
Reagan defends her man.
U.S. News   Mar 9, 1987   p. 14

Coverup. To protect the President, NSC
staffers say Don Regan ordered them to
conceal the early approval of arms sales
to Iran by Ronald Reagan. This week the
Tower Commission will tell how the
president changed his story.
Newsweek   Mar 2, 1987   p. 20

TOWER, JOHN

Wine, women and politics. Tower's
troubles.
Newsweek   Mar 6, 1989   p. 16

The Tower fiasco. Bush faces his first
crisis.
Time   Mar 6, 1989   p. 18

TOWNS

See CITIES AND TOWNS

TOXIC WASTE

See HAZARDOUS WASTES

TOYOTA MOTOR CORP.

Toyota's fast lane. Japan's biggest
company is out to overtake GM.
Business Week   Nov 4, 1985   p. 42

TOYS

Turned-on-toys.
Newsweek   Dec 11, 1978   p. 76

TRADE POLICY

Free-trade fight. Time to raise the bridge?
U.S. News   Sep 23, 1985   p. 46

See Also INTERNATIONAL TRADE

TRADE POLICY - BUSH ADMINISTRATION

Trade warrior. Carla Hills has one of the
toughest jobs in Washington this year:
Negotiate trade policy with Japan and
Europe without succumbing to
protectionist pressure.
Business Week   Jan 22, 1990   p. 50

The Textile and Apparel Trade Act.
Congressional Digest Jan 1989   p. 1

**TRADE POLICY - REAGAN
ADMINISTRATION**

Proposed foreign trade legislation.
Congressional Digest Aug 1986   p. 193

Trade wars. Congress pushes for
protectionism. Reagan holds fast against
barriers.
Time   Oct 7, 1985   p. 22

Controversy over foreign policy export
controls.
Congressional Digest Jun 1983   p. 163

Proposed automobile "domestic content"
legislation.
Congressional Digest Feb 1983   p. 34

TRAFFIC ACCIDENTS

Our deadliest highways.
Life   May 30, 1969   p. 24

TRAFFIC CONGESTION

Gridlock.
Time   Sep 12, 1988   p. 52

Honk! Why you'll be wasting more time in traffic.
U.S. News   Sep 7, 1987   p. 20

TRAMPOLINES

Trampoliners in California.
Life   May 2, 1960   p. 34

TRANSCENDENTAL MEDITATION

Meditation: The answer to all your problems?
Time   Oct 13, 1975   p. 71

TRANSPLANTATION OF ORGANS, TISSUES, ECT.

Gift of a human heart. A dying man lives with a dead girl's heart.
Life   Dec 15, 1967   p. 24

A second chance at life. The miracle of transplants. On a gray afternoon two weeks before Christmas, my doctor told me I was dying.
Newsweek   Sep 12, 1988   p. 52

Medical miracles. But how to pay the bill?
Time   Dec 10, 1984   p. 70

How transplants save lives. The replaceable body.
Newsweek   Aug 29, 1983   p. 38

Replacing the heart.
Discover   Feb 1983   p. 13

Liver transplants. A breakthrough in lifesaving surgery.
Life   Sep 1982   p. 22

The tragic record of heart transplants. A new report on an era of medical failure.
Life   Sep 17, 1971   p. 56

New hearts for old. The promise and perils of transplant surgery.
Newsweek   Dec 18, 1967   p. 86

The transplanted heart. Dr. Christiaan Barnard.
Time   Dec 15, 1967   p. 64

TRANSPORTATION

Mass transit: The expensive dream.
Business Week   Aug 27, 1984   p. 62

The decaying of America. Our dams, bridges, roads and water systems are falling apart.
Newsweek   Aug 2, 1982   p. 12

The great American transportation mess.
U.S. News   Aug 31, 1981   p. 18

Changes in the way you will travel.
U.S. News   Jul 2, 1979   p. 48

TRAVEL

The ultimate travel guide. Exploring Haiti's voodoo underground. Hunting for mammoths in South Dakota. A day at a robot factory. Riding the world's most terrifying roller coasters. Borneo's wild orangutan watch.
Omni   Mar 1989   p. 42

Travel '76. Discovering America.
Time   Jun 28, 1976   p. 59

Summer nomads. The fun and frustrations of Americans on the move.
Life   Aug 14, 1970   p. 20

Life Italian style. Europe's biggest season.
Newsweek   Jul 19, 1965   p. 57

Summertime '61: Vacations off the beaten track.
Newsweek   Jul 3, 1961   p. 45

Travel: The faraway places.
Time   May 19, 1961   p. 70

The Caribbean: Palmy, balmy vacations in the sun.
Newsweek   Jan 9, 1961   p. 46

On the go-'60: A Newsweek spotlight on business.
Newsweek   Jun 13, 1960   p. 81

TRAVELERS, AMERICAN

Off they go! The world's a bargain for U.S. tourists.
Time   Apr 22, 1985   p. 48

Travel. Americans everywhere.
Time   Jul 25, 1983   p. 40

Summer '70. Young Americans abroad.
Newsweek   Aug 10, 1970   p. 44

TRAVOLTA, JOHN

Travolta fever.
Time   Apr 3, 1978   p. 82

TREATIES

The intermediate-range and shorter-range missiles treaty.
Congressional Digest Apr 1988   p. 97

The ABM Treaty controversy.
Congressional Digest Nov 1987   p. 257

Proposed ratification of the Genocide Treaty.
Congressional Digest Dec 1984   p. 289

Law of the Sea Treaty.
Congressional Digest Jan 1983   p. 2

TREES

The miracle of trees. They give us shade, beauty, the air we breathe. If we let them, they could even save our environment.
Life   May 1990   p. 26

TREVINO, LEE

Golf's biggest money winner. Lee Trevino.
Newsweek   Jul 19, 1971   p. 57

Trevino: Golf's new superstar.
Time   Jul 19, 1971   p. 47

TRI QUANG

War within a war. Buddhists Tri Quang and Phap Tri.
Newsweek   May 30, 1966 p. 38

South Viet Nam: The Buddhist bid for power. Thich Tri Quang
Time   Apr 22, 1966 p. 25

TRIALS

You the jury. Can you trust an eyewitness? Hypnosis: How reliable is it? Law and language.
Psychology Today Feb 1984   p. 22

TRIALS (CONSPIRACY)

Verdict in Chicago.
Newsweek   Mar 2, 1970   p. 22

TRIALS (MURDER)

Courtroom pictures of the Klan murder trial.
Life   May 21, 1965 p. 32

TRUDEAU, G. B.

Inside Doonesbury's brain. Garry Trudeau finally talks.
Newsweek   Oct 15, 1990   p. 60

Doonesbury is back! Mike and J.J. are married—and other exciting surprises.
Life   Oct 1984   p. 55

Doonesbury. Politics in the funny papers.
Time   Feb 9, 1976   p. 57

TRUDEAU, PIERRE

Canada in crisis.
Newsweek   Nov 2, 1970   p. 41

TRUMAN, HARRY S.

Harry Truman by Margaret Truman. Mellow, busy days after the White House.
Life   Dec 1, 1972   p. 68

TRUMP, DONALD

Trump. The fall.
Newsweek   Jun 18, 1990   p. 38

This man may turn you green with envy - or just turn you off. Flaunting it is the game, and Trump is the name.
Time   Jan 16, 1989   p. 48

Trump. A billion-dollar empire and an ego to match.
Newsweek   Sep 28, 1987   p. 50

Trump. What's behind the hype? Donald Trump has conquered New York real estate, he's America's biggest casino operator—and he has enough cash to worry Corporate America.
Business Week   Jul 20, 1987   p. 92

TRUST

Creating trust and intimacy in the age of divorce.
Psychology Today May 1989   p. 27

TRW INC.

TRW's team leads a revolution in managing technology.
Business Week   Nov 15, 1982 p. 124

U

U-2 INCIDENT

The Cold War gets hotter. The high-flying U-2 & the cloudy summit. Pilot Francis Powers.
Time   May 16, 1960   p. 15

U2 (MUSICAL GROUP)

U2. Rock's hottest ticket.
Time   Apr 27, 1987   p. 72

UEBERROTH, PETER

Man of the year. Peter Ueberroth. The achievement was Olympian.
Time   Jan 7, 1985   p. 20

UFO

Missing time: A new look at alien abductions.
Omni   Dec 1987   p. 52

UFOs. Converting the disbelievers with science.
Omni   Feb 1985   p. 70

UFO mystery. Explaining the Hudson Valley sightings.
Discover   Nov 1984   p. 18

UGANDA

Idi Amin's reign of terror.
Newsweek   Mar 7, 1977   p. 28

The wild man of Africa. Uganda's Idi Amin.
Time   Mar 7, 1977   p. 19

UGGAMS, LESLIE

New star Leslie Uggams: The Negro in show business.
Newsweek   Jul 17, 1967   p. 63

ULBRICHT, WALTER

East Germany's Ulbricht.
Time   Aug 25, 1961   p. 20

ULLMANN, LIV

Liv Ullmann in "A Doll's House."
Newsweek   Mar 17, 1975   p. 61

Hollywood's new Nordic star. Liv Ullmann.
Time   Dec 4, 1972   p. 77

ULTRALIGHT AIRCRAFT

The bird men.
National Geographic Aug 1983   p. 198

UN

See UNITED NATIONS

UNDERCLASS

See POOR

UNDERGROUND ECONOMY

The underground economy's hidden force. Masking growth. Distorting policy. Undermining government.
Business Week   Apr 5, 1982   p. 64

UNDERGROUND RAILROAD

Underground railroad. Escape from slavery.
National Geographic Jul 1984   p. 3

UNEMPLOYED

Left out. The human cost of the collapse of industrial America.
Newsweek   Mar 21, 1983   p. 26

America's wandering jobless.
U.S. News   Jan 17, 1983   p. 23

Young Blacks out of work. Time bomb for U.S.
U.S. News   Dec 5, 1977   p. 22

"Okies" of the '70s. Mass migration in search of jobs.
U.S. News   Mar 24, 1975   p. 16

Out of work.
Newsweek   Jan 20, 1975   p. 54

UNEMPLOYMENT

Stress: Effects of unemployment.
USA Today   Feb 1985   p. 1

Jobs. How to get America back to work.
Newsweek   Oct 18, 1982   p. 78

Jobs. A million that will never come back.
U.S. News   Sep 13, 1982   p. 53

Unemployment. The biggest worry.
Time   Feb 8, 1982   p. 22

Jobs. A look at the nation's most nagging
problem - and some ways to solve it.
U.S. News   Feb 21, 1977   p. 54

Unemployment in America.
Newsweek   Apr 1, 1963   p. 58

See Also EMPLOYEE DISMISSAL

UNGARO, EMMANUEL

The heat is on. Fashion goes feminine -
and Ungaro leads the way.
Newsweek   Apr 4, 1988   p. 54

UNION CARBIDE CORPORATION

Union Carbide fights for its life.
Business Week   Dec 24, 1984   p. 52

Can it happen here? Poison gas victims in
India.
Newsweek   Dec 17, 1984   p. 26

India's disaster. The night of death. A
global worry.
Time   Dec 17, 1984   p. 20

UNIONS

See LABOR UNIONS

UNITED AUTO WORKERS

Showdown in Detroit. Auto talks will
shape the industry—and the UAW.
Business Week   Sep 10, 1984   p. 102

UNITED FLIGHT 232 DISASTER, 1989

Finding God on Flight 232. Gripping
stories told by the passengers who faced
death for a chilling 41 minutes.
Life   Sep 1989   p. 28

UNITED MINE WOKERS OF AMERICA

The big raise. Labor & inflation.
Time   Nov 25, 1974   p. 22

UNITED NATIONS

Crisis ahead for United Nations?
U.S. News   Sep 17, 1979   p. 61

The outspoken Andrew Young. At the
U.N.
Newsweek   Mar 28, 1977   p. 24

Giving them hell at the U.N. Pat
Moynihan.
Time   Jan 26, 1976   p. 26

China joins the world.
Newsweek   Nov 8, 1971   p. 22

The troubled U.N. Secretary-General U
Thant.
Newsweek   Oct 3, 1966   p. 35

Secretary-General U Thant. Crisis over
the U.N.
Newsweek   Jan 29, 1962   p. 33

Storm over the U.N. Can it survive?
Newsweek   Oct 2, 1961   p. 17

When Dag died. Inside the Congo. Inside
the U.N.
Life   Sep 29, 1961   p. 42

The U.N. in crisis.
Time   Sep 29, 1961   p. 20

The U.N. meets. Disarmament, Berlin,
Red China, Katanga.
Newsweek   Sep 25, 1961   p. 23

The rising Congo crisis. Can the U.N.
survive?
Newsweek   Feb 27, 1961   p. 17

Embattled Dag—U.N.'s gravest hour.
Life   Feb 24, 1961   p. 16

The Russian offensive against the U.N. &
U.S.
Time   Feb 24, 1961   p. 16

Eisenhower's historic speech at U.N.
Life   Oct 3, 1960   p. 22

The score. Ike vs. Khrushchev. Nixon vs.
Kennedy.
Newsweek   Oct 3, 1960   p. 19

The nations.
Time   Oct 3, 1960   p. 11

The 'invasion' of Manhattan. (Special section: Is it 'make-or-break' for the U.N.?)
Newsweek   Sep 26, 1960   p. 31

The U.N. & the Congo. Out of chaos a legal precedent. Dag Hammarskjold.
Time   Aug 22, 1960   p. 18

UNITED STATES

The best of America. Politics. Philanthropy. Craftsmanship. Innovation. Education. Research.
U.S. News   Aug 26, 1991   p. 50

High anxiety. Looming recession, government paralysis and the threat of war are giving Americans a case of the jitters.
Time   Oct 15, 1990   p. 30

Trends: America still has a place in the world.
USA Today   Aug 1990   p. 1

The best of America. The year's most outstanding people, places, products, and ideas.
U.S. News   Jul 9, 1990   p. 43

Back home. Where we grew up: A portrait of America.
U.S. News   Dec 18, 1989   p. 44

Is government dead? Unwilling to lead, politicians are letting America slip into paralysis.
Time   Oct 23, 1989   p. 28

How Reagan changed America.
Newsweek   Jan 9, 1989   p. 12

What Reagan has meant to America. Behind-the-scenes photos of the president at work and play.
U.S. News   Jan 9, 1989   p. 18

What he will do. The President's opportunities and the menaces he faces.
U.S. News   Nov 14, 1988   p. 20

25 years later. JFK's vision and what has come of it.
U.S. News   Oct 24, 1988   p. 30

After Reagan. America's agenda for the 1990s.
Business Week   Feb 1, 1988   p. 56

America's agenda after Reagan. Change in the weather.
Time   Mar 30, 1987   p. 28

A letter to the year 2086. "Do you see starlight? So do we. Smell the fire? We do too. Draw close. Let us tell each other a story."
Time   Dec 29, 1986   p. 24

A day in the life of America. A picture portfolio by the world's best photographer.
Newsweek   Oct 27, 1986   p. 43

American best.
Time   Jun 16, 1986   p. 26

Are you better off now than you were 4 years ago? Yes. No.
U.S. News   Oct 15, 1984   p. 30

I love U.S. America's upbeat mood.
Time   Sep 24, 1984   p. 10

10 forces reshaping America. From Eisenhower to Reagan - it is a span of only 20 years, yet a period of change so dramatic that it has left many Americans both dazzled and bewildered.
U.S. News   Mar 19, 1984   p. 40

Waiting for better days. A nationwide mood survey.
U.S. News   Oct 18, 1982   p. 24

An uneasy America. Nationwide mood survey.
U.S. News   May 24, 1982   p. 34

American renewal.
Time   Feb 23, 1981   p. 34

Rediscovering America.
Time   Jul 7, 1980   p. 20

Ten years that shook America...now, the '80s.
Newsweek   Nov 19, 1979   p. 84

America. Declining power?
U.S. News   Nov 27, 1978   p. 56

America's adults.   In search of what?
U.S. News   Aug 21, 1978   p. 56

America's mood. A new confidence.
U.S. News   Jun 13, 1977   p. 24

America's Mood. Hopeful - sort of.
Time   Jan 24, 1977   p. 8

America's third century. A look ahead.
U.S. News   Jul 5, 1976   p. 37

Young builders of America. 8 who have
made their mark.
U.S. News   Feb 9, 1976   p. 42

What kind of future for America?
U.S. News   Jul 7, 1975   p. 44

Into a new era. How your life will change.
1975...2000.
U.S. News   Mar 3, 1975   p. 32

New directions. Lower taxes. Uphill road
for business. Less worry about oil.
Overhaul of social security.
U.S. News   Feb 17, 1975   p. 13

How America is changing.
U.S. News   Feb 25, 1974   p. 30

The cooling of America.
Time   Feb 22, 1971   p. 10

The spirit of '70. Six historians on the
'American crisis.'
Newsweek   Jul 6, 1970   p. 19

To heal a nation. Special section: The
task before the President.
Time   Jan 24, 1969   p. 16

UNITED STATES - DEFENSES

Shrinking the military. Weapons,
missions and manpower: What to keep,
what to cut.
U.S. News   Oct 14, 1991   p. 24

Defending defense. Budget battles and
star wars.
Time   Apr 4, 1983   p. 8

Defending America. How to cut the
Pentagon's budget - and keep the nation
strong.
Newsweek   Dec 20, 1982   p. 22

Reagan's defense buildup. Does it make
sense? Can we afford it?
Newsweek   Jun 8, 1981   p. 28

Is America strong enough?
Newsweek   Oct 27, 1980   p. 48

How strong is Russia? How prepared is
U.S.?
U.S.News   Feb 11, 1980   p. 17

Defense. How much is enough?
Time   May 23, 1977   p. 14

The great missile debate.
Time   Mar 14, 1969   p. 22

As the test ban approaches: The size &
condition of the U.S. atomic arsenal.
Time   Aug 23, 1963   p. 11

Arms & diplomacy. Re-examing U.S.
military might.
Time   Apr 7, 1961   p. 20

America's firepower: The defense puzzle.
Newsweek   Feb 1, 1960   p. 17

**UNITED STATES - ECONOMIC
CONDITIONS**

See ECONOMIC CONDITIONS - UNITED
STATES

UNITED STATES - ECONOMIC HISTORY

The new America. The nation's changing
demography—and what it means. Six
key trends of the 1990s. Economic
prospects for the year 2000.
Business Week   Sep 25, 1989   p. 90

UNITED STATES - FOREIGN OPINION

What Japan thinks of us. A nation of
crybabies?
Newsweek   Apr 2, 1990   p. 18

How the world views America.
U.S. News   Jul 15, 1985   p. 27

What the world thinks of America.
Loved, hated but always imitated - a new
poll shows how America's image is
changing.
Newsweek   Jul 11, 1983   p. 44

UNITED STATES - FOREIGN POLICY

Uncle Sam as world policeman. Time for
a change?
USA Today   Jan 1991   p. 20

U.S. foreign policy: How to relate self-interest and the preservation of freedom. Senator Fulbright.
Time   Jan 22, 1965   p. 14

UNITED STATES - FOREIGN RELATIONS

Showing muscle. More conflict ahead?
U.S. News   Apr 7, 1986   p. 18

Can Reagan pull the alliance together?
U.S. News   Jun 7, 1982   p. 22

Where are America's allies?
U.S. News   Jan 18, 1982   p. 22

Hobbled giants.
U.S.News   Jun 30, 1980   p. 15

High noon for America's allies.
Time   Apr 28, 1980   p. 10

Diplomacy in crisis. Hostages in Bogotá. Suspense in Iran. Fiasco at the U.N.
Time   Mar 17, 1980   p. 28

Has America lost it clout?
Newsweek   Nov 26, 1979   p. 34

America's world of woes. Feeling helpless.
Newsweek   Feb 26, 1979   p. 22

Crescent of crisis. Troubles beyond Iran.
Time   Jan 15, 1979   p. 18

Man on the move. Secretary of State Cyrus Vance.
Time   Apr 24, 1978   p. 12

Secretary of State Kissinger. "We are moving into a new world."
U.S. News   Jun 23, 1975   p. 23

A world of woes.
Newsweek   Apr 7, 1975   p. 18

America and the world. "A moment of danger."
Time   Apr 7, 1975   p. 10

UNITED STATES - HISTORY

Who are we? American kids are getting a new—and divisive—view of Thomas Jefferson, Thanksgiving and the Fourth of July.
Time   Jul 8, 1991   p. 12

The Patowmack Canal. Waterway that led to the Constitution.
National Geographic Jun 1987   p. 716

A crucial U.S. debate on our national purpose.
Life   May 23, 1960 p. 22

UNITED STATES - HISTORY - CIVIL WAR

The Civil War remembered. A stunning TV series sparks old passions and new controversies.
Newsweek   Oct 8, 1990   p. 58

Reliving the Civil War. Why America's bloodiest conflict still grips us 125 years later.
U.S. News   Aug 15, 1988 p. 48

The Civil War. A new six-part series on our nation's bloodiest drama. I: Deeds of glory. II: Great battles. III: The soldier's life. IV: The war that changed war. V: The home front. VI: The war lives on.
Life   Jan 6, 1961   p. 48

UNITED STATES - HISTORY - REVOLUTION

The makers of America.
U.S. News   Jul 8, 1974   p. 30

UNITED STATES - HISTORY - WAR OF 1812

Ghost ships of the War of 1812.
National Geographic Mar 1983   p. 289

UNITED STATES - JOINT CHIEFS OF STAFF

U.S. Joint Chiefs of Staff. Thinkers and managers replace the heroes.
Time   Feb 5, 1965   p. 22

UNITED STATES - POLITICS AND GOVERNMENT

Throw the bums out! Government is paralyzed, and voters are angry. Is there any way out of the political mess?
U.S. News   Oct 22, 1990   p. 28

How our government works.
U.S. News   Jan 28, 1985   p. 37

At the crossroads.
Time   Jul 23, 1979   p. 20

ABC's of the great game of politics.
U.S. News   Sep 18, 1978   p. 37

ABC's of how your government works.
U.S. News   May 9, 1977   p. 43

How to get America moving again. 20 leaders tell what's needed.
U.S. News   Nov 29, 1976   p. 48

Big government.
Newsweek   Dec 15, 1975   p. 34

Mood of America. "Where do we turn?"
U.S. News   Oct 6, 1975   p. 12

Walter Lippmann on Kennedy.
Newsweek   Jan 21, 1963   p. 24

Special issue. U.S. politics.
Life   Jul 4, 1960   p. 12

UNITED STATES - POPULAR CULTURE

Dirty words. America's foul-mouthed pop culture.
Time   May 7, 1990   p. 92

Pop! It's what's happening in art, fashion, entertainment, business.
Newsweek   Apr 25, 1966   p. 56

Mad new world of Batman, Superman and Marquis de Sade.
Life   Mar 11, 1966   p. 22

UNITED STATES - POPULATION

America's changing colors. What will the U.S. be like when whites are no longer the majority?
Time   Apr 9, 1990   p. 28

UNITED STATES - SOCIAL CONDITIONS

The simple life. Rejecting the rat race, Americans get back to basics.
Time   Apr 8, 1991   p. 58

Thought police. Watch what you say. There's a 'Politically Correct' way to talk about race, sex and ideas. Is this the new enlightenment – or the new McCarthyism?
Newsweek   Dec 24, 1990   p. 48

Twentysomething. Laid back, late blooming or just lost? Overshadowed by the baby boomers, America's next generation has a hard act to follow.
Time   Jul 16, 1990   p. 56

The rat race. How America is running itself ragged.
Time   Apr 24, 1989   p. 58

Taking America's pulse. Prices. Energy. White House. Taxes. Congress.
U.S. News   May 28, 1979   p. 22

America's adults. In search of what?
U.S. News   Aug 21, 1978   p. 56

Springtime mood of America. Inflation. Carter. Bureaucracy. Taxes. Schools.
U.S. News   May 8, 1978   p. 19

America's mood. A new confidence.
U.S. News   Jun 13, 1977   p. 24

UNITED STATES - SOCIAL LIFE AND CUSTOMS

Cocktails '85. America's new drinking habits.
Time   May 20, 1985   p. 68

UNITED STATES - SOCIAL POLICY

Save the children. Too many problems, too little help.
U.S. News   Nov 7, 1988   p. 34

No free lunch. The high cost of entitlements.
Time   Oct 12, 1981   p. 32

A decade of the Great Society. Success or failure?
U.S. News   Jun 9, 1975   p. 26

Can the Great Society be built and managed? H.E.W. Secretary Gardner.
Time   Jan 20, 1967   p. 16

UNITED STATES - SOCIAL VALUES

Morality test. Do you cut corners on your taxes? Is gambling immoral? Are Americans too sexually permissive? Is lying ever justified? Does it pay to be moral?
U.S. News   Dec 9, 1985   p. 52

What Americans think they see in their future.
Psychology Today   Sep 1981   p. 36

Searching for self-fulfillment in a world turned upside down.
Psychology Today   Apr 1981   p. 35

What's happening to America's values. A conversation with Claire Booth Luce.
U.S. News   Jun 24, 1974   p. 52

Anything goes. The permissive society.
Newsweek   Nov 13, 1967   p. 74

UNITED STATES - TREATIES - PANAMA
Panama. A doomed treaty?
U.S. News   Sep 19, 1977   p. 18

Getting out of the canal (slowly).
Time   Aug 22, 1977   p. 8

UNIVERSE
Parallel universes. The new reality—from Harvard's wildest physicist.
Discover   Jul 1990   p. 46

When galaxies collide. The splendid violence of creation.
Discover   Feb 1990   p. 50

The all-creating eye. According to a radical tenet of physics, the universe exists only because it has been, is being, and will be observed.
Discover   May 1987   p. 90

Future universe. The evolution of life over the next one hundred billion years.
Omni   Aug 1986   p. 36

How the universe began. Looking beyond the Big Bang.
Discover   Jun 1983   p. 92

The once and future universe.
National Geographic Jun 1983   p. 704

Mysteries of the universe. Frontiers in physics.
Newsweek   Mar 12, 1979   p. 46

UNIVERSE, END OF
The end of the universe. How and when.
Discover   Jul 1987   p. 82

UNIVERSITY OF CALIFORNIA
University of California. Where things happen first.
Newsweek   Nov 23, 1970   p. 83

UNMARRIED COUPLES
Living together.
Newsweek   Aug 1, 1977   p. 46

UPDIKE, JOHN
Going great at 50. Writer John Updike.
Time   Oct 18, 1982   p. 72

The adulterous society. Author John Updike.
Time   Apr 26, 1968   p. 66

UPPER CLASSES
What it's like today in society.
Time   Jul 20, 1962   p. 45

URBAN RENEWAL
Pittsburgh. Innovative American city.
USA Today   Mar 1986   p. 22

Enterprise zones.
Congressional Digest May 1985   p. 131

Controversy over proposed "Urban Enterprise Zones."
Congressional Digest Mar 1982   p. 69

Urban renewal. Remaking the American city.
Time   Nov 6, 1964   p. 60

UTOPIAS
Utopia. According to Jonas Salk, Oprah Winfrey, Kurt Vonnegut, Tammy Faye Bakker, David Rockefeller, Coretta Scott King.
Omni   Apr 1988   p. 36

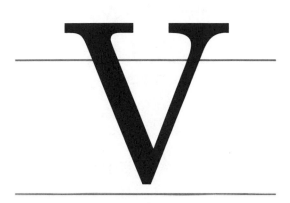

V-E DAY, 1945

May 8, 1945. "Never a greater day." But
Reagan opens old wounds.
Time　　　　Apr 29, 1985　p. 18

VACATIONS

Vacations USA. This is the year! Special
guide on where to go.
U.S. News　　May 5, 1986　p. 46

The great escape: 10 super vacations on
the water.
Ms.　　　　Mar 1982　　p. 77

Tips for winter vacations.
U.S. News　　Nov 7, 1977　p. 39

Travel '76. Discovering America.
Time　　　　Jun 28, 1976　p. 59

Sun spots. The latest resorts.
Newsweek　　Jan 5, 1976　p. 44

Summer nomads. The fun and
frustrations of Americans on the move.
Life　　　　Aug 14, 1970　p. 20

Summertime '61: Vacations off the beaten
track.
Newsweek　　Jul 3, 1961　p. 45

VALDEZ

See EXXON VALDEZ (SHIP) OIL SPILL,
1989

VALUE

Value marketing. It's the way to sell in
the 90's.
Business Week　　Nov 11, 1991　p. 132

VALUES

See UNITED STATES - SOCIAL VALUES

VAMPIRES

Pop culture's occult boom: The sudden,
curious allure of vampires.
Psychology Today　Nov 1989　　p. 31

VAN PALLANDT, NINA

Nina. The singing baroness in the Hughes
affair. Nina van Pallandt traveled with
Clifford Irving.
Life　　　　Feb 11, 1972　p. 30

VANCE, CYRUS

A surprise for State. Senator Edmund
Muskie.
Time　　　　May 12, 1980　p. 12

Man on the move. Secretary of State
Cyrus Vance.
Time　　　　Apr 24, 1978　p. 12

VENEREAL DISEASES

See SEXUALLY TRANSMITTED
DISEASES

VENEZUELA

Latin America. The real builders.
Venezuela's President Betancourt.
Time　　　　Feb 8, 1960　　p. 34

VENTURE CAPITAL

The new entrepreneurs. Lots of startups
give America an edge in product
development. Big corporations try to
imitate the entrepreneurial spirit.
Business Week　　Apr 18, 1983　p. 78

VENUS

The secrets of Venus. Earth's sister planet
helps us understand our own world.
U.S. News　　May 13, 1991　p. 60

VENUS (PLANET)

Venus: What Mariner saw.
Time　　　　Mar 8, 1963　　p. 76

Vietnam. Hard road to peace.
National Geographic Nov 1989   p. 561

New era in North Viet Nam. Ho Chi Minh.
Time   Sep 12, 1969   p. 22

Military coup in Viet Nam. General Duong Van Minh.
Time   Nov 8, 1963   p. 28

South Viet Nam's Madame Nhu.
Time   Aug 9, 1963   p. 21

VIETNAM - POLITICS AND GOVERNMENT

Can Vietnam stand alone?
Newsweek   Dec 16, 1968   p. 40

War within a war. Buddhists Tri Quang and Phap Tri.
Newsweek   May 30, 1966   p. 38

Vietnam—Crippling Buddhist revolt.
Life   Apr 22, 1966   p. 28

South Viet Nam: The Buddhist bid for power. Thich Tri Quang
Time   Apr 22, 1966   p. 25

Turmoil in Vietnam.
Newsweek   Apr 18, 1966   p. 24

Maxwell Taylor in Vietnam: Soldier on the spot.
Newsweek   Sep 21, 1964   p. 43

Vietnam: The coup in pictures.
Life   Nov 15, 1963   p. 34

Vietnam: The showdown. Gen. Duong Van Minh.
Newsweek   Nov 11, 1963   p. 27

McNamara's mission; Mme. Nhu on the road. Vietnam climax.
Life   Oct 11, 1963   p. 22

Vietnam's Madame Nhu.
Newsweek   Sep 9, 1963   p. 33

Holding Southeast Asia. South Vietnam's Diem: A strong man at bay.
Newsweek   May 22, 1961   p. 36

VIETNAM AND THE UNITED STATES

Vietnam 15 years later. In America, the pain endures. In Cambodia, the killing continues.
Time   Apr 30, 1990   p. 18

Untold story of the road to war in Vietnam.
U.S. News   Oct 10, 1983   p. 40

Southeast Asia: "Where the borders are less guarded, the enemy harder to find."
Time   Aug 4, 1961   p. 18

VIETNAM VETERANS MEMORIAL (WASHINGTON, D.C.)

Vietnam memorial.
National Geographic May 1985   p. 552

VIETNAM WAR, 1957-1975

The legacy of Vietnam.
Newsweek   Apr 15, 1985   p. 32

Vietnam. Ten years later.
Time   Apr 15, 1985   p. 16

What Vietnam did to us. A combat unit relives the war and the decade since.
Newsweek   Dec 14, 1981   p. 46

Have the scars healed? 5 years later.
U.S.News   Apr 28, 1980   p. 30

The new Americans.
Newsweek   May 12, 1975   p. 26

The victor.
Time   May 12, 1975   p. 6

The end in Vietnam.
U.S. News   May 12, 1975   p. 16

End of an era.
Newsweek   May 5, 1975   p. 20

Hanoi's triumph.
Time   May 5, 1975   p. 12

The last battle.
Newsweek   Apr 28, 1975   p. 16

Getting out.
Newsweek   Apr 21, 1975   p. 20

Last exit from Viet Nam.
Time   Apr 21, 1975   p. 6

The sorrow and the pity.
Newsweek   Apr 14, 1975   p. 18

Collapse in Viet Nam.
Time   Apr 14, 1975   p. 6

The great retreat.
Newsweek   Mar 31, 1975   p. 16

The last retreat.
Time   Mar 31, 1975   p. 30

The cease-fire.
Time   Feb 5, 1973   p. 10

After the bombs, what peace?
Time   Jan 8, 1973   p. 9

The war that won't go away.
Newsweek   Apr 17, 1972   p. 16

Vietnam: The big test.
Time   Apr 17, 1972   p. 30

The war: Getting in deeper to get out faster?
Time   Feb 15, 1971   p. 24

The troubled army in Vietnam.
Newsweek   Jan 11, 1971   p. 29

The Cambodian campaign. Was it worth it?
Newsweek   Jul 13, 1970   p. 16

Nixon's Cambodian gamble.
Newsweek   May 11, 1970   p. 22

The new war. Will Nixon's gamble work?
Time   May 11, 1970   p. 11

Now it's the Indochina war.
Newsweek   May 4, 1970   p. 21

Vietnamization. Will Nixon's plan work?
Newsweek   Feb 9, 1970   p. 31

The faces of the American dead in Vietnam.
Life   Jun 27, 1969   p. 20

The war: Nixon's big test.
Newsweek   Mar 31, 1969   p. 20

Viet Nam: When can the U.S. begin to leave?
Time   Mar 28, 1969   p. 18

Can Vietnam stand alone?
Newsweek   Dec 16, 1968   p. 40

As the bombing stops—this girl Tron.
Life   Nov 8, 1968   p. 26

Prospects for peace.
Newsweek   Apr 22, 1968   p. 40

Man on the spot. Gen. William Westmoreland.
Newsweek   Feb 19, 1968   p. 33

The enemy lets me take his picture. A remarkable day in Hué.
Life   Feb 16, 1968   p. 22

Suicide raid on the Embassy. New frenzy in the war. Vietcong terrorize the cities.
Life   Feb 9, 1968   p. 22

How goes the war?
Newsweek   Jan 1, 1968   p. 17

Inside the cone of fire at Con Thien. David Douglas Duncan photographs the Marines.
Life   Oct 27, 1967   p. 28

Inside the Viet Cong.
Time   Aug 25, 1967   p. 21

Big Lew Walt. The Marines' Marine on Vietnam's hottest spot.
Life   May 26, 1967   p. 77

Gen. Westmoreland before Congress.
Time   May 5, 1967   p. 17

North Vietnam under siege.
Life   Apr 7, 1967   p. 33

The Delta. Fertile swamp of suspicion. New U.S. front in the widening Vietnam war.
Life   Jan 13, 1967   p. 48

General Westmoreland. A recipe for victory?
Newsweek   Dec 5, 1966   p. 49

LBJ in Vietnam.
Newsweek   Nov 7, 1966   p. 24

The other side's dilemma. North Viet Nam's General Giap.
Time   Jun 17, 1966   p. 32

Viet Nam & the class of '66.
Time   Jun 3, 1966   p. 21

Turmoil in Vietnam.
Newsweek   Apr 18, 1966   p. 24

Captain Pete Dawkins keeps on winning.
Army's All-America Rhodes Scholar, now
in Vietnam.
Life   Apr 8, 1966   p. 91

Vietnam. A searching assessment. The
plus side. The strategy. The dissent.
Life   Feb 25, 1966   p. 27

South Viet Nam's Premier Ky.
Time   Feb 18, 1966   p. 26

The war goes on.
Life   Feb 11, 1966   p. 20

The blunt reality of war in Vietnam.
Life   Nov 26, 1965   p. 50

Mary Martin in Vietnam. Vietcong
ambush.
Life   Oct 22, 1965   p. 32

The turning point in Viet Nam.
Time   Oct 22, 1965   p. 28

Premier Ky: Who rules Vietnam?
Newsweek   Sep 27, 1965   p. 32

The fleet lashes out. In action with the
Navy off Vietnam.
Life   Aug 6, 1965   p. 16

Viet Nam: The intransigent North. Ho
Chi Minh.
Time   Jul 16, 1965   p. 24

Vietnam: The new war. General
Westmoreland.
Newsweek   Jul 5, 1965   p. 30

Deeper into the Vietnam War.
Life   Jul 2, 1965   p. 30

Americans in action. U.S. advisor Capt.
Charles B. Huggins.
Newsweek   May 24, 1965   p. 40

Who's fighting in Viet Nam. A gallery of
American combatants.
Time   Apr 23, 1965   p. 22

Profile of the Viet Cong.
Newsweek   Apr 12, 1965   p. 40

Vietnam.
Newsweek   Feb 22, 1965   p. 32

Escalation in Viet Nam.
Time   Feb 19, 1965   p. 16

Vietnam: Any way out?
Newsweek   Jan 18, 1965   p. 28

Vietnam. A report on the Americans
working and fighting there as the crisis
gets worse.
Life   Nov 27, 1964   p. 30

At Vietnam border General Khanh eyes
the enemy.
Life   Aug 21, 1964   p. 26

The U.S. stand in Asia.
Time   Aug 14, 1964   p. 11

South Viet Nam: The long look north.
Premier Khanh.
Time   Aug 7, 1964   p. 23

Ugly war in Vietnam. U.S. officer heads a
patrol.
Life   Jun 12, 1964   p. 34

The war in Asia: Decision point. Face of
the enemy. Ho Chi Minh.
Newsweek   Jun 8, 1964   p. 24

McNamara's mission; Mme. Nhu on the
road. Vietnam climax.
Life   Oct 11, 1963   p. 22

Laos and Vietnam.
Newsweek   Jul 15, 1963   p. 36

The vicious fighting in Vietnam.
Life   Jan 25, 1963   p. 22

War in Vietnam.
Newsweek   Dec 10, 1962   p. 32

South Viet Nam: What it takes to win.
U.S. General Paul Harkins.
Time   May 11, 1962   p. 24

Vietnam: What price victory?
Newsweek   Apr 30, 1962   p. 36

Vietnam: Our next showdown.
Life   Oct 27, 1961   p. 36

VIETNAM WAR, 1957-1975 - MISSING IN ACTION

Hoping against hope. The MIA mystery. A generation after Vietnam, the families refuse to give up—despite a trail of hoaxes and broken dreams.
Newsweek   Jul 29, 1991   p. 20

VIETNAM WAR, 1957-1975 - PEACE AND MEDIATION

Peace.
Newsweek   Feb 5, 1973   p. 16

How solid a peace?
Newsweek   Jan 29, 1973   p. 16

What went wrong? Presidential adviser Kissinger.
Newsweek   Jan 1, 1973   p. 8

'Peace is at hand.' Good-bye Vietnam.
Newsweek   Nov 6, 1972   p. 33

The shape of peace.
Time   Nov 6, 1972   p. 14

Nixon's Vietnam deal. Hanoi's POW pledge.
Newsweek   Oct 30, 1972   p. 24

On the brink of peace?
Time   Oct 30, 1972   p. 13

Peace talks: The scenario in Paris.
Time   May 10, 1968   p. 21

Behind the peace feelers. 1,000 leads that failed. Exclusive account of a bizarre hoax. Ho Chi Minh implacable—and why.
Life   Mar 22, 1968   p. 32

The chances for peace. Hanoi's Ho Chi Minh.
Newsweek   Feb 20, 1967   p. 25

U.S. envoys deploy around the world. Peace drive aimed at these two men. North Vietnam's President Ho Chi Minh and Prime Minister Pham Van Dong at Presidential Palace in Hanoi.
Life   Jan 14, 1966   p. 22

The U.S. peace offensive and the Communist response. Johnson & advisers at ranch. Shelepin & Ho in Hanoi.
Time   Jan 14, 1966   p. 30

VIETNAM WAR, 1957-1975 - PRISONERS OF WAR

Home at last!
Newsweek   Feb 26, 1973   p. 16

The prisoners return. Welcome home daddy.
Time   Feb 19, 1973   p. 13

Questions for a peace. 543 POWs: what shape are they in? 1,271 MIAs: how many are alive? Where does it leave us?
Life   Nov 10, 1972   p. 32

The battle of the POW's.
Newsweek   Oct 9, 1972   p. 24

P.O.W. wife. As Hanoi releases three fliers, anger and agony over a husband still gone.
Life   Sep 29, 1972   p. 32

The plight of the prisoners.
Time   Dec 7, 1970   p. 15

U.S. prisoners in North Vietnam and visits with their families at home.
Life   Oct 20, 1967   p. 21

Secret struggle to free Gus Hertz from the Vietcong. Heartbreaking effort to get back kidnaped U.S. official—if he is still alive.
Life   Jul 21, 1967   p. 22

VIETNAM WAR, 1957-1975 - PROTESTS AND DEMONSTRATIONS

The May Day arrests.
Newsweek   May 17, 1971   p. 24

Rebel priests: The curious case of the Berrigans.
Time   Jan 25, 1971   p. 12

Nixon's home front.
Newsweek   May 18, 1970   p. 26

Protest!
Time   May 18, 1970   p. 6

The day of dissent. The impact of the nation's Vietnam protest.
Life   Oct 24, 1969   p. 32

Which way out?
Newsweek   Oct 20, 1969   p. 26

Moratorium: At war with war.
Time   Oct 17, 1969   p. 17

Protest! Protest! Protest! Protest! A week
of antiwar demonstrations.
Time　　　　　　　Oct 27, 1967　p. 23

The demonstrators. Who? Why? How
many?
Newsweek　　　　　Nov 1, 1965　p. 25

**VIETNAM WAR, 1957-1975 - PUBLIC
OPINION**

The Vietnam War and American life.
Newsweek　　　　　Jul 10, 1967　p. 16

The home-front war. General
Westmoreland before Congress.
Newsweek　　　　　May 8, 1967　p. 31

**VIETNAM WAR, 1957-1975 - RELIEF
WORK**

To keep a village free. The 'Other War' in
Vietnam.
Life　　　　　　　Aug 25, 1967　p. 24

**VIETNAM WAR, 1957-1975 - REPORTERS
AND REPORTING**

The media on trial. Westmoreland vs.
CBS.
Newsweek　　　　　Oct 22, 1984　p. 60

Westmoreland vs. CBS. Story behind the
battle.
U.S. News　　　　Oct 1, 1984　　p. 44

VIETNAM WAR, 1957-1975 - SOLDIERS

Men at war.
Newsweek　　　　　Aug 1, 1966　p. 28

**VIETNAM WAR, 1957-1975 - SPECIAL
FORCES**

The case of the Green Berets.
Newsweek　　　　　Aug 25, 1969　p. 26

VIETNAM WAR, 1957-1975 - STRATEGY

Nixon's gamble.
Newsweek　　　　　May 22, 1972　p. 18

Nixon strikes back.
Time　　　　　　　May 22, 1972　p. 11

The agony of Khe Sanh.
Newsweek　　　　　Mar 18, 1968　p. 25

VIETNAM WAR, 1957-1975 - VETERANS

Viet Nam vets. Fighting for their rights.
Time　　　　　　　Jul 13, 1981　　p. 18

Our forgotten wounded.
Life　　　　　　　May 22, 1970　p. 24

VIETNAMESE IN THE UNITED STATES

Troubled odyssey of Vietnamese
fishermen.
National Geographic Sep 1981　　　p. 378

VIOLENCE

Violence goes mainstream. Movies,
music, books—are there any limits left?
Newsweek　　　　　Apr 1, 1991　　p. 46

Special report: Everyday violence against
women.
Ms.　　　　　　　Sep 1990　　　p. 33

The epidemic of violent crime.
Newsweek　　　　　Mar 23, 1981　p. 46

The curse of violent crime.
Time　　　　　　　Mar 23, 1981　p. 16

VIOLENCE IN MOTION PICTURES

Violence goes mainstream. Movies,
music, books—are there any limits left?
Newsweek　　　　　Apr 1, 1991　　p. 46

VIRTUAL REALITY

Virtual reality: Life in a computer.
Omni　　　　　　Jan 1991　　　p. 16

VIRUSES

Viruses. Keys to life and death. Aids:
new research, new danger.
Time　　　　　　　Nov 3, 1986　p. 66

Man vs. virus. Fighting the flu.
Newsweek　　　　　Jan 20, 1969　p. 62

Medicine's newest discoveries about
viruses—and how your body fights them.
Life　　　　　　　Feb 18, 1966　p. 56

Medicine gains on viruses.
Time　　　　　　　Nov 17, 1961　p. 60

Tricky viruses on the loose. (A special
medicine report on the ever-changing
menace.)
Newsweek　　　　　Jan 25, 1960　p. 51

VISION

How we really see. The multi-screen
theater in our brain.
Discover　　　　　May 1991　　　p. 50

How we see color. New clues from the
brain.
Discover   Dec 1988   p. 52

VITAMINS

The vitamin diet that makes you young.
Omni   Apr 1982   p. 68

VO NGUYEN GIAP

The big red blitz. North Viet Nam's
General Giap.
Time   May 15, 1972 p. 24

The other side's dilemma. North Viet
Nam's General Giap.
Time   Jun 17, 1966 p. 32

VOLCANOES

The volcano experiment. To forecast
deadly eruptions, scientists are wiring up
the world's most dangerous mountains.
Discover   Jun 1991   p. 60

Volcano! Fiery messages from inside the
earth.
Discover   Jun 1984   p. 88

VOLCANOES - COLOMBIA

Colombia's agony.
Time   Nov 25, 1985 p. 46

VOLCANOES - UNITED STATES

Mount St. Helens. Mountain with a death
wish.
National Geographic Jan 1981   p. 3

The big bang.
Newsweek   Jun 2, 1980   p. 22

The big blowup.
Time   Jun 2, 1980   p. 26

VOLCKER, PAUL

Will he stay? Paul Volcker's term at the
Federal Reserve has four months to go.
Suddenly reappointment looks much
more likely.
Business Week   Mar 30, 1987 p. 76

The second most powerful man in
America. A revealing profile of federal
reserve chairman Paul Volcker.
Newsweek   Feb 24, 1986 p. 46

The fed's plan for economic recovery. Is
Chairman Paul Volcker aiming too low?
Business Week   Dec 13, 1982 p. 90

VOLKSWAGEN

Can VW regain its magic touch? The auto
giant and Germany share deep problems.
Business Week   Aug 6, 1984   p. 50

VOLUNTEERS

The new volunteers. America's unsung
heroes. A talk with Barbara Bush.
Newsweek   Jul 10, 1989 p. 36

America needs you. The push for
voluntary national service.
U.S. News   Feb 13, 1989 p. 20

The do-gooders.
Time   Dec 27, 1971 p. 12

VOTER REGISTRATION

Voter registration.
Congressional Digest Apr 1990   p. 98

VOYAGER (AIRPLANE)

The incredible Voyager. Heading around
the world without a stop.
Newsweek   Dec 29, 1986 p. 34

VOYAGES

In the wake of Sindbad.
National Geographic Jul 1982   p. 2

VOYAGES AROUND THE WORLD

Around the world in the 'Gipsy Moth.'
One man's stirring conquest of the sea.
Sir Francis Chichester's own story and
pictures.
Life   Jun 9, 1967   p. 28

W.R. GRACE & COMPANY

J. Peter Grace. Building a new company Wall Street ignors.
Business Week   Oct 5, 1981   p. 80

WAGE-PRICE CONTROLS

The freeze. What next?
Newsweek   Jun 25, 1973   p. 62

Living with controls.
Newsweek   Oct 18, 1971   p. 26

Fight over the freeze. AFL-CIO's George Meany.
Newsweek   Sep 6, 1971   p. 46

Nixon's economic gamble.
Time   Aug 30, 1971   p. 4

Game plan for the dollar.
Life   Aug 27, 1971   p. 20

WAGES AND SALARIES

1990 career guide. Best jobs for the future. Exclusive salary survey.
U.S. News   Sep 25, 1989   p. 60

Are you making what you're worth? What others earn in 120 jobs. Strategies for getting more.
U.S. News   Jun 23, 1986   p. 60

WAITZ, GRETE

Staying fit for life! How Grete Waitz is getting better.
Ms.   Aug 1985   p. 28

WALESA, LECH

Man of the year. Poland's Lech Walesa.
Time   Jan 4, 1982   p. 12

Challenge to Moscow.
Newsweek   Dec 8, 1980   p. 40

WALKER, ALICE

Gloria Steinem and Mary Helen Washington on Alice Walker.
Ms.   Jun 1982   p. 35

WALKER FAMILY ESPIONAGE CASE

The spy scandal grows. "There are very serious losses." -Caspar Weinberger.
Time   Jun 17, 1985   p. 18

A family of spies. How much did they tell Moscow? The epidemic of Soviet espionage.
Newsweek   Jun 10, 1985   p. 32

WALL STREET

See STOCK MARKET

WALLACE, GEORGE

George Wallace fights back.
Life   Nov 24, 1972   p. 38

The Wallace shooting. Cornelia Wallace embraces her husband.
Life   May 26, 1972   p. 4

Democrats in disorder. The wild card of politics '72. George Wallace.
Newsweek   Mar 27, 1972   p. 22

The revolt of the right: Wallace and LeMay.
Time   Oct 18, 1968   p. 15

The third party threat. Alabama's George C. Wallace.
Newsweek   Sep 16, 1968   p. 25

The spoiler from the South. Wallace—coming on fast. Nixon and Reagan try to slow him down but polls show Wallace in the saddle at home and raiding North.
Life   Aug 2, 1968   p. 17

Alabama: Civil rights battlefield.
Governor Wallace.
Time   Sep 27, 1963   p. 17

WALRUSES

Seals and their kin.
National Geographic Apr 1987   p. 475

WALT DISNEY COMPANY

Why is this mouse smiling? Because
Michael Eisner's magic has transformed
Disney into a $3 billion kingdom.
Time   Apr 25, 1988   p. 66

Disney's magic. It's back! Corporate
profits are surging as Chairman Michael
Eisner launches new theme parks and
broadens the company's role in movies
and television.
Business Week   Mar 9, 1987   p. 62

WALT, LEW

Big Lew Walt. The Marines' Marine on
Vietnam's hottest spot.
Life   May 26, 1967   p. 77

WALTERS, BARBARA

Today's woman. Barbara Walters.
Newsweek   May 6, 1974   p. 56

WANG LABORATORIES, INC.

Wang Labs' run for a second billion.
One-man rule will fade into professional
management.
Business Week   May 17, 1982   p. 100

WAR

Wars without end.
Newsweek   Jun 28, 1982   p. 20

WAR EMERGENCY POWERS

The War Powers Act and the Persian
Gulf.
Congressional Digest Dec 1987   p. 289

WARHOL, ANDY

Art for money's sake. On the block: The
Warhol collection. The booming art
market.
Newsweek   Apr 18, 1988   p. 60

WARREN COMMISSION

The Warren Commission. Probing
Kennedy's death.
Time   Feb 14, 1964   p. 16

WARREN COMMISSION REPORT

A matter of reasonable doubt. Did
Oswald act alone? Amid controversy
over the Warren Report Governor
Connally examines for LIFE the Kennedy
assassination film frame by frame.
Life   Nov 25, 1966   p. 38

The assassination. The Warren
Commission report.
Newsweek   Oct 5, 1964   p. 32

The Warren report. How the commission
pieced together the evidence. Told by
one of its members.
Life   Oct 2, 1964   p. 40

The Warren Commission: No conspiracy,
domestic or foreign. Lee Harvey Oswald.
Time   Oct 2, 1964   p. 45

WARREN, EARL

The Warren Court: Ten momentous
years.
Newsweek   May 11, 1964   p. 24

Bigger voice for big cities. The Supreme
Court decision. Chief Justice Earl Warren.
Newsweek   Apr 9, 1962   p. 29

WARSHIPS

Are big ships doomed? The Falklands
fallout.
Newsweek   May 17, 1982   p. 28

WASHINGTON (D.C.)

Washington vs. New York. Why they
hate each other. Why America hates
them both.
Newsweek   Jun 20, 1988   p. 16

Washington. Gold coast on the Potomac.
U.S. News   Aug 28, 1978   p. 18

**WASHINGTON PUBLIC POWER SUPPLY
SYSTEM**

The fallout from 'whoops.' A legal
precedent scares the bond market.
Business Week   Jul 11, 1983   p. 80

WASHINGTON (STATE)

The Pacific Northwest. Washington
Governor Dixy Lee Ray.
Time   Dec 12, 1977   p. 26

Watergate dynamite. How much damage?
Time May 28, 1973 p. 20

Indicted. John Mitchell.
Newsweek May 21, 1973 p. 16

The inquest begins. John Mitchell.
Time May 21, 1973 p. 16

Can he stay afloat?
Newsweek May 14, 1973 p. 28

How much did he know?
Time May 14, 1973 p. 17

The White House in turmoil.
Newsweek May 7, 1973 p. 22

Nixon and Watergate.
Newsweek Apr 30, 1973 p. 16

Watergate breaks wide open.
Time Apr 30, 1973 p. 11

Showdown over secrecy. Senate v. White House. Watergate prober Sam Ervin.
Time Apr 16, 1973 p. 10

The Watergate mess.
Newsweek Apr 2, 1973 p. 14

WATERLOO, BATTLE OF, 1815
Waterloo. The great battle 150 years ago. Move by move—how the victory hung in the balance.
Life Jun 11, 1965 p. 68

WATT, JAMES
Interior's James Watt. Hero or villain?
U.S. News Jun 6, 1983 p. 51

Watt's land rush. Digging up the last frontier? Interior Secretary James Watt.
Newsweek Jun 29, 1981 p. 22

WATTLETON, FAYE
Repro woman. Pro-choice champion Faye Wattleton talks tough.
Ms. Oct 1989 p. 50

WATTS (LOS ANGELES, CALIFORNIA)
Watts still seething. 1965—When the riot cry was 'Burn, baby, burn!' 1966—Why the ghetto today is close to flashpoint.
Life Jul 15, 1966 p. 34

WATTS RIOTS
See RIOTS - WATTS (CALIFORNIA)

WAYNE, JOHN
John Wayne. Memories of a G-rated cowboy.
Life Jan 28, 1972 p. 42

John Wayne.
Time Aug 8, 1969 p. 53

A choice of heroes. Dusty and the Duke.
Life Jul 11, 1969 p. 36

After a bout with cancer John Wayne is back in action.
Life May 7, 1965 p. 69

WEALTH
The new way to get rich. Never before have so many people stood to inherit so much money.
U.S. News May 7, 1990 p. 26

Wealth. Can you ever have enough? The death of the leisure class.
Psychology Today Apr 1989 p. 27

How to measure your financial health. Saving: 12 ways to build a fortune. Retirement: What to do now to quit early. Real estate: How to make your home pay off. Investing: Risk-taking strategies that work.
U.S. News Jun 8, 1987 p. 52

Flaunting wealth. It's back in style.
U.S. News Sep 21, 1981 p. 61

WEAPONS
The new science of war. High-tech hardware: How many lives can it save? Countdown to a ground strike.
Newsweek Feb 18, 1991 p. 38

Best and worst weapons. The winners and losers in the military's arsenal of planes, missiles, tanks and submarines.
U.S. News Jul 10, 1989 p. 22

'Smart weapons.' How they see and kill. What's ahead: Computer-generated imagery displayed in a U.S. pilot's helmet.
U.S. News Mar 16, 1987 p. 26

The MX missile.
Congressional Digest Jun 1985 p. 163

Killer electronic weaponry. Fighting in Lebanon and the Falklands opens a new era in weapons.
Business Week   Sep 20, 1982   p. 74

WEATHER
See CLIMATE

WEATHER FORECASTING
Predicting storms. How scientists are improving our weather forecasts.
U.S. News   Jul 24, 1989   p. 48

WEAVER, ROBERT
First Negro in the cabinet. Trying to save the cities. Secretary Weaver.
Time   Mar 4, 1966   p. 29

WEAVER, SIGOURNEY
Horrors! The summer's scariest movie. Sigourney Weaver and she-monster in *Aliens*.
Time   Jul 28, 1986   p. 54

WEBBER, ANDREW LLOYD
Magician of the musical. After the triumphs of Evita and Cats, Andrew Lloyd Webber brings *Phantom* to Broadway.
Time   Jan 18, 1988   p. 54

WEBSTER, WILLIAM H. (INTERVIEW)
Webster's CIA. An exclusive interview with the new director. Cleaning up Casey's mess.
Newsweek   Oct 12, 1987   p. 24

WEDDINGS
The weddings. A Kennedy gala. A royal pageant. Memorable moments.
Life   Sep 1986   p. 38

Weddings around the world.
Life   Jun 16, 1961   p. 36

WEIGHT LIFTING
Women muscle in. They join men in body-building, the sport of the '80s.
Life   Oct 1982   p. 46

WEILL, SANFORD
The return of Sandy Weill. He built Shearson but ran into trouble at American Express. Now he's tapping Primerica's money to attempt a big Wall Street comeback.
Business Week   Dec 4, 1989   p. 88

American Express: The golden plan. Now it has to make its financial empire work.
Business Week   Apr 30, 1984   p. 118

WEINBERG, ROBERT
The year in science. Scientist of the year. [Robert Weinberg]
Discover   Jan 1983   p. 62

WELCH, JACK
GE's Jack Welch. How good a manager is he?
Business Week   Dec 14, 1987   p. 92

The dynamo. Jack Welch is often described in three words: tough, tough, and tough. He's determined to transform GE. So far, so good.
Business Week   Jun 30, 1986   p. 62

WELCH, RAQUEL
Raquel Welch. Fit, firm & 41, she is Broadway's newest bombshell.
Life   Jul 1982   p. 74

Raquel. On skates as a derby demon.
Life   Jun 2, 1972   p. 48

Raquel Welch. Can today's sex symbol find happiness as Myra Breckinridge.
Time   Nov 28, 1969   p. 85

WELD, TUESDAY
Tuesday Weld. A star learns to be as young as she really is.
Life   Jul 26, 1963   p. 47

WELFARE
See PUBLIC WELFARE

WEST GERMANY
See GERMANY (WEST)

WEST, MAE
Mae West going strong at 75.
Life   Apr 18, 1969   p. 60

WEST POINT (MILITARY ACADEMY)
What price honor? The West Point scandal.
Time   Jun 7, 1976   p. 18

WESTERN STATES
The war for the West. Fighting for the soul of America's mythic land.
Newsweek   Sep 30, 1991   p. 18

WILDLIFE CONSERVATION

A shameful harvest. America's illegal wildlife trade.
National Geographic Sep 1991   p. 106

The natural world of Aldo Leopold.
National Geographic Nov 1981   p. 682

WILDLIFE CONSERVATION - CHINA

Secrets of the giant panda.
National Geographic Mar 1986   p. 284

Pandas in the wild.
National Geographic Dec 1981   p. 735

WILLIAMS, ROBIN

Funny man. The comic genius of Robin Williams.
Newsweek   Jul 7, 1986   p. 52

WILLIAMS, TENNESSEE

Tennessee Williams.
Time   Mar 9, 1962   p. 53

WILLIS, BRUCE

Sly and sexy. TV's fun couple. Moonlighting's Bruce Willis and Cybill Shepherd.
Newsweek   Sep 8, 1986   p. 46

WILLS, MAURY

Wild west Dodgers.
Life   Sep 28, 1962   p. 49

WILSON, CHARLES KEMMONS

The man with 300,000 beds. Innkeeper Kemmons Wilson.
Time   Jun 12, 1972   p. 77

WILSON, FLIP

On the road with Flip Wilson.
Life   Aug 4, 1972   p. 38

TV's first black superstar. Comedian Flip Wilson.
Time   Jan 31, 1972   p. 56

WILSON, GARY

The fly boys. Finance aces Gary Wilson and Al Checchi won Northwest Airlines. Now what? More deals, of course.
Business Week   Mar 5, 1990   p. 54

WILSON, HAROLD

The surprising socialist. Britain's Harold Wilson.
Time   Apr 30, 1965   p. 35

Britain's Harold Wilson. Will Labor win?
Newsweek   Sep 28, 1964   p. 44

What Labor offers England. Britain's Harold Wilson.
Time   Oct 11, 1963   p. 34

Britain's Harold Wilson. The next Prime Minister?
Newsweek   Apr 15, 1963   p. 42

WINE AND WINEMAKING

American wine: There's gold in them thar grapes.
Time   Nov 27, 1972   p. 76

WINE INDUSTRY

Creating a mass market for wine.
Business Week   Mar 15, 1982   p. 108

WINFREY, OPRAH

Oprah, Inc. Mogul with a mission.
Ms.   Nov 1988   p. 50

WINGER, DEBRA

Wild Debra Winger. Why the star of 'An Officer and a Gentleman' is such an outrageous free spirit.
Life   May 1983   p. 110

WINTER SPORTS

Excitement on the ice.
Life   Jan 19, 1962   p. 54

WIVES OF POLITICIANS

The ordeal of political wives.
Time   Oct 7, 1974   p. 15

The wives of Washington. Martha Mitchell.
Time   Nov 30, 1970   p. 31

WIVES OF THE PRESIDENTS

The Silver Fox. Barbara Bush brings a refreshing new style to the White House.
Time   Jan 23, 1989   p. 22

White House co-star. Nancy Reagan's growing role.
Time   Jan 14, 1985   p. 24

The First Lady's world.
Newsweek   Dec 21, 1981   p. 22

Nancy Reagan's role.
U.S. News   Jun 1, 1981   p. 46

The President's partner.
Newsweek   Nov 5, 1979   p. 36

The First Lady.
Newsweek   Dec 28, 1964   p. 11

Lady Bird Johnson.
Time   Aug 28, 1964   p. 20

Jacqueline Kennedy.
Newsweek   Jan 1, 1962   p. 31

Jacqueline Kennedy.
Time   Jan 20, 1961   p. 18

WIVES, RUNAWAY
   See RUNAWAY ADULTS

WODAABE TRIBESPEOPLE
   Niger's Wodaabe: "People of the taboo."
   National Geographic Oct 1983   p. 483

WOLVES
   Return of the wolf. The fabled animal is
   back, scaring ranchers and mobilizing
   environmentalists. Caution: 'Wolf-dogs'
   may be hazardous.
   Newsweek   Aug 12, 1991   p. 44

   At home with the arctic wolf.
   National Geographic May 1987   p. 562

WOMEN
   The daughter track. The average
   American woman spends 17 years raising
   children and 18 years helping aging
   parents.
   Newsweek   Jul 16, 1990   p. 48

   Women face the '90s. In the '80s they
   tried to have it all. Now they've just plain
   had it. Is there a future for feminism?
   Time   Dec 4, 1989   p. 80

   The women (and men) who made us
   laugh, cheer, cry, and cringe in '88.
   Celebrating our Women of the Year.
   Ms.   Feb 1989   p. 67

   Women of the year.
   Ms.   Jan 1988   p. 41

Are women fed up? A hotly disputed
Hite report says yes - and that men are to
blame.
Time   Oct 12, 1987   p. 68

Women of the year.
Ms.   Jan 1987   p. 39

How women are changing the way
America lives. Life stories about home,
work, love, community & commitment.
Ms.   Apr 1986   p. 33

Women of the Year.
Ms.   Jan 1986   p. 31

Women of the year.
Ms.   Jan 1985   p. 39

She's come a long way - or has she?
U.S. News   Aug 6, 1984   p. 44

Superiority of the female brain.
Omni   Aug 1983   p. 26

Women and power. The drives. The
hang-ups. The joys. The price.
Ms.   Dec 1982   p. 39

Coming on strong. The new ideal of
beauty.
Time   Aug 30, 1982   p. 72

American women. The climb to equality.
Time   Jul 12, 1982   p. 20

Liberated women. How they're changing
American life.
U.S. News   Jun 7, 1976   p. 46

The American woman. On the move -
but where?
U.S. News   Dec 8, 1975   p. 54

The American woman.
Time   Mar 20, 1972   p. 26

The 'Woman Problem'—then and now.
Life   Aug 13, 1971   p. 40

One-third of a nation. U.S. suburbia, 1960.
Time   Jun 20, 1960   p. 14

WOMEN - CONFERENCES
   After Houston: What next for women?
   Time   Dec 5, 1977   p. 18

Corporate women. What it takes to get to the top.
Business Week   Jun 22, 1987   p. 72

Fast-track kids. A new generation is rising in the ranks of Corporate America. Here are some of the best and the brightest—their attitudes, goals, and problems—and how they'll reshape big business.
Business Week   Nov 10, 1986 p. 90

You don't have to dress (like a man) for success.
Ms.   Apr 1984   p. 35

WOMEN IN HATE GROUPS

A special report. Women in the Klan, Aryan Nation, skinheads. Why?
Ms.   Mar 1991   p. 20

WOMEN IN MOTION PICTURES

Why Thelma & Louise strikes a nerve.
Time   Jun 24, 1991   p. 52

New heroines. The changing role of women in films.
Psychology Today   Jan 1983   p. 18

Hollywood's new heroines. Jane Fonda in 'Julia.'
Newsweek   Oct 10, 1977   p. 78

WOMEN IN POLITICS

Raising hell in Arizona. The women who whipped Governor Mecham.
Ms.   Jun 1988   p. 44

Who's crying now? The unsinkable Pat Schroeder.
Ms.   Feb 1988   p. 44

Will a woman make the difference?
Ms.   Oct 1984   p. 43

Women in 1984: Political time bomb.
Ms.   Jul 1984   p. 51

And for vice president...why not a woman?
Time   Jun 4, 1984   p. 18

Women in politics. Ella Grasso for Governor.
Newsweek   Nov 4, 1974   p. 20

Women in politics. How are they doing? Where are they going?
Life   Jun 9, 1972   p. 46

Women in politics. Maine's senate race. Smith v. Cormier.
Time   Sep 5, 1960   p. 13

WOMEN IN TELEVISION

How women are changing TV. New power on and off the screen.
Newsweek   Mar 13, 1989   p. 48

Are women reporters changing the news? A major investigation of the power and the puffery behind TV news stardom.
Ms.   Dec 1984   p. 45

TV's Superwomen.
Time   Nov 22, 1976   p. 67

WOMEN IN THE ARMED SERVICES

Should women fight to kill?
Newsweek   Aug 5, 1991   p. 22

Women warriors. Sharing the danger.
Newsweek   Sep 10, 1990   p. 14

Academy women. Ready to take command.
U.S.News   May 26, 1980   p. 32

Women in combat. Closer than you think.
U.S.News   Mar 3, 1980   p. 30

Women in the military. Should they be drafted?
Newsweek   Feb 18, 1980   p. 34

Women in uniform. Can they save the military?
U.S. News   Jun 5, 1978   p. 31

WOMEN ROCK MUSICIANS

Rock and roll. Woman power.
Newsweek   Mar 4, 1985   p. 48

Rock women. Pride and passion. Joni Mitchell.
Time   Dec 16, 1974   p. 63

WOMEN SCIENTISTS

A celebration of women in science.
Discover   Dec 1991   p. 36

WOMEN'S MOVEMENT

15th anniversary issue!
Ms.   Jul 1987   p. 1

13th anniversary issue.
Ms.   Jul 1985   p. 35

Women–A new superpower? If women had a foreign policy... Getting ready for the UN Conference in Nairobi. Revolutionary surprises: Voices from Cuba and Chile.
Ms.   Mar 1985   p. 41

Women in 1984: Political time bomb.
Ms.   Jul 1984   p. 51

The young feminists. A new generation speaks for itself.
Ms.   Apr 1983   p. 43

Our 10th anniversary.
Ms.   Jul 1982   p. 77

After Houston: What next for women?
Time   Dec 5, 1977   p. 18

The American woman.
Time   Mar 20, 1972   p. 26

Women arise. The revolution that will affect everybody.
Life   Sep 4, 1970   p. 16

The politics of sex. Kate Millett of women's lib.
Time   Aug 31, 1970   p. 16

Women in revolt.
Newsweek   Mar 23, 1970   p. 71

What role for the educated woman?
Newsweek   Jun 13, 1966   p. 68

WONDER, STEVIE

Music's wonder man. Stevie Wonder.
Newsweek   Oct 28, 1974   p. 59

WOOD, NATALIE

Natalie Wood: Star into actress.
Newsweek   Feb 26, 1962   p. 54

WOODS, ROSE MARY

Rose Mary's boo-boo.
Newsweek   Dec 10, 1973   p. 26

The secretary and the tapes. Rose Mary Woods.
Time   Dec 10, 1973   p. 15

WOODWARD, BOB

The secret wars of the CIA by Bob Woodward. Exclusive book excerpts.
Newsweek   Oct 5, 1987   p. 44

WOOL

Wool. Fabric of history.
National Geographic May 1988   p. 552

WORK

How to stop working like a dog and still get more done. The techniques, the tools, the mindset you need to work smarter, not harder.
Psychology Today   Mar 1989   p. 33

WORK FORCE

Human capital. The decline of America's work force. The nation's ability to compete is threatened by inadequate investment in our most important resource: People.
Business Week   Sep 19, 1988   p. 100

The emerging power of the new collar class. "We're the backbone of America."
U.S. News   Sep 16, 1985   p. 59

A revolution in work rules. New job flexibility boosts productivity.
Business Week   May 16, 1983   p. 100

New breed of workers. Prosperous. Restless. Demanding.
U.S. News   Sep 3, 1979   p. 35

Blue collar power.
Time   Nov 9, 1970   p. 68

WORKING MOTHERS

The mommy track. Coping with career and kids in Corporate America.
Business Week   Mar 20, 1989   p. 126

Making it work. America's mothers. How women balance the demands of jobs and children.
Newsweek   Mar 31, 1986   p. 46

Leading two lives. Women at work and home.
Newsweek   May 19, 1980   p. 72

WORKING PARENTS

Working parents. How to give your kids what they need. By Dr. T. Berry Brazelton.
Newsweek   Feb 13, 1989   p. 66

Two-career couples. How they do it. The commuting alternative, the social life squeeze & other trade-offs.
Ms.   Jun 1984   p. 39

WORLD POLITICS

Prince Philip describes a violent world ahead.
U.S. News   Nov 22, 1976   p. 40

WORLD WAR, 1914-1918

Lusitania. New evidence on the 'unprovoked' sinking that dragged us toward war.
Life   Oct 13, 1972   p. 58

The First World War.
Life   Mar 13, 1964   p. 42

WORLD WAR, 1939-1945

Defying Hitler. World War II. 1940. America on the eve of war. The air battle for Britain.
U.S. News   Aug 27, 1990   p. 44

World War II. When darkness fell. September 1939 Germany invades Poland.
Time   Aug 28, 1989   p. 28

Hitler's war against the world.
U.S. News   Aug 28, 1989   p. 32

Ghosts of war in the South Pacific.
National Geographic Apr 1988   p. 424

The legacies of World War II. Power and prosperity. Life in the Nuclear Age.
U.S. News   Aug 5, 1985   p. 38

May 8, 1945. "Never a greater day." But Reagan opens old wounds.
Time   Apr 29, 1985   p. 18

The men who hit the beaches. Remembering D-Day, 1944.
Newsweek   Jun 11, 1984   p. 18

D-Day. Forty years after the great crusade.
Time   May 28, 1984   p. 10

Khrushchev remembers World War II. The great battles. His fear of execution. Stalin's cowardice.
Life   Dec 4, 1970   p. 48

WORLD'S FAIR, 1962

Out of this world fair in Seattle.
Life   May 4, 1962   p. 30

Fabulous fair in Seattle.
Life   Feb 9, 1962   p. 74

WORLD'S FAIR, 1964

A confidential guide to the New York Fair.
Time   Jun 5, 1964   p. 40

The world's fair opens.
Life   May 1, 1964   p. 26

World's Fair preview. New York's Robert Moses.
Newsweek   Jan 13, 1964   p. 43

WORLD'S FAIR, 1967

Tomorrow soars in at the fair. Expo 67.
Life   Apr 28, 1967   p. 32

WORLD'S FAIR, 1970

Japan. Salesman to the world. Expo '70 in color.
Newsweek   Mar 9, 1970   p. 64

Japan shows off at Expo '70.
Time   Mar 2, 1970   p. 20

WRIGHT, JIM

How Congress really works. Jim Wright and the new capitol culture.
Newsweek   Apr 24, 1989   p. 26

WYETH, ANDREW

Andrew Wyeth's secret obsession. For 15 years he drew the same woman and hid the pictures in an attic. Now they've been sold for millions.
Newsweek   Aug 18, 1986   p. 48

Andrew Wyeth's stunning secret. The Helga paintings: a portfolio.
Time   Aug 18, 1986   p. 48

"I want to show Americans what America is like." Painter Andrew Wyeth.
Time   Dec 27, 1963   p. 44

WYETH, ANDREW (FAMILY)

The Wyeth family.
National Geographic Jul 1991   p. 78

An American vision: Three generations of
Wyeth art.
USA Today   Jan 1988   p. 36

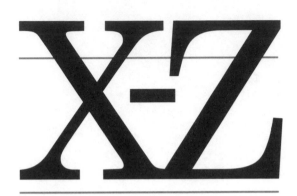

XEROX CORP.

The new lean, mean Xerox. Fending off the Japanese.
Business Week   Oct 12, 1981   p. 126

Copy machine boom. Xerox President Joseph C. Wilson.
Newsweek   Nov 8, 1965   p. 84

YACHTS AND YACHTING

Luxury and languor of Riviera yachting. Aboard some of the world's most elegant yachts.
Life   Jul 9, 1965   p. 46

YAMASAKI, MINORU

Architect Minoru Yamasaki.
Time   Jan 18, 1963   p. 54

YELLOWSTONE NATIONAL PARK

Yellowstone. Crown jewel of the National Park system.
USA Today   Sep 1989   p. 34

The great Yellowstone fires.
National Geographic   Feb 1989   p. 255

YELTSIN, BORIS

The year of Yeltsin. Decade of democracy.
Newsweek   Dec 30, 1991   p. 18

Yeltsin's triumph. How the botched coup will speed Soviet reform.
Business Week   Sep 2, 1991   p. 20

The second Russian Revolution.
Newsweek   Sep 2, 1991   p. 18

The Russian Revolution. August 1991.
Time   Sep 2, 1991   p. 18

Russia's maverick. Boris Yeltsin, the bad boy of Soviet politics, battles Gorbachev in a crucial vote this week.
Time   Mar 25, 1991   p. 26

The Yeltsin challenge. After the summit.
Newsweek   Jun 11, 1990   p. 14

YLVISAKER, WILLIAM

Bill Ylvisaker bets his company on electronics.
Business Week   Nov 2, 1981   p. 86

YORTY, SAM

Mayor Yorty.
Time   Sep 2, 1966   p. 14

YOUNG, ANDREW

The Andrew Young affair.
Newsweek   Aug 27, 1979   p. 14

The outspoken Andrew Young. At the U.N.
Newsweek   Mar 28, 1977   p. 24

YOUNG, JOHN

Can John Young redesign Hewlett-Packard.
Business Week   Dec 6, 1982   p. 72

YOUNG & RUBICAM INC.

Battle in ad land. Will Alex Kroll keep Young & Rubicam on top?
Business Week   Apr 4, 1988   p. 74

YOUNG, WHITNEY

"You've got to give us some victories." Urban League's Whitney Young.
Time   Aug 11, 1967   p. 12

YOUNG WOMEN

The new beauties. Margaux Hemingway
Time   Jun 16, 1975   p. 34

YOUTH

Twentysomething. Laid back, late blooming or just lost? Overshadowed by the baby boomers, America's next generation has a hard act to follow.
Time   Jul 16, 1990   p. 56

Adolescence. Thank goodness, somehow we survive.
Psychology Today   Sep 1987   p. 28

America's youth in search of a cause.
U.S. News   Apr 16, 1984   p. 31

Troubled teenagers.
U.S. News   Dec 14, 1981   p. 40

Yesterday's rebels grow up.
U.S. News   Mar 27, 1978   p. 38

America's youth. Angry...bored...or just confused?
U.S. News   Jul 18, 1977   p. 18

A new generation. Where it's heading.
U.S. News   Sep 6, 1976   p. 45

Summer '70. Young Americans abroad.
Newsweek   Aug 10, 1970   p. 44

California girls spangle the beach.
Life   Jul 10, 1970   p. 46

The youth communes. New way of living confronts the U.S.
Life   Jul 18, 1969   p. 16

Young American nomads abroad.
Life   Jul 19, 1968   p. 20

The teen-agers.
Time   Mar 21, 1966   p. 57

Today's teen-agers.
Time   Jan 29, 1965   p. 56

YOUTH - ATTITUDES

Do you know what your children are listening to?
U.S. News   Oct 28, 1985   p. 46

Man of the year. Twenty-five and under.
Time   Jan 6, 1967   p. 18

The teen-agers.
Newsweek   Mar 21, 1966   p. 57

YOUTH - EMPLOYMENT

The proposed subminimum wage for youth.
Congressional Digest Apr 1985   p. 99

The proposed American Conservation Corps.
Congressional Digest May 1983   p. 131

YOUTH - SEXUAL BEHAVIOR

Safe sex. What you and your children should know.
Newsweek   Dec 9, 1991   p. 52

Kids and contraceptives. A moral dilemma: How to prevent teen pregnancy - and AIDS.
Newsweek   Feb 16, 1987   p. 54

Teenage temptation. Sex & consequences.
Psychology Today   Oct 1986   p. 22

Teen sex. Too much, too soon?
Ms.   Jul 1983   p. 42

Mother daughter sex-talk...do feminists do it better?
Ms.   May 1982   p. 41

Teen age sex. The new morality hits home.
Newsweek   Sep 1, 1980   p. 48

Sex & the teenager.
Time   Aug 21, 1972   p. 34

High school pregnancy.
Life   Apr 2, 1971   p. 34

YOUTH - SOVIET UNION

Russia's new generation. Soviet poet Evtushenko.
Time   Apr 13, 1962   p. 28

YOUTH - UNITED STATES

Teenage America. Saturday night: The scene. The dizzying whirl of a high school senior. The anguish of an eighth grader's abortion.
Life   Mar 1986   p. 28

YOUTH - VOTING

How will youth vote?
Newsweek   Oct 25, 1971   p. 28

Chronology

OF COVER STORIES

1960 – 1991

User's Guide to the Chronology

The Chronology is a tool for those who wish to browse and get a feel for what captured the attention of the media and the public at a given time. The Chronology contains the three news magazines: *Newsweek, Time,* and *U.S. News and World Report.*

The stories are listed in chronological order, side by side, so the news for a week can be seen by reading the titles across the page. A story can easily be followed in this way as it develops through several months or even years.

There are several characteristics the user will note when browsing through the stories. On most covers, the subject of the story is told in both words and picture. Sometimes they work together so that the full meaning can be understood only when the cover is seen. For example, *Time* ran a cover story entitled, He's 50! Unless the reader sees that Superman appears on the cover, there is no way of guessing who just turned 50. Wherever the words by themselves do not convey the meaning, the subject or focus of the story has been put in brackets.

Occasionally, combined issues were published covering a two-week period. The cover story of the single issue is listed under the dates for both weeks. *U.S. News* consistently does this at the end of each year. Others do it on rare occasions, such as a presidential election.

At times, the cover story title exceeded the three or four lines allotted to each citation. Wherever a title has been cropped, an ellipsis(...) appears at the end of the line.

The citations in the Chronology have been abbreviated to make the month-by-month presentation clear and readable. Full titles and page numbers always appear in the Subject Index, making it the best tool for direct access to the cover stories. The Chronology has been created to reflect the time period that surrounds an event and to convey it to the reader.

CHRONOLOGY

Newsweek **January 1980**	*Time* **January 1980**	*U.S. News* **January 1980**
A star for the '80s. Meryl Streep. Jan 7 '80	Man of the year. Ayatullah Khomeini. Jan 7 '80	Outlook '80. Recession. How deep, how long? Elections. Another term for Carter? World. More trouble brewing? Money... Jan 7 '80
A new Cold War. [Afghanistan-Russian invasion] Jan 14 '80	Moscow's bold challenge. [Afghanistan-Russian Invasion] Jan 14 '80	Detente. 1972–1980. Jan 14 '80
America's get-tough strategy. Jan 21 '80	Grain as a weapon. Who winds. Who loses. Jan 21 '80	U.S. economy in '80s. Can we meet the challenge? Jan 21 '80
Should we boycott the Olympics? Jan 28 '80	Squeezing the Soviets. U.S. anger. U.N. condemnation. Olympic threat. Jan 28 '80	America's lonely role. [Soviet Union and the United States] Jan 28 '80

Newsweek **February 1980**	*Time* **February 1980**	*U.S. News* **February 1980**
Bush breaks out of the pack. Feb 4 '80	Taking charge. "An assault will be repelled by any means necessary..." [Soviet Union and the U.S.] Feb 4 '80	It's Carter's turn to cope with Russia. Feb 4 '80
Children of divorce. Feb 11 '80	Good as gold. Lake Placid. [Winter Olympics] Feb 11 '80	How strong is Russia? How prepared is U.S.? Feb 11 '80
Women in the military. Should they be drafted? Feb 18 '80	Operation Abscam. The FBI stings Congress. Feb 18 '80	ABC's of how a President is chosen. Feb 18 '80
A break in the deadlock. Feb 25 '80	The $8,000,000 man. TV news explosion. Feb 25 '80	Our new elite. For better or for worse? Feb 25 '80

Newsweek **March 1980**	*Time* **March 1980**	*U.S. News* **March 1980**
Is inflation out of control? Mar 3 '80	Who is this man? The many faces of Peter Sellers. Mar 3 '80	Women is combat. Closer than you think. Mar 3 '80
Back in the saddle again. Mar 10 '80	Ronnie's romp! And now the real race is on. Mar 10' 80	Washington's lawyers. Rise of the power brokers. Mar 10 '80
DNA's new miracles. How science is retooling genes. Mar 17 '80	Diplomacy in crisis. Hostages in Bogota. Suspense in Iran. Fiasco at the U.N. Mar 17 '80	America's invisible millionaires. A spectacular boom. Mar 17 '80
Carter tilts at inflation. Mar 24 '80	Carter vs. inflation. The President's demand: "Discipline...discipline... discipline." Mar 24 '80	Economy out of control. Mar 24 '80
The credit tumble. Mar 31 '80	Interferon. The IF drug for cancer. Mar 31 '80	Race to top. Is it over? Mar 31 '80

MAGAZINE TITLE

MONTH AND YEAR

SUBJECT HEADING
Bracketed heading used when the subject is not clear from the title

COVER STORY TITLE AND WEEK

Newsweek **January 1960**	*Time* **January 1960**	*U.S. News* **1960**
Rising Phoenix: 'Miracle' in Arizona. Jan 4 '60	Man of the year. Dwight D. Eisenhower. Jan 4 '60	NO COVER STORY. Until 1974, U.S. News reported several stories with equal emphasis.
The lively 'ghost': Adlai Stevenson. Jan 11 '60	That population explosion. Jan 11 '60	
Erle Stanley Gardner. 'Mr. Mystery': After 100 books, Perry Mason wins again. Jan 18 '60	Getting to work. The trials of U.S. commuters. Jan 18 '60	
Tricky viruses on the loose. (A special medicine report on the ever-changing menace.) Jan 25 '60	Japan's Kishi. [Nobusuke Kishi] Jan 25 '60	

Newsweek **February 1960**	*Time* **February 1960**
America's firepower: The defense puzzle. Feb 1 '60	Humphrey for President. Feb 1 '60
France's de Gaulle: The final crisis? Feb 8 '60	Latin America. The real builders. Venezuela's President Betancourt. Feb 8 '60
California's colossal snow show. [Winter Olympics] Feb 15 '60	Washington columnist Scotty Reston. Feb 15 '60
Life in outer space? The search begins. The big 'dishes' seek the answer. Feb 22 '60	The drive for air safety. U.S. Airways boss Quesada. Feb 22 '60
On the road: Salesman K and salesman Ike. [Khrushchev, Eisenhower] Feb 29 '60	Pat Nixon. Feb 29 '60

Newsweek **March 1960**	*Time* **March 1960**
Young wives with brains. Babies, yes - but what else? Mar 7 '60	Kenya's Tom Mboya. Mar 7 '60
The decisive hours of Lyndon Johnson. Mar 14 '60	Movie director Ingmar Bergman. Mar 14 '60
Your color?. . .Your money?. . .Your age - really?. . .The nosey census of '60. Mar 21 '60	Caryl Chessman. Mar 21 '60
Humphrey and Kennedy. Wisconsin - who'll tumble? Mar 28 '60	Skindiving. Poetry, pleasure & self. Jacques Cousteau. Mar 28 '60

Newsweek **April 1960**	*Time* **April 1960**	*U.S. News* **1960**
New German army: The force K fears. Apr 4 '60	Australia. Things are looking up down under. Prime Minister Menzies. Apr 4 '60	NO COVER STORY. Until 1974, U.S. News reported several stories with equal emphasis.
The green thumb means business. [Gardening] Apr 11 '60	R. J. Reynolds' Bowman Gray. Apr 11 '60	
World on 'wheels.' Springtime showing - U.S. and foreign cars. Apr 18 '60	Christian missionaries. From St. Paul to 1960. Apr 18 '60	
De Gaulle. Mission to America. Apr 25 '60	Lyndon Baines Johnson. Apr 25 '60	

Newsweek **May 1960**	*Time* **May 1960**
Yearning for yesterday - America rediscovers Mark Twain. May 2 '60	Arnold Palmer. May 2 '60
Candidate Stu Symington. A second Missouri compromise? May 9 '60	John H. Loudon of Royal Dutch Shell. May 9 '60
Those splitting headaches - How near a cure? May 16 '60	The Cold War gets hotter. The high-flying U-2 & the cloudy summit. Pilot Francis Powers. May 16 '60
Ike and K face to face. Who's on top? Who's in trouble? [Eisenhower, Khrushchev] May 23 '60	The summit. May 23 '60
How safe are we now? Berlin - The U.N. - Ike's task. May 30 '60	Russia's new hard line. Soviet Defense Minister Malinovsky. May 30 '60

Newsweek **June 1960**	*Time* **June 1960**
Sports gambling madness. Jun 6 '60	Rush hour in space. U.S. & Russia take different roads. Jun 6 '60
On the go-'60: A Newsweek spotlight on business. Jun 13 '60	Khrushchev attacks the U.S. Jun 13 '60
The Rockefeller challenge. Will it split the GOP? A 50-state survey. New York's Gov. Rockefeller: It's up to Nixon. Jun 20 '60	One-third of a nation. U.S. suburbia, 1960. Jun 20 '60
Far East fiasco. China's Mao: Will he rule the Pacific? Jun 27 '60	Japan: Cold War cockpit. U.S. Ambassador Douglas MacArthur II. Jun 27 '60

Newsweek **July 1960**	*Time* **July 1960**	*U.S. News* **1960**
Can anybody stop Kennedy? The experts answer - A 50-state listening post. Jul 4 '60	Shakespeare. Midsummer night's box office. Jul 4 '60	NO COVER STORY. Until 1974, U.S. News reported several stories with equal emphasis.
Dawn of the spaceman. The most fascinating story: A special space and atom section. Jul 11 '60	The Kennedy family. Jul 11 '60	
Democrats backstage. F.D.R. - Present but not voting. Jul 18 '60	Democrats in Los Angeles. Battle in the stretch. Lyndon Johnson. Jul 18 '60	
Candidates and crisis. Red pressure - Sizing up the campaigners. Nominee Kennedy and nominee-to-be. . . Jul 25 '60	Those glamour stocks. New ideas & new millionaires. Fairchild Industries' Sherman Fairchild. Jul 25 '60	

Newsweek **August 1960**	*Time* **August 1960**
The '61s roll - The compacts grow. [Automobiles] Aug 1 '60	Republicans: Platform for the '60s. Rockefeller & Nixon. Aug 1 '60
Henry Cabot Lodge: The world's the issue. Aug 8 '60	Communism's western beachhead. Cuba's Che Guevara. Aug 8 '60
Johnson of Texas. Can he swing the South? Aug 15 '60	Comedian Mort Sahl. Aug 15 '60
Africa. Hate...hope. Aug 22 '60	The U.N. & the Congo. Out of chaos a legal precedent. Dag Hammarskjold. Aug 22 '60
The Olympics: Sports summit at Rome. Aug 29 '60	The Olympics. U.S. decathlon star Rafer Johnson. Aug 29 '60

Newsweek **September 1960**	*Time* **September 1960**
Castro and the Reds: Their real goal. Sep 5 '60	Women in politics. Maine's senate race. Smith v. Cormier. Sep 5 '60
The mystery of Joe Kennedy. Speculator...diplomat...bon vivant...and maybe a President's father. Sep 12 '60	Iran: Struggle for stability. Sep 12 '60
A-power: Things to come. Sep 19 '60	New products. [Inventions] Sep 19 '60
The 'invasion' of Manhattan. (Special section: Is it 'make-or-break' for the U.N.?) [United Nations] Sep 26 '60	Henry Cabot Lodge. Sep 26 '60

Newsweek **October 1960**	*Time* **October 1960**	*U.S. News* **1960**
The score. Ike vs. Khrushchev. Nixon vs. Kennedy. [United Nations] Oct 3 '60	The nations. [United Nations] Oct 3 '60	NO COVER STORY. Until 1974, U.S. News reported several stories with equal emphasis.
The TV debates and stormy K. How much influence on the election? [Presidential debates] Oct 10 '60	The Kennedy strategy. Campaign manager Bobby Kennedy. Oct 10 '60	
The First-Lady-to-be: 'Pat' Nixon or 'Jackie' Kennedy. Oct 17 '60	University of California's Clark Kerr. Oct 17 '60	
The 'think machine' - smarter and smarter. [Computers] Oct 24 '60	Michigan candidate Paul Bagwell. Oct 24 '60	
Veep-to-be. The ambassador or the senator? [Henry Cabot Lodge, Lyndon Johnson] Oct 31 '60	Candidate Nixon. Oct 31 '60	

Newsweek **November 1960**	*Time* **November 1960**
Election preview '60. All the pre-balloting trends. Nov 7 '60	Candidate Kennedy. Nov 7 '60
The Eisenhower years in the White House. The President's chair: Mightiest seat in the world. Nov 14 '60	The rough road to Broadway. Lerner & Loewe. Nov 14 '60
Man to see in Washington. Bobby Kennedy's role - The incoming administration. The President-elect's brother... Nov 21 '60	Hong Kong. Nov 21 '60
Today's parents: Trapped in a child-centered world? Nov 28 '60	Business columnist Sylvia Porter. Nov 28 '60

Newsweek **December 1960**	*Time* **December 1960**
The dollar in danger? Dec 5 '60	Nigeria's Prime Minister Balewa. Dec 5 '60
Q and A '61. [Forecasting] Dec 12 '60	U.S. Catholics & the state. John Courtney Murray, S.J. Dec 12 '60
Ford's McNamara: Wanted on the New Frontier. Dec 19 '60	West Germany's Franz Joseph Strauss. Dec 19 '60
We have seen His star... [Christianity] Dec 26 '60	Kennedy's men. The face of the new administration. Secretary of State: Dean Rusk. Dec 26 '60

Newsweek **January 1961**	*Time* **January 1961**	*U.S. News* **1961**
The split-second jet age. Controlling today's traffic jam in the sky. Jan 2 '61	U.S. scientists. Men of the year. Jan 2 '61	NO COVER STORY. Until 1974, U.S. News reported several stories with equal emphasis.
The Caribbean: Palmy, balmy vacations in the sun. Jan 9 '61	Pacific Commander. Harry Felt. Jan 6 '61	
Castro and Cuba. Can they survive? Crisis on our doorstep. Jan 16 '61	Diet & health. Jan 13 '61	
"New Frontier" - special section. [John F. Kennedy] Jan 23 '61	Jacqueline Kennedy. Jan 20 '61	
Douglas Dillon: Republican in the Cabinet and his job. Jan 30 '61	The inauguration of John Fitzgerald Kennedy. Jan 27 '61	

Newsweek **February 1961**	*Time* **February 1961**
New tempo in foreign policy. Kennedy's man Rusk. Feb 6 '61	Return of the airmen. Gambit in the Cold War. [Detained airmen released by Soviet Union].
What makes a prima donna? Eileen Farrell of the Met. Feb 13 '61	Kennedy & Congress. What price victory? Speaker Rayburn. Feb 10 '61
Ribicoff: Health, education - and a welfare state? Feb 20 '61	Oscar Robertson. Feb 17 '61
The rising Congo crisis. Can the U.N. survive? Feb 27 '61	The Russian offensive against the U.N. & U.S. [Soviet support of African independence] Feb 24 '61

Newsweek **March 1961**	*Time* **March 1961**
Can a labor man run labor? Goldberg's real challenge. Mar 6 '61	Kennedy's economic planners. White House economist Walter W. Heller. Mar 3 '61
TV's Huntley and Brinkley: One is solemn, the other twinkly. Mar 13 '61	Soprano Leontyne Price. Mar 10 '61
Arms control. Last chance? Sputtering fuse: Test-ban start again. Mar 20 '61	Laos: Test of U.S. intentions. Mar 17 '61
Adlai Stevenson: A new brand of personal diplomacy. Mar 27 '61	Heyday of the haggle. The buyers' market in cars. Mar 24 '61
	Guilt and anxiety. Mar 31 '61

Newsweek **April 1961**	*Time* **April 1961**	*U.S. News* **1961**
M.I.T. at 100: A race with the future. Apr 3 '61	Arms & diplomacy. Re-examing U.S. military might. Apr 7 '61	NO COVER STORY. Until 1974, U.S. News reported several stories with equal emphasis.
Conservatism. On the campus. In U.S. politics. In the nation. Arizona's Barry. . . Apr 10 '61	Playwright Jean Kerr. Apr 14 '61	
Eichmann on trial. Who is guilty? Who should judge? Apr 17 '61	Man in space. Russia's Yuri Gagarin. Apr 21 '61	
The voyage of Yuri Gagarin. [Soviet space flight] Apr 24 '61	The Cuban disaster. Apr 28 '61	

Newsweek **May 1961**	*Time* **May 1961**
Struggle for Cuba. May 1 '61	Architect Le Corbusier. May 5 '61
C.I.A. - How super the sleuths? Director Allen Dulles: Triumphs and disasters. May 8 '61	"What a beautiful sight." [U.S. space flight] May 12 '61
Caroline in the White House. [Caroline Kennedy] May 15 '61	Travel: The faraway places. May 19 '61
Holding Southeast Asia. South Vietnam's Diem: A strong man at bay. May 22 '61	Can Protestants unite? A Presbyterian proposal. May 26 '61
Neuroses: One psychiatrist's troubled patients. May 29 '61	

Newsweek **June 1961**	*Time* **June 1961**
"We stand for human liberty." "We must be prepared to suffer. . even die. . ." [Civil righ	The South and the freedom riders. [Civil rights movement] Jun 2 '61
Kennedy and Khrushchev: Power and personal diplomacy. Jun 12 '61	President Kennedy. Jun 9 '61
Journey to the moon: U.S. timetable. Jun 19 '61	Making money work. A Texas technique. Jun 16 '61
Shah of Iran: A revolution from the top? Jun 26 '61	Barry Goldwater. Jun 23 '61
	Brazil's President Quadros. Jun 30 '61

Newsweek   **July 1961**

Summertime '61: Vacations off the beaten track.   Jul 3 '61

Hoffa of the teamsters: Driving for more power.   Jul 10 '61

Phil Hill: First world champion from the U.S.? [Automobile racing] Jul 17 '61

Commerce Secretary Hodges: Pro or anti business?   Jul 24 '61

Berlin: Kennedy acts.   Jul 31 '61

Time   **July 1961**

Higher cost of better medicine. How should it be paid for?   Jul 7 '61

Camping: Call of the not so wild. Jul 14 '61

Cartoonist Bill Mauldin. Jul 21 '61

A soldier & the White House. [Maxwell Taylor]   Jul 28 '61

U.S. News   **1961**

NO COVER STORY. Until 1974, U.S. News reported several stories with equal emphasis.

Newsweek   **August 1961**

"We intend to have a wider choice than humiliation or all - out nuclear action. . ." [Berlin

Home run year. Target 60. [Professional baseball]   Aug 14 '61

New bull market...? [Stock market] Aug 21 '61

Barbed wire and bayonets. Berlin report.   Aug 28 '61

Time   **August 1961**

Southeast Asia: "Where the borders are less guarded, the enemy harder to find."   Aug 4 '61

Tough times on the railroads. Aug 11 '61

U.S. money & the Cold War. Aug 18 '61

East Germany's Ulbricht. Aug 25 '61

Newsweek   **September 1961**

"I shall continue to be disatisfied..." - Walter Reuther, Auto Workers' Chief.   Sep 4 '61

Minow of the FCC: Television and the public interest.   Sep 11 '61

USIA's Murrow: Is truth the best weapon?   Sep 18 '61

The U.N. meets. Disarmament, Berlin, Red China, Katanga. Sep 25 '61

Time   **September 1961**

White House & Congress. Power, patronage, and persuasion. Sep 1 '61

Khrushchev.   Sep 8 '61

A private world of love and death. [J.D. Salinger]   Sep 15 '61

Labor & the new frontier. Sep 22 '61

The U.N. in crisis.   Sep 29 '61

Newsweek October 1961	*Time* October 1961	*U.S. News* 1961

Storm over the U.N. Can it survive?   Oct 2 '61

New strength for the West. Europe unites in the Common Market. Oct 6 '61

NO COVER STORY. Until 1974, U.S. News reported several stories with equal emphasis.

Nixon for governor.   Oct 9 '61

The growing U.S. Army in Germany - around the world. Oct 13 '61

For war - the atom - for peace. Seaborg of the AEC: A scientist in command.   Oct 16 '61

Shelters. How soon - how big - how safe. [Backyard bomb shelters] Oct 20 '61

Party Congress: How Russia is ruled.   Oct 23 '61

The aerospace industry.   Oct 27 '61

Sunday's hero. The pro. [Professional football players] Oct 30 '61

Newsweek November 1961	*Time* November 1961

Shelters for survival? [Backyard bomb shelters]   Nov 6 '61

Girls in college: They have scarcely begun to use their brains. Nov 3 '61

New York, N.Y. Can anyone run it? Nov 13 '61

Fallout from Russia. The argument over testing. [Nuclear weapons testing]   Nov 10 '61

Nehru in America: "For us, peace is a passion."   Nov 20 '61

Medicine gains on viruses. Nov 17 '61

Broadway's Robert Morse: Hottest ticket in town.   Nov 27 '61

The art market.   Nov 24 '61

Newsweek December 1961	*Time* December 1961

Thunder on the right. The conservatives. The radicals. The fanatic fringe.   Dec 4 '61

Behind the China debate: Hunger and hate.   Dec 1 '61

Sears. Santa's biggest helper. Dec 11 '61

"The second reformation." [Christian churches]   Dec 8 '61

Those Washington columnists. Dec 18 '61

Christmas shopping.   Dec 15 '61

Peace Corps in action: Ira Gwin. Dec 25 '61

War for the Congo.   Dec 22 '61

Jackie Gleason   Dec 29 '61

Newsweek January 1962	*Time* January 1962	*U.S. News* 1962
Jacqueline Kennedy. Jan 1 '62	Man of the year. John F. Kennedy. Jan 5 '62	NO COVER STORY. Until 1974, U.S. News reported several stories with equal emphasis.
The great American debtor. [Growing personal debt] Jan 8 '62	The new U.S. ambassadors. Reischauer. Kennan. Galbraith. Jan 12 '62	
McCormack of Massachusetts. The new Congress. Jan 15 '62	Head of the House. The other man from Massachusetts. Speaker McCormack. Jan 19 '62	
U.S. Steel's Roger Blough. A strong voice for business. Jan 22 '62	Three-way war in Algeria. Terrorist Salan. Jan 26 '62	
Secretary-General U Thant. Crisis over the U.N. Jan 29 '62		

Newsweek February 1962	*Time* February 1962
Ordeal of a spaceman. [John Glenn] Feb 5 '62	Elections in India. Krishna Menon. Feb 2 '62
The battle of Southeast Asia. Guerrilla warfare. Feb 12 '62	"Where are the Catholic intellectuals?" Notre Dame's President Hesburgh. Feb 9 '62
G.O.P. dark horse. George Romney. The great game of politics. Feb 19 '62	The President's brother: Growing role in foreign policy. Robert Kennedy. Feb 16 '62
Natalie Wood: Star into actress. Feb 26 '62	Japan: Asia's first consumer market. Industrialist Matsushita. Feb 23 '62

Newsweek March 1962	*Time* March 1962
John Glenn: One machine that worked without flaw. Mar 5 '62	The space race is a go. Spaceman Glenn. Mar 2 '62
Defense Secretary McNamara. Mar 12 '62	Tennessee Williams. Mar 9 '62
The race to the moon. Mar 19 '62	Algeria: Birth of a nation. Premier Benkhedda. Mar 16 '62
K vs. Mao. How wide the split? [Soviet-China split] Mar 26 '62	Cities of the '60s. Big, bad and popular. Mar 23 '62
	Democracy's failure in Argentina. Arturo Frondizi. Mar 30 '62

Newsweek April 1962	*Time* April 1962	*U.S. News* 1962

Newsweek — April 1962

Medicare: Who should pay the bill?
Apr 2 '62

Bigger voice for big cities. The
Supreme Court decision. Chief
Justice Earl Warren.   Apr 9 '62

Tax time: Sharp pencils, sharper
machines.   Apr 16 '62

The big steel story. Blough vs.
Kennedy: The price wasn't right.
Apr 23 '62

Vietnam: What price victory?
Apr 30 '62

Time — April 1962

Sophia Loren.   Apr 6 '62

Russia's new generation. Soviet
poet Evtushenko.   Apr 13 '62

"The goal of human life is not
death, but resurrection."
Theologian Karl Barth.   Apr 20 '62

Cuba: Chaos in the economy.
Conflict among the Reds.
Communist. . .   Apr 27 '62

U.S. News — 1962

NO COVER STORY. Until 1974,
U.S. News reported several stories
with equal emphasis.

Newsweek   May 1962

The Pacific tests. [Nuclear weapons
testing]   May 7 '62

New York's Rockefeller. Target '64.
May 14 '62

Stravinsky at 80.   May 21 '62

Farm trouble. Behind the Billie Sol
mess. Agriculture Secretary
Orville Freeman.   May 28 '62

Time   May 1962

U.S. nuclear testing. The shots
heard round the world.   May 4 '62

South Viet Nam: What it takes to
win. U.S. General Paul Harkins.
May 11 '62

The world's biggest manufacturer.
General Motors Chairman
Frederic G. Donner.   May 18 '62

The Billie Sol Estes scandal.
May 25 '62

Newsweek   June 1962

Astronaut Carpenter.   Jun 4 '62

Stock market shock waves.
Jun 11 '62

Arnold Palmer: Perfection under
pressure.   Jun 18 '62

Lolita's creator: Vladimir
Nabokov.   Jun 25 '62

Time   June 1962

Bear v. bull on Wall Street.
Jun 1 '62

The market & economic policy.
White House adviser Walter
Heller.   Jun 8 '62

Nelson Rockefeller.   Jun 15 '62

Spain: Everybody's waiting.
Jun 22 '62

U.S. Open champ Jack Nicklaus.
Jun 29 '62

Newsweek	**July 1962**	*Time*	**July 1962**	*U.S. News*	**1962**

Franco's Spain today.   Jul 2 '62

Consumer spending. Discounting gets respectable. Korvette's Eugene Ferkauf.   Jul 6 '62

NO COVER STORY. Until 1974, U.S. News reported several stories with equal emphasis.

Secretary Rusk. New policies for old problems?   Jul 9 '62

Britain & the Common Market. A historic decision for Europe. Jul 13 '62

Kennedy and his critics. Jul 16 '62

What it's like today in society. [Upper class society]   Jul 20 '62

Too many babies? World population crisis.   Jul 23 '62

Publisher Sam Newhouse. Jul 27 '62

Key to the economy: The mighty U.S. consumer.   Jul 30 '62

Newsweek	**August 1962**	*Time*	**August 1962**

America's Cup: Racing again off Newport.   Aug 6 '62

The retirement city. A new way of life for the old.   Aug 3 '62

Algeria's Ben Bella. Another Castro?   Aug 13 '62

Reaching for the moon. Aug 10 '62

Bertrand Russell.   Aug 20 '62

Congress & Kennedy: Defiance. Aug 17 '62

Russia's men in space.   Aug 27 '62

Russian cosmonauts. Nikolayev & Popovich.   Aug 24 '62

The wall. [Berlin Wall] Aug 31 '62

Newsweek	**September 1962**	*Time*	**September 1962**

Red China today.   Sep 3 '62

Banker David Rockefeller. Sep 7 '62

Number one state. California. Sep 10 '62

Senator Everett Dirksen. Sep 14 '62

The new White House.   Sep 17 '62

The Monroe Doctrine and Communist Cuba.   Sep 21 '62

New showcase for the arts. Lincoln Center. Leonard Bernstein. Sep 24 '62

Teddy Kennedy.   Sep 28 '62

Newsweek **October 1962**	*Time* **October 1962**	*U.S. News* **1962**
Pollsters and politicians. Louis Harris. "We've been asking people all across your state.." Oct 1 '62	The condition of Catholicism. Pope John. Oct 5 '62	NO COVER STORY. Until 1974, U.S. News reported several stories with equal emphasis.
The Space Age. Oct 8 '62	Advertising: The visible persuaders. Oct 12 '62	
The sound and the fury. Oxford, Mississippi. [Riot over school integration] Oct 15 '62	Politics 1962. The campaign in full cry. Pennsylvania's William Scranton. Oct 19 '62	
Castro's Cuba. How U.S. voters feel. Oct 22 '62	Excellence & intensity in U.S. prep schools. Andover's John M. Kemper. Oct 26 '62	
Nixon. Brown. Biggest state's biggest battle. Oct 29 '62		

Newsweek **November 1962**	*Time* **November 1962**
Showdown. 'The cost of freedom is always high...' [Cuban missile crisis] Nov 5 '62	Showdown on Cuba. The evidence that led to action. [Cuban missile crisis] Nov 2 '62
What happened in the Kremlin? [Cuban missile crisis] Nov 12 '62	After Khrushchev's retreat. [Cuban missile crisis] Nov 9 '62
Rockefeller vs. Kennedy. The choice for '64? Nov 19 '62	U.S. politics: The next two years. Republican George Romney. Nov 16 '62
Sid Caesar. The many faces of comedy. Nov 26 '62	Folk singer Joan Baez. Nov 23 '62
	India's lost illusions. Nehru. Nov 30 '62

Newsweek **December 1962**	*Time* **December 1962**
India's Nehru. Reveille for the neutrals. Dec 3 '62	De Gaulle's triumph. Dec 7 '62
War in Vietnam. Dec 10 '62	Adlai Stevenson. Dec 14 '62
The Vatican Council. Reunion and reform. Dec 17 '62	The sport of the '60s. Green Bay coach Vince Lombardi. Dec 21 '62
Ski '63. Europe's 'in' resorts. Dec 24 '62	Toward a world market. The year in business. Dec 28 '62
The world of Walt Disney. Dec 31 '62	

Newsweek	**January 1963**

The Eurocrats. Common Market's Walter Hallstein.   Jan 7 '63

Taxes. To cut or not to cut? Rep. Wilbur Mills. Chairman, Ways and Means.   Jan 14 '63

Walter Lippmann on Kennedy. Jan 21 '63

De Gaulle. Apres moi...?   Jan 28 '63

Newsweek	**February 1963**

Playwright Edward Albee. Odd man in.   Feb 4 '63

Kennedy or de Gaulle. Whose grand design?   Feb 11 '63

Canada's Diefenbaker. Decline and fall.   Feb 18 '63

Hot year for General Motors. Feb 25 '63

Newsweek	**March 1963**

JFK's McGeorge Bundy. Cool head for the Cold War.   Mar 4 '63

Goulart's Brazil: Another New Frontier?   Mar 11 '63

Robert Kennedy. 'It is right...and that's all there is to it.'   Mar 18 '63

Elizabeth Taylor: Cleopatra's fortunes.   Mar 25 '63

Time	**January 1963**

Man of the year. John XXIII. Jan 4 '63

Will your taxes be cut? Congressman Wilbur Mills. Jan 11 '63

Architect Minoru Yamasaki. Jan 18 '63

Britain's troubled mood. Jan 25 '63

Time	**February 1963**

Taxes: All those deductions, loopholes, credits, etc.   Feb 1 '63

The perils of grandeur. De Gaulle. Feb 8 '63

Weapons & diplomacy. Cuba, Canada and Europe. Secretary McNamara.   Feb 15 '63

America's great orchestras. Cleveland conductor George Szell. Feb 22 '63

Time	**March 1963**

Is labor's only weapon a monkey wrench?   Mar 1 '63

Venus: What Mariner saw. Mar 8 '63

Chicago: The new facade. The next election. Mayor Daley.   Mar 15 '63

Cassius Marcellus Clay. Mar 22 '63

"Keep your tents separate and bring your hearts together." - Arab proverb. [Gamal Nasser] Mar 29 '63

U.S. News	**1963**

NO COVER STORY. Until 1974, U.S. News reported several stories with equal emphasis.

| *Newsweek* | **April 1963** | *Time* | **April 1963** | *U.S. News* | **1963** |

Newsweek   **April 1963**

Unemployment in America.
Apr 1 '63

Who manages news? [Presidential press relations]   Apr 8 '63

Britain's Harold Wilson. The next Prime Minister?   Apr 15 '63

Foreign students: Diplomas and diplomacy.   Apr 22 '63

Stocks surge - But where's the public? [Stock market]   Apr 29 '63

Time   **April 1963**

Agriculture Secretary Freeman.
Apr 5 '63

A new nation in Asia. Malaysia's Abdul Rahman.   Apr 12 '63

Canada's Pearson.   Apr 19 '63

Richard Burton.   Apr 26 '63

U.S. News   **1963**

NO COVER STORY. Until 1974, U.S. News reported several stories with equal emphasis.

Newsweek   **May 1963**

Adenauer. End of an era.
May 6 '63

Exploring the secrets of life. Model of DNA molecule.   May 13 '63

Goldwater in '64?   May 20 '63

Astronaut Cooper.   May 27 '63

Time   **May 1963**

If they can operate, you're lucky. [Surgery]   May 3 '63

The individual in America. [Individualism]   May 10 '63

Birmingham and beyond: The Negro's push for equality.
May 17 '63

Astronaut Cooper.   May 24 '63

The rising U.S. economy.
May 31 '63

Newsweek   **June 1963**

The world of John O'Hara.
Jun 3 '63

Pope John XXIII.   Jun 10 '63

World hunger. 10,000 deaths every day.   Jun 17 '63

'We owe them - and we owe ourselves - a better country...' - President Kennedy...   Jun 24 '63

Time   **June 1963**

John XXIII: The last picture.
Jun 7 '63

Candidate-watching in the G.O.P. Can they find a winner? Barry Goldwater.   Jun 14 '63

Civil rights: The moral crisis. "It is time to act in all of our daily lives." Bobby...   Jun 21 '63

Pope Paul VI.   Jun 28 '63

Newsweek **July 1963**	*Time* **July 1963**	*U.S. News* 1963

The new Pope. [Pope Paul VI]
Jul 1 '63

The Peace Corps. A U.S. ideal
abroad. Sargent Shriver.
Jul 5 '63

NO COVER STORY. Until 1974,
U.S. News reported several stories
with equal emphasis.

Smalltown, U.S.A. [Rural towns]
Jul 8 '63

Ireland. New spirit in the Ould Sod.
Jul 12 '63

Laos and Vietnam.   Jul 15 '63

Innkeeper to the world. Conrad
Hilton.   Jul 19 '63

Khrushchev at the crossroads.
Jul 22 '63

The great featherbedding fight.
[Labor unions]   Jul 26 '63

The Negro in America. The first
definitive national survey - who
he is, what he. . .   Jul 29 '63

Newsweek **August 1963**	*Time* **August 1963**

A truce in the Cold War?
Aug 5 '63

Beyond the nuclear agreement.
Aug 2 '63

The rites of fashion.   Aug 12 '63

South Viet Nam's Madame Nhu.
Aug 9 '63

Civil rights: The South's stand.
Georgia's Senator Richard
Russell.   Aug 19 '63

The Anglican communion.
Worldly. Worldwide. Catholic
and Protestant.   Aug 16 '63

Happy and Rocky. Back in the race.
[Nelson Rockefeller]   Aug 26 '63

As the test ban approaches: The size
& condition of the U.S. atomic
arsenal.   Aug 23 '63

The Negro revolution to date.
Aug 30 '63

Newsweek **September 1963**	*Time* **September 1963**

The march on Washington. [Civil
rights movement]   Sep 2 '63

Vistas for the future. Planner
William Pereira.   Sep 6 '63

Vietnam's Madame Nhu.
Sep 9 '63

Red China: The arrogant outcast.
Sep 13 '63

The plight of the urban schools.
Sep 16 '63

Cinema as an international art.
Sep 20 '63

The TV news battle. Walter
Cronkite of CBS.   Sep 23 '63

Alabama: Civil rights battlefield.
Governor Wallace.   Sep 27 '63

Bombing in Birmingham.
[Racial violence]   Sep 30 '63

Newsweek **October 1963**	*Time* **October 1963**	*U.S. News* **1963**
A new German era. Ludwig Erhard. Oct 7 '63	The technology industry. How a whiz kid makes it pay. Litton's "Tex" Thornton. Oct 4 '63	NO COVER STORY. Until 1974, U.S. News reported several stories with equal emphasis.
Catholicism in America. Oct 14 '63	What Labor offers England. Britain's Harold Wilson. Oct 11 '63	
What the white man thinks of the Negro revolt. Oct 21 '63	The college quarterbacks. Navy's Roger Staubach. Oct 18 '63	
Albert Finney in 'Luther.' The new prince of players. Oct 28 '63	Britain's Lord Home. Oct 25 '63	

Newsweek **November 1963**	*Time* **November 1963**
What to do with $14 billion. Bank of America's Rudolph A. Peterson. Nov 4 '63	Germany & the defense of Europe. Ludwig Erhard. Nov 1 '63
Vietnam: The showdown. Gen. Duong Van Minh. Nov 11 '63	Military coup in Viet Nam. General Duong Van Minh. Nov 8 '63
Smoking and health. Nov 18 '63	The man with 1,000,000 children. New York City's Superintendent Calvin Gross. Nov 15 '63
Red China: A paper dragon? Nov 25 '63	Washington hostesses. Nicole Alphand. Nov 22 '63
	President Johnson. Nov 29 '63

Newsweek **December 1963**	*Time* **December 1963**
John Fitzgerald Kennedy. 1917 - 1963. Dec 2 '63	The new administration. A promise of continuity & action. Secretary. . . [Dean Rusk] Dec 6 '63
President Johnson. Dec 9 '63	The search for man's past. Archaeologist Nelson Glueck. Dec 13 '63
Kenya's Kenyatta. From Mau Mau to statehood. Dec 16 '63	The Rothschilds today. Dec 20 '63
Danny Kaye: The entertainer. Dec 23 '63	"I want to show Americans what America is like." Painter Andrew Wyeth. Dec 27 '63
The missionary's new mission. Dec 30 '63	

Newsweek **January 1964**	*Time* **January 1964**	*U.S. News* **1964**
Jacqueline Kennedy. Looking ahead. Jan 6 '64	Man of the year. Martin Luther King, Jr. Jan 3 '64	NO COVER STORY. Until 1974, U.S. News reported several stories with equal emphasis.
World's Fair preview. New York's Robert Moses. Jan 13 '64	Buckminster Fuller. Jan 10 '64	
Walter Lippman: A critique of Congress. Jan 20 '64	Texas: Where myth & reality merge. Governor Connally. Jan 17 '64	
GOP's Scranton. Coming up fast. Jan 27 '64	Sex in the U.S.: Mores & morality. Jan 24 '64	
	The U.S. & Latin America. State Department's Thomas Mann. Jan 31 '64	

Newsweek **February 1964**	*Time* **February 1964**
'After the Fall.' Playwright Arthur Miller. Feb 3 '64	The siren's song. French diplomacy from Richelieu to de Gaulle. Foreign. . . Feb 7 '64
De Gaulle's France: A return to greatness? Feb 10 '64	The Warren Commission. Probing Kennedy's death. Feb 14 '64
Poverty, U.S.A. Feb 17 '64	Breadlines in utopia. Soviet President Leonid Brezhnev. Feb 21 '64
Bugs about Beatles. [The Beatles] Feb 24 '64	Jazz: Bebop and beyond. Jazzman Thelonious Monk. Feb 28 '64

Newsweek **March 1964**	*Time* **March 1964**
Makarios of Cyprus. Mar 2 '64	"A gentleman with innumerable friendships and connections." Bobby Baker. Mar 6 '64
New Hampshire: Rocky, Barry or . . .? The Newsweek poll. Mar 9 '64	From Africa to Viet Nam: New policies in a changing world. Mar 13 '64
Leo D. Welch. Chairman, Communications Satellite Corp. Mar 16 '64	Can Democrats control a Democratic senate? Majority leader Mansfield. Mar 20 '64
GOP's Lodge: Running strong. Mar 23 '64	Author John Cheever. Mar 27 '64
Latin America: The promise and the threat. Venezuela's President Leoni. Mar 30 '64	

Newsweek April 1964	*Time* April 1964	*U.S. News* 1964
Morals on the campus. Apr 6 '64	The U.S. & Southeast Asia. How to cope with never-never land. [Indochina] Apr 3 '64	NO COVER STORY. Until 1974, U.S. News reported several stories with equal emphasis.
The new Hubert Humphrey. LBJ's civil rights whip. Apr 13 '64	Barbra Streisand. Apr 10 '64	
The Mustang. Newest breed out of Detroit. Ford's Lee Iacocca. Apr 20 '64	Ford's Lee Iacocca. Apr 17 '64	
Marx: How Communism has changed. Apr 27 '64	The Communist split. Lenin. Apr 24 '64	

Newsweek May 1964	*Time* May 1964
George Balanchine: 'Ballet is woman...' May 4 '64	The whirlwind President. At garden press conference. [Lyndon Johnson] May 1 '64
The Warren Court: Ten momentous years. May 11 '64	The Methodist church. A concern for religious relevance. Bishop Gerald Kennedy. May 8 '64
Ike and the GOP race. [Presidential candidates] May 18 '64	The Republicans: Can popularity win the prize? Henry Cabot Lodge. May 15 '64
Life and death of the universe. Astrophysicist Fred Hoyle. May 25 '64	Upset in the West. Rockefeller in Oregon. May 22 '64
	The world's biggest company. A.T. & T. chairman Kappel. May 29 '64

Newsweek June 1964	*Time* June 1964
The new Museum of Modern Art. Directors Barr and d'Harnoncourt. Jun 1 '64	A confidential guide to the New York Fair. Jun 5 '64
The war in Asia: Decision point. Face of the enemy. Ho Chi Minh. Jun 8 '64	Barry Goldwater. Jun 12 '64
Can Goldwater be stopped? Jun 15 '64	The Civil Rights Bill. Product of principle and compromise. Jun 19 '64
William Scranton: Eleventh hour bid. Jun 22 '64	The U.S. & Laos. In the jungle of neutralism. General Kong Le. Jun 26 '64
Shastri of India. Jun 29 '64	

Newsweek July 1964	*Time* July 1964	*U.S. News* 1964
Birth control. The pill and the church. Jul 6 '64	Scandinavia today. Denmark's Princess Anne-Marie. Jul 3 '64	NO COVER STORY. Until 1974, U.S. News reported several stories with equal emphasis.
Mississippi. Summer, 1964. Jul 13 '64	Dirksen & Goldwater in Chicago. Jul 10 '64	
Scranton for President. Goldwater for President. GOP convention. Jul 20 '64	The South: View from within. William Faulkner. Jul 17 '64	
'A choice - not an echo.' [Barry Goldwater] Jul 27 '64	The new thrust in American politics. Goldwater accepting nomination. Jul 24 '64	
	Harlem. Jul 31 '64	

Newsweek August 1964	*Time* August 1964
Harlem: Hatred in the streets. Aug 3 '64	South Viet Nam: The long look north. Premier Khanh. Aug 7 '64
The new Rumania. The satellites look west. Aug 10 '64	The U.S. stand in Asia. Aug 14 '64
Vietnam: Widening war? Aug 17 '64	Catholicism in the U.S. A surge of renewal. Boston's Cardinal Cushing. Aug 21 '64
Decision by Robert Kennedy. Aug 24 '64	Lady Bird Johnson. Aug 28 '64
President Johnson. Aug 31 '64	

Newsweek September 1964	*Time* September 1964
The Humphreys. Sep 7 '64	Johnson & Humphrey. Sep 4 '64
America's Cup 1964. Constellation and American Eagle. Sep 14 '64	Baseball: The year they made a game of it. Baltimore manager Bauer. Sep 11 '64
Maxwell Taylor in Vietnam: Soldier on the spot. Sep 21 '64	The Midwestern battleground. Illinois Republican Percy. Sep 18 '64
Britain's Harold Wilson. Will Labor win? Sep 28 '64	The nuclear issue. [Nuclear weapons] Sep 25 '64

Newsweek **October 1964**	*Time* **October 1964**	*U.S. News* **1964**
The assassination. The Warren Commission report. Oct 5 '64	The Warren Commission: No conspiracy, domestic or foreign. Lee Harvey Oswald. Oct 2 '64	NO COVER STORY. Until 1974, U.S. News reported several stories with equal emphasis.
Keating vs. Kennedy. Oct 12 '64	That activist Supreme Court. Justice Black. Oct 9 '64	
Zero Mostel. Broadway's brightest star. Oct 19 '64	Senate races: California & others. Pierre Salinger. Oct 16 '64	
Brezhnev. Shake-up in the Kremlin. Oct 26 '64	The bomb; the overthrow; the squeaker; the scandal. [Jenkins, Brezhnev, Wilson] Oct 23 '64	
	The year of the split ticket. Oct 30 '64	

Newsweek **November 1964**	*Time* **November 1964**
America chooses a president. Nov 2 '64	Election extra. [Presidential election] Nov 4 '64
President Johnson. Nov 9 '64	Urban renewal. Remaking the American city. Nov 6 '64
The GOP: A trunkful of troubles. Nov 16 '64	Post Khrushchev Communism. China's Chou En-Lai greeted by Russia's Kosygin. Nov 13 '64
The Ivy League: Is it still the best? Yale's Kingman Brewster. Nov 23 '64	The fighting Irish fight again. Notre Dame coach Parsceghian. Nov 20 '64
Europe 1964: de Gaulle the defiant. Nov 30 '64	The modern alchemists. Du Pont's Copeland. Nov 27 '64

Newsweek **December 1964**	*Time* **December 1964**
J. Edgar Hoover and the FBI. Dec 7 '64	The Congo massacre. Dec 4 '64
Paul VI. The missionary Pope. Dec 14 '64	Buddhism: Religion and politics. Dec 11 '64
Apollo and the moon men. Dec 21 '64	Building the pavilions of culture. Los Angeles' Buff Chandler. Dec 18 '64
The First Lady. [Lady Bird Johnson] Dec 28 '64	Christian renewal. Dec 25 '64

Newsweek **January 1965**	*Time* **January 1965**	*U.S. News* **1965**
Art in New York. Jan 4 '65	Man of the year. President Johnson. Jan 1 '65	NO COVER STORY. Until 1974, U.S. News reported several stories with equal emphasis.
The state of the Union. President Johnson. Jan 11 '65	The consumer economy. Macy's Jack Straus. Jan 8 '65	
Vietnam: Any way out? Jan 18 '65	The new Congress: Democratic and busy. Jan 15 '65	
The challenge of automation. Jan 25 '65	U.S. foreign policy: How to relate self-interest and the preservation of freedom. . . Jan 22 '65	
	Today's teen-agers. Jan 29 '65	

Newsweek **February 1965**	*Time* **February 1965**
Churchill, 1874-1965. Feb 1 '65	U.S. Joint Chiefs of Staff. Thinkers and managers replace the heroes. Feb 5 '65
Heart and diet. Feb 8 '65	The communist flirtation with profits. Feb 12 '65
The other Asian crisis. Indonesia's Sukarno. Feb 15 '65	Escalation in Viet Nam. Feb 19 '65
Vietnam. Feb 22 '65	The enemy in Asia. Red China's Foreign Minister Chen Yi. Feb 26 '65

Newsweek **March 1965**	*Time* **March 1965**
Inside the White House. Mar 1 '65	Jeanne Moreau. Mar 5 '65
High stakes – U.S. investment in Europe. Mar 8 '65	A Latin American architect of hope. Peru's President Belaúnde. Mar 12 '65
Red China. Mar 15 '65	Martin Luther King. Mar 19 '65
Campus '65. The college generation looks at itself – a Newsweek survey. Mar 22 '65	Outside in space. [Soviet space flight] Mar 26 '65
Voskhod versus Gemini. The space race now. Mar 29 '65	

Newsweek **April 1965**	*Time* **April 1965**	*U.S. News* **1965**
The road from Selma. [Civil rights movement] Apr 5 '65	The computer in society. Apr 2 '65	NO COVER STORY. Until 1974, U.S. News reported several stories with equal emphasis.
Profile of the Viet Cong. Apr 12 '65	Comment in the comics. The world according to Peanuts. Apr 9 '65	
Nureyev: The new Nijinsky. Apr 19 '65	Rudolf Nureyev. Apr 16 '65	
The business of baseball. Apr 26 '65	Who's fighting in Viet Nam. A gallery of American combatants. Apr 23 '65	
	The surprising socialist. Britain's Harold Wilson. Apr 30 '65	

Newsweek **May 1965**	*Time* **May 1965**
The South. Into a new century. May 3 '65	Trying to prevent another Cuba. May 7 '65
Cover girl Jean Shrimpton. May 10 '65	The communications explosion. Early bird - and after. [Satellites] May 14 '65
American foreign policy. Drift or design. May 17 '65	Rock 'n' roll: Everybody's turned on. May 21 '65
Americans in action. U.S. advisor Capt. Charles B. Huggins. May 24 '65	Toward an artificial heart. Surgeon Michael DeBakey. May 28 '65
GOP hope: Lindsay of New York. May 31 '65	

Newsweek **June 1965**	*Time* **June 1965**
Art Buchwald's Washington. Jun 7 '65	"In the Dostoevskian sense, I am the suffering man." Norton Simon. Jun 4 '65
The flight of the Gemini 4. Jun 14 '65	The McDivitt-White flight. Ed White & Jim McDivitt. Jun 11 '65
Back to Earth - Where the trouble is. [Gemini 4 space flight] Jun 21 '65	"I rise to defend /The quite possible She." Phyllis McGinley. Jun 18 '65
The worries of Wall Street Jun 28 '65	The crucial choice. U.S. foreign policy in action. McGeorge Bundy. Jun 25 '65

Newsweek **July 1965**	*Time* **July 1965**	*U.S. News* **1965**
Vietnam: The new war. General Westmoreland. Jul 5 '65	The best resorts. Summer in the U.S.A. Jul 2 '65	NO COVER STORY. Until 1974, U.S. News reported several stories with equal emphasis.
The making of presidents. Author Theodore H. White. Jul 12 '65	The quickest man on wheels. Champion driver Jim Clark. Jul 9 '65	
Life Italian style. Europe's biggest season. Jul 19 '65	Viet Nam: The intransigent North. Ho Chi Minh. Jul 16 '65	
Mariner to Mars. Jul 26 '65	Taking the measure of Mars. Jul 23 '65	
	Chagall. Self-portrait. [Marc Chagall] Jul 30 '65	

Newsweek **August 1965**	*Time* **August 1965**
The politics of power. [Lyndon Johnson] Aug 2 '65	War and the Great Society. How the people feel about Johnson. President Johnson. Aug 6 '65
The bomb. The next twenty years. [Nuclear weapons] Aug 9 '65	India without Nehru. Aug 13 '65
Crime in the streets. Aug 16 '65	The Los Angeles riot. [Watts riot] Aug 20 '65
The water crisis. [Water supply] Aug 23 '65	Flight director Chris Kraft. [U.S. space program] Aug 27 '65
Los Angeles: Why? [Watts riot] Aug 30 '65	

Newsweek **September 1965**	*Time* **September 1965**
Sinatra: Where the action is. Sep 6 '65	The man who wants the government to get off the farm. [Charles Shuman] Sep 3 '65
The war on poverty. Sep 13 '65	The world's need for money. Should the dollar be almighty? [Monetary policy] Sep 10 '65
War over Kashmir. Sep 20 '65	New war in Asia. Pakistan's Ayub v. India's Shastri. Sep 17 '65
Premier Ky: Who rules Vietnam? Sep 27 '65	Pope Paul. Sep 24 '65

Newsweek October 1965	*Time* October 1965	*U.S. News* 1965
Autos: Going like '66. Oct 4 '65	Water: Worldwide use & misuse. Oct 1 '65	NO COVER STORY. Until 1974, U.S. News reported several stories with equal emphasis.
Down to the wire. [Professional baseball] Oct 11 '65	Cuba: The decaying revolution. Oct 8 '65	
The President's operation. [Lyndon Johnson's gall bladder operation] Oct 18 '65	"Education is too important to be left solely to the educators." Commissioner Keppel. Oct 16 '65	
The first year of life. Oct 25 '65	The turning point in Viet Nam. Oct 22 '65	
	The young man next to the President. Bill Moyers. Oct 29 '65	

Newsweek November 1965	*Time* November 1965
The demonstrators. Who? Why? How many? [Anti-Vietnam War demonstrations] Nov 1 '65	The white man in black Africa. Nov 5 '65
Copy machine boom. Xerox President Joseph C. Wilson. Nov 8 '65	The new mayor of New York: "To make our great city once again the empire city of the. . ." Nov 12 '65
Lindsay wins New York. New look for the GOP? Nov 15 '65	The biggest blackout. [Electric power failure] Nov 19 '65
The big blackout. [Electric power failure] Nov 22 '65	Cleveland's Jimmy Brown. Nov 26 '65
What's wrong with newspapers? Nov 29 '65	

Newsweek December 1965	*Time* December 1965
The power in the Pentagon. Defense Secretary McNamara with Joint Chief of Staff. Dec 6 '65	Millionaires under 40. Dec 3 '65
De Gaulle: Once and future king. Dec 13 '65	"The battlefield is a lonely place." General Johnson. Army Chief of Staff. Dec 10 '65
Julie Christie. New darling of the movies. Dec 20 '65	The historian as participant and vice versa. Arthur Schlesinger, Jr. Dec 17 '65
Rendezvous in space. [Gemini 6 and 7 space flights] Dec 27 '65	Rendezvous on the road to the moon. [Gemini 6 and 7 space flights] Dec 24 '65
	Business in 1965: The Keynesian influence on the expansionist economy. . . Dec 31 '65

Newsweek **January 1966**	*Time* **January 1966**	*U.S. News* **1966**

The protesting Protestants. Stanford's Robert MacAfee Brown. Jan 3 '66

Man of the year. General Westmoreland.   Jan 7 '66

NO COVER STORY. Until 1974, U.S. News reported several stories with equal emphasis.

Gross national product. $700 billion plus.   Jan 10 '66

The U.S. peace offensive and the Communist response. Johnson & advisers at ranch. . .   Jan 14 '66

Congress: Consensus or conflict? The Senators Kennedy.   Jan 17 '66

Spain looks to the future. General Franco.   Jan 21 '66

'In Cold Blood.' Truman Capote's hot book.   Jan 24 '66

Troubled India in a woman's hands. Indira Gandhi   Jan 28 '66

Thailand: Next target?   Jan 31 '66

Newsweek   **February 1966**

Time   **February 1966**

Racing to the top. Jim Hall and the Chaparral. [Automobile racing] Feb 7 '66

Doubt & resolution over Viet Nam. Feb 4 '66

Vietnam: The bombers go north. Feb 14 '66

The aerospace industry. Thriving through war but planning for peace.   Feb 11 '66

Australia on the march.   Feb 21 '66

South Viet Nam's Premier Ky. Feb 18 '66

Building the Great Society. HEW's John W. Gardner. Feb 28 '66

Artur Rubinstein.   Feb 25 '66

Newsweek   **March 1966**

Time   **March 1966**

China: How big the threat? Mar 7 '66

First Negro in the cabinet. Trying to save the cities. Secretary Weaver. Mar 4 '66

Foundations. The American way of giving.   Mar 14 '66

Exploring the edge of the universe. Astronomer Maarten Schmidt. Mar 11 '66

The teen-agers.   Mar 21 '66

Eastern Europe. Life under a relaxed Communism.   Mar 18 '66

Politics '66. GOP challenger Ronald Reagan.   Mar 28 '66

Broadway's David Merrick. Mar 25 '66

Newsweek **April 1966**	*Time* **April 1966**	*U.S. News* **1966**
Prime Minister Indira Gandhi. Apr 4 '66	The activated Vice President. Hubert Humphrey. Apr 1 '66	NO COVER STORY. Until 1974, U.S. News reported several stories with equal emphasis.
The draft. Welcome to the United States Army. Apr 11 '66	Is God dead? Apr 8 '66	
Turmoil in Vietnam. Apr 18 '66	London: The swinging city. Apr 15 '66	
Pop! It's what's happening in art, fashion, entertainment, business. Apr 25 '66	South Viet Nam: The Buddhist bid for power. Thich Tri Quang Apr 22 '66	
	Moving the Constitution into the police station. Danny Escobedo. Apr 29 '66	

Newsweek **May 1966**	*Time* **May 1966**
Life in Russia. May 2 '66	Great teachers. May 6 '66
LSD and the mind drugs. May 9 '66	Crossfire in the war on poverty. Sargent Shriver. May 13 '66
Alabama votes. Win for the Wallaces. May 16 '66	What's good for the economy . . . General Motors President Roche. May 20 '66
The Johnson girls. [Lynda and Luci Baines Johnson] May 23 '66	A monarchy fights for freedom. The King and Queen of Thailand. May 27 '66
War within a war. Buddhists Tri Quang and Phap Tri. May 30 '66	

Newsweek **June 1966**	*Time* **June 1966**
Chaplin at 77. [Charlie Chaplin] Jun 6 '66	Viet Nam & the class of '66. Jun 3 '66
What role for the educated woman? Jun 13 '66	The best right arm in baseball. Juan Marichal. Jun 10 '66
The Meredith March. [Civil rights movement] Jun 20 '66	The other side's dilemma. North Viet Nam's General Giap. Jun 17 '66
Police on the spot. Jun 27 '66	Senator Jacob Javits. Jun 24 '66

| *Newsweek* | **July 1966** | *Time* | **July 1966** | *U.S. News* | **1966** |

Newsweek — July 1966

De Gaulle in Russia.   Jul 4 '66

Our sick hospitals. [Hospital finances]   Jul 11 '66

The economy: What's ahead? Presidential adviser Gardner Ackley.   Jul 18 '66

Jim Ryun. How fast the mile? Jul 25 '66

Time — July 1966

Omnis Europa in unam parten? De Gaulle.   Jul 1 '66

Raising the price of aggression. Secretary McNamara.   Jul 8 '66

Indonesia: The land the Communists lost. General Suharto.   Jul 15 '66

What the airlines mean to the country.   Jul 22 '66

The pleasures & perils of middle age.   Jul 29 '66

U.S. News — 1966

NO COVER STORY. Until 1974, U.S. News reported several stories with equal emphasis.

Newsweek   **August 1966**

Men at war. [Vietnam War] Aug 1 '66

Mao and China.   Aug 8 '66

White House wedding. Aug 15 '66

Black and white. A major survey of U.S. racial attitudes today. Aug 22 '66

The SST. Racing for $25 billion. Aug 29 '66

Time   **August 1966**

Getting married in public. Pat & Luci. [Luci Baines Johnson and Pat Nugent]   Aug 5 '66

The psychotic & society. Charles Whitman.   Aug 12 '66

Wall Street: The nervous market. Aug 19 '66

South Africa: The delusions of apartheid.   Aug 26 '66

Newsweek   **September 1966**

How much inflation?   Sep 5 '66

Wall Street: Hitting bottom? Sep 12 '66

The new Met. Rudolf Bing. Sep 19 '66

Campaign '66. How much of the way with LBJ?   Sep 26 '66

Time   **September 1966**

Mayor Yorty. [Los Angeles Mayor Sam Yorty]   Sep 2 '66

The Chinese nightmare. Defense Minister Lin Piao.   Sep 9 '66

Senator Robert Kennedy. Sep 16 '66

Grander days for grand opera. Rudolf Bing.   Sep 23 '66

Canada today: The boom no one noticed.   Sep 30 '66

Newsweek   **October 1966**

The troubled U.N. Secretary-General U Thant. Oct 3 '66

Can the GOP come back? Nixon on the road.   Oct 10 '66

Yugoslavia's Tito. A radical Communist.   Oct 17 '66

The Bobby phenomenon. [Robert F. Kennedy]   Oct 24 '66

The U.S. in Asia.   Oct 31 '66

Newsweek   **November 1966**

LBJ in Vietnam.   Nov 7 '66

Mike Nichols. Lighting up Broadway.   Nov 14 '66

The new GOP galaxy.   Nov 21 '66

Americans abroad. [Americans traveling in foreign countries] Nov 28 '66

Newsweek   **December 1966**

General Westmoreland. A recipe for victory?   Dec 5 '66

Pearl Harbor. 1941 - 1966. Where are they now? Where were they then?   Dec 12 '66

White power in Africa.   Dec 19 '66

Privacy vs. history. Jacqueline Kennedy and "The Death of a President."   Dec 26 '66

Time   **October 1966**

California's governorship race. Ronald Reagan.   Oct 7 '66

The electronic front page. Walter Cronkite.   Oct 14 '66

Two decades of independence in Asia. Philippine President Marcos. Oct 21 '66

The power of talent & teamwork. Notre Dame's Seymour and Hanratty.   Oct 28 '66

Time   **November 1966**

President Johnson.   Nov 4 '66

The relevance of faith & myth in twentieth century life. Bishop Pike. Nov 11 '66

Republican resurgence. Nov 18 '66

What's cooking. Julia Child. Nov 25 '66

Time   **December 1966**

The transformation of Arkansas. Governor-elect Winthrop Rockefeller.   Dec 2 '66

The mood of Germany. [West Germany's political changes] Dec 9 '66

Books by the billion. Bennett Cerf. Dec 16 '66

Julie Andrews.   Dec 23 '66

The U.S. economy, 1967. Concern and confidence. Bank of America's Rudolph Peterson.   Dec 30 '66

U.S. News   **1966**

NO COVER STORY. Until 1974, U.S. News reported several stories with equal emphasis.

Newsweek January 1967

How to build a publishing empire. California's Otis Chandler. Jan 2 '67

The agony of getting anywhere. [Commuting] Jan 9 '67

Must Adam leave Eden? Congressman Adam Clayton Powell. Jan 16 '67

LBJ's problem Congress. Republican leaders Ford and Dirksen. Jan 23 '67

The struggle for China. Jan 30 '67

Newsweek February 1967

The Apollo tragedy. Astronauts Grissom, White and Chaffee. Feb 6 '67

The divorced woman. Feb 13 '67

The chances for peace. Hanoi's Ho Chi Minh. Feb 20 '67

The towering talent of Lew Alcindor. Feb 27 '67

Newsweek March 1967

The message of Marshall McLuhan. Mar 6 '67

Henry R. Luce. 1898 - 1967. Mar 13 '67

How U.S. Catholics view their church. Mar 20 '67

Missiles vs. missiles. $30 billion decision. Mar 27 '67

Time January 1967

Man of the year. Twenty-five and under. Jan 6 '67

China in chaos. Chairman Mao. Jan 13 '67

Can the Great Society be built and managed? H.E.W. Secretary Gardner. Jan 20 '67

The polluted air. Los Angeles at 3:30 P.M. Jan 27 '67

Time February 1967

Astronauts Grissom, White & Chaffee. Feb 3 '67

Island of stability in Asia. Japan's Premier Sato. Feb 10 '67

U.S. Senator Edward Brooke. Feb 17 '67

The CIA and the students. Feb 24 '67

Time March 1967

The pursuit of hedonism. Playboy's Hugh Hefner. Mar 3 '67

Henry R. Luce. Mar 10 '67

Lynn & Vanessa Redgrave. Mar 17 '67

Martin Luther. Mar 24 '67

The industrial conquest of the sky. Aerospaceman James McDonnell. Mar 31 '67

U.S. News 1967

NO COVER STORY. Until 1974, U.S. News reported several stories with equal emphasis.

| *Newsweek* | **April 1967** | *Time* | **April 1967** | *U.S. News* | **1967** |

Newsweek — April 1967

David Rockefeller: New era in banking.   Apr 3 '67

Twiggy.   Apr 10 '67

The defender. Defense attorney F. Lee Bailey.   Apr 17 '67

The new medicine. [Advances in medical technology]   Apr 24 '67

Newsweek — May 1967

Stalin's daughter chooses the U.S. May 1 '67

The home-front war. General Westmoreland before Congress. May 8 '67

Which way for the Negro now? Martin Luther King. Floyd McKissick. . .   May 15 '67

Ronald Reagan: Rising star in the west?   May 22 '67

The speed game. Champion driver Mario Andretti.   May 29 '67

Newsweek — June 1967

The Arabs vs. Israel.   Jun 5 '67

The adventurers. Sir Francis Chichester and Gipsy Moth IV. Jun 12 '67

Victory in the desert. Israeli Defense Minister Moshe Dayan. Jun 19 '67

The U.N. Summit. The Soviet Union's Premier Kosygin. Jun 26 '67

Time — April 1967

The pill. [Birth control]   Apr 7 '67

Weighing in for '68. [Presidential candidates]   Apr 14 '67

Report from Punta del Este: Will Latin America become a success? Brazil's President. . .   Apr 21 '67

Greece: The palace coup. King Constantine.   Apr 28 '67

Time — May 1967

Gen. Westmoreland before Congress.   May 5 '67

The law and dissent. Federal Judge Frank Johnson.   May 12 '67

Humor in the night. Johnny Carson.   May 19 '67

The Negro in Viet Nam. May 26 '67

Time — June 1967

Poetry in an age of prose. Robert Lowell.   Jun 2 '67

Israel: The struggle to survive. Jun 9 '67

How Israel won the war. Jun 16 '67

The precarious future of the private college.   Jun 23 '67

Kosygin & Johnson at Glassboro. Jun 30 '67

U.S. News — 1967

NO COVER STORY. Until 1974, U.S. News reported several stories with equal emphasis.

Newsweek **July 1967**	*Time* **July 1967**	*U.S. News* **1967**
The Glassboro Summit. Jul 3 '67	The hippies. Philosophy of a subculture. Jul 7 '67	NO COVER STORY. Until 1974, U.S. News reported several stories with equal emphasis.
The Vietnam War and American life. Jul 10 '67	The Arabs in the aftermath. Jordan's King Hussein. Jul 14 '67	
New star Leslie Uggams: The Negro in show business. Jul 17 '67	Anatomy of a race riot. Jul 21 '67	
Marijuana. The pot problem. Jul 24 '67	The embattled cities. Urbanologist Pat Moynihan. Jul 28 '67	
Hong Kong under the gun. Jul 31 '67		

Newsweek **August 1967**	*Time* **August 1967**
Battlefield, U.S.A. [Civil unrest and riots] Aug 7 '67	Twelfth Street, Detroit. [Civil unrest and riots] Aug 4 '67
Tax hike. Medicare. Education. Poverty. Space. War. Urban renewal. Highways. Aug 14 '67	"You've got to give us some victories." Urban League's Whitney Young. Aug 11 '67
The Black mood. A Newsweek survey. Aug 21 '67	America's Cup: Ultimate in sailing. Skipper Bus Mosbacher. Aug 18 '67
France's fading hero. Charles de Gaulle. Aug 28 '67	Inside the Viet Cong. Aug 25 '67

Newsweek **September 1967**	*Time* **September 1967**
LBJ in trouble. Sep 4 '67	Sandy Dennis: The star in the $7 dress. Sep 1 '67
The Mideast: Slow boil. Nasser of the U.A.R. Sep 11 '67	Conglomerates: The new business giants. President Harold S. Geneen. Sep 8 '67
Walkout in Detroit. UAW's Walter Reuther. Sep 18 '67	Viet Nam's Thieu. He won under fire. Sep 15 '67
The school crisis. Sep 25 '67	The Beatles / Their new incarnation. Sep 22 '67
	Mr. & Mrs. Guy Smith / An interracial wedding. Sep 29 '67

Newsweek October 1967

Down to the wire. Boston's Carl Yastrzemski.   Oct 2 '67

Jim Ling the merger king. Oct 9 '67

Novelist William Styron. Oct 16 '67

Russia after 50 years.   Oct 23 '67

Trouble in Hippieland. [Hippies and the drug culture]   Oct 30 '67

Newsweek November 1967

Backlash in Boston. Mayoral candidate Louise Day Hicks. Nov 6 '67

Anything goes. The permissive society. [Social values]   Nov 13 '67

The Negro in America. What must be done.   Nov 20 '67

Devaluation. Britain's Harold Wilson. Can Labor last? Nov 27 '67

Newsweek December 1967

Defending the dollar. The federal reserve's William McChesney Martin.   Dec 4 '67

McNamara. Why is he leaving? Dec 11 '67

New hearts for old. The promise and perils of transplant surgery. Dec 18 '67

The nun: Going modern. Dec 25 '67

Time October 1967

Rising doubt about the war. Under fire at Con Thien.   Oct 6 '67

Sculptor Tony Smith. Art outgrows the museum.   Oct 13 '67

For President. Rockefeller of New York. For Vice President. Reagan of California.   Oct 20 '67

Protest! Protest! Protest! Protest! A week of antiwar demonstrations. Oct 27 '67

Time November 1967

William Buckley / Conservatism can be fun.   Nov 3 '67

How Russia survived Marxism: Soviet life today.   Nov 10 '67

Negro election victories. Cleveland's Mayor Stokes. Nov 17 '67

Britain's money crisis. Causes & consequences.   Nov 24 '67

Time December 1967

The miniskirt is here to stay (until spring, anyway). Designer Rudi Gernreich.   Dec 1 '67

The new cinema: Violence...sex...art... Bonnie and Clyde.   Dec 8 '67

The transplanted heart. Dr. Christiaan Barnard.   Dec 15 '67

Christmas in Viet Nam. Bob Hope. Dec 22 '67

The year in business. U.S. industry's global reach. Dec 29 '67

U.S. News 1967

NO COVER STORY. Until 1974, U.S. News reported several stories with equal emphasis.

Newsweek **January 1968**	*Time* **January 1968**	*U.S. News* **1968**
How goes the war? [Vietnam War] Jan 1 '68	Man of the year. L.B.J. as Lear. Jan 5 '68	NO COVER STORY. Until 1974, U.S. News reported several stories with equal emphasis.
Politics '68. Jan 8 '68	Rise of the public universities: Quality as well as quantity. New York's Chancellor. . . Jan 12 '68	
The Howard Hughes puzzle. Jan 15 '68	Conductor Zubin Mehta. The baton is passed to youth. Jan 19 '68	
Consumer crusader. Ralph Nader. Jan 22 '68	Railroads of the future. Jan 26 '68	
The state of LBJ. Jan 29 '68		

Newsweek **February 1968**	*Time* **February 1968**
Seizure at sea. Pueblo prisoners in North Korea. Feb 5 '68	Capture & confrontation. A new threat in Asia. Pueblo skipper Lloyd Bucher. Feb 2 '68
Hanoi on the attack. Feb 12 '68	Days of death on Viet Nam. Hanoi's General Giap. Feb 9 '68
Man on the spot. Gen. William Westmoreland. Feb 19 '68	John Kenneth Galbraith. The all-purpose critic. Feb 16 '68
Megaversity: How good? [Large universities] Feb 26 '68	Russia's navy: A new challenge at sea. Feb 23 '68

Newsweek **March 1968**	*Time* **March 1968**
Faye Dunaway. The new American beauties. Mar 4 '68	Chicago's Bobby Hull. Fastest shot in the fastest game. [Professional hockey] Mar 1 '68
...and then there was Nixon. Can Rocky stop him? Mar 11 '68	The race for the G.O.P. nomination. Mar 8 '68
The agony of Khe Sanh. [Vietnam War] Mar 18 '68	Joffrey Ballet's "Astarte." Mar 15 '68
The fight to dump LBJ. McCarthy and Kennedy. Mar 25 '68	Three's a crowd. The Johnson - Kennedy - McCarthy fight. Eugene McCarthy. Mar 22 '68
	The future of money. Mar 29 '68

Newsweek **April 1968**	*Time* **April 1968**	*U.S. News* **1968**
New look for museums. The Metropolitan's Thomas Hoving. Apr 1 '68	Self-determination for Czechoslovakia. Party boss Dubcek. Apr 5 '68	NO COVER STORY. Until 1974, U.S. News reported several stories with equal emphasis.
The Red Bloc in crisis. Apr 8 '68	President Johnson. Apr 12 '68	
Martin Luther King, Jr., 1929-1968. Apr 15 '68	New man in Viet Nam. General Creighton Abrams. Apr 19 '68	
Prospects for peace. [Vietnam War] Apr 22 '68	The adulterous society. Author John Updike. Apr 26 '68	
Can he stop Bobby? Vice President Humphrey. Apr 29 '68		

Newsweek **May 1968**	*Time* **May 1968**
Student protest. May 6 '68	H • H • H. [Hubert H. Humphrey] May 3 '68
The new GOP race. The Rockefellers. May 13 '68	Peace talks: The scenario in Paris. [Vietnam War] May 10 '68
RFK: Up, up and away? [Robert F. Kennedy] May 20 '68	Poverty in America: Its cause and extent. May 17 '68
French revolution 1968. May 27 '68	Bobby Kennedy. May 24 '68
	France: Beyond the deluge. Charles de Gaulle. May 31 '68

Newsweek **June 1968**	*Time* **June 1968**
The beauty business. [Cosmetic industry] Jun 3 '68	Can you trust anyone under 30? The graduate 1968. Jun 7 '68
Showdown in France. [Charles de Gaulle] Jun 10 '68	Robert Kennedy. Jun 14 '68
Robert F. Kennedy. 1925-1968. Jun 17 '68	The gun in America. Jun 21 '68
A question of guns. [Gun control] Jun 24 '68	The sound of soul. Singer Aretha Franklin. Jun 28 '68

Newsweek **July 1968**	*Time* **July 1968**	*U.S. News* **1968**
Target: Negro jobs. Jul 1 '68	The changing court. Justice Abe Fortas. Jul 5 '68	NO COVER STORY. Until 1974, U.S. News reported several stories with equal emphasis.
The polls. Do they count? Jul 8 '68	Commercials: The best & worst on TV. Jul 12 '68	
The angry Black athlete. Jul 15 '68	The police & the ghetto. Los Angeles Chief Reddin. Jul 19 '68	
The frustrated voter. Can it happen again? We want Wilkie. Jul 22 '68	The challengers. [Presidential candidates] Jul 26 '68	
Defying the Kremlin. Czechoslovakia's Alexander Dubcek. Jul 29 '68		

Newsweek **August 1968**	*Time* **August 1968**
Can Teddy stay out? Senator Edward M. Kennedy. Aug 5 '68	Building for the year 2000. Aug 2 '68
The GOP in Miami. Aug 12 '68	Republicans: The men and the issues. Aug 9 '68
The GOP ticket. Aug 19 '68	The G.O.P. ticket. Aug 16 '68
French actress Catherine Deneuve. Aug 26 '68	Biafra's agony. Colonel Ojukwu. Aug 23 '68
	Invasion. [Soviet invasion of Czechoslovakia] Aug 30 '68

Newsweek **September 1968**	*Time* **September 1968**
The Czech crisis. Sep 2 '68	The Democrats after Chicago. Sep 6 '68
Battle of Chicago. [Demonstrations at the Democratic National Convention] Sep 9 '68	The year of the pitcher. Denny McLain. Sep 13 '68
The third party threat. Alabama's George C. Wallace. Sep 16 '68	Becoming a household word. Spiro Agnew. Sep 20 '68
Bringing up baby. Is Dr. Spock to blame? Sep 23 '68	Russia's dissident intellectuals. Solzhenitsyn. Sep 27 '68
Rebels on the campus. Confrontation at Columbia. Sep 30 '68	

Newsweek October 1968	*Time* October 1968	*U.S. News* 1968

The understudies: Muskie and Agnew.   Oct 7 '68

Law and order.   Oct 4 '68

NO COVER STORY. Until 1974, U.S. News reported several stories with equal emphasis.

Next stop: The moon. Racing the Russians.   Oct 14 '68

Rowan and Martin.   Oct 11 '68

New star on Broadway. James Earl Jones.   Oct 21 '68

The revolt of the right: Wallace and LeMay.   Oct 18 '68

Jackie Onassis. [Jackie Kennedy's marriage to Aristotle Onassis] Oct 28 '68

Jackie's marriage. [Jackie Kennedy's marriage to Aristotle Onassis]   Oct 25 '68

Newsweek November 1968	*Time* November 1968

Countdown for campaign '68. Nov 4 '68

New York: The breakdown of a city. Nov 1 '68

How Nixon won. The President-Elect.   Nov 11 '68

The bombing decision. [Vietnam War]   Nov 8 '68

Can Nixon unite the nation? Nov 18 '68

The election. Richard Nixon. Nov 15 '68

Male plumage '68. [Men's fashion] Nov 25 '68

Rebellion in the Catholic Church. Nov 22 '68

World money crisis.   Nov 29 '68

Newsweek December 1968	*Time* December 1968

The money crisis.   Dec 2 '68

Race for the moon.   Dec 6 '68

The world of Norman Mailer. Dec 9 '68

The Arab commandos. Defiant new force in the Middle East.   Dec 13 '68

Can Vietnam stand alone? Dec 16 '68

The new administration. William Rogers: Nixon's Secretary of State. Dec 20 '68

Changing the guard. [Nixon's executive appointments] Dec 23 '68

Music from the fifth evangelist. Johann Sebastian Bach. Dec 27 '68

To the moon. Astronauts Lovell, Anders and Borman.   Dec 30 '68

Newsweek **January 1969**	*Time* **January 1969**	*U.S. News* **1969**
Apollo triumph. Astronauts Anders, Lovell and Borman. Jan 6 '69	Men of the year. Anders, Borman and Lovell. [U.S. astronauts] Jan 3 '69	NO COVER STORY. Until 1974, U.S. News reported several stories with equal emphasis.
Teddy cracks the whip. [Edward Kennedy] Jan 13 '69	The Democrats regroup. Senator Edward Kennedy. Jan 10 '69	
Man vs. virus. Fighting the flu. Jan 20 '69	Italy: Industrialists as heroes. Fiat's Giovanni Agnelli. Jan 17 '69	
President and Mrs. Richard M. Nixon. Jan 27 '69	To heal a nation. Special section: The task before the President. Jan 24 '69	
	Black vs. Jew. A tragic confrontation. Jan 31 '69	

Newsweek **February 1969**	*Time* **February 1969**
Who is to blame? The Pueblo's Captain: Lloyd M. Bucher. Feb 3 '69	The young actors. Stars and anti-stars. Dustin Hoffman and Mia Farrow. Feb 7 '69
Black mood on campus. Feb 10 '69	New approaches to friends and foes. Presidential adviser Kissinger. Feb 14 '69
Danger! Highly explosive. A talk with Israel's Premier. Feb 17 '69	What's wrong with U.S. medicine. Feb 21 '69
Taxes. How to ease the squeeze. Feb 24 '69	Nixon's trip. The stakes in Europe. Feb 28 '69

Newsweek **March 1969**	*Time* **March 1969**
Mr. Nixon goes to Europe. Mar 3 '69	Takeovers in high gear. Threat or boon to U.S. business? Mar 7 '69
Student rebels. How to tame the turmoil? Mar 10 '69	The great missile debate. Mar 14 '69
The sick, sick cities. Mar 17 '69	Astrology and the new cult of the occult. Mar 21 '69
The assassins. [James Earl Ray and Sirhan Sirhan] Mar 24 '69	Viet Nam: When can the U.S. begin to leave? Mar 28 '69
The war: Nixon's big test. Mar 31 '69	

Newsweek	**April 1969**

Dwight D. Eisenhower. 1890 - 1969.
Apr 7 '69

Sex and the arts.   Apr 14 '69

Beverly Sills. New high for an
American singer.   Apr 21 '69

Challenge from North Korea.
Apr 28 '69

Newsweek	**May 1969**

Universities under the gun.
Militants at Cornell.   May 5 '69

France after de Gaulle. Candidate
Pompidou.   May 12 '69

Abe Fortas. Justice on the spot.
May 19 '69

Janis Joplin. Rebirth of the blues.
May 26 '69

Newsweek	**June 1969**

9.4 miles to the moon. [U.S. space
flight to the moon]   Jun 2 '69

The military industrial complex.
Jun 9 '69

Russia in trouble. [Soviet relations
with China]   Jun 16 '69

Class of '69. The violent years.
Jun 23 '69

Report from Black America.
Jun 30 '69

Time	**April 1969**

Dwight Eisenhower. 1890 - 1969.
Apr 4 '69

The military under attack.
Apr 11 '69

Rage and reform on campus.
Apr 18 '69

Ethel Kennedy.   Apr 25 '69

Time	**May 1969**

Battle plan for the home front.
[Department of Health, Education
and Welfare]   May 2 '69

France after de Gaulle. Georges
Pompidou.   May 9 '69

Deadlock in the Middle East.
Egypt's Nasser.   May 16 '69

The novel is alive and living in
Antiterra. Vladimir Nabokov.
May 23 '69

The Supreme Court. Warren
Burger. Next Chief Justice.
May 30 '69

Time	**June 1969**

The supertourist: Temple Fielding.
Jun 6 '69

Communist summit: Trying to
pick up the pieces.   Jun 13 '69

Starting to go home. [Vietnam
War troop withdrawals]
Jun 20 '69

Is Prince Charles necessary?
Jun 27 '69

U.S. News	**1969**

NO COVER STORY. Until 1974,
U.S. News reported several stories
with equal emphasis.

Newsweek July 1969	*Time* July 1969	*U.S. News* 1969

Newsweek — July 1969

The Moon Age. A special section: How we got there. Where we're going.   Jul 7 '69

Prince Charles: Pomp and circumspection.   Jul 14 '69

The great adventure. Apollo 11 Commander Neil Armstrong. Jul 21 '69

'One giant leap.' [U.S. space flight to the moon]   Jul 28 '69

Time — July 1969

The grapes of wrath, 1969. Mexican-Americans on the march. Cesar Chavez.   Jul 4 '69

The sex explosion. [Sex in the performing arts]   Jul 11 '69

To the moon.   Jul 18 '69

Man on the moon.   Jul 25 '69

U.S. News — 1969

NO COVER STORY. Until 1974, U.S. News reported several stories with equal emphasis.

Newsweek — August 1969

'Should I resign?' Senator Kennedy.   Aug 4 '69

Moonwalk in color.   Aug 11 '69

Advertising's creative explosion. Aug 18 '69

The case of the Green Berets. Aug 25 '69

Time — August 1969

The Kennedy debacle: A girl dead, a career in jeopardy. Edward Kennedy after funeral.   Aug 1 '69

John Wayne.   Aug 8 '69

Nixon rides the waves. [Nixon's relations with Congress] Aug 15 '69

The Mafia v. America.   Aug 22 '69

Shaking up the Pentagon. Defense Secretary Laird.   Aug 29 '69

Newsweek — September 1969

The talk of TV. Merv Griffin. Joey Bishop. Johnny Carson.   Sep 1 '69

Mr. Law-and-Order. Attorney General John Mitchell.   Sep 8 '69

Pro football '69. Namath of the Jets. Sep 15 '69

The great oil hunt. Alaska's North Slope.   Sep 22 '69

Alice's restaurant's kids. Folk singer Arlo Guthrie.   Sep 29 '69

Time — September 1969

The New York Mets: Baseball's wunderkinder.   Sep 5 '69

New era in North Viet Nam. Ho Chi Minh.   Sep 12 '69

Middle East: Toward the brink. Israel's Golda Meir.   Sep 19 '69

Drugs and the young.   Sep 26 '69

Newsweek October 1969	*Time* October 1969	*U.S. News* 1969
The troubled American. Special report on the white majority. Oct 6 '69	The battle for New York. Mario Procaccino. Oct 3 '69	NO COVER STORY. Until 1974, U.S. News reported several stories with equal emphasis.
Nixon in trouble. Oct 13 '69	New leaders for Germany. Socialist Willy Brandt. Oct 10 '69	
Which way out? [Anti-Vietnam War demonstrations] Oct 20 '69	Moratorium: At war with war. Oct 17 '69	
The 747 arrives. Into a new air age. Oct 27 '69	What if we just pull out? [Vietnam War] Oct 24 '69	
	The homosexual in America. Oct 31 '69	

Newsweek November 1969	*Time* November 1969
Lindsay and the fight for New York. Nov 3 '69	California: Here it comes! Nov 7 '69
Hepburn returns to Broadway. Kate and Coco. Nov 10 '69	Agnew: Nixon's other voice. Nov 14 '69
Agnew on the firing line. The Vice President. Nov 17 '69	Counterattack on dissent. [Vice President Agnew's criticism of the media] Nov 21 '69
Does TV tell it straight? Nov 24 '69	Raquel Welch. Can today's sex symbol find happiness as Myra Breckinridge. Nov 28 '69

Newsweek December 1969	*Time* December 1969
Why Haynsworth lost. Dec 1 '69	The massacre. Where does the guilt lie? Lieut. William Calley, Jr. Dec 5 '69
The killings at Song My. Accused: Lt. William L. Calley, Jr. Dec 8 '69	The consumer revolt. Ralph Nader. Dec 12 '69
The dazzling New York Knicks. Dec 15 '69	Will there be a recession? Dec 19 '69
The man in the White House basement. Presidential adviser Henry A. Kissinger. Dec 22 '69	Is God coming back to life? Dec 26 '69
Good-bye to the '60s. Dec 29 '69	

Newsweek **January 1970**	*Time* **January 1970**	*U.S. News* **1970**
Barbra Streisand. Jan 5 '70	Man and woman of the year. The middle Americans. Jan 5 '70	NO COVER STORY. Until 1974, U.S. News reported several stories with equal emphasis.
Can inflation be stopped? The economy in 1970. Jan 12 '70	The new sound of country rock. The Band. Jan 12 '70	
Greece: How the colonels run the country. Jan 19 '70	The superjets take off. Jan 19 '70	
The ravaged environment. Jan 26 '70	Biafra: End of a rebellion. Jan 26 '70	

Newsweek **February 1970**	*Time* **February 1970**
Neil Simon. Last of the red hot playwrights. Feb 2 '70	Environment: Nixon's new issue. Ecologist Barry Commoner. The emerging science of survival Feb 2 '70
Vietnamization. Will Nixon's plan work? Feb 9 '70	The American Indian: Goodbye to Tonto. Feb 9 '70
What's wrong with the high schools? Feb 16 '70	Jane, Henry, and Peter: The flying Fondas. Feb 16 '70
The Panthers and the law. [Black Panthers] Feb 23 '70	The Catholic exodus: Why priests and nuns are quitting. Feb 23 '70

Newsweek **March 1970**	*Time* **March 1970**
Verdict in Chicago. [Chicago Seven Trial] Mar 2 '70	Japan shows off at Expo '70. Mar 2 '70
Japan. Salesman to the world. Expo '70 in color. Mar 9 '70	Retreat from integration. Mar 9 '70
Midi vs. mini. [Women's fashion] Mar 16 '70	Heroin hits the young. Mar 16 '70
Women in revolt. Mar 23 '70	Inefficiency in America. Why nothing seems to work any more. Mar 23 '70
The day the mail stopped. [Postal strike] Mar 30 '70	Postal breakdown: A national crisis. [Postal strike] Mar 30 '70

Newsweek **April 1970**	*Time* **April 1970**	*U.S. News* **1970**
Detroit fights back. Apr 6 '70	Black America 1970. Apr 6 '70	NO COVER STORY. Until 1974, U.S. News reported several stories with equal emphasis.
Abortion and the law. Apr 13 '70	Novelist between the generations. A man who can speak to the young. Germany's Gunter Grass. Apr 13 '70	
The seat Nixon can't fill. Apr 20 '70	The Carswell defeat. Nixon's embattled White House. [Supreme Court nomination] Apr 20 '70	
The saga of Apollo 13. Apr 27 '70	The return. Astronauts praying after splashdown. Apr 27 '70	

Newsweek **May 1970**	*Time* **May 1970**
Now it's the Indochina war. May 4 '70	Who rules Russia? In color: The Soviet military in action. May 4 '70
Nixon's Cambodian gamble. May 11 '70	The new war. Will Nixon's gamble work? May 11 '70
Nixon's home front. [Anti-Vietnam War demonstrations and Kent State riot] May 18 '70	Protest! [Anti-Vietnam War demonstrations and Kent State riot] May 18 '70
Recession. May 25 '70	Sex education for adults. Researchers Masters and Johnson. May 25 '70

Newsweek **June 1970**	*Time* **June 1970**
Russia in the Mideast. Jun 1 '70	Is this slump necessary? [Recession] Jun 1 '70
Wall Street in a whirl. Jun 8 '70	Nixon's palace guard. Kissinger, Mitchell, Haldeman, Ehrlichman. Jun 8 '70
Universities in ferment. Jun 15 '70	"Catch 22" on film. Director Mike Nichols. War as horror-comedy. Jun 15 '70
The music man 1970. Burt Bacharach. Jun 22 '70	Israel and her enemies. Jun 22 '70
The winner. Prime Minister Heath. Jun 29 '70	Upset in Britain. The Tories take over. Prime Minister Edward Heath. Jun 29 '70

Newsweek	**July 1970**

The spirit of '70. Six historians on the 'American crisis.'   Jul 6 '70

The Cambodian campaign. Was it worth it?   Jul 13 '70

The President's preacher. Billy Graham and the surging Southern Baptists.   Jul 20 '70

Is privacy dead? [The right to privacy]   Jul 27 '70

Newsweek	**August 1970**

The Black mayors. How are they doing?   Aug 3 '70

Summer '70. Young Americans abroad.   Aug 10 '70

Can the Mideast truce work? Aug 17 '70

More than you want to know about sex.   Aug 24 '70

Military justice on trial. Aug 31 '70

Newsweek	**September 1970**

Marijuana: Time to change the law?   Sep 7 '70

Showdown in Detroit. [Automobile industry]   Sep 14 '70

The hijack war. [Airplane hijacking]   Sep 21 '70

Explosion in Jordan.   Sep 28 '70

Time	**July 1970**

Fight over the flag: Patriots and put-ons.   Jul 6 '70

Cops v. crime: Ready for a hot summer.   Jul 13 '70

A new job for business: Reform without revolution. Henry Ford II.   Jul 20 '70

Alaska: Last chance for the last frontier.   Jul 27 '70

Time	**August 1970**

Growing old in America. The unwanted generation.   Aug 3 '70

Middle East: Push for peace. Aug 10 '70

How to educate your parents. [Generation gap]   Aug 17 '70

Changing Wall Street. Dreyfus Fund's Howard Stein.   Aug 24 '70

The politics of sex. Kate Millett of women's lib.   Aug 31 '70

Time	**September 1970**

Star for an uptight age. Elliott Gould.   Sep 7 '70

The man behind the midi mania. John Fairchild of "Women's Wear Daily."   Sep 14 '70

Pirates in the sky. [Airplane hijacking]   Sep 21 '70

Showdown in Jordan. The Arab guerrillas.   Sep 28 '70

U.S. News	**1970**

NO COVER STORY. Until 1974, U.S. News reported several stories with equal emphasis.

Newsweek October 1970	*Time* October 1970	*U.S. News* 1970
Trials of a rookie. [Professional football] Oct 5 '70	Facing the Middle East. When to use or not use power. Oct 5 '70	NO COVER STORY. Until 1974, U.S. News reported several stories with equal emphasis.
The Mideast after Nasser. Oct 12 '70	The Arab world after Nasser. Oct 12 '70	
The selling of the candidates 1970. Oct 19 '70	Marxist threat in the Americas. Chile's Salvador Allende. Oct 19 '70	
Angela Davis. Black revolutionary. Oct 26 '70	Battle for the Senate. Oct 26 '70	

Newsweek November 1970	*Time* November 1970
Canada in crisis. Nov 2 '70	The urban guerrillas. [International terrorism] Nov 2 '70
Return of the champ. Muhammad Ali. Nov 9 '70	Blue collar power. Nov 9 '70
The Democrats shape up. Nov 16 '70	New faces of 1970. [Elections] Nov 16 '70
University of California. Where things happen first. Nov 23 '70	Sesame Street. TV's gift to children. Nov 23 '70
Wall Street in trouble. Nov 30 '70	The wives of Washington. Martha Mitchell. Nov 30 '70

Newsweek December 1970	*Time* December 1970
The new movies. Dec 7 '70	The plight of the prisoners. [Vietnam POWs] Dec 7 '70
In search of a foreign policy. Dec 14 '70	The battle of the buck. Worth 73 cents. Dec 14 '70
The quest for identity. Psychoanalyst Erik. H. Erikson. Dec 21 '70	The military goes mod. Admiral Zumwalt. Dec 21 '70
Nostalgia. The vogue for the old. Dec 28 '70	The U.S. family: "Help!" Dec 28 '70

Newsweek **January 1971**	*Time* **January 1971**	*U.S. News* **1971**
The future of rock. Jan 4 '71	Man of the year. Willy Brandt. Jan 4 '71	NO COVER STORY. Until 1974, U.S. News reported several stories with equal emphasis.
The troubled army in Vietnam. Jan 11 '71	The return to romance. Ali MacGraw. Jan 11 '71	
The agony of the commuter. Jan 18 '71	U.S. prisons: Schools for crime. Jan 18 '71	
Who's in charge? [Nixon's relations with Congress] Jan 25 '71	Rebel priests: The curious case of the Berrigans. Jan 25 '71	

Newsweek **February 1971**	*Time* **February 1971**
Dissent in Russia. Feb 1 '71	New Congress v. Nixon. Feb 1 '71
Welfare. There must be a better way. Feb 8 '71	The welfare maze. Feb 8 '71
A wider war? [Vietnam War and Laos] Feb 15 '71	The war: Getting in deeper to get out faster? [Vietnam War and Laos] Feb 15 '71
War against cancer. A progress report. Feb 22 '71	The cooling of America. [Relatively calm social conditions] Feb 22 '71

Newsweek **March 1971**	*Time* **March 1971**
The American Jew. New pride, new problems. Mar 1 '71	The new rock: Bittersweet and low. Mar 1 '71
Justice on trial. [Criminal justice system] Mar 8 '71	The $5,000,000 fighters. Frazer. Ali. Mar 8 '71
The helicopter war. Mar 15 '71	Suburbia: A myth challenged. Mar 15 '71
The art of murder. Detective novelist Ross Macdonald. Mar 22 '71	An actor's art: Rage beneath the surface. George C. Scott. Mar 22 '71
Fashion '71. Anything goes. Mar 29 '71	Kremlin roulette: New faces coming up? Mar 29 '71

Newsweek April 1971	*Time* April 1971	*U.S. News* 1971
How to run a city. Chicago's Mayor Richard J. Daley. Apr 5 '71	After the SST: Picking up the pieces in the aerospace industry. Apr 5 '71	NO COVER STORY. Until 1974, U.S. News reported several stories with equal emphasis.
The Calley verdict. Who else is guilty? Apr 12 '71	Who shares the guilt? [William Calley and the My Lai massacre] Apr 12 '71	
The shape of things to come. [Architecture] Apr 19 '71	The genetics: Man into Superman. Apr 19 '71	
China: A new game begins. Apr 26 '71	China: A whole new game. First color photos. Yanks in Peking. Apr 26 '71	

Newsweek May 1971	*Time* May 1971
The new grade school. Learning can be fun. May 3 '71	That old magic relights Broadway. Alexis Smith in "Follies." May 3 '71
Hoover's FBI. Time for a change? May 10 '71	How to cope with Japan's business invasion. May 10 '71
The May Day arrests. [Anti-Vietnam War demonstrations] May 17 '71	The Middle East riddle. May 17 '71
Corporations under fire. May 24 '71	Now where are the jobs? The graduate, 1971. May 24 '71
What's ahead for TV. May 31 '71	Dixie whistles a different tune. Georgia Governor Jimmy Carter. May 31 '71

Newsweek June 1971	*Time* June 1971
The new Black politics. The House caucus. Jun 7 '71	Wit in the night. [Dick Cavett] Jun 7 '71
White House wedding. Jun 14 '71	White House wedding. Jun 14 '71
Probing the brain. Jun 21 '71	The Jesus revolution. Jun 21 '71
The secret history of Vietnam. Jun 28 '71	Pentagon Papers: The secret war. Jun 28 '71

| *Newsweek* | **July 1971** | *Time* | **July 1971** | *U.S. News* | **1971** |

Newsweek   **July 1971**

The heroin plague.   Jul 5 '71

Victory for the press. [Pentagon papers]   Jul 12 '71

Golf's biggest money winner. Lee Trevino.   Jul 19 '71

Nixon: I will go to China. Jul 26 '71

Newsweek   **August 1971**

Bengal: The murder of a people. Aug 2 '71

Nixon's No. 2 man? Treasury Secretary John Connally. Aug 9 '71

The new woman. Gloria Steinem. Aug 16 '71

A switch in time? John V. Lindsay. Aug 23 '71

Your new dollar. Nixon's recovery plan.   Aug 30 '71

Newsweek   **September 1971**

Fight over the freeze. AFL-CIO's George Meany.   Sep 6 '71

The new face of adoption. Sep 13 '71

JFK's memorial.   Sep 20 '71

The Attica tragedy. [Attica state prison riot]   Sep 27 '71

Time   **July 1971**

The war exposés: Battle over the right to know. Daniel Ellsberg. Jul 5 '71

The Mafia at war.   Jul 12 '71

Trevino: Golf's new superstar. Jul 19 '71

To Peking for peace.   Jul 26 '71

Time   **August 1971**

Pakistan's agony.   Aug 2 '71

Apollo 15: The most perilous journey.   Aug 9 '71

Battle of the economy: Stand pat or do something?   Aug 16 '71

New zip in the old game. Vida Blue.   Aug 23 '71

Nixon's economic gamble. Aug 30 '71

Time   **September 1971**

Labor in the freeze.   Sep 6 '71

Front runner for '72. Senator Edmund Muskie.   Sep 13 '71

B. F. Skinner says: We can't afford freedom.   Sep 20 '71

The bitter lessons of Attica. [Attica state prison riot]   Sep 27 '71

U.S. News   **1971**

NO COVER STORY. Until 1974, U.S. News reported several stories with equal emphasis.

Newsweek **October 1971**	*Time* **October 1971**	*U.S. News* **1971**
Has the Church lost its soul? A survey of U.S. Catholics. Oct 4 '71	It's a tougher world for Japan. Oct 4 '71	NO COVER STORY. Until 1974, U.S. News reported several stories with equal emphasis.
New maestro, new beat. New York Philharmonic's Pierre Boulez. Oct 11 '71	The new spy. Oct 11 '71	
Living with controls. [Wage-price controls] Oct 18 '71	The impact of Phase II. [Nixon's economic policy] Oct 18 '71	
How will youth vote? Oct 25 '71	Jesus Christ Superstar rocks Broadway. Oct 25 '71	

Newsweek **November 1971**	*Time* **November 1971**
Pro football's red-hot Redskins. Coach George Allen. Nov 1 '71	The Nixon court. William H. Rehnquist. Lewis F. Powell, Jr. Nov 1 '71
China joins the world. Nov 8 '71	The Chinese are coming. Nov 8 '71
Battle of the suburbs. Nov 15 '71	The battle over busing. Nov 15 '71
The new espionage. CIA chief Richard Helms. Nov 22 '71	America's queen of opera. Beverly Sills. Nov 22 '71
TV's 'All in the Family.' The Bunkers. Nov 29 '71	Could he win in '72? Ted Kennedy. Nov 29 '71

Newsweek **December 1971**	*Time* **December 1971**
The battle for Bengal. India attacks. Dec 6 '71	Conflict in Asia: India v. Pakistan. Dec 6 '71
Money and politics. Dec 13 '71	Looking for life out there. [Life on other planets] Dec 13 '71
India-Pakistan War. Who's to blame? Dec 20 '71	The bloody birth of Bangladesh. Dec 20 '71
Merry Christmas. Schulz. Dec 27 '71	The do-gooders. [Volunteers] Dec 27 '71

Newsweek **January 1972**	*Time* **January 1972**	*U.S. News* **1972**
From '2001' to 'A Clockwork Orange.' The startling vision of Stanley Kubrick. Jan 3 '72	Man of the year. Richard M. Nixon. Jan 3 '72	NO COVER STORY LISTED. Until 1974, U.S. News reported several stories with equal emphasis.
Who can beat Nixon? Jan 10 '72	Ireland: The tactics of terror. Jan 10 '72	
Amnesty for the war exiles? Jan 17 '72	Super Bowl. Jan 17 '72	
VD. The epidemic. Jan 24 '72	The Hughes mystery. [Howard Hughes] Jan 24 '72	
The economic issue. '1972 will be a very good year.' Richard Nixon. Jan 31 '72	TV's first black superstar. Comedian Flip Wilson. Jan 31 '72	

Newsweek **February 1972**	*Time* **February 1972**
The Vietnam peace offer. Nixon's secret agent. Henry Kissinger. Feb 7 '72	Nixon's secret agent. Henry Kissinger. Feb 7 '72
Winter Olympics in Japan. Feb 14 '72	America's forgotten children. Psychiatrist Robert Coles. Feb 14 '72
The China Nixon will see. Feb 21 '72	Con man of the year. Clifford Irving by Elmyr de Hory. Feb 21 '72
Liza Minnelli in 'Cabaret.' A star is born. Feb 28 '72	The new Miss Show Biz. Liza Minnelli. Feb 28 '72

Newsweek **March 1972**	*Time* **March 1972**
Nixon in China. Mar 6 '72	Nixon's China odyssey. Mar 6 '72
Brando as 'The Godfather.' Mar 13 '72	Is the U.S. going broke? Mar 13 '72
The ITT affair: Politics and justice. Acting Attorney General Richard G. Kleindienst. Mar 20 '72	The American woman. Mar 20 '72
Democrats in disorder. The wild card of politics '72. George Wallace. Mar 27 '72	Now who's on first? [Presidential candidates] Mar 27 '72

Newsweek **April 1972**	*Time* **April 1972**	*U.S. News* **1972**
Bleeding Ireland. Apr 3 '72	Jack Anderson, supersnoop. Washington: Affluence & influence. Apr 3 '72	NO COVER STORY LISTED. Until 1974, U.S. News reported several stories with equal emphasis.
The gambling explosion. Apr 10 '72	What it means to be Jewish. Apr 10 '72	
The war that won't go away. [Vietnam War] Apr 17 '72	Vietnam: The big test. Apr 17 '72	
World trade: Can the U.S. compete? Apr 24 '72	Gang war. The how and why of murder. Apr 24 '72	

Newsweek **May 1972**	*Time* **May 1972**
Heart attack. Curbing the killer. May 1 '72	Nixon at war. May 1 '72
The new Democratic race. May 8 '72	Here comes the prairie populist. Senator George McGovern. May 8 '72
The specter of defeat. [Vietnam War] May 15 '72	The big red blitz. North Viet Nam's General Giap. May 15 '72
Nixon's gamble. [Vietnam War] May 22 '72	Nixon strikes back. [Vietnam War] May 22 '72
The Moscow summit. May 29 '72	The strangest summit. May 29 '72

Newsweek **June 1972**	*Time* **June 1972**
From Russia with hope. [Summit conference] Jun 5 '72	Adding up the summit. Jun 5 '72
The big cleanup. The environmental crisis '72. Jun 12 '72	The man with 300,000 beds. Innkeeper Kemmons Wilson. Jun 12 '72
Can he put the party together? George and Eleanor McGovern. Jun 19 '72	The occult revival. Satan returns. Jun 19 '72
Tennis: The women take over. Jun 26 '72	Here come those great new cameras. Jun 26 '72

Newsweek **July 1972**	*Time* **July 1972**	*U.S. News* **1972**
New life in the American theater. Producer Joseph Papp. Jul 3 '72	Everything you always wanted to know about Woody Allen. Jul 3 '72	NO COVER STORY LISTED. Until 1974, U.S. News reported several stories with equal emphasis.
A spectrum of views on the real issues of '72. Daniel P. Moynihan. Mary McCarthy. . . Jul 10 '72	Baseball's best catcher. Cincinnati's Johnny Bench. Jul 10 '72	
New wave hits Miami. [Democratic National Convention] Jul 17 '72	The battle for the Democratic Party. McGovern's young legions take on the old pros. Jul 17 '72	
Target: Nixon and Agnew. Jul 24 '72	In quest of a second miracle. The Democratic ticket. Jul 24 '72	
Bobby's next move? [Chess and Bobby Fischer] Jul 31 '72	The big chess battle: Knight-Errant v. King. Spassky. Fischer. Jul 31 '72	

Newsweek **August 1972**	*Time* **August 1972**
The Eagleton crisis. Aug 7 '72	The Eagleton affair. Aug 7 '72
All about acupuncture. Aug 14 '72	The Democrats try again. Sargent Shriver. Aug 14 '72
Fall fashions. Ease and elegance designed by Halston. Aug 21 '72	Sex & the teenager. Aug 21 '72
What America really thinks of Nixon. Aug 28 '72	Once more with feeling. [Presidential candidates] Aug 28 '72

Newsweek **September 1972**	*Time* **September 1972**
The Spiro of '76? Sep 4 '72	The global war on heroin. Sep 4 '72
Olympics '72. Sep 11 '72	An Olympian wave. Mark Spitz. Sep 11 '72
The Olympic tragedy. Israel buries its dead. Sep 18 '72	Murder in Munich. [Terrorist attack at the Olympic Games] Sep 18 '72
Show biz in politics. Shirley MacLaine. Sep 25 '72	The new TV season: Toppling old taboos. Fred Sanford. Cousin Maude. Archie Bunker. Sep 25 '72

Newsweek **October 1972**	*Time* **October 1972**	*U.S. News* **1972**
This is Howard Cosell... Oct 2 '72	The two Americas. Is it still a contest? [Presidential campaigns] Oct 2 '72	NO COVER STORY LISTED. Until 1974, U.S. News reported several stories with equal emphasis.
The battle of the POW's. Oct 9 '72	The other campaigners. Pat Nixon. Eleanor McGovern. Oct 9 '72	
Yearning for the fifties. The good old days. Oct 16 '72	Pro football's game plan: Back to the attack. Oct 16 '72	
Black movies. Renaissance or ripoff? Oct 23 '72	A national disgrace: The $400,000,000 election. Oct 23 '72	
Nixon's Vietnam deal. Hanoi's POW pledge. Oct 30 '72	On the brink of peace? [Vietnam War] Oct 30 '72	

Newsweek **November 1972**	*Time* **November 1972**
'Peace is at hand.' Good-bye Vietnam. Nov 6 '72	The shape of peace. [Vietnam War] Nov 6 '72
Four more years. Landslide. [Presidential election] Nov 13 '72	Getting away from it all with Jonathan Livingston Seagull. Nov 13 '72
Global companies. Too big to handle? Nov 20 '72	Landslide. Prospects for the second term. [Presidential election] Nov 20 '72
The new sex therapy. Nov 27 '72	American wine: There's gold in them thar grapes. Nov 27 '72

Newsweek **December 1972**	*Time* **December 1972**
The running backs. [Professional football] Dec 4 '72	Hollywood's new Nordic star. Liv Ullman Dec 4 '72
Love and violence: A vision of America. Novelist Joyce Carol Oates. Dec 11 '72	Building for the Super Bowl. Miami coach Don Shula. Dec 11 '72
Living with crime. Dec 18 '72	Eating may not be good for you. Dec 18 '72
The church faces life. Dec 25 '72	Holiday on skis. The hottest sport, the coolest slopes. Dec 25 '72

Newsweek **January 1973**	*Time* **January 1973**	*U.S. News* **1973**
What went wrong? Presidential adviser Kissinger. [Vietnam War peace talks] Jan 1 '73	Men of the year. Triumph and trial. Henry Kissinger. Richard Nixon. Jan 1 '73	NO COVER STORY. Until 1974, U.S. News reported several stories with equal emphasis.
Coping with depression. Jan 8 '73	After the bombs, what peace? [Vietnam War] Jan 8 '73	
Nixon and the media. Jan 15 '73	Crisis in Congress. Jan 15 '73	
The energy crisis. Jan 22 '73	Sex and death in Paris. Marlon Brando in "Last Tango." Jan 22 '73	
How solid a peace? [Vietnam War] Jan 29 '73	Nixon II: Beyond Viet Nam. Jan 29 '73	

Newsweek **February 1973**	*Time* **February 1973**
Peace. [Vietnam War] Feb 5 '73	The cease-fire. [Vietnam War] Feb 5 '73
The hottest movie. Director Bernardo Bertolucci. Feb 12 '73	Inside pop records. Feb 12 '73
What ever happened to Black America? Feb 19 '73	The prisoners return. Welcome home daddy. [Vietnam POWs] Feb 19 '73
Home at last! [Vietnam POWs] Feb 26 '73	The cheaper dollar. Impact on prices & jobs. George Shultz. Feb 26 '73

Newsweek **March 1973**	*Time* **March 1973**
The high cost of eating. Mar 5 '73	Carlos Castaneda: Magic and reality. Mar 5 '73
The broken family. Mar 12 '73	Europe. America's new rival. Mar 12 '73
Nixon's palace guard. Presidential aide Haldeman. Mar 19 '73	Toward control of cancer. Immunologist Robert Good. Mar 19 '73
Who wants to work? Boredom on the job. Mar 26 '73	The FBI in politics. L. Patrick Gray III. Mar 26 '73

Newsweek **April 1973**	*Time* **April 1973**	*U.S. News* **1973**
The Watergate mess. Apr 2 '73	The Arabs: Oil, power, violence. Libya's strongman Gaddafi. Apr 2 '73	NO COVER STORY. Until 1974, U.S. News reported several stories with equal emphasis.
The meat furor. Apr 9 '73	Food prices: The big beef. Apr 9 '73	
How to stay young. Apr 16 '73	Showdown over secrecy. Senate v. White House. Watergate prober Sam Ervin. Apr 16 '73	
Broadway's music man. Composer Stephen Sondheim. Apr 23 '73	The Jesuits. Catholicism's troubled front line. Apr 23 '73	
Nixon and Watergate. Apr 30 '73	Watergate breaks wide open. Apr 30 '73	

Newsweek **May 1973**	*Time* **May 1973**
The White House in turmoil. May 7 '73	The fastest baton in the West. Chicago's Georg Solti. May 7 '73
Can he stay afloat? [Nixon and the Watergate affair] May 14 '73	How much did he know? [Nixon and the Watergate affair] May 14 '73
Indicted. John Mitchell. [Watergate affair] May 21 '73	The inquest begins. John Mitchell. May 21 '73
Exposing the big cover-up. Watergate witness James McCord. May 28 '73	Watergate dynamite. How much damage? May 28 '73

Newsweek **June 1973**	*Time* **June 1973**
Nixon states his case. [Watergate affair] Jun 4 '73	Nixon fights back. [Watergate affair] Jun 4 '73
Superhorse. Secretariat. Jun 11 '73	Super horse. Secretariat. Jun 11 '73
The country music craze. Jun 18 '73	Nixon's other crisis. [Inflation] Jun 18 '73
The freeze. What next? [Wage-price controls] Jun 25 '73	Brezhnev comes courting. Leonid Brezhnev. Jun 25 '73

Newsweek **July 1973**	*Time* **July 1973**	*U.S. News* **1973**
The accuser. John Dean. [Watergate affair] Jul 2 '73	Dean talks. [Watergate affair] Jul 2 '73	NO COVER STORY. Until 1974, U.S. News reported several stories with equal emphasis.
Dean vs. Nixon. [Watergate affair] Jul 9 '73	Can Nixon survive Dean? [Watergate affair] Jul 9 '73	
Games singles play. Jul 16 '73	Monroe meets Mailer. Jul 16 '73	
Now, pneumonia. Jul 23 '73	In defense of Nixon. 'Speak no evil.' John Mitchell. Jul 23 '73	
The Nixon tapes. [Watergate affair] Jul 30 '73	The Nixon tapes. Playback wanted. [Watergate affair] Jul 30 '73	

Newsweek **August 1973**	*Time* **August 1973**
Showdown! [Watergate tapes] Aug 6 '73	Historic challenge. [Watergate tapes] Aug 6 '73
Chasing the Babe. Hank Aaron. Aug 13 '73	The good life in Minnesota. Gov. Wendell Anderson. Aug 13 '73
The Agnew case. [Spiro Agnew bribery case] Aug 20 '73	Can trust be restored? Adding up Watergate I. Aug 20 '73
Queen of 'The Scene.' Marisa Berenson. Aug 27 '73	Scrambling to break clear. [Nixon and the Watergate affair] Aug 27 '73

Newsweek **September 1973**	*Time* **September 1973**
On the rebound? [Nixon and the Watergate affair] Sep 3 '73	The super Secretary: Ready to shake up State. Henry Kissinger. Sep 3 '73
War for the tapes. Judge John J. Sirica. [Watergate affair] Sep 10 '73	The happy hustler. Bobby Riggs. [Professional tennis] Sep 10 '73
Arab oil squeeze. Sep 17 '73	The hamburger empire. McDonald's. Sep 17 '73
Chile under the gun. Sep 24 '73	After the fall. Allende. [Chile] Sep 24 '73

Newsweek **October 1973**	*Time* **October 1973**	*U.S. News* **1973**
Spiro on the spot. [Spiro Agnew bribery case]　Oct 1 '73	The Agnew crisis. [Spiro Agnew bribery case]　Oct 1 '73	NO COVER STORY. Until 1974, U.S. News reported several stories with equal emphasis.
Spiro fights back. [Spiro Agnew bribery case]　Oct 8 '73	Agnew on the tightrope. [Spiro Agnew bribery case]　Oct 8 '73	
The Mideast erupts.　Oct 15 '73	War in the Middle East. Oct 15 '73	
After Agnew. [Spiro Agnew bribery case]　Oct 22 '73	The new No. 2. Gerald Ford. Oct 22 '73	
The tapes crisis. Archibald Cox. [Watergate affair]　Oct 29 '73	Nixon on the brink. [Watergate affair]　Oct 29 '73	

Newsweek **November 1973**	*Time* **November 1973**
Can he survive? [Nixon and the Watergate affair]　Nov 5 '73	The push to impeach.　Nov 5 '73
What next? [Watergate affair] Nov 12 '73	Nixon's jury: The people. Nov 12 '73
Running out of everything. [Energy crisis]　Nov 19 '73	The oil squeeze. Saudi Arabia's King Feisal.　Nov 19 '73
'I'm not a crook.' [Nixon and the Watergate affair]　Nov 26 '73	TV's year of the cop. Peter Falk as Columbo.　Nov 26 '73

Newsweek **December 1973**	*Time* **December 1973**
How bad a slump? [Energy crisis] Dec 3 '73	The big freeze. Nixon's energy cuts. [Wage-price freeze]　Dec 3 '73
Rose Mary's boo-boo. [Watergate tapes]　Dec 10 '73	The secretary and the tapes. Rose Mary Woods. [Watergate affair] Dec 10 '73
Here comes Bette! The divine Miss Midler.　Dec 17 '73	The new second family. [Vice President Gerald Ford]　Dec 17 '73
The arts in America.　Dec 24 '73	The child's world. Christmas 1973. Dec 24 '73
The coldest winter.　Dec 31 '73	The big car: End of the affair. Dec 31 '73

Newsweek **January 1974**	*Time* **January 1974**	*U.S. News* **January 1974**
How high a price? [Petroleum prices] Jan 71 '74	Man of the year. Judge John Sirica. Jan 7 '74	'74. Special report on a crucial year. Can a recession be avoided? Real peace abroad? An end to fuel crisis? What's in. . . Jan 7 '74
Dylan's back. Jan 14 '74	Inside the brain. Jan 14 '74	Gas shortage - Fact or fiction? Jan 14 '74
Inside Nixon's White House. Ronald Ziegler. Jan 21 '74	Energy crunch: Real or phony? William Simon. Jan 21 '74	What voters tell Congress about: Impeaching Nixon. Pain of high prices. Fuel fiasco. Next November's elections. Jan 21 '74
The telltale tape. [Watergate tapes] Jan 28 '74	The telltale tape. [Watergate tapes] Jan 28 '74	"Cruelest tax." Inflation's bite - Any relief in sight? Jan 28 '74

Newsweek **February 1974**	*Time* **February 1974**	*U.S. News* **February 1974**
The great Redford. Robert Redford in "The Great Gatsby." Feb 4 '74	The impeachment Congress. House leader 'Tip' O'Neill. Feb 4 '74	If Nixon is impeached - what then? Feb 4 '74
The exorcism frenzy. Feb 11 '74	The new arms race. Defense Secretary Schlesinger. Feb 11 '74	Barry Goldwater speaks his mind on Richard Nixon. Feb 11 '74
The Arabs: New pride and power. Feb 18 '74	Exxon: Testing the tiger. Feb 18 '74	Food prices. How much higher? Feb 18 '74
Terror and repression. The hostage. The exile. Feb 25 '74	Alexander Solzhenitsyn. Feb 25 '74	How America is changing. Feb 25 '74

Newsweek **March 1974**	*Time* **March 1974**	*U.S. News* **March 1974**
The big squeeze. [Inflation] Mar 4 '74	The psychics. Mar 4 '74	Political terror in U.S. What next? Mar 4 '74
Indicted. [Watergate defendants] Mar 11 '74	Charging Nixon's men. Special prosecutor Leon Jaworski. Mar 11 '74	No cover story. Mar 11 '74
"I know what I meant." [Nixon and the Watergate affair] Mar 18 '74	The Great Gatsby supersell. Robert Redford & Mia Farrow. Mar 18 '74	Can Nixon withstand new shocks? Mar 18 '74
All about impeachment. Mar 25 '74	Defending Nixon. Mar 25 '74	America's lawyers - "A sick profession?" Mar 25 '74

Newsweek **April 1974**	*Time* **April 1974**	*U.S. News* **April 1974**
Detroit thinks small. [Automobile industry] Apr 1 '74	How Henry does it. [Henry Kissinger] Apr 1 '74	Time for pullback in Europe? Apr 1 '74
The troubled child. Apr 8 '74	World inflation. Apr 8 '74	How safe is the food you eat? Apr 8 '74
Nixon's taxes. Apr 15 '74	Nixon's tax scandal. Apr 15 '74	Alistair Cooke - What TV is doing to America. Apr 15 '74
Bebe and the $100,000. Charles G. Rebozo. Apr 22 '74	Alcoholism. New victims, new treatments. Apr 22 '74	Who runs America? Apr 22 '74
The saga of Patty Hearst. Apr 29 '74	Patty Hearst. Apr 29 '74	America's news industry. Responsible - or reckless? Apr 29 '74

Newsweek **May 1974**	*Time* **May 1974**	*U.S. News* **May 1974**
Today's woman. Barbara Walters. May 6 '74	Country music. Songs of love, loyalty & doubt. Merle Haggard. May 6 '74	Springtime mood at grass roots. On - Nixon ... Inflation ... Politics ... Business ... Morale. May 6 '74
The Nixon papers. [Watergate affair] May 13 '74	Nixon's gamble. Nobody is a friend of ours. I am being the devil's advocate. You could get a million dollars. . . May 13 '74	Nixon's Watergate tapes. May 13 '74
Will he resign? [Nixon and the Watergate affair] May 20 '74	Nixon's shattered presidency. May 20 '74	No cover story. May 20 '74
Patty Hearst. After the shoot-out. May 27 '74	Mid-East massacres. May 27 '74	The Nixon crisis. Where will it lead? May 27 '74

Newsweek **June 1974**	*Time* **June 1974**	*U.S. News* **June 1974**
Women in sports. Jun 3 '74	One-man wild bunch. Oakland's Reggie Jackson. Jun 3 '74	Is Watergate "strangling" U.S. government? Jun 3 '74
It's Super K. [Henry Kissinger] Jun 10 '74	Mideast miracle. Henry Kissinger. Jun 10 '74	What it takes to stop rampant crime. Jun 10 '74
The jury names Nixon. Jun 17 '74	Middle-class Blacks. Making it in America. Jun 17 '74	Inflation. How did it get out of hand? Can you protect yourself? What's the cure? Jun 17 '74
Nixon on tour: 'Welcome, welcome.' Jun 24 '74	Nixon's trip. Seeking a needed lift. Jun 24 '74	What's happening to America's values. A conversation with Claire Booth Luce. Jun 24 '74

Newsweek **July 1974**	*Time* **July 1974**	*U.S. News* **July 1974**
Tennis, everyone! Sweden's Björn Borg. Jul 1 '74	Testing detente. Jul 1 '74	On to Moscow. What's in store for Nixon. Jul 1 '74
Summit of '74. Jul 8 '74	The press: Fair or foul. Jul 8 '74	The makers of America. [U.S. Revolutionary War] Jul 8 '74
Impeachment. Men on the spot. Rodino and Doar. Jul 15 '74	Leadership in America. Special section: 200 rising leaders. Jul 15 '74	Social Security. Promising too much to too many? Jul 15 '74
The evidence. [Nixon and the Watergate affair] Jul 22 '74	Nixon and the court. Watergate: The new evidence. Jul 22 '74	Impeachment crisis - key decisions at hand. Jul 22 '74
How good a case? [Impeachment of Richard Nixon] Jul 29 '74	The G.O.P.'s moment of truth. Jul 29 '74	What stock market is saying. Jul 29 '74

Newsweek **August 1974**	*Time* **August 1974**	*U.S. News* **August 1974**
The impeachment vote. Aug 5 '74	The vote to impeach. Aug 5 '74	Nixon. The case for and against. Aug 5 '74
The eleventh hour. [Nixon presidency] Aug 12 '74	Jack Nicholson. The star with the killer smile. Aug 12 '74	Impeachment. The formal charges. Outlook in the House. Nixon's defense strategy. . . Aug 12 '74
Seven days in August. [Resignation of Richard Nixon] Aug 19 '74	The healing begins. [Resignation of Richard Nixon] Aug 19 '74	What Ford will do as president. Aug 19 '74
The '74 model. Lauren Hutton. Aug 26 '74	Ford on the move. [Gerald Ford] Aug 26 '74	Changeover. Ford sets his course. Aug 26 '74

Newsweek **September 1974**	*Time* **September 1974**	*U.S. News* **September 1974**
The Ford team. [Gerald Ford and Nelson Rockefeller] Sep 2 '74	Nelson Rockefeller. Sep 2 '74	No cover story Sep 2 '74
The big bad bear. [Stock market] Sep 9 '74	Economy. The big headache. Sep 9 '74	A sick economy. What's to be done - Ford's strategy takes shape. Runaway prices. . . Sep 9 '74
Was justice done? [Watergate affair and the Nixon pardon] Sep 16 '74	The pardon. [Watergate affair and the Nixon pardon] Sep 16 '74	No cover story Sep 16 '74
How sick is Nixon? Sep 23 '74	Ford under fire. [Gerald Ford] Sep 23 '74	How Ford runs the White House. Sep 23 '74
Special economic report. What to do? Sep 30 '74	The CIA. Has is gone too far? Director William E. Colby. Sep 30 '74	Mood of America. Prices ... politics ... taxes ... morality. Sep 30 '74

Newsweek **October 1974**	*Time* **October 1974**	*U.S. News* **October 1974**
The operation. Betty Ford. Oct 7 '74	The ordeal of political wives. Oct 7 '74	Politics heats up. Preview of '74 campaign. Now that Ted Kennedy is out - Rockefeller's wealth. The facts about... Oct 7 '74
Julie. The David Eisenhowers. Oct 14 '74	Trying to fight back. Inflation. Recession. Oil. Oct 14 '74	Special report. Squeeze on America's middle class. Oct 14 '74
Photography. Oct 21 '74	New faces, key races. Oct 21 '74	Can Ford win with - Higher taxes. Easier credit. No controls. Oct 21 '74
Music's wonder man. Stevie Wonder. Oct 28 '74	TV's funny girls. Mary Tyler Moore. Valerie Harper. Oct 28 '74	Boston school violence. Turning point in busing? Oct 28 '74

Newsweek **November 1974**	*Time* **November 1974**	*U.S. News* **November 1974**
Women in politics. Ella Grasso for Governor. Nov 4 '74	The emperor of oil. The Shah of Iran. Nov 4 '74	Washington's bureaucrats. "Real rulers of America." Nov 4 '74
Running out of food? [Hunger and world food supply] Nov 11 '74	The Palestinians. Yasser Arafat. Nov 11 '74	What a depression is really like. Scenes from the 1930s. Nov 11 '74
What do we do now? [Democratic party] Nov 18 '74	Now what? [Democratic party] Nov 18 '74	Impact of '74 election - Inflation. Taxes. White House. Business. Jobs. Congress. Nov 18 '74
The new Hollywood. Francis Ford Coppola and the 'Godfathers.' Nov 25 '74	The big raise. Labor & inflation. Nov 25 '74	What Ford sees ahead. Exclusive interview with the President. Nov 25 '74

Newsweek **December 1974**	*Time* **December 1974**	*U.S. News* **December 1974**
How bad a slump? [Recession] Dec 2 '74	Israel besieged. Premier Yitzhat Rabin. Dec 2 '74	No cover story Dec 2 '74
Sizing up Ford. Dec 9 '74	Recession's greetings. P.S. There's some good news too. Dec 9 '74	Straight talk to the U.S. Interview with West German Chancellor Helmut Schmidt. Dec 9 '74
The new gold rush. [Gold as an investment] Dec 16 '74	Rock women. Pride and passion. Joni Mitchell. Dec 16 '74	The losing battle against crime in America. Dec 16 '74
How good is your doctor? Dec 23 '74	The American pet. Dec 23 '74	Merry Christmas. Plus signs in America's future. Dec 23 '74
Christmas '74: Let nothing you dismay. Dec 30 '74	How true is the Bible? Dec 30 '74	Betty Ford's folksy White House. Dec 30 '74

Newsweek **January 1975**	*Time* **January 1975**	*U.S. News* **January 1975**
Wildlife in danger. Jan 6 '75	Man of the Year: King Faisal Jan 6 '75	Betty Ford's folksy White House. Jan 6 '75
The verdict. [Watergate affair] Jan 13 '75	Hypertension. Conquering the quiet killer. Jan 13 '75	"Gold rush." Why the slow start? [Gold as an investment] Jan 13 '75
Out of work. [Unemployment] Jan 20 '75	Trying to turn it around. [Ford economic policy] Jan 20 '75	What it will take to end the recession. Jan 20 '75
Inflation. Recession. Energy. Jan 27 '75	Doctoring the economy. What will work? Jan 27 '75	Ford's new strategy. Can he restore confidence? Jan 27 '75

Newsweek **February 1975**	*Time* **February 1975**	*U.S. News* **February 1975**
Golf's new golden boy. [Johnny Miller] Feb 3 '75	China. Looking beyond Mao. Feb 3 '75	Jobs... Prices... Profits... What next? Feb 3 '75
Oil money. One petrodollar. In oil we trust. Feb 10 '75	Detroit's big gamble. Rebates and smaller cars. Feb 10 '75	$350 billion budget. Spur to recovery. Feb 10 '75
The mad, mad world of Mel Brooks. Feb 17 '75	Scoop out front. Democrat Henry Jackson. Feb 17 '75	New directions. Lower taxes. Uphill road for business. Less worry about oil. Overhaul of social security. Feb 17 '75
How far is down? Feb 24 '75	Hockey. War on ice. Feb 24 '75	A day in the life of the President. Feb 24 '75

Newsweek **March 1975**	*Time* **March 1975**	*U.S. News* **March 1975**
Abortion and the law. Mar 3 '75	Guns for everyone. The world arms trade. Mar 3 '75	Into a new era. How your life will change. 1975...2000. Mar 3 '75
The agony of Cambodia. Mar 10 '75	American Jews and Israel. Mar 10 '75	Ford and Congress. Showdown at hand. Mar 10 '75
Liv Ullmann in "A Doll's House." Mar 17 '75	Cher. Glad rags to riches. Mar 17 '75	Mideast: If Kissinger fails– Mar 17 '75
Ready on the right - Ronald Reagan. Mar 24 '75	Indochina. How much longer? Mar 24 '75	"Okies" of the '70s. Mass migration in search of jobs. Mar 24 '75
The great retreat. [Vietnam War] Mar 31 '75	The last retreat. [Vietnam War] Mar 31 '75	Why courts are in trouble. Mar 31 '75

Newsweek **April 1975**	*Time* **April 1975**	*U.S. News* **April 1975**
A world of woes. [U.S. foreign relations] Apr 7 '75	America and the world. "A moment of danger." Apr 7 '75	Cities in peril. Apr 7 '75
The sorrow and the pity. [Vietnam War and Cambodia] Apr 14 '75	Collapse in Viet Nam. Apr 14 '75	Where U.S. stands after Vietnam debacle. Apr 14 '75
Getting out. [Vietnam War and Cambodia] Apr 21 '75	Last exit from Viet Nam. Apr 21 '75	Who runs America? Apr 21 '75
The last battle. [Vietnam War and Cambodia] Apr 28 '75	Storming the courts. Jimmy Connors. Apr 28 '75	Ford. How he rates now. Kennedy. Democrats' choice after all? Apr 28 '75

Newsweek **May 1975**	*Time* **May 1975**	*U.S. News* **May 1975**
End of an era. [Vietnam War] May 5 '75	Hanoi's triumph. May 5 '75	Things have got to get better. Mood of America. May 5 '75
The new Americans. May 12 '75	The victor. [Vietnam War] May 12 '75	The end in Vietnam. May 12 '75
Ballet at its best. Baryshnikov and Kirkland. May 19 '75	Ballet's new idol. Baryshnikov. May 19 '75	Young genius on the rise in the U.S. [The arts] May 19 '75
The rescue. [Mayaguez incident] May 26 '75	Ford draws the line. [Mayaguez incident] May 26 '75	No cover story. May 26 '75

Newsweek **June 1975**	*Time* **June 1975**	*U.S. News* **June 1975**
Ready for Teddy? [Edward Kennedy] Jun 2 '75	Old age. How to help our parents. Jun 2 '75	What Ford wants in Europe. Jun 2 '75
Malpractice: Doctors in revolt. Jun 9 '75	Mideast. New quest for peace. Jun 9 '75	A decade of the Great Society. Success or failure? Jun 9 '75
Fastest arm in the West. [Nolan Ryan] Jun 16 '75	The new beauties. Margaux Hemingway Jun 16 '75	Health care in America. Progress–and problems. Jun 16 '75
CIA: Who's watching whom? Jun 23 '75	Super shark. "Jaws" on film and other summer thrillers. Jun 23 '75	Secretary of State Kissinger. "We are moving into a new world." Jun 23 '75
Epic of Opry Land. Jun 30 '75	Crime. Why - and what to do. Jun 30 '75	The Attorney General speaks out: Gun control, illegal aliens, marijuana laws, rising crime, death penalty. Jun 30 '75

Newsweek **July 1975**	*Time* **July 1975**	*U.S. News* **July 1975**
Indira's iron fist. [Indira Gandhi and India] Jul 7 '75	Rock's Captain Fantastic. Elton John. Jul 7 '75	What kind of future for America? Jul 7 '75
Bicentennial summer. Jul 14 '75	Can capitalism survive? Don't count me out, folks! Adam Smith. Jul 14 '75	Midyear '75 business outlook. How strong a recovery? Can inflation be stopped? Any cure for high unemployment?. . . Jul 14 '75
The link-up. [Apollo-Soyuz space flight] Jul 21 '75	Space spectacular. Science, politics & show biz. Jul 21 '75	Complaints about lawyers. Are they justified? Interview with a law school dean. Jul 21 '75
Christina Onassis. Poor little rich girl. Jul 28 '75	At ease in the White House. Ford's first year. Jul 28 '75	Big push for detente. Is U.S. moving too fast? Jul 28 '75

Newsweek **August 1975**	*Time* **August 1975**	*U.S. News* **August 1975**
New York's last gasp? Aug 4 '75	Showtime in Helsinki. Presenting: Gerald Ford, Leonid Brezhnev, and an all-star cast in "Goodbye to. . ." Aug 4 '75	Ford probes Brezhnev's Iron Curtain. Aug 4 '75
Food. The new wave. Aug 11 '75	Red threat in Portugal. Lisbon's troika. Aug 11 '75	Ford looks ahead. An interview with the President after his first year. Aug 11 '75
The Hoffa case. Aug 18 '75	Baseball's super showman. Oakland's Charlie Finley. Aug 18 '75	New squeeze on cities by militant workers, money crunch. Aug 18 '75
Kidnapped - Samuel Bronfman II. Aug 25 '75	Mid-East. Is peace at hand? Aug 25 '75	Big change in prisons. Punish - not reform. Aug 25 '75

Newsweek **September 1975**	*Time* **September 1975**	*U.S. News* **September 1975**
Bellow's gift. [Saul Bellow] Sep 1 '75	Forecast: Earthquake. Sep 1 '75	Crisis in the schools. Sep 1 '75
TV's fall season. Sep 8 '75	"I am a homosexual." The gay drive for acceptance. Sep 8 '75	If U.S. does business with Castro - Sep 8 '75
"It didn't go off." 'Squeaky' Fromme after capture. Sep 15 '75	The girl who almost killed Ford. Sep 15 '75	Energy: Higher prices close in on motorists, home-owners, air travelers, manufacturers. Sep 15 '75
Who's raising the kids? Sep 22 '75	Busing battle. [Busing for school integration] Sep 22 '75	Trouble in schools. Will it get worse? Sep 22 '75
The story of Patty Hearst. Sep 29 '75	Apprehended. Patricia Hearst, alias Tania. Sep 29 '75	War on crime by fed-up citizens. Sep 29 '75

Newsweek **October 1975**	*Time* **October 1975**	*U.S. News* **October 1975**
Can the risk be cut? [Presidential protection] Oct 6 '75	Protecting the President. Oct 6 '75	Mood of America. "Where do we turn?" Oct 6 '75
Franco's last hurrah? [Francisco Franco and Spain] Oct 13 '75	Meditation: The answer to all your problems? Oct 13 '75	Rockefeller talks about his job and future. Exclusive interview with the Vice President. Oct 13 '75
Nixon's new life. Oct 20 '75	Brother, can you spare $4 billion? [New York City] Oct 20 '75	If Reagan runs against Ford. Oct 20 '75
Making of a rock star. Bruce Springsteen. Oct 27 '75	Rock's new sensation. Bruce Springsteen. Oct 27 '75	The American family. Can it survive today's shocks? Oct 27 '75

Newsweek **November 1975**	*Time* **November 1975**	*U.S. News* **November 1975**
A right to die? Nov 3 '75	Spain after Franco. Nov 3 '75	No cover story. Nov 3 '75
Ford and New York. Nov 10 '75	Music's wonder woman. Sarah Caldwell. Nov 10 '75	Message from home: Curb the bureaucrats! Nov 10 '75
Ford's big shuffle. [Ford executive appointments] Nov 17 '75	"My guys." [Ford executive appointments] Nov 17 '75	White House shakeup - Meaning for defense, foreign policy, '76 elections. Nov 17 '75
Can he stop Ford? [Ronald Reagan] Nov 24 '75	Ronald Reagan. Heating up the G.O.P. Nov 24 '75	Spiraling crime. How to protect yourself. Nov 24 '75

Newsweek **December 1975**	*Time* **December 1975**	*U.S. News* **December 1975**
Broadway's new kick. Donna McKechnie in "A Chorus Line." Dec 1 '75	U.S. shopping surge. Trendy Bloomingdale's. Dec 1 '75	CIA murder plots. Weighing the damage to U.S. Dec 1 '75
Why Johnny can't write. Dec 8 '75	Pittsburgh's front four. Half a ton of trouble. [Professional football] Dec 8 '75	The American woman. On the move - but where? Dec 8 '75
Big government. Dec 15 '75	Kubrick's grandest gamble. Marisa Berenson in "Barry Lyndon." Dec 15 '75	China to Ford: Protect us from Russia. Dec 15 '75
Ford in trouble. Dec 22 '75	The truth about Hoover. Dec 22 '75	No cover story. Dec 22 '75
Free spirit in the White House. Dec 29 '75	Messengers of love and hope. Living saints. Mother Teresa. Dec 29 '75	The war over taxes. Ford vs. Congress. Dec 29 '75

Newsweek **January 1976**	*Time* **January 1976**	*U.S. News* **January 1976**
Sun spots. The latest resorts. Jan 5 '76	Women of the year. Jan 5 '76	Outlook '76. Year of big decisions. Recovery: Sturdy or frail? Will Ford hold the White House? How far can Russia push?. . Jan 5 '76
Politics '76. Here they come! Jan 12 '76	Soap operas. Sex and suffering in the afternoon. Jan 12 '76	Here comes '76! America's 200 years in pictures. Jan 12 '76
Angola. Detente under the gun. Jan 19 '76	China: Friend or foe? Chou's successor: Teng Hsiao-ping. Jan 19 '76	The power of our judges – Are they going too far? Jan 19 '76
What causes cancer? Jan 26 '76	Giving them hell at the U.N. Pat Moynihan. Jan 26 '76	Back to the cold war? Jan 26 '76

Newsweek **February 1976**	*Time* **February 1976**	*U.S. News* **February 1976**
Patty on trial. [Patty Hearst case] Feb 2 '76	Olympic preview: Artistry on ice. Skater Dorothy Hamill. Feb 2 '76	Big tax changes ahead: Who's helped most. Feb 2 '76
Tatum! The Hollywood kid. [Tatum O'Neal] Feb 9 '76	Doonesbury. Politics in the funny papers. Feb 9 '76	Young builders of America. 8 who have made their mark. Feb 9 '76
The Concorde furor. [Supersonic airplanes] Feb 16 '76	Patty in court. Defense attorney F. Lee Bailey. [Patty Hearst case] Feb 16 '76	New ways to help disturbed minds. Where will it all lead? Feb 16 '76
The payoff scandals. [Lockheed bribery scandal] Feb 23 '76	The big payoff. Lockheed scandal: Graft around the globe. [Lockheed bribery scandal] Feb 23 '76	Why so many wives are running away. Feb 23 '76

Newsweek **March 1976**	*Time* **March 1976**	*U.S. News* **March 1976**
Patty's defense. [Patty Hearst case] Mar 1 '76	Gore Vidal's new novel "1876." Sins of the fathers. Mar 1 '76	ABC's of how a President is chosen. Mar 1 '76
All about Carter. Mar 8 '76	Who is Jimmy Carter? And why do they love/hate him? Mar 8 '76	Is democracy dying? Verdict of 8 leading world scholars. Mar 8 '76
Prince of the tenors. Luciano Pavarotti Mar 15 '76	Americans on the move. [Internal migration] Mar 15 '76	How U.S. sizes up Russia now. Two exclusive interviews. Secretary of Defense, Donald H. Rumsfeld. Secretary of State. . . Mar 15 '76
Rags & riches. Dress designer Diane von Fustenberg. Mar 22 '76	American chic in fashion. Mar 22 '76	Billions of Medicaid ripoffs. Can anyone stop it? Mar 22 '76
Guilty! [Patty Hearst case] Mar 29 '76	Watergate on film. Hoffman & Redford in "All the President's Men." Mar 29 '76	Reverse discrimination. Mar 29 '76

Newsweek **April 1976**	*Time* **April 1976**	*U.S. News* **April 1976**
Nixon's final days. From the new book by Woodward and Bernstein. Apr 5 '76	The porno plague. Apr 5 '76	Are all big cities doomed? Apr 5 '76
How safe is nuclear energy? Apr 12 '76	The Mideast in agony. Special report: How Israel got the bomb. Apr 12 '76	Round 2 begins. [Presidential campaigns] Apr 12 '76
The secret world of Howard Hughes. Apr 19 '76	The Hughes legacy. Scramble for the billions. [Howard Hughes] Apr 19 '76	Who runs America? Apr 19 '76
Who needs college? Apr 26 '76	Baseball springs eternal. Apr 26 '76	Women can make it to the top. 5 tell how. Apr 26 '76

Newsweek **May 1976**	*Time* **May 1976**	*U.S. News* **May 1976**
TV's new craze. Mary Hartman. May 3 '76	Modern royalty. The allure endures. May 3 '76	Sneak preview of '77 cars. May 3 '76
Carter's sweep. [Presidential campaigns] May 10 '76	Jimmy's breakthrough. [Presidential campaigns] May 10 '76	"Revolving door" justice: Why criminals go free. May 10 '76
Jolted! [Presidential campaigns] May 17 '76	Republican rumble. [Presidential campaigns] May 17 '76	People speak their minds. '76 nationwide survey. May 17 '76
Gossip! [Gossip in the mass media] May 24 '76	U.S. Catholicism. A church divided. May 24 '76	What Carter believes. Interview on the issues. May 24 '76
Can anyone stop Carter? May 31 '76	McCartney comes back. May 31 '76	Where Reagan stands. Interview on the issues. May 31 '76

Newsweek **June 1976**	*Time* **June 1976**	*U.S. News* **June 1976**
Can white Africa survive? Jun 7 '76	What price honor? The West Point scandal. Jun 7 '76	Liberated women. How they're changing American life. Jun 7 '76
Capitol capers. [Political ethics] Jun 14 '76	Italy. The Red threat. Jun 14 '76	The vice presidency. Who'll get the No. 2 spots? Jun 14 '76
Carter's game plan. Jun 21 '76	Our next President (pick one). Jun 21 '76	No cover story. Jun 21 '76
Baseball's money madness. Jun 28 '76	Travel '76. Discovering America. Jun 28 '76	Challenge to U.S. 72,000 new jobs needed every week. Jun 28 '76

Newsweek **July 1976**	*Time* **July 1976**	*U.S. News* **July 1976**
Our America. A self-portrait at 200. Jul 4 '76	Birthday issues. The promised land. America's new immigrants. The big 200th bash. Jul 5 '76	America's third century. A look ahead. Jul 5 '76
Life under water. [Scuba diving] Jul 12 '76	The bugs are coming. [Insect control] Jul 12 '76	It was quite a birthday party. [Bicentennial celebration] Jul 12 '76
The coming of Carter. Jul 19 '76	Inside convention city. Jul 19 '76	How Democrats plan to win. Jul 19 '76
Coming on strong. [Jimmy Carter] Jul 26 '76	The Democrats reborn. Jul 26 '76	What Carter would do as President. Jul 26 '76

Newsweek **August 1976**	*Time* **August 1976**	*U.S. News* **August 1976**
A star is born. [Nadia Comaneci] Aug 2 '76	She's perfect. But the Olympics are in trouble. Aug 2 '76	America's press under fire. Aug 2 '76
Reagan's last gamble. Aug 9 '76	Ford closes in. Behind the Reagan gamble. Aug 9 '76	In the next decade - Breakup of communist world? Aug 9 '76
Mystery of the killer fever. [Legionnaire's disease] Aug 16 '76	Tracing the Philly killer. Disease detectives. [Legionnaire's disease] Aug 16 '76	The bureaucracy explosion. Key campaign issue. Aug 16 '76
High noon. [Republican National Convention] Aug 23 '76	The plight of the G.O.P. Looking beyond Kansas City. Aug 23 '76	The Republicans. Can they pull together? Aug 23 '76
The underdogs. [Republican National Convention] Aug 30 '76	The G.O.P. strategy: Give 'em hell. Aug 30 '76	Ford's plan to beat the odds. Aug 30 '76

Newsweek **September 1976**	*Time* **September 1976**	*U.S. News* **September 1976**
Getting your head together. Sep 6 '76	Sex & tennis. The new battleground. Sep 6 '76	A new generation. Where it's heading. Sep 6 '76
Sizing up Carter. Sep 13 '76	Campaign kickoff. Sep 13 '76	Head-to-head on the issues. Exclusive interviews with the candidates - before the TV debates. Sep 13 '76
After Mao. Sep 20 '76	After Mao. Sep 20 '76	Big changes in new cars. Sep 20 '76
The debates. [Presidential debates] Sep 27 '76	The South today. Carter country and beyond. Sep 27 '76	How the U.S. will spend $413 billion in one year. Sep 27 '76

Newsweek **October 1976**	*Time* **October 1976**	*U.S. News* **October 1976**
Stay tuned. "The Governor has also played a little fast and loose with the facts about vetoes." [Presidential debates] Oct 4 '76	The character test. [Presidential debates] Oct 4 '76	After big debate. The picture now. Oct 4 '76
TV news. The new look. Oct 11 '76	Africa. Peace or war. Oct 11 '76	A look into '77. Special section - Business. Oct 11 '76
How good a President? [Gerald Ford] Oct 18 '76	Ford's setback. Oct 18 '76	Betty vs. Rosalynn. Life on the campaign trail. Oct 18 '76
Born again! Evangelicals. Oct 25 '76	Here comes King Kong. Oct 25 '76	Undecided. Why millions wear this button. Oct 25 '76

Newsweek **November 1976**	*Time* **November 1976**	*U.S. News* **November 1976**
Now, the choice. Election guide. Nov 1 '76	Voting your pocketbook. Are things as good as Ford says? Or as bad as Carter says? Nov 1 '76	Who'll win? Results of 50-state survey. Nov 1 '76
The disco whirl. Nov 8 '76	The last pitch. [Presidential campaigns] Nov 8 '76	What the election means to you. Effect on business...jobs, spending, prices...taxes. Nov 8 '76
The new look. Election special. Nov 15 '76	"What I'll do." Special election section. Nov 15 '76	What Carter will do as President. Nov 15 '76
Taking charge. [Jimmy Carter] Nov 22 '76	TV's Superwomen. Nov 22 '76	Prince Philip describes a violent world ahead. Nov 22 '76
Death wish. Convict Gary Gilmore. Nov 29 '76	The joy of art. Rauschenberg by Rauschenberg. Nov 29 '76	How to get America moving again. 20 leaders tell what's needed. Nov 29 '76

Newsweek **December 1976**	*Time* **December 1976**	*U.S. News* **December 1976**
Women at work. Dec 6 '76	Gambling goes legit. Dec 6 '76	Cuban extremists in U.S. A growing terror threat. Dec 6 '76
Picking the new team. [Carter's executive appointments] Dec 13 '76	Howard Hughes. Exclusive: His secret life. Dec 13 '76	Crisis across the borders. [Mexico and Canada] Dec 13 '76
John Denver. The sunshine boy. Dec 20 '76	The great talent hunt. [Carter's executive appointments] Dec 20 '76	White House insiders. How they'll run things. Dec 20 '76
Sugar plum Christmas. The Nutcracker. Dec 27 '76	Stars. Where life begins. Dec 27 '76	Outlook '77. Top questions of the year. Dec 27 '76

Newsweek **January 1977**	*Time* **January 1977**	*U.S. News* **January 1977**
Pictures of '76. Jan 3 '77	Man of the year. Jimmy Carter.. Jan 3 '77	Outlook '77. Top questions of the year. Jan 3 '77
Too much law? Jan 10 '77	Super Bowl. The great American spectacle. Jan 10 '77	What you can expect from Carter's cabinet. Jan 10 '77
Press lord takes city. Murdoch bags New York Post. Battles for mags. Gotham agog! Jan 17 '77	Extra!!! Aussie press lord terrifies Gotham. Rubert Murdoch. Jan 17 '77	No cover story. Jan 17 '77
Guide to the new government. The festivities. The power brokers. The major problems. A talk with Rosalynn. Jan 24 '77	America's Mood. Hopeful - sort of. Jan 24 '77	A new era begins. [Inauguration of Jimmy Carter] Jan 24 '77
'A new spirit.' [Inauguration of Jimmy Carter] Jan 31 '77	The big freeze. [Cold weather] Jan 31 '77	Jimmy Carter takes over. Jan 31 '77

Newsweek **February 1977**	*Time* **February 1977**	*U.S. News* **February 1977**
The gas crisis. Feb 7 '77	The Carters move in. It's a new Washington. Feb 7 '77	A clean America. Will people pay the price? Feb 7 '77
The new actresses. Sissy Spacek. Feb 14 '77	Why 'Roots' hit home. Feb 14 '77	No cover story. Feb 14 '77
What TV does to kids. Feb 21 '77	The dissidents. Challenge to Moscow. Feb 21 '77	Jobs. A look at the nation's most nagging problem - and some ways to solve it. Feb 21 '77
The graying of America. Feb 28 '77	Linda Ronstadt: Torchy rock. Feb 28 '77	Public officials for sale. Now a crackdown. Feb 28 '77

Newsweek **March 1977**	*Time* **March 1977**	*U.S. News* **March 1977**
Idi Amin's reign of terror. Mar 7 '77	The wild man of Africa. Uganda's Idi Amin. Mar 7 '77	"My son, the President." Interview with Lilian Carter. Mar 7 '77
A great American novel. John Cheever's 'Falconer.' Mar 14 '77	Fighting the housewife blues. Mar 14 '77	Moral policeman to the world? Mar 14 '77
Seizing hostages. Scourge of the '70s. Mar 21 '77	Mao's wife tells her story. From actress to empress. Mar 21 '77	Change comes to White House. Interview with the First Lady. Mar 21 '77
The outspoken Andrew Young. At the U.N. Mar 28 '77	New queen of comedy. Lily Tomlin. Mar 28 '77	Uproar over medical bills. Mar 28 '77

Newsweek **April 1977**	*Time* **April 1977**	*U.S. News* **April 1977**
Jewelry's new dazzle. Apr 4 '77	Mr. Energy. Tackling a superproblem. James Schlesinger. Apr 4 '77	Drought. Will history repeat? Apr 4 '77
Rocky KO's Hollywood. Sylvester Stallone. Apr 11 '77	Air travel. How safe? Apr 11 '77	A time of renewal for U.S. churches. Apr 11 '77
Energy. Special report. Apr 18 '77	The DNA furor. Tinkering with life. Apr 18 '77	Who runs America. Apr 18 '77
Fighting pain. [Pain relief] Apr 25 '77	His first big test. [Carter's energy policy] Apr 25 '77 ·	Border crisis. Illegal aliens out of control? Apr 25 '77

Newsweek **May 1977**	*Time* **May 1977**	*U.S. News* **May 1977**
Carter up close. What price energy? May 2 '77	Uncle Jimmy wants you. But will America enlist? May 2 '77	Energy. Will Americans pay the price? May 2 '77
Nixon speaks with David Frost. May 9 '77	Nixon talks. May 9 '77	ABC's of how your government works. May 9 '77
DeNiro: A star for the '70s. In 'New York, New York.' May 16 '77	The Mafia. Big, bad and booming. May 16 '77	Will Europe follow Carter? May 16 '77
Keeping fit. May 23 '77	Defense. How much is enough? May 23 '77	How Americans pursue happiness. May 23 '77
Israel: Day of the hawks. Menahem Begin. May 30 '77	Israel. Trouble in the promised land. Menachem Begin. May 30 '77	The new U.S. challenge to Russia. Exclusive interview with Zbigniew Brzezinski. May 30 '77

Newsweek **June 1977**	*Time* **June 1977**	*U.S. News* **June 1977**
Battle over gay rights. Anita Bryant vs. the homosexuals. Jun 6 '77	The President's boys. Jody Powell. Hamilton Jordan. Jun 6 '77	The President talks tough. Korea. . . Africa. . . Mideast. . . Panama Canal. . .Soviet Union Jun 6 '77
Queen for our day. Elizabeth II and her jubilee. Jun 13 '77	The hot new rich. Jun 13 '77	America's mood. A new confidence. Jun 13 '77
Ray's escape. [James Earl Ray] Jun 20 '77	The escape. James Earl Ray. Jun 20 '77	At last. Alaska's oil flows south. Jun 20 '77
Laetrile and cancer. Should the drug be banned? Jun 27 '77	Spain: Democracy wins. Jun 27 '77	Our junket-happy congress. What secret records disclose. Jun 27 '77

Newsweek **July 1977**	*Time* **July 1977**	*U.S. News* **July 1977**
Everybody's search for roots. Jul 4 '77	Here comes summer. The new swimsuits. Those crowded national parks. Beer: July froth. Amusement parks. . . Jul 4 '77	Time bomb in Mexico. Why there'll be no end to the invasion by "illegals." Jul 4 '77
A beauty named Bisset. [Jacqueline Bisset] Jul 11 '77	Youth crime. Jul 11 '77	How people cheat Uncle Sam out of billions. Jul 11 '77
Life outdoors. Jul 18 '77	Baseball's best hitter. Rod Carew Jul 18 '77	America's youth. Angry...bored...or just confused? Jul 18 '77
Blackout! [Electric power failure] Jul 25 '77	Blackout '77. Once more, with looting. [Electric power failure] Jul 25 '77	Hidden army of Washington lobbyists. Jul 25 '77

Newsweek **August 1977**	*Time* **August 1977**	*U.S. News* **August 1977**
Living together. [Unmarried couples] Aug 1 '77	Why you do what you do. Sociobiology: A new theory of behavior. Aug 1 '77	Brezhnev's nightmare. Breakaway in Europe. Aug 1 '77
Jazz comes back! Aug 8 '77	Carter's foreign policy. Jimmy in the lion's den. Aug 8 '77	The culture boom. [The arts] Aug 8 '77
Seeking other worlds. Astronomer Carl Sagan. Aug 15 '77	Coping with the new New York Times. Aug 15 '77	America's press. Too much power for too few? Aug 15 '77
The sick world of Son of Sam. Aug 22 '77	Getting out of the canal (slowly). [Panama Canal treaty] Aug 22 '77	Inflation. Why can't this headache be cured? Aug 22 '77
The Lance report. Is he home free? [Bert Lance] Aug 29 '77	The Underclass. Minority within a minority. Aug 29 '77	A dying party? 5 Republican leaders speak out. Aug 29 '77

Newsweek **September 1977**	*Time* **September 1977**	*U.S. News* **September 1977**
TV's hot serials. Sep 5 '77	TV's master showman. ABC's Fred Silverman. Sep 5 '77	State fairs. Bigger and brassier than ever. Sep 5 '77
Big city schools. Can they be saved? Sep 12 '77	Sky-high housing. Building up, prices up. Sep 12 '77	TV's new pitch. More sex. Less violence. Sep 12 '77
The Lance affair. What damage to Carter? Sep 19 '77	The Lance affair. What it cost Carter. Sep 19 '77	Panama. A doomed treaty? Sep 19 '77
The furor over 'reverse discrimination.' Sep 26 '77	Diane Keaton. Annie Hall meets Mr. Goodbar. Sep 26 '77	The new cars. Trimmer, slimmer and smaller. Sep 26 '77

Newsweek October 1977	*Time* October 1977	*U.S. News* October 1977
Picking up the pieces. [Jimmy Carter] Oct 3 '77	Master of the spy story. John le Carré strikes again. Oct 3 '77	End of youth culture. Changes it will bring. Oct 3 '77
Hollywood's new heroines. Jane Fonda in 'Julia.' Oct 10 '77	Revolt of the old. The battle over forced retirement. Oct 10 '77	Our armed forces. Ready - or not? Oct 10 '77
The U.S. and Israel. Feeling the strain. Oct 17 '77	Pushing toward Geneva. "The legitimate rights of the Palestinian people must be recognized." "We shall not negotiate. . . Oct 17 '77	America's doctors. A profession in trouble. Oct 17 '77
Super artist. Jasper Johns. Oct 24 '77	The magnificent maestro. Mstislav Rostropovich. Oct 24 '77	Russia's 60 years of Communism. Success or failure? Oct 24 '77
War on terrorism. Oct 31 '77	War on terrorism. Oct 28 '77	"Rights" explosion splintering America? Oct 31 '77

Newsweek November 1977	*Time* November 1977	*U.S. News* November 1977
Is America turning right? Nov 7 '77	How man became man. Anthropologist Richard Leakey with Homo habilis. Nov 7 '77	Tips for winter vacations. Nov 7 '77
Brother Billy. [Billy Carter] Nov 14 '77	High schools in trouble. A tale of three cities. Nov 14 '77	Where China is headed. Nov 14 '77
The UFO's are coming! Hollywood's 'Close Encounters.' Nov 21 '77	South Africa. The defiant white tribe. Nov 21 '77	Best ways to beat inflation. Nov 21 '77
Sadat in Israel. Nov 28 '77	The 'Sacred Mission.' Egypt's President Sadat. Nov 28 '77	Are you eating right? Nov 28 '77

Newsweek December 1977	*Time* December 1977	*U.S. News* December 1977
The Mideast. What next? Dec 5 '77	After Houston: What next for women? [Women's movement] Dec 5 '77	Young Blacks out of work. Time bomb for U.S. Dec 5 '77
Texas! The superstate. Dec 12 '77	The Pacific Northwest. Washington Governor Dixy Lee Ray. Dec 12 '77	Why teachers are under fire. Dec 12 '77
Diet crazes. Dec 19 '77	The cooking craze. Dec 19 '77	How to break logjam in courts. Exclusive inverview with Chief Justice Burger. Dec 19 '77
Pictures of '77. Dec 26 '77	The Evangelicals. New empire of faith. Dec 26 '77	Outlook '78. Key questions of the year. Carter. Will he change course? Business. Can we avoid recession? Peace. . . Dec 26 '77

Newsweek January 1978	*Time* January 1978	*U.S. News* January 1978
Aloha! Sun and fun islands. Jan 2 '78	Man of the year. Anwar Sadat. Jan 2 '78	Outlook '78. Key questions of the year. Carter. Will he change course? Business. Can we avoid recession? Peace. . . Jan 2 '78
Economy '78. A new look? Jan 9 '78	Hollywood's honchos. Burt Reynolds. Clint Eastwood. Jan 9 '78	$100 billion shoot-out. Jan 9 '78
How men are changing. Jan 16 '78	Super Bowl XII. Broncomania v. Cowboy cool. Jan 16 '78	The Carter impact. Jan 16 '78
Humphrey. The happy warrior. [Hubert Humphrey] Jan 23 '78	Congress. Bold & balky. Senate Majority Leader Robert Byrd. Jan 23 '78	The mess in foreign policy. Jan 23 '78
Carter and your money. Can he lift the economy? Jan 30 '78	Trying to build confidence. Treasury Secretary Blumenthal. Jan 30 '78	Carter's pep pill for business. Jan 30 '78

Newsweek February 1978	*Time* February 1978	*U.S. News* February 1978
The CIA: How badly hurt? Feb 6 '78	Mission impossible? [Central Intelligence Agency] Feb 6 '78	Bleak days at Justice Department. Feb 6 '78
Inside Hollywood. High stakes! Fast bucks! Shady deals! Feb 13 '78	Canada. A house divided. Prime Minister Trudeau & Quebec Premier Lévesque. Feb 13 '78	The rush is on. [Presidential candidates] Feb 13 '78
Sex and TV. Feb 20 '78	The computer society. Feb 20 '78	New faces. How they're changing U.S. Feb 20 '78
The best of the book. Haldeman talks. How the Russians almost A-bombed China. The Nixon nobody saw. . . Feb 27 '78	'The Greatest' is gone. Muhammad Ali. Feb 27 '78	The fitness mania. Feb 27 '78

Newsweek March 1978	*Time* March 1978	*U.S. News* March 1978
Coal. Will the deal stick? Mar 6 '78	The all-American model. Cheryl Tiegs. Mar 6 '78	U.S. Navy in distress. Mar 6 '78
Cubans in Africa. Moscow tests Carter. Mar 13 '78	Socialism. Mar 13 '78	Can the dollar be saved? Mar 13 '78
Carter and the Jews. Mar 20 '78	Coal crisis. Mar 20 '78	Chaos in the coal fields. Mar 20 '78
Israel strikes back. Mar 27 '78	Peace: The chances now. Mar 27 '78	Yesterday's rebels grow up. Mar 27 '78

Newsweek **April 1978**	*Time* **April 1978**	*U.S. News* **April 1978**
Comedy's new face. Steve Martin is one wild and crazy guy. Apr 3 '78	Travolta fever. Apr 3 '78	Police. Under fire, fighting back. Apr 3 '78
Burned up over taxes. Apr 10 '78	Those lawyers! Apr 10 '78	Uncle Sam's computer has got you. Apr 10 '78
Furor over the neutron bomb. Apr 17 '78	The fantastic world of Steinberg. [Saul Steinberg] Apr 17 '78	Who runs America. Apr 17 '78
Woody. [Woody Allen] Apr 24 '78	Man on the move. Secretary of State Cyrus Vance. Apr 24 '78	Inflation. How you are being robbed. Apr 24 '78

Newsweek **May 1978**	*Time* **May 1978**	*U.S. News* **May 1978**
Living with dying. May 1 '78	U.S. ballet soars. Gelsey Kirkland. May 1 '78	ABC's of how our economy works. May 1 '78
Fashion '78. Soft and sexy. Designer Calvin Klein. May 8 '78	Attack on the Navy. May 8 '78	Springtime mood of America. Inflation. Carter. Bureaucracy. Taxes. Schools. May 8 '78
Saving the family. May 15 '78	The man who will be King. Britain's Prince Charles. May 15 '78	Crisis in the operating room. May 15 '78
Italy's agony. May 22 '78	Into the jet age. Saudi Arabia's Prince Fahd. May 22 '78	Terror gangs. Is anyone safe? May 22 '78
Inflation. May 29 '78	A born winner. Jockey Steve Cauthen. May 29 '78	U.S. colleges. Life and death struggle. May 29 '78

Newsweek **June 1978**	*Time* **June 1978**	*U.S. News* **June 1978**
Abortion under attack. Jun 5 '78	Africa. A political jungle. Jun 5 '78	Women in uniform. Can they save the military? Jun 5 '78
A new cold war? Carter adviser Brzezinski. Jun 12 '78	How to spend $182 billion. [Federal Health and Human Services budget] Jun 12 '78	Castro. Russia's cat's-paw. Jun 12 '78
Tax revolt! Jun 19 '78	Tax revolt. California's Howard Jarvis. Jun 19 '78	Tug of war over foreign policy. Jun 19 '78
The new royal life. Princess Caroline's wedding. Jun 26 '78	Women in sports. Jun 26 '78	Eavesdropping on the world's secrets. Jun 26 '78

Newsweek **July 1978**	*Time* **July 1978**	*U.S. News* **July 1978**
TV of tomorrow. Jul 3 '78	Mister Hollywood. Warren Beatty. Jul 3 '78	The great national rip-off. Jul 3 '78
After Bakke. No quotas - but race can count. Jul 10 '78	What Bakke means. Quotas: No. Race: Yes. Jul 10 '78	Impact of Bakke decision. Allan Bakke and family. Jul 10 '78
Sister Ruth. Healer Ruth Carter Stapleton. Jul 17 '78	The inflation fighter. Federal Reserve Chairman G. William Miller. Jul 17 '78	Shaking up the Pentagon. Jul 17 '78
Moscow trials - testing Carter. Jul 24 '78	Detente. The trial of Anatoli Shcharansky. Jul 24 '78	Carter's 18 months. What went wrong? Jul 24 '78
Rock tycoon. Impresario Robert Stigwood. Jul 31 '78	The test tube baby. Birth watch in Britain. Jul 31 '78	Poor vs. rich. A global struggle. Jul 31 '78

Newsweek **August 1978**	*Time* **August 1978**	*U.S. News* **August 1978**
That baby. [Fertilization in vitro] Aug 7 '78	Lobbyists. Swarming over Washington. Aug 7 '78	Carter's Mr. Fix-It. Robert S. Strauss. Aug 7 '78
King of country music. Willie Nelson. Aug 14 '78	New era in the air. Cheap fares, crowded flights. Aug 14 '78	Today's "poor" millionaires. Aug 14 '78
After Paul VI. Choosing a new Pope. Aug 21 '78	In search of a Pope. Aug 21 '78	America's adults. In search of what? Aug 21 '78
Flight of the Eagle. [Balloon ascensions] Aug 28 '78	The godfather of the paperback boom. Author Mario Puzo. Aug 28 '78	Washington. Gold coast on the Potomac. Aug 28 '78

Newsweek **September 1978**	*Time* **September 1978**	*U.S. News* **September 1978**
Pope John Paul I. Sep 4 '78	The new Pope. John Paul I. Sep 4 '78	Last chance for peace? [Camp David summit] Sep 4 '78
Son of Star Wars. TV's 'Battlestar Galactica.' Sep 11 '78	Showdown at Camp David. Sep 11 '78	Quest for better schools. Sep 11 '78
Hideaway summit. Sep 18 '78	Iran in turmoil. The Shah. Sep 18 '78	ABC's of the great game of politics. Sep 18 '78
The summit. What next? Sep 25 '78	After the summit. Sep 25 '78	Here they come-the '79s. Sep 25 '78

Newsweek **October 1978**	*Time* **October 1978**	*U.S. News* **October 1978**
Born again! [Camp David summit] Oct 2 '78	Carter's breakthrough. [Camp David summit] Oct 2 '78	Inflation. Where do we go from here? Oct 2 '78
The 34 days of John Paul I. Oct 9 '78	The church in shock. John Paul I. 1912-1978. Oct 9 '78	Politics heats up. Preview of '78 voting. Carter: Help or hindrance? Tax revolt at the polls. Labor takes aim at its. . . Oct 9 '78
The Avedon look. Oct 16 '78	Hispanic Americans. Soon: The biggest minority. Oct 16 '78	Carter's cabinet. How it rates. Oct 16 '78
College humor comes back. John Belushi. Oct 23 '78	Elections '78. The tax slashers. Oct 23 '78	Explosion of new laws. How they affect you. Oct 23 '78
A Polish Pope. John Paul II Oct 30 '78	John Paul II. Oct 30 '78	New alarm over Russian threat. Oct 30 '78

Newsweek **November 1978**	*Time* **November 1978**	*U.S. News* **November 1978**
Inflation fighters. Can they win? Nov 6 '78	The new U.S. farmer. Nov 6 '78	Carter's inflation fighter. A no-win job? Nov 6 '78
Saving the dollar. But risking a recession. [Carter monetary policy] Nov 13 '78	To the rescue! [Carter monetary policy] Nov 13 '78	Where tomorrow's jobs will be. Nov 13 '78
Showdown for the Shah. Nov 20 '78	Big winners. Adding up the results. Mood: Cautious, restless, quirky. Taxing & spending: Stop! Stop! Stop!. . . Nov 20 '78	Election impact on - Business outlook. Carter strategy. Temper of congress. More tax cuts. War on inflation. Labor's. . . Nov 20 '78
The buying of America. [Foreign investments in the U.S.] Nov 27 '78	New American manners. Social arbiter Letitia Baldrige. Nov 27 '78	America. Declining power? Nov 27 '78

Newsweek **December 1978**	*Time* **December 1978**	*U.S. News* **December 1978**
The cult of death. [Jonestown mass deaths] Dec 4 '78	Cult of death. [Jonestown mass deaths] Dec 4 '78	Why everybody is suing everybody. Dec 4 '78
Turned-on-toys. Dec 11 '78	Cosmetics. Kiss and sell. Revlon's Michel Bergerac. Dec 11 '78	China's chant: "Yankee come back." Dec 11 '78
Macho Maestro. Conductor Zubin Mehta. Dec 18 '78	Convention fever. Dec 18 '78	The great American bureaucratic junketing machine. Dec 18 '78
The China breakthrough. Dec 25 '78	Deal with China. Deadlock with Israel. Dec 25 '78	Outlook '79. Top questions of the year. Business. Recession for sure? Carter. Can he tame congress? Money. Where to. . . Dec 25 '78

Newsweek **January 1979**

Superman to the rescue!   Jan 1 '79

Iran in chaos.   Jan 8 '79

Telling all. Memoirs of the stars. Lauren Bacall.   Jan 15 '79

A really super bowl.   Jan 22 '79

The politics of austerity. Jan 29 '79

Time   **January 1979**

Man of the year. Teng Hsiao-p'ing. Visions of a new China.   Jan 1 '79

U.S. architects. Doing their own thing.   Jan 8 '79

Crescent of crisis. Troubles beyond Iran.   Jan 15 '79

America and Russia. Where we stand. Brezhnev: An exclusive interview.   Jan 22 '79

The Colombian connection. Billions in pot & coke.   Jan 29 '79

U.S. News   **January 1979**

Outlook '79. Top questions of the year. Business. Recession for sure? Carter. Can he tame congress? Money. Where to. . .   Jan 1 '79

Carter's juggling act. China. SALT. NATO. Russia. Mid-East. OPEC. Iran.   Jan 8 '79

Working women. Joys and sorrows.   Jan 15 '79

Guns vs. butter. Battle of the year. Jan 22 '79

Illegal aliens. Invasion out of control?   Jan 29 '79

Newsweek   **February 1979**

The new China.   Feb 5 '79

Iran's mystery man. Ayatollah Khomeini.   Feb 12 '79

The coming oil crunch.   Feb 19 '79

America's world of woes. Feeling helpless.   Feb 26 '79

Time   **February 1979**

Teng comes calling. An interview with the Vice Premier.   Feb 5 '79

Iran: Now the power play. Ayatullah Khomeini.   Feb 12 '79

Rediscovering Einstein. His centennial year.   Feb 19 '79

Iran: Anarchy and exodus. Feb 26 '79

U.S. News   **February 1979**

Russia vs. China. Struggle for Asia.   Feb 5 '79

Will U.S. buy China's hard line? Feb 12 '79

Mexico. Carter goes a-wooing. Feb 19 '79

Will inflation tarnish your golden years?   Feb 26 '79

Newsweek   **March 1979**

China's Vietnam gamble. Mar 5 '79

Mysteries of the universe. Frontiers in physics.   Mar 12 '79

Carter's quest for peace. Mar 19 '79

Giving peace a chance. How Carter did it. What's the cost? Will it work?   Mar 26 '79

Time   **March 1979**

Communists at war.   Mar 5 '79

Chaos in television...and what it takes to be No. 1.   Mar 12 '79

Carter's bold mission.   Mar 19 '79

Mideast peace. Its risks and rewards.   Mar 26 '79

U.S. News   **March 1979**

Inside our hospitals.   Mar 5 '79

Runaway inflation. Can Carter corral it?   Mar 12 '79

Carter's fateful move.   Mar 19 '79

Supreme Court. Trials and tribulations.   Mar 26 '79

Newsweek **April 1979**	*Time* **April 1979**	*U.S. News* **April 1979**
Disco takes over. Apr 2 '79	Psychiatry's depression. Apr 2 '79	Saudi Arabia. How true a friend? Apr 2 '79
Nuclear accident. [Three Mile Island nuclear accident] Apr 9 '79	Nuclear nightmare. [Three Mile Island nuclear accident] Apr 9 '79	Energy. Impact. How Carter's plan would hit your pocketbook. OPEC. Ways to foil the oil cartel. Autos. Changes ahead. . . Apr 9 '79
The energy tangle. Apr 16 '79	Islam. The militant revival. Apr 16 '79	Who runs America. Apr 16 '79
The pop politics of Jerry Brown. Apr 23 '79	How gay is gay? Homosexuality in America. Apr 23 '79	Can the world head off a trade war? Apr 23 '79
Legal battle of the sexes. Changing the rules of living together, marriage and work. Apr 30 '79	A comic genius. Woody Allen comes of age. Apr 30 '79	Social Security. Will it be there when you need it? Apr 30 '79

Newsweek **May 1979**	*Time* **May 1979**	*U.S. News* **May 1979**
TV comedy. What it's teaching the kids. May 7 '79	The oil game. May 7 '79	Is worst over for CIA? May 7 '79
Britain turns right. Margaret Thatcher. May 14 '79	Britain's fighting lady. Prime Minister Margaret Thatcher. May 14 '79	Blacks in America. 25 years of radical change. May 14 '79
A long, dry summer? May 21 '79	Now the great debate: Salt II. May 21 '79	Salt II. Can it end the arms race? May 21 '79
Teddy comes on strong. The battle over health care. May 28 '79	Medical costs. Seeking the cure. May 28 '79	Taking America's pulse. Prices. Energy. White House. Taxes. Congress. May 28 '79

Newsweek **June 1979**	*Time* **June 1979**	*U.S. News* **June 1979**
Innovation. Has America lost its edge? Jun 4 '79	The good humor man. Columnist Russell Baker. Jun 4 '79	'80 sweepstakes. At the starting gate. Jun 4 '79
How safe? [Aviation accidents] Jun 11 '79	West Germany. Pride and prosperity. An interview with Chancellor Schmidt. Jun 11 '79	How good...how bad. Bureaucrats. Jun 11 '79
Hollywood's scary summer. Jun 18 '79	Triumphal return. The Pope in Poland. Jun 18 '79	Carter vs. Brezhnev. Face-off in Vienna. Jun 18 '79
The SALT summit. Jun 25 '79	The summit. Jun 25 '79	Third World. Cockpit of turmoil. Jun 25 '79

Newsweek July 1979	*Time* July 1979	*U.S. News* July 1979
Agony of the boat people. Jul 2 '79	The energy mess. Rebellious truckers. Insatiable OPEC. Jul 2 '79	Changes in the way you will travel. Jul 2 '79
Over a barrel. [Petroleum prices] Jul 9 '79	The world over a barrel. OPEC's tightening oil squeeze. Jul 9 '79	America. Still the promised land. Jul 9 '79
The energy crisis. A program for the '80s. Jul 16 '79	Here comes Skylab. Ten years after the moon walk. Jul 16 '79	New adventures in space. Jul 16 '79
To lift the nation's spirit. Jul 23 '79	At the crossroads. [Jimmy Carter] Jul 23 '79	Why Kennedy legend lives on. Jul 23 '79
Carter's juggling act. Jul 30 '79	Now what? [Jimmy Carter] Jul 30 '79	Tightening the belt on energy. Can it be done? Jul 30 '79

Newsweek August 1979	*Time* August 1979	*U.S. News* August 1979
Where have all the heroes gone? Aug 6 '79	Leadership in America. 50 faces for the future. Aug 6 '79	A ray of hope. [Indochinese refugees] Aug 6 '79
Can Chrysler be saved? Aug 13 '79	Hollywood's whiz kids. Aug 13 '79	Fuels for America's future. Aug 13 '79
Secrets of the human cell. Aug 20 '79	Judging the judges. An outsize job - and getting bigger. Aug 20 '79	Young talent on the rise. Aug 20 '79
The Andrew Young affair. Aug 27 '79	The topsy-turvy economy. New ideas to set it right. Aug 27 '79	The great American bureaucratic propaganda machine. Aug 27 '79

Newsweek September 1979	*Time* September 1979	*U.S. News* September 1979
Collision course over the PLO. Sep 3 '79	The master eye. Photographer Ansel Adams. Sep 3 '79	New breed of workers. Prosperous. Restless. Demanding. Sep 3 '79
Probing the planets. Man's closest look at Saturn. Sep 10 '79	Hot on the trail. G.O.P. candidate John Connally. Sep 10 '79	Kids, teachers and parents: "Give us better schools." Sep 10 '79
The angry West. 'Get off our backs Uncle Sam.' Sep 17 '79	Storm over Cuba. Sep 17 '79	Crisis ahead for United Nations? Sep 17 '79
Teddy chips away. [Edward Kennedy] Sep 24 '79	Bravo Pavarotti! Opera's golden tenor. Sep 24 '79	Preachers in politics. Sep 24 '79

Newsweek **October 1979**	*Time* **October 1979**	*U.S. News* **October 1979**
The gold rush of '79. And the economic mess behind it. Oct 1 '79	White House Years by Henry Kissinger. Oct 1 '79	Rocketing inflation. How much worse? Who's hit hardest? Any way to cope? Oct 1 '79
The Pope's historic visit. Oct 8 '79	Mexico: An angry neighbor. President José López Portillo. Oct 8 '79	A Pope on the move. Oct 8 '79
John Paul's triumph. Oct 15 '79	John Paul, superstar. Special: An album of his journey. Oct 15 '79	Challenges of the '80s. Oct 15 '79
Shock treatment for inflation. Oct 22 '79	The squeeze of '79. Tighter money. Higher prices. Wall Street woes. Oct 22 '79	The underground economy. How 20 million Americans cheat Uncle Sam out of billions. . . Oct 22 '79
The talk of TV. Phil Donahue. Oct 29 '79	What price power? Expanding America's arsenal. Oct 29 '79	Crash of '29. Have we learned anything? Oct 29 '79

Newsweek **November 1979**	*Time* **November 1979**	*U.S. News* **November 1979**
The President's partner. [Rosalynn Carter] Nov 5 '79	The Kennedy challenge. Nov 5 '79	Oil profits running wild? Nov 5 '79
Drugs for the mind. Psychiatry's newest weapons. Nov 12 '79	Starvation. Deathwatch in Cambodia. Nov 12 '79	Is the malaise real? Nation's mood in autumn. Nov 12 '79
Ten years that shook America...now, the '80s. Nov 19 '79	Blackmailing the U.S. "America is the great Satan" - Ayatullah Khomeini. Nov 19 '79	White House race. Already a circus. Nov 19 '79
Has America lost it clout? [U.S. foreign relations] Nov 26 '79	The test of wills. [Iran hostage crisis] Nov 26 '79	Test of U.S. resolve. [Iran hostage crisis] Nov 26 '79

Newsweek **December 1979**	*Time* **December 1979**	*U.S. News* **December 1979**
Heading for a showdown. Anti-American mob in Teheran. Dec 3 '79	Attacking America. Fury in Iran. Rescue in Pakistan. Dec 3 '79	U.S. builds for a showdown. Dec 3 '79
Inside the Burger court. Special report on the revealing new book by Woodward & Armstrong.	Center of the storm. Iran's deposed Shah. Dec 10 '79	Islam in ferment. Dec 10 '79
Tightening the screws. [Iran hostage crisis] Dec 17 '79	Rock's outer limits. The Who. Dec 17 '79	A nation aroused. [Iran hostage crisis] Dec 17 '79
Searching for the real Jesus. Dec 24 '79	The cooling of America. Cold wave hits. Fuel prices up. Dec 24 '79	Is Maggie losing the new battle of Britain? Prime Minister Margaret Thatcher. Dec 24 '79
America's vigil. [Iran hostage crisis] Dec 31 '79	Going. . .going. . .gone! The art and antique boom. Dec 31 '79	Outlook '80. Recession. How deep, how long? Elections. Another term for Carter? World. . . Dec 31 '79

Newsweek January 1980	*Time* January 1980	*U.S. News* January 1980
A star for the '80s. Meryl Streep. Jan 7 '80	Man of the year. Ayatullah Khomeini. Jan 7 '80	Outlook '80. Recession. How deep, how long? Elections. Another term for Carter? World. More trouble brewing? Money... Jan 7 '80
A new Cold War. [Afghanistan-Russian invasion] Jan 14 '80	Moscow's bold challenge. [Afghanistan-Russian invasion] Jan 14 '80	Detente. 1972-1980. Jan 14 '80
America's get-tough strategy. Jan 21 '80	Grain as a weapon. Who wins. Who loses. Jan 21 '80	U.S. economy in '80s. Can we meet the challenge? Jan 21 '80
Should we boycott the Olympics? Jan 28 '80	Squeezing the Soviets. U.S. anger. U.N. condemnation. Olympic threat. Jan 28 '80	America's lonely role. [U.S. foreign relations] Jan 28 '80

Newsweek February 1980	*Time* February 1980	*U.S.News* February 1980
Bush breaks out of the pack. Feb 4 '80	Taking charge. "An assault will be repelled by any means necessary..." [Soviet Union and the U.S.] Feb 4 '80	It's Carter's turn to cope with Russia. Feb 4 '80
Children of divorce. Feb 11 '80	Good as gold. Lake Placid. [Winter Olympics] Feb 11 '80	How strong is Russia? How prepared is U.S.? Feb 11 '80
Women in the military. Should they be drafted? Feb 18 '80	Operation Abscam. The FBI stings Congress. Feb 18 '80	ABC's of how a President is chosen. Feb 18 '80
A break in the deadlock. [Iran hostage crisis] Feb 25 '80	The $8,000,000 man. TV's news explosion. [Dan Rather and television news] Feb 25 '80	Our new elite. For better or for worse? [Yuppies] Feb 25 '80

Newsweek March 1980	*Time* March 1980	*U.S.News* March 1980
Is inflation out of control? Mar 3 '80	Who is this man? The many faces of Peter Sellers. Mar 3 '80	Women in combat. Closer than you think. Mar 3 '80
Back in the saddle again. [Ronald Reagan] Mar 10 '80	Ronnie's romp! And now the real race is on. [Ronald Reagan] Mar 10 '80	Washington's lawyers. Rise of the power brokers. Mar 10 '80
DNA's new miracles. How science is retooling genes. Mar 17 '80	Diplomacy in crisis. Hostages in Bogotá. Suspense in Iran. Fiasco at the U.N. Mar 17 '80	America's invisible millionaires. A spectacular boom. Mar 17 '80
Carter tilts at inflation. Mar 24 '80	Carter vs. inflation. The President's demand: "Discipline ... discipline ... discipline." Mar 24 '80	Economy out of control. Mar 24 '80
The credit tumble. Mar 31 '80	Interferon. The IF drug for cancer. Mar 31 '80	Race to top. Is it over? [Presidential campaign] Mar 31 '80

Newsweek	**April 1980**

The billion dollar gambler. Silver king Bunker Hunt.   Apr 7 '80

Top fiddle. Violinist Itzhak Perlman.   Apr 14 '80

The hostage dilemma. Carter's new tack.   Apr 21 '80

Detroit hits the skids - and the recession is on.   Apr 28 '80

Time	**April 1980**

Flying high. $4 billion for the cruise missile. Boeing boss T.A. Wilson.   Apr 7 '80

The Palestinians. Key to a Mideast peace.   Apr 14 '80

Is capitalism working?   Apr 21 '80

High noon for America's allies. [U.S. foreign relations]   Apr 28 '80

U.S.News	**April 1980**

How to survive inflation. Apr 7 '80

Who runs America.   Apr 14 '80

Income taxes. Myth of IRS efficiency. How the honest bear the burden. Now that Uncle Sam has your return.   Apr 21 '80

Have the scars healed? 5 years later. [Vietnam War]   Apr 28 '80

Newsweek	**May 1980**

Fiasco in Iran. [Iran hostage rescue attempt]   May 5 '80

Rescue mission in Washington. [Carter administration] May 12 '80

Leading two lives. Women at work and home.   May 19 '80

The Cuban influx. Can Carter control it?   May 26 '80

Time	**May 1980**

Debacle in the desert. Bulletin: An attempt to rescue the American hostages in Iran was aborted Friday when eight. . .   May 5 '80

A surprise for State. Senator Edmund Muskie.   May 12 '80

The empire strikes back. Star Wars. Archvillain Darth Vader. May 19 '80

Picasso. The show of shows. May 26 '80

U.S.News	**May 1980**

Reagan. What he stands for. May 5 '80

How ready to fight? [U.S. armed forces]   May 12 '80

Powder keg at our doorstep. [Cuba and the Caribbean region] May 19 '80

Academy women. Ready to take command.   May 26 '80

Newsweek	**June 1980**

The big bang. [Mt. St. Helens volcano]   Jun 2 '80

The Anderson factor. Wild card in the game. [John Anderson] Jun 9 '80

Ted Turner's empire. A sports king tackles TV news.   Jun 16 '80

The fight of his life. Sugar Ray Leonard takes on Roberto Duran. Jun 23 '80

Machines that think. Hello, I am your friend Chip. I'm getting smarter all the time. Soon, I will be everywhere. And. . .   Jun 30 '80

Time	**June 1980**

The big blowup. [Mt. St. Helens volcano]   Jun 2 '80

Who'll fight for America? The manpower crisis.   Jun 9 '80

Help! Teacher can't teach. Jun 16 '80

Inside the U.S.S.R.   Jun 23 '80

The incredible tennis machine. Sweden's Bjorn Borg.   Jun 30 '80

U.S.News	**June 1980**

Rage in Miami. A warning? [Race riot]   Jun 2 '80

Detroit fights back. [Automobile industry]   Jun 9 '80

The American family. Bent - but not broken.   Jun 16 '80

Rx for reviving America. Jun 23 '80

Hobbled giants. [U.S. and the Soviet Union]   Jun 30 '80

Newsweek **July 1980**	*Time* **July 1980**	*U.S.News* **July 1980**
The new immigrants. Jul 7 '80	Rediscovering America. Jul 7 '80	Splintered America. Peril or promise. [Ethnic groups] Jul 7 '80
Defending the oil fields. The U.S. military buildup. [Middle East] Jul 14 '80	That aching back. Latest word on the oldest agony. Jul 14 '80	Midyear outlook. When will business bounce back? How much will inflation slow? How steep a drop in profits?. . . Jul 14 '80
Reagan up close. His character. His career. His potential. Jul 21 '80	Feeling super in Detroit. [Republican national convention] Jul 21 '80	Reagan. What kind of President. Jul 21 '80
Photo finish. How the Ford deal fizzled. [Republican national convention] Jul 28 '80	Getting it together. Exclusive: Inside the Ford drama. [Republican national convention] Jul 28 '80	Is '80 a Republican year? Jul 28 '80

Newsweek **August 1980**	*Time* **August 1980**	*U.S.News* **August 1980**
The case of the President's brother. [Billy Carter] Aug 4 '80	Coping with Billy. [Billy Carter] Aug 4 '80	Goodbye to our good life? [Economic conditions] Aug 4 '80
The rebellious Democrats. Aug 11 '80	TV's Dallas. Whodunit? Aug 11 '80	Could he be president? [John Anderson] Aug 11 '80
The Democrats. Can they get it together? Aug 18 '80	The Carter Presidency. Aug 18 '80	Democrats uphill battle. Aug 18 '80
Now for the hard part. [Carter's presidential campaign] Aug 25 '80	Running tough. "A choice between two futures." [Democratic National Convention] Aug 25 '80	Carter's second chance. Aug 25 '80

Newsweek **September 1980**	*Time* **September 1980**	*U.S.News* **September 1980**
Teen age sex. The new morality hits home. Sep 1 '80	Poland's angry workers. Sep 1 '80	Life begins at 55. Sep 1 '80
The productivity crisis. Can America renew its economic promise? Sep 8 '80	Detroit's uphill battle. GM's Murphy. Ford's Caldwell. Chrysler's Iacocca. Sep 8 '80	Union corruption. Worse than ever. Sep 8 '80
Born-again politics. [Religion and politics] Sep 15 '80	The U.S. voter. Wary. Worried. Waiting. Sep 15 '80	Science. America's struggle to stay ahead. Sep 15 '80
The shame of college sports. Sep 22 '80	The poisoning of America. Those toxic chemical wastes. Sep 22 '80	Rebuilding America. It will cost trillions. Sep 22 '80
The Vanessa Redgrave controversy. Sep 29 '80	Supercoach. Alabama's Bear Bryant. Sep 29 '80	Detroit thinks small. Will it pay off? [Automobile industry] Sep 29 '80

Newsweek   October 1980

War in the oil fields.
[Iranian-Iraqi war]   Oct 6 '80

The art of politics.   Oct 13 '80

The Gulf War: Rising risks.
[Iranian-Iraqi war]   Oct 20 '80

Is America strong enough?
Oct 27 '80

Time   October 1980

War in the Gulf.   [Iranian-Iraqi
war]   Oct 6 '80

The jackpot states. Where the
election will be won.   Oct 13 '80

Showman of science. Astronomer
Carl Sagan.   Oct 20 '80

The Gulf. Will it explode?
[Iranian-Iraqi war]   Oct 27 '80

U.S.News   October 1980

Head to head on the issues.
Exclusive interviews with Carter
and Reagan.   Oct 6 '80

Refugees. Stung by a backlash.
Oct 13 '80

The race for First Lady.   Oct 20 '80

Fear stalks the streets. [Crime]
Oct 27 '80

Newsweek   November 1980

And the winner is... [Presidential
candidates]   Nov 3 '80

Breakthrough. [Iran hostage
crisis]   Nov 10 '80

President Reagan.   Nov 17 '80

The riddles of Saturn.   Nov 24 '80

Time   November 1980

Now. The choice. [Presidential
candidates]   Nov 3 '80

The hostage drama. [Iran hostage
crisis]   Nov 10 '80

A fresh start. [Ronald Reagan]
Nov 17 '80

Saturn. Encounter in space.
Nov 24 '80

U.S.News   November 1980

The winner? Results of 50-state
survey.   Nov 3 '80

Election impact. Jobs. Taxes.
Prices. Spending. Energy.
Investing.   Nov 10 '80

What Reagan will do as President.
Nov 17 '80

How to get America back on track.
Reagan's brain trust tells what's
ahead.   Nov 24 '80

Newsweek   December 1980

Wall Street's bad news bulls.
Dec 1 '80

Challenge to Moscow. [Poland]
Dec 8 '80

Poland: The invasion threat.
Dec 15 '80

John Lennon. 1940 - 1980.
Dec 22 '80

Pictures of '80.   Dec 29 '80

Time   December 1980

TV's sunrise serenades.   Dec 1 '80

The robot revolution.   Dec 8 '80

Rocky mountain high. Soaring
prospects for the '80s. [Energy
resources]   Dec 15 '80

When the music died. John
Lennon.   Dec 22 '80

Shaking up communism.
Dec 29 '80

U.S.News   December 1980

What next 20 years hold for you.
Dec 1 '80

Battle of the sexes. Men fight back.
Dec 8 '80

Prosperity without inflation.
Interviews with four Nobel Prize
winners.   Dec 15 '80

Twilight of Communism?
Dec 22 '80

Outlook '81. Reagan. Can he turn
U.S. around? Business. How fast a
recovery? World. New muscle for
America. Money. . .   Dec 29 '80

Newsweek **January 1981**	*Time* **January 1981**	*U.S.News* **January 1981**
The new Mafia. Jimmy 'The Weasel' Fratianno tells the secrets of organized crime. Jan 5 '81	Man of the year. Ronald Reagan. Jan 5 '81	Outlook '81. Reagan. Can he turn U.S. around? Business. How fast a recovery? World. New muscle for America. Money. . . Jan 5 '81
Solid Goldie. Comedienne Goldie Hawn. Jan 12 '81	Aiming high in '81. Space shuttle Columbia. Jan 12 '81	Comeback of the marines. Jan 12 '81
The economy in crisis. Why it's out of control. How to fix it. Jan 19 '81	Reagan's biggest challenge. Mending the economy. Jan 19 '81	Who are these people - and what do they stand for? Jan 19 '81
The hostage deal. [Iran hostage crisis] Jan 26 '81	The hostages. Breakthrough! [Iran hostage crisis] Jan 26 '81	Start of the Reagan era. Jan 26 '81

Newsweek **February 1981**	*Time* **February 1981**	*U.S. News* **February 1981**
A day to remember. [Inauguration of Ronald Reagan] Feb 2 '81	The ordeal ends. And the outrage grows. [Iran hostages return] Feb 2 '81	Reagan starts rolling. Feb 2 '81
A big welcome hug. [Iran hostages return] Feb 9 '81	The '80s look. [Fashion models] Feb 9 '81	China in turmoil - meaning for U.S. Feb 9 '81
Cut, clash, chop. Budget Director David Stockman. Feb 16 '81	Embattled Britain. Prime Minister Thatcher. Feb 16 '81	Turning a tougher face to Russia. Feb 16 '81
Are we running out of water? Feb 23 '81	American renewal. Feb 23 '81	Comeback in space. Feb 23 '81

Newsweek **March 1981**	*Time* **March 1981**	*U.S. News* **March 1981**
Reagan's New Deal. Mar 2 '81	The ax falls. Reagan's plan for a "new beginning." Mar 2 '81	The Reagan revolution. Impact on business taxes... jobs. Investors. Cities. Farmers. Mar 2 '81
After Cronkite. [Television news] Mar 9 '81	Shaping life in the lab. The boom in genetic engineering. Mar 9 '81	Our troubled neighbors - dangers for U.S. [Canada and Mexico] Mar 9 '81
Storm over El Salvador. Mar 16 '81	Taking command. The world according to Haig. Mar 16 '81	The war against Reagan's budget. Mar 16 '81
The epidemic of violent crime. Mar 23 '81	The curse of violent crime. Mar 23 '81	The 9-to-5 presidency. Is it working? Mar 23 '81
Black magic. Novelist Toni Morrison. Mar 30 '81	How Japan does it. The world's toughest competitor. Mar 30 '81	America's middle class. Angry, frustrated and losing ground. Mar 30 '81

Newsweek April 1981	*Time* April 1981	*U.S. News* April 1981
Who's in charge here? Secretary of State Alexander Haig. Apr 6 '81	Abortion. The battle of "life" vs. "choice." Apr 6 '81	Reagan's goal: Cutting Castro down to size. Apr 6 '81
Reagan's close call. The shooting and the surgery. Case history of a gunman. Who's in control. Can the risk be cut? Apr 13 '81	Moment of madness. What happened - and why. Can it never be stopped? [Reagan assassination attempt] Apr 13 '81	What impact? [Reagan assassination attempt] Apr 13 '81
Why public schools are flunking. Part one of a special report. Apr 20 '81	The prince's charmer. Lady Diana is wowing Britain. Apr 20 '81	Income taxes. What happens to your return now. How tough will IRS get? Interview with new chief. Tax cuts you can... Apr 20 '81
'We're in space to stay.' Apr 27 '81	Right on! Winging into a new era. [Columbia space shuttle] Apr 27 '81	Billions down the Pentagon drain. Apr 27 '81

Newsweek May 1981	*Time* May 1981	*U.S. News* May 1981
The cities' Mr. Fixit. Felix Rohatyn. May 4 '81	The money chase. What business schools are doing to us. May 4 '81	Terrorism. Russia's secret weapon? May 4 '81
GM challenges the Japanese. Chevrolet's new 'J' car. May 11 '81	Baseball '81. It's incredible! May 11 '81	Why lawyers are in the doghouse. May 11 '81
The sexes. How they differ - and why. May 18 '81	Troubled Israel. Military tensions. Chaotic economy. Election showdown. May 18 '81	Who runs America. May 18 '81
Again. [Assassination attempt on Pope Paul II] May 25 '81	Terrorist's target. "Why did they do it?" - John Paul II May 25 '81	A crime that shocked the world. May 25 '81

Newsweek June 1981	*Time* June 1981	*U.S. News* June 1981
Can you afford to retire? The Social Security crisis. Turmoil in pension plans. Jun 1 '81	Heart attacks. New insights, new treatments. Jun 1 '81	Nancy Reagan's role. Jun 1 '81
Reagan's defense buildup. Does it make sense? Can we afford it? Jun 8 '81	The savings revolution. Everybody wants your money! Jun 8 '81	We're rallying. America's springtime mood. Jun 8 '81
Cliffhanger classic. 'Raiders of the Lost Ark.' Jun 15 '81	America's mayors. The politics of survival. Ed Koch of New York. Jun 15 '81	The North fights back. [Northeastern states] Jun 15 '81
A dangerous nuclear game. Israel's raid: The inside story. Impact on the Mideast. U.S. policy dilemma. The rush to... Jun 22 '81	Attack - and fallout. The target: Iraq's reactor. Jun 22 '81	The great American immigration nightmare. Jun 22 '81
Watt's land rush. Digging up the last frontier? Interior Secretary James Watt. Jun 29 '81	France's new look. Socialist President François Mitterrand. Jun 29 '81	Water. Will we have enought to go around? Jun 29 '81

Newsweek **July 1981**	*Time* **July 1981**	*U.S. News* **July 1981**
The small town boom. Jul 6 '81	High on cocaine. A drug with status - and menace. Jul 6 '81	9 hours inside the Oval Office. Jul 6 '81
Secrets of sleep. Jul 13 '81	Viet Nam vets. Fighting for their rights. Jul 13 '81	The people's war against crime. Jul 13 '81
Kaddafi. The most dangerous man in the world? Jul 20 '81	Justice - at last. Reagan nominee Sandra O'Connor. Jul 20 '81	The Ottawa summit. Can Reagan keep allies in line? Jul 20 '81
Is big business getting too big? Jul 27 '81	How to spend a trillion. Defense Secretary Caspar Weinberger. Jul 27 '81	Rating Reagan's cabinet. Jul 27 '81

Newsweek **August 1981**	*Time* **August 1981**	*U.S. News* **August 1981**
Royal wedding. [Wedding of Charles and Diana] Aug 3 '81	Three cheers! [Wedding of Charles and Diana] Aug 3 '81	Unruly neighbors. Big worry for Russia. Poland. Afghanistan. China. Aug 3 '81
Smile, please. How the tax cut helps you. Will it hurt the economy? The battered Democrats. Aug 10 '81	Ice cream. Getting your licks. Aug 10 '81	Our endless pursuit of happiness. Aug 10 '81
Who controls the air? Reagan's tough line. The strike's impact. The public's view: A poll. Aug 17 '81	Winging it. Coping without controllers. [Air traffic controllers' strike] Aug 17 '81	Medicine and profits. Unhealthy mixture? Aug 17 '81
Cable TV. Coming of age. Aug 24 '81	Cities are fun. Master planner James Rouse. Aug 24 '81	Hispanics make their move. Aug 24 '81
When doctors play God. The ethics of life-and-death decisions. Aug 31 '81	Wrestling life into fable. Garp creator John Irving strikes again. Aug 31 '81	The great American transportation mess. Aug 31 '81

Newsweek **September 1981**	*Time* **September 1981**	*U.S. News* **September 1981**
The champ you love to hate. John McEnroe. Sep 7 '81	Magic Meryl. Actress Meryl Streep. Sep 7 '81	Signs of hope for our schools. Sep 7 '81
Roadblock to peace? Israel's Menachem Begin. Sep 14 '81	To the right, march! Conservative Senator Jesse Helms. Sep 14 '81	Unions on the run. Sep 14 '81
Reaganomics. The confidence gap. Wall Street votes no. The black-hole budget. The interest-rate squeeze. Sep 21 '81	Reaganomics. Making it work. Sep 21 '81	Flaunting wealth. It's back in style. Sep 21 '81
TV's hottest show. Luke and Laura of 'General Hospital.' Sep 28 '81	We, the jury. That irksome, boring, vital, rewarding experience. Sep 28 '81	Inside Moscow's European empire. What next. Sep 28 '81

Newsweek **October 1981**	*Time* **October 1981**	*U.S. News* **October 1981**
The nuclear arms race. The MX muddle. Reagan's new strategy. Limited war: How it might happen. Oct 5 '81	Broadway blockbuster. Dickens' Nicholas Nickleby. Oct 5 '81	Now the squeeze really starts. [Reagan budget] Oct 5 '81
The new money game. How you can play it. Where it leads the economy. Oct 12 '81	No free lunch. The high cost of entitlements. Oct 12 '81	Our losing battle against crime. Oct 12 '81
'Act of infamy.' The Sadat assassinatin with exclusive color. Oct 19 '81	Mideast turmoil. Anwar Sadat - 1918-1981. [Assassination of Anwar Sadat] Oct 19 '81	Now the shock waves. [Assassination of Anwar Sadat] Oct 19 '81
The survival summit. What the South will ask for. What the North should do. Oct 26 '81	Arming the world. What are the limits? Oct 26 '81	Third World. Uncle Sam's new stand. Oct 26 '81

Newsweek **November 1981**	*Time* **November 1981**	*U.S. News* **November 1981**
Cancer: A progress report. Nov 2 '81	The fitness craze. America shapes up. Nov 2 '81	Reagan's big three. Too much power? [Reagan staff] Nov 2 '81
U.S. foreign policy. The world according to Reagan. Nov 9 '81	AWACS. He does it again! Nov 9 '81	The verdict on Reagan. National mood survey. Nov 9 '81
The storyteller's art. V.S. Naipaul's tales of a troubled world. Nov 16 '81	Golden oldies. Hepburn and Fonda in "On Golden Pond." Nov 16 '81	Probing the heavens. Any real value? Nov 16 '81
The KGB in America. Nov 23 '81	Paradise lost? South Florida. Nov 23 '81	U.S. defense policy. The right direction? Nov 23 '81
The hidden Freud. His secret life. His theories under attack. Nov 30 '81	Europe's fear. And a bold U.S. proposal. Nov 30 '81	The coming industrial miracle. Nov 30 '81

Newsweek **December 1981**	*Time* **December 1981**	*U.S. News* **December 1981**
A new breed of actor. Dec 7 '81	Cats. Love 'em! Hate 'em! Dec 7 '81	America's great new food craze. Dec 7 '81
What Vietnam did to us. A combat unit relives the war and the decade since. Dec 14 '81	The President's men. How the White House works - and doesn't. Dec 14 '81	Troubled teenagers. Dec 14 '81
The First Lady's world. [Nancy Reagan] Dec 21 '81	Libya's hit teams. The specter of terrorism. Colonel Muammar Gaddafi. Dec 21 '81	Is Central America going Communist? Dec 21 '81
Poland's ordeal. Dec 28 '81	Poland's ordeal. The darkness descends. General Jaruzelski. Dec 28 '81	Outlook '82. Recession. When will it end? Reagan. Will he change course? World. Next hot spots for U.S.? Money... Dec 28 '81

Newsweek **January 1982**	*Time* **January 1982**	*U.S. News* **January 1982**
Looking back at '81. Jan 4 '82	Man of the year. Poland's Lech Walesa. Jan 4 '82	Outlook '82. Recession. When will it end? Reagan. Will he change course? World. Next hot spots for U.S.? Money... Jan 4 '82
How life begins. Biology's new frontier. Jan 11 '82	Children of war. Out of the horror, amazing strength. Jan 11 '82	The great propaganda war. Jan 11 '82
The big breakup. Ma Bell loses its phone system. How phone bills will go up. Its coming computer war with IBM... Jan 18 '82	Gronk! Flash! Zap! Video games are blitzing the world. Jan 18 '82	Where are America's allies? Jan 18 '82
Superbowl: Duel of wits. Jan 25 '82	Superdreams. [Super bowl] Jan 25 '82	Marxism in U.S. classrooms. Jan 25 '82

Newsweek **February 1982**	*Time* **February 1982**	*U.S. News* **February 1982**
The Haitians. Refugees or prisoners? Feb 1 '82	The New Deal. FDR's disputed legacy. Feb 1 '82	Taking on an unruly world. Secretary of State Haig. Secretary of Defense Weinberger. National Security Adviser... Feb 1 '82
Reagan's big gamble. Defying the deficits. Can he pass the bucks to the states? Feb 8 '82	Unemployment. The biggest worry. Feb 8 '82	Reagan's new Federalism. How cities and states will be hit. Feb 8 '82
The Keaton charm. Diane Keaton. Feb 15 '82	Striking it rich. America's risk takers. Feb 15 '82	The screw tightens. [Reagan budget] Feb 15 '82
Home is where the computer is. Feb 22 '82	The new baby bloom. [Increased pregnancies] Feb 22 '82	Is Mother Nature going berserk? Feb 22 '82

Newsweek **March 1982**	*Time* **March 1982**	*U.S. News* **March 1982**
The fire next door. Reagan's no-win situation. What can be salvaged. A U.S. poll: Doubts and distrust. Mar 1 '82	Kissinger. Memoirs. The October war. Soviet showdown. Watergate's impact. Mar 1 '82	Communism. The great economic failure. Mar 1 '82
King of the opera. Tenor Placido Domingo. Mar 8 '82	Interest rate anguish. Federal Reserve Chairman Paul Volcker. Mar 8 '82	Can Detroit ever come back? Mar 8 '82
How safe are your savings? Savings and loans crisis. Plans for a bailout. The money-market fund alternative. Mar 15 '82	Salt: A new villain. Mar 15 '82	America's $39 billion heart business. Mar 15 '82
Taking aim at Nicaragua. The propaganda blitz. What U.S. intelligence shows. How real a threat? Mar 22 '82	The peril grows. Central America's agony. A U.S. dilemma. Mar 22 '82	The great nostalgia kick. Mar 22 '82
Mysteries of evolution. Paleontologist Stephan Jay Gould. Mar 29 '82	Thinking the unthinkable. Rising fears about nuclear war. Mar 29 '82	El Salvador. Can it be saved? Mar 29 '82

Newsweek	**April 1982**	*Time*	**April 1982**	*U.S. News*	**April 1982**

Reagan's America. And the poor get poorer.   Apr 5 '82

Giorgio's gorgeous style. Fashion designer Giorgio Armani. Apr 5 '82

How to bring back prosperity. Apr 5 '82

Brezhnev's final days. The succession struggle. Communism in crisis.   Apr 12 '82

Jerusalem. In the eye of the storm - protest and prayer.   Apr 12 '82

Will U.S. shut the door on immigrants?   Apr 12 '82

The empire strikes back. The Falklands crisis.   Apr 19 '82

Battle stations. Showdown in the South Atlantic.   Apr 19 '82

Income taxes. New crackdown by IRS? Interview with top tax man. Underground economy: $100 billion in lost taxes. . .   Apr 19 '82

The nuclear nightmare. The growing outcry over the bomb. How can the arms be halted? Apr 26 '82

The budget brawl.   Apr 26 '82

ABC's of today's economy. Apr 26 '82

Newsweek	**May 1982**	*Time*	**May 1982**	*U.S. News*	**May 1982**

Richard Pryor busts loose. May 3 '82

Computer generation. A new breed of whiz kids.   May 3 '82

America's fitness binge.   May 3 '82

The war is on. [Falkland Islands war]   May 10 '82

The British attack. [Falkland Islands war]   May 10 '82

Who runs America?   May 10 '82

Are big ships doomed? The Falklands fallout.   May 17 '82

Explosive Falklands. Naval war in the missile age. Striving to shape a truce.   May 17 '82

Ahead: A nation of illiterates? May 17 '82

The insanity defense. Should it be abolished? John Hinckley, Jr. May 24 '82

Social Security. What can the nation afford?   May 24 '82

An uneasy America. Nationwide mood survey.   May 24 '82

The British go in. [Falkland Islands war]   May 31 '82

D-day in the Falklands. May 31 '82

The big money questions. Will interest rates drop? When will buying spree start? Where to invest now? What. . .   May 31 '82

Newsweek	**June 1982**	*Time*	**June 1982**	*U.S. News*	**June 1982**

Art imitates life. The revival of realism.   Jun 7 '82

An extraordinary week. Furies in the Falklands. A Pope comes to Britain. Reagan girds for Europe. Jun 7 '82

Can Reagan pull the alliance together?   Jun 7 '82

The Watergate legacy. Ten years later.   Jun 14 '82

Heavyweight hits! Boxing scores one-two punch at the box office. Gerry Cooney fighting champ Larry Holmes. . .   Jun 14 '82

As Reagan barnstorms Europe - Jun 14 '82

Israel's blitz.   Jun 21 '82

Israel's blitz.   Jun 21 '82

Israeli strike. New test for U.S. [Israeli strike into Lebanon] Jun 21 '82

Wars without end.   Jun 28 '82

The spoils of war. Carving up Lebanon. Surrender at Stanley. U.S. frustrations.   Jun 28 '82

End of the permissive society? Jail for drunk drivers! Bring back the death penalty! Raise school standards. . .   Jun 28 '82

Newsweek July 1982	*Time* July 1982	*U.S. News* July 1982
Why Haig quit. Jul 5 '82	Foreign policy shakeup. Out goes Haig. In comes Shultz. Jul 5 '82	America's cults. Gaining ground again. Jul 5 '82
The Iran rescue mission. The untold story. The Pentagon's man in Teheran. Richard J. Meadows. Jul 12 '82	American women. The climb to equality. Jul 12 '82	Who is watching you? Report on privacy. Jul 12 '82
Deathtrap. Can the PLO survive? The U.S. evacuation plan. Jul 19 '82	Beirut under siege. Send in the Marines? Children of war revisited. Jul 19 '82	What next? [Lebanon-Israeli invasion] Jul 19 '82
The joy (and also the tedium, rage and sheer hard work) of gardening. Jul 26 '82	Iran on the march. "This is a war between Islam and blasphemy." - Ayatullah Khomeini. Jul 26 '82	Foreign policy. One more try. Reagan. Schulz. Weinberger. Clark. Jul 26 '82

Newsweek August 1982	*Time* August 1982	*U.S. News* August 1982
The decaying of America. Our dams, bridges, roads and water systems are falling apart. Aug 2 '82	Herpes. Today's scarlet letter. Aug 2 '82	What is TV doing to America? Aug 2 '82
Japan's high-tech challenge. Aug 9 '82	The big TV news gamble. Ted Turner shakes up the networks. Aug 9 '82	Our neglected kids. Aug 9 '82
The Palestinians. Where do they go from here? Aug 16 '82	Destroying Beirut. Israel tightens the noose. Aug 16 '82	Poverty trap. No way out? Aug 16 '82
Allergies. New discoveries, new relief. Aug 23 '82	Going, going...! Land sale of the century. [Sale of federal land] Aug 23 '82	End of the road? [Palestine Liberation Organization] Aug 23 '82
A break in interest rates. How it affects you. Wall Street's wildest week. Aug 30 '82	Coming on strong. The new ideal of beauty. Aug 30 '82	Tax squeeze. What it means to you. Aug 30 '82

Newsweek September 1982	*Time* September 1982	*U.S. News* September 1982
A style of her own. Martina Navratilova. Sep 6 '82	Wall Street. Olé! The economy. Eh? Sep 6 '82	Corporate crime. The untold story. Sep 6 '82
The war on drunk driving. Getting tough with the killers of 26,000 Americans a year. Sep 13 '82	The inmate nation. What are prisons for? Sep 13 '82	Jobs. A million that will never come back. Sep 13 '82
Playing for keeps. A strike threat hangs over the football season. How big business is changing pro sports. Sep 20 '82	Begin digs in. A defiant "No" to Reagan's peace plan. Sep 20 '82	The new army. With new punch. Sep 20 '82
The last fairy tale. Princess Grace, 1929-1982. Sep 27 '82	Massacre in Lebanon. Palestinian civilians are slaughtered. Sep 27 '82	To rebuild America - $2,500,000,000,000 job. Sep 27 '82

Newsweek **October 1982**	*Time* **October 1982**	*U.S. News* **October 1982**

Israel in torment. After the massacre: Can Begin survive? The anguish of American Jews. Oct 4 '82

Israel. A shaken nation.   Oct 4 '82

Mission impossible? [U.S. marines in Lebanon]   Oct 4 '82

The Tylenol scare.   Oct 11 '82

Jimmy Carter's memoirs. Facing up to the Middle East.   Oct 11 '82

As politics heat up - Preview of '82 election. Voters who hold the key. Are Parties falling apart? Oct 11 '82

Jobs. How to get America back to work.   Oct 18 '82

Going great at 50. Writer John Updike.   Oct 18 '82

Waiting for better days. A nationwide mood survey. Oct 18 '82

Guns, grass and money. America's billion-dollar marijuana crop. Oct 25 '82

The PAC men. Turning cash into votes.   Oct 25 '82

Middle Age. The best of times? Oct 25 '82

Newsweek **November 1982**	*Time* **November 1982**	*U.S. News* **November 1982**

Living longer, living better. Growing old without thinking old. How America treats the elderly. Nov 1 '82

The bottom line...busted. De Lorean's shattered dream. Nov 1 '82

American justice. ABC's of how it really works.   Nov 1 '82

America's secret war. Target: Nicaragua.   Nov 8 '82

Catalogues. Delivering the gala goods.   Nov 8 '82

U.S. foreign policy. A change in course?   Nov 8 '82

What course now? [U.S. elections] Nov 15 '82

America's message. Keep on course - but trim the sails.   Nov 15 '82

Election impact. A troublesome congress. Reagan's hard choices. Business outlook now. Tax cuts in danger. The '84 race.   Nov 15 '82

The new boss. A spymaster's rise to power. Will Moscow get tougher? How Reagan should respond. Soviet Party Chief. . .   Nov 22 '82

After Brezhnev. Andropov takes command.   Nov 22 '82

Russia after Brezhnev.   Nov 22 '82

How to deal with Moscow. An exclusive report by Henry Kissinger. Andropov's peace offensive. Reagan. . .   Nov 29 '82

God and the bomb. Catholic bishops debate nuclear morality. Nov 29 '82

Breaking through. Women on the move.   Nov 29 '82

Newsweek **December 1982**	*Time* **December 1982**	*U.S. News* **December 1982**

Infertility. One out of five American couples can't have children. But new drugs and microsurgery. . .   Dec 6 '82

The verdict on Newman: Quite a guy.   Dec 6 '82

Doctor's dilemma. Treat or let die? Dec 6 '82

Man makes a heart. The bold new world of cardiac medicine. Jarvik-7 artificial heart. Dec 13 '82

How Reagan decides. An inside look at the presidency. The qualities a President needs.   Dec 13 '82

Where do we go from here? How strong a recovery. Lasting scars of recession. Next for the stock market. Job outlook for. .   Dec 13 '82

Defending America. How to cut the Pentagon's budget - and keep the nation strong.   Dec 20 '82

Mexico's crisis. "We are in an emergency." New President Miguel de la Madrid.   Dec 20 '82

"See you in court." Our suing society.   Dec 20 '82

The Bible in America. How one book unites us, divides us, and still defines us.   Dec 27 '82

The new missionary. [Christian missionaries]   Dec 27 '82

Outlook '83. Business: How fast a pickup? Reagan: Can he tame congress? Money: Where to invest now? World. . .   Dec 27 '82

Newsweek January 1983	*Time* January 1983	*U.S. News* January 1983

The plot to kill the Pope. The Bulgarian connection. Was the KGB behind it?   Jan 3 '83

Machine of the year. The computer moves in.   Jan 3 '83

Outlook '83. Business: How fast a pickup? Reagan: Can he tame congress? Money: Where to invest now? World...   Jan 3 '83

Splitting up the family. The courts are changing the rules of divorce and child custody - and often making things worse.   Jan 10 '83

The debt bomb. The worldwide peril of go-go lending.   Jan 10 '83

Is U.S. really No. 2?   Jan 10 '83

Portrait of America. The hidden revolution at home and on the job. Jan 17 '83

Making opera grand. James Levine: America's top maestro. Jan 17 '83

America's wandering jobless. Jan 17 '83

Who will pay? The social-security crisis. The growing burden on the young. The mounting worries of the old.   Jan 24 '83

The death penalty. The chair is bolted to the floor near the back of a 12-ft. by 18-ft. room. You sit on a... Jan 24 '83

New hope for the depressed. Jan 24 '83

Arms control. Now or never? Jan 31 '83

Nuclear poker. The stakes get higher and higher.   Jan 31 '83

How to get the country moving again. Advice from six Nobel prize economists. Milton Friedman. Paul Samuelson...   Jan 31 '83

Newsweek February 1983	*Time* February 1983	*U.S. News* February 1983

How the brain works. The human computer.   Feb 7 '83

ABC's gigantic gamble. Robert Mitchum in The Winds of War. Feb 7 '83

Can Reagan keep control? Feb 7 '83

The forgotten. The world's prisoners of conscience suffer harsh jail terms, torture and ruined lives...   Feb 14 '83

The KGB today. Andropov's eyes on the world.   Feb 14 '83

Ready for action - or are they? [U.S. armed forces]   Feb 14 '83

Sharon takes the rap. The politics of the massacre.   Feb 21 '83

Verdict on the massacre. [Israeli massacre in Lebanon]   Feb 21 '83

19 million singles. Their joys and frustrations.   Feb 21 '83

Farewell to M*A*S*H. Will prime-time TV ever be as good? Feb 28 '83

Royalty vs. the press. [Princess Diana]   Feb 28 '83

Cleaner air and water. Can we afford 690 billion dollars? Feb 28 '83

Newsweek March 1983	*Time* March 1983	*U.S. News* March 1983

Cleaning up the mess. The toxic-waste threat to America's health. Chaos at the EPA. Mar 7 '83

U.S. defense spending. Are billions being wasted?   Mar 7 '83

Invasion from Mexico. It just keeps growing.   Mar 7 '83

Sounding the alarm. El Salvador. Washington's hard sell for more aid. The Pope's mission for peace. Mar 14 '83

"To share the pain." The Pope in Central America.   Mar 14 '83

What's wrong with our teachers? Mar 14 '83

Left out. The human cost of the collapse of industrial America. Mar 21 '83

Detroit's comeback kid. Chrysler Chairman Lee Iacocca.   Mar 21 '83

"English sometimes spoken here." Our big cities go ethnic. Mar 21 '83

Bringing up superbaby. Parents are pushing their kids to learn earlier than ever. Does it help or hurt?   Mar 28 '83

Tax cheating. Bad and getting worse.   Mar 28 '83

Spawning new forms of life. Now the payoff starts.   Mar 28 '83

Newsweek **April 1983**	*Time* **April 1983**	*U.S. News* **April 1983**
Star wars. Reagan's new nuclear strategy. Will space be the next battleground? Apr 4 '83	Defending defense. Budget battles and star wars. Apr 4 '83	A search for the sacred. Religion's new turn. Apr 4 '83
Race and politics. Chicago's ugly election. Campaign '84: New black power at the polls. Apr 11 '83	Fighting cocaine's grip. Millions of users. Billions of dollars. Apr 11 '83	Bankers. Everybody's favorite target. Apr 11 '83
Epidemic. The mysterious and deadly disease called AIDS may be the public-health threat of the century. How did. . . Apr 18 '83	Arms control. Making the wrong moves? Apr 18 '83	ABC's of your income tax. What's wrong with the system. Billions the IRS never gets. The games people play. What. . . Apr 18 '83
Is nothing sacred? The low art of parody - spoofing for fun and profit. Apr 25 '83	Spokesman for the elderly. "They deserve much - and need much." Congressman Claude Pepper. Apr 25 '83	Nuclear freeze crusade. Gaining or waning? Apr 25 '83

Newsweek **May 1983**	*Time* **May 1983**	*U.S. News* **May 1983**
Hitler's secret diaries. Are they genuine? How they could rewrite history. Hitler and the Jews. May 2 '83	Hot faces from Europe. Actress Nastassia Kinski. May 2 '83	The $75 billion pork barrel ripoff. May 2 '83
Saving our schools. A scathing report demands better teachers and tougher standards. May 9 '83	Central America. Harsh facts, hard choices. "A vital interest, a moral duty." May 9 '83	What the next 50 years will bring. May 9 '83
Forgery. Uncovering the Hitler hoax. May 16 '83	Forgery. Hitler's diaries join the long list of famous frauds. May 16 '83	How drugs sap the nation's strength. May 16 '83
The male idols. Hollywood's new sex symbols. May 23 '83	Star Wars III. Return of the Jedi. George Lucas & friends wrap it all up. May 23 '83	Who runs America. May 23 '83
Can the recovery last? The Williamsburg summit. May 30 '83	The new economy. Where the jobs will be. Industry winners & losers. Menace of protectionism. May 30 '83	Gambling rage. Out of control? May 30 '83

Newsweek **June 1983**	*Time* **June 1983**	*U.S. News* **June 1983**
The first casualty. Central America. The death of an adviser in El Salvador. The battle for Nicaragua. Reagan's White. . . Jun 6 '83	Stress! Seeking cures for modern anxieties. Jun 6 '83	Interior's James Watt. Hero or villain? Jun 6 '83
Space woman. Sally Ride prepares to make history on shuttle Mission 7. NASA's latest plans for space travel. Jun 13 '83	Los Angeles. America's uneasy new melting pot. Jun 13 '83	How much is enough? Special report on defense. Jun 13 '83
Mission to Poland. The Pope's dramatic pilgrimage. Jun 20 '83	Maggie by a mile. What it means. What she'll do. British Prime Minister Margaret Thatcher. Jun 20 '83	Marriage. It's back in style! Jun 20 '83
Prayer and defiance. The Pope's challenge to Warsaw. Jun 27 '83	Homecoming. The return of the Polish Pope. Jun 27 '83	Turned loose too soon? Criminally insane. Jun 27 '83

Newsweek **July 1983**	*Time* **July 1983**	*U.S. News* **July 1983**
Super computers. The high-stakes race to build a machine that thinks. Can the U.S. beat Japan? Jul 4 '83	Disease detectives. Tracking the killers. The AIDS hysteria. Jul 4 '83	Still the land of opportunity? Jul 4 '83
What the world thinks of America. Loved, hated but always imitated - a new poll shows how America's image is changing. Jul 11 '83	The colossus that works. Big is bountiful at IBM. Jul 11 '83	Next stop-Central America? Jul 11 '83
Feeling the heat. The 'debategate' plot thickens. Who's telling the truth - and will heads roll? Jul 18 '83	Dancing to the music. David Bowie rockets onward. Jul 18 '83	Living without inflation. Where prices are headed. Places to put your money. Tips for consumers. Rent or buy a home. . . Jul 18 '83
Battle over the wilderness. Uncle Sam owns one-third of the country, and Americans are fighting over every acre. Jul 25 '83	Travel. Americans everywhere. Jul 25 '83	"A city without guts." Why Washington is losing the war on waste. J. Peter Grace, Chairman of the President's. . . Jul 25 '83

Newsweek **August 1983**	*Time* **August 1983**	*U.S. News* **August 1983**
Gunboat diplomacy. Reagan gets tougher with Nicaragua. Aug 1 '83	Japan. A nation in search of itself. Aug 1 '83	Lifestyle of the '80s. Anything goes! Aug 1 '83
Gay America. Sex, politics and the impact of AIDS. Aug 8 '83	Central America. The big stick approach. "We don't want war, but..." Maneuvering the military. Uproar over covert aid. Aug 8 '83	Guerrilla warriors. Now the Kremlin feels the heat. Aug 8 '83
What it takes to win. Olympic countdown. Aug 15 '83	Babies. What do they know? When do they know it? Aug 15 '83	Bull market. It's not over yet. Aug 15 '83
Drugs on the job. Aug 22 '83	Seeking votes and clout. A new black drive for political power. Jesse Jackson. Aug 22 '83	Soaring hospital costs. The brewing revolt. Room, $190 a day. Surgeon, $3,500. Anesthesia, $600. Blood, $85 a pint. . . Aug 22 '83
How transplants save lives. The replaceable body. Aug 29 '83	Wheeeeeeee! Chasing thrills and adventure. Aug 29 '83	Are U.S. cars really getting better? Aug 29 '83

Newsweek **September 1983**	*Time* **September 1983**	*U.S. News* **September 1983**
Computer capers. Trespassing in the Information Age - pranks or sabotage? Sep 5 '83	Private violence. Child abuse. Wife beating. Rape. Sep 5 '83	Wanted! 20 million new jobs by 1990. Sep 5 '83
Murder in the air. [Korean Airlines flight 007 incident] Sep 12 '83	Shooting to kill. The Soviets destroy an airliner. Sep 12 '83	Trigger-happy Soviets. A jolt to relations with U.S. [Korean Airlines flight 007 incident] Sep 12 '83
Why Moscow did it. Inquest on Flight 007. The world's outrage. The diplomatic impact. The Soviet stonewall. Sep 19 '83	Putting Moscow on the defensive. "The target is destroyed." Sep 19 '83	Back to school - and back to basics. Sep 19 '83
The Marines under fire. Reagan raises the stakes in Lebanon. Sep 26 '83	Banishing Mao's ghost. Theodore H. White on China. Sep 26 '83	In Lebanon to stay? [U.S. marines in Lebanon] Sep 26 '83

Newsweek **October 1983**	*Time* **October 1983**	*U.S. News* **October 1983**
'The Right Stuff.' Can a movie help make a president? Oct 3 '83	Lebanon. Holding the line. Oct 3 '83	Success! Who has it? How do you get it? What price do you pay? Oct 3 '83
The secret warriors. The CIA is back in business. Oct 10 '83	Shaping up. America's schools are getting better. Oct 10 '83	Untold story of the road to war in Vietnam. Oct 10 '83
To die or not to die. Minutes away from execution on a prison gurney, J.D. Autry won a dramatic reprieve. An account. . . Oct 17 '83	America's Olympics. A gold medal for Los Angeles? Oct 17 '83	In Central America why distrust of U.S. runs deep. Oct 17 '83
Battle over the missiles. Europe's anti-nuclear protests. Oct 24 '83	Making his moves. A shocker for Interior. A shake-up for the NSC. And a big "Why not?" for 1984. Oct 24 '83	The Bell breakup. What it means. To phone users. To competitors. To investors. Oct 24 '83
The Marine massacre. Oct 31 '83	Carnage in Beirut. Mideast madness hits the Marines. Oct 31 '83	War over water. Crisis of the '80s. Oct 31 '83

Newsweek **November 1983**	*Time* **November 1983**	*U.S. News* **November 1983**
Americans at war. [U.S. invasion of Grenada] Nov 7 '83	Worth the price? Tough moves, hard questions. Rescue in Grenada. Sacrifice in Beirut. Nov 7 '83	Agonizing decisions. What next in Grenada? Why stay in Lebanon? How to defuse critics. Nov 7 '83
What makes Jesse run? Presidential candidate Jesse Jackson. Nov 14 '83	J.F.K. How good a President was he? Nov 14 '83	Andropov. A year of failure. Nov 14 '83
TV's nuclear nightmare. Public service or propaganda? How will it affect children? ABC's 'The Day After.' Nov 21 '83	Splitting AT&T. Who wins, who loses - and why. Nov 21 '83	Divorce. How the game is played now. Nov 21 '83
What JFK meant to us. 30 Americans reflect on the man, the myth, the legacy. Nov 28 '83	1984. Big brother's father. Author George Orwell. Nov 28 '83	Rating the colleges. Exclusive national survey. Nov 28 '83

Newsweek **December 1983**	*Time* **December 1983**	*U.S. News* **December 1983**
Nuclear war. Can we reduce the risk? Dec 5 '83	Soviet walkout. A turning point for arms control. Behind the scenes: An exclusive report. Aftermath of "The day after." Dec 5 '83	Machines that think. They're brewing a revolution. Dec 5 '83
What a doll! The Cabbage Patch craze. Marketing a Christmas fad. Dec 12 '83	Accusing the press. What are its sins? Dec 12 '83	Business on a roll. Impact on investors, industry, politics, retailers, taxpayers, borrowers, job hunters. Dec 12 '83
Right men, wrong job? [U.S. marines in Lebanon] Dec 19 '83	Syria. Clashing with the U.S. Bidding for a bigger role. Dec 19 '83	Glut of doctors. Glut of lawyers. Good or bad? Dec 19 '83
Prince of the city. Peter Martins of the New York City Ballet. Dec 26 '83	Video rocks! A musical revolution. Dec 26 '83	Outlook '84. Business. Will it boom? Reagan. Second term a cinch? Money. Where to invest now? President's. . . Dec 26 '83

Newsweek   January 1984

Homeless in America.   Jan 2 '84

Can anyone stop Fritz?
Democratic candidate Walter
Mondale.   Jan 9 '84

El Salvador. The death squads.
Can they be stopped?   Jan 16 '84

Britain rocks America - again.
From the Beatles to Boy George and
beyond.   Jan 23 '84

Can we keep the skies safe? Intense
competition and the drive to cut
costs are making it more difficult.
Jan 30 '84

Newsweek   February 1984

The Reagan magic. Can he make it
work again? 1984.   Feb 6 '84

Going for gold. America's chances.
How TV covers the games.
Feb 13 '84

Pullout in Beirut. Death in
Moscow.   Feb 20 '84

Reagan's retreat. The price of
failure. [Lebanon and the U.S.]
Feb 27 '84

Newsweek   March 1984

The gene doctors. Unlocking the
mysteries of cancer, heart disease
and genetic defects.   Mar 5 '84

Hart's charge. Who he is. What he
stands for. His plan to win.
Mar 12 '84

Stolen children. What can be done
about child abduction.   Mar 19 '84

Showdown. Who's got the beef?
Mar 26 '84

Time   January 1984

Men of the year. Ronald Reagan.
Yuri Andropov.   Jan 2 '84

Why forgive? The Pope pardons
the gunman.   Jan 9 '84

Africa's woes. Coups, conflict and
corruption.   Jan 16 '84

Cashing in big. The men who
make the killings. [Stock market]
Jan 23 '84

Olympic dreams. America's quest
for gold.   Jan 30 '84

Time   February 1984

There he goes again. [Reagan
announced a bid for a second term]
Feb 6 '84

Nuclear power. Bombing out?
Feb 13 '84

The succession. Filling a vacuum,
again. Yuri Andropov 1914-1984.
Feb 20 '84

The Kremlin's new master. What
he might do. His view of the world.
The generation dilemma.
Konstantin. . .   Feb 27 '84

Time   March 1984

That monster deficit. America's
economic black hole.   Mar 5 '84

Now it's a race. [Presidential
candidates]   Mar 12 '84

Michael Jackson. Why he's a
thriller. Inside his world.
Mar 19 '84

Cholesterol. And now the bad news...
Mar 26 '84

U.S. News   January 1984

Outlook '84. Business. Will it
boom? Reagan. Second term a
cinch? Money. Where to invest
now? President's. . .   Jan 2 '84

America. Next target for terrorists?
Jan 9 '84

High tech. Blessing or curse?
Jan 16 '84

Is military taking over the
Kremlin?   Jan 23 '84

It's Reagan vs. the field.   Jan 30 '84

U.S. News   February 1984

Arab world. Where troubles for
U.S. never end.   Feb 6 '84

Drowning in debt. Impact of
another $180 billion deficit.
Feb 13 '84

What next in Russia?   Feb 20 '84

Can't anybody here run a war?
Feb 27 '84

U.S. News   March 1984

When church and state collide.
Mar 5 '84

Fluke or real threat? [Gary Hart]
Mar 12 '84

10 forces reshaping America. From
Eisenhower to Reagan - it is a span
of only 20 years, yet a period of
change so. . .   Mar 19 '84

Your income tax. Standing up to
the IRS. Last-minute tax tips. Tax
changes on the way. What happens
to your return now.   Mar 26 '84

Newsweek **April 1984**	*Time* **April 1984**	*U.S. News* **April 1984**
Under fire. Attorney General-Designate Edwin Meese III. Apr 2 '84	Drawing the line in Central America. Haig looks back. On foreign policy. On Reagan's men. Apr 2 '84	Asian-Americans. Are they making the grade? Apr 2 '84
The decline of Europe. Apr 9 '84	Sex in the '80s. The revolution is over. Apr 9 '84	What next? A world of communications wonders. Apr 9 '84
Tax shelters. How millions of Americans beat the tax man. Apr 16 '84	Computer software. The magic inside the machine. Apr 16 '84	America's youth in search of a cause. Apr 16 '84
Phobias. New drugs and therapies are helping people conquer their fears. Apr 23 '84	Policy collision. Mining Nicaragua's harbors. Apr 23 '84	Bulging prisons. Curbing crime - or wasting lives? Apr 23 '84
The terms of endearment. Reagan goes to China. What the President wants in Peking. Time to play a new China card. . . Apr 30 '84	China's new face. What will Reagan see. Apr 30 '84	Is there a game plan? [U.S. foreign policy] Apr 30 '84

Newsweek **May 1984**	*Time* **May 1984**	*U.S. News* **May 1984**
What Jesse wants. [Jesse Jackson] May 7 '84	The Jackson factor. Black pride, white concerns. [Jesse Jackson] May 7 '84	What Reagan got - and gave. [China and the U.S.] May 7 '84
Sexual abuse. The growing outcry over child molesting. May 14 '84	Getting her kicks at 50. Shirley MacLaine. May 14 '84	Who runs America. May 14 '84
Are the Games dead? [Olympic Games] May 21 '84	Olympic turmoil. Why the Soviets said nyet. May 21 '84	Olympics. Hostage to big-power politics. May 21 '84
The all-star. Robert Redford in 'The Natural.' May 28 '84	D-Day. Forty years after the great crusade. May 28 '84	Is Congress for sale? May 28 '84

Newsweek **June 1984**	*Time* **June 1984**	*U.S. News* **June 1984**
Getting straight. How Americans are breaking the grip of drugs and alcohol. Jun 4 '84	And for vice president...why not a woman? Jun 4 '84	How to make your money grow. Mutual funds. Real estate. Bonds. Stocks. Jun 4 '84
The men who hit the beaches. Remembering D-Day, 1944. Jun 11 '84	Why pain hurts. Unlocking an agonizing mystery. Jun 11 '84	Tomorrow's Europe - friend or foe? Jun 11 '84
Now, the hard part. [Presidential candidates] Jun 18 '84	"I am the nominee." Mondale stakes his claim. Jun 18 '84	Next question: Where's the Veep? Jun 18 '84
Closing the door? The angry debate over illegal immigration. Crossing the Rio Grande. Jun 25 '84	Moscow's hard line. What it means. Reagan's new response. Foreign Minister Andrei Gromyko. Jun 25 '84	Inside CIA. What's really going on. Jun 25 '84

Newsweek **July 1984**	*Time* **July 1984**	*U.S. News* **July 1984**
Breaking out! Dancing the summer away. Jul 2 '84	How Erma copes. Working the house for laughs. "Housework, if you do it right, can kill you." "Why take pride. . . Jul 2 '84	Dynamic elderly. Busier, healthier, happier. Jul 2 '84
The top brass. Can they fight a modern war? Jul 9 '84	What next for Israel? Prime Minister Yitzhak Shamir. Opposition leader Shimon Peres. Jul 9 '84	How safe is your money? Jul 9 '84
The tour. The hype, the hysteria. Michael Jackson in Kansas City. Jul 16 '84	Democratic kickoff. War or peace in San Francisco? Jul 16 '84	Political mania takes over. Jul 16 '84
Making history. What Ferraro stands for. Can she help Mondale win? The man behind the gamble. Jul 23 '84	A historic choice. Geraldine Ferraro. Jul 23 '84	Why it's Ferraro for veep. Jul 23 '84
America's best. Is L.A. ready for the Games? [Olympic Games] Jul 30 '84	America's moment. The Olympics are here! Jul 30 '84	Do they have a chance? [Walter Mondale and Geraldine Ferraro] Jul 30 '84

Newsweek **August 1984**	*Time* **August 1984**	*U.S. News* **August 1984**
The video revolution. How the VCR is changing what you watch. Aug 6 '84	Mexico City. The population curse. Aug 6 '84	She's come a long way - or has she? Aug 6 '84
Gold rush. [Olympic Games] Aug 13 '84	One down! How many more? [Olympic Games] Aug 13 '84	Sports crazy Americans. Aug 13 '84
The spirit lives. [Olympic Games] Aug 20 '84	Sassy Sears. Toasters and tires...and Cheryl Tiegs. Aug 20 '84	Pacific Rim. America's new frontier. Aug 20 '84
How good a President? Aug 27 '84	Republican encore. Coronation in Dallas. Aug 27 '84	What makes great schools great. Aug 27 '84

Newsweek **September 1984**	*Time* **September 1984**	*U.S. News* **September 1984**
The Democrats. Can they come back? Sep 3 '84	Ferraro fights back. [Geraldine Ferraro] Sep 3 '84	A shoo-in? Michener looks at GOP convention. Sep 3 '84
Day care. Who's minding the children? Sep 10 '84	Making babies. The new science of conception. Sep 10 '84	Why unions are running scared. Sep 10 '84
God and politics. Sep 17 '84	Canada changes course. Prime Minister-Elect Brian Mulroney. Sep 17 '84	A trillion for defense. Do we get our money's worth? Sep 17 '84
Why teachers fail. How to make them better. Sep 24 '84	I love U.S. America's upbeat mood. Sep 24 '84	Chernenko's nightmare. An empire in turmoil. Sep 24 '84

Newsweek **October 1984**	*Time* **October 1984**	*U.S. News* **October 1984**
Talking again. Arms control at the crossroads. The fallout on campaign '84. Oct 1 '84	Gromyko comes calling. High stakes in U.S.-Soviet relations. Oct 1 '84	Westmoreland vs. CBS. Story behind the battle. Oct 1 '84
Iacocca. An American legend tells his own story. Oct 8 '84	Decisions, decisions. The high court in transition. Oct 8 '84	ABC's of the great game of politics. Oct 8 '84
Who won? The debate. A Newsweek poll. How the experts called it. Oct 15 '84	Crackdown on the Mafia. Oct 15 '84	Are you better off now than you were 4 years ago? Yes. No. Oct 15 '84
The media on trial. Westmoreland vs. CBS. Oct 22 '84	A real race? [Presidential debates] Oct 22 '84	Peace and war. Exclusive interviews on where they stand. Oct 22 '84
Round two. Who won - and why. [Presidential debates] Oct 29 '84	Showdown. Who won, and why. [Presidential debates] Oct 29 '84	The great superpower spy war. KGB vs. CIA. Oct 29 '84

Newsweek **November 1984**	*Time* **November 1984**	*U.S. News* **November 1984**
Landslide? Interviews with Reagan and Mondale. Nov 5 '84	Mind your manners! The new concern with civility. Nov 5 '84	Here come the baby-boomers. Nov 5 '84
India's crisis. After Indira. Nov 12 '84	"If I die today, every drop of my blood will invigorate the nation." Indira Gandhi. . . Nov 12 '84	After the avalanche. [Ronald Reagan] Nov 12 '84
Megabucks. The billionaire Bass brothers are becoming the new Rockefellers. Nov 19 '84	Reagan's triumph. What it means to America. Nov 19 '84	Four more years! [Ronald Reagan] Nov 19 '84
Famine. Africa's nightmare. The world reaches out. Nov 26 '84	The U.S. in space. What's up, and what's ahead. Nov 26 '84	"Tip" and his Democrats. Where now? Thomas P. O'Neill, Jr., Speaker of the House. Nov 26 '84

Newsweek **December 1984**	*Time* **December 1984**	*U.S. News* **December 1984**
The agony of Alzheimer's disease. Dec 3 '84	America's banks. Awash in troubles. Dec 3 '84	Super dollar. Has it peaked? Dec 3 '84
Tax busters. How the reform plan would help - or hurt. The budget: A freeze or a 'massacre.' Dec 10 '84	Medical miracles. But how to pay the bill? Dec 10 '84	Higher taxes? Who would pay. Dec 10 '84
Can it happen here? Poison gas victims in India. Dec 17 '84	India's disaster. The night of death. A global worry. Dec 17 '84	Space-war era. It's already here. Dec 17 '84
Almighty Bach. The world celebrates a composer for all seasons. Dec 24 '84	VCRs. Santa's hottest gift: The magic box that is creating a video revolution. Dec 24 '84	Welfare in America. Is it a flop? Dec 24 '84
The year of the Yuppie. Dec 31 '84	An old master's new triumph. David Lean directs "A Passage to India." Dec 31 '84	Outlook '85. Reagan. Changes in the wind. Money. Where to invest now. Business. . . Dec 31 '84

Newsweek **January 1985**

Eddie Murphy. Mr. Box Office.
Jan 7 '85

Abortion. The moral dilemma. The medical issues. The turn to violence.   Jan 14 '85

Changing the guard. Tackling the deficit - and arms control. The new White House Chief of Staff Donald Regan.   Jan 21 '85

Encore! [Inauguration of Ronald Reagan]   Jan 28 '85

Time   **January 1985**

Man of the year. Peter Ueberroth. The achievement was Olympian.
Jan 7 '85

White House co-star. Nancy Reagan's growing role.
Jan 14 '85

Shake-up at the White House. Reagan gets a tough new Chief of Staff. Donald Regan.   Jan 21 '85

The second term. A fresh agenda. A new lineup.   Jan 28 '85

U.S. News   **January 1985**

Outlook '85. Reagan. Changes in the wind. Money. Where to invest now. Business. More good times ahead. World. . .   Jan 7 '85

Thaw at last? [Soviet Union and the U.S.]   Jan 14 '85

The big shake-up. What it means for the nation. [Reagan's executive appointments]   Jan 21 '85

How our government works.
Jan 28 '85

Newsweek   **February 1985**

Sharon vs. Time. An absence of malice. [Libel trial]   Feb 4 '85

Defense spending. How much is enough?   Feb 11 '85

Bitter harvest. America's angry farmers. The fight over subsidies.
Feb 18 '85

Cocaine. The evil empire. The explosive Latin connection. Colombia's drug lords. U.S. agents: Targets for terror.   Feb 25 '85

Time   **February 1985**

Discord in the church. The Pope takes a tough line. A radical theology challenges Rome. Women demand. . .   Feb 4 '85

A defector's story. The highest-ranking Soviet diplomat to break with Moscow since World War II describes. . .   Feb 11 '85

Going broke. Tangled policies. Failing farms.   Feb 18 '85

Cocaine wars. South America's bloody business.   Feb 25 '85

U.S. News   **February 1985**

The Marxist world. Lure of capitalism.   Feb 4 '85

The big battle begins. [Reagan's proposed budget]   Feb 11 '85

The English language. Out to conquer the world.   Feb 18 '85

The tax bite. How painful?
Feb 25 '85

Newsweek   **March 1985**

Rock and roll. Woman power.
Mar 4 '85

Apartheid and U.S. policy. How to deal with South Africa.
Mar 11 '85

The war against pornography. Feminists, free speech and the law.
Mar 18 '85

Moscow's new generation. Mikhail Gorbachev   Mar 25 '85

Time   **March 1985**

The takeover game. Corporate raider T. Boone Pickens.
Mar 4 '85

Star Wars. What's at stake in Geneva. The scientific challenge.
Mar 11 '85

Simply the best. Boston's Larry Bird. Edmonton's Wayne Gretzky.   Mar 18 '85

Moscow's new boss. Younger, smoother and probably formidable. Mikhail Gorbachev.   Mar 25 '85

U.S. News   **March 1985**

Happiness. How Americans pursue it.   Mar 4 '85

Farmers up in arms.   Mar 11 '85

Arms race. Any way to muzzle it?
Mar 18 '85

Gorbachev's Kremlin. What now?
Mar 25 '85

Newsweek	**April 1985**

Big media, big money. The ABC takeover. The next targets. Apr 1 '85

Living with cancer. The disease that will strike one in three Americans.   Apr 8 '85

The legacy of Vietnam.   Apr 15 '85

The big thrill. Mystery writers are making a killing. 'Glitz' author Elmore Leonard.   Apr 22 '85

Fury over the Reagan trip. The wounds of war.   Apr 29 '85

Newsweek	**May 1985**

The American family. Who's taking care of our parents? May 6 '85

The Bitburg summit. 'Out of the ashes, hope.'   May 13 '85

Rape and the law. A disturbing case focuses attention on how the legal system deals with the most personal of violent crimes.   May 20 '85

Cosmetic surgery. The quest for new faces and bodies - at a price. May 27 '85

Newsweek	**June 1985**

We are the children. The new wave of sympathy and aid may come too late to save Africa's lost generation. Jun 3 '85

A family of spies. How much did they tell Moscow? The epidemic of Soviet espionage.   Jun 10 '85

Star warriors. The people behind the weapons of the future. Jun 17 '85

Terror on flight 847.   Jun 24 '85

Time	**April 1985**

"I gotta tell ya." America loves listening to Lee. Chrysler's Iacocca. Apr 1 '85

The Goetz case. New charges in the subway shooting. Rising fear of violent crime. Public anger at the justice system.   Apr 8 '85

Vietnam. Ten years later. Apr 15 '85

Off they go! The world's a bargain for U.S. tourists.   Apr 22 '85

May 8, 1945. "Never a greater day." But Reagan opens old wounds. Apr 29 '85

Time	**May 1985**

Did comets kill the dinosaurs? A new theory about mass extinctions. May 6 '85

Reagan in Germany.   "Horror cannot outlast hope."   May 13 '85

Cocktails '85. America's new drinking habits.   May 20 '85

Madonna. Why she's hot. May 27 '85

Time	**June 1985**

Who has the bomb. The nuclear threat is spreading.   Jun 3 '85

Reagan's tax package. What's in it for you.   Jun 10 '85

The spy scandal grows. "There are very serious losses." -Caspar Weinberger.   Jun 17 '85

Hijack terror.   Jun 24 '85

U.S. News	**April 1985**

Nicaragua. Will U.S. squeeze lead to war?   Apr 1 '85

The Yankee trader. Death of a salesman?   Apr 8 '85

Street crime. People fight back. Apr 15 '85

Heroes are back. Young Americans tell why.   Apr 22 '85

The new star system. Executive pay goes sky-high.   Apr 29 '85

U.S. News	**May 1985**

Reagan in Germany. Coming to terms with the past. Eric Sevareid on trusting the Germans. America's stake...   May 6 '85

Who will control TV? And CBS News and 'Dynasty' and 'Today' and Diane Sawyer and Ted Koppel and 'Sportsworld'...   May 13 '85

Who runs America? Hidden influences on the elite. The price of power. Leaders rate their peers. Tomorrow's stars...   May 20 '85

Can you bank on your banker? The latest S & L crisis. How feds back up banks. Banking's dramatic changes.   May 27 '85

U.S. News	**June 1985**

The American male. 'New and improved...' Beyond macho - The search for self. The future of fatherhood...   Jun 3 '85

Taking care of your money. Personal investing. The experts' smart-money advice on stocks, bonds, IRA's...   Jun 10 '85

Lobbyists go for it. How foreign states play for power in Washington. Who pays the lobbyists most...   Jun 17 '85

Mideast terror strikes Americans. Jun 24 '85

| *Newsweek* | **July 1985** | *Time* | **July 1985** | *U.S. News* | **July 1985** |

Newsweek   **July 1985**

Ten ways to fight terrorism. When to retaliate - and how does TV help or hurt?   Jul 1 '85

Striking back. What Reagan might do.   Jul 8 '85

The single parent. By 1990 half of all American families may be headed by only one. . .   Jul 15 '85

Reagan's prognosis. The cancer scare. How swift a recovery? Jul 22 '85

Zero hour. Forty years of the Atomic Age.   Jul 29 '85

Newsweek   **August 1985**

Glory days. Going wild about Bruce. Bruce Springsteen. Aug 5 '85

AIDS. It is the nation's worst public-health problem. No one has ever recovered. . .   Aug 12 '85

Can South Africa save itself? Black rage - and signs of white reforms. Aug 19 '85

Warning. America's sweet tooth may be hazardous to its health. Aug 26 '85

Newsweek   **September 1985**

Cosby. He's No. 1. [Bill Cosby] Sep 2 '85

The comet is coming. Halley's marvel gives scientists and stargazers a. . .   Sep 9 '85

South Africa. What can be done? Sep 16 '85

The fear of AIDS. Ignorance and uncertainty fuel growing public concern.   Sep 23 '85

Mexico. The killer quake. The frantic rescue. The risk in the U.S. Sep 30 '85

Time   **July 1985**

America under the gun. The struggle against terrorism. Jul 1 '85

Immigrants. The changing face of America.   Jul 8 '85

Presenting Steven Spielberg. Magician of the movies.   Jul 15 '85

Reagan's illness.   Jul 22 '85

The Atomic Age. "My God, what have we done?" Captian Robert Lewis co-pilot of. . .   Jul 29 '85

Time   **August 1985**

South Africa. Black rage, white repression. A challenge to U.S. policy.   Aug 5 '85

AIDS. The growing threat. What's being done.   Aug 12 '85

Play ball! ...and nobody plays it like Pete. Cincinnati's wondrous Rose. Aug 19 '85

The fun of American food. Aug 26 '85

Time · **September 1985**

Thunder on the right. The growth of Fundamentalism.   Sep 2 '85

Gorbachev: "The situation in the world today is highly complex, very tense. I would. . .   Sep 9 '85

Cool cops. Hot show. NBC's Miami Vice.   Sep 16 '85

China. Moving away from Marx. Leader Deng Xiaoping.   Sep 23 '85

Mexico's killer quake.   Sep 30 '85

U.S. News   **July 1985**

Reagan's hostage crisis. Revenge or restraint?   Jul 1 '85

What price for freedom? Dealing for American lives.   Jul 8 '85

How the world views America. Jul 15 '85

What are mergers doing to America? Your job. What happens after the sale. Your. . .   Jul 22 '85

The comeback. Reagan's health: Nancy's special role. Impact on the nation and the world. . .   Jul 29 '85

U.S. News   **August 1985**

The legacies of World War II. Power and prosperity. Life in the Nuclear Age.   Aug 5 '85

How Soviets steal America's high-tech secrets. And how U.S. fights back.   Aug 12 '85

The disappearing border. Will the Mexican migration create a new nation?   Aug 19 '85

Can South Africa avoid race war? Aug 26 '85

U.S. News   **September 1985**

U.S. vs. Japan. Can American workers win the battle?   Sep 2 '85

Make or break. Does the Reagan Presidency depend on this man? Chief of Staff. . .   Sep 9 '85

The emerging power of the new collar class. "We're the backbone of America."   Sep 16 '85

Free-trade fight. Time to raise the bridge?   Sep 23 '85

The automobile turns 100. And revs up for the future. Looking ahead. Preview of 1986. . .   Sep 30 '85

Newsweek   October 1985

Ferraro: My story. [Geraldine Ferraro]   Oct 7 '85

Machine gun U.S.A. Nearly 500,000 automatic weapons are now in the hands of collectors - and criminals. Oct 14 '85

Getting even. How Reagan did it. Will justice be done? The risks ahead.   Oct 21 '85

Guess who's coming to dinner. Princess Diana.   Oct 28 '85

Time   October 1985

Trade wars. Congress pushes for protectionism. Reagan holds fast against barriers.   Oct 7 '85

Toxic wastes. The poisoning of America '85.   Oct 14 '85

Turning the tables. The U.S. strikes back at terrorism.   Oct 21 '85

Hijack fallout.   Oct 28 '85

U.S. News   October 1985

Propaganda wars.   Oct 7 '85

Justice under Reagan. New agenda: Ed Meese pushes his program. New judges: An enduring impact. . .   Oct 14 '85

Will Americans still be terrorist targets? 'We want...justice done.' Oct 21 '85

Do you know what your children are listening to?   Oct 28 '85

Newsweek   November 1985

The Philippines. Another Iran? America tries to back away from Marcos.   Nov 4 '85

True West. Sam Shepard. Leading man, playwright, maverick. Nov 11 '85

The mind of a defector. Did Yurchenko fool the CIA? Storm over a Soviet sailor. Vitaly Yurchenko on his. . .   Nov 18 '85

The summit. How to deal with Moscow.   Nov 25 '85

Time   November 1985

Heartland humor. Let's hear it for Lake Wobegon. Author and radio bard Garrison Keillor.   Nov 4 '85

Here they come! Charles and Diana.   Nov 11 '85

The summit. Let's talk.   Nov 18 '85

Colombia's agony.   Nov 25 '85

U.S. News   November 1985

Getting ready for Geneva. At the U.N. Reagan on the offensive. At the White House. The prepping of the President.   Nov 4 '85

Medicine's new triumphs. Surgery that melts, cuts and vaporizes. Solving secrets of the brain. Surviving. . .   Nov 11 '85

Going in strong. Exclusive interview with President Reagan on the Summit, Star Wars and the Soviets.   Nov 18 '85

The best colleges in America. How to pick one. How to pay for it. How to get the most out of it. Poll of 788 college. . .   Nov 25 '85

Newsweek   December 1985

What they said. Behind closed doors. [Summit conference] Dec 2 '85

The Catholics. A church in crisis. Dec 9 '85

Cancer and interleukin-2. The search for a cure.   Dec 16 '85

Showing the flag. Rocky, Rambo, and the return of the American hero. Sylvester Stallone. Dec 23 '85

The video generation.   Dec 30 '85

Time   December 1985

So far, so good. [Summit conference]   Dec 2 '85

Children having children. Teen pregnancy in America.   Dec 9 '85

Skywatch. Halley's comet swings by.   Dec 16 '85

Merger tango. [Corporate mergers] Dec 23 '85

A Christmas story. What Sister Geraldine would have visitors understand is that it is not a matter of how much she. . .   Dec 30 '85

U.S. News   December 1985

Will the smiles last? What's next for the superpowers.   Dec 2 '85

Morality test. Do you cut corners on your taxes? Is gambling immoral? Are Americans too sexually permissive?. . .   Dec 9 '85

The great bull market of '85. Stocks through the roof. Advice from big investors. Where the values still are. . .   Dec 16 '85

Jobs of the future. High tech. Where the best careers are. Executives. Who will be tomorrow's bosses?. . .   Dec 23 '85

A rekindled spirit. Outlook '86. Business. More growth ahead. Nation. The can-do mood in the states. . .   Dec 30 '85

Newsweek January 1986

Abandoned. They are America's castoffs - turned away from mental institutions and into the streets. Who will care for them? Jan 6 '86

Growing up gay. The society's dilemma. One family's crisis. Jan 13 '86

Kaddafi. The 'flaky' fanatic. The Reagan plan to stop him. Jan 20 '86

Calcium. To ward off everything from osteoporosis to cancer, Americans are buying millions of dollars worth of. . . Jan 27 '86

Newsweek February 1986

Staying up late with Letterman. Feb 3 '86

What went wrong? The future of space flight. Tom Wolfe on life at the edge. [Challenger space shuttle explosion] Feb 10 '86

Election mess. What the U.S. can do. Feb 17 '86

The second most powerful man in America. A revealing profile of federal reserve chairman Paul Volcker. Feb 24 '86

Newsweek March 1986

Showdown. The last act in Manila. Mar 3 '86

Woman of the year. Can she clean up the mess Marcos left behind? Should he be allowed to keep his millions? Mar 10 '86

Kids and cocaine. An epidemic strikes middle America. Mar 17 '86

Is Mario Cuomo for real? A profile: The governor, the Italian-American, the Catholic, the candidate. Mar 24 '86

Making it work. America's mothers. How women balance the demands of jobs and children. Mar 31 '86

Time January 1986

Man of the year. Deng Xiaoping. Jan 6 '86

Fare games. Flying has never been cheaper. Jan 13 '86

Slimming down. What works. What won't. What's new. Jan 20 '86

Bad news Bears. Superbowl XX. Jan 27 '86

Time February 1986

What's at stake. The Philippine election. Challenger Aquino. President Marcos. Feb 3 '86

Space shuttle Challenger. January 28, 1986. [Challenger space shuttle explosion] Feb 10 '86

Gospel TV. Religion, politics and money. Feb 17 '86

Fighting on. Philippine opposition leader Corazon Aquino. Feb 24 '86

Time March 1986

Who's this man calling? Influence peddling in Washington. Lobbyist Michael Deaver. Mar 3 '86

Now for the hard part. [Philippine government] Mar 10 '86

Drugs on the job. Mar 17 '86

Sorry, America, your insurance has been canceled. Mar 24 '86

The man who makes Reagan see red. Nicaragua's President Daniel Ortega. Mar 31 '86

U.S. News January 1986

A rekindled spirit. Outlook '86. Business. More growth ahead. Nation. The can-do mood in the states. . . Jan 6 '86

How ordinary people get rich. A million millionaires. Who they are - how they did it. Jan 13 '86

Diet wars. The new science of nutrition. Good for you? Bad for you? How to know what's right for you. Jan 20 '86

What damage claims cost you. Liability lawsuits out of control? Jan 27 '86

U.S. News February 1986

Busting the mob. Feb 3 '86

Challenger. January 28, 1986. 11:39.13 A.M. [Challenger space shuttle explosion] Feb 10 '86

Cuts. The federal budget of the U.S. How the budget will affect you. Feb 17 '86

"My ordeal" by Andrei Sakharov. 'I was seized by KGB men disguised in doctors' white coats. They took me. . . Feb 24 '86

U.S. News March 1986

86 ways to save on your '85 taxes. Mar 3 '86

Can she make it? [Corazon Aquino] Mar 10 '86

Broken lives. America's underclass. Mar 17 '86

Advice. Who gives it. Who listens to it. What it's worth to you. Mar 24 '86

Brave new economy. Mar 31 '86

Newsweek	**April 1986**

'America is our target.' Inside the terror network. Reagan takes on Kaddafi.   Apr 7 '86

You're so vain. Men are primping, preening - and spending millions to look good.   Apr 14 '86

The inside story. David Stockman on the heroes, villains and fatal flaws of the Reagan revolution. Apr 21 '86

Shooting to kill. Did the U.S. go too far - or not far enough? The terrorists strike back. The new threat to air travel.   Apr 28 '86

Newsweek	**May 1986**

Can you pass the job test? From lie detectors to genetic screening. May 5 '86

The Chernobyl syndrome. How the meltdown happened. The Kremlin cover-up. The fall-out: What are the risks?   May 12 '86

He's back. The rehabilitation of Richard Nixon. An exclusive interview.   May 19 '86

Greed on Wall Street. A $12 million stock scandal stuns the financial world - and raises questions about the values of. . .   May 26 '86

Newsweek	**June 1986**

The marriage crunch. If you're a single woman, here are your chances of getting married. Jun 2 '86

Danger in the sun. A good tan may be hazardous to your health. Jun 9 '86

Crack and crime. The drug crisis. Jun 16 '86

South Africa's civil war. The making of a bloodbath.   Jun 23 '86

Reagan's law. By 1989 half of all federal judges will be his appointments. The impact on abortion, civil. . .   Jun 30 '86

Time	**April 1986**

Doctor K. Baseball's hottest pitcher. Dwight Gooden of the Mets. Apr 7 '86

Good news! Cheap oil! Bad news! Cheap oil!   Apr 14 '86

Target Gaddafi. [U.S. attack on Libya]   Apr 21 '86

Hitting home. Tripoli under attack. [U.S. attack on Libya] Apr 28 '86

Time	**May 1986**

Triumph in Moscow. Pianist Vladimir Horowitz.   May 5 '86

Meltdown. Chernobyl reactor. May 12 '86

The baby boomers turn 40. May 19 '86

Ain't she sweet. Teen actress Molly Ringwald.   May 26 '86

Time	**June 1986**

What to make of Mario. New York governor Cuomo.   Jun 2 '86

Fixing NASA.   Jun 9 '86

American best.   Jun 16 '86

Star war games. The stakes go up. Jun 23 '86

Reagan's Mr. Right. Supreme court justice William Rehnquist. Jun 30 '86

U.S. News	**April 1986**

Showing muscle. More conflict ahead? Apr 7 '86

How good is your health care? Revolution in the hospitals - for better or worse.   Apr 14 '86

Texas takes a tumble. [Economic conditions]   Apr 21 '86

America's new war. Can it be won? At what price.   Apr 28 '86

U.S. News	**May 1986**

Vacations USA. This is the year! Special guide on where to go. May 5 '86

Nightmare in Russia. How reckless are the Soviets? Fallout for nuclear power? Can it happen here? Damaged. . .   May 12 '86

High tech anxiety. Why so many disasters.   May 19 '86

Are we failing our kids? New report on American teachers. May 26 '86

U.S. News	**June 1986**

The fear of sex. Why habits are changing.   Jun 2 '86

Make your money grow. Stocks, beating the Dow. Real estate, bargains for buyers. Savings, where to stash your. . .   Jun 9 '86

The CIA. Running strong or running wild?   Jun 16 '86

Are you making what you're worth? What others earn in 120 jobs. Strategies for getting more. Jun 23 '86

Reagan's man in court. Chief Justice-designate William Rehnquist.   Jun 30 '86

Newsweek **July 1986**	*Time* **July 1986**	*U.S. News* **July 1986**
Funny man. The comic genius of Robin Williams. Jul 7 '86	Why is this man so popular? [Ronald Reagan] Jul 7 '86	'Only in America.' [Immigrants in the U.S.] Jul 7 '86
Wow! Portraits of Miss Liberty and her birthday bash. Tom Wolfe on our magical mystery lady. Jul 14 '86	Hail liberty! A birthday party album. Jul 14 '86	Wildcards for the White House. [Presidential candidates] Jul 14 '86
The AIDS doctor. Gerald Friedland has treated nearly 300 men and women with AIDS. More than 200 are dead. The rest. . . Jul 21 '86	Sex busters. [Censorship] Jul 21 '86	U.S. News 100 super-rich owners of American business. Jul 21 '86
Can we save our parks? The stuggle between man and beast. Jul 28 '86	Horrors! The summer's scariest movie. Sigourney Weaver and she-monster in Aliens. Jul 28 '86	Killer drugs. New facts, new enemies. Jul 28 '86

Newsweek **August 1986**	*Time* **August 1986**	*U.S. News* **August 1986**
Playboy. The party's over. Aug 4 '86	Sanctions. Pressuring South Africa. If not now, when? If not this, what? Aug 4 '86	Tough new Navy. 600 ships, an aggressive strategy and a strong top gun. Secretary of the Navy, John F. Lehman, Jr. Aug 4 '86
"Saying No!" The nation's new campaign against users. A poll on drug testing, enforcement and privacy. Aug 11 '86	Voyages to the bottom of the sea. Alvin exploring the Titanic. Aug 11 '86	Easy does it! The new rules of exercise. Life in the slow lane can be good for your health. Aug 11 '86
Andrew Wyeth's secret obsession. For 15 years he drew the same woman and hid the pictures in an attic. Now they've. . . Aug 18 '86	Andrew Wyeth's stunning secret. The Helga paintings: a portfolio. Aug 18 '86	Keeping up is hard to do. The middle-class struggle to hold on. Aug 18 '86
What tax reform means to you. Who pays more, who pays less. New ways to invest your money. Ten hot tax shelters. Aug 25 '86	Breakthrough. Tax reform. Aug 25 '86	Behind the Harvard mystique. Shaping America for 350 years. Who gets in, who doesn't. Where the money comes. . . Aug 25 '86

Newsweek **September 1986**	*Time* **September 1986**	*U.S. News* **September 1986**
No baby on board. Not since the Depression have so many couples decided not to have kids. Sep 1 '86	Selling that sporty look. Polo's Ralph Lauren. Sep 1 '86	Ike: overrated warrior? In a new biography, his grandson answers the critics. Sep 1 '86
Sly and sexy. TV's fun couple. Moonlighting's Bruce Willis and Cybill Shepherd. Sep 8 '86	Harvard. 350 and going strong. Sep 8 '86	China now. 10 years after Mao. Sep 8 '86
Civil war at CBS. The struggle for the soul of a legendary network. Sep 15 '86	Drugs. The enemy within. Sep 15 '86	Frame-up. The Daniloff arrest in Moscow. The threat to superpower relations. Working the Kremlin: journalists beware. . . Sep 15 '86
Can we deal with Moscow? Beyond the Daniloff affair. Sep 22 '86	The man who captured CBS. Loews' Laurence Tisch takes over. Sep 22 '86	Next move? Superpower chess game. Journalist Nicholas Daniloff. Sep 22 '86
Memory. New insights into how we remember and why we forget. Sep 29 '86	Mafia on trial. Crime boss John Gotti. Sep 29 '86	Heavy strains. Washington vs. Moscow. The superpowers grope for ways to repair the damage that threatens. . . Sep 29 '86

Newsweek   October 1986

Inside America's toughest prison.
Oct 6 '86

Danger at the summit? Plus:
What Reagan hopes to get.
Gorbachev's game plan.
Oct 13 '86

Stalemate. The Iceland summit.
Oct 20 '86

A day in the life of America. A
picture portfolio by the world's best
photographer.   Oct 27 '86

Newsweek   November 1986

Have guns, will travel. The secret
world of America's new
mercenaries.   Nov 3 '86

The way we werc. Our Ice Age
heritage: Language, art, fashion,
and the family.   Nov 10 '86

The Iran connection. Reagan's
secret strategy.   Nov 17 '86

AIDS. Future shock. How the
spreading epidemic will affect
health care, government policy,
civil liberties and. . .   Nov 24 '86

Newsweek   December 1986

His biggest blunder. The Iran mess.
Exclusive: How Reagan's
'cowboys' got out of control.
Dec 1 '86

Who knew? The looming
shake-up. Plus: John Ehrlichman
on a White House under siege.
Dec 8 '86

Reagan's role. His secret message to
Iran. His green light to the CIA.
His attempt to contain the damage.
Dec 15 '86

The enduring power of Star Trek.
Dec 22 '86

The incredible Voyager. Heading
around the world without a stop.
Dec 29 '86

Time   October 1986

A novel by Stephen King. As it saw
Eddie looking, its green-black lips
wrinkled back from huge fangs...
Oct 6 '86

Getting down to business.
Appointment in Iceland.
Oct 13 '86

No deal. Star Wars sinks the
summit.   Oct 20 '86

Rock's renaissance man. Singer,
composer, lyricist, guitarist, film
director, writer, actor, video artist,
designer. . .   Oct 27 '86

Time   November 1986

Viruses. Keys to life and death.
AIDS: new research, new danger.
Nov 3 '86

Is it good for America? High-tech
Wall Street.   Nov 10 '86

Reagan's secret dealings with Iran.
Nov 17 '86

Sex education. What should
children know? When should
they know it?   Nov 24 '86

Time   December 1986

Wall St. scam. Making millions
with your money. Investor "Ivan
the Terrible" Boeskey.   Dec 1 '86

How far does it go? Reagan lashes
out. "There is a bitter bile in my
throat."   Dec 8 '86

Neil Simon's best play. "Broadway
Bound". Laughter and tears.
Dec 15 '86

Probing the mess. Fresh money
trails. The CIA role. An interview
with Casey.   Dec 22 '86

A letter to the year 2086. "Do you see
starlight? So do we. Smell the fire?
We do too. Draw close. Let us tell
each. . .   Dec 29 '86

U.S. News   October 1986

Making tax reform work for you.
Smart strategies for families,
homeowners, investors, employees,
entrepreneurs. . .   Oct 6 '86

Back on track? Arms control. What
Reagan and Gorbachev want from
their mini-summit.   Oct 13 '86

The world according to Gorbachev.
After Iceland.   Oct 20 '86

Children under stress. Are we
pushing our kids too hard?
Oct 27 '86

U.S. News   November 1986

Can they do the job? America's
special forces.   Nov 3 '86

Master of terror. Syria's President
Assad.   Nov 10 '86

Taking on American Catholics.
The Pope cracks down.   Nov 17 '86

Taking care of your money. How to
invest, save and earn more under
tax reform.   Nov 24 '86

U.S. News   December 1986

How the stock market is rigged
against you. Wall Street's insider
trading scandal.   Dec 1 '86

Who else knew? Reagan's
damaged presidency.   Dec 8 '86

America's shadow network.
Behind the secret deals with Iran
and the Contras.   Dec 15 '86

Gridlock. You think it's bad now?
Airline delays are going to get
worse.   Dec 22 '86

Outlook 87. What's ahead. Reagan:
Can he make a comeback? World:
Trouble spots for the U.S. Money:
Hot picks for. . .   Dec 29 '86

Newsweek **January 1987**	*Time* **January 1987**	*U.S. News* **January 1987**
Gorbachev's gamble. Opening a closed society. How far will he go? Sakharov on his struggle. Jan 5 '87	Woman of the year. Philippine President Corazon Aquino. Jan 5 '87	Outlook 87. What's ahead. Reagan: Can he make a comeback? World: Trouble spots for the U.S. Money: Hot picks for the. . Jan 5 '87
Hormones. How they affect behavior, growth, sex and health. Jan 12 '87	Air travel. How safe is it? Jan 12 '87	AIDS. What you need to know. What you should do. Jan 12 '87
Mothers for hire. The battle for Baby M. Surrogate mother Mary Beth Whitehead. Jan 19 '87	Those shadowy arms traders. Adnan Khashoggi's high life and flashy deals. Jan 19 '87	U.S. vs. Japan. Is your child getting a first-class education? He is. Jan 19 '87
The revolution in medicine. A special report on how money, machines, and politics are changing. . . Jan 26 '87	Platoon. Vietnam as it really was. Jan 26 '87	The cult of risk taking. Why people go out on a limb. A special test: Are you a risk taker? Jan 26 '87

Newsweek **February 1987**	*Time* **February 1987**	*U.S. News* **February 1987**
Your next boss may be Japanese. Hundreds of thousands are already working for Japan Inc. Feb 2 '87	Why is service so bad? The hapless American consumer. Feb 2 '87	America's competitive drive. Are we losing it? Feb 2 '87
Game shows. America's obsession. TV cashes in. Wheel of Fortune Vanna White. Feb 9 '87	Going for it. America's Cup skipper Dennis Conner. Feb 9 '87	Hostage to terror. What the U.S. can do. Feb 9 '87
Kids and contraceptives. A moral dilemma: How to prevent teen pregnancy - and AIDS. Feb 16 '87	The big chill. How heterosexuals are coping with AIDS. Feb 16 '87	The mutual fund jungle. Your money. Choosing a fund: The do's and don'ts. Picking winners: The top forty. Feb 16 '87
The pressure builds. McFarlane's suicide attempt. The NSC's computer secret. Turmoil in the White House. Feb 23 '87	Africa. An essay. Feb 23 '87	Lying in America. Public concern over honesty and standards of behavior has reached the highest level since Watergate. Feb 23 '87

Newsweek **March 1987**	*Time* **March 1987**	*U.S. News* **March 1987**
Coverup. To protect the President, NSC staffers say Don Regan ordered them to conceal the early approval of arms. . . Mar 2 '87	You Bette! Midler strikes again in Outrageous Fortune. Mar 2 '87	The smart taxpayer's guide. Money saving strategies for 1987. How to avoid an IRS audit. Mar 2 '87
Reagan's failure. Can he recover? Mar 9 '87	Can he recover? [Ronald Reagan] Mar 9 '87	The teflon is gone. A question of competence. Can Howard Baker rebuild a shattered presidency. How Nancy. . . Mar 9 '87
Birth defects. Every parent's nightmare. The father remembers the color of his son's face when he was born. . . Mar 16 '87	Starting over. New White House Chief of Staff Howard Baker. CIA nominee William Webster. National Security. . . Mar 16 '87	'Smart weapons.' How they see and kill. What's ahead: Computer-generated imagery displayed in a U.S. pilot's helmet. Mar 16 '87
Brothers. A vivid portrait of Black men in America. Mar 23 '87	Bang! A star explodes, providing new clues to the nature of the universe. Mar 23 '87	You're fired! Starting over: A survival guide. Mar 23 '87
Les Miserables. Show of shows. Mar 30 '87	America's agenda after Reagan. Change in the weather. Mar 30 '87	The big sting. New information on the Iran affair points to a grand deception, conceived by Ayatolla Khomeini. . . Mar 30 '87

Newsweek	**April 1987**

Holy wars. Money, sex and power. Evangelists Jim and Tammy Bakker.   Apr 6 '87

The return of the French connection. How drug agents broke up the $225 million heroin deal of the decade.   Apr 13 '87

Mad about Max. The making of a video cult. Max Headroom. Apr 20 '87

Finally, an arms deal that can work. But not without some risks. Apr 27 '87

Newsweek	**May 1987**

Depression. The bad news: It's striking more young adults. The good news: Almost all can be helped. May 4 '87

The Secord story. A close-up look at the first witness in the Iran-Contra TV hearings. Will he link Reagan to the. . .   May 11 '87

Sex, politics and the press. Gary Hart self-destructs.   May 18 '87

Genius of the people. A special report celebrating the Constitution. May 25 '87

Newsweek	**June 1987**

Why? The Navy struggles to defend the oil lanes - and itself. The USS Stark after Iraqi attack. Jun 1 '87

Heaven can wait while the holy war heats up.   Jun 8 '87

Q & A. Nightline's Ted Koppel asks all the right questions.   Jun 15 '87

'The Untouchables.' Mob hit. Robert DeNiro as Al Capone. Jun 22 '87

Korea in crisis. The threat to the Olympics.   Jun 29 '87

Time	**April 1987**

Unholy row. TV preacher Jimmy Swaggart and the besieged Bakkers. Apr 6 '87

Trade wars. The U.S. gets tough with Japan.   Apr 13 '87

Spy scandals. Marine Corps woes. High-tech surveillance. Assessing the damage.   Apr 20 '87

U2. Rock's hottest ticket.   Apr 27 '87

Time	**May 1987**

South Africa. Hints of hope. Afrikaners begin to unbend. May 4 '87

Wiring the future. The superconductivity revolution. May 11 '87

Hart's fall. Sex and politics. Democrats in a quandary. Questions about press ethics. May 18 '87

What ever happened to ethics? Assaulted by sleaze, scandals and hypocrisy, America searches for its moral bearings.   May 25 '87

Time	**June 1987**

Stark questions. [Iraqi missile attack on the Stark]   Jun 1 '87

When China went mad. An extraordinary memoir of the Cultural Revolution.   Jun 8 '87

The new Mr. Dollar. Fed nominee Alan Greenspan.   Jun 15 '87

Who's bringing up baby? With both Mom and Dad at work, the big problem is finding quality child care.   Jun 22 '87

Korea's crisis. South Korea President Chun Doo Hwan. Jun 29 '87

U.S. News	**April 1987**

War in the TV pulpits. Can they bind the wounds.   Apr 6 '87

The gene factor. How heredity shapes personality.   Apr 13 '87

AIDS. Should you be tested? Why it's prudent for 30 million Americans. Turmoil in the testing centers. Answers. . .   Apr 20 '87

We did it! The miracle at Philadelphia, 1787. The U.S. Constitution at 200. How it shapes our lives today.   Apr 27 '87

U.S. News	**May 1987**

Drugs. Terror and politics. The deadly new alliance.   May 4 '87

How you can play the global money game. Risks and rewards in volatile markets. Should you buy foreign stocks?   May 11 '87

Private lives. How much are we entitled to know about public figures? The self-destruction of Gary Hart.   May 18 '87

Predicting diseases. New genetic clues to heart disease, cancer, AIDS and other killers could save your life.   May 25 '87

U.S. News	**June 1987**

To catch a spy. Inside a top-secret U.S. agency: A case study of sloppy security. How one spy milked the files at six. . .   Jun 1 '87

How to measure your financial health. Saving: 12 ways to build a fortune. Retirement: What to do now to quit early. . .   Jun 8 '87

The silent war beneath the waves. Submarines and superpowers: A deadly game of hide-and-seek. A conversation with. . .   Jun 15 '87

Are we having enough babies? A controversial new book, The Birth Dearth, by Ben Wattenberg argues that Americans. . .   Jun 22 '87

Taking the pain out of pain. Promising new treatments for headaches, back pain, arthritis, and other ailments. . .   Jun 29 '87

Newsweek	**July 1987**

A celebration of heroes. Past and present.   Jul 6 '87

Oliver North, star witness. Plus Gore Vidal and Pat Buchanan on the hearings.   Jul 13 '87

Ollie takes the Hill. The fall guy becomes a folk hero.   Jul 20 '87

Year of the near miss. How to make air traffic safer.   Jul 27 '87

Time	**July 1987**

We the people. [U.S. Constitution] Jul 6 '87

Front and center. Lieut. Colonel Oliver North.   Jul 13 '87

"I was authorized to do everything that I did" -Oliver North.   Jul 20 '87

Gorbachev's revolution. Can he make it work? Is the Cold War fading?   Jul 27 '87

U.S. News	**July 1987**

Stock market killings. College dropout Bill Gates made $750 million last year. Now he's America's youngest. . .   Jul 6 '87

Ollie's private world. Out of the shadows.   Jul 13 '87

How Ollie stormed the Hill. A TV triumph turns the tables on his critics. Who really gave the orders. Jul 20 '87

Television's blinding power. How it shapes our views.   Jul 27 '87

Newsweek	**August 1987**

Elvis. Ten years after, the legend grows.   Aug 3 '87

The face of AIDS. One year in the epidemic.   Aug 10 '87

How to stay married. The divorce rate drops as couples try harder to stay together.   Aug 17 '87

Lost in space. How to get America off the ground.   Aug 24 '87

Kate. A rare talk with the invincible Hepburn. And exclusive excerpt from her new memoir.   Aug 31 '87

Time	**August 1987**

God & money. Greed, secrecy and scandal: An inside look at Jim and Tammy Bakker's bankrupt empire. Aug 3 '87

Where's the beach? America's vanishing coastline.   Aug 10 '87

Iran vs. the world   Aug 17 '87

Steve Martin: He's off the wall. Aug 24 '87

Those Asian-American whiz kids. Aug 31 '87

U.S. News	**August 1987**

Living alone and learning to love it. A survival guide.   Aug 3 '87

Cars of the 90s. Engine: More power. Steering: Both front and rear wheels turn for tight maneuvering. . .   Aug 10 '87

Defending your health. How to ward off the 5 top killers. Aug 17 '87

How to beat the Japanese. Aug 24 '87

The Bull market. Time to get out? The experts pick the best buys now. How to protect your winnings. Aug 31 '87

Newsweek	**September 1987**

Kids with AIDS. The struggle to care for the epidemic's youngest victims.   Sep 7 '87

Where Bork stands. The battle over the future of the Supreme Court. Sep 14 '87

John Paul. How he's changing the Church.   Sep 21 '87

Trump. A billion-dollar empire and an ego to match.   Sep 28 '87

Time	**September 1987**

U.S. Catholics. A feisty flock awaits the Pope.   Sep 7 '87

The selling of America. Foreign investors buy, buy, buy.   Sep 14 '87

Bork. How a young socialist became a conservative and one of history's most controversial Supreme Court. . .   Sep 21 '87

Cosby, Inc. Funny, famous, fifty - and really rich.   Sep 28 '87

U.S. News	**September 1987**

Honk! Why you'll be wasting more time in traffic.   Sep 7 '87

Judging Bork. Will he change America?   Sep 14 '87

The Pope's foot soldiers. Keeping the faith: Two American priests in a changing church. Catholic priests Raymond Dlugos. . .   Sep 21 '87

What Americans should know (and don't).   Sep 28 '87

Newsweek **October 1987**	*Time* **October 1987**	*U.S. News* **October 1987**

The secret wars of the CIA by Bob Woodward. Exclusive book excerpts.   Oct 5 '87

Moscow takes the lead. An inside look at the Soviet space program.   Oct 5 '87

One out of 6 couples now asks, 'Why can't we have a baby?'   Oct 5 '87

Webster's CIA. An exclusive interview with the new director. Cleaning up Casey's mess.   Oct 12 '87

Are women fed up? A hotly disputed Hite report says yes - and that men are to blame.   Oct 12 '87

Outcast. How AIDS is tearing apart one American community.   Oct 12 '87

Fighting the 'wimp' factor. George Bush.   Oct 19 '87

The heat is on. How the Earth's climate is changing. Why the ozone hole is growing.   Oct 19 '87

A new revolution. Can Gorbachev save a failing system?   Oct 19 '87

Is the party over? A jolt for Wall Street's whiz kids. How to play it safe, by Jane Bryant Quinn.   Oct 26 '87

A day in the life of the Soviet Union. A 38-page portrait of the changing superpower.   Oct 26 '87

America's best colleges. Expert advice on getting and paying for college. SAT scores, school by school.   Oct 26 '87

Newsweek **November 1987**	*Time* **November 1987**	*U.S. News* **November 1987**

After the crash. Robert Samuelson: The specter of depression. Jane Bryant Quinn: Keeping your money safe.   Nov 2 '87

The crash. After a wild week on Wall Street, the world is different.   Nov 2 '87

After the fall. How to protect your money now. Is a recession coming?   Nov 2 '87

Heading off hard times. What the experts think should be done. How to invest for the long term by Jane Bryant Quinn.   Nov 9 '87

Who's in charge? The crash on Wall Street spotlights America's leadership crisis.   Nov 9 '87

How to ride out the bear market. Best strategies for investors. Where interest rates are heading.   Nov 9 '87

Up in smoke. The Ginsburg fiasco. A Newsweek poll on pot and politics: Forgive and forget. Judge Douglas H. Ginsburg.   Nov 16 '87

The thriller is back. In Fatal Attraction , stars Glenn Close and Michael Douglas live a nightmare of the late 1980s.   Nov 16 '87

Jesse Jackson. The man who would be king.   Nov 16 '87

All about twins. Probing the mysteries of a double life.   Nov 23 '87

Bringing the city back to life.   Nov 23 '87

Warning: Medical tests may be hazardous to your health.   Nov 23 '87

Cher. Movie star, video vamp - and all business.   Nov 30 '87

This is one of the 18 million Americans who have a drinking problem. But there is hope: Science is discovering. . .   Nov 30 '87

Alcoholism. Getting the monkey off our backs. Is the addiction inherited? Can it be prevented? Getting help for. . .   Nov 30 '87

Newsweek **December 1987**	*Time* **December 1987**	*U.S. News* **December 1987**

Headaches. New way to cope with the pain.   Dec 7 '87

Om....The New Age. Starring Shirley MacLaine, faith healers, channelers, space travelers and crystals galore.   Dec 7 '87

Last chance to cut your taxes. Money-saving strategies for the end of the year.   Dec 7 '87

Gorbachev in America. How the Soviets see us.   Dec 14 '87

The long road to Washington. Mikhail Gorbachev.   Dec 14 '87

Are we safer now? After the summit: The U.S.-Soviet military balance. A memorandum for the President by Richard Perle.   Dec 14 '87

Behind the smiles. Reagan and Gorbachev: A new era? Kissinger: The dangers ahead.   Dec 21 '87

Famine. Why are Ethiopians starving again? What should the world do - and not do?   Dec 21 '87

Moscow on the Potomac. Is Gorbachev playing a winning hand?   Dec 21 '87

'Broadcast News.' Hollywood scores with love and laughs. Albert Brooks, Holly Hunter and William Hurt.   Dec 28 '87

The grinch who stole Christmas. Will Gary Hart spoil the Democrats' chances?   Dec 28 '87

Outlook '88. What's ahead. Politics: What the candidates aren't telling us. Economy: Getting ready for the. . .   Dec 28 '87

Newsweek **January 1988**	*Time* **January 1988**	*U.S. News* **January 1988**
The 80's are over. Greed goes out of style. Jan 4 '88	Man of the year. Mikhail Sergeyevich Gorbachev. Jan 4 '88	Outlook '88. What's ahead. Politics: What the candidates aren't telling us. Economy: Getting ready. . . Jan 4 '88
The search for Adam & Eve. Scientists explore a controversial theory about man's origins. Jan 11 '88	1968. The year that shaped a generation. Jan 11 '88	The hidden poor. There are 9 million of them, mostly white and working. And their ranks could soon grow. Jan 11 '88
Alcohol and the family. Growing up with alcoholic parents can leave scars for life. Jan 18 '88	Magician of the musical. After the triumphs of Evita and Cats, Andrew Lloyd Webber brings Phantom to Broadway. Jan 18 '88	The new face of organized crime. Asians, Jamaicans and other ethnic gangs are giving the Mafia a run for its money. Jan 18 '88
Miami. America's Casablanca. Jan 25 '88	Iowa. A profile of the feisty folks who have an outsized say in picking the next President. Jan 25 '88	Bush vs. Dole. Winner take all. Jan 25 '88

Newsweek **February 1988**	*Time* **February 1988**	*U.S. News* **February 1988**
Is this any way to elect a president? Adventures in campaignland. Feb 1 '88	Is getting tough the answer? School prinicpal Joe Clark says yes - and critics are up in arms. Feb 1 '88	Rethinking mutual funds. Why you can't take them for granted any more. How small investors can still play the funds game. Feb 1 '88
What you should know about heart attacks. The aspirin breakthrough. The latest on cholesterol, diet. . . Feb 8 '88	The ambush that failed. CBS gunslinger Dan Rather. Feb 8 '88	The new American establishment. Feb 8 '88
Drugs, money and death. The sordid story of Panama's outlaw dictator. Gen. Manuel Antonio Noriega. Feb 15 '88	Winter wonders. Debi Thomas. Can America's sweetheart dethrone East Germany's Katarina Witt. . . Feb 15 '88	The truth about designer diets. Can eating the right foods really prevent heart attacks, cancer, pain - even old age? Feb 15 '88
The Pacific Century. Is America in decline? Feb 22 '88	And now for the fun years. Americans are living longer and enjoying it more - but who will foot the bill? Feb 22 '88	Pat Robertson's amazing race. How he is raising a 'hidden army' to take over the Republican Party. Feb 22 '88
Tax terror. How to survive April 15. Feb 29 '88	Hell-bent for gold. The presidential pack races toward super Tuesday. Feb 29 '88	Finally, hope for the homeless. Five approaches that work. Feb 29 '88

Newsweek **March 1988**	*Time* **March 1988**	*U.S. News* **March 1988**
Black & white. How integrated is America? Mar 7 '88	The drug thugs. Panama's Noriega proves they're a law unto themselves. Mar 7 '88	21st century executive. Four key traits for managers of the future. Rupert Murdoch: On the importance of. . . Mar 7 '88
Sex in the Age of AIDS. Masters & Johnson. Excerpts from their controversial new book. Mar 14 '88	He's 50! [Superman] Mar 14 '88	What puts the whiz in whiz kids. A revealing look at America's best science students. Nurturing talent: What works. . . Mar 14 '88
The power broker. What Jesse Jackson wants. Mar 21 '88	The big Mo. How Bush bounced back. Can the Democrats avoid a deadlock? The secret of Jackson's success. Mar 21 '88	Secret warriors. Inside the covert military operations of the Reagan era. Exclusive: Oliver North's private notebooks. Mar 21 '88
The drug gangs. Waging war in America's cities. Mar 28 '88	Computers of the future. Mar 28 '88	Benefits shock. How to protect yourself from cuts in health care and other benefits. Mar 28 '88

Newsweek **April 1988**	*Time* **April 1988**	*U.S. News* **April 1988**

The heat is on. Fashion goes feminine - and Ungaro leads the way.   Apr 4 '88

Israel. 40 years of achievement. 40 years of conflict.   Apr 4 '88

A house divided. Israel's war with the Palestinians and with itself. Apr 4 '88

Can he win? The Democratic battle. [Jesse Jackson]   Apr 11 '88

Jesse!? [Jesse Jackson]   Apr 11 '88

Inside America's biggest drug bust. A blow by blow account of how the Feds hit the Sicilian Mafia, based on. . .   Apr 11 '88

Art for money's sake. On the block: The Warhol collection. The booming art market.   Apr 18 '88

Butt out! The war over smoking. Apr 18 '88

The military's new stars. Smarter and tougher.   Apr 18 '88

Stress on the job. What you and the boss can do about it.   Apr 25 '88

Why is this mouse smiling? Because Michael Eisner's magic has transformed Disney into a $3 billion kingdom.   Apr 25 '88

1988 career guide. Best jobs for the future. Prospects for MBA's. How to stay ahead. The hot professions. Exclusive. . .   Apr 25 '88

Newsweek **May 1988**	*Time* **May 1988**	*U.S. News* **May 1988**

Yes, our schools can be saved. The story of a school that's getting better.   May 2 '88

The Duke. Can he unite the Democrats?   May 2 '88

The guns of terror. The secret wars of the Middle East: No boundaries, no rules.   May 2 '88

Remembering Bobby. Excerpts from 'Robert Kennedy: In His Own Words.'   May 9 '88

Kids who sell crack. Call him Frog. He says he rakes in $200 a week selling "rock" in East L.A. He brags that he. . .   May 9 '88

Japan moves in. Tokyo Inc.'s bold thrust into the American heartland.   May 9 '88

Preemies. Five years ago, saving a two-pound baby was remarkable. Today, the miracles begin at one pound.   May 16 '88

Astrology in the White House. Excerpts from Don Regan's explosive memoirs.   May 16 '88

The Soviets in space. Why the U.S. should worry about Moscow's conquest of the heavens. May 16 '88

How smart are animals? They know more than you think. May 23 '88

The battle inside your body. New discoveries show how the immune system fights off disease. May 23 '88

The man who beat the KGB. Exclusive book excerpt. Natan (Anatoly) Sharansky spent nine years in Soviet. . .   May 23 '88

His game plan. A talk with Gorbachev.   May 30 '88

Should drugs be made legal? May 30 '88

America's No. 1 doctor. His advice on everything from acupuncture to sex education.   May 30 '88

Newsweek **June 1988**	*Time* **June 1988**	*U.S. News* **June 1988**

Reagan in Moscow.   Jun 6 '88

Raisa. A new image for the Soviet Union's overworked, underappreciated women. Jun 6 '88

Where to invest now. Stocks-bonds-mutual funds. 10 top brokers tell you where to put your money.   Jun 6 '88

Master of the universe. One scientist's courageous voyage to the frontiers of the cosmos. Physicist Stephen. . .   Jun 13 '88

"I never expected to be here." Reagan reflects on his remarkable voyage.   Jun 13 '88

Mothers on the run. The child-abuse crisis. Thousand of fearful women now flee their husbands. . .   Jun 13 '88

Washington vs. New York. Why they hate each other. Why America hates them both.   Jun 20 '88

Paradise found. America returns to the garden.   Jun 20 '88

Super patriot Ross Perot. How he'll make his next billion.   Jun 20 '88

Who is Roger Rabbit? Spielberg and Disney take a $45 million gamble.   Jun 27 '88

Why the fascination with boxing? Heavyweight Mike Tyson. Jun 27 '88

How the brain really works. The new science of memory, thought and emotion.   Jun 27 '88

Newsweek July 1988	*Time* July 1988	*U.S. News* July 1988
Garrison Keillor's Fourth of July. Plus: America's unsung heroes. Jul 4 '88	The big dry. [Drought] Jul 4 '88	The great weapons scandal. How 'Pentagate' weakens our military strength. Jul 4 '88
The greenhouse effect. Danger: More hot summers ahead. Jul 11 '88	Magnifico! Hispanic culture breaks out of the barrio. Actor Edward James Olmos. Jul 11 '88	How to beat breast cancer. What your doctor may not be telling you. Ways men can help. Jul 11 '88
Why it happened. The Gulf tragedy. Time to talk with Iran by Henry Kissinger. Jul 18 '88	Onward to Mars. Jul 18 '88	Smart ways to shape up. How to exercise effectively without wasting time or money. The cure for workout. . . Jul 18 '88
Dukakis. By the people who know him best. Jul 25 '88	The odd couple. Gary Wills: Searching for Dukakis' soul. Jul 25 '88	Dukakis. How good a president? He's cool, shrewd and still trying to prove he's tough. Jul 25 '88

Newsweek August 1988	*Time* August 1988	*U.S. News* August 1988
Don't go near the water. Our polluted oceans. Aug 1 '88	Our filthy seas. Aug 1 '88	Duke's charge. [Democratic National Convention] Aug 1 '88
Tom Clancy, best seller. Master of the techno-thriller. Aug 8 '88	Through the eyes of children. Growing up in America today. Aug 8 '88	Men vs. women. The new debate over sex differences. Aug 8 '88
Miscarriages. As many as 1 in 3 pregnancies fails. Doctors are just beginning to understand why. Aug 15 '88	Who was Jesus? A startling new movie raises an age-old question. Aug 15 '88	Reliving the Civil War. Why America's bloodiest conflict still grips us 125 years later. Aug 15 '88
Bush. High stakes in New Orleans. A revealing interview. Nixon on the race. Aug 22 '88	In search of stature. [George Bush] Aug 22 '88	George Bush. What does he stand for? Aug 22 '88
Shaky start. Questions about Quayle. Can Bush get back on track? Aug 29 '88	The Quayle factor. Aug 29 '88	The keys to election '88. The Quayle affair. The cutting issues. The swing voters. (Double issue) Aug 29 '88

Newsweek September 1988	*Time* September 1988	*U.S. News* September 1988
Will we ever get over the '60s? Sep 5 '88	To give or not to give? Begging in America. Sep 5 '88	The keys to election '88. The Quayle affair. The cutting issues. The swing voters. (Double issue) Sep 5 '88
A second chance at life. The miracle of transplants. On a gray afternoon two weeks before Christmas, my doctor told me. . . Sep 12 '88	Gridlock. [Traffic congestion] Sep 12 '88	The capture of a terrorist. Fawaz Younis is the first accused terrorist to be arrested overseas and brought to the U.S.. . . Sep 12 '88
The best and the brightest. [Olympic Games] Sep 19 '88	To be the best. [Olympic Games] Sep 19 '88	Faster. Farther. Higher. What science reveals about the body's ultimate limits. Sep 19 '88
Hanks hits it big. The dazzling actor scores again in "Punchline." Sep 26 '88	Computer viruses. Sep 26 '88	The new frontiers. The coming shuttle flight opens the way to four remarkable space adventures that NASA is planning. Sep 26 '88

Newsweek **October 1988**	*Time* **October 1988**	*U.S. News* **October 1988**
Hardball. The debate. Dukakis and Bush go on the attack. A Newsweek poll assesses the results. Oct 3 '88	Battle of the handlers. Dukakis' John Sasso. Bush's James Baker. Oct 3 '88	Abortion. America's new civil war. Say that one word, and other words fire like weapons. One side yells bloody murder... Oct 3 '88
To dare again. [Space shuttle missions] Oct 10 '88	Whew! America returns to space. Oct 10 '88	America's best colleges. Exclusive ratings. The 125 top schools. Oct 10 '88
John Lennon. The battle over his memory. Oct 17 '88	Zapped. The networks under attack. Oct 17 '88	The making of a president. 24 hours in the life of the campaign. Oct 17 '88
Mr. Chips. Steve Jobs puts the 'wow' back in computers. Oct 24 '88	1988, you're no 1960. Myth, memory and the politics of personality. Oct 24 '88	25 years later. JFK's vision and what has come of it. Oct 24 '88
Mud in your eye. A nasty race trips up pundits and turns off voters. Oct 31 '88	The nuclear scandal. [Radioactive waste disposal] Oct 31 '88	Planet earth. How it works. How to fix it. Oct 31 '88

Newsweek **November 1988**	*Time* **November 1988**	*U.S. News* **November 1988**
Body & soul. Scientists discover the links between the brain and your health. Nov 7 '88	Death of a narc. U.S. drug agent "Kiki" Camarena's mission was to hunt down Mexico's drug barons... Nov 7 '88	Save the children. Too many problems, too little help. Nov 7 '88
Trash TV. From the lurid to the loud, anything goes. Geraldo Rivera. Nov 14 '88	Who's teaching our children? Nov 14 '88	What he will do. The President's opportunities and the menaces he faces. Nov 14 '88
How Bush won. The inside story of campaign '88. A preview of his Presidency. What's ahead for the Democrats. Nov 21 '88	Election special. President-elect George Bush savors his victory. Nov 21 '88	How he will change the Reagan revolution. Nov 21 '88
Crack. Hour by hour. The junkies, the jailer, the pimps and the tiniest addicts. Nov 28 '88	J.F.K.'s assassination: Who was the real target. Twenty-five years later, a new book argues Oswald was actually out to... Nov 28 '88	The new era of invisible warfare. The Pentagon reveals the B-2 Stealth bomber. Is it a wonder weapon or a costly... Nov 28 '88

Newsweek **December 1988**	*Time* **December 1988**	*U.S. News* **December 1988**
Who would wear this stuff? The fashion revolt. Dec 5 '88	A game of greed. This man could pocket $100 million from the largest corporate takeover in history. Has the buyout craze... Dec 5 '88	Where to put your money now. Dec 5 '88
A tale of abuse. The horrifying Steinberg trial. The psychology of violent relationships. Dec 12 '88	"Good" cholesterol. Encouraging news for your heart. Dec 12 '88	Amazing families. Why gifted parents produce gifted children. Dec 12 '88
The agony. Dec 19 '88	Over to you, George. Gorbachev's newest peace offensive challenges the U.S. to respond. Dec 19 '88	How to respond to Gorbachev. Dec 19 '88
The battle over animal rights. A question of suffering and science. Dec 26 '88	About face. Why Arafat said the magic words. How the U.S. changed course. What next in the Middle East. Dec 26 '88	America enters the new world. Politics. What to expect from the Bush Presidency. Economy. Is America losing... Dec 26 '88

Newsweek **January 1989**	*Time* **January 1989**	*U.S. News* **January 1989**

Newsweek **January 1989**

Explosion in the sky. Tragedy and terror on Pan Am 103. How families cope with sudden loss. Jan 2 '89

How Reagan changed America. Jan 9 '89

Chemical warfare. The fight against 'The Winds of Death.' A showdown with Kaddafi. Jan 16 '89

How to survive on $300 billion a year. Bush's defense dilemma. Jan 23 '89

Can you afford to get sick? The battle over health benefits. Jan 30 '89

Time **January 1989**

Planet of the year. Endangered earth.   Jan 2 '89

Mississippi Burning. A new movie's searing view of racism stirs a debate over fact vs. fiction. Jan 9 '89

This man may turn you green with envy - or just turn you off. Flaunting it is the game, and Trump is the name.   Jan 16 '89

The Silver Fox. Barbara Bush brings a refreshing new style to the White House.   Jan 23 '89

The Bush era begins.   Jan 30 '89

U.S. News **January 1989**

America enters the new world. Politics. What to expect from the Bush Presidency. Economy. Is America losing. . .   Jan 2 '89

What Reagan has meant to America. Behind-the-scenes photos of the president at work and play. Jan 9 '89

The new organization man. The realities of getting to the top of today's corporation. A revealing poll of how executives. . .   Jan 16 '89

The bust of '89. A shocking, inside account of how the government helped create the S&L crisis. Jan 23 '89

'The age of the offered hand.' [Inauguration of George Bush] Jan 30 '89

Newsweek **February 1989**

Hot cities. America's best places to live and work. Providence. St. Paul. Orlando. Ft. Worth. Sacramento. Columbus.   Feb 6 '89

Working parents. How to give your kids what they need. By Dr. T. Berry Brazelton.   Feb 13 '89

Addictive personalities. Who gets hooked on drugs and alcohol - and why. Kitty Dukakis: Her private struggle.   Feb 20 '89

'Satanic' fury. Putting a price on the head of Salman Rushdie. Feb 27 '89

Time **February 1989**

Armed America. More guns, more shootings, more massacres. Feb 6 '89

The velvet hammer. Secretary of State James Baker is a gentleman who hates to lose.   Feb 13 '89

Betrayal. "This was the most scandalous fact of all: that the security of Moscow station. . ." [Espionage]   Feb 20 '89

The Ayatullah orders a hit. He causes an uproar by sentencing author Salman Rushdie to death for his book. . .   Feb 27 '89

U.S. News **February 1989**

The best mutual funds for 1989. Exclusive rankings. How to judge performance.   Feb 6 '89

America needs you. The push for voluntary national service. Feb 13 '89

Allergies. New drugs and more tests are giving sufferers more way to spell relief.   Feb 20 '89

The first humans. Science's new view of who we were and the way we lived.   Feb 27 '89

Newsweek **March 1989**

Wine, women and politics. Tower's troubles. [John Tower] Mar 6 '89

How women are changing TV. New power on and off the screen. Mar 13 '89

Arthritis. 37 million Americans, young and old, suffer from the disease. There's still no cure, but new treatments. . .   Mar 20 '89

How safe is your food?   Mar 27 '89

Time **March 1989**

The Tower fiasco. Bush faces his first crisis. [John Tower] Mar 6 '89

Between two worlds. Middle-class Blacks are making it in white America - but they're paying a price.   Mar 13 '89

Solving the mysteries of heredity. The drive to map human genes could revolutionize medicine but also raises troubling. . .   Mar 20 '89

Is anything safe? How two grapes triggered a panic about what we eat. Mar 27 '89

U.S. News **March 1989**

How Iran's terrorists operate. Are Americans at risk from Khomeini's death threat to Salman Rushdie?   Mar 6 '89

The Soviet empire: Part 1. Soviet military power. How serious a threat?   Mar 13 '89

How animals tamed people. What science tells us about the bonds between man and beast. Mar 20 '89

Best ways to cut your taxes. Last-minute strategies to save money.   Mar 27 '89

CHRONOLOGY

Newsweek	April 1989

Mickey's new magic. Disney World unveils a $1 billion movieland.   Apr 3 '89

The drug warrior. He's ambitious, abrasive and tough. Can he make a difference? [William Bennett]
Apr 10 '89

How kids learn.   Apr 17 '89

How Congress really works. Jim Wright and the new capitol culture.   Apr 24 '89

Newsweek	May 1989

The battle over abortion. The Court confronts Roe vs. Wade. Justice O'Connor's key role. Sandra Day O'Connor.   May 1 '89

The race for fusion. The scientific debate. Why the stakes are so high.
May 8 '89

After the Cold War. Bush's dilemma: How to deal with Gorbachev.   May 15 '89

Lyme disease. A tiny tick is spreading a mysterious illness in 43 states. How to protect yourself this summer.   May 22 '89

Upheaval in China.
[Pro-democracy movement]
May 29 '89

Newsweek	June 1989

An old spy's new game. John le Carré comes in from the cold with 'Russia House.'   Jun 5 '89

Bloodbath. [Tiananmen Square demonstration]   Jun 12 '89

Reign of terror. China's crackdown.   Jun 19 '89

The battle over Time Inc.
Jun 26 '89

Time	April 1989

The college trap. Student athletes earn millions for schools, but are they getting an education?
Apr 3 '89

The new U.S.S.R.   Apr 10 '89

Alaska. The battle for America's last frontier.   Apr 17 '89

The rat race. How America is running itself ragged.   Apr 24 '89

Time	May 1989

Abortion. Will the Court turn back the clock?   May 1 '89

Fusion or illusion? How two obscure chemists stirred excitement - and outrage - in the scientific world.   May 8 '89

Waiting for Washington. The U.S. dithers while Moscow woos Europe. Soviet Foreign Minister Shevardnadze says. . .   May 15 '89

Politics, Panama-style. Noriega bludgeons his opposition, and the U.S. turns up the heat.   May 22 '89

China in turmoil.
[Pro-democracy movement]
May 29 '89

Time	June 1989

People power. Beijing: Defying dictatorship. Moscow: Demanding democracy.
Jun 5 '89

Massacre in Beijing. [Tiananmen Square demonstration]
Jun 12 '89

Revolt against Communism.
China. Poland. USSR.   Jun 19 '89

Kevin Costner. The new American hero - smart, sexy and on a roll.
Jun 26 '89

U.S. News	April 1989

The Soviet Union: Part 3. Revolution and ruin. Hope and anger in a collapsing empire.
Apr 3 '89

Murder zones. America is full of its own Beiruts, where drug lords reign and no cops tread.   Apr 10 '89

What's your home worth? The decision to buy or rent. When to move, when to improve. The latest financing wrinkles.   Apr 17 '89

When mental illness hits home. What we know about depression and schizophrenia. How families cope with their ordeal.   Apr 24 '89

U.S. News	May 1989

Plastic surgery. Who should, who shouldn't. A guide to the procedures.   May 1 '89

Guns. Americans and firearms: The attraction, the debate.
May 8 '89

Outer space. New missions, new discoveries.   May 15 '89

Battle for democracy. The crisis in Panama. The students in the streets of Beijing. Eruptions in the Soviet Republics.   May 22 '89

1989 fitness guide. Shaping up. Four exercise plans to lose weight, firm up and gain energy. How to outfit a home. . .   May 29 '89

U.S. News	June 1989

China. What went wrong. The Communist Party has lost its moral authority to govern.
Jun 5 '89

Dirty air. The losing battle to clean up the atmosphere. What pollution does to your health.   Jun 12 '89

Collapse of Communism. In China, Poland and the Soviet Union, the people defy their leaders.
Jun 19 '89

Jobs. Skills young Americans need to succeed. Why schools and companies are failing them.
Jun 26 '89

Newsweek   **July 1989**

The summer of '69 and how it still plays in '89. Woodstock. Chappaquiddick. Manson. Gay rights.   Jul 3 '89

The new volunteers. America's unsung heroes. A talk with Barbara Bush.   Jul 10 '89

The future of abortion in America. New restrictions: How tough will the states get? A dilemma for doctors. . .   Jul 17 '89

Cleaning up our mess. What works, what doesn't and what we must do to reclaim our air, land and water.   Jul 24 '89

California. American dream. American nightmare.   Jul 31 '89

Time   **July 1989**

Great ball of fire. An angry sun stages a spectacular show.   Jul 3 '89

You bet your life. Pete Rose and the great American obsession. [Gambling]   Jul 10 '89

Death by gun. America's toll in one typical week: 464. The faces behind the statistics. A 28-page portfolio. Jul 17 '89

Fateful voyage. What really happened aboard the Exxon Valdez. Captain Joseph Hazelwood. Jul 24 '89

Doctors and patients. Image vs. reality.   Jul 31 '89

U.S. News   **July 1989**

Battle for the wilderness. The fate of America's pristine land is at stake. Jul 3 '89

Best and worst weapons. The winners and losers in the military's arsenal of planes, missiles, tanks. . .   Jul 10 '89

Building your fortune. Savings. Inheritance. Investments. Insurance.   Jul 17 '89

Predicting storms. How scientists are improving our weather forecasts.   Jul 24 '89

Victims of crime. Why the cops and courts are failing. The emotional and psychological trauma. . .   Jul 31 '89

Newsweek   **August 1989**

The HUD scandal. Anatomy of a ripoff.   Aug 7 '89

Dreams. New lessons from the theater of the mind.   Aug 14 '89

Rhymes with rich. Hotel queen Leona Helmsley battles the tax man. Aug 21 '89

The party's over. Communism crumbles in Poland.   Aug 28 '89

Time   **August 1989**

Is she worth it? ABC bets big on Diane Sawyer.   Aug 7 '89

The hostage agony. A Time poll: Talk, don't shoot. No ransom. Israel went too far.   Aug 14 '89

How Bush decides. He's smarter than Reagan, less driven than Carter and savvy like Nixon. Aug 21 '89

World War II. When darkness fell. September 1939 Germany invades Poland.   Aug 28 '89

U.S. News   **August 1989**

America's doomsday project. The U.S. has a secret survival plan in the event of nuclear war, but would it work?   Aug 7 '89

Retirement. Tips to help you build your nest egg. Mapping out a new career after retirement. A work sheet to chart. . .   Aug 14 '89

Secrets of the sea. New light on the mysteries of the deep. Scientists vs. salvagers: The fight over shipwrecks.   Aug 21 '89

Hitler's war against the world. (Double issue)   Aug 28 '89

Newsweek   **September 1989**

The blue planet. A close encounter with Neptune.   Sep 4 '89

Can the children be saved? One block's battle against drugs and despair.   Sep 11 '89

The Alaska spill. What Exxon leaves behind. Is the damage permanent? Cutting through the hype, hysteria and. . .   Sep 18 '89

Barney Frank's story. A congressman talks about his double life. A Newsweek poll on homosexuality and politics.   Sep 25 '89

Time   **September 1989**

Rock rolls on. Aging stars like the Rolling Stones strut their staying power.   Sep 4 '89

The lonely war. In drug-infested neighborhoods, across America, angry citizens like Detroit's Rantine McKesson. . .   Sep 11 '89

Torching the Amazon. Can the rain forest be saved?   Sep 18 '89

Boardwalk of broken dreams. [Atlantic City]   Sep 25 '89

U.S. News   **September 1989**

Hitler's war against the world. (Double issue)   Sep 4 '89

A family guide. How you can beat drugs. Prevention, treatment and community action.   Sep 11 '89

Alaska's oil spill. The disaster that wasn't. Why the environment will recover. Should Exxon continue the cleanup?   Sep 18 '89

1990 career guide. Best jobs for the future. Exclusive salary survey. Sep 25 '89

Newsweek **October 1989**	*Time* **October 1989**	*U.S. News* **October 1989**
The innovators. 25 Americans on the cutting edge. Science, Technology. Medicine. Business. Education. Fun and. . . Oct 2 '89	A day in the life of China. Oct 2 '89	Endangered species. Can they be saved? Oct 2 '89
Japan invades Hollywood. Sony's $3.4 billion deal for Columbia. Five ways to meet the challenge on trade, takeovers. . . Oct 9 '89	Want a baby? Not all children are equal in the joy and anguish of adoption. Oct 9 '89	Exclusive book excerpt. West Point Story. The class of '66, from Vietnam to the New Army. Oct 9 '89
Amateur hour. The U.S. vs. Noriega. Step by step: Did Bush go too far or not far enough? Oct 16 '89	The ivory trail. From Africa to Asia, a story of greed and slaughter. Oct 16 '89	America's best colleges. Oct 16 '89
Nancy Reagan's 'My Turn.' On astrology. On Don Regan. On Raisa. On her kids. Oct 23 '89	Is government dead? Unwilling to lead, politicians are letting America slip into paralysis. Oct 23 '89	The new refugees. Should America take them in? Oct 23 '89
Bracing for the big one. The lessons of San Francisco. [Earthquake] Oct 30 '89	San Francisco. October 17, 1989. [Earthquake] Oct 30 '89	The next quake. Science's startling new view of the turbulent forces inside the earth. Oct 30 '89

Newsweek **November 1989**	*Time* **November 1989**	*U.S. News* **November 1989**
Scene stealer. Michelle Pfeiffer takes big risks for the right roles. Nov 6 '89	The big break. Moscow lets Eastern Europe go its own way. Nov 6 '89	The selling of America's schools. Big business sees schools as a rich new market. Is that good or bad for your kids? Nov 6 '89
The dirty 300. How Colombia's drug rings operate in America. Nov 13 '89	Arsenio. TV's hip host grabs the post-Carson generation. [Arsenio Hall] Nov 13 '89	America's new boom towns. Hot cities that may surprise you. Nov 13 '89
The wall. 1961-1989. [Berlin wall] Nov 20 '89	Freedom! [Berlin wall] Nov 20 '89	Communist meltdown. The crumbling Iron Curtain. The Soviet economy in ruins. Nov 20 '89
Buried alive. The garbage glut: An environmental crisis reaches our doorstop. Nov 27 '89	Art and money. Who's winning and who's losing as prices go through the roof. Nov 27 '89	The truth about cholesterol. Confused by the claims and counterclaims? Here are answers to the critical health. . . Nov 27 '89

Newsweek **December 1989**	*Time* **December 1989**	*U.S. News* **December 1989**
Can he ride the tiger? With Eastern Europe out of control and his economy in ruins, Gorbachev faces his toughest test. Dec 4 '89	Women face the '90s. In the '80s they tried to have it all. Now they've just plain had it. Is there a future for feminism? Dec 4 '89	Best places for your money. Stocks. Bonds. Real estate. Collectibles. Dec 4 '89
Super partners. An ambitious game plan for a new era. [Summit conference] Dec 11 '89	Building a new world. [Summit conference] Dec 11 '89	After the Cold War. Do we need an army? Of course. But its size and mission are about to change. Dec 11 '89
All about Alzheimer's. What doctors know. How families cope. Dec 18 '89	Money laundering. The trillion-dollar shell game. Dec 18 '89	Back home. Where we grew up: A portrait of America. Dec 18 '89
People of the year. Standing up for freedom. 1989. Changing the course of history. Dec 25 '89	Cruise control. Hollywood's top gun gets serious in a bold new movie about Viet Nam. [Tom Cruise] Dec 25 '89	What's ahead. Politics. Exclusive: George Bush on the '90s. Economy. America's place in a global race. Environment. Dec 25 '89

Newsweek   **January 1990**

Target: Noriega. Bush's invasion. How high a price? How long a stay? Jan 1 '90

The last days of a dictator. A violent end to a year of revolution. Romania.   Jan 8 '90

The Noriega files. His treacherous links with the drug cartel, Castro, Bush and the CIA. Excerpts from a new book...   Jan 15 '90

The Boston murder. Unraveling a grisly hoax. Race, anger and a divided city.   Jan 22 '90

Busting the mayor. Washington's Marion Barry faces cocaine charges.   Jan 29 '90

Time   **January 1990**

Man of the decade. Mikhail Gorbachev.   Jan 1 '90

When tyrants fall. Rumania. A firing squad for Ceausescu. Panama. End of the line for Noriega?   Jan 8 '90

Antarctica. Is any place safe from mankind?   Jan 15 '90

A murder in Boston. How a bizarre case inflamed racial tensions and raised troubling questions about politicians...   Jan 22 '90

Who is the NRA? A look at America's embattled gun lobby. Jan 29 '90

U.S. News   **January 1990**

What's ahead. Politics. Exclusive: George Bush on the '90s. Economy. America's place in a global race. Environment...   Jan 1 '90

The price of victory. College sports vs. education. When the cheering stops, are big-time college athletes adequately...   Jan 8 '90

The collapse of Communism. Is the Soviet Union next?   Jan 15 '90

How doctors decide who shall live and who shall die.   Jan 22 '90

Best ways to fight that cold. Jan 29 '90

Newsweek   **February 1990**

Afflicted? Addicted? Support groups are the answer for 15 million Americans.   Feb 5 '90

My life in hiding. Salman Rushdie talks about his death sentence — and defends 'Satanic Verses'.   Feb 12 '90

Free! Breakthrough in South Africa. [Nelson Mandella released from prison]   Feb 19 '90

A united Germany. The new superpower.   Feb 26 '90

Time   **February 1990**

Mandela: Free at last? After 27 years, a changing South Africa prepares to release its most famous political prisoner.   Feb 5 '90

Scaling down defense. How to really cut military costs.   Feb 12 '90

Starting over. Gorbachev turns his back on Lenin.   Feb 19 '90

Predator's fall. The collapse of Drexel Burnham, the house that junk built, is only the latest of Wall Street's woes...   Feb 26 '90

U.S. News   **February 1990**

Should hunting be banned? Animal-rights activists war on blood sports.   Feb 5 '90

Winners for the 1990s. Annual mutual fund guide. Exclusive rankings. Strong funds in shaky markets...   Feb 12 '90

In the Kremlin, Communism's last stand. Gorbachev's desperate new bid to save his party — and his revolution.   Feb 19 '90

The man who conquered Communism. "The New Europe" by Vaclav Havel, playwright-president of...   Feb 26 '90

Newsweek   **March 1990**

Looking for the fountain of youth. Scientists unlock the secrets of aging.   Mar 5 '90

The future of gay America. Militants versus the mainstream. Testing the limits of tolerance. Mar 12 '90

Rap Rage. Yo! Street rhyme has gone big time. But are those sounds out of bounds?   Mar 19 '90

Prozac. A breakthrough drug for depression.   Mar 26 '90

Time   **March 1990**

Gossip. Where does it come from — and why does America love it? Mar 5 '90

Soviet disunion. Growing cries for independence bring Gorbachev's empire to the breaking point.   Mar 12 '90

The right to die.   Mar 19 '90

The Germans. Should the world be worried?   Mar 26 '90

U.S. News   **March 1990**

Beating depression. New treatments bring success. Mar 5 '90

Inside China. Exclusive: The first interviews with China's leaders since Tiananmen Square. Mar 12 '90

America's best graduate schools. Business. Law. Medicine. Engineering.   Mar 19 '90

When the universe was new. A journey to the beginning of time. The Hubble space telescope: Launching...   Mar 26 '90

Newsweek **April 1990**	*Time* **April 1990**	*U.S. News* **April 1990**
What Japan thinks of us. A nation of crybabies? Apr 2 '90	Nixon. In an emotional memoir, he describes the agony of his exile and his struggle for renewal. Apr 2 '90	Lost empires of the Americas. New finds reveal our ancient past. Inca Emperor Pachacuti. Apr 2 '90
Not just for nerds. How to teach science to our kids. Apr 9 '90	America's changing colors. What will the U.S. be like when whites are no longer the majority? Apr 9 '90	What is your home worth now? The 25 top housing markets. Apr 9 '90
Life on the Mississippi. Huck's river faces all of the nation's environmental problems. Apr 16 '90	Smash! Colossal colliders are unlocking the secrets of the universe. Apr 16 '90	The last days of Jesus. The new light on what happened. Apr 16 '90
Why America love the Simpsons. TV's twisted new take on the family. Apr 23 '90	No joke. This man could be our next president. A probing look by Garry Wills. [Dan Quayle] Apr 23 '90	Death at sea. What blew up the U.S.S. Iowa? A year later, the Navy still blames one 'suicidal' sailor. But that verdict is... Apr 23 '90
Liquid diets. Are they safe? How they work. Apr 30 '90	Vietnam 15 years later. In America, the pain endures. In Cambodia, the killing continues. Apr 30 '90	America's best hospitals. Exclusive ratings. A national guide that helps you choose. Apr 30 '90

Newsweek **May 1990**	*Time* **May 1990**	*U.S. News* **May 1990**
The long shadow. New fears of anti-Semitism in Eastern Europe and the Soviet Union. May 7 '90	Dirty words. America's foul-mouthed pop culture. May 7 '90	The new way to get rich. Never before have so many people stood to inherit so much money. May 7 '90
The 8th grade wonder. Tennis superstar Jennifer Capriati. May 14 '90	Sakharov. Memoirs of a 20th century giant. May 14 '90	Getting slim. How to find the right diet. May 14 '90
Bonfire of the S&L's. How much you will pay. Are the banks next? May 21 '90	Bush's bad cop. From taxes to clean air, John Sununu is the power to reckon with. May 21 '90	The old West. The new view of frontier life. May 21 '90
Guns and dolls. Scientists explore the differences between girls and boys. May 28 '90	Emergency! Overwhelmed and understaffed, medicine's front lines are collapsing across America. May 28 '90	The hidden life of Barbara Bush. May 28 '90

Newsweek **June 1990**	*Time* **June 1990**	*U.S. News* **June 1990**
Why Gorbachev is failing. Jun 4 '90	In the eye of the storm. With his country in a perilous passage, Gorbachev defines his course and answers his critics. Jun 4 '90	The most dangerous man in the world. Saddam Hussein, President of Iraq. Jun 4 '90
The Yeltsin challenge. After the summit. Jun 11 '90	Making crime pay. Scott Turow scores big with a new novel about family, money and the law. Jun 11 '90	Falling star. After the summit: The growing danger for Gorbachev back in the U.S.S.R. Jun 11 '90
Trump. The fall. Jun 18 '90	Child warriors. Burma's Tin Hle is only 13 years old. In war zones around the world, kids like him are fighting... Jun 18 '90	Best ways to stay healthy. The ten most important new developments. Plus the A-to-Z health almanac. Jun 18 '90
Hot tickets. Hollywood's high-stakes summer. Madonna and Warren Beatty go for broke in 'Dick Tracy'. Jun 25 '90	Who gives a hoot? The timber industry says that saving this spotted owl will cost 30,000 jobs. It isn't that simple. Jun 25 '90	The forgotten war. 40 years after Korea. Jun 25 '90

Newsweek **July 1990**	*Time* **July 1990**	*U.S. News* **July 1990**
Art or obscenity? Jul 2 '90	A hero in America. Nelson Mandela. Jul 2 '90	The body at war. New breakthroughs in how we fight disease. Jul 2 '90
Star crossed. The Hubble telescope. NASA's $1.5 billion blunder. Jul 9 '90	Abortion's most wrenching questions. Should parents have a say? What about rape victims? Jul 9 '90	The best of America. The year's most outstanding people, places, products, and ideas. Jul 9 '90
The daughter track. The average American woman spends 17 years raising children and 18 years helping aging parents. Jul 16 '90	Twentysomething. Laid back, late blooming or just lost? Over-shadowed by the baby boomers, America's next... Jul 16 '90	The U.S. vs. Japan vs. Germany. Will America lose out in the new global boom? Jul 16 '90
The mind of the rapist. The psychology of sexual violence. New York's grisly 'Jogger' trial. The fear of AIDS. Jul 23 '90	A long, bloody search for nationhood. The Palestinians. Jul 23 '90	Race and the South. How blacks and whites are remaking the old confederacy. Jul 23 '90
The Bush court. A move to the right. What it means for: Abortion, the death penalty, civil rights. Jul 30 '90	Mr. Germany. The man who pushed his country back together. Jul 30 '90	How to build your fortune. Retirement: A guide for late starters. Investing: Where you should put your... Jul 30 '90

Newsweek **August 1990**	*Time* **August 1990**	*U.S. News* **August 1990**
The most hated man in baseball. The Damned Yankees by George F. Will. George Steinbrenner. Aug 6 '90	Just who is David Souter? Aug 6 '90	How to reverse heart disease. A tough new program to combat America's No. 1 killer. Aug 6 '90
Baghdad's bully. Can he be stopped? The war of the future. Oil shocks ahead. [Iraqi invasion of Kuwait] Aug 13 '90	Iraq on the march. [Iraqi invasion of Kuwait] Aug 13 '90	What America can do about Iraq. The military options. The new oil crisis. Aug 13 '90
Drawing the line. [Iraqi invasion of Kuwait] Aug 20 '90	Showdown. Can Bush make Saddam blink? Aug 20 '90	Target Iraq. Is air power enough? Facing the chemical-weapons threat. Aug 20 '90
Will it be war? [Iraqi invasion of Kuwait] Aug 27 '90	Talk of war. Saddam's foreign pawns. Bush's massive buildup. Diplomacy's last chance. Aug 27 '90	Defying Hitler. World War II. 1940. America on the eve of war. The air battle for Britain. Aug 27 '90

Newsweek **September 1990**	*Time* **September 1990**	*U.S. News* **September 1990**
Horror show. Saddam's prisoners of war. Sep 3 '90	Are we ready for this? [Chemical warfare] Sep 3 '90	Defying Hitler. World War II. 1940. America on the eve of war. The air battle for Britain. Sep 3 '90
Women warriors. Sharing the danger. [Women soldiers in the Middle East] Sep 10 '90	Playing cat and mouse. Saddam sends mixed signals while Bush holds firm. Does diplomacy stand a chance? Sep 10 '90	Desert warriors. How the Gulf is testing the new U.S military. The diplomatic moves to contain Saddam Hussein. Sep 10 '90
The Moscow connection. On the day before the Iraqi invasion, the Kremlin got a CIA alert that the attack was... Sep 17 '90	The rotting of the Big Apple. [New York City] Sep 17 '90	1991 career guide. Best jobs for the future. Exclusive salary survey. The 20 hottest professions. Sep 17 '90
The power to heal. From ancient arts to modern medicine. A photo portfolio. Sep 24 '90	Under the gun. Saudi anxieties. Bush's resolve. The quick-strike option. Sep 24 '90	How to prosper in hard times. The smart investor's guide. Sep 24 '90

Newsweek — October 1990

The real estate bust. "How to survive" by Jane Bryant Quinn. Oct 1 '90

The Civil War remembered. A stunning TV series sparks old passions and... Oct 8 '90

Inside Doonesbury's brain. Garry Trudeau finally talks. Oct 15 '90

Bush league. The President stumbles, Congress bumbles. Boooo! Oct 22 '90

The case against war. The case for war. The Gulf Crisis. How will Bush decide? Oct 29 '90

Time — October 1990

David Lynch. The wild-at-art genius behind Twin Peaks. Oct 1 '90

Do we care about our kids? The sorry plight of America's most disadvantaged... Oct 8 '90

High anxiety. Looming recession, government paralysis and the threat of war... Oct 15 '90

The new jazz age. Oct 22 '90

Can America still compete? With its new Saturn, GM bets the answer is yes. Oct 29 '90

U.S. News — October 1990

Top guns. What America's military commanders think about waging war. Oct 1 '90

Hostage to oil. Why the Gulf showdown is driving up prices. How costs would soar... Oct 8 '90

America's best colleges. Exclusive rankings of 405 universities and colleges. Teaching... Oct 15 '90

Throw the bums out! Government is paralyzed, and voters are angry. Is there any way out... Oct 22 '90

Vietnam story. Twenty-five years ago, soldiers of the U.S. 7th Cavalry fought the first major... Oct 29 '90

Newsweek — November 1990

How safe is your job? The warning signals. How to cope. Nov 5 '90

Chronic fatigue syndrome. A debilitating disease afflicts millions... Nov 12 '90

Letters in the sand. In millions of letters our soldiers tell their story. Nov 19 '90

Should we fight? Americans take sides. "Why we must break Saddam's... Nov 26 '90

Time — November 1990

Reagan. Memoirs: "An American Life." Nov 5 '90

Ready for war. Pentagon partners Dick Cheney and Colin Powell have the troops... Nov 12 '90

The untouchables. America's voters said no to politics as usual. So why are 96%... Nov 19 '90

Hey. Don't miss our really interesting story on the junk mail explosion! Nov 26 '90

U.S. News — November 1990

The roots of language. How modern speech evolved from a single, ancient source. Nov 5 '90

Can your bank stay afloat? How the real-estate crash threatens financial institutions... Nov 12 '90

Death of a nation. U.S.S.R. 1917 – Nov 19 '90

Smart ways to fly. Air traveler's guide. Exclusive airport ratings. On-time airlines... Nov 26 '90

Newsweek — December 1990

The iron lady falls. A greengrocer's daughter who bent a nation... [Margaret Thatcher] Dec 3 '90

'This will not be another Vietnam'. A deadline for diplomacy. And a plan for all-out war. Dec 10 '90

And the children shall lead them. Young Americans return to God. Dec 17 '90

Thought police. Watch what you say. There's a 'Politically Correct' way to talk about... Dec 24 '90

The 90's. A survival guide. Issues, people and predictions for the age of anxiety. Dec 31 '90

Time — December 1990

The lady bows out. What Maggie Thatcher's departure means for the U.S. and Europe. Dec 3 '90

What war would be like. Dec 10 '90

The sleep gap. Too much to do, too little rest. Dec 17 '90

What is Kuwait? And is it worth dying for? Dec 24 '90

The best of '90. Yes, Bart, even you made the list. Dec 31 '90

U.S. News — December 1990

Cops under fire. They are outmanned, outgunned, second-guessed... Dec 3 '90

Who wrote the Bible? The surprising new theories. Dec 10 '90

The 200 best stocks and mutual funds. How to rebuild a battered portfolio. Where to... Dec 17 '90

With the cavalry. Desert Shield exclusive. And with the families back home. Dec 24 '90

Outlook 1991. What's ahead. 24 predictions for the new year. Dec 31 '90

Newsweek **January 1991**	*Time* **January 1991**	*US News* **January 1991**
Saddam's endgame. More than just a madman. Jan 7 '91	Men of the year. The two George Bushes. Jan 7 '91	Outlook 1991. What's ahead. 24 predictions for the new year. Jan 7 '91
Riding out the recession. The 'fear' factor. Jan 14 '91	One American woman in ten will get breast cancer. Why—and what can be done? Jan 14 '91	Desert warfare. If diplomacy fails. How a war would be fought in the air and on the ground. Jan 14 '91
The path to war. 'We'll win, but why rush?' [Persian Gulf War] Jan 21 '91	January 15. Deadline for war. [Persian Gulf War] Jan 21 '91	Showdown. The Gulf crisis. Last-ditch diplomacy. What war won't solve. Jan 21 '91
America at war. [Persian Gulf War] Jan 28 '91	War in the Gulf. [Persian Gulf War] Jan 28 '91	America at war. Operation Desert Storm. Jan 28 '91

Newsweek **February 1991**	*Time* **February 1991**	*US News* **February 1991**
Hard days ahead. A brutal war on the ground? The POWs: Torture and torment. Saddam's environmental terror. Feb 4 '91	Stalking Saddam. [Persian Gulf War] Feb 4 '91	The coming ground war. Operation Desert Storm. Feb 4 '91
Heat of battle. The showdown in the sand. [Persian Gulf War] Feb 11 '91	Saddam's weird war. [Persian Gulf War] Feb 11 '91	War power. Inside the air war. Our man in charge. Feb 11 '91
The new science of war. High-tech hardware: How many lives can it save? Countdown to a ground strike. Feb 18 '91	The war comes home. Lance Cpl. Thomas Jenkins, 21, killed in action in Saudi Arabia. . . Feb 18 '91	Saddam Hussein. The real target? [Persian Gulf War] Feb 18 '91
Saddam on the ropes. [Persian Gulf War] Feb 25 '91	Beginning of the end. The ground war: How it will be fought. Inside Iraq: Photos of the bombing. Feb 25 '91	Saddam's desperate hours. Facing a crushing military defeat, Iraq's dictator hopes a political offensive will save his skin. Feb 25 '91

Newsweek **March 1991**	*Time* **March 1991**	*US News* **March 1991**
Bush's battle plan. Target: Total victory. [Persian Gulf War] Mar 4 '91	Into Kuwait! Tightening the noose around Saddam. The inside story of Soviet diplomacy. Mar 4 '91	The last act. [Persian Gulf War] Mar 4 '91
Victory! And what comes next. [Persian Gulf War] Mar 11 '91	Kuwait City. Feb. 27, 1991. [Persian Gulf War] Mar 11 '91	Knockout. [Persian Gulf War] Mar 11 '91
The secret history of the war. [Persian Gulf War] Mar 18 '91	A moment to savor. And the lessons of victory. Inside Kuwait: Anger and chaos. Mar 18 '91	The U.S. military reborn. After the triumph of Desert Storm. Mar 18 '91
Revolt in Iraq. Bush keeps the pressure on. [Iraqi Kurds revolt] Mar 25 '91	Russia's maverick. Boris Yeltsin, the bad boy of Soviet politics, battles Gorbachev in a crucial vote this week. Mar 25 '91	The rekindling of hell. Religion in the '90s. Record numbers of Americans now believe in a netherworld. . . Mar 25 '91

Newsweek **April 1991**	*Time* **April 1991**	*US News* **April 1991**
Violence goes mainstream. Movies, music, books—are there any limits left? Apr 1 '91	Law and disorder. Why cops turn violent. Apr 1 '91	What your home is worth. The 25 top housing markets. The outlook for prices this year. Strategies for buyers and sellers. Apr 1 '91
Arms for sale. After the war, business as usual? Apr 8 '91	The simple life. Rejecting the rat race, Americans get back to basics. Apr 8 '91	Kids who kill. What's behind the epidemic of teenage murder. Apr 8 '91
'Why won't he help us?' Exodus of the Kurds. Bush's dilemma. [Iraqi Kurds revolt] Apr 15 '91	Saddam's latest victims. Can Bush avoid a human tragedy? [Iraqi Kurds revolt] Apr 15 '91	Saddam's revenge. Iraq's killing fields: Should the U.S. stop the slaughter? Apr 15 '91
Poison Pen. Kitty vs. Nancy. The boom in trash biography. [Kitty Kelley and Nancy Reagan] Apr 22 '91	Is she that bad? What's true–and not true–in Kitty Kelley's slasher biography of Nancy Reagan. Apr 22 '91	History's hidden turning points. How Paul made Christianity. Who says Columbus discovered America? Apr 22 '91
Victims of rape. Should their names be kept secret? Privacy, the media and the Kennedy case. Apr 29 '91	Nuclear power. Do we have a choice? Apr 29 '91	America's best graduate schools. Business. Law. Medicine. Engineering. Apr 29 '91

Newsweek **May 1991**	*Time* **May 1991**	*US News* **May 1991**
The new politics of race. May 6 '91	Scientology. The cult of greed. How the growing dianetics empire squeezes millions from believers worldwide. May 6 '91	Storm clouds over the recovery. America's troubled economy. Why too much debt threatens your pocketbook. . . May 6 '91
The reluctant warrior. Doubts and divisions on the road to war. Gen. Colin Powell. May 13 '91	Crack kids. Their mothers used drugs, and now it's the children who suffer. May 13 '91	The secrets of Venus. Earth's sister planet helps us understand our own world. May 13 '91
The Quayle handicap. Is he a lightweight—or smarter than you think? May 20 '91	Five who could be Vice President. Bush's heart scare stirs old doubts about Dan Quayle. May 22 '91	Best ways to stay healthy. Exercise and your heart. A live-longer diet. Surgery without knives. May 20 '91
Fed up! Is there anything left we can eat? [Nutrition] May 27 '91	Orlando. Where fantasy meets reality. [Disney World] May 27 '91	Making kids smarter. How magnet education is giving children the edge they need. May 27 '91

Newsweek **June 1991**	*Time* **June 1991**	*US News* **June 1991**
Heavens! Black holes, quasars, starquakes: Astronomers launch a new age of discovery. Jun 3 '91	Date Rape. Jun 3 '91	The new spy wars. Is the CIA ready? Jun 3 '91
Tackling a taboo. Spike Lee's take on interracial romance. Mixed couples on love and prejudice. Jun 10 '91	Evil. Does it exist — or do bad things just happen? Jun 10 '91	Sex and religion. Churches, the Bible and the furor over modern sexuality. Jun 10 '91
Secret warriors. Behind Iraqi lines. How SEALS and Scud-hunters helped win the war. Jun 17 '91	The gift of life. Little Marissa was born to provide lifesaving bone marrow to her big sister Anissa. . . Jun 17 '91	The executive suite. Why women can't, won't, don't want to make it to the top. Jun 17 '91
What do men really want? Drums, sweat and tears. Now they have a movement of their own. Jun 24 '91	Why Thelma & Louise strikes a nerve. [Motion picture] Jun 24 '91	Where emotions come from. Unlocking the biological secrets of joy, fear, anger and despair. Jun 24 '91

Newsweek **July 1991**	*Time* **July 1991**	*US News* **July 1991**
Doctors with AIDS. Jul 1 '91	Cocaine Inc. The new drug kings. Cold-blooded and efficient. . . Jul 1 '91	The odd couple. How George Bush has become a true believer in Mikhail Gorbachev. Jul 1 '91
How far right? Abortion, crime & quotas: The court that will change America. Jul 8 '91	Who are we? American kids are getting a new—and divisive— view. . . [Americans] Jul 8 '91	America before Columbus. The untold story. Jul 8 '91
Lead and your kids. Disturbing new evidence about the threat to their health. . . Jul 15 '91	Misleading labels. Why Americans don't know what they're eating. Jul 15 '91	Where to invest now. The top 50 small stocks. The top 65 mutual funds. . . Jul 15 '91
Video vigilantes. Cops, crooks, adulterers: No one is safe from the camera's eye. Jul 22 '91	The Colorado. The West's lifeline is now America's most endangered river. Jul 22 '91	Black & white in America. Race and the troubled state of integration. Jul 22 '91
Hoping against hope. The MIA mystery. A generation after Vietnam. . . Jul 29 '91	The world's sleaziest bank. How B.C.C.I. became a one-stop shopping center. . . Jul 29 '91	Is your water safe? The dangerous state of drinking water in America. Jul 29 '91

Newsweek **August 1991**	*Time* **August 1991**	*US News* **August 1991**
Should women fight to kill? Aug 5 '91	Was it worth it? The mess in Kuwait. Saddam's staying power. [Persian Gulf War] Aug 5 '91	America's best hospitals. Exclusive rankings. How to find care in 15 specialties. . . Aug 5 '91
Return of the wolf. The fabled animal is back, scaring ranchers. . . Aug 12 '91	Busybodies & crybabies. What's happening to the American character? Aug 12 '91	Alzheimer's. New advances in the battle against a terrifying disease. Aug 12 '91
Halcion. It's the most widely prescribed sleeping pill in the world. But is it safe? Aug 19 '91	Why now? Who's next? Hostages. John McCarthy's release. . . [Hostages in Lebanon] Aug 19 '91	The men who created crack. The history of the drug plaguing America's cities. Aug 19 '91
Choosing death. More doctors are helping the very sick die gently. Aug 26 '91	Science under siege. Tight money, blunders and scandal plague America's researchers. Aug 26 '91	The best of America. Politics. Philanthropy. Craftsmanship. Innovation. . . Aug 26 '91

Newsweek **September 1991**	*Time* **September 1991**	*US News* **September 1991**
The second Russian Revolution. [Attempted Soviet coup] Sep 2 '91	The Russian Revolution. August 1991. [Attempted Soviet coup] Sep 2 '91	Russia reborn. [Attempted Soviet coup] Sep 2 '91
Crackup. [Breakup of the Soviet Union] Sep 9 '91	Power vacuum. Breaking from the past. Struggling for the future. [Attempted Soviet coup] Sep 9 '91	The end of the empire. [Breakup of the Soviet Union] Sep 9 '91
Judging Thomas. The life and contradictions of the Supreme Court nominee. Sep 16 '91	Can this man save our schools? Education Secretary Lamar Alexander. Sep 16 '91	Early man. The radical new view of where we came from. Sep 16 '91
Was Cleopatra black? Afrocentrism. Facts or fantasies—a debate rages. . . Sep 23 '91	Lost tribes, lost knowledge. When native cultures disappear, so does a trove of scientific. . . Sep 23 '91	Wonder cures? New respect for fringe medicine. Acupuncture. Hypnosis. Biofeedback. Sep 23 '91
The war for the West. Fighting for the soul of America's mythic land. Sep 30 '91	How a dazzling array of medical breakthroughs has made curing infertility. . . Sep 30 '91	America's best colleges. How top experts rate 455 schools. The best buys. . . Sep 30 '91

Newsweek   October 1991

The future of the bomb. Will Bush's plan work? Can we trust the Soviets? What is Saddam hiding? Oct 7 '91

No bull. The campaign America needs—but won't get. [Presidential campaigns]   Oct 14 '91

Anita Hill: 'I had to tell the truth.' Clarence Thomas: 'It is a high-tech lynching.'   Oct 21 '91

How dinosaurs lived. Sex, day care and fast food—100 million years ago.   Oct 28 '91

Newsweek   November 1991

The bite on the middle class. What recovery?   Nov 4 '91

The October surprise. The charge: Treason. The evidence: Myth. Reagan, Bush and the Iran hostage release.   Nov 11 '91

'Even me'—Magic Johnson. [Johnson announces he is HIV positive]   Nov 18 '91

Remembering Pearl Harbor. Nov 25 '91

Newsweek   December 1991

The 10 best schools in the world. And what we can learn from them. Dec 2 '91

Safe sex. What you and your children should know.   Dec 9 '91

What you don't see. Behind the drama at the Smith rape trial. Dec 16 '91

The twisted truth of 'JFK.' Why Oliver Stone's new movie can't be trusted.   Dec 23 '91

The year of Yeltsin. Decade of democracy.   Dec 30 '91

Time   October 1991

Defusing the nuclear threat. What Bush did NOT give up. What Gorbachev stands to gain. Oct 7 '91

A director is born. Jodie Foster. Oct 14 '91

Sex, lies & politics. America's watershed debate on sexual harassment.   Oct 21 '91

"Reagan knew everything." Ollie North tells his story.   Oct 28 '91

Time   November 1991

The new age of alternative medicine. Why biofeedback and other offbeat treatments are catching on.   Nov 4 '91

Somebody's watching. How business, government and even the folks next door are tracking your secrets.   Nov 11 '91

California. The endangered dream.   Nov 18 '91

10 ways to cure the health care mess. Nov 25 '91

Time   December 1991

Day of infamy. December 7, 1941. Pearl Harbor.   Dec 2 '91

One nation, under God. Has the separation of church and state gone too far?   Dec 9 '91

The smile of freedom. Terry Anderson's terrible ordeal. The inside story of the hostage release. Dec 16 '91

Gorbachev says he'll fight on, but he's already a man without a country.   Dec 23 '91

The search for Mary. Was the most revered woman in history God's handmaid — or the first feminist? Dec 30 '91

US News   October 1991

The Bible's last secrets. Deciphering the mysteries of the Dead Sea Scrolls.   Oct 7 '91

Shrinking the military. Weapons, missions and manpower: What to keep, what to cut.   Oct 14 '91

Sex and justice. The Thomas affair. The furor over sexual harassment. Oct 21 '91

The great gold scandal. A billion-dollar giveaway is ravaging the American West. Oct 28 '91

US News   November 1991

Genetic miracles. How a medical revolution is saving lives–and raising fears.   Nov 4 '91

Best jobs for the future. 1992 career guide. Exclusive salary survey. The hottest professions.   Nov 11 '91

The rich in America. How they made their money. The populist assault on them.   Nov 18 '91

Saddam's bomb. The secrets of Iraq's nuclear weapons program. Nov 25 '91

US News   December 1991

Pearl Harbor. America fights back. Dec 2 '91

The flight from public schools. Five leading alternatives: Parochial. For-profit schools. Prep. Afrocentric. . .   Dec 9 '91

Grandparents. The silent saviors. Protecting millions of children from troubled parents, drugs and abuse.   Dec 16 '91

The creation. Religion's search for a common ground with science. Dec 23 '91

What's ahead. 24 predictions for the new year. Money. Election '92. Health. Business.   Dec 30 '91

Subject Headings

OF THE COVER STORY INDEX

1960 — 1991

Subject Headings

Aaron, Hank
Abdul-Jabbar, Kareem
Abortion
Abrams, Creighton
Abscam Bribery Scandal, 1980
Abu Simbel, Temples of
Abzug, Bella
Academy Awards (Motion Pictures)
Achille Lauro Ship Hijacking, 1985
Acid Rain
Ackley, H. Gardner
Acupuncture
Adams, Ansel
Addictive Behavior
Adenauer, Konrad
Adoption
Adventure and Adventurers
Advertising
Advertising Agencies
Advertising in Schools
Advice
Aerospace Industry
Aetna Life and Casualty Co.
Afghanistan-Russian Invasion, 1979-1989
Africa
Africa - Race Question
Africa and the United States
Africa, Southern
Afrocentrism
Age Groups
Aggressiveness (Psychology)
Aging
Agnelli, Giovanni
Agnew, Spiro
Agriculture
Agriculture Policy - Johnson
  Administration
Agriculture Policy - Kennedy
  Administration
Agriculture Policy - Reagan
  Administration
Aids (Disease)
Air Traffic Control
Air Travel

Air Travel - Accidents
Air Travel - Safety
Air Travel - Security
Airborne Warning and Control
Aircraft Carriers
Airline Industry
Airplanes, Jet
Airplanes, Military
Airplanes, Supersonic
Akers, John
Alaska
Albee, Edward
Alcoa Aluminum Co.
Alcoholics' Families
Alcoholism
Alda, Alan
Alexander the Great
Algeria - Politics and Government
Ali, Muhammad
Aliens, Illegal
Allegheny International Inc.
Allen, George
Allen, Woody
Allende, Salvador
Allergies
Allied Corp.
Alphand, Nicole
Alsop, Joseph
Alternative Medicine
Altman, Robert
Alzheimer's Disease
AM International
Amax Inc.
Amazon
America - Antiquities
America's Cup Race
American Airlines, Inc.
American Broadcasting Company
American Can Company
American Express Co.
American Telephone & Telegraph
Americans
Americans in Foreign Countries
Americans with Disabilities Act

Amin Dada, Idi
Amnesty
Amusement Parks
Anastasia, Grand Duchess of Russia
Anchorage (Alaska)
Anders, William
Anderson, Jack
Anderson, John
Anderson, Terry
Andretti, Mario
Andrews, Julie
Andropov, Yuri
Anger
Angkor, Kampuchea
Angola
Angola and the United States
Anheuser-Busch, Inc.
Animal Behavior
Animal Communication
Animal Experimentation
Animal Intelligence
Animals
Animals - Training
Animals and Civilization
Ann-Margret
Anne, Princess of Great Britain
Antelope
Anthropocentrism
Anthropology
Anti-Ballistic Missile Treaty, 1972
Anti-Nuclear Movement - Catholic
   Church
Anti-nuclear Movement - Europe
Anti-nuclear Movement - United States
Antimatter
Anxiety
Apartheid
Apes
Apollo Project
Apollo Testing Accident
Apollo-Soyuz Flight, 1975
Apple Computer Inc.
Aquino, Corazon
Arab Countries
Arabs
Arafat, Yasir
Aransas National Wildlife Refuge, Texas
Archaeology
Architecture
Arctic Exploration
Arctic Peoples
Arctic Regions
Argentina - Economic Conditions
Argentina - Politics and Government
Armani, Giorgio
Armed Forces - Soviet Union
Armed Forces - United States

Armed Forces - United States -
   Demobilization
Arms Control
Arms Dealers
Arms Race
Arms Sales
Armstrong, Louis (Interview)
Armstrong-Jones, Antony
Army - United States
Arnault, Bernard
Arson
Art
Art, American
Art and Children
Art - Museums
Art - Prices
Art, Rococo
Arthritis
Artificial Insemination
Artificial Intelligence
Arts
Arts - Federal Aid
Ashe, Arthur
Asia and the United States
Asian-Americans
Aspirin
Assad, Hafez
Assassination Attempt
Assassinations
Assembly Line
Asthma
Astrology
Astronauts
Astronomy
Athletes
Atkinson, Rick
Atlantic City (New Jersey)
Atlantic Coast
Attica State Prison - Riot, 1971
Audubon, John James
Austin (Texas)
Australia
Australian Aborigines
Automated Teller Machines
Automation
Automobile Dealers
Automobile Industry
Automobile Ownership
Automobile Racing
Automobiles
Automobiles - Fuel Efficiency
Automobiles, Experimental
Avedon, Richard

Baby Boom Generation
Baby M Case
Bacall, Lauren
Bach, Johann Sebastian

Bach, Richard
Bacharach, Burt
Backaches
Baez, Joan
Bagwell, Paul
Bahamas
Bailey, F. Lee
Bailey, Pearl
Baker, Anita
Baker, Bobby
Baker, Carroll
Baker, James
Baker, Russell
Bakke, Allan, Case
Bakker, Jim
Balance of Trade
Balanced Budget - Constitutional
  Amendment
Balanchine, George
Baldrige, Letitia
Baldwin, James
Balewa, Abubakar Tafawa
Balin, Ina
Ball, Lucille
Ballard, Robert
Ballet
Balloon Ascensions
Baltic Sea Region
Band (Musical Group)
Bangladesh
Bank of Credit and Commerce
  International
Bankamerica
Banks and Banking
Banks and Banking, International
Bardot, Brigitte
Barth, Karl
Baryshnikov, Mikhail
Baseball, Professional
Basketball, Professional
Basques
Bass Family
Bass, Robert
Bay of Pigs Invasion, 1961
Beatles (Musical Group)
Beatty, Warren
Bees
Beggars and Begging
Begin, Menachem
Begin, Menachem (Interview)
Behavior (Psychology)
Beirut Airplane Hijacking, 1985
Belaunde, Ferando
Bellow, Saul
Belmondo, Jean-Paul
Belushi, John
Bench, Johnny
Benedict, Gamble

Benkhedda, Benyoussef
Bennett, Michael
Bennett, William
Benton, Thomas Hart
Bentsen, Lloyd
Berenson, Marisa
Berg, Paul
Bergen, Candice
Bergman, Ingmar
Bergman, Ingrid
Berkowitz, David
Berlin Crisis, 1961
Berlin (East Germany)
Berlin (Germany)
Berlin Wall
Bernstein, Leonard
Berrigan, Daniel
Berrigan, Philip
Bertolucci, Bernardo
Betancourt, Romulo
Bhopal Poisonous Gas Disaster
Bible
Bicentennial Celebration - United States
Bing, Rudolf
Bingham, Sallie
Biofeedback
Biological Rhythms
Biotechnology
Bird, Larry
Birds
Birmingham (Alabama)
Birth
Birth Control
Birth Control - Catholic Church
Birth Defects
Birth Rate
Bisset, Jacqueline
Black Actors and Actresses
Black Athletes
Black Entertainers
Black Holes
Black, Hugo
Black Men
Black Panthers
Black Students
Black Students - Protests and
  Demonstrations
Blacks
Blacks - Civil Rights
Blacks - Economic Conditions
Blacks - Education
Blacks - Employment
Blacks - History
Blacks - Integration
Blacks - Protests and Demonstrations
Blacks and Jews
Blacks in Motion Pictures
Blacks in Politics

Blood Flow
Blough, Roger
Blue, Vida
Blues Music
Blumenthal, Werner (Interview)
Bocuse, Paul
Body, Human
Body Image
Boeing Company
Boesky, Ivan
Boise Cascade Corp.
Bomb Shelters
Bombeck, Erma
Borg, Bjorn
Bork, Robert
Borman, Frank
Botswana
Botti, John
Boulez, Pierre
Bowie, David
Boxing
Brady, Nicholas
Brain
Brando, Marlon
Brandt, Willy
Brazelton, T. Berry
Brazil
Brazil and the United States
Break Dancing
Breast Cancer
Brewing Industry
Brewster, Kingman
Brezhnev, Leonid
Brezhnev, Leonid (Interview)
Bribery
Bricker, William
Brinkley, David M.
Broadcast Journalism
Broadcasting
Brokerage Industry
Brokers
Bronfman, Edgar Jr.
Bronfman, Samuel
Bronze Age
Brooke, Edward W.
Brooklyn Bridge (New York)
Brooklyn (New York) - Social Conditions
Brooks, Mel
Brown, Edmund G. "Pat"
Brown, Jerry
Brown, Jim
Bryant, Anita
Bryant, Louise
Bryant, Paul "Bear"
Brzezinski, Zbigniew
Brzezinski, Zbigniew (Interview)
Bucher, Lloyd M.
Buchwald, Art

Buckley, Robert
Buckley, William F.
Buckley, William F. (Family)
Buddhism
Budget - Bush Administration
Budget - Carter Administration
Budget - Ford Administration
Budget - Reagan Administration
Budget - United States
Bullfights
Bundy, Mcgeorge
Bunting, Mary
Bureaucracy
Burger, Warren E.
Burger, Warren E. (Interview)
Buried Treasure
Burke, Chris
Burke, James E.
Burnett, Carol
Burr, Donald
Burton, Richard
Bush, Barbara
Bush, Barbara - Pets
Bush, George
Bush, George - Inauguration
Bush, George (Interview)
Business
Business Management
Business Schools
Busing for School Integration
Byrd, Harry
Byrd, Robert
Byrne, David
Byzantine Empire

Cabbage Patch Kids
Cabinet - Carter Administration
Cabinet - Ford Administration
Cabinet - Reagan Administration
Caesar, Sid
Calcium (Mineral Supplements)
Caldwell, Sarah
California
Calley, William
Camarena, Enrique, Murder
Cambell Soup Co.
Cambodian Conflict
Cambodian - Vietnamese Conflict
Cameras
Campaign Financing
Camping
Canada
Canada - Economic Conditions
Canada - Politics and Government
Canada and the United States
Canals
Cancer
Cancer Patients

Canion, Rod
Cannes Film Festival
Cape Kennedy (Florida)
Capital Punishment
Capitalism
Capitalists
Caplin, Mortimer
Capote, Truman
Carbohydrates
Carew, Rod
Caribbean Region
Carlson, Paul
Caroline, Princess of Monaco
Caron, Leslie
Carpenter, Scott
Carson, Johnny
Carswell, Harold
Carter, Billy
Carter, Jimmy
Carter, Jimmy - Inauguration
Carter, Jimmy - Public Relations
Carter, Jimmy - Staff
Carter, Jimmy - Visit to Mexico, 1979
Carter, Jimmy - Visit To the Middle East, 1979
Carter, Jimmy (Interview)
Carter, Lilian (Interview)
Carter, Rosalynn (Interview)
Casey, William
Cash, Johnny
Cassidy, David
Castaneda, Carlos
Castro, Fidel
Caterpillar Tractor Co.
Catholic Church
Catholic Church - Clergy
Catholic Church - United States
Cats
Cauthen, Steve
Caves
Cavett, Dick
Cells
Cellular Phones
Censorship
Census
Central America
Central Intelligence Agency
Cerf, Bennett
Chagall, Marc
Challenger (Space Shuttle)
Chamberlain, Wilt
Chandler, Buff
Chandler, Otis
Chanel, Gabrielle
Chang, Niem
Chaos (Science)
Chaplin, Charlie
Chaplin, Geraldine

Charles, Prince of Wales
Charterhouse J. Rothschild
Chartres Cathedral
Chase Manhattan Corp.
Chavez, Cesar
Checchi, Al
Cheever, John
Chemical and Biological Warfare
Cher
Chernenko, Konstantin
Chernobyl Nuclear Accident, 1986
Chess
Chessman, Caryl
Chevalier, Maurice
Chicago (Illinois)
Chichester, Sir Francis
Child Abuse
Child Care
Child, Julia
Child Psychology
Child Rearing
Childbirth
Childlessness
Children
Children - Diseases
Children and War
Children, Emotionally Disturbed
Children, Gifted
Children of Alcoholics
Children of Divorced Parents
Children, Terminally Ill
Chile
China
China - Cultural Revolution,
China - Economic Conditions
China - Foreign Relations
China - History
China - Nuclear Weapons
China - Politics and Government
China - Social Conditions
China - Social Life and Customs
China and Hong Kong
China and the Soviet Union
China and the United States
China and Vietnam
Chocolate
Cholesterol
Christianity
Christie, Julie
Christmas
Christmas Business
Chrysler Corp.
Church and State
Church of England
Churches
Churchill, Sir Winston L.
Circus
Citicorp

Cities and Towns
Civil Defense
Civil Rights
Civil Rights Movement
Clancy, Tom
Clark, Jim
Clark, Joe
Class Reunions
Clean Air Act
Climate
Clones (Biology)
Close, Glenn
Clowns
Coal Industry
Coastal Changes
Coca-Cola Company
Cocaine
Colby, William E.
Cold Fusion
Coles, Robert
College Athletes
College Education
College Graduates
College Students
College Students - Sexual Behavior
Colleges and Universities
Colleges and Universities - Faculty
Colleges and Universities - Graduate
  Schools
Colleges and Universities - Research
Collins, Joan
Color Perception
Colorado River
Columbia Broadcasting System, Inc.
Columbia, South Carolina
Columbia (Space Shuttle)
Columbus, Christopher
Comaneci, Nadia
Comets
Comic Books, Strips, etc.
Communal Living
Communes
Communication
Communication Satellites
Communism
Communist Countries
Communist Countries - Economic
  Conditions
Communist Parties
Communist Party - Italy
Commuting
Compaq Computer Corp.
Competitiveness
Comprehensive Education and Training
  Act
Computer Chips
Computer Crimes
Computer Industry

Computer Industry - Health Aspects
Computer Industry - Japan
Computer Industry - Standards
Computer Networks
Computer Software
Computer Stores
Computer Viruses
Computers
Computers - Banking Use
Computers - Medical Use
Computers - Musical Use
Computers - Psychological Aspects
Computers and Children
Computers, Government Use of
Computers in Motion Pictures
Computers, Personal
Congress
Connally, John
Conner, Dennis
Connors, Jimmy
Conservation
Conservation Corps, American
Conservatism
Constantine II
Constitution - United States
Constitutional Convention, 1787
Consumer Protection
Continental Telephone
Contras (Nicaragua)
Conventions
Conversation
Cooke, Alistair (Interview)
Cooking
Cooking, American
Cooley, Denton
Cooney, Gerry
Cooper, Gordon
Cooper, Trudy
Copeland, Lammot Du Pont
Coppola, Francis Ford
Cormier, Lucia Marie
Cornell University, Ithaca (New York)
Corning Inc.
Corporate Promotions
Corporate Social Responsibility
Corporations
Corporations - Acquisitions and Mergers
Corporations - Corrupt Practices
Corporations - Directors
Corporations - Divestiture
Corporations - Finance
Corporations, International
Cosby, Bill
Cosell, Howard
Cosmetic Industry
Cosmetic Surgery
Cosmic Rays
Cosmology

Cost of Living
Costner, Kevin
Counterculture
Counterfeits and Counterfeiting
Country Music
Courts
Cousteau, Jacques Yves
Couve De Murville, M.
Cox, Archibald
Crack (Cocaine)
Cray, Seymour
Creation
Creationism
Creativity
Credit
Credit Cards
Crime
Crime Prevention
Crime, Victims of
Criminal Justice, Administration of
Criminal Procedure
Cro-Magnon Man
Cronkite, Walter
Crosby, Bing
Crown, Lester
Cruise, Tom
Crusades
Cryonics
Crystal, Billy
Cuba
Cuba - Politics and Government
Cuba and the United States
Cuban Missile Crisis, 1962
Cubans in the United States
Cults
Cultural Literacy
Cummins Engine Co.
Cuomo, Mario
Cushing, Richard James, Cardinal
Customer Service
Cypress Semiconductor Corp.
Cyprus - Politics and Government
Czechoslovakia - Politics and
   Government
Czechoslovakia - Russian Invasion,
Czechoslovakia and the Soviet Union

D-Day Invasion, 1944
Daley, Richard
Daniloff-Zakharov Espionage Case,
Darman, Richard
Dating (Social Customs)
David-Weill, Michel
Davis, Angela
Dawkins, Peter
Day, Doris
De Benedetti, Carlo
De Gaulle, Charles

De Lorean, John
De Vosjoli, Thyraud
Dead Sea Scrolls
Dean, John
Dean Witter Reynolds Inc.
Death
Deaver, Michael
Debakey, Michael
Debategate Case
Debt
Debt, Corporate
Decision Making
Defectors, Political
Defense Contracts
Defense Policy - Kennedy
Defense Policy - Reagan
Defense Spending
Defense Spending - Bush
Defense Spending - Carter
Defense Spending - Reagan
Deficit Financing
Delta Air Lines, Inc.
Democracy
Democratic National Convention, 1960
Democratic National Convention, 1964
Democratic National Convention, 1968
Democratic National Convention, 1972
Democratic National Convention, 1976
Democratic National Convention, 1980
Democratic National Convention, 1984
Democratic National Convention, 1988
Democratic Party
Deneuve, Catherine
Deng Xiaoping
Deng Xiaoping (Interview)
Denial (Psychology)
Deniro, Robert
Dennis, Sandy
Denver, John
Department of Defense
Department of Education
Department of Health and Human
   Services
Department of Health, Education and
   Welfare
Department Of Housing and Urban
   Development - Scandal
Department Of Justice
Department Of Treasury
Depression (Financial), 1929-1939
Depression (Mental)
Deregulation
Deserts
Design, Industrial
Detective and Mystery Stories
Developing Countries
Diamond Shamrock Corp.
Diana, Princess of Wales

Diefenbaker, George
Dieting
Digestive System
Digital Equipment Corp.
Diller, Barry
Dillon, Douglas
Dinosaurs
Diplomacy
Diplomats
Dirksen, Everett
Disco Music
Discotheques
Discount Stores
Discrimination in Employment
Discrimination in Housing
Diseases
Disney, Walt
Disney World
Dissenters
Divorce
Dlugos, Raymond
DNA Fingerprints
Dog Sleds and Sledding
Dogs
Dolphins
Domingo, Placido
Dominican Republic and the United States
Donahue, Phil
Donner, Fred G.
Doonesbury (Comic Strip)
Douglas-Home, Sir Alec
Down, Lesley-Anne
Dreams
Drexel Burnham Lambert Inc.
Drinking of Alcoholic Beverages
Drinking Water
Droughts
Drug Abuse
Drug Enforcement Administration
Drug Testing
Drug Trafficking
Drugs - Laws and Regulations
Drugs and Artists
Drugs and Crime
Drugs and Employment
Drugs and Gangs
Drugs and Infants
Drugs and Youth
Drugs (Pharmaceutical)
Drunk Driving
Du Pont Corporation
Dubcek, Alexander
Dukakis, Michael
Dunaway, Faye
Duong Van Minh
Duran, Roberto
Dylan, Bob

Eagleton, Thomas
Earth
Earth - Photographs from Space
Earthquake Prediction
Earthquakes
Earthquakes - Alaska, 1964
Earthquakes - Armenia, 1988
Earthquakes - Iran, 1962
Earthquakes - Mexico, 1985
Earthquakes - San Francisco (California), 1989
Easter
Eastern Europe
Eastern Europe - Economic Conditions
Eastern Europe and the Soviet Union
Eastman Kodak Co.
Eastwood, Clint
Eating Disorders
Eavesdropping
Eclipses, Solar
Economic Assisstance
Economic Competition
Economic Conditions - Europe
Economic Conditions - United States
Economic Conditions - World
Economic Forecasting
Economic Policy - Bush
Economic Policy - Carter
Economic Policy - Ford
Economic Policy - Johnson
Economic Policy - Kennedy
Economic Policy - Nixon
Economic Policy - Reagan
Economics
Education
Education - Federal Aid
Education - Multicultural
Education, Bilingual
Education, Elementary
Education, Higher
Education, Secondary
Efficiency, Industrial
Egypt
Egypt - Foreign Relations
Egypt, Ancient
Egypt and the United States
Ehrlich, Thomas (Interview)
Eichmann, Adolf
Einstein, Albert
Eisenhower, Dwight D.
Eisenhower, Julie (Nixon)
Eisenstaedt, Alfred
Eisner, Michael
El Niño (Ocean Current)
El Salvador and the United States
Election Laws
Elections
Elections - Germany (West)

Elections - Great Britain, 1979
Elections - Panama, 1989
Elections - Philippines, 1986
Elections - United States, 1970
Elections - United States, 1974
Elections - United States, 1978
Elections - United States, 1982
Elections - United States, 1984
Elections - United States, 1988
Electric Power Failures
Electric Utilities
Electronic Industry
Electronic Office Machine Industry
Electronic Warfare
Electronics - Military Use
Electronics in Criminal Investigations,
    Espionage, Etc.
Elephants
Elite
Elizabeth II, Queen of Great Britain
Ellis Island (New York)
Ellsberg, Daniel
Embargo - Soviet Union
Embryology
Emerson Electric
Emotions
Employee Benefits
Employee Dismissal
Employee Morale
Employee Rights
Employee Stock Ownership Plans
Employment Tests
End of the World
Endangered Species
Endorphin
Endowments
Energy
Energy Conservation
Energy Crisis
Energy Policy
Energy Policy - Bush Administration
Energy Policy - Carter
Energy Resources
Engineering
English Language
English Language - Errors
Entertainment Industry
Entrepreneurs
Environment
Environment - Eastern Europe
Environmental Policy - Bush
    Administration
Environmental Protection Agency
Envy
Erhard, Ludwig
Erikson, Erik
Erikson, Erik (Interview)
Ervin, Sam

Escobedo Ruling
Eskimos
Espionage
Espionage, Industrial
Esslinger, Hartmut
Estes, Billie Sol
Estonia - Nationalism
Estrogen
Ethics
Ethiopia
Ethnic Groups
Etiquette
Etosha National Park, Namibia
Europe
Europe - Defenses
Europe - Economic Conditions
Europe - Politics
Europe and the United States
European Economic Community
Euthanasia
Evangelicalism
Evers, Medgar W.
Evolution
Evolution - Study and Teaching
Evtushenko, Evgeny
Executive Appointments - Carter
Executive Appointments - Ford
Executive Appointments - Kennedy
Executive Appointments - Nixon
Executive Appointments - Reagan
Executive Power - United States
Executive Search Consultants
Executives
Executives - Relocation
Executives - Salaries, Pensions, Etc.
Executives - Training
Exercise
Exorcism
Expo '70 (Osaka, Japan)
Extinct Animals
Exxon Corp.
Exxon Valdez (Ship) Oil Spill,

Face
Fairchild, John
Fairchild, Sherman
Fairs
Faisal, King of Saudi Arabia
Falkland Islands War, 1982
Family
Family and Medical Leave
Family Violence
Famines
Fantasy
Farmers and Farming
Farrell, Eileen
Farrow, Mia
Fashion

Fast Food Restaurants
Fathers
Fathers and Sons
Faulkner, William
Fear
Federal Bureau of Investigation
Federal Communications Commission
Federal Deficit
Federal Express
Federal Reserve Board
Federal Reserve System
Federal-City Relations
Federal-State Relations
Felt, Harry Donald
Ferkauf, Eugene
Ferraro, Geraldine
Fertilization *in Vitro*, Human
Fetus
Fetus - Surgery
Fidelity Investments
Fielding, Temple
Fifth Force (Physics)
Finance, Personal
Financial Services
Finch, Robert
Finley, Charles
Finney, Albert
Firestone Tire & Rubber Co.
Fireworks
Fischer, Bobby
Fishing
Flag Burning
Flags - United States
Fleming, Ian
Fleming, Peggy
Floods
Floods - Italy
Florence (Italy)
Florida
Flu (Disease)
Folklore - United States
Fonda, Henry
Fonda, Jane
Fonda, Peter
Food
Food - Labeling
Food Contamination
Food Industry
Food Stamp Program
Food Supply
Football, College
Football, Professional
Ford, Betty
Ford, Betty (Interview)
Ford, Cristina
Ford, Eileen
Ford, Gerald
Ford, Gerald - Assassination Attempts

Ford, Gerald - Protection
Ford, Gerald - Relations with Congress
Ford, Gerald - Staff
Ford, Gerald - State of the Union
    Message
Ford, Gerald - Visit to Europe, 1975
Ford, Gerald (Family)
Ford, Gerald (Interview)
Ford, Henry II
Ford Motor Co.
Forecasting
Foreign Policy - Bush Administration
Foreign Policy - Carter Administration
Foreign Policy - Johnson Administration
Foreign Policy - Kennedy Administration
Foreign Policy - Nixon Administration
Foreign Policy - Reagan Administration
Forest Fires
Forest Products Industry
Forests and Forestry
Forgiveness
Fortas, Abe
Foster, Jodie
Fourth of July Celebration
Fowler, Joe
Fox Broadcasting
Fractals
France
France - Economic Conditions
France - Foreign Relations
France - Politics and Government
France - Riots
France and the Soviet Union
France and the United States
Franco, Francisco
Frank, Barney
Frankenstein
Franklin, Aretha
Fraud
Frawley, Brian
Frazier, Joe
Freedom of Information
Freeman, Orville
Freud, Sigmund
Friedland, Gerald
Friendship
Fromme, Lynette
Frondizi, Arturo
Frontier and Pioneer Life
Frost, Robert
Fuel - Conservation
Fulbright, William
Fuller, R. Buckminster
Fundamentalism
Furstenberg, Diane Von

Gable, Clark
Gable, John Clark

Gagarin, Yuri
Galaxies
Galbraith, John Kenneth
Galleons
Gambling
Gandhi, Indira
Gandhi, Indira - Assassination
Gangs
Gardening
Gardner, Erle Stanley
Gardner, John W.
Garr, Teri
Gasoline Prices
Gasoline Supply
Gates, Bill
Gates, Robert
Gay Men and Women
Gay Rights
Gebel-Williams, Gunther
Gemini 4
Gemini 5
Genealogy
Geneen, Harold S.
Genentech Inc.
General Dynamics Corp.
General Electric Co.
General Electric Credit Corp.
General Motors Corp.
Generation Gap
Genetic Engineering
Genetic Mapping
Genetic Research
Genetic Research - Ethical Aspects
Genius
Genocide
Geology
Gere, Richard
German Reunification
Germany
Germany (West)
Germany (West) and the United States
Germany (West) - Armed Forces
Germany (West) - Politics and
  Government
Gerstner, Louis
Ghana - Politics and Government
Giamatti, Bart
Gift Giving
Gilligan, Carol
Gilmore, Gary
Ginsburg, Douglas
Givens, Robin
Gleason, Jackie
Glenn, John
Glenn, John (Family)
Glueck, Nelson
God
Goetz, Bernhard, Subway Shooting

Goizueta, Robert C.
Gold
Gold As an Investment
Gold Mines and Mining
Goldberg, Arthur
Goldwater, Barry
Goldwater, Barry (Interview)
Gone With the Wind (Book) - Sequel
Good and Evil
Gooden, Dwight
Gorbachev, Mikhail
Gorbachev, Mikhail - Visit to the United
  States, 1988
Gorbachev, Mikhail (Interview)
Gorbachev, Raisa
Gossip
Goulart, Joao
Gould, Elliott
Gould Inc.
Gould, Sam
Gould, Stephen Jay
Government Bonds
Government Investigations
Government Publicity
Government Spending Policy
Grace, J. Peter
Grace, J. Peter (Interview)
Grace, Princess of Monaco
Graham, Billy
Grandma Moses
Grandparents
Grass, Gunter
Grasso, Ella
Gravity
Gray, Bowman
Great Britain - Economic Conditions
Great Britain - Politics and Government
Great Britain - Social Conditions
Greece
Greece - Politics and Government
Greece, Ancient
Greed
Greenhouse Effect
Greenland
Greenspan, Alan
Greer, Germaine
Grenada-American Invasion, 1983
Gretsky, Wayne
Griffith, Melanie
Grissom, Virgil
Grizzly Bears
Gromyko, Andrei
Gross, Calvin
Guatemala - Antiquities
Guatemala - Politics and Government
Guevara, Ernesto "Che"
Guidebooks
Guided Missiles - Defenses

Gulf Oil Corp.
Gun Control
Guns in the United States
Guthrie, Arlo

Haggard, Merle
Haig, Alexander
Haitians in the United States
Haldeman, H. R.
Hall, Arsenio
Hall, Jim
Halley's Comet
Halloween
Hallstein, Walter
Hallucinations and Illusions
Hallucinogenic Drugs
Halston
Hamill, Dorothy
Hammarskjold, Dag
Handicapped
Hanks, Tom
Hannah, Daryl
Hanratty, Terry
Happiness
Hare Krishna
Harkins, Paul
Harlem (New York)
Harper, Valerie
Harriman, W. Averell
Hart, Gary
Harvard University
Hatch Act of 1939 - Amendments
Hatcher, Richard
Hate Groups
Hawaii
Hawking, Stephen
Hawn, Goldie
Haynsworth, Clement
Hazardous Wastes
Headaches
Health
Hearst, Patricia, Case
Heart - Diseases
Heart, Artificial
Heart Attacks
Heath, Edward
Hefner, Hugh
Helicopters
Hell
Heller, Walter W.
Helms, Jesse
Helmsley, Leona
Hemingway, Ernest
Hemingway, Margaux
Hendrix, Jimmy
Henson, Jim
Hepburn, Katharine
Heredity

Heroes and Heroines
Heroin
Herpes
Hertz, Gustav Crane
Hesburgh, Theodore
Hesselbein, Frances
Hewlett-Packard Co.
Hibernation, Human
Hicks, Louise Day
High Definition Television
High Schools
Hijacking, Airplane
Hijacking, Ship
Hill, Anita
Hill, Phil
Hills, Carla
Hilton, Conrad
Himalaya, Asia
Hinckley, John, Jr.
Hippies
Hiroshima (Japan) - Bombing, 1945
Hispanic-Americans
History
History, Teaching of
Hitler, Adolf
Hitler, Adolf - Forgeries
Ho Chi Minh
Hockey, Professional
Hodges, Luther
Hoffa, Jimmy
Hoffman, Dustin
Hollywood (California)
Holmes, Larry
Holography
Home Equity Loans
Home Shopping
Homeless
Homosexuality
Honda Motor Co.
Honesty
Hong Kong
Hoover, J. Edgar
Hope, Bob
Hopper, Dennis
Hormones
Hormones, Sex
Horne, Lena
Hornung, Paul
Horowitz, Vladimir
Horse Racing
Hospitals
Hostages - Lebanon
Hot Air Balloons
Hotels, Motels, etc.
Houghton, James R.
Housing
Housing - Construction
Housing - Costs

Hoving, Thomas
Hoyle, Fred
Hubble Space Telescope
Hudson, Rock
Hughes, Howard
Hull, Bobby
Human Relationships
Humor
Humphrey, Hubert H.
Hunger
Hunt, Nelson and Bunker
Huntington's Disease
Huntley, Chet
Hurd, Gale Anne
Hurricanes
Hussein, King of Jordan
Hussein, Saddam
Hutton, Lauren
Hydrogen Bomb
Hyperspace
Hypertension
Hypnotism

Iacocca, Lee
Ibn Battula, Mohammed
Icahn, Carl
Ice Age
Ice Cream
Iceland
Identity (Psychology)
Illegal Aliens
Immigrants in the United States
Immigration and Naturalization
Immune System
Imports and Exports
Imports and Exports - Korea (South)
In Search of Excellence (Book)
Income Distribution
Income Tax
India
India - History
India - Politics and Government
India and Pakistan
India-Pakistan War, 1971
Indians of North America
Indians of North America - Pottery
Individualism
Indonesia
Industrial Design
Industrial Management
Industrial Relations
Industry
Industry - Government Policy
Industry - Social Aspects
Infants
Infants, Premature
Infertility
Inflation (Financial)

Influenza
Information Services
Information Technology
Innovations
Insane, Criminally
Insanity Defense
Insect Control
Insider Trading
Insurance Companies - Finance
Insurance, Health
Insurance, Liability
Insurance, Life
Insurance, Malpractice
Integration, Racial
Intel Corp.
Intelligence
Interactive Video
Interest Rates
Internal Revenue Service
International Business Machines
International Businesses
International Geophysical Year
International Harvester Co.
International Telephone and Telegraph
International Trade
International Trade with China
International Trade with Japan
International Trade with Mexico
Interpersonal Relations
Interracial Marriages
Intuition
Inventions
Investment Advisors
Investment Banking
Investments
Investments, Foreign
Iowa
Iran
Iran - Foreign Relations
Iran - Politics and Government
Iran and the United States
Iran Hostage Crisis, 1979-1981
Iran Hostage Rescue Attempt, 1980
Iran-Contra Affair
Iranian Air Downing, 1988
Iranian-Iraqi War, 1979-1988
Iraq
Iraq - Defenses
Iraq - Politics and Government
Ireland
Irish-Americans
Irish Unification Question
Irving, Clifford
Irving, John
Islam
Israel
Israel - History
Israel - Politics and Government

Israel and Lebanon
Israel and the United States
Israeli-Arab Relations
Israeli-Arab Wars, 1967-
Israeli-Arab Wars, 1967 - Peace and
　Mediation
Israeli-Egyptian Treaty, 1979
Italy - Antiquities
Italy - Industries
Ivory Trading

J.P. Morgan & Co., Inc.
Jackson, Henry "Scoop"
Jackson, Jesse
Jackson, Michael
Jackson, Reggie
Jade
Jagger, Mick
Japan
Japan - Defenses
Japan - Economic Conditions
Japan - Social Conditions
Japan - Technology
Japan and the United States
Japanese
Jaruzelski, Wojciech
Javits, Jacob
Jaworski, Leon
Jazz Music
Jealousy
Jellyfish
Jenkins, Thomas
Jenkins, Walter - Scandal
Jerusalem
Jesuits
Jesus Christ
Jesus Christ Superstar (Rock Musical)
Jesus People
Jewelry
Jews
Jews - Persecutions
Jews in the United States
Job Satisfaction
Job Training
Jobs
Jobs, Steve
John, Elton
John F. Kennedy Center for the
　Performing Arts
John Paul I, Pope
John Paul II, Pope
John Paul II, Pope - Assassination Attempt
John Paul II, Pope - Visit to Central
　America, 1983
John Paul II, Pope - Visit to Great Britain,
　1982
John Paul II, Pope - Visit to Poland, 1979

John Paul II, Pope - Visit to Poland, 1983
John Paul II, Pope - Visit to the United
　States, 1979
John XXIII, Pope
Johns, Jasper
Johnson, Don
Johnson, Frank
Johnson & Johnson
Johnson, Keith
Johnson, Lady Bird
Johnson, Luci Baines
Johnson, Lynda
Johnson, Lyndon B.
Johnson, Lyndon B. (Family)
Johnson, Lyndon B. - Inauguration
Johnson, Lyndon B. - Pets
Johnson, Lyndon B. - Relations with
　Congress
Johnson, Lyndon B. - Staff
Johnson, Lyndon B. - State of the Union
　Message
Johnson, Lyndon B. - Visit to Asia, 1966
Johnson, Magic
Johnson, Ned
Johnson, Rafer
Johnson, Sonia
Joint Ventures
Jonathan Livingston Seagull
Jones, James Earl
Jones, Jim
Jones, Tom
Jonestown, Guyana, Mass Deaths, 1978
Joplin, Janis
Jordan
Jordan, William Hamilton
Journalistic Ethics
Journalists
Joyner-Kersee, Jackie
Juan Carlos I, King of Spain
Judges
Junk Bonds
Jury
Justice
Justice, Administration of

Kappel, Fred
Kaye, Danny
Keating, Ken
Keaton, Diane
Keillor, Garrison
Kelley, Kitty
Kemper, John M.
Kennecott Corp.
Kennedy, Caroline
Kennedy, Edward M.
Kennedy, Edward M. - Chappaquiddick
　Accident, 1969
Kennedy, Ethel

Kennedy, Gerald
Kennedy, John F.
Kennedy, John F. - Assassination
Kennedy, John F. (Family)
Kennedy, John F. - Inauguration
Kennedy, John F. - Relations With
  Congress
Kennedy, John F. - Visit to Mexico, 1962
Kennedy, Joseph P.
Kennedy, Robert F.
Kennedy, Robert F. - Assassination
Kennedy, Rose
Kent State University - Riot (May 4, 1970)
Kenya
Kenyatta, Jomo
Keppel, Frank
Kerr, Clark
Kerr, Jean
Keynes, John Maynard
Keys, Ancel
KGB
Khmer Rouge
Khomeini, Ruhollah
Khrushchev, Nikita S.
King, Martin Luther, Jr.
King, Martin Luther, Jr. - Assassination
King, Stephen
Kinski, Nastassia
Kirkland, Gelsey
Kishi, Nobusuke
Kissinger, Henry A.
Kissinger, Henry A. (Interview)
Kittinger, Joseph
Klaben, Helen
Klein, Calvin
Kleindienst, Richard G.
Knoll, Alex
Koch, Ed
Kohlberg Kravis Roberts & Co.
Koko (Gorilla)
Kong Le
Koop, C. Everett
Koppel, Ted
Korea (North) and the United States
Korea (South) - Economic Conditions
Korea (South) - Politics and Government
Korea (South) - Protests and
  Demonstations
Korean Airlines Flight 007 Downing, 1983
Kosygin, Aleksei
Koufax, Sandy
Kravis, Henry
Krishna Menon, V. K.
Ku Klux Klan
Kubrick, Stanley
Kurds
Kuwait
Kuwait-Iraqi Invasion, 1990-1991

Kwan, Nancy

Labor
Labor Contracts - Coal Industry
Labor Productivity
Labor Supply
Labor Unions
Labrecque, Thomas
Laetrile
Laird, Melvin R.
Lakonia (Ship)
Lance, Thomas Bertram
Land, Edwin
Landon, Michael
Landsbury, Angela
Laos and the United States
Laragh, John
Lasers
Lasers - Medical Use
Lasser, Louise
Last Supper in Art
Latin America - Politics and Government
Latin America and the United States
Latvia - Nationalism
Lauper, Cyndi
Lauren, Ralph
Lawsuits
Lawyers
Lawyers - Washington, D.C.
Lazard Freres & Co.
Le Carre, John
Le Corbusier
Leachman, Cloris
Lead Poisoning
Leadership
Leadership (Survey)
Leakey, Richard
Learning, Psychology of
Lebanon
Lebanon - Israeli Invasion, 1982
Lebanon - Massacre, 1982
Lebanon - United States Marine Corps
Lebanon - United States Marine Corps-
  Terrorist Attack, 1983
Lebanon and the United States
Legal Assistance for the Poor
Legionnaire's Disease
Lehman, John F.
Leigh, Janet
Lemurs
Lennon, John
Lennox, Donald D.
Leonard, Elmore
Leonard, Sugar Ray
Leopards
Leopold, Aldo
Lerner, Alan Jay
Letterman, David

Leveraged Buyouts
Levi, Edward H. (Interview)
Levine, James
Libel and Slander
Libyan-American Conflict, 1986
Libyan-American Conflict, 1989
Lie Detectors and Detection
Liedtke, Hugh
Life (Biology) - Origin
Life on Other Planets
Life (Periodical)
Lifestyles
Lightning
Lincoln, Abraham
Lindsay, John V.
Ling, James
Lions
Lippmann, Walter
Literacy
Lithuania - Nationalism
Liz Claiborne Inc.
Lobbyists and Lobbying
Lockheed Corporation
Lodge, George
Lodge, Henry Cabot
Loewe, Frederick
Lombardi, Vince
London
Longevity
Loons
Lopez Portillo, Jose - Visit to the United
    States, 1979
Loren, Sophia
Lorenzo, Frank
Los Angeles (California)
Loudon, John H.
Love
Lovell, James
Lowell, Robert
Loyalty
LSD
Lucas, George
Luce, Claire Booth (Interview)
Luce, Henry R.
Lusitania (Ship)
Luther, Martin
Lying
Lyme Disease

Ma Sitson
MacArthur, Douglas II
MacDonald, Ross
MacGraw, Ali
MacLaine, Shirley
Madonna
Madrid Hurtado, Miguel De La
    (Interview)

Magnet Schools
Mail Order Business
Mailer, Norman
Makarios II, Archbishop
Malaysia
Malcolm X - Assassination
Malinovsky, Rodion
Malone, John C.
Man
Man - Influence on Nature
Man - Origin
Man, Prehistoric
Management
Manatees
Manchester, William
Manila (Philippines) - History
Mann, Thomas C.
Mansfield, Michael J.
Manson, Charles
Mantle, Mickey
Manufacturing Industries
Manzu, Giacomo
Mao Zedong
Mao Zedong, Mme.
Marcos, Ferdinand
Margaret, Princess of Great Britain
Marichal, Juan
Marijuana
Marine Animals
Marine Corps
Marine Pollution
Mariner 2
Mariner 4
Marketing
Marriage
Mars (Planet)
Martin, Steve
Martins, Peter
Marxism
Mary, Mother of Jesus
Mass Media
Mass Media and Youth
Mass Transit
Massachusetts Institute of Technology
Master of Business Administration
    Degree
Materialism
Materials Research
Matsushita, Konosuke
Matter
Mauldin, William
Max Headroom (Fictional)
Max, Peter
Mayaguez Incident, 1975
Mayas
Mayas - Art
Mayors

Mboya, Tom
McArthur, John
McAuliffe, Christa
McCarthy, Eugene
McCartney, Paul
McCaw, Craig
McColl, Hugh
McCormack, Edward
McCormack, John
McDonald's Corp.
McDonnell, James
McEnroe, John
McFarlane, Robert
McGinley, Phyllis
McGovern, Eleanor
McGovern, George
McGowan, William
McKone, John
McLain, Denny
McLuhan, Marshall
McNamara, Robert S.
McNealy, Scott
McQueen, Steve
Meat
Mecham, Evan
Medical Care
Medical Care - Fraud
Medical Care, Cost of
Medical Care Industry
Medical Ethics
Medical Technology
Medical Testing
Medicare
Meese, Edwin
Mehta, Zubin
Meir, Golda
Memory
Men
Mental Illness
Mentally Handicapped
Menzies, Robert Gordon
Mercenary Soldiers
Merck & Co.
Mercouri, Melina
Meredith, James
Merrick, David
Merrill, Dina
Merrill Lynch & Co., Inc.
Mevacor (Medication)
Mexicans in the United States
Mexico
Mexico - Economic Conditions
Mexico and the United States
Mexico City (Mexico)
Meyerson, Bess
Miami (Florida)
Michelangelo Buonarroti, 1475-1564

Micro Marketing
Micromechanics
Microsoft Corp.
Middle Age
Middle Class
Middle East
Middle East - History
Middle East - Politics and Government
Middle East - Strategic Aspects
Middle East and the United States
Middle Western States
Midler, Bette
Migration, Internal
Military Assistance, Cuban-Africa
Military Law
Military Operations, Covert
Military Personnel
Military Service, Compulsory
Military-Industrial Complex
Milken, Mike
Miller, Arthur
Miller, G. William
Miller, Johnny
Millett, Kate
Milliken & Co.
Millionaires
Mills, Hayley
Mills, Wilbur
Mimieux, Yvette
Mind
Minelli, Liza
Mines and Mineral Resources - United
 States
Minimum Wage
Mining Industry
Minnesota
Minnesota Mining & Mfg. Co.
Minow, Newton
Miracles
Miscarriages
Miss Piggy (Muppet)
Missing Children
Missionaries, Christian
Mississippi
Mississippi - Race Relations
Mitchell, John
Mitchell, Joni
Mitchell, Martha
Mitsubishi Group Companies
Mitterrand, Francois
Mobil Corp.
Models, Fashion
Mogul Empire
Mohammed Reza Pahlevi, Shah of Iran
Monaco - Royal Family
Mondale, Walter
Monetary Policy

Monetary Policy - United States
Money - International Aspects
Money Laundering
Monk, Thelonious
Monkeys
Monnet, Jean
Monroe Doctrine
Monroe, Marilyn
Monsoons
Montana, Joe
Montand, Yves
Monterey Bay (California)
Moon
Moore, Mary Tyler
Moore, Paul
Moore, Sara Jane
Morale, National
Morality
Moreau, Jeanne
Morgan, Marabel
Mormons
Moro, Aldo, Kidnapping
Morrison, Toni
Morse, Robert
Mostel, Zero
Mothers
Mothers and Sons
Motion Picture Actors and Actresses
Motion Picture Industry
Motion Picture Producers and Directors
Motion Pictures
Motion Pictures - Special Effects
Motorola, Inc.
Mount Everest (China and Nepal)
Mount St. Helens, Washington (State)
Mountaineering
Moving
Moyers, Bill
Moynihan, Daniel Patrick
Moynihan, Pat
Mulroney, Brian
Mummies
Municipal Bonds
Municipal Finance
Municipal Government
Murder
Murdoch, Rupert
Murphy, Eddie
Murray, John Courtney
Murray River (Australia)
Murrow, Edward R.
Muscular System
Museum of Modern Art (New York)
Music
Music Recording Industry
Musicians
Muskie, Edmund

Muslims in the United States
Mutual Funds
My Lai Massacre, 1968
Myerson, Bess
Mysticism
Mythology - Social Aspects
Mythology, Greek

Nabisco Company
Nabokov, Vladimir
Nader, Ralph
Naipaul, V. S.
Namath, Joe
Namibia
Nanotechnology
Napoleon
Nasser, Gamal Abdel
National Aeronautics and Space
   Administration
National Broadcasting Company
National Gallery of Art (Washington,
   D.C.)
National Geographic Society
National Guard
National Parks and Reserves
National Rifle Association
National Security Agency
National Service
Nationalism
Native Americans
Native Peoples
Natural Disasters
Natural Gas Industry
Navratilova, Martina
Navy - Soviet Union
Navy - United States
NCBN Corp.
Ndebele Tribespeople
Neff, Tom
Nehru, Jawaharlal
Nelson, Willie
Neptune (Planet)
Neutron Bombs
New Age Movement
New Deal Legislation
New York (City)
New York Times
Newhouse, Sam
Newman, Paul
News Media
Newspaper Publishers and Publishing
Next Inc.
Ngo Dinh Diem
Ngo Dinh Diem - Assassination, 1963
Ngo Dinh Nhu, Mme.
Nguyen Cao Ky
Nguyen Khanh

Nguyen Van Thieu
Nhu, Mme Dinh Ngo
Nicaragua - Politics and Government
Nicaragua and the United States
Nichols, Mike
Nicholson, Jack
Nicklaus, Jack
Niger - Native Peoples
Nigeria
Nineteen Hundred and Eighties
Nineteen Hundred and Eighty
Nineteen Hundred and Eighty-Eight
Nineteen Hundred and Eighty-Five
Nineteen Hundred and Eighty-Four
Nineteen Hundred and Eighty-Nine
Nineteen Hundred and Eighty-One
Nineteen Hundred and Eighty-Seven
Nineteen Hundred and Eighty-Six
Nineteen Hundred and Eighty-Three
Nineteen Hundred and Eighty-Two
Nineteen Hundred and Fifties
Nineteen Hundred and Forty
Nineteen Hundred and Nineties
Nineteen Hundred and Ninety
Nineteen Hundred and Seventies
Nineteen Hundred and Seventy-One
Nineteen Hundred and Seventy-Six
Nineteen Hundred and Seventy-Two
Nineteen Hundred and Sixties
Nineteen Hundred and Sixty
Nineteen Hundred and Sixty-Eight
Nineteen Hundred and Sixty-Nine
Nippon Telegraph & Telephone
Nixon, Pat
Nixon, Richard M.
Nixon, Richard M. (Family)
Nixon, Richard M. - Health
Nixon, Richard M. - Impeachment
Nixon, Richard M. - Inauguration
Nixon, Richard M. - Income Taxes
Nixon, Richard M.   (Interview)
Nixon, Richard M. - Pardon
Nixon, Richard M. - Relations with
   Congress
Nixon, Richard M. - Resignation
Nixon, Richard M. - Staff
Nixon, Richard M. - Visit to China, 1972
Nixon, Richard M. - Visit to Europe,
   1969
Nixon, Richard M. - Visit to the Middle
   East, 1974
Nixon, Tricia
Nobility
Nonprofit Institutions
Nordenstrom, Bjorn
Norell, Norman
Noriega, Manuel

Norodom Sihanouk
North Atlantic Treaty Organization
North Dakota
North, Oliver
North Pole
Northeastern States
Northrop Corp.
Nostalgia
Nuclear Energy
Nuclear Freeze Movement
Nuclear Fusion
Nuclear Power Plants
Nuclear Power Plants - Accidents
Nuclear Propulsion
Nuclear Submarines
Nuclear Test Ban
Nuclear Warfare
Nuclear Weapons
Nuclear Weapons - Iraq
Nuns
Nureyev, Rudolf
Nutrition

Oates, Joyce Carol
Obrien, Lawrence
Obscenity (Law)
Occult
Occupational Health and Safety
Ocean Mining
Oceanographic Submersibles
Oceanography
OConnor, Sandra Day
Office Buildings
OHara, John
Oil Well Drilling
OKeeffe, Georgia
Old Age
Older Americans
Olmos, Edward James
Olmstead, Freeman
Olsen, Kenneth
Olson, James E.
Olympic Athletes
Olympic Games, 1960
Olympic Games, 1964
Olympic Games, 1972
Olympic Games, 1976
Olympic Games, 1980
Olympic Games, 1984
Olympic Games, 1988
Olympic Games (Winter), 1960
Olympic Games (Winter), 1964
Olympic Games (Winter), 1972
Olympic Games (Winter), 1976
Olympic Games (Winter), 1980
Olympic Games (Winter), 1984
Olympic Games (Winter), 1988

Police
Political Action Committees
Political Campaigns, 1974
Political Campaigns, 1978
Political Candidates, 1960
Political Candidates, 1962
Political Candidates, 1964
Political Candidates, 1966
Political Candidates, 1967
Political Candidates, 1970
Political Candidates, 1974
Political Candidates, 1978
Political Candidates, 1984
Political Cartoons and Caricatures
Political Conventions
Political Prisoners
Politics
Pollen
Pollution
Pollution - Eastern Europe
Pollution, Air
Pollution, Marine
Pollution, Radioactive
Pollution, Water
Pompidou, Georges
Poor
Popes - Election
Population - United States
Population - World
Pork Barrel Legislation
Pornography
Porter, Sylvia
Portugal
Porumbeanu, Andrei
Postal Service
Posters
Poverty
Powell, Adam Clayton
Powell, Colin
Powell, Joseph "Jody"
Power
Power Resources
Powers, Francis Gary
Pregnancy
Presidential Campaign Issues, 1964
Presidential Campaign Issues, 1972
Presidential Campaign Issues, 1976
Presidential Campaign Issues, 1988
Presidential Campaigns
Presidential Campaigns, 1960
Presidential Campaigns, 1964
Presidential Campaigns, 1968
Presidential Campaigns, 1972
Presidential Campaigns, 1976
Presidential Campaigns, 1980
Presidential Campaigns, 1984
Presidential Campaigns, 1988

Presidential Candidates, 1960
Presidential Candidates, 1964
Presidential Candidates, 1968
Presidential Candidates, 1972
Presidential Candidates, 1976
Presidential Candidates, 1980
Presidential Candidates, 1984
Presidential Candidates, 1988
Presidential Candidates, 1992
Presidential Debates, 1960
Presidential Debates, 1976
Presidential Debates, 1984
Presidential Debates, 1988
Presidential Election, 1960
Presidential Election, 1964
Presidential Election, 1968
Presidential Election, 1972
Presidential Election, 1976
Presidential Election, 1980
Presidential Election, 1980
Presidential Election, 1984
Presidential Election, 1988
Presidential Elections
Presidents - Children
Presidents - United States
Presidents - United States - Press
  Relations
Presley, Elvis
Presley, Lisa
Press
Press and Politics
Price, Leontyne
Primates
Primerica
Prions
Privacy, Right of
Pro-Democracy Movement
Pro-Democracy Movement - Romania
Pro-Democracy Movement - China
Pro-Democracy Movement - Eastern
  Europe
Pro-Democracy Movement - Germany
Pro-Democracy Movement - Poland
Pro-Democracy Movement - Soviet Union
Procaccino, Mario
Procrastination
Procter & Gamble Co.
Program Trading (Securities)
Propaganda
Prosperity
Protestant Churches
Protestantism
Protests and Demonstrations
Prozac
Prudential-Bache Securities Inc.
Pryor, Richard
Psychiatry

Psychoanalysis
Psychology
Psychopharmacology
Psychotherapy
PTL Scandal
Public Employees - Political Activity
Public Lands
Public Officials
Public Opinion
Public Opinion Polls
Public Schools
Public Welfare
Public Works
Publishers and Publishing
Pueblo Indians
Pueblo (Warship) Incident, 1968
Puzo, Mario
Pyramids

Qaddafi, Muammar Al-
Quadros, Janio
Quality Control
Quality of Life
Quantum Theory
Quayle, Dan
Quebec (Canada)
Quinlan, Karen Anne
Quinlan, Michael
Quintuplets

R.H. Macy and Co.
R.J. Industries, Inc.
Rabin, Yitzhak
Race Relations - United States
Racketeering
Radicals and Radicalism
Radio Industry
Radio Programs
Radioactive Waste Disposal
Radner, Gilda
Radziwill, Lee
Ragghianti, Marie
Rahman, Abdul
Railroads
Rain Forests
Rainwater, Richard
Ramsey, Arthur (Archbishop)
Rap Music
Rape
Rather, Dan
Rauschenberg, Robert
Rawl, Larry
Ray, Dixy Lee
Ray, James Earl
Rayburn, Sam
RCA Corp.
Reagan, Nancy

Reagan, Nancy (Interview)
Reagan, Ronald
Reagan, Ronald - Assassination Attempt
Reagan, Ronald - Executive
  Appointments
Reagan, Ronald - Health
Reagan, Ronald - Inauguration
Reagan, Ronald - Staff
Reagan, Ronald - State of the Union
  Message
Reagan, Ronald - Visit to West Germany,
  1985
Reagan, Ronald (Interview)
Real Estate Business
Rebozo, Charles G. "Bebe"
Recession
Redford, Robert
Redgrave, Lynn
Redgrave, Vanessa
Reducing
Reed, John
Refugees
Refugees, Cambodian
Refugees, Indochinese
Refugees, Kurdish
Refugees, Vietnamese
Refuse and Refuse Disposal
Regan, Donald
Regional Planning
Rehnquist, William
Reichmann, Paul
Relativity (Physics)
Religion
Religion and Politics
Religion and Social Problems
Religion in Public Schools
Remick, Lee
Reporters and Reporting
Reproduction
Republican National Convention, 1960
Republican National Convention, 1964
Republican National Convention, 1968
Republican National Convention, 1972
Republican National Convention, 1976
Republican National Convention, 1980
Republican National Convention, 1984
Republican National Convention, 1988
Republican Party
Research
Resnick, Pat
Reston, James "Scotty"
Retail Trade
Retirement
Retirement Communities
Reuther, Walter
Revlon, Inc.
Revolutions

Reynolds, Burt
Rheault, Robert
Rhythmic Gymnastics
Ribicoff, Abraham
Rich
Ride, Sally
Riggs, Bobby
Right and Left (Political Science)
Right to Die
Righter, Carl
Ringwald, Molly
Riots - Boston (Massachusetts)
Riots - Detroit (Michigan)
Riots - Harlem (New York)
Riots - Kent State University (Ohio)
Riots - Miami (Florida)
Riots - Newark (New Jersey)
Riots - Oxford (Mississippi)
Riots - United States
Riots - Watts (California)
Ripley, Alexander Braid
Risk Taking (Psychology)
Rites and Ceremonies
RJR Nabisco, Inc.
Robberies and Assaults
Robertson, Oscar
Robertson, Pat
Robinson, James
Robots
Robots, Industrial
Roca, Blas
Rock Music
Rock Videos
Rockefeller, David
Rockefeller, John
Rockefeller, Nelson
Rockefeller, Nelson (Family)
Rockefeller, Nelson (Interview)
Rockefeller, Winthrop
Rockettes
Rodgers, T.J.
Rohatyn, Felix
Rolling Stones (Musical Group)
Romania
Romania - Politics and Government
Rome, Ancient
Romney, George
Ronstadt, Linda
Rooney, Mickey
Roosevelt, Franklin D.
Rose, Pete
Rosellini, Isabella
Ross, Diana
Ross, Steven J.
Rostropovich, Mstislav
Rothschild Family
Rothschild, Jacob

Rouse, James
Rubella
Rubinstein, Artur
Rumsfeld, Donald H. (Interview)
Runaway Adults
Runaways
Running
Rushdie, Salman
Rusk, Dean
Russell, Bertrand
Russell, Charles M.
Russell, Donald
Russell, Richard
Ryan, Nolan
Ryun, Jim

Sadat, Anwar
Sadat, Anwar - Assassination, 1981
Sadat, Anwar - Visit to Israel, 1977
Sagan, Carl
Sahel (Region), Africa
Sahl, Mort
Sakharov, Andrei
Salan, Raoul
Salinger, J. D.
Salinger, Pierre
Salomon Inc.
Salt in the Body
Samana Cay, Bahama Islands
Sanctions (International Law)
Sarah, Duchess of York
Satellites
Sato, Eisaku
Saturn (Planet)
Saudi Arabia
Saudi Arabia and the United States
Saving and Savings
Savings and Loan Associations
Savings and Loan Associations - Federal
  Aid
Savings and Loan Scandal
Sawyer, Diane
Saxbe, William B. (Interview)
Scandinavians
Schacht, Henry
Schank, Roger
Schirra, Walter
Schizophrenia
Schlesinger, Arthur M.
Schlesinger, James
Schlumberger Ltd.
Schmidt, Helmut (Interview)
Schmidt, Maarten
School Choice
School Integration
Schools - New York City
Schools, Private

Schroeder, Pat
Schulhof, Michael
Schulz, Charles
Schweitzer, Albert
Science and Law
Science and Scientists
Science Talent Search
Scientology
Scott, George C.
Scranton, William
Scuba Diving
Sculley, John
Sculpture
Seaborg, Glenn T.
Seagram Co.
Seals (Animals)
Sears, Roebuck and Co.
Secord, Richard
Secretariat (Horse)
Self Help Groups
Sellers, Peter
Selling
Semiconductor Industry
Semiconductors
Senses and Sensation
Serengeti National Park (Tanzania)
Serial Murders
Sex and Religion
Sex and Television
Sex (Biology)
Sex Differences
Sex Differences (Psychology)
Sex Discrimination
Sex Education
Sex in the Arts
Sex Therapy
Sexual Behavior
Sexual Harassment
Sexually Transmitted Diseases
Seymour, Jim
Shakespeare, William, 1564-1616
Shakespeare, William - Drama
Sharansky, Natan (Anatoly)
Sharks
Sharon, Ariel
Shastri, Lal Bahadur
Shelley, Mary
Shepard, Alan
Shepard, Sam
Shepherd, Cybill
Shevardnadze, Eduard
Shevchenko, Arkady N.
Shields, Brooke
Shipwrecks
Shore, Dinah
Shrimpton, Jean
Shriver, Sargent

Shula, Don
Shultz, George
Shuman, Charles
Siberia (Soviet Union)
Sichuan Province (China)
Sickness
Sills, Beverly
Silver
Silverman, Fred
Simon, Neil
Simon, Norton
Simon, William (Interview)
Simpsons (Fictional Character)
Sinatra, Frank
Sinatra, Frank, Jr.
Sindbad the Sailor
Single Parent Families
Single People
Single Women
Singleton, Henry
Sino-indian War, 1962
Sirhan, Sirhan
Sirhan Trial, 1969
Sirica, John J.
Sistine Chapel, Vatican City
Skateboarding
Skeletal System
Skiing
Skiing and Skiers
Skin Cancer
Skinner, B. F.
Skyscrapers
Slavery - United States
Sleep
Slim, Mongi
Smell
Smith, Fred
Smith, Margaret Chase
Smith, Roger
Smith, William Kennedy
Smoking
Smoking - Laws and Regulations
Snakes
Snowmobiles
Soap Operas
Social Security
Socialism
Sociobiology
Solar System, End of
Solti, Georg
Solzhenitsyn, Alexander
Somalia
Sondheim, Stephen
Sony Corp.
Souter, David
South Africa
South Africa - Native Peoples

South Africa - Race Relations
South Africa and the United States
Southeast Asia
Southeast Asia and the United States
Southern States
Soviet Union
Soviet Union - Armed Forces
Soviet Union - Armed Forces In Cuba
Soviet Union - Breakup of the Union
Soviet Union - Civil Rights
Soviet Union - Coup Attempt, 1991
Soviet Union - Defenses
Soviet Union - Economic Conditions
Soviet Union - Foreign Relations
Soviet Union - Politics and Government
Soviet Union and China
Soviet Union and Eastern Europe
Soviet Union and the Middle East
Soviet Union and the United States
Soybeans
Space Exploration
Space Flight
Space Flight - Japan
Space Flight - Soviet Union
Space Flight - United States
Space Flight to Mars
Space Flight to the Moon
Space Flight to Venus
Space Sciences
Space Shuttle Missions
Space Stations
Space Stations - Skylab Missions
Space Vehicles
Space Weapons
Spacek, Sissy
Spain
Spain - Economic Conditions
Spain - History
Spain - Politics and Government
Special Forces
Speculation
Speed Limits - Laws and Legislation
Spielberg, Steven
Spirituality
Spitz, Mark
Sports
Sports - Economic Aspects
Sports and Business
Spring (Season)
Springsteen, Bruce
Squaw Valley (California)
Stalin, Svetlana
Stalin, Svetlana (Family)
Stallone, Sylvester
Standard of Living
Standard Oil Company of California
Stapleton, Ruth Carter

Star Trek
Stark (Warship) - Missile Attack, 1987
Stars
State Government - Finance
Statue of Liberty
Statue of Liberty - Centennial
   Celebration, 1986
Staubach, Roger
Stealth Bomber
Steel Industry
Steinberg, Saul
Steinbrenner, George
Steinem, Gloria
Stempel, Robert
Stevenson, Adlai
Stigwood, Robert
Stingrays (Fish)
Stock Brokers
Stock Index Futures
Stock Market
Stock Market - Insider Trading
Stock Market - Tokyo
Stock Market Crash, 1929
Stock Market Crash, 1987
Stockman, David
Stokes, Carl Burton
Strategic Arms Limitation Talks
Strategic Defense Initiative
Strauss, Franz Joseph
Strauss, Robert S.
Stravinsky, Igor
Streep, Meryl
Streisand, Barbra
Stress
Strikes
Strikes - Air Traffic Controllers
Strikes - Airline Employees
Strikes - Automobile Workers
Strikes - Coal Miners
Strikes - Farm Workers
Strikes - Postal Service
Strikes - Teachers
Stuart, Charles - Murder Case, 1990
Student Loans
Student Movement
Students
Students - Protests and Demonstrations
Students, Foreign
Style
Styron, William
Subconsciousness
Submarine Warfare
Suburban Life
Success
Sudan
Suez Canal
Sugar in the Body

Sugar Substitutes
Sukarno (President)
Suleiman I, Sultan of the Turks, 1495-1566
Summer
Summer Resorts
Summit Conference, 1960
Summit Conference, 1967
Summit Conference, 1972
Summit Conference, 1974
Summit Conference, 1975
Summit Conference, 1978
Summit Conference, 1979
Summit Conference, 1981
Summit Conference, 1982
Summit Conference, 1983
Summit Conference, 1985
Summit Conference, 1986
Summit Conference, 1987
Summit Conference, 1988
Summit Conference, 1989
Summit Conference, 1990
Sun
Sun Microsystems Inc.
Suntan
Sununu, John
Super Bowls
Superconducting Supercolliders
Superconductors and Superconductivity
Superfund - Government Policy
Superman (Fictional Character)
Supernatural
Superstring Theory (Physics)
Supply-Side Economics
Supreme Court
Surgery
Surgery, Cosmetic
Suruga Bay (Japan)
Swimming
Symbionese Liberation Army
Symington, Stuart
Syria and the United States
Szell, George

Talk Shows
Tanganyika - Politics and Government
Tanzania
Tax Evasion
Tax Reform
Tax Shelters
Taxation
Taxation - California
Taylor, Elizabeth
Taylor, James
Taylor, Maxwell Davenport
Teachers
Teamsters Union
Technological Innovations

Technology
Technology - Economic Aspects
Technology - Japan
Teenage Pregnancy
Telecommunications
Teledyne Inc.
Telephone Industry
Telescopes
Television
Television - Comedy Programs
Television - Game Shows
Television - News
Television - Religious Programs
Television Advertising
Television and Children
Television, Cable
Television, Cable - Laws and Regulations
Television in Politics
Television Industry
Television Programs
Tenneco Inc.
Tennessee - Industries
Tennessee Board of Pardons and Paroles
Tennis
Teresa, Mother
Terrorism
Terrorists, Arab
Terrorists, German
Terrorists, Italian
Texas
Texas Instruments
Textile Industry
Thailand
Thant, U
Thatcher, Margaret
Theater
Thomas, Clarence
Thomas, Debi
Thorton, Charles
Thought and Thinking
Tiananmen Square (China) Student
    Demonstration, 1989
Tiegs, Cheryl
Tiger International Inc.
Tigers
Time
Time Inc.
Time Travel
Time Warner Inc.
Time's Machine of the Year
Time's Man of the Decade
Time's Man/Woman of the Year
Time's Planet of the Year
Tisch, Laurence
Titanic (Steamship)
Tobacco Industry
Tomlin, Lily

Tomography
Tornadoes
Touch
Tourist Trade
Tower Commission Report, 1987
Tower, John
Toyota Motor Corp.
Toys
Trade Policy
Trade Policy - Bush Administration
Trade Policy - Reagan Administration
Traffic Accidents
Traffic Congestion
Trampolines
Transcendental Meditation
Transplantation of Organs,
Transportation
Travel
Travelers, American
Travolta, John
Treaties
Trees
Trevino, Lee
Tri Quang
Trials
Trials (Conspiracy)
Trials (Murder)
Trudeau, G. B.
Trudeau, Pierre
Truman, Harry S.
Trump, Donald
Trust
TRW Inc.
Tsai, Gerald
Tshombe, Moise
Turkey - History
Turner Broadcasting System Inc.
Turner, Stansfield (Interview)
Turner, Ted
Turow, Scott
Twain, Mark
Twenty-First Century
Twiggy
Twins
Two Thousand and One
Tylenol Poisoning Case, 1982
Tyson, Mike

U-2 Incident
U2 (Musical Group)
Ueberroth, Peter
UFO
Uganda
Uggams, Leslie
Ulbricht, Walter
Ullmann, Liv
Ultralight Aircraft

Underground Economy
Underground Railroad
Unemployed
Unemployment
Ungaro, Emmanuel
Union Carbide Corporation
United Auto Workers
United Flight 232 Disaster, 1989
United Mine Wokers of America
United Nations
United States - Defenses
United States - Economic History
United States - Foreign Opinion
United States - Foreign Policy
United States - Foreign Relations
United States - History
United States - History - Civil War
United States - History - Revolution
United States - History - War of 1812
United States - Joint Chiefs of Staff
United States - Politics and Government
United States - Popular Culture
United States - Population
United States - Social Conditions
United States - Social Life and Customs
United States - Social Policy
United States - Social Values
United States - Treaties - Panama
Universe
Universe, End of
University of California
Unmarried Couples
Updike, John
Upper Classes
Urban Renewal
Utopias

V-E Day, 1945
Vacations
Value
Vampires
Van Pallandt, Nina
Vance, Cyrus
Venezuela
Venture Capital
Venus
Venus (Planet)
Veruschka
Vesuvius (Italy)
Veto (Presidential)
Vice-Presidential Candidates, 1964
Vice-Presidential Candidates, 1968
Vice-Presidential Candidates, 1976
Vice-Presidential Candidates, 1984
Vice-Presidential Candidates, 1988
Vice-Presidents - United States
Vidal, Gore

Widows
Wilderness Survival
Wildlife
Wildlife - Africa
Wildlife - Texas
Wildlife Conservation
Wildlife Conservation - China
Williams, Robin
Williams, Tennessee
Willis, Bruce
Wills, Maury
Wilson, Charles Kemmons
Wilson, Flip
Wilson, Gary
Wilson, Harold
Wine and Winemaking
Wine Industry
Winfrey, Oprah
Winger, Debra
Winter Sports
Wives of Politicians
Wives of the Presidents
Wodaabe Tribespeople
Wolves
Women
Women - Conferences
Women - Education
Women - Employment
Women - Health
Women - Legal Status, Laws, etc.
Women - Saudi Arabia
Women - Social Conditions
Women - Soviet Union
Women Athletes
Women Executives
Women in Hate Groups
Women in Motion Pictures
Women in Politics
Women in Television
Women in the Armed Services
Women Rock Musicians
Women Scientists
Women's Movement
Wonder, Stevie
Wood, Natalie
Woods, Rose Mary
Woodward, Bob
Wool
Work
Work Force
Working Mothers
Working Parents
World Politics
World War, 1914-1918
World War, 1939-1945
World's Fair, 1962
World's Fair, 1964

World's Fair, 1967
World's Fair, 1970
Wright, Jim
Wyeth, Andrew
Wyeth, Andrew (Family)

Xerox Corp.

Yachts and Yachting
Yamasaki, Minoru
Yellowstone National Park
Yeltsin, Boris
Ylvisaker, William
Yorty, Sam
Young, Andrew
Young, John
Young & Rubicam Inc.
Young, Whitney
Young Women
Youth
Youth - Attitudes
Youth - Employment
Youth - Sexual Behavior
Youth - Soviet Union
Youth - United States
Youth - Voting
Youth and Crime
Youth as Actors and Actresses
Yugoslavia
Yugoslavia - Politics and Government
Yuppies
Yurchenko, Vitaly

Zaire
Zhou Enlai
Ziegler, Ron
Zimbabwe
Zimbabwe - Race Relations
Zoos
Zumwalt, Elmo Russell, Jr.

About the Editor

Robert Skapura taught math, physics and English before becoming a librarian more than fifteen years ago. He is a frequent speaker at state and national library conferences and for three years chaired the Technology Committee for American Association of School Librarians (AASL). He has designed computer software for both library automation and bibliographic instruction and, published two student term paper manuals, one on researching and writing about history, the other covering literature. In 1990 he edited the first volume of *The Cover Story Index*.

Mr. Skapura is addicted to spy novels and plays fullback on a soccer team. He lives with his wife and children near San Francisco where he is the librarian for Clayton Valley High School.